De remediis i. Beginning of Dialogue 1. Earliest printed text. Strassburg, Heinrich Eggesteyn, 1468. Cf. Fiske (1888), no. 6; and Mann (1971), p. 1, n. 4. Courtesy Petrarch Collection, Cornell University. Photo Cornell Libraries.

❖

Petrarch's Remedies for Fortune Fair and Foul:
A Modern English Translation of
De remediis utriusque Fortune,
with a Commentary

in five volumes

❖

Publication of this work was assisted
by a grant from the Publications Program of the
National Endowment for the Humanities, an independent
federal agency; and by a grant from the Andrews Foundation.

PETRARCH'S
Remedies for
Fortune Fair and Foul

VOLUME 2

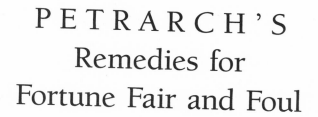

PETRARCH'S
Remedies for
Fortune Fair and Foul

A Modern English Translation of
De remediis utriusque Fortune,
with a
Commentary

BY

CONRAD H. RAWSKI

Volume 2

BOOK I   Remedies for Prosperity

Commentary

INDIANA UNIVERSITY PRESS
Bloomington & Indianapolis

Manufactured in the United States of America

Library of Congress Cataloging-in-Publication Data

Petrarca, Francesco, 1304–1374.
  [De remediis utriusque fortunae. English]
  Petrarch's Remedies for fortune fair and foul : a modern English
translation of De remediis utriusque fortune, with a commentary / by
Conrad H. Rawski.
    p.   cm.
  Includes bibliographical references.
  Contents: v. 1. Book I—Remedies for prosperity, translation—v.
2. Book I—Remedies for prosperity, commentary—v. 3. Book II—
Remedies for adversity, translation—v. 4. Book II—Remedies for
adversity, commentary—v. 5. References—bibliography, indexes,
tables and maps.
    ISBN 0-253-34844-7 (v. 1)
    I. Rawski, Conrad H.   II. Title.
PQ4496.E29D413   1991   v. 2
189'.4—dc20   88-46015

ISBN 0-253-34844-7 (v. 1 : alk. pa.)
ISBN 0-253-34845-5 (v. 2 : alk. pa.)
ISBN 0-253-34846-3 (v. 3 : alk. pa.)
ISBN 0-253-34847-1 (v. 4 : alk. pa.)
ISBN 0-253-34848-X (v. 5 : alk. pa.)
ISBN 0-253-34849-8 (set)

1 2 3 4 5   95 94 93 92 91

Quia sicut voluimus non potuimus,
quam melius potuimus voluimus.

We could not do what we wished to do,
but we wish we could have done better what we did.

—ABBOT SUGER

Nec pigebit autem nos, sicubi haesitamus, quaerere,
nec pudebit, sicubi erramus discere . . . parati
corrigi, si fraterne et recte reprehendimur; parati
etiam, si ab inimico, vera tamen dicente, mordemur.

I shall not be reluctant to search if I am in doubt,
I shall not be ashamed to learn if I am in error . . .
ready to be corrected if criticized justly and in
friendly fashion, ready even, if hurt intentionally
by any enemy, as long as he speaks the truth.

—AUGUSTINE, *De trin.* i, 2, ii, 9,
paraphrased in *Fam.* xxii, 2, 29.

CONTENTS

List of Illustrations

EDITOR'S NOTE

In the text of the Commentary, the terms "Antiquity" and "ancient" designate a time period from approximately 1000 B.C. to the collapse of the Roman Empire at the end of the fifth century A.D. The terms "Middle Ages" and "medieval" designate the period from the collapse of the Roman Empire to the end of the Trecento; and the term "Renaissance," an overlapping period extending from the mid-1300s to the early 1600s.

All references to the translation are uniformly made by book, dialogue, and line in the Latin text established by the editor and described in the Introduction iii. In the translation, the line count in 10s is indicated in brackets.

All bibliographic references in the text of the Commentary are by author, editor, or title, followed by year of publication in parentheses. Petrarch's works and most works by ancient and medieval authors are referred to by abbreviations or short titles listed in the Bibliography i and ii.

All scriptural passages in Latin are from *Biblia Sacra juxta Vulgatam Clementinam,* Rome, Paris, Desclée, 193The Psalms are cited in accordance with the numbering in this edition. The pre-Tridentine text, consulted when needed, was Basel, Joh. Froben, 1495. All passages in English are from the Douay-Challoner revision of the Old Testament and the Rheims-Challoner revision of the New Testament. My text, Baltimore, John Murphy, 1899.

The orthography of Latin titles and texts is that of their immediate source. All independent transcriptions of manuscript abbreviations, contractions, and sigla comply with the standards of the *Oxford Latin Dictionary* (1982).

Most foreign-language texts are followed by an English translation. Sources and translators are indicated immediately following the English texts. All translations without such citations are mine.

For detailed text references to the *Familiares* and *Bucolicum carmen,* the reader is referred to the concordances by Bernardo (1976) and Mann (1984). A large number of the textual relationships between the *De remediis* and other Petrarchan writings have been previously established by Heitmann (1958).

All chronological data pertaining to Petrarch and his writings are based on the work of the late Ernest Hatch Wilkins (see Bibliography iii) if not indicated otherwise.

INTRODUCTION TO THE COMMENTARY

i. ❖ PETRARCH'S *DE REMEDIIS UTRIUSQUE FORTUNE*

The present edition of Petrarch's *De remediis utriusque Fortune*[1] is the first complete version of the work in more than a century, offering, to the best of my knowledge, for the first time a fully annotated text. The last complete edition of the Latin text was published in Budapest in 1756.[2] The only English translation of the entire text, *Phisicke against Fortune, aswell prosperous, as aduerse,* by Thomas Twyne, appeared in London in 1579. Giovanni da San Miniato's Quattrocento translation of the work into Italian was edited in 1867–1868 by Casimiro Stolfi.[3]

The neglect of the *De remediis* (henceforth abbreviated as *DR*) is linked to a waning interest in Petrarch's Latin works, which, though never quite as popular as his Italian poems, were pushed aside by the veritable flood of editions and translations that offered the *Rime* and the *Trionfi* to a seemingly insatiable public ever since the 1470s.[4] The decline of the "Latin Petrarch" came to a halt during the second half of the eighteenth century. Eventually, the vagaries of reader predilection and an increasing stress on the *total* Petrarch,[5] led to a renewed interest in the Latin texts, which culminated in the publications of the Edizione nazionale (since 1926), and such editions as the *Prose* (1955) volume in the series *La letteratura italiana: Storia e Testi,* as well as a number of modern translations.[6] The *DR* was not included in this revival. The work remained sidelined, as it were: *quella più abbandonata dagli studiosi*[7]—limited to the publication of the old Italian translation already mentioned and to a number of casual selections from the Latin text or in translation.

Yet, besides the collections of his letters, the *DR* is Petrarch's largest and most ambitious work—the *magnum opus* of his later years. Beyond this important place in the canon of Petrarch's works, the *DR* is historically noteworthy. Immediately popular,[8] it held a position of fundamental importance in the culture of Europe from the outgoing fourteenth century to the mid-1600s. For contemporary readers—among them scholars and intellectuals such as Boccaccio, Lapo da Castiglionchio, Jan ze Středa, and Salutati, and princes, secular as well as clerical, such as Emperor Charles IV, Charles V of France, Cardinal Ammannati, and, probably, Jean Birel, Grand Prior of the Carthusians[9]—the book dealt with timeless topics of human significance—an essay of bitter truth[10] and consolation in the medieval tradition, but direct, forceful, and keenly astute in its all-inclusive Trecento outlook: a useful mirror and practical helpmate when it came to moral choice and independent action.[11] The DR was not just another tortuous scholastic summa or popular compendium of moral theology and catechesis.[12] With its stress on individual choice and responsibility, its method of argument by contraries inviting the participation of the reader, and its trenchant maxims, examples, stories, and historical vignettes, the text may have appealed once again through that "familiar novelty" Ernest Hatch Wilkins spoke of in connection with another work by Petrarch[13] as it substantiated the author's psychological intent to offer remedies against what people call Fortune—remedies . . . soothing and helpful to the mind,[14] and desperately needed and longed for in an age of insecurity, lawlessness and civil strife, war, pestilence, fires, earthquakes, anxiety, and terror.[15]

Apart from his historico-classical scholarship,[16] which is all but unique, the Petrarch of the DR is essentially a protean summarizer, a virtuoso practitioner of imitatio-aemulatio in the widest and best sense of the ancient notion,[17] which he repeatedly discussed.[18] He accepts the medieval intellectual and literary tradition, follows its res and verba often with a closeness that is surprising to us today. But he does so attuned to the temper of his age, with an original perspective rich in aspects and interpretations that open new vistas, spawn new directions. As physician for the mind who discerns the wounds, diagnoses perceptively, and medicates with understanding, Petrarch instigated ideas, viewpoints, and ends in which a future generation would recognize and find itself, through the ways in which he applied the practices of the past.

Nicholas Mann's checklist of the manuscripts of Petrarch's DR shows that the work "is preserved in at least 150 manuscripts; another 94 at least contain abridgements, excerpts and translations; at least a further 70 which once existed have not yet been identified."[19] The list shows an initial group of Italian manuscripts, followed, since about 1425, by manuscripts from France, "the Low Countries, the Germanic countries and the East of Europe, England and the Iberian peninsula. By 1500 the presence of the text is attested all over Europe within an area bounded roughly speaking by York, Cracow, Naples and Alcobaça." Interest in the DR, Mann continues, "is thus truly a European phenomenon, and yet it is one that one would do well not to consider synonymous with Humanism. All the evidence suggests that the manuscripts of the De remediis are the milestones in the progress of a great medieval moralist."[20]

ii. ✤ THE WRITING OF THE *DE REMEDIIS*: THE MAJOR DOCUMENTS

The historical circumstances of the writing of the *DR* have been discussed primarily by Arnaldo Foresti (1928/1977), Pier Giorgio Ricci (*Prose* [1955], pp. 1169–1171), Klaus Heitmann (1957), and Ernest Hatch Wilkins (1958 and later).[21] Thanks to Wilkins' fundamental inquiries, the major documents bearing directly on these circumstances may be presented in roughly chronological order as follows:

1. 1354. June. *Sen.* xvi, 9 (1581: 961–963) to Jean Birel, Grand Prior of the Carthusian Order.[22]

This letter is a reply to a nonextant letter to Petrarch by Jean Birel, in which the Grand Prior asked Petrarch to undertake the completion of Pope Innocent III's work on the state of man by writing the sequel to *De miseria conditionis humane,* announced by Innocent in his *prologus* of A.D. 1195, which was to describe, *Christo favente*—Christ willing—*dignitatem humane nature . . . quatinus ita per hoc humilietur elatus, ut per illud humilis exaltetur*—the dignity of human nature, so that just as in [*De miseria*] the proud man is humbled, so in this [book] the humble man would be exalted.[23]

Petrarch replies that he is unequal to *uirum illum, quem uirtus & ingenium, ante tempus ad Romani pontificatus apicem euexerunt*—a man whose virtue and genius elevated him to the summit of the Roman pontificate before the usual time—and a work *quod illum uel noluisse, uel timuisse, uel nequiuisse compertum est*—which, we know, this man either fought shy of, or feared, or could not bring himself to take in hand: *sed quis ego sum, aut quae est in me facultas? Ut apud Ciceronem ait Laelius. Ergo ego, quod ille uir exhorruit, securus aggrediar?*—And who am I? or what skill have I? as Laelius says in Cicero [*De amic.* v, 17. On *facultas,* Cicero, *De fin.* ii, 1, and *De or.* i, 102; and LCL, Falconer, pp. 126–127]. And I, then, should confidently undertake what such a man dreaded?—Not only do you bid me to be equally creative than a man of such authority, such powers of intellect, but you assign me the contrary topic, to *human misery,* and so, *quod nemo dubitat, quae illi prona fuit, & facilis, mihi difficilis, & maligna materia sit. Amplissima est enim humana miseria, breuis & perangusta foelicitas . . .*—which no one will deny, what was simple and easy for him, will be difficult and nasty for me because human misery is most plentiful, but happiness is short and hard to come by . . .[24] Continuing with equal rhetorical verve—which may not have been altogether lost on the venerable Grand Prior, Petrarch states that he is too busy—involved in numerous other tasks imposed upon him by *operosum ocium, & literarum sitis inexplebilis*—toilful leisure and an insatiable thirst for scholarship.[25] *Itaque sicut nihil tibi negatum uelim, sic uiribus meis maiora promittere non ausim*—And thus, although I do not wish to deny you anything, I do not dare to promise a major work considering the strength I have.

Petrarch reports, however, on literary activities, *non tam ingenio meo, quam orationibus tuis fisus*—which depend less on my inclination than on your words:

> Et dicam tibi, quorsum processerim dictu mirum, cum adhuc nihil inceperim. Est mihi liber in manibus, de Remediis ad utranque Fortunam in quo pro uiribus nitor, & meas, & legentium passiones animi mollire, uel si datum fuerit extirpare, forte autem ita accidit, ut dum de tristitia miseriaque tractatus uenisset, ad calamum, essemque in eo occupatus, ut eiusmodi tristitia, nullis certis ex causis ortam, quam aegritudinem animi Philosophi appellant, obiectu contrarii consolarer, quod nullo melius modo fit, quam causas laetitiae conquirendo. Id uero nihil est aliud, quam humanae conditionis exquirere dignitatem, eo ipso die, tua superuenit epistola, hoc ipsum uehementer expostulans, quasi quid tunc agerem sciens, ultro currenti stimulum tuae exhortationis adiiceres. Feci igitur & diligentius institi, non aliter quam si scribenti assidue, immineres, & tibi in silentio respondebam. Facio ecce quod iubes, hic rerum & arbitror summa est, qua[m] si ornare, diligentiusque distinguere, uel uitae breuitas, uel uerum impedimenta uetuerint, hoc tibi saltem nullus eripiet, haec hactenus.

And I am able to tell you how far I have proceeded, which is remarkable because I had not begun anything up to now. I have in hand a book *de Remediis ad utranque Fortunam,* in which I strive with what strength I have to relieve or, if it is granted unto me, to eradicate the afflictions of my mind as well as the minds of those who read it. It so happens, that I had put the pen to the text on *tristitia et miseria*—sadness and misery [DR ii, 93]—and was trying to console by juxtaposing contraries the kind of sadness that stems from uncertain causes and is viewed by the philosophers as a sickness of the mind. This is done best by searching for the causes of happiness. Actually it is nothing else but inquiring into the dignity of the human condition. On that very day your letter arrived, forcefully demanding this, as if you knew what I was doing and wanted to add from afar the spur of your exhortation to my efforts already under way. Thus I have undertaken and diligently begun exactly what you long for, writing so pointedly, and thus have silently answered you. You see, I am doing what you tell me to do and believe this to state the gist of a matter, the elegant and detailed treatment of which is made impossible by the shortness of this life and the difficulties of arriving at the truth. Of this, at least, you have not been deprived. And so much for this.

2. 1354–1360 (?).[26] Boccaccio's references to the *DR* in his *Genealogie deorum gentilium.*

xiv, 10:

> Nemo edepol sui satis compos assenciet; et longe minus qui uiderunt que scripserit soluto stilo in libro solitarie uite et in eo quem titulauit *De remediis ad utramque fortunam,* ut alios plures omictam! In quibus, quicquid in moralis philosophie sinu

potest sanctitatis aut perspicacitatis assummi, tanta uerborum maiestate percipitur, ut nil plenius, nil ornacius, nil maturius, nil denique sanctius ad instructionem mortalium dici queat.

No man in his right mind will agree that these [i.e., skilled fictitious narratives] were his final object; much less, if he considers his prose treatise on the solitary life, or the one which he calls *On the Remedies for either Fortune,* not to mention others. Herein all that is clear and holy in the bosom of moral philosophy is presented in so majestic a style, that nothing could be uttered for the instruction of mankind more replete, more mature, nay, more holy.[27]

xv, 6: Boccaccio lists "many memorable works from [Petrarch's] hand in prose and verse . . . First his divine poem *Africa* . . . [which] still lies in his drawer awaiting publication. Second is his *Bucolics,* famous the world over. Third, the book of metrical epistles to his friends. Fourth are two great volumes of letters in prose, so replete with thought and fact, so resplendent with artistic embellishment, that no fair-minded reader would judge them in any respect inferior to Cicero's. Fifth are his *Invectives against the Physician.* Sixth his book *On the Solitary Life.* And then

qui paucis post diebus in lucem nouissimum uenturus est, *De remediis ad utranque fortunam.*

the latest one which will see the light within a few days, *De remediis ad utranque fortunam.*"[28]

3. 1360. December 1. *Fam.* xxiii, 12, to Guido Sette, Archbishop of Genoa, 13–14:

. . . in hoc unum et philosophi omnes et experientia et veritas ipsa consentiunt: in rebus asperis, seu mala seu incommoda dici mavis, patientie unicum esse remedium; indignatio enim et querele et muliebris eiulatio et luctus, preterquamquod viros dedecent, ipsum quoque dolorem non leniunt sed acerbant. Sicut contra prosperis in rebus, seu bona illa seu commoda dici placet, unum est remedium, modestia, cuius freno letitie gestientis impetum teneamus; de quibus simul remediis ambobus nuper nescio quid latiusculum ut scriberem, mens incidit et feci. Quem libellum habuisses, nisi quia et ego iam scribendi fessus et adiutor nullus.

. . . but all philosophers, all experience, and truth itself agree on this: In times of hardship—you may prefer to speak of "ills" or *incommoda*—disadvantages—the one remedy is patience. Indignation, complaints and effeminate wailing and grieving not only are unbecoming to a man [Cicero, *Tusc. disp.* ii, 13, 31]; they also do not soothe, but aggravate the pain. Just as against times of prosperity—you may wish to speak of "goods" or *commoda*—advantages [cf. DR ii, 114, note 28]—the only remedy is *moderation* [Fam. i, 8, 9, as in DR i, 41, note 7] that allows us to bridle the ardor of excessive pleasure [DR ii, 90, note 53. On the whole statement, DR i, Pref., note 41]. It has come to my mind—I do not know how recently—that I should write somewhat more extensively about both these remedies. And now I have done it. You would have this little book [cf. Rawski (1967), p. 1, and n. 2], were it not for the fact that I am now tired of writing and without an assistant.[29]

4. 1361. Paris. Petrarch's congratulatory mission to King John of France on behalf of Galeazzo Visconti.[30]

On January 13, Petrarch delivered his oration in the royal palace in the presence of the king and Prince Charles. He spoke of Fortune as

> magnum aliquid et magne potencie, quam in concutiendo statum ac requiem summi regis et regni omnium maximi, quorum vexacio et adversitas totum pene terrarum orbem et omnium fidelium ac bonorum corda concussit,

> something momentous and of great power, as she shatters the position and the peace of mind of his supreme Majesty and all other great kings, whose distress and misfortune upsets nearly the entire world and the hearts of all loyal and good people,

referred to *constantia fortune ad utramque partem*—the perseverance of Fortune of either kind,[31] and presented the king with two rings, as gifts from Galeazzo.[32]

5. 1362. March. Emperor Charles IV invited Petrarch to visit him in Prague. In a separate letter, LAP no. 69, the imperial chancellor Jan ze Středa urged Petrarch to accept the invitation:

> Veniat, queso, tecum liber ille qui loquitur utriusque fortune remedium. Veniant et alia arche tue grata pigmentaria, quibus melius nosti imbecilles animos sacre tue doctrine remedio confoveri.[33]

> I beg you to bring with you the book called *utriusque fortune remedium*. And to bring also any other soothing ointments in your medicine chest which, as you are able to judge best, will strengthen our faltering minds with the remedy of your sacred doctrine.

6. 1366. September 1. *Sen.* v, 4 (1581: 801) to Donato Albanzani, his life-long Venetian friend (Wilkins [1961], esp. pp. 200, 210, 223), who translated *De vir. ill.* into Italian (Razzolini [1874, 1879]):

> Ea ipsa hora, qua litterae illae uenerunt tuae, in libello meo de Remediis, animo simul ac digitis intentus eram, festino enim, ut eum tibi si detur absolutum feram, & iam fini proximus sum. Casus autem fuit, ut tunc maxime tractatum illum scriberem, qui est de Auditu perdito. Itaque nullus, nisi quae ibi dicta ueram transcribendi labor erat, gratia illi, qui largitor sensuum, seruatorque, te nostri remedii non egentem fecit, meque dubium an ad tempus euenisse gaudeam.

> At the very hour your [two] letters arrived, I was with mind and hand at work on my little book *de Remediis*. I am hurrying, so that, God willing, I can have it for you in finished form. And I am already close to the end. Just then, it so happened that I was writing the chapter on the Loss of Hearing [DR ii, 97]. Yet none that I wrote is worth the bother to transcribe, thanks to Him, the giver and protector of our senses, who created you not in want of our remedy—and I still enjoy being in doubt when that time will come for me.[34]

7. The Fossadolce explicit of 1398. Venice, Biblioteca Marciana, Zan. lat. 475.[35]

When Petrarch had finished his work on the *DR*, he dated his manuscript with an explicit at the end of his text, which has been preserved by a later copyist:

Deo gracias. Scriptus et completus manu/ mea francisci[ni] de fossadulci notarij ciuis tarui/ sini. Taruisij anno Nativitatis dominice Millesi/ motrecentesimononagesimo octauo. Indictione sexta. die Martis. XII. Nouembris. hora septima Ex/ origina[li] proprio scripto manu Indelende me/ morie domini Francisci petrarce dignissimi laureati/ et per eum ipsum ad exitum perducti. Ticini. anno Do/ mini MCCCLXVI. IIIJ nonas Octobris hora tertia./ Amen.[36]

Thanks to the Lord. Written and completed with my hand by me, Franceschino da Fossadolce, notary and citizen of Treviso. Treviso, in the year of the Lord 1398, sixth *indictio*,[37] Tuesday, November 12, at the seventh hour. [about 1 p.m.]. From the original, written with his own hand by Francesco Petrarca, the most revered Laureate of everlasting memory, and finished by him, at Pavia, in the year of the Lord 1366, on the fourth day before the Nones of October, at the third hour [October 4, 1366, at about 9 a.m.]. Amen.

The Fossadolce Explicit. Tuesday, November 12, 1398. Venice, Bibl. Marc., Zan. lat. 475 (= 1660). Foto Toso.

8. 1367. November 9. *Sen.* viii, 3 (1581: 836–838; and, in part, *DR* ii, Pref., note 91):

. . . ego autem peccator, & utrumque secularibus olim studiis occupatus, millies
nomen. Hoc literulis meis inseruisse uideor, nempe quo & uulgi ora, & doctorum
libros hominum plenos noceram, quin etiam adeo me nominis huius non poenituit, ut
nouissime de utriusque fortunae remediis, libellum scripserim, non fortunam
duplicem, sed bifrontem statuens, de quo libro quid aliis uideatur, eorum sit iuditium,
qui audierint, aut legerint. Ego ex quo ad exitum ductus est, nec ex illo profunde
aliquid degustaui, nec experiri fuit, quantum meis ipse consiliis adiuuare, eo tamen
mihi probatior factus est, quo illum quibusdam magnis ingeniis gratum ualde, &
optatum sensi.

I, a sinner, engaged only in secular studies, have been known to insert [the name of
Fortune] a thousand times into my insignificant writings, since I knew it was in the
mouths of the crowd and in many books by learned men. In fact, that name worries
me so little that I used it in a small book I have written most recently on remedies for
both fortunes, which refers not to two kind of fortunes, but to Fortune's two faces [cf.,
e.g., Machaut, *Remede de Fortune* 2407–2410 and 2779–2780]. What others may
think of the book is for them to decide, as they hear it read or read it themselves. I,
who have seen it through to completion, do not find anything profound in it, nor
much to aid me in my own considerations. However, it has become somewhat more
acceptable to me, since I understand that it appears most pleasing and desirable to
some great minds.[38]

9. 1367 or later. *Sen.* viii, 7 (1581: 841–842), to Federigo Aretino.

This letter to a minor poet deals with the advantages of country life as compared to
life in the city, that rural

uita illa de qua olim, dum ea frui licuit,[39] non pauca disserui.

life about which I had quite a few things to say in the old days, when I was allowed to
enjoy it.[40]

The text refers to topics and topical sequences in the *DR,* Books i and ii, without
specific reference, but uses the phraseology of the *DR.*[41] It addresses Federigo's
complaint that *non perdius modo, sed pernox, ac perpetuus clangor te anserum in-
quietat*—not just all day long, but throughout the night, the constant honking of the
geese bothers you—pointing to the historical significance of the watchfulness of
the geese that awakened M. Manlius Capitolinus in time to repel the night attack of
the Gauls on the Roman Capitol (390 B.C.), and stressing the much greater annoy-
ance caused by a raucous mob. It suggests that Federigo imagine he hears instead
the angelic trumpet (*DR* i, Pref., note 56) summoning him to resist vice in *saluber-
rima cogitatio*—wholesome reflection—a remedy[42] that suggested itself *quod nuper
dum de remediis scriberem* . . . —as I recently wrote *de remediis* . . . [43]

    As summarized in table 1 (below, vol. v, *References*) this evidence suggests that
Petrarch began writing the *DR* sometime in 1354, apparently not long before he
received Jean Birel's letter.[44] If we admit *indirect evidence,* and accept the incum-

bent risks of interpretation, which at present are rather high as far as Petrarch's Latin texts are concerned, it would seem possible that Petrarch's planning, if not writing, activities began a few years earlier, probably after the plague of 1348–1349.[45]

Boccaccio may have seen the manuscript, titled *De remediis ad utranque (utramque) fortunam*,[46] on one of his visits to Petrarch, possibly the one in 1359, when he copied the *Bucolicum carmen*.[47] This first version of the *DR* was complete by the end of 1360 and, most likely, was prefaced by the dedicatory letter to Azzo da Correggio. Petrarch continued to work on the book, revising and rearranging the text,[48] and, perhaps, adding some new dialogues—*Sen.* v, 4, item 6, above, seems to suggest the latter. Further revisions may have been made after 1366.[49] That the work on the *DR* must have been intermittent is indicated by Petrarch's other activities between 1354 and 1366 (table 2, below, vol. v, *References*), which provide a highly realistic basis for Boccaccio's hyperbolic statement that

> quo neminem magis redimentem non dicam tempus set quoscumque temporis laben-tis athomos noscimus.

> no one has saved and employed to better advantage—I will not say, his time, but every crumb of it, than [Petrarch].[50]

On September 1, 1366, writing *DR* ii, 97—possibly to be inserted together with dialogues *DR* ii, 94–96 and 98–104 between *DR* ii, 93, *De tristitia et miseria* and the group of dialogues devoted to the seven deadly sins (*DR* ii, 105–111), within the area of the text where, presumably, he had started twelve years earlier (item 1)—he was *fini proximus*—close to the end (item 6). Slightly more than a month later, Petrarch completed the manuscript of this second version, which he had titled prior to March 1362 (item 5), and perhaps as late as after his return from Paris (item 4), *De remediis utriusque Fortune*. He dated the manuscript at Pavia, in the morning of October 4, 1366 (item 7). Since 1367, Petrarch referred to the "recent" writing of the *DR* as a past event.

iii. ❖ THE TEXT, THE TRANSLATION, AND THE NOTES

PETRARCH'S LATIN TEXT

In the absence of a critical edition of the *DR*,[51] I established somewhat extem-pore a working text primarily based on a collation of the Cremona edition of 1492 and the *Opera* of 1581.[52] A comparison with the printed independent editions of 1468[53] and 1490,[54] which is a second edition, reprinting even the major errors of 1468, and the versions in the *Opera* of 1496, which relies on 1492, and of 1501, which all but reprints the text of 1496,[55] implemented the basic text. At a later date, the text was checked against three manuscript sources: Venice, Marc. Zan. lat 475—the Fossadolce ms. of 1398;[56] the related ms. Florence, Laur. Strozz. 90,[57] as a neat early Quattrocento example of Ricci's redaction *W*; and Florence, Laur. Plut. 26, sin. 8, copied by Fra Tedaldo della Casa in 1379,[58] which represents Ricci's redaction *Z*.[59] Thanks to the courtesy of Professor Aldo S. Bernardo, I was also able to examine in 1983 the State University of New York at Binghamton manuscript of the *DR*—a mid- to late fifteenth-century text, apparently of Ricci's redaction *W*, described in Dziedzic (1981).

Notwithstanding its obvious limitations, this modest source material furnished a basic text of reasonable stability. It also led to certain conclusions, which, at the present stemma-less state of the *DR* manuscripts and casual filiation of early printed texts, are of a distinctly ancillary nature—yet in the absence of less parochial information useful enough to be briefly reported here.

A comparison of the texts in the independent *editio princeps* of 1468 and its offshoot of 1490, as well as of the *DR* texts in the collected works of 1496 and 1501, reveals the significance of the now neglected Cremona edition of 1492, which is superior to 1468 and 1490, and is the model followed in 1496 and, through the latter, also in 1501. D. W. Fiske thought that 1492 offered *virtually the text since followed* in all later editions.[60] Closer examination requires a less sweeping assessment, yet without challenge to the unexpected centrality of 1492 in the repertory of late fifteenth- and early sixteenth-century texts of the *DR*.[61]

This 1492 edition[62] was edited by Niccolò Lucaro of Cremona (d. January 8, 1515), a professor of eloquence, historian, and editor,[63] who tells us in his epistolary preface addressed to Marchesino Stanga, secretary to Lodovico Sforza, that he collated two copies of the *DR*, one

> superiori anno deformis concisus: & imperfectus,

> unsightly because of its great age, mutilated, and incomplete,

that fell into his hands and now goes forth to Marchisino, his former pupil, *reforma/tum redintegratumque*—transformed and restored[64]—and another one, brought to Cremona by Gian Filippo Melio, *iampridem*—long ago—and furnished to Lucaro, *non precario Sed sponte*—not on request, but because of his own inclination—by Gian Filippo's son, Gian Francesco. In this way, Lucaro recalls,

> quantum a publicae lectoris officio uacare li/ cuit ad integram lectionem reuocare conatus sum.

> as often as I could free myself from the duties of a public lecturer, I tried to restore the text in its entirety.[65]

If we accept this story, which is uncomfortably similar to that of Franciscus Caymus of Milan in his epistolary preface to the third edition of 1498 of *De vita solitaria,* and his

> neglected manuscript, worm holed and moth eaten, whose leaves fell apart as soon as he began to handle it,[66]

the question of text provenance suggests itself. Did Lucaro use manuscript or printed texts? If his first copy was in fact ancient, it had to be a manuscript. If in the early 1490s the Melio copy was from "long ago," it may also have been an older manuscript, although the Strasbourg edition could have been available in printed or longhand form.[67] Be that as it may, it is certain that at least one of the two exemplars must have offered a fairly sound text close to or identical with that of Venice, Marc. Zan. lat. 475, and Ricci's ms. group *W,* which seems to be followed more or less throughout 1492. Lucaro's text dominates in subsequent issues, particularly in the independent editions, nearly to 1600. It is, however, superseded in the *Opera* of 1554, edited by Johannes Herold of Basel,[68] who, while continuing to rely on the old 1492 text in large measure, used also another source (or sources) containing a different text, which might have been related to that of Ricci's ms. group *Z* but certainly was not identical with it.[69]

The Translation

As I stated in one of my earliest Petrarchan efforts nearly twenty years ago,

> the first objective in making the translation . . . was to render the Latin original in simple modern English. To do this in close adherence to Petrarch's text was a second, subordinate objective.[70]

These tasks, quite obviously, involve Petrarch's Latin text, the translator, and the resulting translation. The translator has to establish what the text says and what that which it says means, and, having negotiated this *brute ontological fact,*[71] as far as his source and its language is concerned, has to produce a statement of meaning in the target language that is adequate in terms of both the text it translates and the readers of the translation.[72] In this encounter success or failure of the translation depend on the translator's ability to bring to fruition the contact of minds involved,[73] to understand and, in a process of inward mimesis as it were, to express fittingly in the target language the *materia*—subject matter of his source, its *res* and *verba*—that which is being said and how it is being said, as well as the *aptum* ("what is fitting")[74]—the notion of appropriateness that governs the text.[75] This holds for any text.[76] But it poses particular problems with texts in which *res, verba,* and *aptum* reflect a distinctly different basic stance, a different structuring of experience, a different cosmos.[77]

In Petrarch's case this involves his meaning requirements—linguistic, referential, and emotive[78]—and his intellectual native grounds with its subjects, topics, trends, and modes, as well as the established meaning requirements, and the intellectual native grounds of his age. The translator is first and foremost confronted by Petrarch's text, its manifest vocabulary, syntax, phraseology, usage, techniques of formulation and text development, expository devices, patterns of imagery, and the literary genre used.[79] Yet even here, at the outer surface of the text, we face the challenge of meaning beyond mere lexicality. Pithy phrases, loaded terms, allusions, not to speak of irony and humor, have to be recognized as such, which creates a need to seek out, grasp, and express what is not stated in the words of the text but is nevertheless there—ever tentative for us today but exasperatingly overt and self-understood for Petrarch and his reader. Thus translation becomes *commentary in action,*[80] with an omnipresent residual risk of misprision[81]—and at the end of a long day with a long text a tired translator is ready to entertain views akin to Roger Bacon's and Dante's negative assessment of all translation.[82]

The present effort toward an English translation of Petrarch's *DR* proceeded in close adherence to Petrarch's text, and tried to negotiate the challenge of its multi-layered difficulties by comparing it with other, related texts, Petrarchan or otherwise; by seeking out textual parallels and echoes; by observing the topical nodes and verbal intersections in this network; and by preparing as best as my competencies allowed the grounds for a reasonably sound reading of the text—this not without awareness that even such a careful procedure involves "acts of more or less conscious, or more or less declared, restatement and interpretation."[83]

The translation attempts to be responsive to the text and my reading of it. I have tried to keep the English vocabulary consistent and to parallel the syntactic and rhetorical characteristics and figures of diction of the original as much as possible. But I have avoided casting the English text into nonidiomatic patterns, even though this required changing, with varying degrees of empathy and skill, the sentence structure of certain passages. Similarly, I observed, and sometimes laboriously collated, text passages to determine Petrarch's usage, but refrained from quasi-scientific procedures to fix exact Latin-English word equivalents and to force the English text into a straitjacket that fails to do justice to the subtle chiaroscuro of Petrarch's choice of words.

In sum, the dominant purpose in making this translation was to *present* Petrarch's work to the English reader—to make it possible for the reader to encounter Petrarch's thought and manner of organizing and expressing it in a key document of the late Trecento—and to do so on Petrarch's terms. Yet, notwithstanding my care and dedication as translator, this version is not exempt from the *caveat* of a prefatory note Horace Rackham included in the monumental translation of Pliny's *Naturalis historia*:

This translation is designed to afford assistance to the student of the Latin text; it is not primarily intended to supply the English reader with a substitute for the Latin.[84]

THE NOTES

Besides serving the customary purposes of identifying citations, references, and allusions, supplying explanatory commentary and bibliographic information for those who wish to pursue further the subject matter under consideration, and providing needed cross references in the text, the notes for the DR must furnish support for both Petrarch's text as it stands and Reason's avowed purpose in that text as far as her discussant and the reader are concerned. The two issues are interdependent.

Unlike other Petrarchan Latin texts, such as the *Secretum,* the text of the DR has still not received adequate attention by modern scholars. Consequently, we remain ill equipped to read the DR.[85] Apart from the limited indexes in the early editions,[86] which are geared to another intellectual and educational climate, and difficult to access and use for today's reader, and several later summaries of varying accuracy and value, we actually lack the immediate wherewithal to read the dialogues as they are. The only inclusive effort "of any substance"[87] in our times is Heitmann (1958)—and even that magisterial study is hard to use and not necessarily responsive to the inquisitive reader's specific questions concerning such matters as topics, maxims, examples and their patterns, phraseology, imagery, and, above all, historical and literary source materials and backgrounds. These difficulties are increased by the polymath scope of Petrarch's work and its encyclopedic approach—which only too often forced me to trespass into specialized fields far removed from my academic upbringing and experience. Yet, without taking such risks, a useful modern edition of Petrarch's *Remedies* is simply not possible.

In the dialogues Reason often refers to subject matter, examples, and so on, in a, to us, curiously brief, allusive way, for example, by naming only a main protagonist or a place, with the stated intent that her discussants and the readers recall the stories or situations so labeled from their well-stocked memories[88] or learn more about them by consulting books or persons able to enlighten them.[89] Without this added dimension of related information, Reason's exemplification often deteriorates into tedious listing which does not illustrate[90] but beclouds the argument—at least as far as today's reader is concerned.[91] The present edition supplies in the notes much of the needed information from the text sources Petrarch knew and used, or indicates where this information can be found in the literature, in an attempt to make it possible for us, so unprepared for pre-Cartesian argument by analogy and the holistic protocol of the medieval house of intellect, to come a little closer to reading the *DR* as Petrarch intended it to be read.[92] The indexes should also be helpful in this respect.

Petrarch's reader reads—and rereads—slowly, thoughtfully, as an active partner, engaged in continuous dialogue with a text that often demands not only casual acquaintance with the historical scenes, authors, and works referred to but also a thorough knowledge of specific texts and text passages. Not infrequently Reason's allusions require the grasp of a textual phrase (for example, a line by Virgil, or a scriptural snippet) for a meaningful reading or a savoring of an artful passage. Petrarch and his contemporaries admired the tenacious memory and sensitive ear this required,[93] and Reason's idiom challenges the modern reader (including an editor, painfully aware of his shortcomings in this respect) *sub specie ludi*—as a game, in the full sense of Huizinga's *sinnvoller Funktion* and *geistiger Betaetigung.*[94]

This is the first reason for including in the notes the full text of many passages and background materials in order to assist the reader. A second one was to make possible a sampling of the literary ecology, as it were, of Petrarch's house of intellect and to provide a smattering of the web of thought that, for Petrarch and his contemporaries, linked ideas, topics, and notions over the centuries, and entailed the silent contexts of a "literacy" which, to a large degree, today's educated readers are lacking. A sturdier practicality, but wholly consonant with the purposes of this edition, speaks from Daniel Georg Morhof's grounds for a similar arrangement in his long-lived *Polyhistor:*[95]

> Loca Scriptorum saepe integra adduxi, non ut chartas implerem, sed iis subvenirem, qui libris destituuntur, & pleniorem ex ipsorum Scriptorum verbis sensum excuterent lectores.

> I cite passages from the literature in their entirety, not to fill my pages, but to assist those who are deprived of books, and readers who seek a better understanding based on the author's own words.

The bibliographic apparatus in the notes (listed by author, editor, or title, followed by publication date in parentheses) brings together a selection of relevant materials prior to 1986. It cannot be limited to English-language publications, but gives preference to them. In most instances the cited works contain further significant bibliographic and source information, a fact seldom indicated in the notes, but important to remember, since, in the case of the *DR*, scope and size of the pertinent literature are enormous—and had to be sharply limited. A similar constraint holds for parallel and background texts from antique and medieval sources, as well as Petrarch's own works.[96]

iv. ❖ THE ILLUSTRATIONS

Book illustration serves a number of purposes, although there is inevitably a pictorial penumbra—aesthetic, artistic, decorative—that attaches to the object equipped with illustrations. Like glosses and notes, illustrations can function as supportive tools strengthening the position of the reader vis-à-vis a text.

For today's reader of the *DR*, such a visual dimension is of particular importance. Not only does it afford concrete contact and a resultant measure of familiarity with the artifacts, objects, and artistic traits and inclinations directly related to a text that, for us, is distant and strange in many respects—it may also suggest the visual vocabulary the educated reader of Petrarch's time would have associated with certain subjects, concepts, topics, and notions as he encountered them in the *DR*—and thus assist us further in our bid for shared reason and recognition.[97] On the other hand, the direct link with the text may help overcome the unrelated side-by-side of pictorial specifics. Text and illustrations may combine to body forth the world of the *DR* and to make it more accessible for us.[98]

In order to make this possible, our small *musée imaginaire*[99] includes mostly items prior to 1400, among them many artifacts and objects Petrarch did see or could have seen. The far-flung panorama of the *DR* provides many more places for illustrations than could possibly be filled. I only hope that those offered here will indeed "illustrate" the text, as they assist us in our exploration of Petrarch's great book—and widen our perspective with glimpses of a past that may now be *a foreign country*,[100] but has much to offer . . .

NOTES

INTRODUCTION TO THE COMMENTARY

1   Petrarch's spelling of his title varies. I have adopted the capitalized form *Fortune* in keeping with his remarks in *Sen.* viii, 3, Introduction ii, item 8; and the spelling in *Sen.* xvi, 9, ibid., item 1.

2   The book was reissued unchanged in Eger, 1758. Cf. Fiske (1888), no. 28.

3   The full title of Twyne's translation is

> Phisicke / against For/ tune, aswell pro/ sperous, as aduerse, con/ teyned in two/ Bookes./ Whereby men are instructed, with lyke in/ differencie to remedie theyr affections, aswell in/ tyme of the bryght shynyng sunne of pros-peritie,/ as also of the foule lowryng stormes of aduer/ sitie. Expedient for all men, but most ne/ cessary for such as be subiect to any/ notable insult of eyther extre/ mitie. Written in Latine/ by Frauncis Petrarch, a/ most famous Po/ et, and Ora/ tour./ And now first Englished by/ Thomas Twyne./ At London, printed by Richard/ watkyns. An. Dom./ 1579.

On the Twyne and Da San Miniato translations, Fiske (1888), no. 51; Fowler (1916), pp. 18, 24; P. G. Ricci in *Prose* (1955), pp. 1169–1171; and Rawski (1967), pp. 13–15. There is a second Italian translation, *De rimedi de l'una et l'altra fortuna,* by Remigio Nannini da Firenze, Venice, Gabriel Giolito de Ferrari, 1549, reissued 1584, 1589, and 1607 (Fowler [1916], pp. 24–25; Ricci, ibid., p. 1071). On translations of the *DR* into Czech, Dutch, French, German, Hungarian, and Spanish, cf. Fowler (1916), pp. 17–26; and *Petrarch* (1974), pp. 23–28.

4   Cf. Wilkins (1955), chap. 12. —A rough count of full text editions between 1470 and 1756 shows some 27 printings of the *DR* as compared to more than 200 issues of the *Rime* and the *Trionfi* (Fiske [1888]; Fowler [1916], pp. 12–15, 71–118; *Petrarch* [1974], pp. 19–22, 93–129). Note also Mann (1971), pp. 57–58, and n. 4; and Heitmann (1958), pp. 11–14. On the Quattrocento editions of the Canzoniere and the *Triumphs,* Wilkins (1951), chap. 24. For Petrarch's own opinion on *hoc vulgare et vulgatum genus*—this

common and widely accepted kind of [vernacular] poetry—*Sen.* v, 2 (1581: 793–796); Wilkins (1951), pp. 291–292; Mann (1984), pp. 54–55; and Foster (1984), esp. pp. 27–28, 33–34.

5   On this, E. Bonnora in Binni (1962), i, pp. 124–141; and Handschin (1964), chap. 3, 1.

6   Cf. below, Bibliography.

7   P. G. Ricci in *Prose* (1955), p. 1169.

8   Wilkins (1954), p. 91; Jasenas (1974), p. 14.

9   Cf. Boccaccio, *Geneal. deor.* xiv, 10, as below, ii, item 2. On Lapo da Castiglionchio, Piur (1925), pp. 333–334. On Jan ze Středa and Emperor Charles IV, Burdach (1929), pp. 28–40; and Piur (1933), pp. xlii, xlvi–xlvii, and no. 29, 29–31 (= LAP no. 69), as ii, item 5, below. Coluccio Salutati referred to the *DR* as a *sacrum opus* (*Epistolario* i [1891], p. 180). —The earliest translation of the *DR*, into French, was made by Jean Daudin for King Charles V in 1378 (Mann [1969], pp. 9–13; Fowler [1916], p. 18; Fiske [1888], no. 54). On Cardinal Ammannati, Voigt, i (1880), p. 153. On Jean Birel, Wilkins (1961), pp. 138–140; and ii, item 1, below.

10   Cf. *Fam.* xxiii, 15, 2:

> . . . veri potius appetens, licet acris, quam blandi alloquii ac mulcentis.

> . . . to have the truth, though it be bitter, rather than flattering and soothing encouragement.

Note also *Fam.* iii, 13, 11, as in *Dramatis personae,* note 19.

11   Cf. *Dramatis personae*; and Rawski (1967), pp. 5–9. On the *DR*, the basic Petrarchan studies by E. H. Wilkins listed in the Bibliography, and the summary in Wilkins (1961), pp. 138–140, 173, 178, 182, 205; Heitmann (1958); and Gerosa (1966); Diekstra (1968), pp. 16–31; Deyermond (1961), chap. 1, and the literature cited there; Schottlaender (1975), pp. 9–45; and Koerting (1878), pp. 542–564. Note also Bergin (1970), pp. 130–134; P. O. Kristeller in Hempfer (1983), pp. 116–121; Foster (1984), esp. pp. 158–161; Scheidig (1955), pp. 12–13; and the references in Trinkaus (1970) and Johannes von Tepl, *Ackerm.*, Bernt & Burdach (1917).

12   On this, Wenzel (1984), pp. 6–8; H. F. North in Wiener (1973), iv, pp. 365–378; and Lottin, iii (1949), pp. 154–194. Note also Sarton (1949), C. N. J. Mann in Bolgar (1971), chap. 22; Meinel (1972); and Gruber (1978), pp. 24–29.

13   Wilkins (1962), p. v, observes regarding the *Trionfi* that their

> extraordinary immediate success came to them because to their first readers they seemed at once familiar and novel—familiar in their concern with love and in their visionary character, novel in their vivid evocation of dimly remembered persons and processions of the ancient world.

In many respects Wilkins' oxymoron holds true also of other Petrarchan works, foremost among them, the *Secretum*; the *De viris illustribus,* and the *Rerum memorandarum libri* (Martellotti [1983], pp. 375–376). —Note Mann (1984), pp. 20–22.

14 *Sen.* viii, 3 (1581: 837), as in DR ii, Pref., note 91. The therapeutic value of statements of moral analysis and advice was widely accepted in Petrarch's time. Cf. *Dramatis personae,* note 19; and DR i, 11, note 19, and ii, 84, note 1.

15 Cf., e.g., the "dark picture of the conditions in Italy" in *Fam.* xix, 9, written April 24, 1355, to Guido Sette, Wilkins (1958), pp. 94–95, Wilkins (1961), p. 146.

16 On this, among a large number of publications, Nolhac (1907); B. L. Ullman (1955), chap. 6; Gerosa (1966); Martellotti (1983), chaps. 41 and 47; and the remarkable study *La Tradizione del Testo di Livio e le Origini dell' Umanesimo* by Giuseppe Billanovich.

17 Nolhac (1907), i, p. 16; Curtius (1953), p. 467; Bolgar (1954), pp. 252–255; Mann (1984), esp. pp. 18, 28; Lowenthal (1985), pp. 72, 81–84.

18 DR i, 29, note 17, i, 44, note 3, i, Pref., note 34.

19 Mann (1971), pp. 58–59.

20 Ibid. Note also idem (1975), pp. 139–141, and the manuscript texts listed and described in the catalogue of this work. The corpus of Florence manuscripts is briefly analyzed by P. G. Ricci in *Prose* (1955), pp. 1170–1171; and Ricci (1955). For mss. in the U.S. (Jasenas [1974]), France, West Germany, the Vatican library, Biblioteca civica, Trieste, and the libraries of Leningrad, see the volumes of the Censimento dei codici Petrarcheschi, edited by Giuseppe Billanovich since 1964 for the Ente nazionale Francesco Petrarca and the Commissione per l'Edizione nazionale through Antenore, Padua.

21 Cf. Bibliography iii.

22 Cf. Wilkins (1958), pp. 65–72.

23 Lewis (1978), pp. 92–93. On this, Gerosa (1966), pp. 151–153.

24 Cf. DR ii, 93, 26-35, and note 7.

25 Cicero, *De off.* iii, 1, 1; *De vita sol.* ii, as in DR i, 21, note 6.

26 Cf. Osgood (1930), p. xiii, n. 2; Branca (1976), p. 109.

27 Reedy (1978), pp. 46–47; Osgood (1930), pp. 53–54. On this, Bergin (1981) pp. 238–239. The translation *remedies for* is based upon contemporary usage, which is *remedia fortunae,* as in DR version 2, or *remedia ad,* as in *DR,* version 1; and *remedia contra*—remedies against—as in *Sen.* viii, 3, note 14, above. Twyne (1579) has *Phisicke against* in the title and the running heads for Book ii, but *Phisicke for* in the running heads for Book i.

28 *Genealogia,* Romano (1951), ii, p. 710; Osgood (1930), p. 116.

29 On this, note *Fam.* iii, 16, to Paganino da Bizzozzero of Milan, as in DR ii, 67, note 31. Paganino died of the plague, May 23, 1349 (Wilkins [1961], p. 83). The letter is of uncertain date; the phraseology is that of the 1350s. On *patientia* and *modestia,* DR i, Pref., note 40.

30   Wilkins (1958), pp. 220–225; idem (1961), pp. 173–176.
31   Barbeu du Rocher (1854), pp. 216–219; Godi (1965), pp. 45–83.
32   On this, *DR* i, 37, note 32.
33   Piur (1933), no. 29, p. 139.
34   In his first letter, Donato had reported that he was ill and losing his hearing; in his second, that he had recovered (Wilkins [1959], pp. 102, 107).
35   Mann (1971), no. 132.
36   Cf. Koerting (1878), p. 542, n. 1; Voigt (1880), i, p. 135, n. 2; Heitmann (1957), p. 17; Wilkins (1958), pp. 235–236; Sambin (1958), p. 368; Wilkins (1959), p. 108; Rawski (1967), pp. 2 and 98, nn. 11, 12; and the moot debate between Alberto del Monte and Pier Giorgio Ricci (Ricci [1955], pp. 165–166). Even a superficial examination of the Venice manuscript reveals a number of traits that deserve paleographic and text-critical analysis much closer than that so far accorded it.
37   The indictio pontificalis is a number which indicates the place of a given year within a cycle of 15 years, predicated on 3 B.C. (Thus A.D. 1398, plus 3 = 1401, divided by 15 = 93, with a remainder of 6; hence the *indictio* for 1398 is 6, i.e., 1398 is the sixth year in the ninety-third cycle of *indictiones*). Leist (1893), pp. 281–284; Grotefend (1872), p. 64.
38   Cf. *Fam.* xx, 7, 6, on Moggio dei Moggi, to Francesco Nelli, Milan, April 11, 1359:

> . . . nugellas meas, quas epystolas quidam vocant quasque nunc maxime cuiusdam ingeniosi hominis et amici digitis coacervo . . .

> . . . my trifles—some call them letters—that I am now collecting with the help of a gifted man and friend . . .

Bernardo (1985), p. 142; on this, Billanovich (1947), p. 22. —On a similar approval by great personages of the *De vita solitaria,* cf. Wilkins (1959), p. 103; and idem (1961), p. 204. Note also *Sen.* xvii, 3 (1581:540): *quae licet a multis & laudata, & expetita fuerit*—since my version [of *Griselda*] has been praised and requested by a number of readers.

39   Cf. Augustine, *De doct.* i, 4, 4, *PL* 34, c. 20:

> Frui enim est amore alicui rei inhaerere propter seipsam. Ubi autem, quod in usum venerit ad id quod amas obtinendum referre, si tamen amandum est.

> For to enjoy a thing is to rest with satisfaction in it for its own sake. To use, on the other hand, is to employ whatever means are at one's disposal to obtain what one desires, if it is a proper object of desire.

J. F. Shaw in *Augustine* (1952), p. 625. On *frui* and *uti, DR* i, 10, note 19.
40   A reference to *de vita solitaria,* begun in 1346 (Wilkins [1961], esp. pp. 54–55).

41   For example:

Sen. viii, 7	and, in the same sequence,	DR ii. Pref.:
cicadae stridulae		*cicadae stridulae*
rudentes aselli		*rudentes aselli* ...
vulgi fragor ac strepitus		*vulgaris clamor*

Fortuna ergo haec quae dicitur non thesauros, discussed in *DR* i, 55	
nec munitas arces,	i, 35
nec instructas classes,	i, 98
nec prevalidos horret exercitus	i, 97

42   As in *DR* ii, 90, 13–17 or 47–52. Note also *DR* ii, Pref. 220–231.

43   Petrarch's use of *nuper* is casual. In our documents, *nuper* appears in items 3 and 9. The stretch of *nuper* (with 1366 as year of reference) is shown by these examples: *DR* i, Pref. 162–164, mentioning rulers *et exules nuper captivos,* such as King John of France, captured by the English in the Battle of Poitiers, September 19, 1356 (item 4, above; *DR* i, 37, notes 31 and 32); *in acie caesos,* such as John, blind King of Bohemia, in the battle of Crécy, August 26, 1346 (*DR* ii, 96, 125–135, and notes 25, 26); *& laqueo enectos foedeque laniatos,* such as Andrew of Hungary, King of Naples, in 1345 (cf. *Fam.* vi, 5) and Cola di Rienzo (*DR* i, 89, 19–23), October 8, 1354; or *DR* i, 88, *apud vos nuper,* referring to the earthquakes which devastated Rome in 1349 and Basel, October 18, 1356. A similar *nuper* occurs in a second referral to the Basel earthquake in *DR* ii, 91. *DR* i, 89, describes the end of Cola di Rienzo as *nuper. Sen.* x, 2, written in 1367 (Wilkins [1959], pp. 129–131; Prose [1955], p. 1090), mentions Paris, *quo sum nuper ex negotio rediissem*—whereto, recently, I returned on an official mission (*Prose* [1955], p. 1108)—which took place 1360–1361. A prompt *nuper* opens the invective *Contra eum,* written in March 1373, with reference to events that occurred some months earlier (Wilkins [1959], pp. 237–240), but is followed by a reference to Cola di Rienzo and his *recent* attempt to buttress the republic with his weak shoulders (1581: 1071; Cosenza [1913], p. 244). For other examples, see Wilkins (1959), p. 158, n. 6; and Rico (1974), pp. 7, n. 1, 113, 186–188, 322, n. 242, 341, 405. An instructive sample of Boccaccio's usage is offered by C. G. Osgood, who points out that Petrarch's coronation as poet laureate in 1341 was referred to by Boccaccio about 1360 as *nuper* in *Genealogie* xv, 6, vi, 35; but in ibid. vii, 29, as *iam pridem*—a long time ago (Osgood [1930], pp. 191–192).

44   Petrarch's *cum adhuc nihil inceperim*—because I had not begun anything up to now—may indicate that *DR* ii, 93, was one of the first dialogues he wrote (P. G. Ricci in Prose [1955], p. 1169; Wilkins [1958], pp. 66, 70–71). —The date of *Sen.* xvi, 8 and 9, both to Jean Birel, has been established by Foresti, Ricci, and Wilkins as 1354 (Wilkins [1958], pp. 69–72). Heitmann (1957)

argued at length that the two letters were written in 1357. His argument is summarized in Wilkins (1958), pp. 69–71, where it is shown that 1354 is the more probable date (ibid., pp. 71–72; also Baron [1968], p. 97). Furthermore, Heitmann's assumption, shared by Foresti (1977, pp. 338–339), that the *DR* dialogues were written in the order in which they stand, is wholly at odds with (a) Petrarch's usual work procedure (cf., e.g., Wilkins [1951], esp. chaps. 8, 9; Ullman [1955], chap. 7; and Bergin [1977], Introd.); and (b) the fact that between the writing of *DR* ii, 93, and ii, 97, by Heitmann's chronology, nine years would have elapsed (with the remaining 38 dialogues to have been written between September 1 and October 4, 1366?). Nor is Heitmann's suggestion that the first version of the *DR* ended with *DR* ii, 93 supported by external or internal evidence: e.g., his *cesura molto profonda* in theme and treatment separating *DR* ii, 93, from the subsequent dialogues becomes much less incisive when viewed from a vantage point prior to ii, 93, such as ii, 82 or 90. *DR* ii, 92, clearly anticipates the dialogues on death beginning with ii, 117, as a topic, Reason says, *de quo nobis . . . antequam res desinat disceptandum reor*—I intend to discuss before we end these talks.

45   An overview of the texts affording—not fancifully posited and eloquently argued, but reliably established—indirect internal evidence would require the kind of careful study the present edition of the *DR* is, it is hoped, designed to encourage. At present, a modest sampling must suffice.

(a) Possible early references to the *DR* as such may be found in

Fam. vi, 3, 51, dated May 30, 1342 (Wilkins [1958], pp. 31–35; Foresti [1977], pp. 43, 99–100, 145):

> Et de paupertate quidem remedioque quod illa secum habet, hactenus. De animi autem moderatione patientiaque longior sermo est autoritatibus rationibus et exemplis instructus;

> But enough about poverty and the remedy it provides. Concerning moderation and patience [cf. *DR* i, Pref., note 41], however, a longer discourse is required—replete with authentic reasons and examples;

and in *Fam.* i, 9, 1, dating from August 1350 (Billanovich [1947], pp. 48–55):

> Animi cura philosophum querit, eruditio lingue oratoris est propria; neutra nobis negligenda, si nos, ut aiunt, humo tollere et per ora virum volitare propositum est. Sed de priore alibi; magna enim res est et labor ingens, sed messis uberrima.

> The care of the mind calls for a philosopher, instruction in the use of language is the domain of the orator [cf. *Sen.* iii, 8]. We must not neglect either one if, as they say, we are to *rise from earth and fly [victorious] upon the lips of men* [Virgil, *Georg.* iii, 9, LCL, Fairclough, p. 155]. But I shall deal with the care of

the mind elsewhere; for it is a great undertaking and an enormous labor, though very rich in harvest.

(On the Ciceronian distinction philosopher-orator, Seigel [1968], pp. 30, 39. n. 25, and chap. 2.) —Similar evidence is afforded in *Secretum* ii and iii.

Prose (1955), p. 122; Rico (1974), pp. 235–236; Baron (1985), p. 167; Baron (1968), pp. 96–98:

> [*Augustinus*]: Quotiens legenti salutares se se offerunt sententie, quibus vel excitari sentis animum vel frenari, noli viribus ingenii fidere, sed illas in memorie penetralibus absconde multoque studio tibi familiares effice; ut, quod experti solent medici, quocunque loco vel tempore dilationis impatiens morbus invaserit, habèas velut in animo conscripta remedia.

> [*Augustinus*]: Whenever you encounter in your readings any wholesome maxims by which you feel your spirit stirred or restrained [*DR* i, Pref., note 41], do not rely merely on the resources of your wits, but remand them to the inmost recesses of your memory, and make them familiar to you through hard effort, so that, like an experienced physician, no matter when or where some urgent case of illness arises, you have the remedy written, so to speak, in your head.

(Based on Draper [1911], pp. 99–100.) E. Carrara (*Prose* [1955], ibid.) refers to this passage as the argument *in nuce* of the *DR*.

Prose (1955), p. 128; Rico (1974), pp. 245–246; Baron, ibid.:

> [*Franciscus*]: Possum utique, si modo aliquid esset fortuna. Nam ut vides, inter graium et nostrum poetam hac de re tanta dissensio est ut, cum ille fortunam in operibus suis nusquam nominare dignatus sit, quasi nichil eam esse crederet, hic noster et sepe eam nominet et quodam in loco omnipotentem etiam vocet. Cui sententie et historicus ille nobilis favet et orator egregius. Nam et Crispus Salustius dominari profecto ait in re qualibet fortunam; et M. Tullius humanarum rerum dominam asseverare non timuit. Ego autem quid sentiam, aliud forte tempus ac locus alter fuerit dicendi.

> [*Franciscus*]: Yes, I am able, supposing always that there is any such thing as fortune at all. For I notice the two Greek and Latin Poets are so little of one mind on this point that the one [i.e., Homer] has not deigned to mention the word even once in all his works, whereas the other [i.e., Virgil] mentions the name of fortune often and even reckons her Almighty [*Aeneid* viii, 334; on this, Macrobius, *Saturn.* v, 16, 8]. And this opinion is shared by a celebrated historian and a famous orator. Sallust has said of fortune that "all things are under her dominion" [*Catil.* viii, 1]. And Cicero has not scrupled to affirm that "she is the mistress of human affairs" [*Pro Marc.* ii, 7]. For myself, perhaps I will declare what I think on the subject at some other time and place.

Draper (1911), pp. 104–105. Cf. *Sen.* viii, 3, as in *DR* ii, Pref., note 91. Note also *Prose* (1955), p. 112: *et extrema perpessis* . . . , Rico (1974), p. 211; *Prose* (1955), p. 120: *hec enim parcius* . . . ; and, weaker yet, p. 194: *Quid tamen tam grande* . . . —Unfortunately, none of these passages can be dated reliably. Petrarch revised the *Secretum,* begun in 1347 (on this, Baron [1985], esp. chaps. 1 and 2, 1), as late as 1358 (Wilkins [1961], p. 162; Wilkins [1958], pp. 176, 234; on the ongoing debate about the writing of the *Secretum* and the dates involved, Rico [1974], Martellotti [1983], chap. 42; Rico [1978], Martinelli [1982], Rico [1984], Foster [1984], pp. 179–185, Baron [1985]). Thus it is difficult to use any of the *Secretum* passages as points of reference for the progress of work on the *DR.* (On Petrarch as a writer *senza storia,* Bosco [1946], pp. 9–12, and Martellotti [1983], pp. 311–314; Binni [1954], pp. 159–160; Heitmann [1958], pp. 249–250; Baron [1968], pp. 10–13; and idem [1985], p. 69.)

Also into the group of hard-to-interpret references fall opaque text passages such as Nelli's letter xiv, to Petrarch of August 18, 1354 (Cochin [1892], pp. 220–221; Cochin [1901], pp. 126–127; Nolhac [1907], i, pp. 189–190), as quoted in Wilkins (1958), pp. 74–75:

> Dic michi quando te in Africa tua legam? quando in bucolicis omnibus? quando in comediis? et dyalogo? nec non et compendio illo et paratissimo ad ystorias generosas itinere?

> Tell me, when may I read you in your *Africa*? when, in all of the Bucolics? when in the comedies? and the Dialogue? and when, indeed, in that remarkable guide to the study of the histories of the eminent?

Wilkins, ibid., n. 16, points out:

> There is no reason to think that Petrarch ever wrote any comedy other than the lost *Philologia* [cf. *DR* ii, 83, note 40]. Cochin suggests that the "dialogue" may have been the *Secretum*: it is possible also that Nelli may have heard of the beginning of Petrarch's work on the *De remediis.* The "compendium" was doubtless the *De viris.*

(b) Striking anticipations of concepts and topics, phraseology, and quotations used in the *DR* occur in

Fam. vi, 3 of May 30, 1342, above;

Fam. vi, 5 of August 1, 1346;

Fam. iii, 16 of May 23, 1349—a short statement regarding patience (*DR* ii, 67, note 31), which seems to foresee related passages in *Fam.* xxi, 9 (as in *DR* ii, 84, note 13), of January 23, 1359—a veritable cento of *DR* phraseology and quotes; or references to *DR* topics, such as the one to *ingens ac multiplex leticia animi*—immoderate and manifold pleasure (cf. Cicero,

Tusc. disp. iii, as in *Dramatis personae*, note 11; DR ii, 90, note 53; and the diagram in DR i, Pref., note 41)—in

Fam. vii, 8, dating from December 1, 1352 (Di Benedetto [1949], pp. 61–62).

One of the seemingly "obvious" anticipatory texts,

Fam. xvii, 3, to Guido Sette, Milan, mid-September, 1353 (DR ii, Pref., note 82),

illustrates both the degree of close textual relationship and the related problem of interpretation:

Fam. xvii, 3

3	Heraclitic *nowhere on earth is life peaceful* (DR ii, Pref.)
5	Seneca and Cicero on suicide (DR ii, 118)
6	life assigned as is a soldier's duty (ibid.)
	patience overcomes (cf. DR i, Pref., note 41; ii, 84, note 13)
8	body as prison (DR i, 2, note 22)
10	to live in moderation, patience, and humility (DR i, Pref., note 41)
12–14	the greedy mind of the covetous
	contempt for riches (e.g., DR ii, 13)
20	forgetful of the human condition (e.g., DR i, 58, note 13)
22	error, companion of prosperity
23	Dame Reason
25	nothing remains the same for long (e.g., DR ii, 83, note 19)
27 and 33	Fortune's wheel
28	the victor vanquished (e.g., DR i, 22, note 7)
31 and 42	cities live longer than people, but they, too, age (DR ii, 69)
31	*utranque fortune faciem [vidisse]*
42	all that is born must die (Sallust, *Jug.* ii, 3)
46	*ubi sunt?* (DR i, 15, note 40)
48	even kingdoms are mortal (DR ii, 69, i, 16, note 4; note *Secretum* ii, Prose [1955], pp. 118, 120)

All these materials are familiar fare in the *DR*; some phrases are identical, and the same quotations recur. But are these the indications of a writer's stepwise progress as he works on his book, or are they, all or some, derived from an established repertory, hence not indicative of historical sequence? The contemporary stock of topics, maxims, examples, and quotations, coupled with the paramount need to rely on memory and association patterns much more so than in our times of "ready access," provides a static stratum which in its innate redundancy is puzzling and misleading in many ways when it comes to historical becoming and inference. Thus, for instance, the tracing of quotations, such as the Aristotle phrase in *DR* ii, Pref., 328–331, which occurs also in SN 6, "certainly written on 31 March . . . 1352" (Wilkins [1955], p. 111, n. 42), or Virgil, *Aeneid* viii, 334: *Fortuna omnipotens et ineluctabile fatum* . . . in *Fam.* vi, 5, 1 (1346)—*Fam.* xix, 9, 4γ (1355)—*Secretum* ii (*Prose* [1955], p. 128)—*Sen.* viii, 3 (1367), indicates hardly more than Petrarch's long-standing acquaintance with and continued attention to these lines.

Similarly, *Sen.* viii, 3 of November 9, 1367, offers in its second part (1581: 836–838; as in *DR* ii, Pref., note 91) an *ex post facto* summary of the Fortune topic a year or so after the completion of the *DR* in its revised form, which rehearses one of Petrarch's established topical repertories in great detail without revealing much information about its diachronic growth (cf. above, the *Secretum* passage, *Prose* [1955], p. 128). In this inclusive discussion, the conflicting opinions of Homer and Virgil are cited, followed by *omnipotens, Aeneid* viii, 334; and Sallust, Cicero, Augustine, and Juvenal are adduced, most of this appearing in Lactantius (*Div. inst.* iii, 29), whose subsequent commentary is quoted in Petrarch's text—which exemplifies the problem of provenance in the evidential interpretation of quotations of and allusions to earlier texts. (On Petrarch and Lactantius, Gerosa [1966], p. 161; and Nolhac [1907], e.g., i, pp. 183–184.)

46   The title phrase (cf. items 1, 2, 4, above) echoes Cicero, *De off.* ii, 6, 19:

> Magnam vim esse in fortuna in utramque partem, vel secundas ad res vel adversas, quis ignorat?

> Who fails to comprehend the enormous, twofold power of Fortune for weal and for woe?

LCL, Miller, p. 187. Quoted in Lactantius, *Div. inst.* iii, 29; Petrarch's Paris oration (1361), and *Sen.* viii, 3, above; and alluded to in *Fam.* iii, 16, as in *DR* ii, 67, note 31. Cf. *DR* i, Pref., note 39. —Niccolò Lucaro of Cremona, the learned editor of the 1492 edition of the *DR*, promptly noted in his prefatory letter to his former pupil Marchesino Stanga, secretary to Lodovico Sforza (1492, f. a, recto):

> . . . de remediis utriusque fortunae: cuius magnam uim esse in utramque partem a nemine ignorari ait Cicero.

> On the remedies for either Fortune, whose enormous, twofold power, said Cicero, no one can ignore.

—A surprising recurrence of *De remediis ad utramque fortunam* occurs in the abridged version, Brit. Mus., Landsdowne 781 (ca. 1400), Mann (1971), no. 170; Mann (1975), no. 128.

47   Wilkins (1961), pp. 163–164.

48   The revisions—which, in the light of Petrarch's work habits and other activities, seem to have been changes and additions in the text of version 1 rather than a total recasting (Baron [1985], pp. 80–86; note 44, above [a])—included the interpolation of references to events that took place after the writing of the original text, such as Petrarch's mission to Paris in *DR* ii, 37, and the second Lateran fire in *DR* ii, 55—both in 1361.

49   E.g., the St. Romuald reference in *DR* ii, 88, 57–59. —Petrarch's manner of revision may also be reflected in the two manuscript redactions, first pointed out convincingly—but never broadly established—by Pier Giorgio Ricci (*Prose* [1955], pp. 1170–1171, and Ricci [1955]; on this, also Billanovich [1947], pp. xxi, and 343), and exemplified in *DR* ii, 53, 56–62, and note 11. It is probable that the text changes in Ricci's ms. group W and, perhaps, some in his group Z (Ricci [1955], pp. 165–166) were introduced after 1366.

50   Boccaccio, *Geneal. deor.* xiv, 10, 38–40; Reedy (1978), p. 46; Osgood (1930), p. 53.

51   On Alberto del Monte's efforts toward a first critical edition of the Latin text for the Edizione Nazionale of Petrarch's works, cf. Rawski (1967), p. 98, n. 13; Ricci (1955), and Del Monte (1956); Heitmann (1957); and Mann (1971), p. 58.

52   Fiske (1888), nos. 8 and 5; Fowler (1916), pp. 13 and 1.

53   The *editio princeps,* Strassburg, Heinrich Eggesteyn, Fiske (1888), no. 6, *Petrarch: Catalogue* (1974), pp. 19–20; date in accordance with Mann (1971), pp. 57–58, n. 4.

54   Fiske (1888), no. 7; Fowler (1916), pp. 12–13; Mann, ibid.

55   Fiske (1888), nos. 1 and 2; Fowler (1916), pp. 1–3. On the Basel edition of 1496, and the use of sources printed in Italy by the publisher Johannes Amerbach, as well as Andrea Torresani's Venice edition of 1501, cf. Handschin (1964), pp. 68–73. On the contents of the two editions, also Deyermond (1961), chap. 2.

56   Mann (1971), no. 132; above, Introduction ii, item 7.

57   Mann (1971), no. 33.

58   Mann (1971), no. 28.

59   On this, *Prose* (1955), pp. 1170–1171; Ricci (1955); Mann (1971); and Dziedzic (1981). —Sincere thanks are due the Hill Monastic Manuscript Library, St. John's Abbey and University, Collegeville, Minnesota, and its director, Julian G. Plante, without whose ready and effective assistance this phase of my text preparation could not have been carried out. An enlarged, documented version of this Latin working text is now being prepared for publication.

60   Fiske (1888), p. 8.
61   Cf., e.g., the often reprinted 1515 edition, Venice, Alexander Paganinus
      (Fiske [1888], nos. 9–17; Fowler [1916], pp. 13–14), whose editor certainly
      knew the 1492 text.
62   The Cremona 1492 edition may be described as follows:

[f. i]		blank
[ii]r.		Tabula Rubricarum praecedentis libri. &c.
		[Dialogues 1–123, due to a printer's error: Dialogue cxv is fol-lowed by cxvii.]
[iii]r.		Explicit tabula Liber primus .d. Francisci Petrarcae de remediis utriusque fortunae.
[iii]v.		Incipit Tabula secundi libri.
		[Dialogues 124–255]
[iv]v.		Explicit Tabula. Liber secundus .d. Fra[ncisci]. Petrarcae de remediis utriusque fortunae.

[Gathering]

a.	r.	Ad magnificum splendidissimum uirum Marchisinum stangham: Ducalem Se/cretarium Nicolai Lucari Cremonensis Epistola.
a2.	r.	Francisci Petrarcae poetae oratorisque. Clarissimi de Remediis utriusque fortu/ nae: ad Azonem. Liber primus. Incipit.
a4.	v.	[BOOK I: Dialogues] i–ix.
b.	r.	10–xviiii
c.	r.	xx–xxviii
d.	r.	xxix–xxxii; followed by xxx. *De numeroso famulatu*; and xxxiv-xxxvii
e.	r.	xxxvii [ctd.]–xliii
f.	r.	xliii [ctd.]–li
g.	r.	lii–lxiii; followed by liiii. *De auiariis auibus loquacibus*
h.	r.	liiii [ctd.]; followed by lxv–lxxiii
i.	r.	lxxiiii–lxxxvii; followed by lxxxix and lxxxx. *De tranquillo statu*; followed by
k.	r.	lxxxx. *De Votiua portus apprehensione*–lxxxxiiii; followed by lxxxxvi. *De occupata tyrannide*; and lxxxxvi. *De regno et imperio*; followed by lxxxixviii [*sic*]. *De exercitu armato*; followed by
l.	r.	lxxxxviii. *De classe instructa*; and xcix–cix
m.	r.	cix [ctd.]–cxi; followed by cxiii, *De promissis aruspicum*; cxiii [re-peated]. *De laeto rumore*; and cxiiii. *De filii uel amici expectatione*; followed by an *unnumbered dialogue, De expectatione meliorum temporum*; followed by cxvii–cxx
n.	r.	cxxi–cxxiii. FINIS
n2.	r.	Clarissimi poetae et oratoris Francisci Petrarcae de/remediis for-tunae aduersae secundus liber incipit.

[BOOK II: Dialogues] cxxiiii–cxxv (All other text versions examined by me did not employ continuous numbering of the dialogues but, in Book ii, started again with Dialogue i.)

o. r. cxxvi–cxxvii; followed by cxxviii–cxxxii

p. r. cxxxiii–cxl

q. r. cxli–cli

r. r. clii–clxiiii

s. r. clxv–clxviii. *De discordi fratre*; followed on s2.v. by clxviii [repeated]. *De amisso patre*; and clxx. *De ammissa matre*; clxxi–clxxviii. *De incendio*

t. r. clxxix; followed on t. v. by clxxviii [repeated from above]. *De duro itinere*; followed on t2. v. by clxxxi. *De sterilitate annua*; and clxxxii–clxxxvii; followed by clxxxiii. *De tormentis,* repeating the number of the preceding [clxxxiii.] *De furtis*; and clxxxix–clxxxx

u. r. clxxxxi–cciiii

x. r. cciiii [ctd.]; ccv–ccxi

y. r. ccxii–ccxviiii

z. r. ccxx–ccxxxi

A. r. ccxxxii–ccxl

B. r. ccxl [ctd.]; ccxli–ccxlii; followed by ccxx. *De morte ante diem,* repeating the number of the preceding [ccxx.] *De auditu perdito*; and ccxliiii; followed by ccxl. *De ignominiosa,* repeating the number of the preceding.[ccxl.] *De metu mortis*

C. r. ccxlvi–ccliiii.

[EXPLICIT:] Accipe tandem candidissime lector diuinum Francisci Petrarcae: opus/ Nicolai Lugari industria sollerti Nitidissimum: Bernardini. de misintis Papiensis/ac Caesaris Parmensis sociorum diligenti opera. Impressum Cremonae. Anno/ Incarnationis dominice. 1492. die. 17. mensis Nouembris.

[Printer's mark]

63 Fiske (1888), p. 8.
64 1492: a. verso.
65 1492: ibid.
66 Fowler (1916), p. 31; Zeitlin (1924), pp. 16–17.
67 On the distribution of the early Petrarch editions, cf. Handschin (1964), esp. pp. 58–64, 69–70.
68 Fiske (1888), no. 4; Fowler (1916), p. 1. On this edition and its editor, Handschin (1964). pp. 78–80.
69 Cf. *DR* ii, 53, 56–62, and note 11. A case in point is ms. Florence, Laur. Plut. 26, sin. 8, which shows some of Ricci's readings for his group Z but offers a text identical with Venice, Marc. Zan. lat 475, the Fossadolce ms. of 1398,

and 1492 for *DR* ii, 53, 56–62. On the mss. related to Laur. Plut. 26, sin. 8, cf. Billanovich (1947), p. xxi.

70 Rawski (1967), p. 21.

71 Hirsch (1967), p. 210:

> The critic is right to think that the text should speak to us. The point which needs to be grasped clearly by the critic is that a text cannot be made to speak to us until what it says has been understood. This is not an argument in favor of historicism as against criticism—it is simply a brute ontological fact.

72 On this, e.g., Kelly (1979), chap. 4.

73 On the contact of minds in argumentation, Perelman (1969), pp. 14–17.

74 Cicero, *Orator* xxii, 74:

> decere quasi aptum esse consentaneumque tempori et personae; quod cum in factis saepissime tum in dictis valet, in voltu denique et gestu et incessu . . .

> 'Propriety' is what is fitting and agreeable to an occasion or person; it is important often in actions as well as in words, in the expression of the face, in gesture and in gait . . .

LCL, Hubbell, p. 361.

75 Rawski (1975), pp. 257–260; Rawski (1977), p. 2, and n. 9.

76 Cf., e.g., *Groupe μ* (1981).

77 Von den Steinen (1959), p. 5. —All this has often been explained and discussed—nowhere more comprehensively and felicitiously than in Steiner (1975).

78 Cf. Nida (1964), pp. 41–43, and chaps. 4, 5.

79 On Petrarch's latinity, Martellotti (1983), chap. 26; and Rawski (1967), p. 116, n. 129. Note also Baxandall (1971), chap. 1; and Scaglione (1972), chap. 2.

80 Steiner (1984), pp. 214, 294.

81 Von den Steinen (1959), p. 6:

> . . . Das Verstaendnis unsrer Vergangenheiten, das echte Gespraech mit ihnen ist unendlich schwer geworden.

Note also T. M. Greene in Rimanelli (1976), pp. 208–221.

82 On this, Kelly (1979), esp. pp. 214–218; and *Fam.* xviii, 2, 6, referring to a manuscript of Homer in Greek, which Petrarch received from Nicholas Sygeros in 1353, as

> non in alienum sermonem violento alveo derivatum, sed ex ipsis greci eloquii scatebris purum et incorruptum et qualis primum divino illi perfluxit ingenio.

> not in a strange language, as though funneled through a crude tideway, but pure and undefiled, from the very wellsprings of Greek eloquence, and as it originally flowed from [Homer's] divine mind.

—On Petrarch's own free translation into Latin of Boccaccio's story of the patient Griselda (*Decameron* x, 10), cf. *Sen.* xvii, 3, 4 (1581: 540–547); Wilkins (1961), pp. 236–238; and Bryan & Dempster (1958), pp. 288–331.

83 Steiner (1984), p. 294.

84 Pliny, *Nat. hist.*, LCL, ii, p. vii.

85 Rawski (1967), p. 23. Note also Mann (1971), p. 2.

86 Rawski (1967), p. 117, n. 131. On the index to the Latin works of 1496, Deyermond (1961), chap. 2. The later editions of the *Opera* have a somewhat spotty *rerum ac uerborum memorabilium, index utilissimus* (5 pp. in 1581), covering all the Latin works.

87 Mann (1971), ibid.

88 Cf. *DR* i, 8, esp. notes 2 and 12; and *DR* ii, 101, and note 4.

89 Cf., e.g., *DR* ii, 72, 12–14.

90 Cf., e.g., *De vita sol.* i, as in *Dramatis personae*, note 14.

91 On this, Lewis (1964), pp. 198–203. Note also L. H. Loomis in Bryan & Dempster (1958), pp. 550–559, on the catalogue lists in Chaucer's *Canterbury Tales,* Tale of Sir Thopas.

92 Cf. *Dramatis personae,* notes 17 and 18.

93 Cf. Petrarch's enthusiastic report to Boccaccio on the talents in this regard of the youthful Giovanni Malpaghini in *Fam.* xxiii, 19. Cf. also *Prose* (1955), pp. 1014–1021; and Rawski (1967), pp. 77–81.

94 Huizinga (1938), esp. pp. 1–44, 236–253.

95 Luebeck, Peter Boeckmann, 1688, *Ad lectorem.*

96 On this, also Rawski (1967), pp. 23–24. For the scope of coverage regarding Petrarch's own writings, cf. below, Works by Petrarch Referred to in the Commentary, vol. 5, *References.*

97 For a recent example of such an approach, cf. Eco (1983).

98 On this, cf., e.g., the notable essays of Von den Steinen (1965); and Evans (1948).

99 André Malraux on *le musée imaginaire* in Malraux (1949), chap. 1.

100 Lowenthal (1985).

TO THE MODERN READER

1 Huizinga (1930), chap. 1.

2 *De vita sol.* ii, *Prose* (1955), p. 556:

Libros ... paratos ... et confabulari, et iocari, et hortari, et solari, et monere, et arguere, et consulere, et docere secreta rerum, monimenta gestorum, vite regulam mortisque contemptum, modestiam in prosperis, fortitudinem in adversis, equabilitatem in actionibus atque constantiam. . . .

3   *Fam.* vi, 4, 7; *Sen.* xvii, 3 (1581: 540), cf. Boccaccio, *Decameron,* Singleton (1982), p. 27. Also, *De vita sol.* ii, *Prose* (1955), p. 580:

Sed bene habet; non hi sunt hominum mores neque tam patulas vulgus aut tam faciles honestis consiliis aures prebet; paucis utinam persuaserim.

But it is all right. The disposition of men at large is not of such a sort: the multitude does not lend ears so alert and wide open to honest advice. I shall be glad if I persuade a few.

Zeitlin (1924), p. 310. On reading the *DR*, cf. Sarton (1949).

4   Von den Steinen (1965), vol. i, p. 173:

Denn die Tatsache ist da, dass auch wir die Sonne auf-und untergehn und nicht die Erde rollen sehen; dass auch fuer uns, solang wir auf unsern Fuessen laufen, der Weg von Schleswig bis Rom weit ist; dass auch fuer uns trotz unsrer, staendig gebrauchten Milliardenziffern unser Hunger unser Hunger und jeder Tag ein Tag ist: kurz, dass all unser Wissen und Koennen an dem, was wir sind, nichts Wesentliches aendert. Der Abstand zwischen den schier grenzenlosen Leistungen unsres Hirns und dem, was klar und schoen in unsern beseelten Leib eingeht, klafft mit jedem Fortschritt naturgesetzlich weiter auseinander, und das Unbekoemmliche, Naturwidrige davon erfaehrt im Grunde jeder. Die Aufgabe steht auch heute da, dass wir unsern nun einmal begrenzten Erdenstunden Sinn und Wert verleihen. (Um nicht zu sagen, dass wir, wie der Grieche es suchte, schoen seien, oder dass wir, wie Christus es forderte, vollkommen seien.)

Sowie wir solcherart geistig mit unserm eignen Jahrhundert Schritt halten, tut das Tor zur Geschichte sich auf. Wir bemerken, dass vergangene Zeiten, mit all ihren sachlich widerlegten Weltvorstellungen, in einem Gleichgewicht lebten, das wir preisgeben. Ihr Wissen hielt sich in den Grenzen des Menschenmasses, des Augenmasses—und war damit mathematisch eo ipso falsch. Denn in den exakten Wissenschaften gilt kein Augenmass. Aber nur sekundaer lag dies "falsch" am Fehlen unsrer Entdeckungen und Kenntnisse; primaer lag es daran, dass man die grundlegende Voraussetzung der modern-mathematischen Forschung, naemlich die methodische Spaltung von Subjekt und Objekt oder von Wissen und Liebe, nicht aufkommen liess. Ein Wissen galt, wenn es dem Denken Verantwortlichkeit, dem Leben Tiefe und Wuerde gab: was auch heute jedem genauer Denkenden am Herzen liegt. Weil die Kunst des Mittelalters bewusst wie unbewusst das notwendige Zusammenklingen des Menschen mit dem All bezeugt, ist es nicht von ungefaehr, dass sie uns anspricht.

PETRARCH ON HIS WORK

1   Quantulum enim vel ingenium vel scientia, vel eloquentia profuerit, nullum
     lacerantibus animum morbis afferens remedium!

   Prose (1955), p. 78.

2   . . . . . . Poterunt discussis forte tenebris
                 Ad purum priscumque iubar remeare nepotes.

3   Ego scribam, ueritas dictabit, humanum genus omne testabitur, iudex esto
     posteritas, nisi forte tuis malis oppressa, nostris intendere non potes.

   1581: 717. Zacour (1973), p. 63.

4   . . . quamuis uulgatum & publicatum loquendi modus secutus, id fecerim
     quod mihi ad uulgares saepius, quam ad philosophos sermo esset.

   1581: 837.

5   Sed delectat in questione nova, que michi de rebus vetustissimis orta est,
     veterum ludere sententiis.

6   Nos in hac re inque aliis ad hunc modum abditis opinari possumus, certi
     aliquid scire qui possumus inexperti? Ubi quidem poetice ludimus, libertate
     nostra uti nequaquam prohibemur; hoc autem loco—quod sine temeritate arro-
     gantiaque licet—aliquot exempla proferemus ex illustribus historiis.

7   Magna enim res est et labor ingens, sed messis uberrima.

   Bernardo (1975), p. 47.

8   . . . quam solicitus inquisitor sim. Ad quam licet enim studio semper aspirem,
     vereor tamen nequando michi vel illius latebre, vel mee cure, vel tarditas
     quedam obstet ingenii, ut sepe res querens opinionibus implicer. Hec ergo non
     diffinitor, sed scrutator vestigatorque tractaverim. Nam et diffinire sapientis est
     proprium, et ego nec sapiens nec proximus sapienti; sed, ut Ciceronis verbum
     utar, "magnus sum opinator." Contra autem paucos quibus loquor, affuturos
     scio preter numerum superiores rebus omnibus atque victores.

   Prose (1955), p. 588. Cf. Cicero, *Acad.* ii, 66. Note *Tusc. disp.* ii, 1, 4: *Est
   enim philosophia paucis contenta iudicibus* . . . —For philosophy is content
   with few judges . . . (LCL, King, p. 149).

DRAMATIS PERSONAE: THE ARGUMENT OF THE BOOK

1 Augustine, *De trin.* x, 10, 14, *PL* 42, c. 981:

   Vivere se tamen et meminisse et intelligere et velle et cogitare et scire et
   iudicare quis dubitet?

On the other hand who would doubt that he lives, remembers, understands, wills, thinks, knows, and judges?

McKenna (1963), p. 308; Javelet (1967), ii, p. 33, n. 258.

2   On the topic, which is at least as old as Euripides (*Hippolytus* 380: *by teaching and experience we learn the right but neglect it in practice* [Oates (1938), i, pp. 773–774]), cf. Rom. 7, 19:

> Non enim quod volo bonum, hoc facio; sed quod nolo malum, hoc ago.

For the good which I will, I do not; but the evil which I will not, that I do.

In both subject and figurative language, the medieval key text on this psychological conflict is Augustine, *Conf.* viii, 5, 10–12; *PL* 32, cc. 753–754:

> . . . Velle meum tenebat inimicus, et inde mihi catenam fecerat, et constrinxerat me. Quippe ex voluntate, perversa, facta est libido: et dum servitur libidini, facta est consuetudo; et dum consuetudini non resistitur, facta est necessitas. Quibus quasi ansulis sibimet innexis, unde catenam appellavi, tenebat me obstrictum dura servitus. Voluntas autem nova quae mihi esse coeperat ut te gratis colerem, fruique te vellem, Deus sola certa iucunditas, nondum erat idonea ad superandam priorem vetustate roboratam. Ita duae voluntates meae, una vetus, alia nova, illa carnalis, illa spiritualis, confligebant inter se, atque discordando dissipabant animam meam.
>
> Sic intelligebam, meipso experimento, id quod legeram, quomodo caro concupisceret adversum spiritum, et spiritus adversus carnem. Ego quidem in utroque; sed magis ego in eo quod in me approbabam, quam in eo quod in me improbabam. Ibi enim magis iam non ego; quia ex magna parte id patiebar invitus, quam faciebam volens. Sed tamen consuetudo adversus me pugnacior ex me facta erat, quoniam volens, quo nollem, perveneram. Et quis iure contradiceret, cum peccantem iusta poena sequeretur? Et non erat iam illa excusatio, qua videri mihi solebam propterea nondum me contempto saeculo servire tibi, quia incerta mihi esset perceptio veritatis: iam enim et ipsa certa erat. Ego autem adhuc terra obligatus, militare tibi recusabam; et impedimentis omnibus sic timebam expediri, quemadmodum impediri timendum est.
>
> Ita sarcina saeculi, velut somno assolet, dulciter premebar; et cogitationes quibus meditabar in te, similes erant conatibus expergisci volentium, qui tamen superati soporis altitudine remerguntur. Et sicut nemo est qui dormire semper velit, omniumque sano iudicio vigilare praestat; differt tamen plerumque homo somnum excutere, cum gravis torpor in membris est; cumque iam displicentem carpit libentius, quamvis surgendi tempus advenerit: ita certum habebam esse melius tuae charitati me dedere, quam meae cupiditati cedere; sed illud placebat et vincebat; hoc libebat et vinciebat. Non enim erat quod tibi responderem dicenti mihi, *Surge qui dormis, et exsurge a mortuis; et illuminabit te Christus*: et undique ostendenti vera te dicere, non erat omnino quod responderem veritate convictus, nisi tantum verba lenta et somnolenta: "Modo." "ecce modo." "sine paululum." Sed, "modo et modo," non habebant modum; et "Sine paululum," in longum ibat. Frustra condelectabar legi tuae

secundum interiorem hominem, cum lex alia in membris meis repugnaret legi mentis meae, et captivum me duceret in legem peccati, quae in membris meis erat. Lex enim peccati est violentia consuetudinis, qua trahitur et tenetur etiam invitus animus, eo merito quo in eam volens illabitur. Miserum ergo me quis liberaret de corpore mortis huius, nisi gratia tua per Jesum Christum dominum nostrum?

My will was the enemy master of, and thence had made a chain for me and bound me. Because of a perverse will was lust made; and lust indulged in became custom; and custom noι resisted became necessity. By which links, as it were, joined together (whence I term it a "chain"), did a hard bondage hold me enthralled. But that new will which had begun to develop in me, freely to worship Thee, and to wish to enjoy Thee, O God, the only sure enjoyment, was not able as yet to overcome my former wilfulness, made strong by long indulgence. Thus did my two wills, one old and the other new, one carnal, the other spiritual, contend within me; and by their discord they unstrung my soul.

Thus came I to understand, from my own experience, what I had read, how the flesh lusteth against the Spirit, and the Spirit against the flesh [Gal. 5, 17]. I lusted both ways; yet more in that which I approved in myself, than in that which I disapproved in myself. For in this last it was now rather not "I" [Rom. 7, 20], because in much I rather suffered against my will than did it willingly. And yet it was through me that custom became more combative against me, because I had come willingly whither I willed not. And who, then, can with any justice speak against it, when just punishment follows the sinner? Nor had I now any longer my wonted excuse, that as yet I hesitated to be above the world and serve Thee, because my perception of the truth was uncertain; for now it was certain. But I, still bound to earth, refused to be Thy soldier; and was as much afraid of being freed from all embarrassments, as we ought to fear to be embarrassed.

Thus with the baggage of the world was I sweetly burdened, as when in slumber; and the thoughts wherein I meditated upon Thee were like the efforts of those desiring to awake, who, still overpowered with a heavy drowsiness, are again steeped therein. And as no one desires to sleep always, and in the sober judgment of all waking is better, yet does a man generally defer to shake off drowsiness, when there is a heavy lethargy in all his limbs, and, though displeased, yet even after it is time to rise with pleasure yields to it, so was I assured that it were much better for me to give up myself to Thy charity, than to yield myself to my own cupidity; but the former course satisfied and vanquished me, the latter pleased me and fettered me. Nor had I aught to answer Thee calling to me, *Awake, thou that sleepest, and arise from the dead, and Christ shall give thee light* [Eph. 5, 14]. And to Thee showing me on every side, that what Thou saidst was true, I, convicted by the truth, had nothing at all to reply, but the drawling and drowsy words: "Presently, lo, presently"; "Leave me a little while." But "presently, presently" had no present; and my "leave me a little while" went on for a long while. In vain did I delight in Thy law after the inner man, when another law in my members warred against the law of my mind, and brought me into captivity to the law of sin which is in my members. For the law of sin is the violence of custom, whereby the mind is drawn and held, even against its will; deserving to be so held in that it so willingly falls into it. O wretched man that I am! who shall deliver me from the body of this death but Thy grace only, through Jesus Christ our Lord [Rom. 7, 22–24]?

J. G. Pilkington in Oates (1948), i, pp. 116–117. Note also Ovid, *Metam.* vii, 19–21; Petrarch's translation of Ovid's line 21 in his canzone *I' vo pensando* (*Rime* [1951], p. 343, line 136); and Prudentius, *Psychomachia,* 902–915. On the dialogue within, Rawski (1967), pp. 104–105, n. 37; Tateo (1965); and below, *DR* i, 11, note 10, ii, Pref. note 85. On the related Augustinian notion of the exterior and interior man (*Fam.* ii, 9, 17) Gilson (1960), pt. ii, chap. 1; Ladner (1959), esp. pp. 182–192; Javelet (1965), i, pp. 59, 243–245, ii, xxi, n. 5, p. xxv, n. 23; on *bellum intestinum*—internal war (Augustine, *De civ. Dei* xix, 4, LCL, Greene, p. 128)—as "the root of all allegory," Lewis (1938), pp. 68–70.

3   On *Fortuna* and the literature on Fortune, Trompf (1979); Cioffari in Wiener (1973), ii, pp. 225–236; Pickering (1970); Fleming (1969), pp. 124–126; Heitmann (1958), esp. part i, A; Patch (1935); and idem (1927). For Aristotle's view, Randall (1960), pp. 181–184.

4   Inherent in this primal confrontation are man's self and his world. George Steiner describes with keen perception the structure of this contraposition, which *is at once universal and local*:

Self-definition and the agonistic recognition of 'otherness' (of *l'autre*) across the threatened boundaries of self, are indissociable. The polarities of masculinity and femininity, of ageing and of youth, of private autonomy and of social collectivity, of existence and mortality, of the human and the divine, can be crystallized only in adversative terms (whatever the many shades of accommodation between them). To arrive at oneself—the primordial journey—is to come up, polemically, against 'the other'. The boundary-conditions of the human person are those set by gender, by age, by community, by the cut between life and death, and by the potentials of accepted or denied encounter between the existential and the transcendent.

But 'collision' is, of course, a monistic and, therefore, inadequate term. Equally decisive are those categories of reciprocal perception, of grappling with 'otherness', that can be defined as erotic, filial, social, ritual, and metaphysical. Men and women, old and young, individual and *communitas,* living and deceased, mortals and gods, meet and mesh in contiguities of love, of kinship, of commonality and group communion, of caring remembrance, of worship. Sex, the honeycomb of generations and of kinship, the social unit, the presentness of the departed in the weave of the living, the practices of religion, are the modes of enactment of ultimate ontological dualities. In essence, the constants of conflict and of positive intimacy are the same. When man and woman meet, they stand against each other as they stand close. Old and young seek in each other the pain of remembrance and the matching solace of futurity. Anarchic individuation seeks interaction with the compulsions of law, of collective cohesion in the body politic. The dead inhabit the living and, in turn, await their visit. The duel between man and god(s) is the most aggressively amorous known to experience. In the physics of man's being, fission is also fusion.

(Steiner [1984], pp. 231–232, 233.) This core conflict of the human condition and its interlocking relationships with the demands of living, posed by the surrounding world and faced by each and every one, dominated Petrarch's thought during his later years.

5 Cf. Chalcidius' definition, *Comm. Tim.* vii, 159, Waszink (1962), p. 193; Boethius, *Cons. phil.* ii, 1–3, esp. P 2, as in *DR* ii, 9, note 2 (Pickering 1970, pp. 187–191); Thomas Aquinas, 2 *anal.* 9l, 2 *phys.* 8d, etc.; and Dante, *Div. Comm.*, Inf. vii, 67–96.

6 Cf. *DR* i, 16, note 7.

7 Lady Reason, Cicero's *mistress and queen of the world* (*Tusc. disp.* ii, 21, 47), and prominent colloquist in Augustine's *Soliloquies* and the *Roman de la Rose* (Fleming [1969], esp. pp. 112–122), is identified by Augustine as representing "that in the mind which the act of looking is in the eyes" (C. C. Starbuck in Oates [1948], i, p. 266; Misch, i, 2 [1950], p. 642). In *Fam.* xvii, 3, 23, Petrarch notes:

> Illa in consilium advocanda, quod inimica eius prosperitas non sinebat; illa stupori nostro dolorique medebitur; illa nobis fortune mores constantiamque monstrabit.

> It is she who now must be invited for counsel [*Fam.* xix, 9, 4]—which her enemy Prosperity never did permit. She will cure our numbness and our pain; she will teach us both the habits of Fortune and steadfastness.

In order to involve and/or persuade the reader, Reason, as well as her equally emblematic interlocutors, speak for themselves (Reason says so in *DR* ii, 18, 16–19), expressing viewpoints that may or may not be shared by the author. Similarly, the *Franciscus* and *Augustinus* of the *Secretum* are participants in Petrarch's dialogue, engaged in a dynamics of sorts which allows the author to manipulate topics, viewpoints, and identities—to write *a kind of cryptic poem* (SN, Praef., Piur [1925], p. 64; Rico [1974], p. 510, n. 194, of *Bucolicum carmen,* probably Eclogue 7, Zacour [1973], p. 28, n. 3) and to remain a teller of tales without directly committing himself. On this, Rico (1974), esp. pp. 30–38, 510–511, 531–535; Mann (1984), esp. pp. 67–68, 91–92; Baron (1985), esp. pp. 174–175; Pelikan, iv (1984), pp. 20–22; Trinkaus (1970), i, p. 4; and Tateo (1965). Note also Tripet (1967), pp. 104, 166–176; and Foster (1984), p. 162. On the autobiographical fallacy, which in varying degrees bedevils a significant portion of Petrarchan studies, Fleming (1969), esp. pp. 112–114; and Piur (1925), i, chap. 6. Cf. also

Green (1979), pp. 218–222; Calin (1974), esp. pp. 38, 47–49, 115–118, 143–145, 166–172, 196–198; Colie (1966), esp. pp. 74–89; Spitzer (1959), sect. i, 8; Mazzaro (1981); and the essays on allegory, Lewis (1938), chap. 2, and Jackson (1964). —Here should be noted also the extension of the narrative "I" in *Secretum,* Prohem., *Prose* (1955), p. 26, which states explicitly what Dante seems to imply in the much discussed opening lines, *Div. Comm.,* Inf. i, 1–2 [*Nel mezzo del cammin di* nostra vita/ mi ritrovai . . . Singleton, *Commentary* (1970), pp. 3–4; Spitzer (1959), p. 104]:

> Ubi multa licet adversus seculi nostri mores, deque comunibus mortalium piaculis dicta sint, ut non tam michi quam toti humano generi fieri convitium videretur, ea tamen, quibus ipse notatus sum, memorie altius impressi.

> Though we talked of many things much against the manners of this age, and on faults and failures common to mankind, in such wise that the reproaches of the Master [i.e., *Augustinus*] seemed in a sense more directed against men in general than against myself, yet those which to me came closest home I have graven with more especial vividness on the tablet of my memory.

Draper (1911), p. 5. —On Chaucer as author/narrator or participant in his narrative, Robinson (1933), pp. 881–882; Donaldson (1970), pp. 1–3; and Spearing (1972), p. 14. On Guillaume de Machaut, Calin (1974), esp. p. 38. —On Petrarch's *Augustinus,* also Foster (1984), esp. pp. 162–167; Seigel (1968), chap. 2; Tateo (1965); and Heitmann (1960).

8   Most of the dialogues are not explicitly argued, self-contained exchanges between two discussants confronting each other—they present, often in starkly schematic form, a topic, thesis, and antithesis for the benefit of a third party, the reader/listener/patient. There is no dramatic confrontation. Georg Misch, with an eye on Augustine's *Soliloquies* (e.g., ii, 14), speaks of a *Form des Dialoges als ein verkleidetes Selbstgespraech* (Misch, i, 2 [1950], pp. 639–645, iii, 2 [1976], p. 72, ii [1955], p. 595; cf. also Lerer [1985], pp. 46–56, 69–71). —On the dialogue within, e.g., DR ii, 81, 151, ii, 97, 42, 77, ii, 102, 53, ii, 103, 23, ii, 114 (*sermo intimus*), and ii, 126, 17.

9   The synonym indicates that this is ἐπιθυμία—desirous expectation, wishful thinking, or concupiscent hope (*Secretum* ii, *Prose* [1955], p. 94)—not the theological virtue described in DR i, 109, 66–73. When listing the passions, Isidore, *Diff.* ii, 40, 159, *PL* 83, c. 95, refers with Augustine simply to *cupiditas*—desire. Cf. also Isidore, *Lib. num.* v, 23, *PL* 83, c. 184; Lactantius, *Inst. div.* vi, 16, *PL* 6, cc. 692–693; and Fontaine (1959), ii, pp. 700–702. On the four passions, the Stoic tetrad of πάθη—affects (Cicero, *Tusc. disp.* iii, 4, 7–8), φόβος, ἐπιθυμία, λύπη, ἡδονή—fear, hope or desire, sorrow, and joy (= Virgil, *Aeneid* vi, 733, as note 11, below), which, in the DR, furnishes Reason's discussants, Pohlenz, i (1959), p. 148, Johannes von Tepl, *Ackerm.,* Bernt & Burdach (1917), pp. 301–303; and below, DR i,

Pref., note 60. On Augustine's reinterpretation of the Stoic notions regarding the tetrad, Pohlenz, ibid., p. 457; and Augustine, *De civ. Dei* xiv, 6, as below, note 12. Note also De Lubac, ii, 2 (1964), pp. 26–32, on number 4. On the personal metaphor, note Curtius (1953), pp. 131–134; and below, *DR* i, Pref., note 60.

10   Who, in their contrariety, signify *concordia discors*—the disharmonic harmony—implicit in Fortune, fair and foul, the mistress whom they serve. On *concordia discors, DR* i, 11, note 19.

11   *Secretum* i, *Prose* (1955), pp. 64, 66:

> *Augustinus*: Audi ergo. Animam quidem tuam, sicut celitus bene institutam esse non negaverim, sic ex contagio corporis huius, ubi circumsepta est, multum a primeva nobilitate sua degenerasse ne dubites; nec degenerasse duntaxat, sed longo iam tractu temporis obtorpuisse, factam velut proprie originis ac superni Conditoris immemorem. Nempe passiones ex corporea commistione subortas oblivionemque nature melioris, divinitus videtur attigisse Virgilius, ubi ait:
>
> > Igneus est illis vigor et celestis origo
> > seminibus, quantum non noxia corpora tardant
> > terrenique hebetant artus, moribundaque membra.
> > Hinc *metuunt cupiuntque dolent gaudentque,* neque auras
> > respiciunt, clause tenebris et carcere ceco.
>
> Discernis ne in verbis poeticis quadriceps illud monstrum nature hominum tam adversum?
>
> *Franciscus*: Discerno clarissime quadripartitam animi passionem, que primum quidem, ex presentis futurique temporis respectu, in duas scinditur partes; rursus quelibet in duas alias, ex boni malique opinione, subdistinguitur; ita quattuor velut flatibus aversis humanarum mentium tranquillitas perit.
>
> *Augustinus*: Rite discernis, atqui verificatum est in vobis illud apostolicum: "Corpus, quod corrumpitur, aggravat animam, et deprimit terrena inhabitatio sensum multa cogitantem." Conglobantur siquidem species innumere et imagines rerum visibilium, que corporeis introgresse sensibus, posquam singulariter admisse sunt, catervatim in anime penetralibus densantur; eamque, nec ad id genitam nec tam multorum difformiumque capacem, pregravant atque confundunt. Hinc pestis illa fantasmatum vestros discerpens laceransque cogitatus, meditationibusque clarificis, quibus ad unum solum summumque lumen ascenditur, iter obstruens varietate mortifera.
>
> *Augustinus*: Then listen. It was from Heaven your soul came forth: never will I assert a lower origin than that. But in its contact with the flesh, wherein it is imprisoned, it has lost much of its first splendour. Have no doubt of this in your mind. And not only is it so, but by reason of the length of time it has in a manner fallen asleep; and, if one may so express it, forgotten its own beginning

and its heavenly Creator. And these passions that are born in the soul through
its connection with the body, and that forgetfulness of its nobler nature, seem
to me to have been touched by Virgil with pen almost inspired when he
writes—

> The souls of men still shine with heavenly fire,
> That tells from whence they come, save that the flesh
> And limbs of earth breed dullness, hence spring *fears,*
> *Desire, and grief and pleasures* of the world,
> And so, in darkness prisoned, they no more
> Look upward to heaven's face.

[Virgil, *Aeneid* vi, 730–734, and *Comm. Enn.,* pp. 91–92, 121. Cf. Horace, *Ep.*
i, 6, 12; Ovid, *Fasti* iii, 362; Augustine, *De civ. Dei* xiv, 3; 7; 8; xxi, 3; 13;
Macrobius, *Comm.* i, 8, 11; Boethius, *Cons. phil.* i, M 7; Isidore, *Diff.* ii, 50, 159,
and *Lib. num.* v, 23, *PL* 83, cc. 95, 184; *Fam.* ii, 5, 4, xx, 12, 2; *Sen.* iii, 1; *aequo
despicere spes metusque, gaudia & dolores; Sen.* x, 4: *specs & metus, & gaudia, &
dolores* (1581: 766, 876); SN 4, Piur (1925), p. 183, 19–28, Zacour (1973), p.
56; *Secretum* ii, Prose (1955), p. 124; *DR* ii, Pref., 401; ii, 64, 10–13.] Do you
not in the poet's words discern that monster with four heads so deadly to the
nature of man?

Franciscus: I discern very clearly the fourfold passion of our nature, which,
first of all, we divide in two as it has respect to past and future, and then
subdivide again in respect of good and evil. And so, by these four winds dis-
traught, the rest and quietness of man's soul is perished and gone.

Augustinus: You discern rightly, and the words of the Apostle [i.e., Paul] are
fulfilled in us, which say: "The corruptible body presseth down the soul, and
the earthly tabernacle weigheth down the mind that museth upon many
things." [Sap. 9, 15. The erroneous attribution to Paul is probably due to a
misreading of Augustine, *De civ. Dei* xiv, 3. On this, Rico (1974), p. 108. Note
also Augustine, *Conf.* vii, 17.] Of a truth the countless forms and images of
things visible, that one by one are brought into the soul by the senses of the
body, gather there in the inner centre in a mass, and the soul, not being akin to
these or capable of learning them, they weigh it down and overwhelm it with
their contrariety. Hence that plague of too many impressions tears apart and
wounds the thinking faculty of the soul, and with its fatal, distracting complex-
ity bars the way of clear meditation, whereby it would mount up to the threshold of the One Chief God.

Draper (1911), pp. 41–43; italics and commentary mine. The "fourfold passion of our nature" and its division are Ciceronian.

Cicero, *Tusc. disp.* iii, 11, 24–25:

Nam cum omnis perturbatio sit animi motus vel rationis expers vel rationem aspernans vel rationi non obediens, isque motus aut boni aut mali opinione citetur bifariam, quattuor perturbationes aequaliter distributae sunt: nam duae sunt ex opinione boni, quarum altera, voluptas gestiens, id est, praeter modum elata laetitia, opinione praesentis magni alicuius boni, altera quae est immoderata appetitio opinati magni boni rationi non obtemperans, vel cupiditas recte vel libido dici potest. Ergo haec duo genera, voluptas gestiens et libido, bonorum opinione turbantur, ut duo reliqua, metus et aegritudo, malorum. Nam et metus opinio magni mali impendentis et aegritudo est opinio magni mali praesentis et quidem recens opinio talis mali, ut in eo rectum videatur esse angi; id autem est, ut is, qui doleat, oportere opinetur se dolere.

For as all disturbance is a movement of the soul, either destitute of reason, or contemptuous of reason, or disobedient to reason, and as such a movement is provoked in two ways, either by an idea of good or idea of evil, we have four disturbances equally divided. For there are two proceeding from an idea of good, one of which is exuberant pleasure, that is to say, joy excited beyond measure by the idea of some great present good; the second is the intemperate longing for a supposed great good, and this longing is disobedient to reason, and may be rightly termed desire or lust. Therefore these two classes, exuberant pleasure and lust springing from the idea of good, disturb the soul just as the two remaining, fear and distress, cause disturbances by the idea of evil. For fear is the idea of a serious threatening evil and distress is the idea of a serious present evil and indeed an idea freshly conceived of an evil of such sort that it seems a due reason for anguish; now that means that the man who feels the pain believes that he *ought* to feel pain.

LCL, King, p. 255. Related, ibid. 1v, 6, 11–12. On this, Fontaine (1959), ii, pp. 698–702; Heitmann (1960); idem (1958), pp. 89–94; and Rawski (1967), pp. 2, 99–100, n. 15. Cf. also Augustine's psychological approach, *De civ. Dei* xiv, 6; and *Boethius, Cons. phil.* i, M 7, 25–28, Gruber (1978), p. 181, *25ff.* On combat by debate of allegorical *personae*, Taylor (1925), ii, p. 128; Artelt (1934); Bloomfield (1952), p. 65; and Panofsky (1962), p. 154 and fig. 111. On poetic debates, Manitius, iii (1931), pp. 944–963; and Raby (1934), ii, pp. 282–308. Note also Burdach (1926/1932), pp. 440–452; and Marsh (1980), on Cicero's dialogue *in utramque partem* and Petrarch's revival of the genre.

12   In the *DR, virtus,* if used in a general sense, denotes a redeeming force attainable through man's God-given ability to will and to know (Augustine, *Conf.* vii, 3; Gilson [1960], p. 157; Pohlenz, i [1959], pp. 457–458). This *virtus* implies the two ways of life, or the potential for them, decency of action and conduct, and belief in God (below, *DR* ii, 114, note 48), of which Lactantius speaks (Pohlenz, ibid., pp. 442–443; idem, ii [1955], p. 217). It constitutes the essence of self-fulfillment, the ideal "virility" (*ex viro virtus*—Cicero, *Tusc. disp.* ii, 18, 43, as in *DR* i, Pref., note 53, cited in *Fam.* xxiii, 2, 28), open to all—men, women (*DR* ii, 48, 23–26), freemen, slaves

(Pohlenz, i [1959], pp. 127–129. Related, Javelet [1967], i, pp. 236–245. Note Lactantius, *Div. inst.* iii, 25, as in *SVF* iii, 253). In this sense also must be read the military terminology (e.g., life is a combat [Seneca, *Ep.* 96, 5, and Lewis (1938), pp. 59–73; Job 7, 1, as in *DR* i, 48, 16; John of Salisbury, *Policrat.* ii, 27, *PL* 199, c. 471; *Fam.* i, 1, 26, xvi, 6, 2, xxi, 9, 7; and *DR* i, 48, note 3]), which is in evidence throughout our text. On this, Martellotti (1983), p. 184, n. 10. —Cf. Augustine, *De civ. Dei* xiv, 6:

> De qualitate voluntatis humanae, sub cuius
> iudicio affectiones animi aut pravae habentur
> aut rectae

Interest autem qualis sit voluntas hominis, quia si perversa est, perversos habebit hos motus, si autem recta est, non solum inculpabiles verum etiam laudabiles erunt. Voluntas est quippe in omnibus, immo omnes nihil aliud quam voluntates sunt. Nam quid est cupiditas et laetitia nisi voluntas in eorum consensione quae volumus? Et quid est netus atque tristitia nisi voluntas in dissensione ab his quae noluimus? Sed cum consentimus appetendo ea quae volumus, cupiditas, cum autem consentimus fruendo his quae volumus, laetitia vocatur. Itemque cum dissentimus ab eo quod accidere nolumus, talis voluntas metus est, cum autem dissentimus ab eo quod nolentibus accidit, talis voluntas tristitia est. Et omnino pro varietate rerum quae appetuntur atque fugiuntur, sicut allicitur vel offenditur voluntas hominis, ita in hos vel illos affectus mutatur et vertitur.

Quapropter homo, qui secundum Deum, non secundum hominem vivit oportet ut sit amator boni, unde fit consequens ut malum oderit. Et quoniam nemo natura, sed quisquis malus est vitio malus est, perfectum odium debet malis qui secundum Deum vivit, ut nec propter vitium oderit hominem nec amet vitium propter hominem, sed oderit vitium, amet hominem. Sanato enim vitio, totum quod amare, nihil autem quod debeat odisse remanebit.

> On the character of the human will, whose judgement
> determines whether the dispositions of the mind are
> considered wrong or right

Moreover, the character of a man's will makes a difference. For if it is wrong, these emotions will be wrong; but if it is right, they will be not only not blameworthy but even praiseworthy. The will is indeed involved in them all, or rather, they are all no more than acts of will. For what is *desire* or *joy* but an act of will in sympathy with those things that we wish, and what is *fear* or *grief* but an act of will in disagreement with the things that we do not wish? When our sympathy, however, is indicated by a pursuit of the things that we wish, it is called desire, but when it is indicated by an enjoyment of these things that we wish, it is called joy. Similarly, when we disagree with that which we do not wish to happen, such an act of will is fear, but when we disagree with that which happens to us against our will, such an act of will is grief. And generally, even as a man's will is attracted or repelled in accordance with the diverse character of the objects that are pursued or avoided, so it shifts and turns into emotions of one sort or the other.

Therefore, the man who lives according to God and not according to man is bound to be a lover of the good, and the consequence is that he hates evil. Moreover, since no one is evil by nature, but whosoever is evil is so because of some defect, the person who lives according to God owes to those who are evil a perfect hatred [Ps. 139, 22], that is, he should neither hate a man because of his defect nor love a defect because of the man, but he should hate the defect and love the man. For once the defect is mended, only what he should love and nothing that he should hate will remain.

LCL, Levine, pp. 285, 287. (Italics mine.)

13　　Beside *virtus generaliter sumpta*—virtue as such (below, *DR* i, Pref., note 7; the description of virtue *DR* ii, 9, 16–25; and the address to the allegorical figure, *DR* ii, 25, 104–11)—the text of the *DR* refers to the *moral virtues* and the *theological virtues* (e.g., *DR* i, 122, 8–9), faith, hope, and charity (*DR* i, 109, 70). The moral virtues comprise the four *cardinal virtues* in Ciceronian order (*DR* i, Pref., note 2) and, not consistently identified, the remaining moral virtues of Aristotle, "which are about the passions" (Thomas Aquinas, *Summa theol.* i, II, Q.59, a.l, Pegis [1945], ii, p. 449; Ferguson [1954], p. 174), and mostly identical with the modes in Cicero's paradigm (cf. Thomas Aquinas, ibid., Q.60, a.5, Pegis, ii, p. 465). The *intellectual virtues*—wisdom, including prudence, which is both intellectual and moral/cardinal; science, in the sense of subject knowledge, and art; and understanding—are dealt with in separate dialogues and referred to, but without categorization. (On this, Thomas Aquinas, Cayré, ii [1940], pp. 562–565, 601–607; Dante, Toynbee [1968], art. Virtù; Kantorowicz [1957a], pp. 468–469; and Boyde [1981], pp. 169–171.) On the other hand, Reason's clinical therapy prescribes the practice of such virtues as moderation and patience, humility and courage as specific remedies (cf. below, *DR* i, Pref., note 41). On this second series of virtues, which became prominent in moral theology during the twelfth and thirteenth centuries, Wenzel (1984), pp. 7–8; and H. F. North in Wiener (1973), iv, pp. 371–375. Size and scope of the contemporary literature on the virtues and vices are indicated by Bloomfield (1979). Cf. also Tuve (1966), esp. chap. 3; Heitmann (1958), part i, B; Bloomfield (1952), esp. pp. 64–66; Lottin (1942–1960); and Zoeckler (1904).

14　　Cf. *Sen.* xvi, 9 (1581: 963), about *DR* ii, 93: *obiectu contrarii consolarer*—I soothe by juxtaposing contraries. Note also *DR* ii, Pref., 279–282, ii, 6, 46, ii, 58, 2, ii, 71, 23; and *De vita sol.* i, *Prose* (1955), pp. 300, 326:

> . . . vel ratione vel contrariorum collatione monstratum est, et mox exemplis illustribus astruetur.

. . . which has been shown by rational argument as well as by reference to contraries, and, before long, shall be confirmed with examples from illustrious lives.

On *disputatio in utramque partem,* in order to sharpen our eyes for truth, Cicero, *Acad.* i, 12, 45–46, and ii, 3, 7. Cf. also *Tusc. disp.* i, 7, 13–14, ii, 3, 9; and *De fin.* ii, 1, 2–3. Cf. Solmsen in G. E. L. Owen (1968), p. 54; Marsh (1980), chap. 1, esp. pp. 2–3; and Lerer (1985), pp. 32–45. Cicero comments on his *Tusculan Disputations* (i, 4, 8):

Fiebat autem ita, ut cum is, qui audire vellet, dixisset quid sibi videretur, tum ego contra dicerem. Haec est enim, ut scis, vetus et Socratica ratio contra alterius opinionem disserendi. Nam ita facillime quid veri simillimum esset inveniri posse Socrates arbitrabatur. Sed quo commodius disputationes explicentur, sic eas exponam, quasi agatur res, non quasi narretur.

The procedure was that, after the would-be listener had expressed his view, I opposed it. This, as you know, is the old Socratic method of arguing against your adversary's position; for Socrates thought that in this way the probable truth was most readily discovered; but in order that the course of our discussions may be more conveniently followed I shall put them before you in the form of a debate and not in narrative form.

LCL, King, p. 11. Quoted, Lerer (1985), p. 40.

15   Abelard, *Sic et non,* Prol. 338–339, Boyer & McKeon (1977), p. 103. On this, Seigel (1968), pp. 190–192; and Von den Steinen (1959), pp. 288–293. Note also Augustine, *De trin.* x, 10, 14, *PL* 42, c. 981; Stock (1983), chap. 4, 1, esp. pp. 335, 343, on Anselm; and Javelet (1967), i, pp. 59–60, ii, p. 33, n. 258.

16   Cf. Seneca, *Dial.* viii, De otio, 7, on the three kinds of life devoted to pleasure, contemplation, and action; and Augustine, e.g., *De civ. Dei* viii, 4, and *Enarr. in Ps.* 51, 6. On the Augustinian interpretation of *vita activa* and *vita contemplativa,* Gilson (1960), pp. 117–119. Note also Ullman (1977), chap. 6; Baron (1955), pp. 89–101; J. Zeitlin's discussion in his translation of Petrarch's *De vita solitaria,* Zeitlin (1924), pp. 24–92; and Mann (1984), chap. 3.

17   Petrarch's reader is expected to read for action: to engage in a continuing internal dialogue in quest of knowledge that can and should be put to use. Books supply text and context, as it were, the facts, issues, and aspects, and their expression in a verbal medium—which permit the reader to search for and arrive at the truth and to translate it into action (e.g., *Secretum* ii, *Prose* [1955], p. 72; and *DR* i, 44, 49–56, ii, 8, 42). Thus the dialogues of the *DR* are meant to occur in two places: the fictive pro and con of the *text* involving Reason and the Passions—and the "real" debate ensuing *in his own bosom,* when the thoughtful reader reacts, weighs, argues, and assesses for

action the substantive issues presented to him *obiectu contrarii.* On this thoughtful reader, e.g., *Secretum* ii, *Prose* (1955), p. 122; and *Fam.* xxiv, 1, 9–10. Note also Anselm, *Orationes sive Meditationes,* prol., as cited in Stock (1983), p. 332, n. 13; and Steiner (1984), pp. 290–292. —*Vera philosophia*—the true philosophy expounding the morality of the deed (below, *DR* i, Pref., 52–54, and note 16)—serves a kindred purpose. Cf. also *believing others rather than oneself.* —It is possible that Petrarch's thoughts were influenced by the integral vision of monastic life, which his brother Gherardo experienced and adhered to in the Carthusian charterhouse of Montrieux (cf. *Fam.* x, 3, x, 4, x, 5, xvi, 2, xvii, 1, xviii, 5), and that the *DR* may represent an attempt to create and foster such an integral vision of the *vita activa* for the denizens of the secular world.

18   In *De ocio* ii, Rotondi, p. 71, addressing the Carthusian monks of Montrieux (Wilkins [1961], pp. 58–59), Petrarch discusses his citation practices:

> . . . iuvat tamen cuiusdam clarissimi viri testimonium inserere, quod ipsum licet late cognitum atque ideo multis supervacuum videri possit, vobis tamen in heremo degentibus solique sacrarum literarum studio deditis forte vel novitate vel autoritate certe vel veritate vel ipse saltem varietate probabitur, cuius studio ut interdum oratione soluta inter seculares sacris stilum testimoniis condire soleo, sic inter ecclesiasticos et religiosos viros secularibus literis delector, que et prime et aliquandiu michi sole fuerunt et ubi consonant nostris, nescioquid oportuni admodum, licet peregrini, auxilii videtur accedere.

> . . . yet it is pleasing to insert the testimony of some great man. Even though it is widely known and may appear superfluous to many, it will be accepted by you who live in a monastery, solely dedicated to the study of the Scriptures, perhaps for its novely, certainly for its authority or truth, or, at least, for variety's sake. With such quotations I relish to season the style of my prose writings, those addressed to laymen with sacred ones, and in those for ecclesiastics and religious men I enjoy citing the secular texts that were with me alone at first and for some time—and if they agree with our beliefs, they may seem to provide help—I know not how relevant, and, admittedly, from foreign quarters.

On this, *Fam.* xxii, 10; and Trinkaus (1970), i, pp. 42–43. Petrarch found his views on the practical usefulness of literary quotations, *sententiae,* and analogous examples, be they now from Judaeo-Christian or pagan sources, or just exemplary stories, anticipated by a number of writers, among them John of Salisbury, who expressed his views in the prologue to his *Policraticus, PL* 199, c. 387:

> Quae vero ad rem pertinentia a diversis auctoribus se animo ingerebant, dum conferrent, aut juvarent, curavi inserere, tactitis interdum nominibus auctorum; tum quia tibi, utpote exercitatio in litteris, pleraque plenissime nota esse noveram; tum ut ad lectionem assiduam magis ascenderetur ignarus. In quibus si quid a fide veri longius abest, mihi veniam deberi confido, qui non

omnia, quae hic scribuntur, vera esse promitto; sed sive vera, seu falsa sunt, legentium usibus inservire. . . . . . . Haec quoque ipsa, quibus plerumque utor, aliena sunt, nisi quia quidquid ubique bene dictum est, facio meum, et illud nunc meis ad compendium, nunc ad fidem et auctoritatem alienis exprimo verbis. Et quia semel coepi revelare mentis arcana, arrogantiam meam plenius denudabo. Omnes ergo qui mihi in verbo aut opere philosophantes occurrunt, meos clientes esse arbitror, et quodque maius est, mihi vindico in servitutem; adeo quidem ut in traditionibus suis se ipsos pro me linguis obiiciant detractorum.

I have been careful to insert pertinent text passages by various authors that came to mind as helpful and gratifying, sometimes without naming the authors—this because I know they are all familiar to you (i.e., Thomas Becket, Archbishop of Canterbury), who are exceptionally versed in literature, and might induce those who are less knowledgeable to further assiduous reading. If in these texts there should be anything that is far removed from the truth of the faith, I believe that I should be forgiven, since I do not promise that all that is written here is true, but, rather, that it will be useful to the reader, whether it is now true or false. . . . . . . The greater part of what I present here belongs to others, save for the fact that I make my own whatever is well said somewhere else, and express it in my own words for brevity's sake, or in the words of the original for reasons of authenticity. And since I have started to reveal the secrets of my mind—let me disclose my arrogance still further: I consider all those whose words or deeds I encounter in the field of philosophy to be my vassals and, what is more, claim them as my servants, so that they, and what they stood for, oppose the cries of my detractors, rather than myself.

Petrarch (whose remark, *sententiam . . . meam facio,* in *Fam.* xvii, 3, 3, as below, *DR* ii, Pref., note 82, or flourish in *Fam.* v, 18, 5, may indicate kindred feelings), discussed his penchant for examples in *Fam.* vi, 4, as below, *DR* i, Pref., note 52. Note also the exchange between Augustinus and Franciscus, *Secretum* iii, *Prose* (1955), pp. 178, 180; Rico (1974), pp. 357–360; the reference to the lessons of the past in *Fam.* xvii, 3, 43; and the discussion of *historicorum finis* in the Prohemium of *De vir. ill.,* Martellotti (1983), pp. 479–481; and the debate by examples in *Buc. carm.* xii, 90–115. In the *Rerum memorandarum libri,* Petrarch followed Valerius Maximus by grouping his *exempla* into *Romana* and *Externa,* i.e., non-Roman ones, but added *Moderna,* examples from later history and his own times (G. Billanovich in his edition of *Rer. mem. libri* [1943], pp. ccxxviii–ccxxix; Martellotti [1983], p. 476). On the use of such "modern" examples, which were difficult to come by and to present in an age without ready access to up-to-date recorded information (cf. *DR* ii, 96, 136–137), *Roman de la Rose* 6631–6632:

And if you give no value to these proofs taken from old stories, you have others from your own recent times, proofs from fresh, beautiful battles . . .

(Dahlberg [1971], pp. 128–129.) —Cf. Dornseiff (1927); Kornhardt (1936); Von den Steinen (1959), pp. 15, 147, 335–343; De Lubac, i, 2 (1959), pp. 467–470; Gardner (1977), pp. 140–145; P. von Moos in Wilks (1984), pp. 207–261, on John of Salisbury's *Policraticus;* Preminger (1965), art. Exemplum; Rawski (1967), pp. 10–13; and, on the contemporary adaptation of antique material, clearly evident in the *DR,* Panofsky (1960), pp. 84–85. On *res* and *verba,* e.g., *DR* i, 8, 42–44, and C. H. Rawski in Scaglione (1975), pp. 258–260. Note also Boethius, *Cons. phil.* iii, P 12, 65. On Petrarch's notion of "visual" literacy, note the beginning of *Var.* 60, Fracassetti (1863), iii, p. 473; and Trinkaus (1970), i, p. 12. On analogy in medieval thought, Marrou (1938), pp. 116–117; idem (1956), pp. 12–13, 169, 235, 285; A. Maurer in Wiener (1973), i, pp. 64–67; Trompf (1979), pp. 241–243; Berman (1983), pp. 282–286; and also Porphyry (Warren [1975], pp. 20–21). For an instructive text demonstrating the depth of interpretation associated with medieval argument by example, note, e.g., Ramon Llull, *Felix,* esp., vii [Book of the Beasts], 38–40, Bonner (1985), pp. 787–802. On the related genre of *fable,* briefly, but authoritatively, B. E. Perry in his LCL edition of Babrius and Phaedrus (1965), pp. xix–xxxiv. —In his epistolary preface to the 1492 edition of the *DR,* Niccolò Lucaro (1492: *a* verso) "comes right to the point":

> nihil in perpetuo opere sine sententiarum pondere exemplorumque ua/rietate inter legendum reperies.

> As you read [the *DR*] you do not find in the entire work anything that is not supported by notable maxims or a variety of examples.

19 *Fam.* iii, 13, 11:

> Alter tibi adsum Ypocras: amarum forte sed salubre farmacum offertur.

> As another Hippocrates I offer you this pill: bitter perhaps, but wholesome.

Cf. Nicholas of Lynn, *Kalendarium,* Canon pro medicinis dandis, Eisner (1980), p. 213, 424–434:

> Et sic quicquid confortat fortitudinem unius debilitat fortitudinem alterius, secundum apparet de duobus congredientibus ad pugnam. Cum igitur secundum astrologos Jupiter confortat res naturales, eo quod amicus est omni nature, qui vult evacuare humorem quando fortificatur natura humoris per influenciam ipsius Jovis abreviatur, opus eius et eius effectus minuitur. Exemplum ponit Haly, dicens: "Odorifera inquit confortant naturam et ideo in ipso impetu medicine debilitant effectum eius, et hinc est quod in multis medicinis applicanda sunt naribus fetida et amara."

> And thus whatever promotes strength in one weakens the strength of the other, just as is evident with two contestants in a fight. According to the

astrologers, therefore, since Jupiter strengthens natural things because he is a friend to all nature, the one who wishes to evacuate a humor when the nature of the humor is strengthened by the influence of Jupiter himself has his work cut short and his effect minimized. Haly gives an example, saying: "Pleasant odors," he says, "strengthen nature and for that reason in the very impact of the medicine weaken its effect, and this is why the constituents that are fetid to the nose and bitter are to be included in many medicines."

Eisner (1980), p. 212. —Reason acts as *medicus spiritualis*—physician for the mind (Alain de Lille, *PL* 210, c. 257. Note Augustine, *De civ. Dei* v, 14: *medicus mentium*. Cf. *DR* ii, 93, 188). Her approach is clinical: the operational argument is aimed at reasonable credibility, not philosophical or theological intelligibility. "Virtue" denotes aspects of one's state of mind, such as moderation or patience, designed to offset the cravings of the passions (*DR* i, Pref., note 41). They are inalienably man's and allow him to cope with "Fortune"—life's events as they occur—without having to despair in the individual's mission on the road to life eternal, where human virtue finds its true rewards (Lactantius, *Div. inst.* iii, 27, *PL* 6, cc. 433–436. Cf. *Sen.* viii, 3, as below, *DR* ii, Pref., note 91; and *Fam.* xxi, 12, 21, on resorting to *virtus, incorrupti fons iudicii et rationis arx inexpugnabilis atque invicta*—Virtue, the font of incorruptible judgment, and the impregnable and, indeed, invincible citadel of reason).

For his contemporaries, Petrarch's "remedies" combined both altogether new medication and tried and proven nostrums, and a bedside manner, considered original and extremely effective (cf. LAP 69; and Guido Sette on *Fam.* vi, 3, Wilkins [1958], p. 219, and *Fam.* xxiii, 12, 26–27, and 37). —Medical terminology concerning the ills of the mind and soul was used throughout Antiquity (Gruber [1978], esp. pp. 32–38). It was well known to the Christian fathers (note Jerome, e.g., *Ep.* 60, 7, and 77, 5, LCL, Wright, pp. 276, 320; Cassian, Cayré, i [1936], pp. 595–596, 598; and Wenzel [1984], esp. p. 8, and n. 11), and continued to be popular during the Middle Ages. Cf. Rabbow (1914, 1954); Auer (1947); Pohlenz (1959, 1955); Tateo (1965), pp. 36–37; and Misch, e.g., iii, 2 (1979), pp. 1171–1178. Note also Olson (1982), esp. chap. 2. —Among the many examples of medical imagery Petrarch must have encountered are those in texts by Cicero, Seneca, and Augustine. Also Boethius, *Cons. phil.,* e.g., i, P 2, 1, i, P 5, 40, i, P 6, 23–24 and 56, ii, P 1, 19–25, ii, P 5, 1–2, or iii, P 1, 7 (Pickering [1970], p. 188; Rand [1941], pp. 165–168; Burdach [1933]); Leo the Great, e.g., *Sermo* 95, 1–2, *PL* 54, cc. 461–462; John of Salisbury, *Policrat.* vii, 15, *PL* 199, c. 672; and the vocabulary of popular guides such as the *Summa virtutum de remediis animae,* the thirteenth-century source for the description of the remedial virtues opposing the seven deadly sins in Chaucer's Parson's Tale (Wenzel [1984]). Note *Sen.* x, 4 (1581: 875–876); and below, *DR* ii, 93, 188–189.

On eloquent exhortation and silent meditation, Seigel (1968), chap. 2; and Trinkaus (1970), i, pp. 11–13.

20   On *spectaculum mundi*—spectacle of the world—and *theatrum mundi*—theater of the world—Cicero, *De fin.* i, 15, 49; i Cor. 4, 9; Boethius, *Cons. phil.* ii, P 3; John of Salisbury, *Policrat.* iii, 7 and 8, *PL* 199, cc. 487–492; and Curtius (1953), pp. 138–140.

21   Cf. Krautheimer (1956, 1982), pp. 218–219. On Petrarch's visual response, e.g., *Fam.* ii, 12, iv, 1, xiii, 8, xvii, 5; and *Sen.* iv, 3, as below, *DR* i, 30, note 1. But note Krautheimer (1956, 1982), pp. 294–296, on Petrarch's approach to the monuments and sights of Antiquity.

22   (Ioan. 15, 5:)

> quia sine me nihil potestis facere.

> for without me you can do nothing

—stressed by Reason throughout the *DR* (e.g., ii, 66, 25).

23   In a way, the *DR* bodies forth the quest of *chevalerie célestienne,* which Rosemond Tuve described when speaking of Christine de Pizan's *Épitre d'Othéa* and Frère Lorens' *Somme le roi:*

> It does not at all preclude . . . an attention to the Good Knight's earthly combats with vices. But I think it may be apparent that the large literature of virtues battling with vices, which we are accustomed to think of solely as a great tableau of the psychomachia we call the moral struggle, had running through it another kind of image as well—the spirit's quest for a lost but native noblesse, regainable ultimately but not here, a noblesse which every soul had as belonging to the "kin" of the sons of God.

Tuve (1966), p. 44. —On the term *humana dignitas* (e.g., John of Salisbury, *Metalog.* i, 7, *PL* 199, cc. 834–835), Kamerbeek (1957). Innocent III, *De miseria cond. hum.,* prol., Lewis (1978), p. 93, distinguishes between *vilitas humane condicionis* and *dignitas humane nature*—the vileness of the human condition and the dignity of human nature. The latter was to be the topic of the sequel to Innocent's work of 1195, which Jean Birel, Grand Prior of the Carthusian Order, had asked Petrarch to write (above, Introduction ii, item 1). On Gianozzo Manetti and his mid-fifteenth-century reply to Innocent, cf. Kristeller (1956), pp. 284–285; Kristeller (1979), p. 170; and Trinkaus (1940), pp. 70–73.

Within the allegorical framework of the *DR,* the real emphasis is not upon some abstract encounter of "Fortune" and "Virtue" (as presented in Heitmann [1958], *passim*), but upon the old polarities of Augustine and Boethius—God and His Providence, and man with a free will—man, who is, knows, and wills (Augustine, *Conf.* xiii, 11, 12; *De trin.* x, 10, 13), and the action habits he espouses as Fortune happens; whether responding to the conditions and circumstances of life, he rises to virtue and its aspects as advocated by Reason or gives in to his natural impulses, the Passions, when he acts and "takes his chances." (Trinkaus [1979], p. 121, reaches a similar conclusion.)

Petrarch thus seems to restate the Augustinian notion of the *novus homo,* or *novus Adam*—new man, or new Adam (Col. 3, 9–10; Augustine, *De vera rel.* xxvi, 48–51 [on Petrarch's copy, Gerosa (1966), pp. 47–48, n. 15, 167; Ullman (1953), p. 129]; *pseudo*-Hugh of St. Victor, *De fructu carnis et spiritus, PL* 176, cc. 997–1006; but referred to much earlier, e.g., in the ninth-century hymn *O virgo, princeps virginum, AH* ii, 61; Dreves [1909], ii, pp. 265–266), along thoroughly human lines—not as a symbolic figure, but as contemporary man standing with both feet in life, deciding, acting, and making the choices he has to make. *Var.* 50 and 61 support this assumption. The allegorical tree and its devices Petrarch describes and interprets in the two letters (summarized in Wilkins [1958], pp. 104–105, 109) are the medieval tree of virtues (Macrobius, *Comm.* i, 8, 3–11), which, together with its counterpart, the tree of vices, dates back to John Cassian, Boniface, and *pseudo*-Hugh and was carefully described by Laurent d'Orleans in his popular *Somme le roi* (1279). Cf. Bloomfield (1952), pp. 70, 79–80, 84, 125; Jackson (1958); Fisher (1964), chap. 4, i; and Mâle (1984), pp. 108–110,

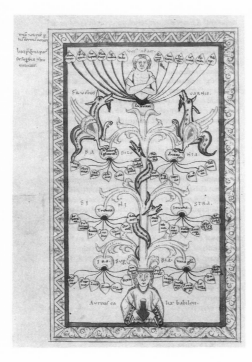

Tree of Vices. First half of 12th c. Andernach, Augustinian convent St. Maria (later, St. Thomas). Koeln, Historisches Stadtarchiv, W. f. 276a (A), f. llv. Photo Stadtarchiv.

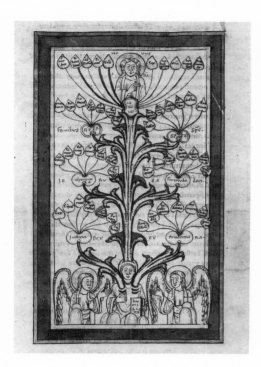

Tree of Virtues. First half of 12th c. Andernach, Augustinian convent St. Maria (later, St. Thomas). Koeln, Historisches Stadtarchiv, W. f. 276a (A), f. 12r. Photo Stadtarchiv.

192–194. Judging from Petrarch's text in *Var.* 50 and 61, as well as other iconographic references (e.g., *DR* i, 16, 71–75), we may assume that he was familiar with some of the many contemporary pictorial representations (Mâle [1984], pp. 108–110; Meiss [1951], p. 153, fig. 162; Katzenellenbogen [1939], pls. 40–41) of the trees, hence of the two Adams, *vetus* and *novus*— old and new—unregenerate and reborn in Christ, who, as a rule, appear in illustrations such as the miniatures in a twelfth-century manuscript of the *Speculum virginum* (Bernards [1955], pl. 2 and 3, and the literature cited there, note 126, pp. 27–29. Note also Ladner [1979]; or the trees in *De fructibus carnis et spiritus*, Gombrich (1972), fig. 141. Petrarch's transformation of the *novus Adam* into the common man, who is God's greatest creation (*Fam.* v, 4, 10, citing Ps. 135, 4; but note *Asclepius* 6, as pointed out in Kristeller [1979], p. 307, note 3), yet who must steer the course of his life choosing between the arguments of Reason and the Passions, anticipates one of the basic themes of humanist thought. Cf. Cassirer (1927), pp. 79–82 *et passim*; Kristeller (1956), pp. 264–265; idem (1979), chap. 9; Saxl (1957), i, pp. 68–69; Mazzeo (1965), chap. 1; Javelet (1967), chap. vii, 1, i, pp. 246–251, and pp. 20, 122, 299, 308, 314, 351, 458, ii, pp. 14, n. 124, 35, n. 281, 100, n. 151, 218, n. 114; Trinkaus (1970), esp. i, parts 1 and 2;

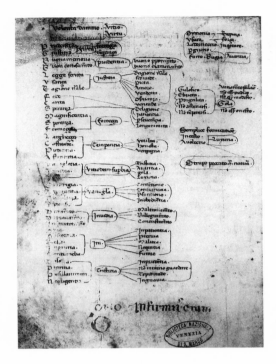

Page from Bono Giamboni, *Libro de'Vizi e delle Virtudi.* 13th c. Venice, Bibl. Marc., ms. It. li, 73, f. 46v. Foto Toso.

idem in Wiener (1973), iv, art. Renaissance Idea of the Dignity of Man; and Pickering (1970), II, iii. On the topic in Dante, Mazzotta (1979), pp. 18, 31, 38–40; and Kantorowicz (1957a), chap. 8. On the Augustinian ideas of reform and the perfectibility of man, Ladner (1959), chap. 5, esp. pp. 155–159, 185–203; and Passmore (1970), esp. chaps. 4–6. On the Augustinian notion of mankind as *lapides vivi*—living stones—of the spiritual house (i. Petr. 2, 5; *De civ. Dei* viii, 24, xviii, 45 and 48; and, earlier, Origen, *Tom.* x, 20, *PG* 14, cc. 370–371), Gilson (1960), p. 168; Frankl (1960), p. 212; and De Lubac, ii, 2 (1964), chap. vii, 2, esp. pp. 53–54.

✣

Francesco Petrarca
(1304–1374)

De remediis utriusque Fortune

B O O K I Remedies for Prosperity

Commentary

NOTES TO CONTENTS: BOOK I

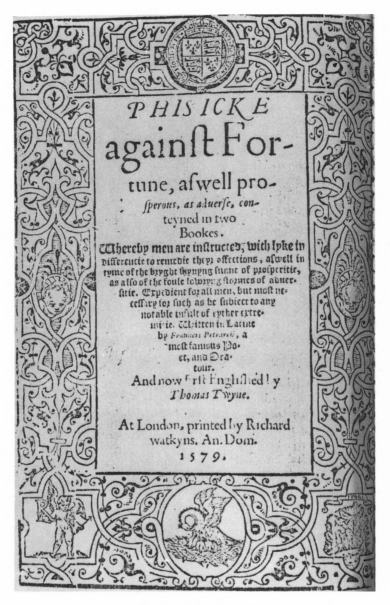

PHISICKE
againſt For-
tune, aſwell pro-
ſperous, as aduerſe, con-
teyned in two
Bookes .

Whereby men are inſtructed, with lyke in
differencie to remedie theyr affections, aſwell in
tyme of the bryght ſhynyng ſunne of proſperitie,
as alſo of the foule lowryng ſtormes of aduer-
ſitie. Expedient foz all men, but moſt ne-
ceſſary foz ſuch as be ſubiect to any
notable inſult of eyther extre-
mitie. Written in Latine
by *Frances Petrarch*, a
moſt famous Po-
et, and Ora-
tour.
And now firſt Engliſhed by
Thomas Twyne.

At London, printed by Richard
watkyns. An. Dom.
1579.

Thomas Twyne's English Translation of the *De remediis*. Title page.

NOTES TO PREFACE

1   On Azzo da Correggio, sometime lord of Parma and governor of Verona, Bigi (1866; note Wilkins [1978], pp. 139–140); Koerting (1878), pp. 99–102, 185–188, 214–216; Foresti (1977), pp. 227–231, 321–324, 339, 432–435; Burdach (1929), pp. 226–235; Masnovo (1934); Billanovich, introduction to the *Rerum memorandarum libri* (Ediz. naz., xiv, 1943), pp. xcii–xciv; Wilkins (1961), esp., pp. 26, 44–53, 61, 137, 173, 188; Rawski (1967), p. 100, n. 17; and, for the older literature, Chevalier (1960), i, c. 402. The foremost Petrarchan texts which relate to Azzo are the Pre-Chigi form of the *Canzoniere* of 1358, now lost, which "might also be called the Correggio form" (Wilkins [1951], p. 154, and chap. vi); a canzone, *Quel c'ha nostra natura,* celebrating the conquest of Parma by Azzo and his three brothers, May 23, 1341 (on this, *Fam.* iv, 9), and an epigram, *Turris parmensis,* referring to *Corrigie splendor* and Azzo as *princeps Parme* (*Rime* [1951], pp. 619–624, 848, and below, *DR* ii, 90, note 21); *Bucolicum carmen* viii, 49–50, 107–108; *Met.* iii, 27: *Perdit amice operam,* esp. 70–74; *Rer. mem. libri* ii, 13; *Var.* 28, and *Var.* 19, on Azzo's death (on or before November 17, 1362; Foresti [1977], pp. 90–91). Note also *Posteritati, Sen.* xviii, 1, *Prose* (1955), p. 16; *Fam.* ix, 5, 31–34; *Fam.* v, 10 (Foresti [1977], chap. 28; Wilkins [1961], pp. 48–51); Foresti (1977), chap. 11, on *Rime* 238; and Wilkins (1978), pp. 256, 267–270, 281.

2   Petrarch refers to Aristotle's "fifth element" in Cicero, *Tusc. disp.* i, 10, 22:

>   Aristoteles longe omnibus—Platonem semper excipio—praestans et ingenio et diligentia, cum quattuor nota illa genera principiorum esset complexus, e quibus omnia orerentur, quintam quandam naturam censet esse, e qua sit mens: cogitare enim et providere et discere et docere et invenire aliquid et meminisse, et tam multa alia, amare odisse, cupere timere, angi laetari; haec et similia eorum in horum quattuor generum inesse nullo putat: quintum genus adhibet vacans nomine . . .

>   Aristotle, who far excels everyone—always with the exception of Plato—in genius and industry, after grasping the conception of the well-known four classes of elements [i.e., fire, air, water and earth, e.g., *DR* i, 11, note 19; i, 18,

note 15] which he held to be the origin of all things, considers that there is a special fifth nature from which comes mind; for mind reflects and foresees and learns and teaches and makes discoveries and remembers and a multitude of other things: mind loves, hates, descries, fears, feels pain and joy; these and similar activities are to be found, he thinks, in none of the four first classes: he employs a fifth class without a name . . .

LCL, King, pp. 27, 29. Similar, the quotation from Cicero's lost *Consolatio,* ibid., i, 27, 66–67, on the nature of the human mind. Note also Alcuin, *Disp. de rhet.,* Howell (1941), p. 146, 1220–1226; and Boccaccio, *Decameron* x, 10, Singleton (1974), 109v, B, 51–54:

> . . . il senno de mortali non consiste solamente nellavere ad memoria le cose preterite / o conoscere le presenti / ma per luna et per laltra di queste sapere antiveder le future . . .

> . . . the understanding of mortals consists not only in having in memory things past and taking cognizance of things present; but in knowing, by means of the one and the other of these, to forecast things future . . .

Singleton (1982), pp. 791–792.

In *De inv.* ii, 53, 159–54, 165, Cicero defines virtue as *animi habitus naturae modo atque rationi consentaneus*—a habit of mind in harmony with reason and the order of nature—which has four parts, subdivided as follows:

PRUDENTIA	IUSTITIA	FORTITUDO	TEMPERANTIA
Wisdom or Prudence	*Justice*	*Courage or Fortitude*	*Restraint or Moderation*
The knowledge of what is good, what is bad, and what is neither good nor bad.	A habit of mind which gives every man his desert while preserving the common advantage.	The quality by which one undertakes dangerous tasks and endures hardships.	A firm and well-considered control exercised by reason over lust or other improper impulses of the mind.
MEMORIA—Memory INTELLIGENTIA—Intelligence PROVIDENTIA—Foresight	RELIGIO—Religion PIETAS—Devotion GRATIA—Gratitude VINDICATIO—Revenge OBSERVANTIA—Reverence VERITAS—Truth	MAGNIFICENTIA—High-mindedness FIDENTIA—Confidence PATIENTIA—Patience PERSEVERANTIA—Perseverence	CONTINENTIA—Continence CLEMENTIA—Mercy MODESTIA—Modesty

All these qualities are desirable for their own sake. Their contraries are to be avoided. Each virtue and its modes have a related vice, which is either its opposite, such as injustice and justice, or borders on it, such as stubbornness, which borders on perseverance, or superstition, which is akin to religion. In regard to the aspects of *prudentia,* Cicero explains (ibid., 160):

> Memoria est per quam animus repetit ille quae fuerunt; intelligentia, per quam ea perspicit quae sunt; providentia, per quam futurum aliquid videtur ante quam factum est.

> Memory is the faculty by which the mind recalls what has happened. Intelligence is the faculty by which it ascertains what is. Foresight is the faculty by which it is seen that something is going to occur before it occurs.

LCL, Hubbell, pp. 327, 329, 331, 333. Cf. Cicero, *De fin.* v, 23, 67; *Ad Herenn.* iii, 2, 3: . . . *prudentiam, iustitiam, fortitudinem, modestiam*: Jerome, *Ep.* 52, LCL, Wright, p. 222; and Isidore, *Etym.* ii, 24, 6:

> Ethicam Socrates . . . dividens . . . in quattuor virtutibus animae, id est prudentiam, iustitiam, fortitudinem, temperantiam.

> Socrates . . . divides ethics into four virtues of the mind, namely, prudence, justice, courage, and restraint.

On this, Fontaine (1959), ii, pp. 698–702, and the literature cited there. —In his edition of the *Rer. mem. libri,* pp. cxxiv–cxxx, Billanovich has shown that the Ciceronian paradigm of virtue and, in particular, the *prudentia* scheme of *preteritorum memoria, presentium intelligentia,* and *futurorum providentia,* which plays an important part in the *DR,* provided also the basic plan for Petrarch's earlier work. On Cicero's paradigm, Macrobius, *Comm.* i, 8; Thomas Aquinas, *Summa theol.* i, II, Q. 55. o. 5, Pegis (1945), ii, p. 426; and Brunetto Latini, *Li livres dou tresor* ii, 53–113, Carmody (1948), pp. 228–295. On *prudentia* and its three modes, Augustine, *De trin.* xiv, 11, *PL* 42, c. 1047, and *De div. quaest.* 31, 1, *PL* 40, c. 20; Pierre Bersuire, *Reductorium morale,* based on Pseudo-Seneca (Martin of Braga), *De quattuor virtutibus* (= *Formula vitae honestae,* Barlow [1950], pp. 235–250), Fabricius, v (1736), pp. 117–121; Manitius, i (1911), pp. 110–111; Panofsky (1955), pp. 148–151; Wilkins (1978), chap. xi; Tuve (1966), esp. pp. 61–62; and Suchomski (1975), pp. 37–40. Petrarch identified Martin as the author of the widely known tract in *Sen.* ii, 4 (1581: 761; Nolhac [1907], ii, pp. 120–121). On Petrarch's longtime friend Pierre Bersuire, Wilkins (1961), pp. 19, 174–176; Wilkins (1958), p. 222; Smalley (1960), pp. 261–264; and Allen (1970), esp. pp. 168–173. *De vita sol.* i, 4, *Prose* (1955), pp. 340, 342, outlines the *fourfold distinction* of the virtues based upon Plotinus-Macrobius. On the whole topic, H. F. North in Wiener (1973), iv, art. Temperance.

3   *vita: quae si rite ageretur: foelicissima prorsus ac iocundissima rerum erat.* Cf.
Sen. viii, 7 (1581) 841):

> Sic tu uitam . . . aequanimitate ac patientia, non modo tolerabilem iucundam
> efficis ac foelicem . . .

> So can you, through calmness of mind and patience, make this life not only
> tolerable, but gratifying and happy.

4   Cf. *Var.* 61, Fracassetti, iii (1863) p. 476:

> malefida enim voluptatis statio, ad quam velut ad portum mundus iners con-
> fluit, ut blandos introitus sic moestos habet ac praecipites egressus . . .

> Treacherous is the place where pleasure dwells, whereto all mankind numbly
> drifts as it if were a safe haven, so that what had such a pleasant entrance ends
> with such sad and sudden exits.

On this, Wilkins (1958), p. 107. Note also *Sen.* viii, 2 (1581: 831):

> tota uita error ac uanitas est.

> all of life is error and deception.

Here, and in many other places in the *DR,* the text seems to echo Augustine,
De civ. Dei ix, 8, quoting Apuleius, *De deo Socratis* 4:

> "Igitur homines," inquit, "ratione gaudentes, oratione pollentes, immortalibus
> animis, moribundis membris, levibus et anxiis mentibus, brutis et obnoxiis
> corporibus, dissimilibus moribus, similibus erroribus, pervicaci audacia, per-
> tinaci spe, casso labore, fortuna caduca, singillatim mortales, cuncti tamen
> universo genere perpetui, vicissim sufficienda prole mutabiles, volucri tem-
> pore, tarda sapientia, cita morte, querula vita terras incolunt."

> "So men," he says, "dwell upon the earth, proud of their reasoning faculty,
> gifted with speech, with immortal spirits but mortal members, their minds
> fickle and worried, their bodies stupid and vulnerable, unlike in their ways,
> alike in their failures, irrepressible in their audacity, unyielding in their hope,
> their toil unavailing, their fortune precarious, mortal as individuals, yet collec-
> tively persisting as a race, successively moving on as new generations replace
> the old, their time winging swiftly by, their wisdom arriving late, their death
> speedy, their life a lamentation."

LCL, Wiesen, pp. 179, 181. —On error, and *the countless roads that lead to it*
(*Fam.* iv, 2, 4), also *Fam.* ii, 2, 20, v, 17, 13, xiii, 5, 11, xvii, 3, 22, xxi, 12, 12,
xxii, 7, 16; and below, *DR* i, 11, note 1.

5   Innocent III, *De miseria cond. hum.* i, 21, Lewis (1978), p. 131:

> Semper mundane letitie tristicia repentina succedit, et quod incipit a gaudio
> desinit in merore. Mundana quippe felicitas multis amaritudinibus est respersa.

Noverat hoc ille qui dixerat: "Risus dolore miscebitur, et extrema gaudii luctus occupat."

George Gascoigne, *The Droomme of Doomes day* (1576), i, Cunliffe (1910), ii, p. 209:

> Always some sodeyne sorrowes doo succede and folow after worldly joye: And he which beginneth in joye, endeth in griefe. For the worldly felicitie is mingled with many sorrowes and sharpe mishappes, as he well knewe which sayd: "Thy laughter shall be mingled with sorrow, & lamentacion comes in th'end of rejoycing" (Prov. 14, 13).

The scriptural passage is cited *Sen.* xv, 3 (1581: 935), as below, *DR* i, 23, note 11. On the topic of "laughter," note Suchomski (1975), chap. 1.

6   *bellum quamque perpetuum quod cum fortuna gerimus:* (echoing Boethius, *Cons. phil.* ii, P 8, 1–2: . . . *inexorabile contra fortunam gerere bellum* . . .). —Cf. *Fam.* xvii, 3 (to Guido Sette, September 1353), 48:

> fortune blanditias minasque contemnito . . . Acri et implacabili cum hoste bellum gerimus; pacem sperare non possumus, victoriam possumus nisi cedimus, nisi falsis opinionibus locum damus.

> We must despise the allurements and threats of Fortune . . . We fight a war with a fierce and implacable foe; we cannot hope for peace, but we can expect victory, if we do not yield and do not pay heed to false opinions.

Note also *Fam.* xvi, 6; and *Sen.* viii, 7 (1581: 841): *tecum contra illam virtus militet*—virtue fights against Fortune with you.

7   This is the virtue Fortune cannot take away (Seneca, *Dial.* ii, 4–5)—*virtus generaliter sumpta*—virtue as such—"a generally admirable quality in human action rather than the sum of particular qualities ('virtues') which conformed to religious or philosophical prescriptions" (J. E. Seigel in Wiener [1973], iv, p. 477; and above, *Dramatis personae,* note 13). Cf. the unidentified statement, *Fam.* xi, 3, 10: *que virtutem esse ait recte sentire de Deo et recte inter homines agere*—which defines virtue as thinking right about God and acting right toward men; and the related *Sen.* vi, 8 (1581: 555): *qui recte prorsus opinarentur . . . et recte agerent*—those who, in short, thought right . . . and acted right. Note Aristotle, *Eth. Nic.* ii, 6, 1106a, 20, 1106b, 35, Barnes (1984), pp. 1747, 1748; Cicero, *De inv.* ii, 53, as note 1 above; Augustine, e.g., *De lib. arb.* ii, 19, *PL* 32, c. 1268, and *De civ. Dei* iv, 21: *ars quippe ipsa bene recteque vivendi virtus definita est*—virtue was in fact defined [by the ancients] as the art of living rightly and well (LCL, Green, p. 75); and *Glossa ordinaria,* on Job 4, 6, *PL* 113, c. 764. On the identification of Hercules as a representative of *virtus generaliter sumpta* in Trecento Italy, Panofsky (1960), pp. 149–150, n. 4; and idem (1962), p. 157. On the whole subject, Seigel, op. cit., pp. 476–486; and Heitmann (1958), Part i, B. In *Secretum* i, Augustinus' initial argument runs as follows:

1. a. *sola virtus animum felicitat*—only virtue can bring happiness to the human mind (*Prose* [1955], pp. 32, 34; cf. Cicero, *Tusc. disp.* v, 1, 1, *et passim*; and *De fin.* v, 26, 77); which implies *ut nichil quoque nisi virtutis oppositum a felicitate dimoveat*—that nothing is opposed to happiness except what is also opposed to virtue (*Prose,* ibid., p. 34). Hence

   b. *nisi vitio miserum non esse neque fieri*—no one can become or be unhappy except through his own fault (*Prose,* ibid.).

2.   *Ad evadendum huius nostre mortalitatis angustias ad tollendumque se se altius*—To avoid the distresses of this mortal life and rise up to higher things,

   a. *primum veluti gradum obtinere meditationem mortis humaneque miserie*—the first step is to meditate on death and on man's misery;

   b. *secundum vero desiderium vehemens studiumque surgendi*—the second, to have a vehement desire and purpose to rise (*Prose,* ibid.), always aware of the fact that

3.   *in animis hominum perversa quedam et pestilens libido, se ipsos fallendi*—in the minds of men there is a perverse and dangerous inclination to deceive themselves (*Prose,* ibid., p. 36).

(Based on Draper [1911], pp. 12–15.) On this, Koerting (1878), pp. 630–631; and Heitmann (1960), pp. 34–38. These topics are addressed throughout the *DR*.

8   [*Fortuna*] . . . *de nobis ludit:* —Seneca Rhetor, *Controv.* v, 1 (243M): *ludit de suis Fortuna muneribus.* Note Horace, *Carm.* i, 1, 3, iii, 29, 49–52, and *Sat.* ii, 8, 62–63; Seneca, *Ep.* 74, 7: *ludos facere fortunam* (similar, idem, Dial. ix, De tranqu. 11, 5, xi, Ad Polyb. 16, 2; and Pliny the Younger, *Ep.* iv, 11, 3); Statius, *Theb.* xii, 35; also Ovid, *Ex pont.* iv, 3, 49; and Boethius, *Cons. phil.* ii, P 1, 35–37, P 2, 29, Gruber (1978), pp. 164, 3, 175, 9.

9   Dante, *Div. Comm.,* Purg. i, 1–3:

> Per correr miglior acque alza le vele
>   omai la navicella del mio ingegno,
>   che lascia dietro a sé mar sì crudele . . .

> To course over better waters the little bark
>   of my genius now hoists her sails, leaving behind her
>   a sea so cruel . . .

Singleton (1973), p. 3. On this, idem, *Commentary* (1973), p. 3.

10   Seneca, *Ep.* 5, 7–9.

> Quemadmodum eadem catena et custodiam et militem copulat, sic ista, quae tam dissimilia sunt, pariter incedunt; spem metus sequitur. Nec miror ista sic ire; utrumque pendentis animi est, utrumque futuri exspectatione solliciti. Maxima autem utriusque causa est, quod non ad praesentia aptamur, sed

cogitationes in longinqua praemittimus. Itaque providentia, maximum bonum condicionis humanae, in malum versa est. Ferae pericula, quae vident, fugiunt; cum effugere, securae sunt; nos et venturo torquemur et praeterito. Multa bona nostra nobis nocent, timoris enim tormentum memoria reducit, providentia anticipat. Nemo tantum praesentibus miser est.

Just as the same chain fastens the prisoner and the soldier who guards him, so hope and fear, dissimilar as they are, keep step together; fear follows hope. I am not surprised that they proceed in this way; each alike belongs to a mind that is in suspense, a mind that is fretted by looking forward to the future. But the chief cause of both these ills is that we do not adapt ourselves to the present, but send our thoughts a long way ahead. And so foresight, the noblest blessing of the human race, becomes perverted. Beasts avoid the dangers which they see, and when they have escaped them are free from care; but we men torment ourselves over that which is to come as well as over that which is past. Many of our blessings bring bane to us; for memory recalls the tortures of fear, while foresight anticipates them. The present alone can make no man wretched.

LCL Gummere, pp. 23, 25. Cf. Pohlenz, i (1959), p. 322, ii (1955), p. 160.
11 *cum Cerbero tricipiti hoste luctandum est.* —Cerberus, the three-headed Hound of Hell, whose capture was the twelfth labor of Hercules (Virgil, *Aeneid* vi, 417–423; Boethius, *Cons. phil.* iii, M 12, 29–30, iv, M 7, 19, Gruber (1978), pp. 317, *29f*, 375, *19*; Isidore, *Etym.* xi, 3, 33: [*Cerberus*] . . . *tria capita habentem* = Hrabanus Maurus, *De univ.* vii, 7, *PL* 111, c. 198; Dante, *Div. Comm.,* Inf. vi, 13–18; Graves [1955], i, 31, 34, ii, 134). On Cerberus as a symbol of the three modes of time (past, present, future) and of Prudence (memory, intellect, foresight; note 1 above), Panofsky (1955), chap. 4.

In the *Africa,* Petrarch described, among other representations of the gods in the palace of King Syphax of Numidia, a sculpture of Apollo based on Macrobius' discussion of the Serapis cult in Hellenistic Egypt and Serapis' three-headed creature, which Plutarch had equated with Cerberus (*De Iside et Osiride* 78; Panofsky, ibid., pp. 152–153):

Macrobius, *Saturn.* i, 20, 13–15

quod exprimit medio eodemque maximo capite leonis effigiem, dextra parte caput canis exoritur mansueta specie blandientis, pars vero laeva cervicis rapacis lupi capite finitur, easque formas animalium draco conectit volumine suo, capite redeunte ad dei dexteram qua compescitur monstrum. Ergo leonis capite monstratur praesens tempus, quia condicio eius inter praeteritum futurumque actu praesenti valida fervensque est. Sed et praeteritum tempus lupi capite signatur, quod memoria rerum transactarum rapitur et aufertur. Item canis blandientis effigies futuri temporis designat eventum, de quo nobis spes, licet incerta, blanditur. Tempora autem cui nisi proprio famularentur auctori?

The middle head of this figure, which is also the largest, represents a lion's; on the right a dog raises its head with a gentle and fawning air; and on the left the neck ends in the head of a ravening wolf. All three beasts are joined together by the coils of a serpent whose head turns to the god's right hand which keeps the monster in check. The lion's head, then, is a symbol of time present, which midway between the past and the future, has the strength and ardor of immediate action; time past is represented by the head of the wolf, because the memory of things that are over and done is swiftly borne away; so too the likeness of a fawning dog indicates the issue of time to come, the object of our hopes, which are uncertain but flatter us. And indeed times and seasons are surely the servants of the power that creates them.

Davies (1969), p. 139.

Africa iii, 156–164

> Proximus imberbi specie crinitus Apollo:
> Hic puer, hic iuvenis, nec longo tempora tractu
> Albus erat sacer, ante pedes rapidusque, fremensque
> Stabat equus, quatiensque solum mandebat habenas.
> At iuxta monstrum ignotum, immensumque trifauci
> Assidet ore sibi, placitum blandumque tuenti
> Dextra canem, sed laeva lupum fert atra rapacem
> Parte leo medio est, simul hoc serpente reflexo
> Iunguntur capita, & fugientia tempora signant. . . .

> Next comes beardless Apollo with flowing hair:
> Here a boy, there a young man, but in short
>   time with all white hair.
> Before him stands his sacred horse,
> Swift-footed, neighing, champing at the bit.
> Next to the god a huge, strange monster sits,
> Its triple-throated face turned up to him
> In friendly manner. On the right it looks
> A dog and on the left, a grasping wolf.
> Midway a lion. And a curling snake
> Conjoins these heads; they mean the fleeting times. . . .

Panofsky (1955), p. 155.

In Seznec's analysis of the image of Apollo as described in the *Libellus de imaginibus deorum* (Seznec [1953], p. 178),

Apollo, sometimes with the face of a child, or that of a young man, always beardless, or again as an old man;

Bows, arrows, and quiver in right hand; in left, the zither;

Apollo and the Muses. Ca. 1420. *Libellus de imaginibus deorum*. Rome, Bibl. Vat., lat. 1290, f. lv. Photo Library.

Three-headed monster beneath the god's feet . . .

Under the laurel tree, the nine Muses forming a choir;

At a slight distance, the great serpent Python . . .

all are Petrarchan images (*Africa* iii, 156–171).

The translation of Cerberus is complete in miniatures such as the one in the fifteenth-century *Livre des échecs amoureux* (Paris, B.N. f. frç. 143), which shows Pluto and Proserpina, the rulers of the underworld, attended by Cerberus, replete with heads of a dog, lion, and wolf. Seznec (1953), p. 196, fig. 80.

On the use of Petrarch's text by Bersuire, who endowed the *tricipitium*—triple head—with a *corpus serpentinum*—serpent's body—and its significance in Renaissance mythography and imagery, Panofsky, ibid., pp. 156–168; Seznec, ibid., pp. 94–95, 172–179; and Wilkins (1978), pp. 71–85.

12 Some of Petrarch's remarks recall Seneca's "*Quid est homo?*" *Dial.* vi, Ad Marciam, 11. —Blaise Pascal wrote in the late 1650s:

We do not rest satisfied with the present. We anticipate the future as too slow in coming, as if in order to hasten its course; or we recall the past, to stop its too rapid flight. So imprudent are we that we wander in the times which are

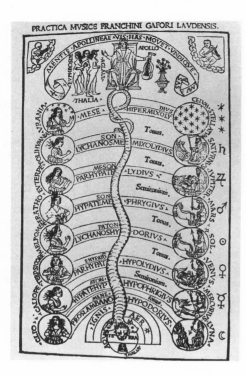

Franchinus Gaffurius, *Practica musicae* (1496). Title page. Photo T. G. Morris.

not ours, and do not think of the only one which belongs to us; and so idle are we that we dream of those times which are no more, and thoughtlessly overlook that which alone exists. For the present is generally painful to us. We conceal it from our sight, to see it pass away. We try to sustain it by the future, and think of arranging matters which are not in our power, for a time which we have no certainty of reaching.

Let us each one examine his thoughts, and he will find them all occupied with the past and the future. We scarcely ever think of the present; and if we think of it, it is only to take light from it to arrange the future. The present is never our end. The past and the present are our means; the future alone is our end. So we never live, but we hope to live; and, as we are always preparing to be happy, it is inevitable we should never be so.

Trotter (1941), *Pensées* 172, pp. 60–61.

13   *Fam.* xxi, 12, 23:

Nil mortalibus arduum, ait Flaccus. Ita est; quedam nobis impossibilia torpor fecit, nichil prorsus impervium est virtuti; multa possumus, nisi desperata priusquam tentata liquissemus.

Nothing is too hard for mortal men, said Horace [*Carm.* i, 3, 37]. And he is quite right. It is sloth that makes things impossible for us; nothing can resist strength of mind. There are many things we could do if we didn't renounce them in despair without making an effort.

Bishop (1966), p. 174.

14 *Learned men are scarce*—an often recurring topic in the *DR*. Cf. *Fam.* xxiv, 12, 34–37; or *Fam.* xiv, 2, 6–7:

> Docti autem enim semper pauci, nostra etate paucissimi; cito autem, nisi sapientia divina providerit, nulli erunt.

> The learned, who are always scarce, are extremely scarce in our age, and soon, unless divine wisdom provides otherwise, there will be none.

15 In *Met.* i, 6 (to Giacomo Colonna, Bishop of Lombez, Vaucluse, c. 1338), 181–183, 189–197 (*Rime* [1951], pp. 736, 738), Petrarch mentions that secret friends—his books—are always with him:

> . . . . comitesque latentes,
> quos michi de cuntis simul omnia secula terris
> transmittunt . . . .
> . . . . et multa canunt et multa loquuntur.
> Nature secreta alii, pars optima vite
> consilia et mortis, pars inclita gesta priorum,
> pars sua, preteritos renovant sermonibus actus.
> Sunt qui festivis pellant fastidia verbis,
> quique iocis risum revehant, sunt omnia ferre
> qui doceant, optare nichil, cognoscere se se;
> sunt pacis, sunt militie, sunt arva colendi
> artifices strepitusque fori pelagique viarum.

> They come to me from every century
> And every land . . . .
> Sometimes they sing for me;
> Some tell me of the mysteries of nature;
> Some give me counsel for my life and death;
> Some tell of high emprise, bringing to mind
> Ages long past; some with their jesting words
> Dispel my sadness, and I smile again;
> Some teach me to endure, to have no longing,
> To know myself. Masters are they of peace,
> Of war, of tillage, and of eloquence,
> And travel o'er the sea.

Wilkins (1961), pp. 20–21. Similar, *Fam.* iii, 18, 3:

> . . . libri medullitus delectant, colloquuntur, consulunt et viva quadam nobis atque arguta familiaritate iunguntur, neque solum se se lectoribus quisque suis insinuat, sed et aliorum nomen ingerit et alter alterius desiderium facit.

But books thrill you to the marrow; they talk to you, counsel you, admit you to their living, speaking friendship. Nor do they insinuate themselves alone into the reader's spirit; they introduce other books; each one creates a desire for another.

Bishop (1966), p. 40. Note also below, *DR* i, 44, note 19. —On the nautical metaphor of the text, e.g., *Fam.* xxiv, 5, 5–9; and *DR* i, 109, note 16.

16   On *vera philosophia*—the true philosophy—and its detractors, e.g., *Fam.* ii, 4, 28, vi, 2, 4, 16, xii, 3, 10, xvi, 14, 11; and *De sui ipsius,* as below, *DR* ii, 97, note 13. On medieval academic disputations, Kenny and Pinborg in Kretzmann (1982), pp. 21–33; and Von den Steinen (1959), pp. 293–295.

17   1492: Nam te . . . fecerat: fortuna . . .
      1581: Natura te . . . fecerat, fortuna . . .

18   *turbido quodam ac profundo negociorum: & curarum pelago.* Cf. *DR* ii, 76, 14, Fortuna as *pelagus procellosus.*

19   Cf. the anonymous entry in *Rer. mem. libri* ii, 13. *De memoria*—On Memory:

> . . .   . . . ab adolescentia ad hanc etatem tam multis et domus et patrie laboribus periculisque iactatus est, ut otiosum ferme nullum tempus invenerit. Quo nichil huic de qua loquimur facultati potest esse funestius: vaga enim mens multa complectitur, pauca stringit. Ceterum huic inter varias et innumerabiles ac discerpentes animum curas inexhaustam quandam memoriam militarem insitam animadverti, que me crebro in horrorem compulit cogitantem quanto uberior fuisset, si eam sibi—quod studiosi homines solent—circumvallare ac fulcire quotidiana lectione licuisset. Vidisse semel vel audisse sat est, nunquam obliviscitur; nec res modo meminit, sed verba tempusque et locum ubi quid primum accepit. Sepe totos dies aut longas noctes colloquendo transegimus: audiendi namque cupidior nemo est; post annos vero suborta earundem rerum mentione, siquid forte plus minus ve aut aliter dixissem, submissa voce confestim admonebat hoc me aut illud verbum immutare; mirantique et unde hoc nosset percunctanti non solum tempus quo id ex me audivisset, sed sub cuius ilicis umbraculo, ad cuius undam fluminis, in cuius maris litore, cuius montis in vertice—longinquas enim secum oras circuivi—me singula recognoscente memorabat. Quod iterum et iterum expertus, fateor, ad loquendum illo presente vel cautior certe vel tardior factus sum. Et hec quidem memoria sub armis, at sequens sub amictu religionis inter libros habitat.

> . . .   . . . from youth to his present age [Azzo] was thrown into so many troubles and dangers at home as well as in public life that he found hardly any time for quiet leisure—and nothing is more detrimental to the faculty we are talking about. A roving mind covers much, but retains little. Yet I must note the unsurpassed memory he displayed as a soldier amidst countless different and distracting cares of the mind—and many times I have been awestruck when I thought how much more productive his memory could have been had he, like others given to intellectual pursuits, been able to protect and fortify himself with daily readings. To see or to hear was enough for him. He never forgot. Not

only did he remember the subject matter, but the words, the time, and the place where he first heard it. Often we spent entire days and long nights in conversation. Nobody is more eager to listen than he. And if, years after the time some matter had been mentioned, I would refer to it with more, or less, or different words, he, without fail, would quietly point out where I had changed the story or some word; and when, surprised, I asked him how he knew all this, he would tell me not only the time when he first heard it from me, but where—in what shady grove, at what rushing stream, at what ocean shore, on top of what mountain—recalling all the distant places I visited with him, as I recognized each single detail. Having experienced this again and again, I confess, I have become much more cautious and more careful when I say things in his presence. And, indeed, this remarkable memory, which now dwells amidst arms, has also dwelt among books, garbed in the cloth of the Faith.

Azzo's memory is still mentioned in Morhof (1747), i, p. 369. On Azzo's clerical state, Koerting (1878), p. 101. —Note also the echoes of our text, lines 57–61, in *Fam.* xxiii, 18, 2.

20 Paraphrased in *Fam.* xx, 8, 22. —Petrarch thought well of proverbs, the truth value of which appeared to him as *great and self-evident*. Cf. *Fam.* vi, 5, 5, xx, 8, 19.

21 Cf. *Ad Herenn.* iv, 54, 68; and Curtius (1953), Exc. 13. The topic recurs in *Fam.* xx, 11, 1: *sententiosa brevitas*; and *De vir. ill.,* Prohem. 6. —On brevity in Boethius, Lerer (1985), pp. 73–74, 81–84. On Isidorean *brevitas*—brevity and conciseness—Fontaine (1959), ii, pp. 766–770. Note also Alcuin, *Disp. de rhet.,* Howell (1941), 1194–1198; and Hugh of St. Victor, *Didasc.* iii, 11:

> memoria hominis hebes est, et brevitate gaudet, et, si in multa dividitur, fit minor in singulis. Debemus ergo in omni doctrina breve aliquid et certum colligere, quod in arcula memoriae recondatur, unde postmodum, cum res exigit, reliqua deriventur.

> The memory of man is dull and likes brevity, and, if it is dissipated upon many things, it has less to bestow upon each of them. We ought, therefore in all we learn, to gather brief and dependable abstracts to be stored in the little chest of the memory, so that later on, when need arises, we can derive everything else from them.

Taylor (1961), p. 94. —In Hugh's time (he died in 1141), and well into the fourteenth century, *brevitas compendiosa*—in-sum-brevity (e.g., *CS* I, p. 136b)—was associated with *modernitas. Gaudent brevitate moderni*—moderns prize brevity—a formulaic phrase occurring in the Franconian treatises on musical notation (e.g., ms. Saint Victor 813, f. 272, Coussemaker [1852], p. 265; *CS* I, pp. 292, 303, 383), had broader significance; cf. the opening of Thomas le Myésier's early-fourteenth century *Breviculum seu parvum Electorium*:

> Domine, moderni gaudent brevitate considerabilium . . .

Hillgarth (1971), p. 179, pl. xi. On *modernitas,* also Walter Map, *De nugis curialium,* as quoted in Chenu (1968), pp. 320–321; Curtius (1953), pp. 251–255; Ladner (1959), p. 45 and n. 38; and Stock (1983), pp. 517–521. On Petrarch as a *modernus,* Mann (1984), esp. pp. 19–22, 105–109.

22 *in ordinario ut ita dicam fortunae certamine.* Compare Boethius, *Consol. phil.* iv, P 7, 40: *quotiens in fortunae certamen adducitur.* Note Seneca, *Ep.* 113, 27–28; and related, Cicero, *Tusc. disp.* i, 45, 109: *cum fortuna bella,* as below, *DR* i, 92, note 11.

23 1492: Difficilius esse tristia sustinere quam a delectabilibus abstinere
    1581: Difficilius esse tristitia sustinere quam delectabilius abstinere

Aristotle, *Eth. Nic.* iii, 9, 1117a, 34, Barnes (1984), p. 1764. On good and ill fortune, *idem, Phys.* ii, 197a, 25–32.

24 Seneca, *Ep.* 66, 49:

> Maius est enim difficilia perfringere quam laeta moderari.

LCL, Gummere, p. 33. 1492 and 1581 read *Maius est difficilia perstringere . . .*

Durum quidem: & temeritatis parata suspicio novo homini vĕtūstă¹ tăngēntĭ. This is *cursus planus* and may serve as an example of the use of rhythmic *cursus* endings in our text. On this system of rhythmical clausulae, Scaglione (1972), pp. 98–105, and in Murphy (1978), pp. 261–262; and Murphy (1974), *passim,* esp. pp. 160–161, and the literature cited there. On Petrarch's use of *cursus,* Billanovich (1947), pp. 193–198; Wilkins (1951), p. 323; Martellotti (1983), chap. 16; and C. H. Rawski in Scaglione (1975), esp. p. 272, Detail 2 (where in the column *clausulae* the symbols for lines 1, 5, 8, 10, 11, 13, 14, 18, 23, and 26 should be deleted). The assumption that Petrarch "threw away" the *cursus* (Von den Steinen [1959]) has never been tested on a broad scale.

26 Cicero, *Brutus Letters* xvii, 6:

> neque enim impetrari potest, quin, quale, quidque videatur ei, talem quisque de illo opinionem habeat.

LCL, Cary, p. 681.

27 During the Middle Ages and the Renaissance, the favorite Ciceronian reference on the virtues was *De inv.* ii, 53–54 (Tuve [1966], chap. 2; Yates [1966], pp. 20–21); cf. note 2, above. Yet Petrarch seems to allude to Cicero's remarks in *Tusc. disp.* iii, 8, 16–18:

> Veri etiam simile illud est, qui sit temperans, —quem Graeci σώφρονα appellant eamque virtutem σωφροσύνην vocant, quam soleo equidem tum temperantiam, tum moderationem appellare, non nunquam etiam modestiam, sed haud scio an recte ea virtus frugalitas appellari possit, quod angustius apud Graecos valet, qui frugi homines χρησίμους appellant, id est, tantum modo

utiles; at illud est latius; omnis enim abstinentia, omnis innocentia—quae apud
Graecos usitatum nomen nullum habet, sed habere potest αβλάβειαν: nam est
innocentia adfectio talis animi, quae noceat nemini—reliquas etiam virtutes
frugalitas continet; quae nisi tanta esset et si iis angustiis, quibus plerique
putant, teneretur, numquam esset L. Pisonis cognomen tanto opere laudatum.
Sed quia nec qui propter metum praesidium reliquit, quod est ignaviae, nec qui
propter avaritiam clam depositum non reddidit, quod est iniustitiae, nec qui
propter temeritatem male rem gessit, quod est stultitiae, *frugi* appellari solet,
eo tris virtutes, fortitudinem, iustitiam, prudentiam, frugalitas complexa est—:
etsi hoc quidem commune est virtutum: omnes enim inter se nexae et iugatae
sunt—: reliqua igitur est, quarta virtus ut sit, ipsa frugalitas. Eius enim videtur
esse proprium motus animi appetentis regere et sedare semperque adver-
santem libidini moderatam in omni re servare constantiam: cui contrarium
vitium nequitia dicitur. *Frugalitas,* ut opinor, a *fruge,* qua nihil melius e terra,
nequitia ab eo—etsi erit hoc fortasse durius, sed temptemus; lusisse putemur,
si nihil sit—, ab eo, quod *nequidquam* est in tali homine, ex quo idem *nihili*
dicitur. Qui sit frugi igitur vel, si mavis, moderatus et temperans, eum necesse
est esse constantem; qui autem constans, quietum; qui quietus, perturbatione
omni vacuum, ergo etiam aegritudine; et sunt illa sapientis; aberit igitur a
sapienti aegritudo.

It is also probable that the temperate man—the Greeks call him σώφρων, and
they apply the term σωφρωσύνη to the virtue which I usually call, sometimes
temperance, sometimes self-control, and occasionally also discretion; but, it
may be, the virtue could rightly be called 'frugality,' the term corresponding
to which has a narrower meaning with the Greeks, who call 'frugal' men
χρήσιμοι, that is to say simply useful; but our term has a wider meaning, for it
connotes all abstinence and inoffensiveness (and this with the Greeks has no
customary term, but it is possible to use αβλάβεια, harmlessness; for inoffensiveness is a disposition of the soul to injure no one)—well, 'frugality' em-
braces all the other virtues as well; had its meaning not been so comprehensive
and had it been confined to the narrow limits of ordinary acceptation, it would
never have become the much eulogized surname of L. Piso (i.e. Lucius
Calpurnius Piso, surnamed Frugi, consul 133 B.C.). But because neither the man
who through fear has deserted his post, which is proof of cowardice, nor the
man who through avarice has failed to restore a trust privately committed to
him, which is a proof of unrighteousness, nor the man who through rashness
has mismanaged a business transaction, which is a proof of folly, are usually
called 'frugal,' 'frugality' has come to include the three virtues of fortitude,
justice and prudence: (though this is a feature common to the virtues; for they
are all mutually linked and bound together). Therefore I count 'frugality' by
itself as left to be the fourth virtue. For it seems to be its special function to
guide and compose the eager impulses of the soul and, by a constant opposition to lust, to preserve on every occasion a tempered firmness: and the vice
which is its opposite is 'worthlessness.' 'Frugality,' as I think, is derived from
'fruit' and nothing better comes from the earth: 'worthlessness' is derived (the
derivation, it may be, will be somewhat harsh; but all the same let us make the

attempt; let it be taken as a jest if it should come to nothing) from that which is *nequidquam,* 'for nothing,' in a man of that kind; hence he is also said to be 'good for nothing.' The man therefore who is 'frugal' or, should you prefer it, self-restrained and temperate must be firm; the firm man must be calm; the calm man must be free from all disturbance, therefore free from distress as well. All these are characteristic of the wise man. Therefore distress will keep far away from the wise man.

LCL, King, pp. 243, 245, 247. *Modestia* and its synonyms, *temperantia* (Alain de Lille: *temperantia vel modestia, PL* 210, c. 161; and note 2, above), *frugalitas, sobrietas,* occur frequently in the *DR*. Note also below, *DR* i, 2, note 25; and ii, 99, note 2. On *frugalitas/modestia, Sen.* viii, 7 (1581: 841), *DR* i, 41, 38; and i, 96, 197. On the order of listing the cardinal virtues (from *Ad Herenn.* iii, 2, 3, and Cicero, *De inv.* ii, 53, 159, to Isidore, *Etym.* ii, 24, 6), Fontaine (1959), ii, pp. 698–700.

28 1492: ut sic opiner

1581: ut sic opinor

29 Boethius, *Cons. phil.* ii, P 8:

Etenim plus hominibus reor aduersam quam prosperam prodesse fortunam. Illa enim semper specie felicitatis cum uidetur blanda, mentitur; haec semper uera est, cum se instabilem mutatione demonstrat. Illa fallit, haec instruit, illa mendacium specie bonorum mentes fruentium ligat, haec cognitione fragilis felicitatis absoluit. Itaque illam uideas uentosam, fluentem suique semper ignaram, hanc sobriam succinctamque et ipsius aduersitatis exercitatione prudentem. Fostremo felix a uero bono deuios blanditiis trahit, aduersa plerumque ad uera bona reduces unco retrahit.

I am convinced that adverse fortune is more beneficial to men than prosperous fortune. When Fortune seems kind, and seems to promise happiness, she lies. On the other hand, when she shows herself unstable and changeable, she is truthful. Good fortune deceives, adverse fortune teaches. Good fortune enslaves the minds of good men with the beauty of the specious goods which they enjoy; but bad fortune frees them by making them see the fragile nature of happiness. You will notice that good fortune is proud, insecure, ignorant of her true nature; but bad fortune is sober, self-possessed, and prudent through the experience of adversity. Finally, good fortune seduces weak men away from the true good through flattery; but misfortune often turns them around and forcibly leads them back to the true good.

Green (1962), p. 40. Based on this is *Roman de la Rose,* lines 4837–4864, 4893–4895:

And now that we come to Fortune . . . I should like to tell you a great marvel of which I don't believe you have ever heard the like. I don't know if you'll be able to credit it, but it is true nevertheless, and one may find it written, that perverse, contrary Fortune is worth more and profits men more than does pleasant and agreeable Fortune. If this idea seems doubtful to you, it still can be proved by reasoning. Pleasant, agreeable Fortune lies to men, tricks them, and makes fools of them. Like a mother, she suckles them, and does not seem to give bitter milk. She gives them the appearance of being loyal when she distributes among them her delights—riches and honor, dignities and author-ity—and promises them stability in a condition of mutability; and when she places them on her wheel, she feeds them all on vain glory in worldly prosper-ity. . . .   . . . But when contrary, perverse Fortune turns them from their high estate and tumbles them around the wheel from the summit toward the mire; when like a mother-in-law, she places on their hearts a painful plaster moistened, not with vinegar, but with unhappy, meager poverty; then she shows that she is sincere and that no one should trust himself to prosperous Fortune, in whom there is no security whatever. . . .

Dahlberg (1971), pp. 102–103, and his note, p. 377. Note also *Stimulus con-scientie* (translated, perhaps by Richard Rolle, as *The Pricke of Conscience*), citing Gregory I:

> si omnis fortuna timenda est, magis tamen prospera quam adversa

> though all Fortune is to be feared, prosperity should be feared more than adversity.

Ed. R. Morris (1863), 1311–1312. On this, *Fam.* vi, 3, 41, xii, 2, 4–6, xx, 8, 20; *Sen.* ii, 3 (1581: 758); *Rer. mem. libri* iii, 33, 1; and *De vita sol.* i, *Prose* (1955), pp. 376, 378. On *robur animi*—strength of mind—note below, *DR* ii, 51, 76, ii, 114, *passim.* —Among Petrarch's encounters with *those overthrown by prosperous Fortune* was his acquaintance in the 1340s and 1350s with Cola di Rienzo, the ill-fated Tribune August of the Romans (below, *DR* i, 89, 14–22). —On *robur animi,* cf. below, *DR* ii, 51, note 11.

30   Perhaps deliberately, Petrarch uses time-honored and, probably, widely known phraseology. Cf. the remarks of Emperor Frederick II in his letter to the people of Bologna about the Goddess Fortuna, more than a century ear-lier, Kantorowicz (1957b), pp. 670–671. Also Seneca, *Dial.* xii, *Ad Helviam matrem* 5, 4–5:

> Neminem adversa fortuna comminuit, nisi quem secunda decepit. Illi qui munera eius velut sua et perpetua amaverunt, qui se suspici propter illa volu-erunt, iacent et maerent, cum vanos et pueriles animos, omnis solidae voluptatis ignaros, falsa et mobilia oblectamenta destituunt; at ille, qui se laetis rebus non inflavit, nec mutatis contrahit. Adversus utrumque statum invictum animum tenet exploratae iam firmitatis; nam in ipsa felicitate, quid contra infelicitatem valeret, expertus est.

> No man is crushed by hostile Fortune who is not first deceived by her smiles. Those who love her gifts as if they were their very own and lasting, who desire to be esteemed on account of them, grovel and mourn when the false and fickle

delights forsake their empty, childish minds, that are ignorant of every stable pleasure; but he who is not puffed up by happy fortune does not collapse when it is reversed. The man of long-tested constancy, when faced with either condition, keeps his mind unconquered; for in the very midst of prosperity he proves his strength to meet adversity.

LCL, Basore, p. 427. —On pertinent *exempla,* Heitmann (1958), p. 154; and below, *DR* i, 37, 97, ii, 90, 185, etc. On *oblivious to his real condition,* cf. *DR* ii, 79, note 18.

31 *In proverbium venit magni laboris esse: ferre prosperitatem.* Echoed in *La Celestina* xi, 2, Marciales (1985), ii, p. 191; Simpson (1955), p. 125.

32 I.t.: Flaccus

33 Horace, *Carm.* iii, 27, 74–75:

> . . . bene ferre magnam
> disce fortunam:

34 *Sed quoniam & virtus & veritas publicae sunt*: cf. Seneca, *Ep.* 33, 11, and 71, 16; and Billanovich (1960), p. 10. —*Outdoing the ancients,* although and because we are late heirs to classical Antiquity, is an important notion in the medieval tradition

> graphically summarised by a twelfth-century scholar, Bernard of Chartres, who had described his contemporaries as dwarfs on the shoulders of giants, able to see further than their predecessors, but only because they were raised up upon their colossal shoulders [cf. John of Salisbury, *Metalog.* iii, 4, Webb (1929), p. 136]. The humanist (in the original sense of classical scholar) of the twelfth century, as indeed his fourteenth-century successor, was constantly aware of all that made his elevated position possible, yet also of the implications of that elevated position: he was uniquely placed to outshine his models. To progress beyond the tradition from which he had sprung is a fundamental Petrarchan aspiration, and his efforts to achieve this are a familiar topic in his writings.

Mann (1984), p. 20. On this, also Lowenthal (1985), pp. 75–87; Stock (1983), pp. 33, 497–498, 517–521; Berschin (1980), pp. 13, 27, n. 2; Jeauneau (1967); Merton (1965); Kantorowicz (1957a), p. 277, n. 7; and Ghellinck (1945). —Note *Sen.* v, 2 (1581: 795):

> O aetas ingloria, tu ne antiquitatem matrem tuam, honestarum omnium artium repertricem, spernis? Teque illi non aequare tantum, sed praeferre audes?

> O inglorious time! Do you spurn Antiquity, your mother, the discoverer of all honest arts and crafts? Do you dare to proclaim yourself not merely the equal but the superior of Antiquity?

Bishop (1966), p. 245. Related, *imitatio, DR* i, 29, note 12; and *aemulatio, DR* i, 44, note 3.

35 Petrarch has reference to the *De remediis fortuitorum,* a brief dialogue, for centuries ascribed to Seneca (Haase, iii [1886], pp. 446–457, and Bloomfield [1979], no. 2956; attributed to Martin of Braga [d. A.D. 579] in Toynbee [1965], arts. Martinus Dumiensis, and *Fortuitorum remedia,* but not included in the critical edition of Martin's *opera omnia,* ed. Barlow [1950]), in which *Ratio* and *Sensus*—Reason and Feeling—discuss remedies for adverse Fortune, such as death, exile, affliction, and sorrow. The book is addressed to Seneca's brother Gallio, to whom is also inscribed Seneca's essay *De beata vita.* On this, Kristeller (1984), pp. 116–117; Nolhac (1907), ii, pp. 119–120; and Fabricius, ii (1773), pp. 118, 121, 123. In *Sen.* ii, 4 (1581: 761, Barlow [1950], p. 205), Petrarch identified Martin of Braga as the real author of the *Formula vitae honestae* (identical with *De quatuor virtutibus,* Bloomfield [1979], no. 4457), long considered a work by Seneca (note Hortis [1879], esp. pp. 22–24, 33–34; and Sabbadini, i [1905], pp. 185, 220, ii [1914], pp. 14, 57, 250). —The *De remediis fortuitorum,* which is cited as Seneca by Tertullian (*Apologet.* 50), and quoted as such by Vincent of Beauvais (*De eruditione filiorum nobilium* xvii, 174, xli, 123; and *Speculum hist.* viii, 116 and 123), Dante (*Ep.* iii, 4, 8), and Salutati (*De lab. Herc.* iii, 14, 18), appears in the list of Petrarch's favorite books among the Seneca entries (Ullman [1955], pp. 122, 124). The numerous passages in our text relating to the *De remediis fortuitorum* and its *additiones* (Haase [1859]; Haase, iii [1886], pp. xvi–xx; Hortis [1879]) are indicated where they occur. *De rem. fort.* iv, 2, paraphrased below, *DR* ii, 120, 43, turns up also in *Fam.* xxiv, 1, 30. *De rem. fort.* vii, 2, is quoted in *Fam.* xiv, 4, 4, as *illud Senece*—a line by Seneca.

36 *qui paucissimis diebus coeptum perfectumque opus admirans videris.* Cf. the similar, though less exaggerating, formulaic reference to *De vita solitaria* as *paucissimis mensibus scriptum opus*—a work written in just a few months—in *Sen.* v, 1, to Boccaccio, Pavia, December 22, 1365 (1581: 792). On this, Ullman (1955), p. 153.

37 Isidore, *Quaest. in Gen.,* praef. 2, *PL* 83, c. 207:

> veterumque ecclesiasticorum sententias congregantes, voluti ex divorsis pratis flores lectos ad manum fecimus.

> We have collected the maxims of the ancient Fathers and brought them together *ad manum*—in convenient fashion—like flowers gathered in various meadows.

On this, Fontaine (1959), note 21, above. Cf. *Secretum* i, *Prose* (1955), p. 54; and below, *DR* ii, 95, note 13.

38 *Secretum* ii, *Prose* (1955), p. 122:

> Quotiens legenti salutares se se offerunt sententie, quibus vel excitari sentis animum vel frenari, noli viribus ingenii fidere, sed illas in memorie penetralibus absconde multoque studio tibi familiares effice; ut, quod experti solent

medici, quocunque loco vel tempore dilationis impatiens morbus invaserit, habeas velut in animo scripta remedia. Sunt enim quedam sicut in corporibus humanis sic in animi passiones, in quibus tam mortifera mora est ut, qui distulerit medelam, spem salutis abstulerit. Quis enim ignorat, exempli gratia, esse quosdam motus tam precipites ut, nisi eos in ipsis exordiis ratio frenaverit, animum corpusque et totum hominem perdant, et serum sit quicquid post tempus apponitur?

Whenever you read and encounter wholesome maxims by which you feel your mind is stirred or restrained, do not entrust them to the powers of your intellect alone, but store them in the recesses of your memory and make them familiar to you by careful study, so that like an experienced physician you know the remedy as if it were written in your mind, no matter where or at what moment an urgent case of illness may occur. For, as with the human body, there are afflictions of the mind, in which delay is deadly, and who puts off the remedy takes away any hope for recovery. Who, for instance, fails to realize that certain impulses of the mind are so precipitous that, unless Reason checks them as they arise, they destroy mind and body, the whole man—and whatever is supplied after this moment is in vain.

On this, Heitmann (1958), p. 10; and Rico (1974), pp. 234–236. Cf. Cicero, *Tusc. disp.* iv, 10 (Thomas Aquinas, *Summa theol.* i, II, Q.59, a.2, o.2, Pegis [1945], ii, p. 450, etc.); and Cicero, ibid. iv, 13, 28:

Quo modo autem in corpore est morbus, est aegrotatio, est vitium, sic in animo

Now as the body is liable to disease, to sickness, to defect, so is the soul.

LCL, King, p. 357. Note Thomas Aquinas, ibid. Q. 55, a.2, o.1, Pegis (1945), ii, p. 414. On the notion of *remedia* and the medical terminology of the penitential literature, Bloomfield (1952), pp. 67, 353, nn. 196, 197. Cf. above, *Dramatis personae,* note 19.

39   1492: facies
       1581: acies

On *utraque fortuna*—a topical expression based on Cicero, *De off.* ii, 6, 19, cited in Petrarch's Paris oration (January 13, 1361; Barbeu du Rocher [1854], p. 219) and, six years later, in *Sen.* viii, 3, as below, *DR* ii, Pref., note 91, and other ancient models, such as Livy, vi, 24, 9; Seneca Rhetor, *Controv.* x, 5, 22 (of Timagenes); Seneca the Philosopher, *Nat. quaest.* iii, Praef. 13, and *Ep.* 71, 37; and Boethius, *Cons. phil.* i, M 4, 3 (Heitmann [1958], p. 28, n. 17), and alluded to line 156, below—e.g., *Fam.* viii, 1, 36, xii, 2, 9, xiv, 1, 21, xvii, 3, 31, xviii, 16, 13, xix, 9, 4γ; *Collatio* 24, Martellotti (1983), pp. 317, 340, and *Contra eum* (1581: 1076). Related, *dulcia/amara, DR* i, 89, note 1. —On the image of two-faced Fortune, *Fam.* viii, 1, 36, xi, 8, 7, xvii, 3, 31; *Sen.* viii, 3, Rawski (1967), pp. 102–103, n. 26; and below, *DR* ii, Pref., note 91. Note Tubach (1969), no. 2154; and Patch (1927), esp. chap. 2.

40   Cf. Ambrose, *De virg.* 15, 96, *PL* 16, c. 304; and Bernards (1955), p. 99, and the literature cited there. Note also the horse-related metaphors discussed in Dahlberg (1971), pp. 25–26; and Robertson (1963), pp. 30, 194, 253–254, 394, 476.

41   *utraque fortunae facies metuenda uerumtamen utraque toleranda est: & haec quidem freno indiget: illa sollacio: hic animi elatio reprimenda. Illic refouenda: ac subleuanda fatigatio.* On "bridle" (*frenum/frenare*—bridle, bit/to bridle, curb, restrain) as topical expression (e.g., Lactantius, *Div. inst.* vi, 16; Augustine, *De civ. Dei* xiv, 19, as below, *DR* ii, 75, note 8, xix, 4, LCL, Greene, p. 126; and Isidore, *Etym.* ii, 24, 6) and iconographic device, e.g., *Fam.* iii, 18, 2, v, 3, 4, xvii, 3, 9, xxi, 9, 8, as in *DR* ii, 84, note 13, xxii, 7, 17, xxiii, 12, 13, xxiv, 5, 6; *Secretum* ii, *Prose* (1955), p. 122, as in Introduction to the Commentary, note 45, and *De vita sol.* ii, *Prose* (1955), p. 574; *DR* i, 30, note 15; Heitmann (1958), p. 136, n. 236; Rico (1974), p. 81, n. 94; and H. F. North in Wiener (1973), iv, pp. 374–375. —Petrarch introduces here the Christian modification and simplification of the ancient virtue system, which stresses *modestia, patientia,* and *humilitas*—moderation (*ne quid nimis*—nothing in excess—*DR* i, 5, note 1), self-knowledge (*nosce te ipsum*—know thyself—*DR* ii, 73, note 12), and self-restraint (e.g., *DR* i, 89, 31); relentless patience ("patience, with an indomitable mind," *Fam.* xxi, 9, as in *DR* ii, 84, note 13); and humility (*DR* i, 10, 17)—and may be ultimately based on Col. 3, 12:

> Induite vos ergo sicut electi Dei, sancti, et dilecti, viscera misericordiae, benignitatem, humilitatem, modestiam, patientiam . . .

> Put ye on therefore, as the elect of God, holy, and beloved, the bowels of mercy, benignity, humility, modesty, patience . . .

These concepts had been widely discussed in the Christian ethical literature since patristic times (cf., e.g., Quasten, ii [1953], pp. 97, 298, 359, 406, iii [1963], pp. 215, 510; and Cayré, ii [1940], doctrinal index, nos. 107–114) and had long been popularized in form of maxims, such as

> *nulla virtus sufficit sine temperantia*—without moderation no virtue is adequate (Bloomfield [1979], no. 4618; related, Whiting [1968], M 455);

> *patientia vincit omnia*—patience conquers all (Bloomfield [1979], no. 4864; Whiting [1968], P 61; cf. *Fam.* xvii, 3, 6);

> *patientia omnium virtutum maxima est*—patience is the greatest of all virtues (Lactantius, *Div. inst.* vi, 18, *PL* 6, c, 700; Whiting [1968], P 56–58; S 86);

> *humilitas genitrix virtutum*—humility, mother of the virtues (Hugh of St. Victor? Bloomfield [1979], no. 4689); and

> *prima virtus fuit humilitas*—the foremost virtue was humility (Bloomfield [1979], no. 4089).

During Petrarch's century, catastrophes and disasters may have contributed to a deepening interest in these topics.

The terminology in the *DR*, which has been studied by Klaus Heitmann (Heitmann [1958]) is inconsistent, at least in a modern reader's judgment. Reason's vocabulary uses the commonplaces of Antiquity and a number of later terms in a variety of senses—some of them as synonyms, the terms of synonymy not always being evident to us today. Nevertheless, Reason's usage, as a whole, hews close to the deceptively simple formulation in *Fam.* xxiii, 12, 13 (above, Introduction to the Commentary, ii, 3):

> in rebus asperis, seu mala seu incommoda dici mavis, patientie unicum esse remedium . . . Sicut contra prosperis in rebus, seu bona illa seu commoda dici placet, unum est remedium, modestia, cuius freno letitie gestientis impetum teneamus.

> In times of hardship—you may prefer to speak of "ills" or *incommoda*—disadvantages—the one remedy is *patience*. . . . Just as against times of prosperity—you may wish to speak of "goods" or *commoda*—advantages [cf. *DR* ii, 114, note 28]—the only remedy is *moderation* [Fam. i, 8, 9, as below, *DR* i, 41, note 8] that allows us to bridle the ardor of excessive pleasure [*DR* ii, 90, note 53].

(Note the early formulation in *Fam.* vi, 3, 51, as above, Introduction to the Commentary, note 45; *Fam.* xix, 16, 12, on moderation; and the paraphrase, below, *DR* ii, 66, 23–24. Petrarch's idea is anticipated in Isidore, *Synon.* ii, 26, *PL* 83, c. 851: *habeto temperamentum in prosperis, habeto patientiam in adversis*—practice moderation in prosperity, practice patience in adversity.) —Throughout the *DR, moderation* and *patience* are cardinal points. Accompanied by *humilitas*—humility—and *fortitudo*—courage—sometimes in superordinate, sometimes in subordinate function, they form sum and substance of Reason's multifaceted argument by contraries, which is crudely sketched by the following therapeutic paradigm:

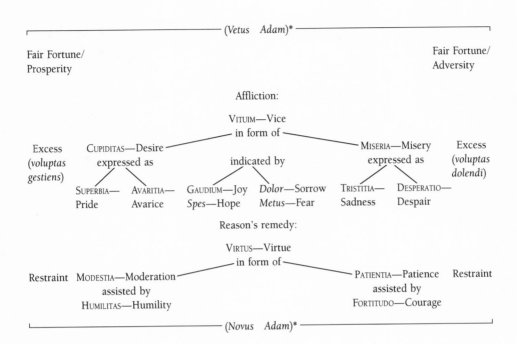

*Based on Augustine, *De vera rel.* xxvi, 48–50; cf. *Dramatis personae*, note 23.

On *cupiditas*—man's innate desire for the "good" and happiness—e.g., *Fam.*
iii, 7, 4; iii, 18, on Petrarch's craving for books; ix, 16, 1; xvii, 3, 3–14; and
xvii, 8, xxi, 13, 2 on *cupiditas literarum*. The functions of *Humility* and *Courage* (Cicero, *Tusc. disp.* ii, 18, 43, and *De fin.* i, 15, 49) are anticipated in
Cyprian's chiastic isocolon of the Breviary (Dom. iv post Pascha, in II Noct.,
Lect. vi):

> Patientia est, quae nos . . . facit humiles in prosperis, in adversis fortes . . .

> Patience . . . makes us humble in prosperity, in adversity, courageous.

which, in turn, invokes Job 4, 6:

> Ubi est timor tuus, fortitudo tua? patientia tua et perfectio viarum tuarum?

> Where is thy fear, thy fortitude, thy patience, and the perfection of thy ways?

On this, cf. *Glossa ordinaria, PL* 113, c. 764; also Tertullian, *De pat.* i, *PL* 1, cc. 1249–1274; Ambrose, *In Ps.* 118, *PL* 15, cc. 1379, 1587; Jerome, *In Eccli., PL* 23, c. 1123; etc.; note also *Fam.* ii, 9, 3–4. For an extension of the function of patience to steadfastness/equanimity, cf. Lactantius, *Div. inst.* v, 23; and Gregory I, *Hom. in Ev.* ii, 24, as in *DR* ii, 7, note 8, and ii, 84, note 13. For Reason's views, *DR* i, 89, 31, and note 5. Petrarch seems to summarize in *Fam.* xvii, 3 (to Guido Sette, Milan, September 1353, Wilkins [1958], p. 31), 10:

> mentibus precor in celo, corporibus hic simus sobrie patienter humiliter, et iniquitatem locorum equitate animi molliamus.

> I pray that we live with our minds in heaven and our bodies here on earth in moderation, patience, and humility, and relieve the adversity of circumstances with intrepidness of mind.

On Petrarch's *great breviary,* the only one of his books mentioned in his testament, Mommsen (1957), p. 83.

42   Cicero, *De sen.* i, 2:

> Sed mihi, cum de senectute *vellem aliquid scribere, tu occurrebas dignus eo munere, quo uterque nostrum communiter uteretur.*

> But when I resolved *to write something on this theme you* continually *came before my mind as worthy of a gift which both of us might enjoy together.*

LCL, Falconer, p. 11.

43   *in utramque partem*—cf. Cicero, *De off.* ii, 6, 19; and note 39, above.

44   The Wheel of Fortune (Herodotus, i, 207; Aristotle, *Eth. Nic.* i, 10, 1100b; Cicero, *Piso* 22; Ovid, *Ex ponto* ii, 3, 55–56; Pseudo-Callisthenes, 189, 197, Wolohojian [1969], pp. 99, 104; Boethius, *Cons. phil.* ii, P 1, 59–62, P 2, 29, as below, *DR* ii, 9, note 2; John of Salisbury, *Policrat.* v, 4, *PL* 199, cc. 545–546; Dante, *Div. Comm.,* Inf. xv, 94–96; *Roman de la Rose* 3980–3990; Chaucer, *Troilus and Criseyde* iv, 1–7) is often represented with four men in its quadrants. Proceeding clockwise from the top, the *tituli* of this *formula of four* (Patch [1927], pp. 164–166) usually are *Regno, Regnavi, Sum sine regno, Regnabo*—I reign, I have reigned, I am without reign, I shall reign (cf. Boccaccio, *L'Amorosa visione* xxxi).

> Regno sits smugly for his moment's glory at the top, his crowned head jutting out most immoderately over the confines of the border at the top of the minia-ture. Regnavi slides head over heels on the same road to misery represented by the wretched (Sum sine regno), now crushed below the wheel which once elevated him to his tawdry glory. Finally Regnabo, slowly being raised toward his brief day of worldly prosperity, proves the existence of a frantic kind of fortune.

Wheel of Fortune. Ca. 1330. Holkham Bible Picture Book.
English. London, British Museum, ms., Add. 47682, f. lv.
Courtesy Trustees of the British Museum.

Fleming (1969), p. 124. Fleming describes a miniature in the copy of the
Roman de la Rose, Oxford, Bodl. Douce 332, f. 38r (ibid., fig. 30); and Mâle
(1984), pp. 95–98, a rose window in the south porch of the cathedral of
Amiens. For other examples, see Schmeller (1847), p. 1, also in Zeydel
(1966), frontisp.; and the frequently reproduced *Imago mundi,* Cambridge,

Wheel of Fortune. 12th c. Added drawing in Gregory, *Moralia in Hiob.*
Spanish, late 9th c. Manchester, John Ryland's Library, Latin ms. 83, f.
214v.

Corp. Christi MS 66, f. 66r, showing Fortune and Sapience (e.g., Patch
[1927], pl. 5). For the iconography of Fortune, see De Laborde (1909), plates;
Johannes von Tepl, *Ackerm.,* Bernt & Burdach (1917), pp. 250–251; Patch
(1927), chap. v; Siciliano (1934); Patch (1935); Stammler, iii (1962), cc. 671–
674; Courcelle (1967); and Pickering (1970), part II, iii, and plates 1a–8b. Cf.
also Doren (1922–1923); Robinson (1946); and Trompf (1979). The late-
twelfth-century *De nugis curialium* by Walter Map offers this imaginative
connection of Fortune's wheel and the four passions (above, *Dramatis personae,* notes 9, 11) in v, 7:

> Yxion ibi uoluitur in rota, sibi sepe dissimilis, super subter, hinc et illinc.
> Habemus et nos Yxiones, quos sorte sua uolubilis fortuna torquet. Ascendunt
> ad gloriam, ruunt in miseriam, sperantque deiecti, supremi gaudent, infimi
> lugent; dextri sperant, sinistri metuunt; cumque sit undique timendum in rota,
> nullus in ea sine spe locus est, et cum ipsam spes metus gaudium luctusque
> participent, sola sibi familiam spes facit et detinet. Tota terribilis est, contra
> consciencias tota militat, nec inde minus appetitur.

The Four Figures. Ca. 1429. Domenico di Niccolò (?). Wooden inlay door. Siena, Palazzo Publico, Capella del Consiglio. Alinari/Art Resource.

Ixion there is rolled round on his wheel, often unlike himself, up, down, hither and thither [cf. below, *DR* i, 24, note 5]. We too have our Ixions, whom rolling fortune torments with their lot. They climb to glory and fall to wretchedness, when down they hope, when at the top they exult, when at the bottom they mourn; when on the right hand they are in hope, when on the left they are in fear. And though on every side of the wheel there is room for fear, there is in it no place which is devoid of hope; and as it is shared by hope, fear, joy and grief, it is hope alone that makes and keeps together its occupants. It is all terrible, all in fight against conscience, but none the less for that is it sought after.

James et al. (1983), pp. 502–505. —Petrarch mentioned frequently the wheel of Fortune, e.g., *Fam.* v, 3, 19, xi, 6, 4, xvii, 3, 27, 33, xxiii, 5, 15; *Sen.* iv, 4, xii, 2 (1581: 808, 907); SN 4 (1581: 714; Piur [1925], p. 180); *Met.* iii, 19; *Rime* (1951), pp. 798, 800; *Africa* vii, 329; *Buc. carm.* xii, 159; and below, *DR* i, 16, 84, i, 17, 32, i, 85, 75–79, i, 90, 6, i, 91, 44.

45   Seneca, *Ep.* 83, 13:

Sibi quisque nunc nominet eos, quibus scit et vinum male credi et sermonem bene, unum tamen exemplum, quod occurrit mihi, referam, ne intercidat. Instruenda est enim vita exemplis inlustribus. Non semper confugiamus ad vetera.

So let each one call to mind those who, to his knowledge, can be ill trusted with wine, but well trusted with the spoken word; and yet one case occurs to my mind, which I shall relate, lest it fall into oblivion. For life should be provided with conspicuous illustrations. Let us not always be harking back to the dim past.

LCL, Gummere, p. 267. The juxtaposition of *vetera* and *nova*—ancient and modern—examples remained customary; cf., e.g., Jerome, *Ep.* 54, 18, LCL, Wright, p. 262.

46   Such as King John II of France, captured September 19, 1356, at Poitiers and imprisoned in England (*Sen.* x, 2, *Prose* [1955], p. 1110; *De vita sol.* ii, ibid., p. 486; *De ocio,* ibid., p. 596; and below, *DR* i, 37, 199–205); blind King John of Bohemia, who fell in the battle of Crécy, August 26, 1346 (below, *DR* ii, 96, 124); King Edward II of England, forced to abdicate in 1326 and horribly murdered in 1327; King Andrew, who was hanged in Naples, September 18, 1345 (cf. Petrarch's report to Barbato da Sulmona, *Fam.* vi, 5, August 1, 1346; Wilkins [1955], pp. 222–223); and Cola di Rienzo (below, *DR* i, 89, 19–23). The reference may include other local rulers, such as Alberigo da Romano, torn to pieces and dragged to death by a mob at Treviso (Salimbene, Coulter [1972], p. 248), or Passerino Bonaccolsi, Lord of Mantua, killed by the citizenry in 1328. Cf. *Quel c'ha nostra* 75, *Rime* (1951), p. 622.

47   Petrarch repeats—perhaps as a nostalgic reminder—the play on words "regal heart"—(Lat.) *cor regium* = Correggio, Azzo's family name, which he had

used in the canzone *Quel c'ha nostra* 49, written in celebration of the conquest of Parma (above, note 1):

> COR REGIO fu, sì come suona il nome,
> quel che venne sicuro a l'alta impresa
> per mar per terra e per poggi e per piani, . . .

Rime (1951), p. 621; Foresti (1977), p. 92. For a similar play on the name Colonna, *Rime* 10 and 53, as below, *DR* i, 35, note 9. Note also Petrarch's remarks on the names of *Sagremor* de Pommiers (*Fam.* xxi, 2, 9, xxi, 5, 1, xxi, 7, 4); Enrico *Capra* (*Fam.* xxi, 11, 8); and the Doge Laurentius *Celsus* (*Sen.* iv, 3 [1581: 782]).

48   Augustine, e.g., *Conf.* x, 28:

> Hei mihi! Domine, miserere mei. Contendunt moerores mei mali cum gaudiis bonis, et ex qua parte stet victoria nescio. Hei mihi! Domine, miserere mei. Hei mihi! ecce vulnera mea non abscondo: medicus es, aeger sum; misericors es, miser sum.

> Woe is me! Lord, have pity on me. My evil sorrows contend with my good joys; and on which side the victory may be I know not. Woe is me! Lord, have pity on me. Woe is me! Lo, I hide not my wounds; Thou art the Physician, I the sick; Thou merciful, I miserable . . .

Pilkington in Oates (1948), i, p. 167. Note also Augustine, *De civ. Dei* iv, 16, *Conf.* vii, 21, and *Serm.* 23a (*Corpus Christianorum, Ser. Latina*, 41, 321–323). On *Christus medicus*, Ladner (1959), p. 311, and the literature cited there. Cf. above, *Dramatis personae*, note 19.

49   *insolitae gravitatis.* Petrarch may have had in mind the Ciceronian dignity of character, e.g., Cicero, *De nat. deor.* i, 1, 1, or *Ad Quintum* i, 1, 23; another passage of this letter is cited *DR* ii, 53, 42–43. Cf. also *DR* ii, 118, 105; *Sen.* xvi, 4, as below, *DR* i, 37, note 16; and *Sen.* xiv, 1, to Francesco Carrara, Arquà, November 28, 1373 (1581: 384):

> Tu mediocri cultu contentus incedis, ut te dominum non uestis, non elatio, sed sola morum grauitas, & frontis probet auctoritas.

> You are satisfied with a modest appearance, since your nobility as a ruler is indicated not by your attire, not by ceremonial glorification, but merely by the commanding presence of your grave deportment and countenance.

Note also Boethius, *Cons. phil.* iv, 1, 1; and Gruber (1978), pp. 42–43, 320.

50   The whole passage is a reference to the experience of Azzo at the time of the uprising in Verona, Spring 1354. Cf. Wilkins (1958a), p. 235.

51   Probably proverbial. Cf. Whiting (1968), F634, P418.

52   This kind of hyperbolic mannerism, which originated in the poetry of late Antiquity, recurs throughout the medieval literature. On this and its use in

Dante (e.g., *Div. Comm.,* Inf. xxv, 94–138), Curtis (1953), pp. 162–165. Note also De Lubac, i, 2 (1959), pp. 541–542. —Both Gaius Marius, the victor over Jugurtha (107 B.C.) and the Teutones and Cimbri (102 and 101 B.C.), and Gnaeus Pompeius, who defeated Mithridates (66 B.C.), were self-made men (Seneca Rhetor, *Controv.* i, 6, 4), and suffered prosecution and exile. Marius died apparently insane; Pompey was murdered in Egypt. For the "ups and downs of Marius," cf., e.g., Seneca Rhetor, *Controv.* i, 1, 3 and 5; and Alain de Lille, *Anticlaud.* viii, 1, *PL* 210, c. 560. —Fleming (1969), p. 35, notes:

> Medieval men, including, incidentally, nominalist philosophers of the fourteenth century, seem to have been capable of referring literary fictions and historical events to abstract moral concepts for verification. The reality of the story . . . . . . was not that it concerned real people and actual events, but that it exemplified a real principle.

(Cf. John of Salisbury, as above, *Dramatis personae,* note 18.) —Years before his work on the *DR,* Petrarch defended his use of *exempla* in *Fam.* vi, 4, 1 and 3–4:

> Exemplis abundo, sed illustribus, sed veris, et quibus, nisi fallor, cum delectatione insit autoritas. Possem, aiunt, paucioribus uti. . . . . . . Veruntamen si ratio queritur cur exemplis interdum affluam, curioseque in his videar immorari, dicam: puto lectorem eo animo esse quo sum ego. Me quidem nichil est quod moveat quantum exempla clarorum hominum. Iuvat enim assurgere, iuvat animum experiri an quicquam solidi habeat, an generosi aliquid atque adversus fortunam indomiti et infracti an sibi de se mentitus sit. Id sane, preter experientiam que certissima magistra rerum est, nullo melius modo fit, quam si eum his quibus simillimus esse cupit, admoveam. Itaque, sicut omnibus quos lego, gratiam habeo, si michi sepe propositis exemplis hanc experiendi facultatem dederint, sic michi gratiam habituros spero qui me legent. Fallor forsan in hac spe; tu tamen in hac narratione non falleris; hec enim una vera rei causa est.

> I do use great numbers of examples but they are all illustrious, true, and, unless I am mistaken, contain both pleasure and authority. People say that I should use fewer. . . . . . . Nevertheless if anyone asks why I sometimes overflow with examples, and seem to linger lovingly over them, I shall answer as follows: I believe the reader is of the same mind as myself. There is nothing that moves me as much as the examples of outstanding men. They help one to rise on high and to test the mind to see whether it possesses anything solid, anything noble, anything unbending and firm against fortune, or whether it lies to itself about itself. Next to experience itself which is the best teacher of things, I would wager there is no better way to learn than by having the mind desire to emulate these greats as closely as possible. Therefore, just as I am grateful to all those authors I have read who afford me this opportunity to test myself with appropriate examples, so do I hope that those who read me will be

grateful. I am perhaps wrong in hoping for this; but I am not deceiving you with these words, for in this hope rests the one true reason for my practice.

Bernardo (1975), p. 314. — . . . *sicut vultus ad speculum, sic mores hominum ad exemplar facillime corriguntur*—just as a face in the mirror (e.g., Cicero, *Piso* 29, 71, *De fin.* v, 22, 61, and *De re publ.* ii, 42, 69; Terence, *Adelphoë* iii, 415; Seneca, *De clem.* i, 1, 1; Augustine, *PL* 34, c. 889), the *mores* of mankind are most easily corrected by way of example: *Rer. mem. libri* iii, 42, 4. Cf. also *De vir. ill.,* Prohem. 6–7; *Fam.* x, 3, 48, xix, 18, 44; also *Fam.* viii, 4, 17; *Sen.* iv, 1, viii, 5, xvii, 2 (1581: 387, 839, 966); and above, *Dramatis personae,* note 18. On examples as mirror, Grabes (1982), pp. 92–93. Note also De Lubac, i, 2 (1959), pp. 569, 625, 635, n. 4; and note 55, below. On the related topic of *imitatio, DR* i, 29, note 17.

53   Cf. Cicero, *Tusc. disp.* ii, 18, 43:

> Appellata est enim ex viro virtus; viri autem propria maxime est fortitudo, cuius munera duo sunt maxima mortis dolorisque contemptio.

> For it is from the word for 'man' that the word 'virtue' is derived; but man's peculiar virtue is fortitude, of which there are two main functions, namely scorn of death and scorn of pain.

LCL, King, p. 195; cf. *Fam.* xxiii, 2, 28. Related, e.g., *Tusc. disp.* ii, 13, 32, iii, 7, 14, iv, 24, 53; *De off.* iii, 33, 117; *De fin.* v, 23, 67. Cf. note 2 above. Note also Boethius, *Cons. phil.* iv, P 7, 38–55. —Lactantius, *Div. inst.* vii, 5, *PL* 6, c. 754, speaks of courage as *malorum victrix*—the conqueress of ills. Augustine, *In Ps.* 83, 11, *PL* 37, c. 1065, notes:

> Fortitudo dicitur qua omnia molesta toleramus.

> It is called "courage" when we withstand all troubles.

On *fortitudo*—the shield against all sallies of Fortune (*Fam.* xxi, 9, 8, as in *DR,* ii, 84, note 13; *Sen.* vi, 4 [1581: 808])—as a mode of *patientia* in adversity, note 41 above; and, with a warning reference to unrestrained courage as rashness, *DR* i, 73, 8. Note *Fam.* ii, 4, 17, v, 17, 14, viii, 1, 10, ix, 1, 6, xvii, 3, 6, xvii, 4, 13–14; and *Fam.* xvi, 6, xxiii, 12, on courage and equanimity (cf. Isidore, *Etym.* ii, 24, 6: *Fortitudo, qua adversa aequanimiter tolerantur*). Also *Sen.* viii, 7 (1581: 841); and *De vita sol.* ii, Prose (1955), p. 556:

> . . . modestiam in prosperis, fortitudinem in adversis, equabilitatem in actionibus atque constantiam.

> . . . moderation in prosperity, fortitude in adversity, equanimity and steadfastness in all our actions.

Zeitlin (1924), p. 291. Similar, *Fam.* xiv, 5, 15.

54   Fortune and *varietas mundana*—the whims of this world are also the adver-

saries of *triplex fortitudo*—courage in poverty, sickness, and tyranny, in Alain de Lille, *Ars. praed.* xxiv, *PL* 210, cc. 159–161.

> With Petrarch the question of Fortune resumes its moral significance. Petrarch's philosophy of life is directly related to his views on the influence of Fortune in human affairs . . . Fortune is God's will and as such it must prevail, whether we like it or not. The problem is how to best conduct one's life in view of the unquestioned existence of the fortuitous element in human affairs. . . . Accepting the traditional view that material goods constitute the domain of Fortune, Petrarch explains that these material goods are God's gifts and their goodness depends on the use which man makes of them. Evil arises not from their possession but from their misuse. The root of bad luck is not any natural disposition, but the blame which Man bears for misusing God-given gifts. The Stoic concept of Fortune as a test of man's fortitude runs throughout Petrarch's views, but in the Stoics the test has no significance for the afterlife, whereas in Petrarch the test is viewed as a preparation for eternity.

V. Cioffari in Wiener (1973), vol. ii, p. 234.

55   Cf. *De vita sol.*, Pref. Ep., *Prose* (1955), p. 294:

> Adesto igitur; audies quid michi de toto hoc solitario vite genere cogitanti videri soleat: pauca quidem ex multis, sed in quibus parvo velut in speculo totum animi mei habitum, totam frontem serene tranquilleque mentis aspicias.

> Attend, therefore, and hear what ideas I am accustomed to entertain when I reflect on this whole subject of the solitary life. I shall set down but a few of the many thoughts that occur to me, but in these, as in a little mirror, you shall behold the entire disposition of my soul, the full countenance of a serene and tranquil mind.

Zeitlin (1924), p. 102. Similar, Alain de Lille, *De planctu nat.*, *PL* 210, c. 431: *velut in speculo*. Note also *Sen.* iv, 1, viii, 5 (1581: 387, 839); *Trionfi*, Tr. temp. 55–60; and *Secretum* iii, *Prose* (1955), p. 184, citing Seneca, *Nat. quaest.* i, 17, 4: *inventa sunt specula ut homo ipse se noscet*—mirrors are invented in order that man may know himself (LCL, Corcoran, p. 91); on this, Rico (1974), p. 367. —On the topic of the mirror which "shows things that are in front of it, without cover, in their true colors and shapes" (*Roman de la Rose,* Dahlberg [1971], p. 51; Chaucer, *Rom. of the Rose,* 1585–1588, Robinson [1933], p. 679), Grabes (1982), esp. chaps. 4 and 7, and p. 386; Curtius (1953), pp. 336–337; Tripet (1967), pp. 22–23, n. 9; and Rawski (1967), p. 103, n. 28. Note also Evans (1983), pp. 150–151; Huizinga (1930), pp. 293–294, on i Cor. 13, 12: *per speculum in aenigmate; tunc autem facie ad faciem,* and Javelet (1967), i, pp. 376–390; De Lubac, i, 2 (1959), pp. 569–571, 625–628. On *speculum* as a metaphoric book title, Lehmann, v (1962), pp. 72–84; Bernards (1955), pp. 1–6; Grabes (1982), pp. 93–100; and Bradley (1954).

56   *sed paratus ad omnia: promptus ad singula: dulcia pariter & amara despicias.*

Similar, *Fam.* v, 17, 14, xvii, 4, 13, xxi, 9, 7–11; *Sen.* xii, 1, xiii, 13, xiv, 1 (1581: 903, 926, 379); and *Fam.* xxi, 10, 24:

> Paratique simus [*Sen.* iii, 1 (1581: 770)] non ad hoc aut illud mali genus, sed ad omnia.

> And we should be prepared, not for this or that kind of trouble, but for anything.

De ocio (1581: 299):

> intentissimos & paratissimos tamen ad omnia esse oportet

> Nevertheless, it is necessary to be utterly watchful and wholly prepared for anything.

Note also *Sen.* xiv, 1 (1581: 379); *Var.* 32, Fracassetti, iii (1863), pp. 381–382, 392–393; and *Sen.* x, 4 (1581: 874):

> ne deficeres animo & ut aiunt ante tubam tremeres, sed inter spem ac metum rectus incederes, paratus ad utrumlibet . . .

> lest you lose courage and, as the saying goes, tremble at the sound of the trumpet; that you should remain undaunted by both hope and fear, prepared for either one . . .

(On the terrifying trumpet, Virgil, *Aen.* ix, 503–504 after Ennius [in Priscian, Vahl: Ann. v, 452]; as summons for sinners, e.g., Matth. 24, 27–31; i Cor. 15, 51–53; Dante, *Div. Comm.,* Inferno vi, 94–96; Praetorius [1614–1615; facs. 1959], i, pp. 122–123, 126; and Hammerstein [1962], pp. 210–211.) —Compare also Seneca, *Dial.* 5, *De ira* iii, 37, 4, and *Ep.* 107, 3–4, as below, *DR* ii, 114, note 43. The topic of *paratus ad omnia* is frequently referred to in the *DR*; cf., e.g., *DR* ii, 45, 18–20, ii, 49, 2–3, ii, 51, 39–41, ii, 59, 15–16, ii, 64, 13–17, ii, 83, 181–183, ii, 113, 39–41, ii, 117, 127–130, 151–157.

57 I.t.: Maronianum illud
58 Fitzgerald (1983), p. 163. The answer of Aeneas to the Sibyl's prophecy, Virgil, *Aeneid* vi, 103–105:

> . . . . . . non ulla laborum
> o virgo, nova mi facies inopinave surgit;
> omnia praecepi atque animo mecum ante peregi.

1492 and 1581 have *percepi* for *peregi,* which is an acknowledged alternate reading (Schrevelius [1661], p. 580). Compare Seneca, *Ep.* 76, 33–35:

> Si rectis oculis gladios micantes videt et si scit sua nihil interesse, utrum anima per os an per iugulum exeat, beatum voca; si cum illi denuntiata sunt corporis tormenta et quae casu veniunt et quae potentioris iniuria, si vincula et exilia et vanas humanarum formidines mentium securus audit et dicit:

non ulla laborum
o virgo, nova mi facies inopinave surgit;
omnia praecepi atque animo mecum ipse peregi.

Tu hodie ista denuntias; ego semper denuntiavi mihi et hominem paravi et ad humana. Praecogitati mali mollis ictus venit. At stultis et fortunae credentibus omnis videtur nova rerum et inopinata facies; magna autem pars est apud imperitos mali novitas. Hoc ut scias, ea quae putaverant aspera, fortius, cum adsuevere, patiuntur. Ideo sapiens adsuescit futuris malis et quae alii diu patiendo levia faciunt, hic levia facit diu cogitando. Audimus aliquando voces imperitorum dicentium: "sciebam hoc mihi restare"; sapiens scit sibi omnia restare. Quicquid factum est, dicit: "sciebam."

If a man can behold with unflinching eyes the flash of a sword, if he knows that it makes no difference to him whether his soul takes flight through his mouth or through a wound in his throat, you may call him happy; you may also call him happy if, when he is threatened with bodily torture, whether it be the result of an accident or of the might of the stronger, he can without concern hear talk of chains, or of exile, or of all the idle fears that stir men's minds, and can say:

"O maiden, no new sudden form of toil
springs up before my eyes; within my soul
I have forestalled and surveyed everything. (Virgil, *Aeneid* vi, 103–105.)

Today it is you who threaten me with these terrors; but I have always threatened myself with them, and have prepared myself as a man to meet man's destiny." If an evil has been pondered beforehand, the blow is gentle when it comes. To the fool, however, and to him who trusts in fortune, each event as it arrives "comes in a new and sudden form," and a large part of evil, to the inexperienced, consists in its novelty. This is proved by the fact that men endure with greater courage, when they have once become accustomed to them, the things which they had first regarded as hardships. Hence, the wise man accustoms himself for coming trouble, lightening by long reflection the evils which others lighten by long endurance. We sometimes hear the inexperienced say: "I knew that this was in store for me." But the wise man knows that all things are in store for him. Whatever happens, he says: "I knew it."

LCL, Gummere, pp. 167, 169. Petrarch quoted from this passage in *Fam.* ii, 1, 36, iv, 12, 21.

59   Rom. 10, 17:

Ergo fides ex auditu, auditus autem per verbum Christi.

Faith then cometh by hearing: and hearing by the words of Christ.

Cited also in *De sui ipsius* (1581: 1044; *Prose* [1955], p. 726; Nachod in Cassirer [1949], p. 79). Cf. Augustine, *De civ. Dei* xvii, 16. The hearing of false opinions is to be replaced by the *auditus fidei*—hearing of the faith—the truths of faith that are known only by revelation—considered the basis of positive theology in the Middle Ages (Cayré, ii [1940], p. 355; and the remarks in Ong [1967], pp. 186–188, 268–270). Cf. Alain de Lille, *Regulae de sacra theol.*, *PL* 210, cc. 622–623, and *Anticlaudianus* v, 5, ibid., c. 534 (Sheridan [1973], p. 146), where Prudence discards her cart and team, and mounted on the horse *Auditus*—Hearing—follows her guide, Theology (De Bruyne [1946], ii, pp. 289–290; Lewis [1938], p. 101); and Alain on Prov. 20, 12, *PL* 210, c. 714. Note also the *audio* passage in *De vita sol.* ii, *Prose* (1955), p. 426.

60   Cf. the four-headed monster in *Secretum* i, as above, *Dramatis personae,* note 11; *Fam.* xx, 12, 3; *Sen.* i, 5; iii, 1 (1581: 743, 766), x, 4 (1581: 876): *spes, metus, gaudia, dolores,* and *Rime* 252, 1–2: *or piango o canto / E temo e spero*; and below, *DR* ii, Pref., 402–406. Note *Rer. mem. libri* iii, 84, 2. —Personal metaphors such as these usually involve female agents with Latin nouns of feminine gender as names (Patch [1927], pp. 48–49; Bloomfield [1952], p. 129 *et passim*; Curtius [1953], pp. 131–134; and Wenzel [1967], p. 79; also Huizinga [1930], pp. 292–308; Lewis [1938], pp. 93, 100; and Fletcher [1964], pp. 26–35). *Fortuna, Prosperitas, Adversitas, Ratio, Virtus*—Fortune, Prosperity, Adversity, Reason, and Virtue (addressed in *DR* ii, 25, 104–111)— are women. In the literature, Reason's four discussants, the children of the sisters Prosperity and Adversity, have been frequently referred to as "sisters" or "daughters" (Koerting [1878], p. 545; Heitmann [1958], pp. 89–90)—this perhaps because they have been considered female as *passiones*—passions (a feminine noun in Latin). But only one of their names, *Spes sive cupiditas,* is routinely feminine (*Gaudium* being neuter; *Metus,* masculine or sometimes feminine; *Dolor,* masculine). The sex of the allegorical person is not always indicated by the gender of its name (e.g., Job 17, 14:

> Putredine dixi: Pater meus es;
> Mater mea, et soror mea, vermibus,

> I have said to rottenness: Thou art my father;
> to worms, my mother and my sister,

putredo being feminine and *vermis* masculine). Yet throughout the *DR,* Reason's discussants seem to serve as emblematic figurative designations, pictorial *tituli,* as it were, signifying the emotional mood that motivates and is expressed by a thoroughly human speaker, who views life and the world as a male. On this, Schlosser (1964), pp. 34–38; Auerbach (1959), "Figura," esp. pp. 53–56; and Mommsen (1952).

61   Petrarch uses the image of *arx rationis* (Cicero, *Tusc. disp.* i, 10, 20) often, e.g., *Secretum* ii, and *Prose* (1955), p. 106: *in arcem rationis evado*—I retreat to the castle of Reason (Rico [1974], p. 206); ibid., p. 122: *rationem in capite*

velut in arce—reason in one's head as in a castle; *Fam.* vii, 12, 16, xi, 11, 2, xii, 14, 2, xviii, 15, title, xix, 10, 5, xix, 11, 2, xx, 1, 15, xxi, 12, 21; *Sen.* iv, 5, x, 4, xvi, 4 (1581: 789, 877, 954), xvii, 2; and *Secretum* ii, *Prose* (1955), pp. 1152, 122; etc. On the topic of *arx capitis* and its numerous extensions (*arx rationis*, —*simplicitatis*, —*philosophiae*, —*Stoicorum*) Fontaine (1959), ii, pp. 684–686, and the literature cited there; to which may be added Cicero, *Tusc. disp.* ii, 24, 58, and *De div.* i, 6, 10; Seneca, *Dial.* ii, De const. 6, 8; Augustine, *De civ. Dei* xiv, 19, *De beata vita* ii, 10, and *De ord.* i, 11, 32, *PL* 32, cc. 964, 994; Boethius, *Cons. phil.* i, P 3, 43–46, iv, M 3, 34 and P 6, 25, Gruber (1978), pp. 108–109; John of Salisbury, *Metalog.* iv, 17, *PL* 199, c. 926; Cornelius (1930); and Rawski (1967), pp. 191–192. Note also the allegorical sermon by Hugh of St. Victor discussed in Bloomfield (1952), pp. 85, 117, 363, n. 127, 368, n. 164; and below, *DR* ii, 93, note 46.

62   1492: sed coelesti magno auxilio
     1581: sed coelesti magis auxilio

63   Similar imagery related to *castra Christi*—the armed encampments of Christ—is used in *De ocio* i (1581: 299). On the ancient device of allegorical battle and the ensuing *psychomachia* fought by female combatants, Fletcher (1964), chap. 3, esp. pp. 157–161; Katzenellenbogen (1933) and (1939); Mâle (1984), pp. 99–132; and Bloomfield (1952), p. 65 *et passim*. On the attacks of the vices upon man, Alain de Lille, *Anticlaud.* ix, *PL* 210, cc. 565–574, Sheridan (1973), pp. 203–216. Cf. also Smith (1976), pp. 126–132 *et passim*; Saville (1972), chap. 1; Bloomfield, ibid., pp. 117–118, 141, 149, 175, 200–201; Cornelius (1930); and Taylor (1925), ii, pp. 120–129. The allegorical castle returns as late as the end of the sixteenth century in Spenser's *Faerie Queene,* Book ii, Canto 11. On *God's help, DR* ii, 66, note 4.

64   Sap. 11, 21:

     sed omnia in mensura, et numero, et pondere disposuisti.

     But thou hast ordered all things in measure, and number, and weight.

This was the key sentence for the ancient topic of the harmonious, i.e., proportionate, composition of everything beautiful (Isidore, *Etym.* iii, 4; Fontaine [1959], i, pp. 344, 369, 373; Grant [1974], p. 4; cf. Augustine, *De civ. Dei* xi, 30, xii, 18, and the literature cited in Javelet (1967), ii, p. 198, n. 471; and *Roman de la Rose* 16747–16767, Dahlberg [1971], p. 282). Alain de Lille paraphrased it in the *Anticlaudianus* v, 5, *PL* 210, c. 534:

     Summe parens, aeterne Deus, ...

     . . . .
     Omnia sub numero claudens, sub pondere sistens
     Singula, sub stabili mensura cuncta coercens . . .

     Father in the highest, eternal God, ...

. . .   .
Encompassing every single thing according to number,
Placing it according to weight, and ordering all
In its entirety according to enduring measure . . .

On this, Gilson (1960), pp. 211–213; Ladner (1959), pp. 213–216; Javelet (1967), ii, p. 90, n. 82, p. 105, n. 15, pp. 113–114, n. 103, p. 122, n. 189, p. 174, n. 303; De Lubac, ii, 2 (1964), pp. 10–11; Robertson (1963), pp. 114–137; Curtius (1953), pp. 504–505; De Bruyne (1946), e.g., i, chap. 1, 2; Von Simson (1956), pp. 22, 32–33; and Rawski (1967), p. 131, n. 6. Note also White (1971), p. 189; and Paul Frankl's discussion of the culture of the Middle Ages in Frankl (1960), pp. 205–234.

NOTES TO THE DIALOGUES

1 ❖ PRIME OF LIFE

1   *Prose* (1955), pp. 606–613. Dialogues 1–14 deal with attributes of the happy man.

2   1492: Gaudium: Spes: & Ratio / Gaudium & Spes
    1581: Gaudium et Spes, Ratio / Gaudium & Spes

3   *aetas florida:* cf. Catullus, 68, 16: *iucundum quum aetas florida ver agerat.* Similar: *Sen.* xvii, Bryan & Dempster (1958), p. 298, line 40.

4   Cf., e.g., *Fam.* ix, 5–6, xvii, 3, 42; *Secretum* i, *Prose* (1955), p. 60, Rico (1974), pp. 102–104; and *De ocio* (Rotondi, p. 64).

5   Reason uses a contemporary image of long standing (Ps. 102, 15; Jac. 1, 10; Whiting [1968], F 326, G 436, L243, M220, M 663). Cf., e.g., *Fiori e vita di filosafi . . .* xxviii, Secundus, *La prosa del duecento* (1959), p. 530:

> Che è la bellezza?

> La bellezza èe fiore fracido, beatitudine carnale, desiderio de li genti;

and Chaucer, *Troilus and Criseyde* v, 1835–1841:

> O yonge, fresshe folkes, he or she,
> In which that love up groweth with youre age,
> Repeyreth hom fro worldly vanyte,
> And of youre herte up casteth the visage
> To thilke God that after his ymage
> Yow made, and thynketh al nys but a faire
> This world, that passeth soone as floures faire.

On the Augustinian metaphor *florida iuventus,* Isidore, *Etym.* i, 37, 4; and Fontaine (1959), i, pp. 144–145.

6   *aetas integra:* Terence, *Andria* i, 73: *egregia forma atque aetate integra.*

7   Ps. 89, 10:

> dies annorum nostrorum in ipsis septuaginta anni.
> Si autem in potentatibus octoginta anni,
> et amplius eorum *labor et dolor;*

> the days of our years in them are three-score and ten years.
> But if in the strong they be fourscore years:
> and what is more of them is *labour and sorrow.*

Cf. Innocent III, *De miseria* i, 9; and Lewis (1978), pp. 106–109.

8   Eccli. 18, 8:

> Numerus dierum hominum, ut multum centum anni.

9   *Fam* xxiv, 1, 27:

> Continue morimur, ego dum hec scribo, tu dum leges, alii dum audient dum-
> que non audient; ego quoque dum hec leges moriar, tu moreris dum hec scribo,
> ambo morimur, omnes morimur, semper morimur, nunquam vivimus dum hic
> sumus, nisi quandiu virtuosum aliquid agentes sternimus iter nobis ad veram
> vitam, ubi contra nemo moritur, vivunt omnes et semper vivunt, ubi quod
> semel placuit semper placet, cuius ineffabilis et inexauste dulcedinis nec mo-
> dus animo capitur, nec mutatio sentitur, nec timetur finis.

> We all are constantly dying, I while writing these words, you while reading
> them, others while hearing or not hearing them; I too shall be dying while you
> read this, you are dying while I write this, we both are dying, we all are dying,
> we are always dying; we never live here except when doing something virtu-
> ous to pave our path to the true life, where in contrast no one dies, everyone
> lives and will live forever, where what once pleased will ever be pleasing,
> whose unutterable and infinite charm can scarcely be contained in the spirit,
> where there are no change and no reason to fear its ending. [Note *Africa* ii,
> 415–426.]

Bernardo (1985), pp. 312–313. —*The omnipresence of death* is one of Reason's opening topics. Throughout the *DR,* Reason, in accordance with contemporary literacy practice, relies on a large repertory of topics of varying
origin and age, which I have attempted to identify and list in the special
index of topics and maxims. On topics (motifs, *loci,* commonplaces, Walter
Ong's "purple patches") and related meta-statements and examples, cf. Curtius (1953), esp. chaps. 3, 7, 5; Ong (1958), pp. 116–118; Lechner (1962);
and Ong (1967), esp. pp. 79–87. On the indexes to the *sententiae* in the early
collected editions of Petrarch's Latin works, Fowler (1916), pp. 2–4, on Basel,
1496, Venice 1501, 1503; and, in considerable detail, Deyermond (1961),
chap. 2, on 1496.

10   1492: pedetentim
      1581: pedentim

11   On *ascensus/descensus* and the related figures of "up" and "down," "high"
      and "low" (Trompf [1979], pp. 65–66 *et passim*), *Fam.* i, 3, 11:

> scio me ascendere ut descendam, virere ut arescam, ut senescam adolescere,
> vivere ut moriar.

I know that I ascend to descend, blossom to wither, grow up to grow old, live to die.

Bernardo (1975, p. 24; cf. Eccli, 33, 15, as in Isidore, *Etym.* ii, 21, 5. Also *Fam.* i, 6, 14, v, 17, 13, vii, 6, 3, xiv, 1, 30, xx, 4, 17; *Sen.* ix, 2 (1581: 959); *Secretum* i, as cited *DR* ii, 95, note 13; *De vita sol.* ii, *Prose* (1955), pp. 542, 544; and *DR* i, 5, 44–47, i, 17, 19–29, i, 90, 4–6, i, 96, 255 *et passim,* i, 107, 13–14, and note 8. On pride and humility, also Augustine, *Conf.* iv, 12; and *De civ. Dei* xiv, 13, as cited *DR* i, 13, note 9. On the up/down antitheton in Dante, e.g., *Div. Comm.*, Purg. x, 34–99, cf. below, *DR* i, 24, note 3; and the imagery of Par. vii, which culminates (97–120):

> Non potea l'uomo ne' termini suoi
> mai sodisfar, per non potere ir giuso
> con umiltate obediendo poi,
> quanto disobediendo intese ir suso;
> e questa è la cagion per che l'uom fue
> da poter sodisfar per sé dischiuso.
> Dunque a Dio convenia con le vie sue
> riparar l'omo a sua intera vita,
> dico con l'una, o ver con amendue.
> Ma perché l'ovra tanto è più gradita
> da l'operante, quanto più appresenta
> de la bontà del core ond' ell' è uscita,
> la divina bontà che 'l mondo imprenta,
> di proceder per tutte le sue vie,
> a rilevarvi suso, fu contenta.
> Né tra l'ultima notte e 'l primo die
> si alto o sì magnifico processo,
> o per l'una o per l'altra, fu o fie:
> ché più largo fu Dio a dar se stesso
> per far l'uom sufficiente a rilevarsi,
> che s'elli avesse sol da sé dimesso;
> e tutti li altri modi erano scarsi
> a la giustizia, se 'l Figliuol di Dio
> non fosse umiliato ad incarnarsi.

> Man, within his own limits, could never make
> satisfaction, for not being able to descend
> in humility, by subsequent obedience, so far
> as in his disobedience he had intended to ascend;
> and this is the reason why man was shut off from
> power to make satisfaction by himself. Therefore
> it was needful for God, with His own ways, to
> restore man to his full life—I mean with one way,
> or else with both. But because the deed is
> so much the more prized by the doer, the more it

> displays of the goodness of the heart whence it issued,
> the divine Goodness which puts its imprint on the
> world, was pleased to proceed by all Its ways
> to raise you up again; nor between the last night
> and the first day has there been or will there be
> so exalted and so magnificent a procedure, either
> by one or by the other; for God was more bounteous
> in giving Himself to make man sufficient to uplift
> himself again, than if He solely of Himself had remitted;
> and all other modes were scanty in respect to justice,
> if the Son of God had not humbled himself
> to become incarnate.

Singleton (1975), pp. 77, 79. Note the similar perception in *Fam.* x, 3, 54. Cf. also below, *DR* i, 90, 64–68, and note 16, ii, 5, 84–87, etc. —On ascent and descent in Christian existence, Balthasar (1982), chap. 100.

12   *Tusc. disp.* i, 31, 76; *volat enim aetas* (LCL, King, pp. 88–89). Cf. *Sen.* xii, 1 (1581: 898); and *Fam.* i, 3, 2:

> "volat enim etas," ut ait Cicero, et "omnino nichil est aliud tempus vite huius quam cursus ad mortem; in quo," ut ait Augustinus, "nemo vel paulo stare vel aliquanto tardius ire permittitur; sed urgentur omnes pari motu nec diverso impelluntur accessu. . . . "

> As Cicero says, "life time flies away," "so that our present life," as Augustine says [*De civ. Dei* xiii, 10, LCL, Levine, p. 165], "is nothing but a race toward the goal of death—a race in which no one is allowed either a brief pause or the slightest slackening of pace, but all are propelled with a uniform motion and driven along with no variation in the rate of progress. . . . "

Petrarch was fond of Augustine's metaphoric *cursus ad mortem*: cf. *Africa* ii, 340 *et sequ.*: *DR* ii, 117, 18; and *Sen.* xiii, 13 = *Var.* 15, Fracassetti, iii (1863), p. 336. Note also *Fam.* i, 6, 13, ii, 5, 2. On the topic of *fuga temporis, Fam.* xxiv, 1.

13   Virgil, *Aeneid* v, 217:

> . . . . . . celeris neque commovet alas.

LCL, Fairclough, p. 461. 1492, 1581 read *celeres*, which is also the reading in Schrevelius (1661), p. 523.

14   George Gascoigne, *The Grief of Joye*, 1576, Song i, 29–30:

> The heavens on highe perpetually doe move/
> By mynutes meale, the howre dothe steale awaie/
> By howres, the daie, by daies, the monethes remove/
> And then by monethes, the yeares as fast decaie/
> Yea, *Virgills* verse, and *Tully,* truth do saie,
> *That tyme flieth on, and never claps her wings,*

> But rides on clowdes, & forward still she flinges.
> Muche lyke to them, who (sitting in a shipp)
> Are borne forthright, and feele no footing sturr./
> In silent sleepes, the tyme awaie dothe slipp./

Reason's simile (Lucretius, iv, Oates [1940], p. 144) recalls the discussion of relative motion by contemporary scientists such as Campanus of Novara (c. 1205–1296), John Buridan (c. 1300–c. 1358) and Nicole Oresme (c. 1325–1382), which reappears in Nicholas of Cues' *De docta ignorantia* (ii, 12) of 1440 (Frey [1929], pp. 99–100) and in Copernicus' *De revolutionibus* . . . (i, 8) of 1543 (Grant [1974], pp. 501, 503–505, 511). The ship argument was still used by Galileo and Newton. Cf. Grant (1971b), pp. 65–69; B. Hoffmann in Wiener (1973), iv, pp. 76–77; J. Bronowski in Gingerich (1975), pp. 180–181; and Durham (1983), pp. 137–139. Note also below, *DR* ii, 48, 7–10.

15   *prima aetas*—the first age (Cicero, *De off.* ii, 13). According to J. G. Kempf in the *Thesaurus linguae latinae,* i (1900, cc. 1123–1138) *aetas* donotes human life in general; the various ages in the life of humans; or a historical era or age. The ages of life were variously apportioned, but comprised usually *infantia, pueritia, adolescentia, iuventus,* and *senectus,* the latter divided into *gravitas* and *senectus* by Augustine, *In Ps.* 70, 2, 4. On this, Aulus Gellius, x, 28, xv, 20; Augustine, *De div. quaest.* 58, 2, *PL* 40, c. 43, and Ladner (1959), pp. 222–235, on both life ages and world ages; and Isidore, *Etym.* xi, 2, and Fontaine (1959), i, pp. 377–378. Note also the interesting discussion of five ages in Marbod of Rennes, *Liber decem capitulorum,* Langosch (1968), pp. 238–249. On Dante's four ages, *Convivio* vi, 24, as below, *DR* ii, 83, note 7; and Mazzotta (1979), chap. 1. —Death coming at different times is discussed in *Secretum* iii, *Prose* (1955), pp. 138, 140. Cf. Rico (1974), pp. 276–286.

16   1492: durus
      1581: impurus

17   Such intervention in execution is the subject of Boccaccio, *Decameron* v, Stories 6 and 7. George Gascoigne's translation of the passage, *The Grief of Joye,* 1576, Song i, 18, Cunliffe, ii (1910), p. 520, eliminates this possibility:

> Unlesse (percase) of two condempnd to death,
> The ladd wch last, dothe clyme the gallow tree,
> (Because a while, he hath prolonged breath)
> Maie seeme (to some) the happier to be/
> And yet who lyst, to harken unto me,
> I saie hee seemes, moore paine for to endure
> Which lyngers lyfe, and is to dye most sure./

18   *animus ingens,* often used by Seneca, e.g., *Dial.* ii, 15, 2, *Nat. quaest.* vi, 32, 3, and *Ep.* 111, 2. Cf. Cicero's use of *animus magnus, De off.* i, 27, 94, and *Sen.* vii, 1 (1581: 824), *magnanimus.* On *altus animus, Fam.* vi, 3, 54, and *De vita*

sol. i, *Prose* (1955), p. 380. Note the documentation of related terms, Heitmann (1958), p. 205, n. 9.

19   Cf. Is. 26, 19; 32, 3:

> Expergiscimini, et laudate,
> qui habitatis in pulvere . . .

> Non caligabunt oculi videntium,
> et aures audientium diligenter auscultabunt.

> awake, and give praise,
> ye that dwelt in the dust . . .

> The eyes of them that see shall not be dim,
> and the ears of them that hear shall hearken diligently

Cf. Augustine, *Conf.* viii, 5, 10–12, as above, *Dramatis personae*, note 2.

20   1492: nobiscum
      1581: uobiscum

21   1492: relinquamur
      1581: relinquamini

Reason echoes the Augustinian time scheme which stresses the transitory nature of earthly life. In constant flux, ever changing, everything is either past or future. A true, i.e., stable, present, true joy that men long for, can be found only in eternity (e.g., *De trin.* xiii, 8, 11). On this, Gilson (1960), part iii, chap. 1; Urs von Balthasar (1967), pp. 1–42; Saville (1972), chap. 4; and Quinones (1972), chap. 3. Note also Boethius, *Cons. phil.* iii, P 8, 17, as below, *DR* i, 2, note 14; and the perceptive remarks in Steiner (1975), chap. 3, sect. 2.

22   1492: raperis. &c.
      1581: raperis.

Fam. xix, 16 (June 1357, to Guido Sette, Archbishop of Genoa, Wilkins [1958], pp. 138–140), 1:

> Statum meum vis audire; atqui si a stando status dicitur, nullus hic homini status est, sed fluxus iugis ac lapsus atque ad ultimum ruina.

> You want to hear about my state; well, if 'state' comes from *stare*, to stand still, there is no standing still for man here below; there is nothing but continual flow and down-slipping and at the end the collapse of all.

Bishop (1966), p. 161. —Pascal noted in *Pensées* 72:

> We sail within a vast sphere, ever drifting in uncertainty, driven from end to end. When we think to attach ourselves to any point and to fasten to it, it wavers and leaves us; and if we follow it, it eludes our grasp, slips past us, and vanishes forever. Nothing stays for us. This is our natural condition, and yet

most contrary to our inclination; we burn with desire to find solid ground and an ultimate sure foundation whereon to build a tower reaching to the Infinite. But our whole groundwork cracks, and the earth opens to abysses. Let us therefore not look for certainty and stability. Our reason is always deceived by fickle shadows.

Trotter (1941), p. 25.

2 ❖ A SPLENDID BODY

1   *Prose* (1955), pp. 612–619.
2   1492: umbrae in morem
      1581: umbrae in mortem

The phrase echoes Job 14, 2:

> Qui quasi flos egreditur et conteritur,
> et fugit velut umbra, et nunquam in eodem statu permanet.

> Who cometh forth like a flower, and is destroyed,
> and fleeth as a shadow, and never continueth in the same state.

3   Reason expounds school knowledge on particulars (Gerosa [1966], p. 187). Accidents have no independent existence (Martianus Capella iv, 347, 361–362); "they are not predicated essentially of the subject but rather qualifying it." (Porphyry, *Isag.* 3, 5–15; Bocheński [1961], p. 136; cf. Aristotle, *Top.* i, 5, 102b, 4–7.)

> Accidens autem non solet dici, nisi quod aliqua mutatione ejus rei cui accidit amitti potest. . . . sicuti est capillis hominum nigritudo, quoniam dum capilli sunt possunt albescere, separabile accidens dicitur: sed diligenter intuentibus satis apparet, non separatione quasi emigrare aliguid a capite dum canescit, ut nigritudo inde candore succedente discedat et aliquo eat, sed illam qualitatem coloris ibi verti atque mutari.

> The term accident is usually applied only to that which can be lost through some kind of change in a thing to which it belongs. . . . Thus, for example, the blackness of Men's hair, as long as the hair remains, can become white and, therefore, is called a separable accident. But if we observe carefully it becomes sufficiently clear that this is not really a separation. It is not as though

something leaves the hair when it becomes white, so that as the blackness departs and goes somewhere, the whiteness takes its place. What happens is that the quality of color in this instance has been turned and changed.

(Augustine, *De trin.* v, 4, *PL* 42, c. 913; McKenna [1963], pp. 178–179). Petrarch's sources included also Cassiodorus, *Inst.*ii, 3, 8; and Isidore, *Etym.* ii, 25, 7, 26, 11–15. On Isidore, Fontaine (1959), ii, pp. 629–631. Note also *Roman de la Rose* 16955–16957, Dahlberg (1971), pp. 285, 410.

4   On *qualitas*, Isidore, ibid. ii, 26, 7.

5   1492: prunia
     1581: pruina

6   1492: uenit ecce
     1581: uenit certe

7   1492: quanti esset forma uiui Hominis mors ostendit
     1581: quanti etiam sit forma uiui hominis mox ostendit

8   Cf. Boethius, *Cons. phil.* iii, P 8, 17–31:

Respicite caeli spatium, firmitudinem, celeritatem et aliquando desinite uilia mirari. Quod quidem caelum non his potius est quam sua regitur ratione mirandum. Formae uero nitor ut rapidus est, ut uelox et uernalium florum mutabilitate fugacior! Quod si, ut Aristoteles ait, Lynceis oculis homines uterentur, ut eorum uisus obstantia penetraret, nonne introspectis uisceribus illud Alcibiadis superficie pulcherrimum corpus turpissimum uideretur? Igitur te pulchrum uideri non tua natura sed oculorum spectantium reddit infirmitas. Sed aestimate quam uultis nimio corporis bona, dum sciatis hoc quodcumque miramini triduanae febris igniculo posse dissolui!

Fix your gaze on the extent, the stability, the swift motion of the heavens, and stop admiring base things. The heavens are not more remarkable in these qualities than in the reason by which they are governed. The beauty of your person passes swiftly away; it is more fleeting than spring flowers. And if as Aristotle says [probably in the lost *Protrepticus*], men had the eyes of Lynceus [cf. *DR* ii, 96, note 11] and could see through stone walls, would they not find the superficially beautiful body of Alcibiades to be most vile upon seeing his entrails? It is not your nature which makes you seem fair but the weak eyes of those who look at you. You may esteem your bodily qualities as hightly as you like as long as you admit that these things you admire so much can be destroyed by the trifling heat of a three-day fever.

LCL, pp. 252, 254; Green (1962), p. 55. Cf. Gruber (1978), pp;. 268–270.

9   Suetonius, viii, Dom. 18, 2:

Scias nec gratius quicquam decore nec brevius.

LCL, Rolfe, p. 381. Quoted in *Fam.* i, 3, 10, v, 18, 5; *Rer. mem. libri* iii, 35, 3 and *Secretum* ii, *Prose* (1955), p. 78.

10   1492: quod quamuis sit durabile
      1581: quamuis etiam si durabile
11   On *vera bona* which justify *gaudium verum* (*DR* i, 90, 10-11) and constitute
      vera felicitas (*Rer. mem. libri* iv, 24, 2–3): *Fam.* ii, 4, 11, as below, *DR* ii, 114,
      note 1, iii, 6, 1, iv, 17, 3, v, 18, 1, vi, 8, 1, xv, 7, 21, xxi, 9, 13, xxii, 12, 5;
      Trionfi, Tr. temp. 40–45, *Rime* (1951), p.549; and below, *DR* i, 9, 26–29, i,
      58, 15–18, ii, 6, 48–53, ii, 51, 67–70 ii, 55, 17–24, ii, 64, 2–6, ii, 73, 62–64,
      ii, 74, 16–17, ii, 83, 265–267, ii, 114, 5–7. Note also *DR* i, 109, note 12; and
      ii, 64, note 1.
12   On this, *Secretum* iii, "Cogita . . . ," *Prose* (1955), pp. 186–189; Rawski
      (1977), pp. 38–41. —On *birdlime on your wings*, cf. *Fam.* x, 3, 26.
13   1492: quantum uero inter comendum tempus effunditur
      1581: quantum uero interea commodum effunditur
14   Boethius, *Cons. phil.* iii, p 5, 41 (echoing Cicero, *Ver.* ii, 1, 15, which is quoted
      in Augustine, *De civ. Dei* xix, 5):

      Quae vero pestis efficacior ad nocendum quam familiaris inimicus?

      And what plague is able to hurt more than a familiar enemy?

      LCL, Stewart-Rand, p. 247. Cf. *Secretum* i, *Prose* (1955), p. 36; *Ps. poen.* vii.
      Note *La Celestina* (1499), i, 11, Marciales (1985), ii, p. 53; and Simpson
      (1955), p. 31. For other quotations of Petrarchan texts in the *Celestina*, cf.
      Deyermond (1961), chaps. ii–iv, and Appendix ii.
15   1492: fomenta libidinum
      1581: tormenta libidinum
16   1492: odiosus uiris aut forte suspectus. Nulla re magis quam forma corporea
      1581: odiosus uiris, aut forma corporea
17   1492: rata est
      1581: rara est
18   *oris habitus* = Cicero, *De fin.* iii, 17, 56. *flava caesaries* = Juvenal, 13, 165.
      reliqua albescent = Horace, *Carm.* iii, 14, 25. *serenam frontem* = Cicero, *Tusc.
      disp.* iii, 15, 31; Apuleius, *Metam.* ix, 27 (cf. Virgil, *Aeneid* iv, 477). *arabunt
      rugae* = Virgil, *Aeneid* vii, 417.
19   1492: faces
      1581: facies

      On *oculorum faces et . . . sidera* Propertius, ii, 3, 14; and Statius, *Ach.* i, 164.
      On *sidera oculi,* also Ovid, *Am.* ii, 16, 44, iii, 3, 9. On *scaber situs,* Ovid,
      Metam. viii, 802. On this, also *Sen.* vii, 2 (1581: 830), *passim.*
20   Matth. 12, 10: *homo habens manum aridam*; Marc. 3, 1: *homo manum habens
      aridam.* On *curva senecta,* Ovid, *Ars amat.* ii, 670. Note *Sen.* x, 1, as below,
      DR i, 90, note 16; and *Ps. poen.* v.
21   *te in speculo non agnoscas* = *La Celestina* iv, 5; Deyermond (1961), p. 58. Cf.
      Fam. xxiv, 1. 4:

sed legebam apud Flaccum:

> Insperata tue cum veniet pluma superbie
> Et, que nunc humeris involitant, deciderint come,
> Nunc et qui color est punicee flore prior rose
> Mutatus Ligurinum in faciem verterit hispidam;
> Dices: 'heu' quotiens te in speculo videris alterum . . .

but I read in Horace (*Carm.* iv, 10, 2-6; LCL, Bennett, p. 325):

> When unexpected down shall come upon thy pride
> And the locks have fallen that now wave upon thy shoulders,
> And the bloom that now outvies the blossom of the crimson rose
> Has faded, Ligurinus, and changed to a shaggy visage,
> Then as often as thou gazest in the mirror on thy altered features,
> Thou shalt say "Alas!" . . .

Note Innocent III, *De miseria cond. hum.* i, 9, Lewis (1978), pp. 107, 109:

Pauci nunc ad quadraginta, paucissimi ad sexaginta annos perveniunt. Si quis, autem, ad senectutem processerit, statim cor eius affligitur et capud concutitur, languet spiritus et fetet anhelitus, facies rugatur et statura curvatur, caligant oculi et vacillant articuli, nares effluunt et crines defluunt, tremit tactus et deperit actus, dentes putrescunt et aures surdescunt. Senex facile provocatur et difficile revocatur, cito credit et tarde discredit, tenax et cupidus, tristis et querulus, velox ad loquendum et tardus ad audiendum, set non tardus ad iram; laudat antiquos et spernit modernos, vituperat presens et commendat preteritum, suspirat et anxiatur, torquetur et infirmatur. Audi poetam: "Multa senem circumveniunt incommoda" et cetera. Porro nec senes contra iuvenem glorientur, nec insolescant iuvenes contra senem, quia quod sumus iste fuit, erimus quandoque quod hic est.

Gascoigne translated Innocent's driving *homoeoptoton* in *The Droomme of Doomes day*, 1576 (Cunliffe [1910], p. 222):

For now a dayes, men doe lyve forty yeares, and very fewe doe reache sixtie yeares. But if man doe attayne unto age, immediately his hart is afflicted, his head is troubled, his spirites languishe, his breath stincketh, his face is wrinckled, his body is bowed, his eyes are daseled, his feeling faylleth, and his quicknesse quayleth, his teeth become rotten, and his eares are closed up. An olde man is soon provoked, but hardly revoked, beleaving quickly, and mistrustinge laysurely: covetous, and greedy, heavy, and needy. Swyft to speake, and slowe to heare, praysing thinges of antiquitie, and dispysinge what is used presently, blaminge the tyme present, and allowing the tyme past, he sigheth and is vexed, he waxeth weake and is astonied, as Horace sayth. *Multa senem circumveniunt incomoda* [many ills beset an old man; *Ars poet.* 169]. To conclude, neyther let olde men glory against yonge men, nor yet let younge men waxe insolent and disdayne olde men, for they have been as we are, and we shall one daye be as they now are.

Cf. also *Roman de la Rose* 339–406. On the topic, Coffman (1934), pp. 249–258.

22   Cf. Virgil, *Aeneid* i, 142:

> Sic ait, et dicto citius tumida aequora placat

> Thus he speaks, and swifter than his word he calms the swollen
> seas . . .

LCL, Fairclough, p. 251. On the whole passage, cf. *Secretum* ii, *Prose* (1955), p. 80:

> Siquando autem vultus tui species tentare animum forte ceperit, occurrat qualia mox eadem futura sint membra que nunc placent, quam feda, quam tristia, quam tibi ipsi, si revidere possis, horrenda; tecumque hec inter philosophicum illud frequenter ingemina: "Ad maiora sum genitus quam ut sim mancipium corporis mei." Profecto enim summa insania est hominum, se se negligentium, corpus autem et, in quibus habitant, membra comentium. Siquis in carcerem tenebrosum atque humentem olentemque pestifere ad breve tempus intrusus sit, nonne, si non desipiat, intactum se, quam possibile fuerit, ab omni parietum et soli contagione servabit et, iamiam egressurus, intentis auribus liberatoris sui expectabit adventum? Quod si, his curis abiectis cenoque et horrore carceris delibutus, exire metuat, ac pingendis ornandisque circa se menibus omnem curam studiosus impendat, loci stillantis naturam frustra superare meditans, nunquid non merito insanus videatur et miser? Nempe vos carcerem vestrum et nostis et amatis, ah miseri! et mox vel educendi certe vel extrahendi heretis in eo exornando soliciti quem odisse decuerat. Sicut tu ipse in *Africa* tua Scipionis illius magni patrem loquentem induxisti:

>> odimus et laqueos et vincula nota timemus
>> libertatis onus: quod nunc sumus illud amamus.

> Preclare quidem, modo quod alios dicere facis ipse tibi diceres.

> If by any chance the fashion of your countenance should at any time have stirred the least motion of conceit, then I beg you to reflect what soon those bodily members must become, though now they please your eye: think how their destiny is to be foul and hideous, and what repulsion they would cause even in yourself were you able to see them then. Then call often to mind this maxim of the philosopher: "I was born for some higher destiny than to be the slave of my body" (Seneca, *Ep.* 65, 21). Assuredly it is the very climax of folly to see men neglect their real selves in order to cosset the body and limbs in which they dwell. If a man is imprisoned for a little while in some dungeon, dark, damp and dirty, would he not seem to have lost his senses if he did not shield himself as far as he was able from any contact with the walls and soil?

And with the expectation of freedom would he not eagerly listen for the foot-steps of his deliverer? But if giving up that expectation, covered with filth and plunged in darkness, he dreads to leave his prison; if he turns all his attention to painting and adorning the walls which shut him in, in a vain endeavour to counteract the nature of his dripping prison-house, will he not rightly be counted a wretched fool? Well, you yourself know and love your prison house, wretched that you are! And on the very eve of your issuing or being dragged therefrom you chain yourself more firmly in it, labouring to adorn what you ought to despise, if you would follow the advice you yourself had tendered to the father of the great Scipio in your poem called *Africa:*

> The bonds and fetters known and suffered long,
> The clogs on liberty are hateful to us,
> And the new freedom now attained we love.

(*Africa* i, 329–330.) Wonderful is it if you made others give the counsel you yourself refuse!

Draper (1911), pp. 58–59. On the Platonic notion of the body as prison of the soul (*Phaedo* 62b, 66b–67b, 82e; *Cratylus* 400c; Courcelle [1965]; on Petrarch's *Phaedo*, below, DR ii, 119, note 17), cf. Virgil, *Aeneid* vi, 724–751; Cicero, *Tusc. disp.* i, 19, 44, i, 30, 72 and 74; *De re publ.* vi, 14, 14, as in DR ii, 117, note 6, vi, 15, 15, and 26, 29; Seneca, *Ep.* 65, 16 and 21, and 120, 14; *Dial.* ix, De tranqu. 11, 1; Prudentius, *Psychomachia* 902–915; Macrobius, *Comm.* i, 11, 3, i, 12, 7 and 16, i, 13, 5, i, 14, 14, ii, 17, 12; and Boethius, *Cons. phil.* ii, P7, 82. On this, and the many Petrarchan references, Heitmann (1958), pp. 121–125; Foster (1984), esp. pp. 162–166; and below, DR ii, 117, note 23. —The mind-body topic and its facets recurs throughout the DR. For an overview, cf., e.g., A. L. Long in Wiener (1973), iv, pp. 1–9; and K. R. Popper in Popper-Eccles (1971), pp. 148–209. For Augustine's ideas on the subject, Gilson (1960), pp. 56–65; and Armsrtong (1967), chap. 22. Note also Javelet (1967), chap. vi.

23   Apuleius, *Florida* x, 5;

expecta paulisper et non erit.

24   Cicero, *Tusc. disp.* iv, 13, 30–31:

sunt enim in corpore praecipua, pulcritudo, vires, valetudo, firmitas, velocitas, sunt item in animo. Ut enim corporis temperatio, cum ea congruunt inter se, e quibus constamus, sanitas, sic animi dicitur, cum eius iudicia opinionesque concordant, eaque animi est virtus, quam alii ipsam temperantiam dicunt esse, alii obtemperantem temperantiae praeceptis et eam subsequentem nec habentem ullam speciem suam, sed, sive hoc sive illud sit, in solo esse sapiente. Est autem quaedam animi sanitas, quae in insipientem, etiam cadat, cum curatione medicorum conturbatio mentis aufertur. Et ut corporis est quaedam apta figura membrorum cum coloris quadam suavitate eaque dicitur pulcritudo, sic in animo opinionum iudiciorumque aequabilitas et constantia cum firmitate quadam et stabilitate virtutem subsequens aut virtutis vim ipsam continens pulcritudo vocatur. Itemque viribus corporis et nervis et efficacitati similes similibus quoque verbis animi vires nominantur. Velocitas autem corporis celeritas appellatur, quae eadem ingenii etiam laus habetur propter animi multarum rerum brevi tempore percursionem.

For the chief blessings of the body are beauty, strength, health, vigour, agility; so are they of the soul. For as in the body the adjustment of the various parts, of which we are made up, in their fitting relation to one another is health, so health of the soul means a condition when its judgments and beliefs are in harmony, and such health of soul is virtue, which some say is temperance alone, others a condition obedient to the dictates of temperance and following close upon it and without specific difference, but whether it be the one or the other, it exists, they say, in the wise man only. There is furthermore a certain kind of health of the soul which the unwise too can enjoy, when agitation of the mind is removed by medical treatment. And as in the body a certain symmetrical shape of the limbs combined with a certain charm of colouring is described as beauty; so in the soul the name beauty is given to an equipoise and consistency of beliefs and judgments, combined with a certain steadiness and stability, following upon virtue or comprising the true essence of virtue. And so strength of soul resembling the strength and sinews and effectiveness of the body is also described by similar terms. Agility of body again is termed quickness, and the same term is held to imply praise when applied to the intellect as well, because of the soul's rapid survey of a number of things in a short space of time.

LCL, King, pp. 359, 361. Note also, *DR* i, Pref., note 27. On properties of the beautiful, *DR* i, Pref., 244; and below, *DR* i, 66, note 2, ii, 2, 48, and note 13.

25 On *mediocritas*—moderation—the Aristotelean Peripatetic μεσόης, which "in all kinds of Fortune is like gold" (= Horace, *Carm.* ii, 10, 5–8), "is best" (Cicero, *Tusc. disp.* iv, 20, 46; *De off.* i, 36, 130, ii, 17, 59): *Fam.* iii, 7, 4, vii, 6, 4, xx, 8, 16; *Sen.* vi, 8 (1581: 552); *Secretum* ii, *Prose* (1955), p. 114; and *Fam.* iii, 14, 7, xii, 11, 14, xix, 5, 4, xx, 8, 16; *Sen.* ii, 2, vi, 8 (1581: 757, 552); *De vita sol.* ii, *Prose* (1955), p. 516. Also *Fam.* i, 3, 6–7, i, 10, 4, iii, 1, 5, iii, 20, 10, v, 17, 9, viii, 4, 1–8 and 24, xiv, 4, 10, xix, 16, 12, xix, 17, 1, xxiii, 12, 13, as above, *DR* i, Pref., note 41; *Sen.* viii, 7, xii, 1 (1581: 841, 903); *Var.* 55, as below, *DR* ii, 99, note 2, and 64, Fracassetti, iii (1863), pp. 456, 482; *Africa* v, 487, viii, 297, viii, 808; *Secretum* ii; *De vita sol.* i and ii, *Prose* (1955), pp. 88, 310, 318, 506, 556, 574; Rawski (1967), pp. 131–132, n. 7; and Baron (1988), i, pp. 172–174. Note Aristotle, *Eth. Nic.* ii, 6, Randall (1960), pp. 267–268; Cicero, *Tusc. disp.* iii, 10, 22; and *Fam.* xxiii, 2, 42. — On moderation as one of Reason's remedies for both Fortunes, cf. above, *DR* i, Pref., note 41.

26 On *alieno gloriari, Fam.* viii, 1, 37, xv, 7, 22; and below, *DR* i, 16, i, 58, 21–24,

i, 79, 30–33, i, 80, 2, ii, 6, 17–19, ii, 9, 2–3 and note 2, ii, 13, 17–22, ii, 127, 60–66.

27   *Trionfi,* Triumph. pudic. 187–189, *Rime* (1951), p. 516:

> e'l giovene Toscan che non ascose
> le belle piaghe che 'l fer non sospetto
> del comune nemico in guardia pose . . .

> And there to guard the common foe she [i.e., Chastity] set
> The Tuscan youth who in his face displayed
> The wounds that made him not a cause for fear.

Wilkins (1962), p. 47. Both our text and this refer to the story of Spurina,

> excellentis . . . pulchritudinis adulescens . . . cum mira specie con-
> plurium feminarum inlustrium sollicitaret oculos ideoque viris ac parentibus
> earum se suspectum esse sentiret, oris decorem vulneribus confudit deformi-
> tatemque sanctitatis suae fidem quam forman inritamentum alienae libidinis
> esse maluit.

> an exceedingly handsome young man whose admirable looks attracted the
> eyes of many distinguished women, so that, because he felt himself suspected
> by their husbands and parents, he disfigured with wounds the beauty of his
> face, for he preferred ugliness and the integrity of his honor to attractiveness
> provoking improper desires.

Valerius Maximus iv, 5, 6, Ext. 1. Twyne, f. 4r, refers to Spurina as female.

28   Seneca, *Ep.* 66, 2:

> Errare mihi visus est, qui dixit,
>   gratior et pulchro veniens e corpore virtus.
> Non enim ullo honestamento eget; ipsa magnum sui decus est et corpus suum
> consecrat.

> The poet who sang
>   Worth shows more pleasing in a form that's fair (Virgil, *Aeneid* v, 344)
> is, in my opinion, mistaken. For virtue needs nothing to set it off; it is its own
> great glory, and it hallows the body in which it dwells.

LCL, Gummere, p. 3. 1492 has *ueniens in* as in all Virgilian manuscripts; 1581 has *ueniens e.*

29   Augustine, *De civ. Dei* xix, 3:

> Omnium autem bonorum vel animi vel corporis nihil sibi virtus omnino prae-
> ponit. Haec enim bene utitur et se ipsa et ceteris, quae hominem faciunt
> beatum, bonis. Ubi vero ipsa non est, quamlibet multa sint bona, non bono eius
> sunt cuius sunt, ac per hoc nec eius bona dicenda sunt cui male utenti utilia
> esse non possunt. Haec ergo vita hominis, quae virtute et aliis animi et corporis
> bonis, sine quibus virtus esse non potest, fruitur, beata esse dicitur; si vero et

aliis, sine quibus esse virtus potest, vel ullis vel pluribus, beatior; si autem prorsus omnibus, ut nullum omnino bonum desit vel animi vel corporis, beatissima. Non enim hoc est vita, quod virtus, quoniam non omnis vita, sed sapiens vita virtus est; et tamen qualiscumque vita sine ulla virtute potest esse, virtus vero sine ulla vita non potest esse. Hoc et de memoria dixerim atque ratione, et si quid tale aliud est in homine. Sunt enim haec et ante doctrinam, sine his autem non potest esse ulla doctrina, ac per hoc nec virtus, quae utique discitur. Bene autem currere, pulchrum esse corpore, viribus ingentibus praevalere et cetera huius modi talia sunt ut et virtus sine his esse possit et ipsa sine virtute; bona sunt tamen, et secundum istos etiam ipsa propter se ipsa diligit virtus, utiturque illis et fruitur, sicut virtutem decet.

Now of all goods, whether of soul or of body, virtue prefers none at all to herself. For virtue makes good use both of herself and of all the other goods that go to make man happy; but where she is lacking, however many goods a man has, they do him no good, and so must not be called his "goods"; since he uses them ill, they cannot be useful to him. Here, then, is the sort of human life that is termed happy, a life that enjoys virtue and the other goods of soul and body without which virtue cannot exist; a life is called happier, if it enjoys one or more of the goods that virtue can lack and still exist; and happiest, if it enjoys absolutely all goods, so that it lacks not one of the goods either of soul or body. For life is not identical with virtue, since not every life, but only a wisely conducted life, is virtue; in fact, there can be life of a sort without any virtue, though there can be no virtue without some life. I might say as much of memory and reason and any other such human faculties; these exist before instruction, but without them there can be no instruction, and therefore no virtue, since virtue is in any case imparted by instruction. But swiftness in running, and physical beauty and victories won by unusual strength and the like, can exist without virtue, as virtue without them; yet they are goods, and according to these philosophers, even these are sought by virtue herself for their own sake, and are used and enjoyed by her in her own becoming way.

LCL, Greene, pp. 119, 121.

3 ❖ GOOD HEALTH

1   1492: de forma modo diximus
     1581: de forma non diximus

2   1492: accersere
      1581: arcessere
3   1492: peius quam in sano
      1581: peius sano in
4   1492: habitat. &c.
      1581: habitat.

Cf. Juvenal, x, 356:

orandum est ut sit mens sana in corpore sano.

You should pray for a sound mind in a sound body.

LCL, Ramsay, p. 219. Cf. *De vita sol.* i, *Prose* (1955), p. 304.

4 ✣ HEALTH RESTORED

1   1492: mortales bona uestra uix
      1581: mortales uestra uix
2   Virgil, *Aeneid* vi, 425, calls the Styx *ripam irremeabilis undae*—stream
      whence none return (LCL, Fairclough, p. 535).
3   1492: aequi
      1581: aeque

5 ✣ STRENGTH

1   Cf. Terence, *Andria* i, 61:

Ne quid nimis.

Beware of too much.

Cited below, *DR* i, 22, 21, i, 43, 26 (Rawski [1967], p. 131); and *Fam.* xi, 3, 3,
xvii, 1, 37; *Var.* 43, Fracassetti, iii (1863), p. 414; *Rer. mem. libri* iii, 64, 3.

2   Note the proverb *omne quod est nimium vertitur in vicium*—That that is overdoon is wol nat preeve/ Aright . . . , Chaucer, *Cant. Tales* viii, G, 645–646, Robinson (1933), p. 256. On moderation, above, *DR* i, 2, note 25. On *virtus in medio*—virtue as the mean (Aristotle, *Eth. Nic.* ii, 6, 1107a, Barnes [1984], p. 1748; cited in Chaucer, *LGW*, F 165–166, and referred to in his *Rom. of the Rose* 6525–6528; proverbial: *in medio stat virtus,* Whiting [1968], V 45), *Fam.* i, 10, 4, iii, 1, 14, xii, 2, 12, xviii, 1, 30, xxiii, 2, 43; *Sen.* vi, 7 (1581: 549); *Secretum* ii, *Prose* (1955), pp. 90, 114; and below, *DR* i, 69, 71, i, 94, 35. Note also Alcuin, *Disp. de rhet.,* Howell (1941), p. 144, 1179–1198.

3   Pliny, *Nat. hist.* vii, 20, 83:

> Milonem athletam cum constitisset nemo vestigio educebat, malum tenenti nemo digitum corrigebat.

> When the athlete Milo took a firm stand, no one could make him shift his footing, and when he was holding an apple no one could make him straighten out a finger.

LCL, Rackham, p. 561.

4   Hercules died poisoned by a robe smeared with the blood of the Centaur Nessus, whom he had shot with an arrow dipped in the poisonous blood of the Hydra.

5   Valerius Maximus, ix, 12, Ext. 9:

> Milo Crotoniates, cum iter faciens quercum in agro cuneis adactis fissam uidisset, fretus uiribus accessit ad eam insertisque manibus diuellere conatus est. Quas arbor excussis cuneis in suam naturam reuocata conpressit eumque cum tot gymnicis palmis lacerandum feris praebuit.

> When Milo of Croton, walking along, saw in a field an oak tree split and held open by driven wedges, he approached it and, confident of his strength put his hands into the crack trying to tear the tree apart. But as soon as the wedges fell out, the tree, reverting to its nature, clasped and held that athlete of so many victories until wild animals tore him to pieces.

6   1492: eximium sine exemplo
     1581: eximium corporis sine exemplo

7   George Gascoigne, *The Grief of Joye,* 1576, Song iii, 15–17:

> *Mylo* was stronge, and few men stronger founde
> But many wyser, and, muche more esteemdd/
> For every greate thing going on the grownde,
> Ys nott therefore, the better alwaies deemd./
> Thes *Oliphants* (in tyme past) peerless seemd,
> Because their sturdy joyntes did seldome bowe,
> But smaller beastes can overcome them nowe./

> And what great good, gott *Milo* by his strengthe,

Although in games, he gayned somtymes a gawde?
A smalle clefte oke, gan holde hym fast at lengthe,
Untyll wth beasts, hee were bothe champt & chawed/
Yea *Hercules,* whose might was never awed,
By womans wyles (yet) weakely lost his lyfe/
"Suche toyes (to tame the strongest men) are ryfe.

"For fortune fights not as thes fencers doe,
"Withe equall blades, or weapones of assise/
"But markes her tyme, and takes her vaūtage to,
"And in awaite, full waryly Shee lyees/
"Yea when Shee lyst, Shee can suche blowes devise,
"As (unawares) doe give some sodeyne patt,
"And overthrowe, a Gyant wth a gnatt./"

8   1492: apertius
     1581: aptius

George Gascoigne, ibid., 26:

"At last they dye, who thought longe tyme to lyve,
"At last they fade, whiche seemed freshe and fayre,
"At last they yeelde, w^ch (withe their strengthe) did strive
"And downe they fall, owt of theire stately chayre/
"They must descende, (but by unequall stayre)
"For he that clombe, as soft as snayles can slyde,
"Cõmes headlong downe, and maye no longer byde."

Cf. *Secretum* iii, *Prose* (1955), p. 208:

Ad hec, dum tibi occurrunt quos modo pueros vidisti, ascendentes etatum gradibus, recordare te interim alio calle descendere eoque celerius quo secundiore natura fit omnis gravium casus.

Moreover, when you meet with those whom you knew but yesterday as children, and see them now growing up in stature to their manhood, stage by stage, remember how you in like manner, in the same lapse of time, are going down the hill, and at a greater speed, by that law in nature under which things that are heavy tend to fall.

Draper (1911), p. 186. Note above, *DR* i, 1, note 11.

9   The lion "makes sure to cover all his footprints / Dragging dust with his tail wherever he steps / Either dust or mud, so he cannot be tracked" (Elliott [1971], *Leo*). Cf. Isidore, *Etym.* xii, 2; Bartholomaeus Anglicus, *De propr. rer.* xviii, 65 (Trevisa [1975], ii, p. 1214); Brunetto Latini, *Li Livres dou Tresor* i, 173, 10 (Carmody [1948], p. 155); and Goldstaub (1892), pp. 24 (8, 2–3), 287.

10   Cf. *Secretum* ii, as above, *DR* i, 2, note 22.

11   Virgil, *Aeneid* x, 740: nec longum laetabere . . . , LCL, Fairclough, p. 221.
12   1492: conqueritur. &c.
      1581: conqueritur.

He who was so strong and whom I mentioned twice is Milo.

6 ❖ RUNNING SWIFTLY

1   Cf. Augustine, *De civ. Dei* xiii, 10; and above, *DR* i, 1, note 12. Note also
      Boethius, *Cons. phil.* iii, P 8.
2   Cf. Pliny, *Nat. hist.* ii, 68, 173–175, as cited below, *DR* i, 92, note 4.
3   1492: perfecte
      1581: profecto
4   1492: confragia
      1581: confragra
5   According to John Trevisa's translation of Bartholomaeus Anglicus, xviii, 8
      and 83, the ass

> is a symple beste and a slowe . . . . . . The parde hatte pardus, as Ysidorus
> [*Etym.* xii, 2, 10] seiþ, and is þe moste swyfte beste . . .

(Trevisa [1975], ii, pp. 1120, 1235). Cf. Hrabanus Maurus, *De univ.* vii, *PL* 111,
c. 212A; White (1954), pp. 82, 13; etc.
6   1492: metuit. &c
      1581: metuit.
      George Gascoigne, *The Grief of Joye,* 1576, Song iv, 39–40:

> I wyll not spare to speake as *Petrark* spake,
> Who sayd that leapers (leap they never so well)
> Cannott withe Squyrells full compare (yett) make/
> Nor he whose rooñyng alwaies wyñes the bell,
> Shall therein seeme, a hare (yet) to excell/
> Nor he that vaults, or gambolds best in shape,
> Can coome abowt (yet) nymbly lyke an Ape./
>
> A lambe can leape, full lightly in his yowthe,
> Which afterwards, proves heavie heeelde and slowe,
> For loompyshe age, the lightest lyñes ensewth,/
> And (at an ynche) doth, followe where they goe/

> Then he that rooñes so fast, or leapeth so,
> Where wyll he light, but in the lappe of death?
> And (streynyng force) he seemes to shorten breath./

Cunliffe, ii (1910), pp. 555–556.

7 ❖ A GOOD MIND

1 Reason distinguishes between *animus,* the reasonable part of the human soul, and *ingenium,* intellectual aptitude (Quintilian, *Inst. orat.* x, 2, 12, x, 1, 130). Hugh of St. Victor, *Didasc.* iii, 6, *PL* 176, c. 771:

> ingenium invenit et memoria custodit sapientiam. Ingenium est vis quaedam naturaliter animo insita, per se valens. Ingenium a natura proficiscitur, usu juvatur, immoderato labore retunditur et temperato acuitur exercitio.

> Aptitude gathers wisdom, memory preserves it. Aptitude is a certain faculty naturally rooted in the mind and empowered from within. It arises from nature, is improved by use, blunted by excessive work, and is sharpened by temperate practice.

Taylor (1961), p. 91. On this, John of Salisbury, *Metalog.* i, 11, *PL* 199, c.838; De Bruyne (1946), ii, pp. 384–385; and Fontaine (1959), ii, pp. 686–689, 691. For the later history of *ingenium,* Pareyson (1947–49).

2 *onerosa: periculosa: laboriosa*

3 Virgil, *Georg.* iv, 246–247:

> aut invisa Minervae
> laxos in foribus suspendit aranea cassis.

> or the spider, hateful to Minerva,
> hangs in the doorway her loose-woven nets.

LCL, Fairclough, pp. 213, 215.

4 Reason refers to Pallas Athene's encounter with Arachne,

> a princess of Lydian Colophon—famed for its purple dye— . . . so skilled in the art of weaving that Athene herself could not compete with her. Shown a cloth into which Arachne had woven illustrations of Olympian love affaires, the goddess searched closely to find a fault but, unable to do so, tore it up in a cold, vengeful rage. When the terrified Arachne hanged herself from a rafter,

Athene turned her into a spider—the insect she hates most—and the rope into a cobweb, up which Arachne climbed to safety.

Graves (1955), 25.h. and 6. Cf. Ovid, *Metam.* vi, 1–145; and Dante, *Div. Comm.*, Purg. xii, 43–45;

> O folle Aragne, sì vedea io te
> già mezza ragna, trista in su li stracci
> de l'opera che mal per te si fé.

5   1492: uersatile
     1581: uersabile

6   Reason alludes to what Petrarch called *triplex Catonis laus*—the threefold praise of Cato, in Pliny, *Nat. hist.* vii, 27, 100:

> Cato primus Porciae gentis tres summas in homine res praestitisse existimatur, ut esset optimus orator, optimus imperator, optimus senator . . .

> Cato the first of that name in the Gens Porcia is deemed to have exemplified the three supreme human achievements, excelling alike as orator, as general and as senator.

LCL, Rackham, p. 571. The passage is quoted in *De vir. ill.* xxii, 5; *Fam.* xix, 18, 20; and, in different sequence, below, *DR* i, 57, 25. On Petrarch's annotation in his copy of Cicero, *De orat.* iii, 333, 135, Nolhac (1907), i, p. 243. Note also ibid., ii, pp. 109–110.

7   This may be a reference to the fact that *excello*—to excel, surpass, be eminent—can be used in both a good and a bad sense. Compare, e.g., Cicero, *Tusc. disp.* ii, 18, 43, with his *De leg.* i, 19, 51; and note Cornelius Nepos, *De exc. duc.* vii, 1:

> . . . nihil illo fuisse excellentius vel in vitiis vel in virtutibus.

> . . . that (Alcibiades) was never excelled either in faults or in virtues.

LCL, Rolfe, p. 435. Aulus Gellius has a chapter on words used in both a good and a bad sense in his *Noctes Atticae* xii, 9.

8   I.t.: Crispus

9   Sallust, *Cat.* 5:

> L. Catilina, nobili genere natus, fuit magna vi et animi et corporis, sed ingenio malo pravoque.

> Lucius Catilina, scion of a noble family, had great vigour both of mind and of body, but an evil and depraved nature.

LCL, Rolfe, p. 9.

10   1492: prodiere. &c.
      1581: prodiere.

On *in magnis ingeniis magni errores,* cf. also below, *DR* i, 7, 35.

8 ❖ MEMORY

1   1492: formosarum
     1581: fumosarum

atrium fumosarum imaginum = Boethius, *Cons. phil.* i, P 1, 16. Cf. also Cicero *Piso* i; Seneca, *Ep.* 44, 5; *De benef.* iii, 28, 2; and, below, *DR* ii, 5, note 24.

2   A reference to memory as the house of images, which resembles ancient architecture but stresses irregular shapes and places. It is filled with images of a very personal kind, human figures, beautiful or grotesque, distinct or shadowy. Cf. *Ad Herenn.* iii, 18–19 *et passim.* Augustine, *Conf.* x, 8, *PL* 32, c. 784, refers to *aula ingenti memoriae meae*—the vast chamber of my memory; *penetrale amplum et infinitum*—an inner chamber large and boundless—and *campos et lata praetoria memoriae, ubi sunt thesauri innumerabilium imaginum de cuiuscemodi rebus sensis invectarum*—the fields and roomy chambers of my memory, where are the treasures of countless images, imported into it from all manner of things by the senses (Oates [1948], i, pp. 152–153). Cf. above, *DR* i, Pref., note 21. For Augustine on memory, cf. Yates (1966), esp. pp. 46–49; and Armstrong (1967), pp. 370–373. On memory in Dante's *Divina Commedia,* Mazzotta (1979), pp. 260–267. Note also the mnemonic echoes *(loci, sedem)* in Aristotle, *Topics* viii, 163b, 27–31; and Boethius, *Cons. phil.* i, P 5, 20–24.

3   Dante, *Div. Comm.,* Inf. v, 121–123:

> E quella a me: "Nessun maggior dolore
> che ricordarsi del tempo felice
> ne la miseria; e ciò sa 'l tuo dottore . . . "

> And she to me, "There is no greater sorrow
> than to recall, in wretchedness, the happy time;
> and this your teacher knows . . . "

Singleton (1970), p. 55. Cf. Boethius, *Cons. phil.* ii, P 4, 3–6; and Singleton (1970), *Commentary,* p. 93.

4   1492: cogitatio
     1581: cogitationem
5   1492: delectatio
     1581: delectationem
6   1492: iocunda
     1581: iucundam
7   1492: sed incolumis: sed liber: carcerem: sed solutus: uincula: sed reuersus:
         exilium [*destroying the* isocolon *figure* disiunctio]
     1581: sed incolumis, seruitutem sed liber, carcerem sed solutus, exilium sed
         reuersus

Augustine, *Conf.* x, 14, *PL* 32, c. 788:

> Aliquando et e contrario tristitiam meam transactam laetus reminiscor, et tris-
> tis laetitiam.

> Again, on the contrary, I at times remember when joyous my past sadness, and
> when sad my joy.

J. G. Pilkington in Oates (1948), i, p. 157. Cf. *De vita sol.* i, *Prose* (1955), p.
378. Note also Euripides, *Andromeda,* quoted in Cicero, *De fin.* ii, 32, 105.

8   1492: in recordatione multiplici multiplex
     1581: in recordatione multiplex
9   1492: accidit
     1581: accidunt
10   Pliny, *Nat. hist.* vii, 24, 89: *inventa est a Simonide melico* . . . Cf. Cicero, *De
     orat.* ii, 86: Quintilian, *Inst. orat.* xi, 2, 11; and Yates (1966), chap. i.
11   *malle se oblivionis artem quam memoriae discere.* The passage adheres closely
     to *Rer. mem. libri* ii, 9. The story is from Cicero, *De orat.* ii, 74, 299. But
     Themistocles' answer, as given here, is, in fact, Antony's rephrasing of this
     answer, Cicero, *De orat.* ii, 86, 351: *oblivionis artem quam memoriae malim.*
     Note also Cicero, *De fin.* ii, 32, 104; and *Acad.* ii, 1, 2, Cf. Yates (1966), p. 17.
12   Artificial memory—Cicero's *memoria technica* (*Acad.* ii, 1, 2)—includes
     loci—places—and *imagines*—images. A *locus* is a place easily grasped by the
     natural memory, such as a house, hall, or arch; images are forms, marks,
     signs, or portraits of what we wish to remember. The art of memory is like an
     inner writing:

> For the places are very much like wax tablets or papyrus, the images like the
> letters, the arrangement and disposition of the images like the script, and the
> delivery (i.e., when we say what we recall) is like reading.

Ad Herenn. iii, 17, 30; Yates (1966), pp. 4–12. *Imagines rerum et verborum*—
images of things and words—refers to the two kinds of images which help us
remember: images of things (*res*), the subject matter of speech; images of
words (*verba*), the language in which this subject matter is being presented.

Cf. *Ad Herenn,* iii, 16–24; Rawski (1975), pp. 257–260. —For a succinct overview of the subject of artificial memory, cf. Spence (1984), chap. 1. On the later history of artificial memory and related *subsidia memoriae*—aids to memory—also Morhof (1747), i, 2, 6, pp. 366–385.

13 Reason alludes to the two kinds of memory, *naturalis*—natural—and *artificiosa,* or *artificialis*—the product of art.

> Naturalis est ea quae nostris animis insita est et simul cum cogitatione nata; artificiosa est ea quam confirmat inductio quaedam et ratio praeceptionis.

> The natural memory is that memory which is imbedded in our minds, born simultaneously with thought. The artificial memory is that memory which is strengthened by a kind of training and system of discipline.

Ad Herenn, iii, 16, 28, LCL, Caplan, p. 207.

14 1492: si qua
    1581: si quae

9 ❖ ELOQUENCE

1 Cf. above, *DR* i, 2, note 25.
2 I.t.: Crispus. —Sallust, *Cat.* v, 4, reads in all the best mss. *satis eloquentiae sapientiae parum.* Petrarch uses here and (slightly varied) in *De sui ipsius* (1581: 1039; Nachod, p. 61), the phrase discussed by Aulus Gellius (i, 15, 18), in a chapter on

> What a tiresome and utterly hateful fault is vain and empty loquacity, and how often it has been censured in deservedly strong language by the greatest Greek and Latin writers.

Gellius relates that Valerius Probus, a famous grammarian, insisted that Sallust wrote *satis loquentiae, sapientiae parum*—

> quod 'loquentia' novatori verborum Sallustio maxime congrueret, 'eloquentia' cum insipientia minime coveniret.

> since the word *loquentia* was very characteristic of Sallust, an innovator in diction, while *eloquentia* was not at all consistent with lack of discretion.

LCL, Rolfe, p. 79. Cf. Pliny the Younger, *Ep.* v, 20, 5: [Julius Cordus] solet dicere, aliud esse eloquentiam, aliud loquentiam.

used to say, *eloquentia*—eloquence—is one thing, *loquentia*—loquacity—another.

3   1492: in homine illo scelestissimo
     1581: in homine illo Catilina

4   Reason alludes to the Gellius story, note 2 above, as *altiore iudicium*.

5   This refers to Cato's definition, Quintilian, *Inst. orat.* xii, 1, 1 and 44 (cf. Seneca Rhetor, *Cont.* i, Praef. 9; Cassiodorus, *Inst.* ii, 2, 1; Isidore, *Etym.* ii, 3, 1, and Fontaine [1959], i, pp. 233–236; and Rawski [1967], p. 186), which is identified in our text, lines 31–32, below; and in *De sui ipsius* (1581: 1039; Nachod, p. 61).

6   *Fam.* i, 3, 7:

quoniam paucis bene loqui, bene vivere autem omnibus datum est . . .

since to speak well is possible only for a few, but to live well is possible for all . . .

7   On virtue and wisdom, cf. Seneca, *Ep.* 98, 9. Note also *DR* ii, 114, note 1; and *Posteritati,* Prose (1955), p. 6:

Ego, modo bene vixissem, qualiter dixissem parvi facerem: ventosa gloria est de solo verborum splendore famam querere.

If only I have lived well, I make small account of how I have spoken. To seek reputation by mere elegance of language is only vainglory.

Bishop (1966), p. 7.

8   *orator est vir bonus dicendi peritus.* Discussed at length in Quintilian, *Inst. orat.* i, Praef. 9, xii, 1, 1 and 44. Cf. Fontaine (1959), i, pp. 233–236, 332–334. Note also the takeoff on Cato's definition reported by the younger Pliny, *Ep.* iv, 7:

Herennius Senecio mirifice Catonis illud de Oratore . . . e contrario vertit, Orator est vir malus dicendi imperitus.

Herennius Senecio inverted marvelously Cato's saying on the orator: An orator is a bad man unskilled in speaking.

9   Cicero, *De part. or.* xxiii, 79:

Nihil enim est aliud eloquentia, nisi copiose loquens sapientia.

10   On the title orator, *DR* i, 46, 61–72.

11   Reason refers to elementary dialectic as expounded, e.g., in Cassiodorus, *Inst.* ii, 3, 12 = Isidore, *Etym.* ii, 9, 1–8 and 28; and Fontaine (1959), i, pp. 255–275.

12   1492: principium essentiale
       1581: praecipuum essentiale—i.e., the essential mentioned lines 34–36,
       above.

According to Aristotle, *Topics* i, a definition is a phrase signifying a thing's
essence (Bocheński [1961], 11. 07). If this essence is missing, the defintion
collapses. Petrarch's source probably was Cassiodorus, *Inst.* ii, 3, 14 = Isidore, *Etym.* ii, 29, 1–16. On this, Fontaine (1959), ii, pp. 622–624, 634–638.
—Reason continues to answer in quasi-formal fashion, as if to oppose her
"clenched fist" of logical syllogism to the "open palm" of rhetorical *enthymema*, by shifting from Joy's impulsive assertions on eloquence to the
aspects of rigorous logical argument. Petrarch was well aware of Cassiodorus,
Inst. ii, 3, 2, = Isidore, *Etym.* ii, 23, 1–2, Mynors (1937), p. 109:

> Dialecticam et Rhetoricam Varro in novem disciplinarum libris tali similitudine
> definivit: 'Dialectica et Rhetorica est quod in manu hominis pugnus adstrictus
> et palma distensa: illa verba contrahens, ista distendens.' Dialectica siquidem
> ad disserendas res acutior: Rhetorica ad illa quae nititur docenda facundior. Illa
> ad scholas nonnunquam venit: ista iugiter procedit in forum. Illa requirit raris-
> simos studiosos: haec frequenter et populos.

> In his nine books of *Disciplines* [now lost] Varro distinguishes dialectic and
> rhetoric by using the following comparison: 'Dialectic and rhetoric are like
> man's closed fist and open palm [cf. Cicero, *De fin.* ii, 6, 17; Quintilian, *Inst.
> orat.* ii, 20, 7], one contracting its language, the other extending it.' If indeed
> dialectic is more subtle for the discussion of questions, rhetoric is more elo-
> quent for the teaching of its objectives. One sometimes comes to the schools;
> the other constantly proceeds to the forum. One seeks a few studious men; the
> other the great mass.

L. W. Jones (1946), p. 159; Fontaine (1959), i, p.211. The *Invective contra
medicum* takes an opposite approach, employing the weapon of narrative
vituperative eloquence (*Fam.* i, 7, 6: *armatum enthimemate bisacuto*—armed
with double edged enthymemas) against the physician's syllogistic demon-
strations. On this, Rawski (1975), pp. 256–257.

13   On *know yourself*, below, DR ii, 73, note 12.

14   1492: oblisci caepit iam non
       1581: obliuisci coeperit non iam

15   1492: pateficit
       1581: patefecit

16   I.e., Sallust, note 2, above; and the sententious quotation, *Fam.* xviii, 1, 48,
       Piur (1933), no. 6, p. 38, n. 291.

17   1492: esse non posse
       1581: esse posse

18   This is a paraphrase of Cicero, *De inv.* i, 1:

eloquentiam vero sine sapientia nimium obesse plerumque, prodesse numquam.

that eloquence without wisdom is generally highly diadvantageous and is never helpful.

LCL, Hubbell, p. 3. On this, *Fam.* i, 9; Augustine, *De doct.* iv, 5, 7; and Seigel (1968), pp. 34–36, 47–48, and chap. 2. Reason refers to Cicero's *rhetorics,* i.e., his incomplete *De inventione* and, as the *rhetorica secunda,* or *rhetorica nova, Ad Herennium,* ascribed to Cicero since the days of St. Jerome. Cf. *Ad Herenn.,* LCL, Caplan, pp. vii–ix.

19   1492 and 1581 read *nostros*—us (i.e., Romans)—although Reason, as a rule, would use *vestros*—yourselves. Twyne, f. 9v, translates *Latines.*

20   All three were great orators. Demosthenes, who had agitated against Macedonia and was pursued by Antipater's henchmen, took poison, 322 B.C.; Cicero's Philippics against Antony led to his murder by Antony's agents, December 7, 43 B.C.; Marcus Antonius—the grandfather of Shakespeare's Antony—was killed by partisans of Marius, 87 B.C.

21   Prov. 18, 21:

Mors et vita in manu linguae

22   1492 and 1951 read *attonitum;* Twyne, f. 9v. has *Aconitum.* According to the Greeks, Aconite or Wolfsbane was created from the froth of the three-headed Cerberus that Hercules dragged up from hell (Graves [1955], i, 97.c; Ovid, *Metam.* vii, 404–424). Cf. above, *DR* i, Pref., note 11.

10 ❖ VIRTUE

1   1492: non saltem licet de uirtute gloriari
    1581: non saltem de uirtute licet gloriari

Seneca, *Dial.* vii, Ad Gall., 20, 1–5, describes a man striving for virtue as follows:

Studiorum salutarium etiam citra effectum laudanda tractatio est. Quid mirum, si non escendunt in altum ardua adgressi? Sed si vir es, suspice, etiam si decidunt, magna conantis. Generosa res est recipientem non ad suas sed ad naturae suae vires conari, alta temptare et mente maiora concipere, quam quae etiam ingenti animo adornatis effici possunt. Qui sibi hoc proposuit: "Ego mortem eodem voltu comoediamque videbo. Ego laboribus, quanticumque illi erunt, parebo animo fulciens corpus. Ego divitias et praesentis et absentis aeque contemnam, nec si aliubi iacebunt, tristior, nec si circa me fulgebunt, animosior. Ego fortunam nec venientem sentiam nec recedentem. Ego terras omnis tamquam meas videbo, meas tamquam omnium. Ego sic vivam quasi sciam aliis esse me natum et naturae rerum hoc nomine gratias agam; quo enim melius genere negotium meum agere potuit? Unum me donavit omnibus, uni mihi omnis. Quicquid habebo, nec sordide custodiam nec prodige spargam. Nihil magis possidere me credam quam bene donata. Non numero nec pondere beneficia nec ulla nisi accipientis aestimatione perpendam; numquam id mihi multum erit, quod dignus accipiet. Nihil opinionis causa, omnia conscientiae faciam. Populo spectante fieri credam quicquid me conscio faciam. Edendi mihi erit bibendique finis desideria naturae restinguere, non implere alvum et exinanire. Ero amicis iucundus, inimicis mitis et facilis. Exorabor, antequam roger, et honestis precibus occurram. Patriam meam esse mundum sciam et praesides deos, hos supra me circaque me stare factorum dictorumque censores. Quandoque aut natura spiritum repetet aut ratio dimittet, testatus exibo bonam me conscientiam amasse, bona studia, nullius per me libertatem deminutam, minime meam"—qui haec facere proponet, volet, temptabit, ad deos iter faciet, ne ille, etiam si non tenuerit,

                    Magnis tamen excidit ausis.

The pursuit of salutary studies is praiseworthy, even if they have no practical result. What wonder that those who essay the steep path do not mount to the summit? But if you are a man, look up to those who are attempting great things, even though they fall. The man that measures his efforts, not by his own strength, but by the strength of his nature, that aims at high things, and conceives in his heart greater undertakings than could possibly be accomplished even by those endowed with gigantic courage, shows the mark of nobility. The man who has set before himself such ideals as these: "As for me, I shall look upon death or a comedy with the same experssion of countenance. As for me, I shall submit to all hardships, no matter how great they be, staying my body by the spirit. As for me, I shall despise riches alike when I have them and when I have them not, being neither cast down if they shall lie elsewhere, nor puffed up if they shall glitter around me. As for me, I shall pay no heed to Fortune, either when she comes or when she goes. As for me, I shall view all lands as my own, my own as belonging to all others. As for me, I shall always live as if I were aware that I had been born for service to others, and on this account I shall render my thanks to Nature: for how could she better have served my interest? She has given me, the individual, to all men and all men to me, the individual. Whatever I may possess, I shall neither hoard as a miser, nor as a spendthrift squander. Nothing shall seem to me so truly my possessions as the gifts I have wisely bestowed. I shall not estimate my benefactions by their number, nor by their size, nor by anything except my estimation of the recipient; never shall what a worthy man receives seem great in my eyes. Nothing shall I ever do for the sake of opinion, everything for the sake of my conscience. Whatever I shall do when I alone am witness I shall count as done beneath the gaze of the Roman people. In eating and drinking my aim shall be to quench the desires of Nature, not to fill and empty my belly. I shall be agreeable to my friends, to my enemies mild and indulgent. I shall give pardon before it is asked, and hasten to grant all honourable requests. I shall know that the whole world is my country, that its rulers are the gods, and that they abide above me and around me, the censors of my words and deeds. And whenever Nature demands back my breath, or my reason releases it (referring to suicide), I shall depart, bearing witness that I have loved a good conscience and all good endeavour, that I have been guilty of nothing that impaired the liberty of any man, least of all my own"—the man who shall resolve, shall wish, and shall essay to do these things will be following the path toward the gods—ah! such a man, even if he shall not reach them,

> Yet fails in a high emprise

(Ovid, *Metam.* ii, 328).

LCL, Basore, pp. 149, 151, 153.

2   1492: creditur
     1581: credi
3   1492: adsit
     1581: absit
4   1492: illi
     1581: ei
5   *Fam* xvi, 3, 4:

> . . . si avaritie credidero, pauperrimus ac mendicus videar; luxuria et avaritia et ambitio nullis finibus sunt contente.

> . . . if I were to listen to greed, I should think I were the poorest beggar. Excess and greed and ambition know no bounds.

6   1492: morem
     1581: morem est.
7   1492: uirtus
     1581: uirtutis
8   *Fundamentum verae virtutis humilitas:* Cf. Alain de Lille, *Ars praedic.,* citing Gregory the Great. (*Hom. in Ev.* i, 7, 4, *PL* 76, c. 1103), *PL* 210, c. 132:

> qui sine humilitate virtutes congregat, quasi in ventum pulverem portat.

> He who collects virtues without humility is like one who carries dust into the wind (Ps. 1, 4).

In one of his *sententiae* (*PL* 210, c. 264), Alain refers to humility with a lyrical anaphora as

> virtutum nutrix, virtutum gloria, virtutum vita, nomen et meritum.

the virtues' wetnurse, the virtues' glory, the virtues' life, fame, and value.

Cf. *Fam.* vii, 2, 3, on *humilitas virtus altissima*—humility, the highest virtue; and *Fam.* xx, 4, 1:

humilitas, optima dos animi et ad virtutem veramque gloriam primus gradus.

Humility, the best endowment of the mind, and the first step toward virtue and true glory.

Note Augustine, *De civ. Dei* xiv, 13, as below, *DR* i, 13, note 9; *Fam.* i, 8, 10–16, ii, 9, 11, vii, 2, xxi, 5, 5, xxiii, 10; *Sen.* viii, 6, viii, 7, xiii, 2 (1581: 840, 841, 916, Wilkins [1959], p. 172); *Secretum* ii, *Prose* (1955), p. 70: *Que, quanquam grandia . . . ,* Draper (1911), p. 49; etc. —On *humilitas* as a mode of *modestia* in prosperity, above, *DR* i, Pref., note 41.

9   I Tim. 3, 6:

ne in superbiam, elatus, in iudicium incidat diaboli.

lest being puffed up with pride, he fall into the judgment of the devil.

10   1492: non obscurus tantum
      1581: non obscuris tantum
11   I.e., Lucifer—Satan,

> Vedea colui che fu nobil creato
>   più ch'altra creatura, giù dal cielo
>   folgoreggiando scender, da l'un lato.

> I saw, on the one side, him who was created nobler
> than any other creature fall as lightning from heaven.

Dante, *Div Comm.*, Purg. xii, 25–26, Singleton (1973), p. 123 and *Commentary* (1973), p. 246. Note also Parad. xix, 46–48. Cf. Augustine, *De civ. Dei* xi, 33 (LCL, pp. 560–563); Innocent, *De miseria* ii, 31, Lewis (1978), pp. 185, 187; and below, *DR* ii, Pref., note 61.

12   1492 miratrix
      1581: moratrix
13   1492: semper
      1581: semperque
14   1492: peruenisse credit
      1581: peruenisse se credit
15   *Quisquis ad summam pervenisse credit. In hoc primum fallitur: quod ubi credit esse non est.* Note *Fam.* xvii, 8 (to Brother Matteo Como, probably late in 1353), 3:

Nemo se satis extimet profecisse, nunquam enim nitetur ut ad summum veniat qui pervenisse confidit.

Let no one believe that he has made sufficient progress, for that man never strives to reach the summit who thinks he has reached it.

(Bernardo [1985], p. 27); and *Contra med.* ii, Ricci (1950), p. 53, 499–501:

cum nunquam propinquaveris, pervenisse te putas.

though you never got near it, you fancy that you have arrived.

The vocabulary of these passages points to Seneca, *Dial.* ix, De tranqu. i, 16:

Puto multos potuisse ad sapientiam pervenire, nisi putassent se pervenisse, nisi quaedam in se dissimulassent, quaedam opertis oculis transiluissent.

I fancy that many men would have arrived at wisdom if they had not fancied that they had already arrived, if they had not dissembled about certain traits in their character and passed by others with their eyes shut.

LCL, Basore, p. 211. Note *Secretum* i, *Prose* (1955), p. 36; and Tateo (1965), pp. 25–26.

16   1492: magna parantibus obstitit iamque alta praehesantibus [*obscuring the homoeoteleuton figure*]
     1581: magna parantibus obsistit, iamque alta pensantibus

On the road metaphor, cf. *Secretum* ii, *Prose* (1955), p. 96.

17   1492: uis mediocritas
     1581: uix mediocritas

18   Augustine, *De doct.* i, 22, 20; *PL* 34, c. 26: *solo deo fruendum*—we must enjoy God alone. "Virtue, then, means to will what we should will, i.e., to love what we should love," out of love for Him (Gilson [1960], p. 135). Cf. Anselm of Canterbury, *Cur deus homo* i, 15, Allers (1936), p. 457; Von den Steinen (1959), p. 267; and Thomas Aquinas, *Summa theol.* i, II, Q.55, a.l.o.4, Pegis (1945), ii, p. 412.

19   Reason refers to Augustine's teachings on the Christian life and, in particular, to his—Ciceronian (e.g., *De. nat. deor.* ii, 60, 152)—distinction between things that are to be enjoyed *(frui)* and things that are to be used *(uti)*. Gilson (1960), p. 169, summarizes *De doct.* i, 4, 4; *PL* 34, c. 20:

When the different ways in which man conducts himself towards things are reduced to their simplest forms, they are found in final analysis to be but two: man either enjoys things or uses them. Enjoying a thing means fixing one's will upon it out of love for the thing itself; using a thing means utilizing it as a means of obtaining something else. We enjoy what we think of as an end; we use what we look upon only as a means.

On this, Cayré, i (1936), pp. 620–621; and Huppé (1959), pp. 6–7. Note also the early reference in Augustine's *De div. quaest.*, q. 30, and *De civ. Dei* xi, 25, xix, 3, as above, *DR* i, 2, note 29, xix, 17, xv, 7:

Boni quippe ad hoc utuntur mundo, ut fruantur Deo; mali autem contra ut fruantur mundo uti volunt Deo . . .

For whereas the good make use of the world in order to enjoy God, the wicked would like to make use of God in order to enjoy the world . . .

LCL, Levine, p. 441. Among Petrarchan references to *frui* and *uti* are, below, *DR* i, 21, 6–7; *De ocio*, Rotondi, p. 69; *Fam.* xii, 4, 2, xxii, 10, 6–10; *Sen.* viii, 7, as in Introduction to the Commentary, ii, item 9; and *De vir. ill.* xvii, Hanibal, 44, and *Fam.* iii, 3, 6, both citing Florus, i, 22, 21. One the Augustinian topic, Robertson (1963), pp. 65–66; Heitmann (1958), pp. 197–199; Battenhouse (1955), pp. 380–381; Rawski (1967), pp. 152–153; in Dante, Mazzotta (1979), pp. 165–166; and in Bernard of Clairvaux, Brian Stock in Murdoch (1975), pp. 226–227.

20 Reason refers to the two contrary modes of anticipation, *spes gaudendi (sperare gavisurum)* hope to enjoy—and *metus dolendi (ut metuas doliturum)*—fear to be sorry. Cf., e.g., below, *DR* i, 109, 9, i, 116, 2–3, ii, 128 *passim*; *Fam.* iv, 12, 28, xi, 3, 9, xx, 2–3; and *Sen.* ix, 1 (1581: 845). *Spes* and *metus* were familiar to the medieval reader as standard rhetorical devices in deliberative exposition (Quintilian, *Inst. orat.* iii, 8, 15–55; Isidore, *Etym.* ii, 4, 4, Fontaine [1959], i, p. 239; for dramatic effects, *Ad Herenn.* i, 8, 13, and Cicero, *De inv.* i, 19, 27). On this, Finke (1951). Note also above, *Dramatis personae,* notes 9 and 11.

11 ❖ REPUTATION

1 *Opinio rem non mutat* (*La Celestina* ii, 2, Marciales [1985], ii, p. 58; Simpson [1955], p. 33) = *DR* i, 69, 78, and *Fam.* xviii, 1, 46. In this letter of November 23, 1353, to Emperor Charles IV, the statement occurs among a number of *sententiae*—maxims—the source of which is not clear (Piur [1933], pp. 34, 38, n. 277). Related is *Fam.* xxi, 12, 12: *siquidem error omnis non in rebus sed in opinione consistit*—since all error dwells not in the things but in your opionion; and Cicero's proverbial phrase, *De leg.* i, 16, 45: *nec arboris nec equi virtus . . . in opinione sita est, sed in natura*—the strength of a tree or of a horse is not determined by opinion but by nature. Reason distinguishes between the thing itself and our belief about the thing, which, as Cicero observes, *non natura exoriatur, sed iudicio, sed opinione*—did not originate in

nature, but in an act of judgement, of opinion (*Tusc. disp.* iii, 33, 82). Cicero uses similar phraseology when he discusses the Stoic states of disorder (*perturbatio*—πάθος—as δόξα, i.e., *opinio, Tusc. disp.* iv, 7, 1, iv, 38, 82; *De fin.* iii, 10, 35).

> Sunt enim ingeniis nostris semina innata virtutum, quae si adolescere liceret, ipsa nos ad beatam vitam natura perduceret: nunc autem, simul atque editi in lucem et suscepti sumus, in omni continuo pravitate et in summa opinionum perversitate versamur, ut paene *cum lacte nutricis* errorem *suxisse* videamur.

> The seeds of virtue are inborn in our dispositions and, if they were allowed to ripen, nature's own hand would lead us to happiness of life; as things are, however, as soon as we come into the light of day and have been acknowledged [by our fathers], we at once find ourselves in a world of iniquity amid a medley of wrong beliefs, so that it seems as if *we drank in deception with our nurse's milk.*

Tusc. disp. iii, 1, 2; LCL, King, p. 227. Note also Lactantius, *Div. inst.* vi, 14, *PL* 6, c. 688; and Prudentius, *Symm.* i, 201–202. Petrarch quoted the italicized words in *Fam.* v, 17, 13; again, when he annotated his copy of the commentary on Plato's *Timaeus* by Chalcidius (Paris, B.N., lat. 6280, f. 41r; Nolhac [1907], ii, pp. 146–147; cf. Waszink [1962], p. 196); and paraphrased them in *Fam.* xx, 4, 33, and *Sen.* x, 4 (1581: 876). —This view is echoed by Reason's ancestress *Philosophy* in Boethius, *Cons. phil.*, who contrasts *rebus quidem rectus ordo*—the true order of things—i.e., the reality to be known, with *opinioni perversa confusio*—the perverse confusion of personal or public opinion—not supported by the evidence of reflective inquiry (ibid., iv, P 6, 133; and the passages cited in Gruber [1978], pp. 26, 158, and 260). Based on these texts, Petrarch explains in *Fam.* ii, 2, 6:

> vides itaque—quod saepe dicere soleo, nec mea solum est, sed illustrium philosophorum sententia—quicquid in hac vita patimur molesti, non tam ex ipsa rerum natura, quam ex nostre mentis imbecillitate sive, ut eorum etiam verbis utar, ex opinionum perversitate.

> And thus you can see—what I often say, which is not only my observation, but a maxim of distinguished philosophers—that whatever grievous experience we suffer in this life is not so much due to the nature of things, as to the weakness of our mind, or, to use the works of these philosophers, the result of the perversity of opinion.

Related, Seneca, *Ep.* 13, 4, and 16, 9; and *Fam.* ii, 2, 14. On *opinionum perversitas*—the διαστροφή of Aristotle's ὀρθὸς λόγος—*recta ratio* (Cicero, *Tusc. disp.* iv, 15, 34; *De leg.* i, 16, 45)—healthy reason (Pohlenz, i [1959], p. 305, ii [1955], pp 35–36, 152; Heitmann [1958], pp. 101–102), cf., e.g., *Fam.* i, 8, 22, ii, 2, 6, ii, 3, 3, xvi, 3, 4; *Sen.* vi, 8 (1581: 555); *Secretum, Prose*

(1955), pp. 34, 36, 94, 114, 116; *De ocio*, Rotondi, p. 70; and *DR* i, Pref., 229–230, i, 93, 20, ii, 81, 115, ii, 124, 28, etc. The *opinionum pestifera vis, que totum orbem vastat atque inficit*—the pestiferous power of opinion, which ravages and corrupts all the world—and *opinionum infinita perversitas*—the infinite perversity of opinion—are mentioned in *Sen.* viii, 3 (1581: 835). Note also, above, *DR* i, Pref., note 7. —Related to the topic and well known to Petrarch is Isidore, *Etym.* ii, 24, 2, clearly based on Lactantius' discussion of *scientia* and *opinatio* in his *Div. inst.* iii, 3, *PL* 6, cc. 354–356; Fontaine (1959), ii, pp. 607–609.

2   Prov. 22, 1:

> melius est nomen bonum quam divitiae multae.

On formulaic phrases, such as *quidam sapiens vir,* below, *DR* ii, 79, 98, and note 24.

3   Eccl. 7, 1:

> melius est nomen bonum quam unguenta preciosa.

4   1492: imperii
    1581: impii
5   Prov. 10, 7:

> nomen impiorum putrescet.

6   II Cor. 1, 12:

> gloria nostra haec est testimonium conscientiae nostrae.

7   *e radice mala nihil boni oritur*
8   1492: neque hinc ortum
    1581: neque hinc igitur ortum
9   *in utranque partem*
10   *intus in anima*—a reference to Augustine's notion of the "mind's innerness." Cf. Gilson (1960), pp. 70–71:

> Whether we know an intelligible or a sense object, our knowing is effected within and from within, without the introduction of anything from the outside. Thus in both orders of knowledge, Augustine's doctrine seems to find the same law, which we might call the law of the mind's innerness. Outside the soul there may be, and indeed there should be, things to warn and advise, or signs to invite the soul to enter into itself and consult the truth there; but its own spontaneity remains inviolable, for even though it seizes upon such signs in order to interpret them, it is always from within that it derives even the substance of what it seems to receive.

See also the discussion of *sensus interior,* and of the "inner master," ibid., pp. 14, 65, and chap. v; De Lubac, ii, 1 (1959), pp. 508–510; Javelet (1967), esp. i, pp. 84–86, 338–339, and chap. ix, and ii, p. 58, n. 141, p. 231, n. 255; and

Rawski (1967), p. 162. Note Nicole Oresme, *De config.* i, 31, Clagett (1968), pp. 249–251; *De ocio* (1581: 308); *Contra med.* iv, as below, *DR* ii, 29, note 7; and *DR* i, 4, 7.

11 In *Secretum* i, *Prose* (1955), p. 36, Augustine castigates the *perversa . . . et pestilens libido*—the perverse and pestiferous craving of mortals to deceive themselves. Cf. above, *DR* i, Pref., note 7. On this, Rico (1974), pp. 59–60. On the topic of self-deception, Augustine, *Conf.* viii, 7, *PL* 32, cc. 756–757. Note also Lewis (1938), p. 71.

12 1492: nunc te autem
    1581: num te autem

13 Cf. Boethius, *Cons. phil.* iii, P 6, 5–8:

> Plures enim magnum saepe nomen falsis uulgi opinionibus abstulerunt; quod quid turpius excogitari potest? Nam qui falso praedicantur, suis ipsi ncesse laudibus erubescant. Quae si etiam meritis conquisita sit, quid tamen sapientis adiecerit conscientiae qui bonum suum non populari rumore, sed conscientiae ueritate metitur?

> For many men have achieved a great name based on the false opinion of the masses; and what is more disgraceful than that? Those who are falsely praised must blush when they hear the applause. And, even if the praise is merited, what does it matter to the wise man who measures his virtue by the truth of his conscience, not by popular esteem.

Greene (1962), pp. 52–53.

14 1492: uobis *throughout the sentence*
    1581: nobis *throughout the sentence*

15 *To believe others rather than oneself* is an ever recurring theme in Petrarch's work; ct., e.g., *DR* i, 12, 62, i, 45, 16 (Rawski [1967], p. 59), i, 109, 48; *Secretum* i, *Prose* (1955), p. 36; and *Fam.* ii, 4, 20, ix, 5, 6. In *Fam.* i, 3, 11, Petrarch remarks *cogito non quid aliis videor, sed quid sum*—I do not consider what I seem to others, but what I am (Bernardo [1975], p. 24); in *Sen.* xvii, 2 (1581: 967), *Prose* (1955), p. 1152, perhaps somewhat mellowed by age, *ultro alienis testimoniis acquiescam et, qui mos est publicus de me aliis credam*—beyond this, I am content with the statements of other poeple and, in the common fashion, believe others about myself. On this, Rawski (1967), pp. 162–163. Cf. Horace, *Ep.* i, 16, 19: *sed vereor ne cui de te plus quam tibi credas*—but I fear, as touching yourself, that you may give more credit to others than to your own judgment (LCL, Fairclough, p. 353); and Seneca, *Dial,* ix, De tranqu. an. xv, 6: *ex aliena opinione pendere*—depending on the opinion of others (LCL, Basore, p. 275). Petrarch may also have remembered the verse *one learned as a child*, as John of Salisbury notes (*Policrat.*, *PL* 199, c. 484), i.e, Cato's distich:

> Quum te aliquis laudat, iudex tuus esse memento:
> Plus aliis de te, quam tu tibi credere noli.

> When someone praises you, be judge alone:
> Trust not men's judgment of you, but your own.

Dicta Catonis i, 14, LCL, Duff, p. 599. Cf. Henry of Settimello, *De diversitate fortunae et philosophiae consolatione* ii, 85–86, Leyser (1721), p. 479.

16   I.t.: *Flacci sententiam*

17   Paraphrasing Horace, Ep. i, 16, 39:

> falsus honor iuvat et mendax infamia terret.

> False honor delights and lying infamy frightens.

18   Among the many references to the old topic of the vulgar crowd and its *consuetudo*—ingrained habits (e.g., Cicero, *De leg.* ii, 17, 43; Boethius, *Cons. phil.* i, P 3 *et passim;* Hildegard of Bingen, *PL* 197, c. 336; and Huizinga [1931], pp. 78–87) are *Fam.* ii, 2, 20, ii, 4, 13, x, 3, 13, xxi, 10, 7; *Sen.* v, 2, xii, 1 (1581: 795, 905); *Africa* ii, 344–347; *Secretum, Prose* (1955), pp. 34, 94, 114, 116; *Trionfi,* Tr. mortis ii, 31–33, *Rime* (1951), p. 524; *DR* i, 12, 47–49, i, 19, 38, i, 30, 110–112; i, 38, 66–69, i, 40, 47–51, i, 69, 123–126, ii, 10, 16–19; etc. Cf. Rawski (1967), pp. 189–190.

19   *contraria contrariis gaudent*—because *nullum adeo contrarium est sine contrario altero*—as a matter of fact, no opposite is conceivable without something to oppose it (Chrysippus, *On Providence,* as told by Aulus Gellius, vii, 1, 4, LCL, Rolfe, p. 91). *By his contrarie is every thyng declared* (Chaucer, *Troilus* i, 637; cf. below, *DR* ii, 58, note 2). Cf. Aristotle, *Eth. Nic.* v, 1, 1129a, 18, Barnes (1984), ii, p. 1782; Thomas Aquinas, *In Meta.* iv, 4, 1004b, 30, lect. 4, 581; idem, *Summa theol.* i, Q. 77, a. 3, ad 2; Pegis (1945), i, p. 725; and the curious echo in *Fam.* vi, 3, 4. Contraries and their dynamics were among the root concepts of ancient philosophy (e.g., Heraclitus [Jones], frag. 43, 45, 46, 56; Plato, *Lysis* 215e: "for everything . . . craves for its contrary"; Aristotle, based on Thales, Pythagoras, and Empedocles, *Categ.* viii, x–xi; *Phys.* i, 5, 188a, etc.; Randall [1960], pp. 179–180; and Boyde [1981], chap. 2). Medieval thought saw the interplay of opposites in every aspect of God's order—*concordia discors*—discordant concord (Horace, *Ep.* i, 12, 19; Ovid, *Metam.* i, 433; Lucan, i, 98; Seneca, *NQ* vii, 27, 4; Lactantius, *Div. inst.* ii, 9, 17; Joh. Scotus Erigena, *De div. nat.* iii, 6, v, 36, as below, *DR* ii, 93, note 19; Alain de Lille, *De planctu nat., PL* 210, c. 443), from the beauty of creation, descending, as it were, to the specifics of mind and body, and the inanimate world, all composed

> ex imparibus scilicet et paribus. Hic enim stabilitas, illic instabilis variatio, hic inmobilis substantiae robur, illic mobilis permutatio; hic definita soliditas, illic infinita congeries multitudinis.

> obviously of uneven and even ones. Here stability, there instable variation;

here the mass of immovable matter, there quick moving change; here mono-lithic unity, there an infinite cluster of variety.

(Boethius, *De arith.* ii, 32, 19–21; De Bruyne [1946], i, pp. 13–15; note also, ibid., ii. pp. 299–301, and Colie [1966], pp. 32–33)—as Augustine had said:

ita quasi ex antithesis quodammodo, quod nobis etiam in oratione iucundum est, id est, ex contrariis, omnium simul rerum pulchritudo figuratur.

as if caused, somehow, by an antithesis, which also pleases us in speech, namely, the employment of contraries that bring about the beautiful in all things.

(*De ord.* i, 6, 18, *PL* 32, c.986).

His antithesis et Paulus apostolus in secunda ad Corinthios epistula illum lo-cum suaviter explicat, ubi dicit:
Per arma iustitiae dextra et sinistra: per gloriam et ignobilitatem, per infamiam et bonam famam; ut seductores et veraces, ut qui ignoramur et cognoscimur; quasi morientes, et ecce vivimus, ut coherciti et non mortifi-cati; ut tristes, semper autem gaudentes, sicut egeni, multos autem di-tantes, tamquam nihil habentes et omnia possidentes.
Sicut ergo ista contraria contrariis opposita sermonis pulchritudinem reddunt, ita quadam non verborum, sed rerum eloquentia contrariorum oppositione saeculi pulchritudo componitur. Apertissime hoc positum est in libro ecclesias-tico isto modo:
Contra malum bonum est et contra mortem vita;
sic contra pium peccator.
Et sic intuere in omnia opera Altissimi,
bina bina, unum contra unum.

These antitheses are gracefully demonstrated by the Apostle Paul too, in his second letter to the Corinthians, where he says:
With the weapons of righteousness for the right hand and for the left; in honour and dishonour, in ill repute and in good repute; treated as impos-ters, and yet truthful; as unknown, and yet well known; as dying, and behold we live; as punished, and yet not killed; as sorrowful, and yet always rejoicing; as poor, yet making many rich; as having nothing, and yet possessing everything (ii Cor. 6, 7–10).
So, just as beauty of language is achieved by a contrast of opposites in this way, the beauty of the course of this world is built up by a kind of rhetoric, not of words but of things, which employs this contrast of opposites. This is very clearly stated in the book of Ecclesiasticus as follows:
Good is the opposite of evil, and life the opposite of death;
so the sinner is the opposite of the godly.
And so you are to regard all the works of the Most High:
two by two, one the opposite of the other (Eccli. 33, 14–15).

De civ. dei xi, 18, LCL, Wiesen, pp. 495, 497. *Eccli.* 33, 14–15, is the text of the *Vetus latina,* quoted also in Isidore, *Etym.* ii, 21, 5. On God's symbols representing "like through unlike," Gombrich (1972), pp. 150–152; and Von den Steinen (1959), p. 14. Isidore, *Etym.* ii, 31, discusses opposites and their subset, contraries, based on Cicero and Martianus Capella (Fontaine [1959], ii, pp. 640–644). Cf. also Bartholomaeus Anglicus, *De propr. rer.* viii, 1, Trevisa (1974), p. 443, etc.; Chaucer, *Canterbury Tales,* Nun's Priest's Tale, 3279–3280; and Elbow (1975).

In the *DR,* much of Reason's argument relies upon *contentio*—opposition of contraries—as described in *Ad Herenn.,* iv, 15, 21; Cicero, *Part. orat.* vi, 21; and Quintilian, *Inst. orat.* ix, 3, 81, etc., recalling Aristotle's discussion of argument from contraries (*Rhet.* ii, 19, 1392a, 9) and his endorsement of this form of expression:

> Such a form of speech is satisfying, because the significance of contrasted ideas is easily felt, expecially when they are thus put side by side, and also because it has the effect of a logical argument; it is by putting two opposing conclusions side by side that you prove one of them false.

(*Rhet.* iii, 9, 1410a, 20, Barnes [1984], p. 2249; among the many examples of *antitheton* in Petrarch's writings is *Rime* 134, *Pace non trovo, e non ho da far guerra*). —As physician for the mind, Reason is aware of the Aristotelian contraries warm/cold, dry/wet, and the four elements, fire, water, air, earth, contraries themselves, and their humors (cf. Lewis [1964], pp. 94–96, 169–174; Sarton, i, [1952], pp. 338–339; Durham [1983], pp. 44, 53–54; and below, *DR* i, 18, note 15; ii, Pref., notes 4, 84), as well as therapy by contraries—this in accordance with age-old interpretive tradition (cf., e.g., Javelet [1967], i, p. 303, ii, p. 251, nn. 39, 40; and Olson [1982], chap. 2, esp. pp. 48–55). *Fam.* vii, 17, 5, cites as *vetus medicorum regula*—ancient rule of physicians—the classical phrase of the Hippocratic corpus: *contraria contrariis curari*—opposites are cures for opposites (Hippocrates, *Breaths* i, 33–34, LCL, Jones, pp. 228–229; Temkin [1973], p. 18; Aristotle, *Eth. Nic.* ii, 3, 1104b, 15, Barnes [1984], p. 1745), which recurs *Sen.* xii, 2 (1581: 912). Cf. also *Fam.* vii, 9, 4. Both the Hippocratic writer and Petrarch include sample remedies in their texts; Petrarch's are psychological (e.g., for pleasure, the remedy is sadness; cf. below, *DR* ii, 43, note 4); those of the Hippocratic writer, physical (e.g., for hunger, eating; for thirst, drink; for fatigue, rest). On this, note also *Sen.* v, 4 (1581: 801); and above, *Dramatis personae,* notes 14 and 19. On the related tetradic division of the ages of man, cf. below *DR* ii, 83, note 7.

20   1492: uentus
      1581: uetus

Cf. Virgil, *Aeneid* vii, 646: *Ad nos vix tenuis famae perlabitur aura*—to us scarcely is wafted some scant breath of fame (LCL, Fairclough, p. 47); below, *DR* ii, 88, note 20; and the maxim in Seneca, *Ep.* 123, 16: *Gloria vanum et volucre quiddam est auraque mobilius*—Glory is an empty and fleeting thing, lighter than air (LCL, Gummere, p. 435). Based on this, Dante, *Div. Comm.*, Purg. xi, 100–102:

> Non è il mondan romore altro ch'un fiato
> di vento, ch'or vien quinci e or vien quindi,
> e muta nome perché muta lato.

> A breath of wind is all there is to fame
> here upon earth: it blows this way and that,
> and when it changes quarter it changes name.

Ciardi (1977), p. 245. Note *Fam.* i, 2, as below, *DR* ii, 25, note 14; *Fam.* x, 6, 1; *Secretum* iii, *Prose* (1955), p. 190; and Rico (1974), p. 382, n. 466.

21   *radices agent: & propagabuntur: At si ficte celeriter tanquam flosculi decident*—paraphrasing Cicero, *De off.* ii, 12, 43:

> Vera gloria radices agit atque etiam propagatur, ficta omnia celeriter tamquam flosculi decidunt, nec simulatum potest quicquam esse diuturnum.

> True glory strikes deep root and spreads its branches wide; but all pretences soon fall to the ground like fragile flowers, and nothing counterfeit can be lasting.

LCL, Miller, p. 213.

22   *insanorum sermunculis gloriare*—cf. *Fam.* ii, 4, 21: *ignorantium sermunculi.* The phrase *i nunc, i nunc et, ite nunc,* used as a "formula introducing an ironical command which, in the face of what has just been said, is held to be absured or unreasonable" (Glare [1982], p. 610, 10b), and, e.g., Plautus, *Aulularia* 828; Horace, *Ep.* i, 7, 71, ii, 2, 76, as quoted in *Secretum* ii, *Prose* (1955), p. 120 (note also ibid., p. 72: *I nunc, et ingenio gloriare!*); Ovid, *Ars amat.* ii, 122, and *Ex pont.* i, 3, 61; Seneca, *De benef.* iv, 38, 2, *Ep.* 88, 38, *Herc. fur.* 89–90, and *Medea* 650 (= Boethius, *Cons. phil.* iv, M 7, 32–33) and 1007–1008; and Juvenal, vi, 306, *Contra eum* (1581: 1074, line 13), *De vir. ill.* xvi, 33, *Buc. carm.* xii, 160, and *Sen.* v, 2 (1581: 796, line 7); etc., occurs frequently in the *DR,* e.g., *DR* i, 14, 40, i, 21, 73, i, 34, 36, i, 37, 145, i, 64, 31, i, 78, 9, and i, 112, 109. Similar, *DR* i, 69, 103.

1492: gloriare &c.
1581: gloriare.

12 ✤ WISDOM

Beatum cui etiam in senectute contigerit ut sapientiam verasque opiniones

assequi possit: Plato, *Laws* 653a, as quoted in Cicero, *De fin.* v, 21, 58.
2   Cf. *Fam.* x, 5, 10, xv, 14, 4; *Sen.* xvi, 3 (1581: 952); *Rer. mem. libri* iii, 99, 2; and *DR* ii, 40, 32–34.
3   I.e., Saint Paul in Phil. 3, 12:

> Non quod iam acceperim aut iam perfectus sim.

> 1492: quod inde acceperim perfectus sim
> 1581: quod iam acceperim aut perfectus sim

4   Phil. 3, 13:

> Ego me non arbitror comprehendisse.

5   Ps. 138, 16:

> Imperfectum meum viderunt oculi tui.

6   In *La Celestina* ix, 2, Marciales (1985), ii, p. 163; Simpson (1955), p. 105; Deyermond (1961), p. 59.
7   The text is not clear. Both 1492 and 1581 have:

> Vos qui legitis non ueros modo: sed citra uerum sistere illos rati: publico errore fallimini.

Twyne, f. 13r, translates:

> You that reade them, and thynke them not only to be true, but somewhat inferiour to the trueth, are deceyued by a common errour.

8   Cf. *DR* i, 11, 58–61, above.
9   *Put your life before your eyes:* cf. above, *DR* i, 10, 39–42.
10   1492: uere licet pauci
      1581: uerum licet pauci
11   *Learned men are scarce:* cf. above, *DR* i, Pref., note 14.
12   Pliny, *Nat. hist.* vii, 40, 131:

> Quid quod nemo mortalium omnibus horis sapit? utinamque falsum hoc et non ut a vate dictum quam plurimi incident!

> What of the proverb that none among mortals is wise all the time? And would

that as many men as possible may deem this proverb false, and not as the utterance of a prophet!

LCL, Rackham, pp. 593, 595. Note also Augustine, *Prof. fid.* 28, Oates (1948), i, p. 420.

13   According to Cant. 7, 7: *threescore queens and fourscore concubines,* i.e., at a given time. Iii Reg. 11, 3 notes *he had seven hundred wives as queens, and three hundred concubines: and the women turned away his heart.*

14   Iii Reg. 11, 4–8:

> Cumque jam esset senex, depravatum est cor ejus per mulieres, ut sequeretur deos alienos; nec erat cor ejus perfectum cum Domino Deo suo sicut cor David patris ejus. Sed colebat Salomon Astarthen, deam Sidoniorum, et Moloch, idolum Ammonitarum. Fecitque Salomon quod non placuerat coram Domino, et non adimplevit ut sequeretur Dominum, sicut pater ejus. Tunc aedificavit Salomon fanum Chamos, idolo Moab, in monte qui est contra Jerusalem, et Moloch, idolo filiorum Ammon. Atque in hunc modum fecit universis uxoribus suis alienigenis, quae adolebant thura et immolabant diis suis.

> And when he was now old, his heart was turned away by women to follow strange gods: and his heart was not perfect with the Lord his God, as was the heart of David his father.
> But Salomon worshipped Astarthe the godess of the Sidonians, and Moloch the idol of the Ammonites.
> And Salomon did that which was not pleasing before the Lord, and did not fully follow the Lord, as David his father.
> Then Salomon built a temple for Chamos the idol of Moab, on the hill that is over-against Jerusalem, and for Moloch the idol of the children of Ammon.
> And he did in this manner for all his wives that were strangers, who burnt incense, and offered sacrifice to their gods.

Isidore defined *ironia*—irony, which is used frequently in the *DR,* as *sententia per pronuntiationem contrarium habens intellectum*—a sentence composed and spoken in a manner suggesting that the apparent meaning is the contrary to the real meaning. *Etym.* i, 37, 23; Fontaine (1959), i, p. 152; Green (1979), pp. 3–11. Note also Chaucer, *Troilus* v, 897–899. On the rhetorical trope *ironia,* Perelman (1969), pp. 207–209 *et passim;* and Lausberg (1960), pp. 302–303, 729–731. On *pronuntiatio,* ibid., pp. 527, 787. On irony in medieval texts, Green (1979).

15   Cicero, *De amic.* ii, 6–7:

> Sunt ista Laeli; . . . sed existimare debes omnium oculos in te esse coniectos unum; te sapientem et appellant et existimant. Tribuebatur hoc modo M. Catoni . . .

> What you say is true, Laelius; . . . But you should realize that all men have fixed their eyes on you alone; you it is whom they both call and believe to be wise. Recently this title was given to Marcus Cato . . .

LCL, Falconer, p. 113. Cf. also *De vir. ill.* xxii, Cato, 1.

16   1492: Meriodoro
     1581: Metrodoto

17   1492: qualis qualis gloria
     1581: qualis gloria

18   The lists naming the Seven Sages of ancient Greece vary (Sarton, i [1952], pp.
     168–169). They usually include Bias of Priene, Chilo of Sparta, Cleobolus of
     Lindos in Rhodes, Periander of Corinth, Pittacus of Mitylene, Solon of Athens,
     and Thales of Miletus (Diogenes Laertius, i; Augustine, *De civ. Dei* xviii, 25;
     Ausonius, *Lud. sept. sap.*). On the Seven, *Rer. mem. libri,* esp. Book iii; and
     Rime (1951), p. 572, nn. 22, 23.

     Reason's story comes from Cicero, *De fin.* ii, 3, where Cicero replies to
     Lucius Torquatus, who advocates the hedonistic statements of Epicurus:

> nec est quod te pudeat assentiri qui se unus, quod sciam, sapientem profiteri sit
> ausus. Nam Metrodorum non puto ipsum professum, sed, cum appeleretur ab
> Epicuro, repudiare tantum beneficium noluisse: septem autem illi non suo sed
> populorum suffragio omnium nominati sunt.

> And you have no reason to be ashamed of sharing the opinions of a Wise Man,
> who stands alone, so far as I am aware, in venturing to arrogate to himself that
> title. For I do not suppose that Metrodorus himself claimed to be a Wise Man,
> though he did not care to refuse the compliment when the name was bestowed
> upon him by Epicurus; while the Seven Wise Men of old received their appel-
> lation not by their own votes, but by the universal suffrage of mankind.

LCL, Rackham, pp. 85, 87. Cf. *Fam.* i, 2, 17.

19   The oracle at Delphi pronounced Socrates to be the wisest man of Greece
     (Cicero, *Acad.* i, 4, 16; Pliny, *Nat. hist.* vii, 119) because he said, "I alone of
     all the Greeks know that I know nothing." Cf. Cicero, *De amic.* ii, 7.

> . . . sapientem, qualem in Graecia reliqua neminem—nam qui septem appel-
> lantur, eos qui ista subtilius quaerunt in numero sapientium non habent—
> Athenis unum accepimus et eum quidem etiam Apollinis oraculo sapientis-
> simum iudicatum.

> And in this sense we have understood that no one in all Greece was "wise"
> except one in Athens, and he [i.e., Socrates], I admit, was actually adjudged
> "most wise" by the oracle of Apollo—for the more captious critics refuse to
> admit those who are called "The Seven" into the catagory of the wise.

LCL, Falconer, p. 115. On this, *De vir. ill.* xxii, Cato, 4.

20   1492: unum illum
     1581: uirum illum

21   1492: Hoc de antiquis
     1581: Haec de antiquis

22   *Fam*. i, 2, 16–18:

> Aspice istos purpuratos, qui ingenti strepitu populorum in se ora convertunt, qui se sapientes dici volunt et quos sapientes vulgus appellat, singulis civitatibus ascribens sapientum greges; cum tamen illa florens olim studiorum mater, Grecia, non amplius quam septem sapientum nominibus glorietur; quod ipsum posteris importune nomen arrogantie visum est. Sed qui eos excusant, aiunt non id eis cognomen proprio iudicio, sed populorum suffragiis obtigisse. Unus ex omnibus seculis Epycurus sapientem se profiteri ausus: intoleranḑa superbia, seu potius ridiculosa dementia, cuius, secundo *De Finibus bonorum et malorum,* meminit Cicero. Hodie in nostrorum causidicorum grege furor ille vulgaris est. Respice et hos qui in altercationibus et cavillationibus dyalecticis totum vite tempus expendunt seque inanibus semper questiunculis exagitant; et presagium meum de omnibus habeto: omnium nempe cum ipsis fama corruet unumque sepulcrum ossibus sufficiet ac nomini. Cum enim mors frigidam linguam stare coegerit, non modo ut sileant necesse est, sed ut de his etiam sileatur.

> Consider those who like to dress in purple and who with loud outcries draw to themselves the attention of the people. They wish to be known as wise men and are called such by the multitude which assigns swarms of wise men to each city. Compare this to that once flourishing mother of studies, Greece, that gloried in having no more than seven such wise men, a reputation that seemed even to posterity a sign of arrogance. But those who try to justify them say that the reputation fell to them not because of their personal judgment, but through the judgment of the people. Throughout the centuries Epicurus dared to declare himself a wise man, an intolerable arrogance indeed or rather a ridiculous madness to which Cicero refers in the second book of his *De Finibus bonorum et malorum* [ii, 3, 7]. Today that madness has become common amidst the swarms of our lawyers. Just consider those who spend every minute of their life in debates and dialectical scoffing and who are constantly stirred up by inane trifling questions. Observe them well and believe my prediction about all of them: the fame of all of them will disappear with their deaths and a single grave will suffice for their bones and their names. When death compels their cold tongues to remain still, not only must they be silent, but there will also be silence about themselves.

Bernardo (1975), p. 18.

23   1492: praeceptores illum sui illum praedicant
      1581: praeceptores illum sui praedicant

24   1492: tunc maiores
      1581: nunc maiores

25   1492: niger pannuus
      1581: niger pannus

26   I.e., the *liripipium*—the black teacher's hood. On the academic ceremonial described here, Powicke (1936), i, pp. 226–231, 287.

27   Referring to Ovid's *Metamorphoses*.

28 This satirical description of a graduation ceremony, which reappears in the
fifteenth-century compilation *De vera sapientia* (Hain 13138; cf. Rawski
[1967], p. 118, n. 145), is anticipated in Geoffrey of Vinsauf, *Poetria nova*, ca.
1200 (Leyser [1721], pp. 885–887), example of *apostrophe*, lines 435–447.
Related, John of Salisbury, *Metalog.* i, 3, *PL* 199, cc. 828–830, as pointed out
in Gerosa (1966), pp. 190–191. Note also *Carmina Burana*, Schmeller
(1847), no. 69, 1–5; and Hilka-Schumann, i (1930), p. 7:

> Florebat olim studium,
> nunc vertitur in tedium;
> iam scire diu viguit,
> sed ludere prevaluit.
>
> Iam pueris astutia
> .contingit ante tempora,
> qui per 'malevolentiam'
> excludunt sapientiam.
>
> Sed retroactis seculis
> vix licuit discipulis
> tandem 'nonagenarium'
> quiescere post studium.
>
> At nunc decennes pueri
> decusso iugo liberi
> se nunc magistros iactitant
> ceci cecos precipitant.
>
> Inplumes aves volitant,
> Brunelli chordas incitant,
> boves in aula salitant,
> stive precones militant . . .

> Learning that flowered in days of yore
> in these our times is thought a bore.
> Once knowledge was a well to drink of;
> Now having fun is all men think of.
>
> Today mere striplings grow astute
> Before their beards begin to shoot—
> Striplings whose truant dispositions
> Are deaf to wisdom's admonitions.
>
> Yet it was true in ages past
> No scholar paused from toil at last
> Nor shrank from studies the most weighty
> Till his years numbered more than eighty.
>
> Now boys you'd think were barely ten
> Throw off the yoke and pose as men,

Nay, even plume themselves as masters:
Blind lead the blind to swift disasters [Matth. 15, 14].

Our birds unfledged must now take wing,
Our donkeys tune the lyre and sing,
Bulls dance in hall, and herald's calling
Is mocked by knaves at the plow-tail bawling . . .

Whicher (1949), p. 143. On this, Curtius (1953), pp. 94 –95. On ὄνος λύρας
(Varro, *Menipp. Sat.,* fragm. 348–369B, based on Phaedrus [Brenot], app. 12,
1–7)—the proverbial *ass to the harp* (Aulus Gellius, iii, 16, 13; Jerome, *Ep.* 27,
2; Boethius, *Cons. phil.* i, P4 = Chaucer, *Boece* i, 4, 2–3; Whiting [1968], A
227; Tubach [1969], no. 378; Martianus Capella, viii, 807; Wille [1967], pp.
410–411; Gruber [1978], pp. 113–114, *1*)—*Fam.* xx, 6, 6; *Sen.* v, 4 (1581:
801, Wilkins [1959], p. 102. Cf. Mâle (1978), pp. 340–341; Hammerstein
(1974), pp. 73–75; and Robertson (1963), p. 493. On the implied paradox,
Colie (1966), Intr., Curtius (1953), chap. v, 7. —On yet another parallel
between a statement by Petrarch (*Sen.* xvii, 3 [1581: 540]) and Geoffrey of
Vinsauf's *Poetria nova*, lines 1906–1912 (Leyser [1721], p. 968; Faral [1924],
pp. 255–256; Nims [1967], p. 85), see Olson (1982), pp. 218–219.

29   Cf. *DR* i, 10, 39–42.

30   Cf. Petrarch's *strive and rise up* to Donato Albanzani's fourteen-year-old son,
Antonio. *Sen.* xi, 7, missive form, Burdach-Piur ii, 2, (1928), p. 358; Rawski
(1967), p. 202, n. 32; *De vita sol.* ii, *Prose* (1955), pp. 568, 570, 572; *Secretum*
i, as quoted in *DR* i, Pref., note 7. —On *ad altum niti*—to reach for on high—
linked with the topics of *homo erectus, homo ex humo,* and *homo divinum et
coeleste animal,* cf. Lactantius, *Div. inst.* vii, 9, *PL* 6, esp. cc. 765–766. Note
also Von den Steinen (1965), i, pp. 105–110; and Von den Steinen (1959),
esp., pp. 103–107.

31   An Augustinian notion. The way to reach the truth is *prima humilitas; secunda
humilitas; tertia humilitas*—humility first, last, and always. (Augustine, *Ep.*
118, 3, 22, and *PL* 33, c. 442; Gilson [1960], pp. 227, 359, n. 2. Note Foster
[1984], pp. 161–162. Cf. also Augustine, *Serm.* 23a (*Corpus Christianorum,
Ser. Latina* 41, 321–323), on the path of humility, and *De civ. Dei* xiv, 13,
cited below, *DR* i, 13, note 9.)

13 ❖ RELIGION

1   Dialogues 13–30 are devoted to personal circumstances, and to pleasures and
pastimes.

2   1492: religio optima est ac perfecta una est supra Christi nomen
    1581: religio optima ac perfecta una est, supra Christo nomen
3   The *most firm rock* is Christ's legacy, i.e., the Church. Matth. 16, 18:

> Et ego dico tibi, quia tu es Petrus, et super hanc petram aedificabo Ecclesiam
> meam, et portae inferi non praevalebunt adversus eam.

> And I say to thee: That thou art Peter and upon this rock I will build my
> church, and the gates of hell shall not prevail against it.

Note Gerosa (1966), pp. 361–362.

4   1492: retribui
    1581: tribui
5   *Fam.* vi, 2, to Giovanni Colonna O.P., 1341, 1–4:

> Deambulabamus Rome soli. Meum quidem obambulandi perypateticum
> morem nosti. Placet; nature moribusque meis aptissimus est; ex opinionibus
> quedam placent, alie autem minime; non etenim sectas amo, sed verum.
> Itaque nunc perypateticus, nunc stoicus sum, interdum achademicus; sepe
> autem nichil horum, quotiens quicquam occurrit apud eos, quod vere ac
> beatifice fidei adversum suspectum ve sit. Ita enim philosophorum sectas
> amare et approbare permittimur, si a veritate non abhorrent, si nos a nostro
> principali proposito non avertunt; quod ubi forte tentaverint, seu ille sit
> Plato seu Aristotiles seu Varro seu Cicero, libera contumacia contemnantur
> omnes atque calcentur. Nulla disputationum argutiam nulla verborum
> lenitas, nulla nominum nos tangat autoritas: homines fuerunt, quantum hum-
> ana inquisitione fieri potuit et notitia rerum docti et eloquio clari et naturali
> ingenio felices, sed supremi et ineffabilis obiecti privatione miserabiles et, ut
> qui viribus suis fiderent veramque lucem non requirerent, cecorum in morem
> sepe lapsi, sepe ad lapidem offendentes. Itaque sic illorum miremur ingenia,
> ut ingenii veneremur auctorem; sic illorum compatiamur erroribus, ut nostre
> gratie gratulemur, et cognoscamus nos gratuito, sine ullis meritis, honoratos
> prelatosque maioribus ab Illo qui archanum suum, quod sapientibus abscon-
> dit, parvulis revelare dignatus est; denique sic philosophemur, ut, quod
> philosophie nomen importat, sapientiam amemus. Vera quidem Dei sapientia
> Cristus est; ut vere philosophemur, Ille nobis in primis amandus atque
> colendus est.

> You and I have walked all over Rome. You know my peripatetic habit of
> prowling around. I enjoy this and find it most appropriate to my nature and
> inclinations. Of the opinions of the Peripatetics, some please me, others hardly
> so. I really do not love sects, but the truth. Thus I am at one time a Peripatetic,
> at another a Stoic, and now and then an Academic. Often, however, I am
> neither, especially whenever something occurs in their texts which is suspect
> or outright contrary to the true and blessed faith. We are permitted to love and
> espouse philosophical schools as long as they do not turn us from the primary
> tenets of the faith. But when they attempt this, whether it be Plato, or Aristotle,

or Varro, or Cicero, they must be condemned with utter firmess and altogether eradicated. Neither brilliance of argument, nor sweetness of style, or authority of name must affect us. They all were human and, within the limits of human abilities, of great factual learning, clear expression, and blessed with intellectual gifts. But they were wretched in their lack of the highest and ineffable good, and, not feeling the lack of the true light, had to rely upon their own strength. Like the blind they often fell down, or "dashed their foot against a stone" [Ps. 90, 12 = Matth. 4, 6]. Consequently, we should admire their genius in such a way that we venerate the author of this genius. Let us have compassion for their errors as we rejoice in our grace and realize that costless—without doing anything to deserve it—we have been honored and have been raised above the men of old by Him Who deemed it worthy to *reveal to the little ones* the mystery *He hid from the wise* [Matth. 11, 25 = Luc. 10, 21]. In sum, let us philosophize as the very name 'philosophy' suggests, by loving wisdom. The true wisdom of God is Christ; and all true philosophizing requires that, above all, we love and cherish Him.

On this, Krautheimer (1956/1982), pp. 294–295.
6   *Placere sibi superbire est.* —Cf. ii Petr. 2, 10. Similar: *Secretum* ii, *Prose* (1955), p. 70; *Sen.* xiii, 13 (1581: 927).
7   1492: quae te deo religat: deum tibi
    1581: quae te Deo, & Deum tibi religat
8   1492: tanto sis melior
    1581: tanto sis humilior
9   Petrarch read in Augustine, *De civ. Dei* xiv, 13:

Est igitur aliquid humilitatis miro modo quod sursum faciat cor, et est aliquid elationis quod deorsum faciat cor. Hoc quidem quasi contrarium videtur, ut elatio sit deorsum et humilitas sursum. Sed pia humilitas facit subditum superiori: nihil est autem superius Deo, et ideo exaltat humilitas quae facit subditum Deo. Elatio autem, quae in vitio est, eo ipso respuit subiectionem et cadit ab illo quo non est quicquam superius, et ex hoc erit inferius et fit quod scriptum est: *Deiecisti eos cum extollerentur.* Non enim ait: "Cum elati fuissent," ut prius extollerentur et postea deicerentur; sed cum extollerentur, tunc deiecti sunt. Ipsum quippe extolli iam deici est.

Accordingly, strange as it may seem, there is something in humility to uplift the mind, and there is something in exaltation to abase the mind. It does indeed appear somewhat of a paradox that exaltation abases and humility uplifts. But religious humility makes the mind submissive to what is superior; hence, since nothing is superior to God, humility elevates the mind in making it submissive to God. On the other hand, exaltation that is connected with a fault automatically scorns subordination and lapses from him who is supreme. This will bring it lower, and the words of Scripture come to pass: "Thou hast cast them down when they were being exalted." (Ps. 72, 18.) Scripture does not say: "When they had been exalted," and thus imply that they were first exalted and afterwards cast down; but at the very moment that they were being exalted, then were they cast down. For the very act of being exalted is already an act of being cast down.

LCL, Levine, p. 339. Note the possibly ironic *tamque sublimis humilitas*—such lofty humility—in *Fam.* xxiii, 10, 1, to Jan ze Středa, the Imperial Chancellor of Charles IV. Cf. *DR* i, 1, note 11, i, 24, note 3.

10   1492: ex hac mortali uita
1581: ex hac mortalitate

11   1492: custodi
1581: custode

12   *pietas est sapientia* occurs also in *DR* i, 46, 17–18; *Fam.* x, 5, 8; and *De sui ipsius, Prose* (1955), p. 718 (with incorrect note 4). It is not in the Vulgate. Rawski (1967), pp. 172–174, shows that it is a pre-Vulgate version of Job 28, 28: *ecce pietas est sapientia*—behold piety that is wisdom—frequently cited by Augustine (e.g., *Conf.* v, 5, as below, *DR* i, 46, note 15, viii, 1, *PL* 32, cc. 709, 749; *Ench.* i, 2; *Enarr. in Ps.* 135, 8; *De trin.* xii, 14, xiv, 1). The same old text appears in Jerome's *Hexaplar Liber Hiob, PL* 29, c. 98. On this, Rotondi (1943), p. 126; Gerosa (1966), p. 172, n. 79; Ceglar (1971), pp. 71–75, 234; and Foster (1984), pp. 152–153. Cf. also below, *DR* ii, 42, note 7. — *initium sapientiae timor Domini* is Ps. 110, 1 = Eccli. 1, 16.

13   This is *Asclepius* (below, note 14), but seems to echo the Lord's Prayer (Matth. 6, 13), *sed libera nos a malo*—but deliver us from evil.

14   Affirmat . . . Hermes eos qui cognoverunt deum non tantum ab incursibus demonum tutos esse. Verum etiam ne fato quidem teneri. Una inquit custodia pietas. Et enim pius homo: neque demoni pessimo: neque fato subiacet. Deus enim liberat pium ab omni malo. Namque unicum atque solum bonum est hominibus pietas. Quid sit autem pietas ostendit alio loco his verbis. Pietas enim scientia est dei. Eandemque sententiam Asclepium in sermone quodam regio latius explicasse confirmat.

The entire passage comes from Lactantius, *Div. inst.* ii, 16; *PL* 6, cc. 335–336:

Denique affirmat eos Hermes, qui cognoverint Deum, non tantum ab incursibus daemonum tutos esse, verum etiam ne fato quidem teneri. Μία, inquit, φυλακὴ εὐσέβεια᾽ εὐσεβοῦς γὰρ ἀνθρώπου οὐ δαίμων κακός; οὔτε εἱμαρμένη κρατεῖ. Θεὸς γὰρ ῥύεται τὸν εὐσεβῆ ἐκ παντὸς κακοῦà τὸ γὰρ ἐν καί μόνον ἐν ἀνθρώποις ἐστὶν ἀγαθόν εὐσέβεια.* Quid sit autem εὐσέβεια, alio loco his verbis testatur, dicens: ἡ γὰρ εὐσέβεια γνῶσίς ἐστι τοῦ Θεοῦ.** Asclepius quoque auditor eius, eamdem sententiam latius explicavit in illo sermone perfecto, quem scripsit ad regem.
    *Latine: Una, inquit, custodia pietas: pios enim homines nec daemon malus, nec fatum tenet. Nam Deus liberat pium ab omni malo: quod enim unum et solum in hominibus bonum, est pietas.
    **Latine: Pietas enim scientia est Dei.

Lactantius follows his paraphrasing sentence with the Greek text from the *Asclepius,* a Neoplatonic dialogue dating probably from the second or early third century A.D. and attributed to Hermes Trismegistus—Milton's "thrice-great Hermes" (Yates [1964], p. 14). Cicero, *De nat. deor.* iii, 22, 56 refers sarcastically to five Mercuries, one of whom took refuge in Egypt and *gave letters and laws to the Egyptians.* According to Lactantius, this Egyptian Hermes-Mercury,

> qui tametsi homo, fuit tamen antiquissimus, et instructissimus omni genere doctrinae: adeo ut ei multarum rerum et artium scientia Trismegisto cognomen imponeret. Hic scripsit libros, et quidem multos, ad cognitionem divinarum rerum pertinentes, in quibus majestatem summi ac singularis Dei asserit, iisdemque nominibus appellat, quibus nos, Deum et patrem.

> although he was a man, was of great antiquity, and most fully versed in every kind of learning, so that the knowledge of this many subjects and arts earned him the by-name Trismegistus. He wrote books, and among them many relating to the knowledge of divine things, in which he asserts the majesty of the supreme and only God, and refers to Him by the same names we use: God and Father.

Div. inst. i, 6, *PL* 6, c. 139. —Lactantius thought Hermes Trismegistus was much more ancient than Plato or Pythagoras (*De ira* xi, *PL* 7, cc. 112–113; but cf. Augustine, *De civ. Dei* xviii, 39).

Petrarch's text follows the medieval Latin translation of the *Asclepius* (Nock [1945], ii, pp. 296–355), used by Augustine (e.g., *De civ. Dei* viii, 23), which has been transmitted among the works of Apuleius of Madaura, but is not by him. The last sentence, however, is changed. Lactantius refers to the explanation by Asclepius in *illo sermone perfecto*—i.e., *The Perfect Word,* which is the correct title of the *Asclepius,* ostensibly written for the king. Petrarch has in *sermone quodam regio,* without clear reference to the hermetic title. On the *Asclepius,* also *Sen.* xv, 3 (1581: 935).

Lactantius, *a man of great learning* (below, *DR* ii, 9, 132), was one of Petrarch's favorite patristic authors (cf. *De ocio* i [Nolhac (1907), ii, p. 111]; *Fam.* xxiv, 6, 6; etc.).

15 Reason's remark recalls Augustine's criticism (*De civ. Dei* viii, 23) referring to Hermes Trismegistus, who in his admiration for Egyptian idolatry was blind and whose prophecy of its passing came from the devil (Yates [1964], p. 10). Nevertheless, Reason's extensive quotation introduces both an important hermetic text (one of the few known during the Latin Middle Ages prior to the introduction, about 1460, of the Greek *corpus hermeticum* to Italy and Marsilio Ficino's translation for Cosimo de' Medici, 1463, 1471 [Kristeller (1956), pp. 22–26]) and its foremost apologist among the Christian Fathers, Lactantius—anticipating the great surge of Renaissance Hermetism during the fifteenth and sixteenth centuries. On this, Yates (1964), pp. 35–38, where the *Asclepius* is summarized; Lietzmann, iii (1952), pp. 48–52, 174–177; and C. Trinkaus in Wiener (1973), iv, p. 139.

16   1492: circumuolant
       1581: circumuelant

14 ❖ LIBERTY

1   1492: fiditis
      1581: fidimus
2   *quia dominum nullum habes* = Seneca, *Ep.* 47, 12; Macrobius, *Saturn.* i, 11, 7;
      John of Salisbury, *Policrat.* viii, 12, *PL* 199, cc. 756–757.
3   Seneca, ibid.:

> Bona aetas est; forsitan habebis. Nescis, qua aetate Hecuba servire coeperit,
> qua Croesus, qua Darei mater, qua Platon, qua Diogenes?

LC, Gummere, pp. 307, 309. —Hecuba was the wife of Priam and mother of
Hector, Paris, and many other children. "After the fall of Troy she fell to the
lot of the hated Odysseus" (Harvey [1974], art. Hecuba). Croesus, the last
king of Lydia, was captured by Cyrus (Herodotus i, esp. 29–33 and 86–89).
The mother of Darius, Sisygambis, was captured at Issus, 333 B.C. Her humane treatment by Alexander the Great (Quintus Curtius, iii, 11, 24 through
12, 27 = *De vir. ill.* xv, 3) was celebrated in the medieval Alexander literature
as a shining example of a knight's chivalry (Huizinga [1931], p, 93; Cary
[1956]; Fox [1980], pp. 181–182). On Hecuba, Croesus, and Sisygambis, *Roman de la Rose*, 6774–6776. On Plato, sold into slavery by Dionysius I of
Syracuse, Cornelius Nepos, *De exc. duc.* x, 2, 3; and Lactantius, *Div. inst.* iii,
25, *PL* 6, cc. 430–431. On the servitude of Diogenes the Cynic, Aulus Gellius, ii, 18, 9–10; Lactantius, ibid.; and Macrobius, *Saturn.* i, 11, 42.
4   On the republican hero M. Atilius Regulus (Horace, *Carm.* i, 12, 37; Cicero,
De off. i, 39, iii, 99-115, and *De sen.* xx, 75; Valerius Maximus, i, 1, 14, ix, 1,
4, ext. 1; Aulus Gellius, vii, 4; Augustine, *De civ. Dei* i, 15; etc.), who was
taken prisoner by the Carthaginians in the First Punic War, sent back to
Rome to negotiate an exchange of prisoners (250 B.C.) and, in accordance
with his pledge to the enemy, returned to Carthage to face extreme torture
and death, Livy, xviii, Perioch., as below, *DR* i, 21, note 6; *DR* ii, 15, note 14;
and Hadas (1956), pp. 29–30. The Regulus story inspired Horace, *Carm.* iii,
5. Boccaccio retells it in *De casib.*, Hall (1962), ff. 48r–49r. On emperor
Valerian, who was captured by Sapor I, the Sassanid king of the Persians, A.D.

259 or 260, and died in captivity (Orosius, *Hist. adv. pag.* vii, 22), Hadas, ibid., p. 168.

5   Perseus, last king of Macedonia, was defeated by Aemilius Paulus at Pydna, 168 B.C. Jugurtha was put to death in Rome, 104 B.C. Petrarch told the story of Syphax in his *Africa* (esp. iii, 87–90, v, 385–485, ix, 481–490). *Fam.* xxii, 14, refers to the examples of Regulus, Perseus, Syphax, and Jugurtha. Each of them is frequently mentioned separately in the *Familiares*. Twyne, f. 15r., omits Jugurtha.

6   1492: e regia trusit in carcerem eundemque una hora
    1581: regum trusit in carcerem eosdemque una hora

This is probably a reference to King John II of France, captured by the English in the battle of Poitiers, September 19, 1356. On Petrarch's division of ancient and later history, *Fam.* vi, 2, 16, xx, 8, 11; Mommsen (1942); Ferguson (1948), pp. 8–9; and Yates (1960), pp. 70–71.

7   Cf. Plato, *Theaetetus* 174e–175a, as referred to in Seneca, *Ep.* 44, 4.

8   Compare, e.g., *Fam.* xxii, 14, 1:

> Mutantur assidue res humane et ut reliquarum sic militie gloria preterfluit ac de gente in gentem sedes transfert; denique una est horum que videmus omnium stabilitas, non stare; una fides, fallere; una requies, circumvolvi.

> Man's affairs change continually and, as everything else, the glories of the military move on and pass from nation to nation [Ps. 104, 13]. In short, all we see has one stability—namely, to be unstable; one trustworthiness—to deceive; one steady state—to move about.

Africa ii, 344–354:

> Omnia nata quidem pereunt, et adulta fatiscunt:
> Nec manet in rebus quicquam mortalibus, unde
> Vir etenim sperare potest, populusve, quod alma
> Roma nequit facili labuntur secula passu.
> Tempora diffugiunt, ad mortem curritis, umbra,
> Umbra estis, pulvisque levis, vel in aethere fumus
> Exiguus, quem ventus agat, quo sanguine parta
> Gloria? quo tanti mundo fugiente labores?
> Stare quidem vultis, sed enim rapidissima coeli
> Vos fuga praecipitat, cernis quam parva pudendi
> Imperii pateant circum confinia nostri?

> All that is born
> must die and after ripeness comes decay;
> no thing of earth endures, wherefore what man
> or race of men can hope for what's denied
> even to cherished Rome? In hasty flight

the ages pass; all time is swept away,·
and ye who rush towards death, ye are but shades
and only shades, light dust or wisps of smoke
tossed by the wind. This blood-stained glory, then,
what boots it? And what purpose, say, is served
by arduous effort on a transient earth?
Though fain you'd tarry there, a breathless flight
bears you to Heaven. See what little room
within its bounds our sorry empire fills . . .

Bergin (1977), pp. 34–35, lines 446–459. Or *Trionfi,* Tr. etern. 46–51; *Rime* (1951), pp. 555–556:

O felice colui che trova il guado
di questo alpestro e rapido torrente
ch'à nome vita e a molti è sì a grado!
    Misera la volgare e cieca gente
che pon qui sue speranze in cose tali
che'l tempo le ne porta sì repente!

Happy indeed is he who finds the ford
To cross the torrent, mountainous and swift,
That is called life, to many men so dear!
    Wretched indeed the blind and common folk
Who set their hopes upon the things of earth,
That Time so suddenly doth bear away!

Wilkins (1962), p. 109; and the many references in the *DR*, e.g., *DR* i, Pref. 13–15, i, 1, 68–76, i, 90, 8, etc. Similar, Pascal, *Pensées* (1670), 72, as above, *DR* i, 1, note 22.

9   1492: duxeris
     1581: dixeris
10   1492: uenundarus
     1581: uenundatus
11   1492: uobis
     1581: nobis
12   1492: fingi potest
     1581: figi potest
13   Blindness, traditionally ascribed to fickle Fortune (Boethius, *Cons. phil.* ii, P 1, 33–34), strikes also anyone favored by her. "Blind" and "blindness" (*Var.* 56, Fracassetti, iii [1863], p. 462) are often used by Reason in this context. Cf. *Africa* vii, 329–330, Bergin (1977), p. 153, lines 431–437, a passage which, as pointed out in Heitmann (1958), p. 173, n. 113, echoes Cicero, *De amic.* xv, 54, quoted in turn in *Contra quendam*, Ricci (1949), 372. Blindness as *caecitas cordis*—blindness of the heart (Marc. 3, 5)—is a scriptural topic. Cf., e.g., Matth. 15, 14, and 23, 16–24. Related, Panofsky (1960), pp. 10–11.

14   Among the many references to *Fortuna* and *virtus* in Petrarchan texts, note *Fam.* xvii, 3, 33; *Var.* 53 and 60, Fracassetti, iii (1863), pp. 449, 472; *Secretum* ii, *Prose* (1955), p. 92; and *DR* ii, 5, 84–87, 130–132, ii, 9, 7–14, ii, 25 *passim*, esp. 105–111, ii, 32, 3, ii, 76, 13–20, ii, 104. Cf. also *DR* ii, 1, note 14.

15   1492: externum
      1581: extremum

15 ✤ A GLORIOUS NATIVE COUNTRY

1   Dialogues 15–21 deal with personal circumstances.
2   1492: hebet
     1581: habet
3   Boötes (*Fam.* xix, 7, 2; *Buc. carm.* xi, 23) is the northern constellation that contains the bright star Arcturus; Lucifer, the planet Venus as the Morning Star (Isidore, *Etym.* iii, 71, 8–9 and 18, Fontaine [1959], ii, pp. 527–530; Barthol. Anglicus viii, 23 and 14). Reason interprets *gloriosus* and *gloria, claritas, fulgor*, etc., in terms of light and radiance, which invoke the medieval ideas of the luminosity of the universe (De Bruyne [1946], iii, chap. 1). John the Scot had transmitted the Platonizing notions of the Pseudo-Areopagite (*De coelesti hierarchia*), which designated God, the Creator of the world, as *pater luminum*—the father of the lights. Augustine, too, had declared that "light" is the proper name for God (*De Gen. ad litt.* iv, 28, 45).

> Thus the whole material universe becomes a big 'light' composed of countless small ones as of so many lanterns (. . . *universalis huius mundi fabrica maximum lumen fit, ex multis partibus veluti ex lucernis compactum.*)

PL 122, c. 129, Panofsky (1946), p 20. Cf. also Gilson (1955), e.g., pp. 155–156. As Dante explained in his Letter to Can Grande (*Ep.* xiii, 64):

> quod divinus radius sive divina gloria, "per universum penetrat et resplendet:" penetrat, quantum ad essentiam; resplendet quantum ad esse.

> The divine ray or divine glory *pierces and reglows* through the universe. It pierces as to essence; it reglows as to being.

Singleton (1975), Comm., p. 5. Cf. also Toynbee (1968), art. "Luce." For Christian Platonism, light becomes

> the principle of order and value. The objective value of a thing is determined by the degree to which it partakes of light.

Von Simson (1956), p. 52. The medieval mind had little difficulty with the shift of meaning from physical light to "a transcendental light, only symbolically invested with the qualities of physical light" (ibid., p. 54), or vice versa.

4   1492: uirtutum hospes
      1581: uirtutum hospites

5   1492: hoc tuum
      1581: hoc tuum est

6   1492: ducitis
      1581: dicitis

7   1492: Romana
      1581: Romanam

8   *felix prole virum*: Virgil, *Aeneid* vi, 784.

9   1492: eque latebris eruet
      1581: eque lateribus eruet

10   1492: in luce letaberis
      1581: in luce notaberis

11   I.t.: Gaius

12   *patria*—country—and *urbs magna*—a large city—are used interchangeably because, often, the superordinate governing authority of *patria* was vested in the medieval city state.

13   1492: Inter tot oculos: nullae sunt latebrae
      1581: tot inter oculos mille sunt latebrae

14   1492: per te fulxeris
      1581: per te fulseris

15   1492: Est quae suas
      1581: Est qui suas

16   non eum sua: sed patriae gloria clarum esse: neque hercle ait. Aut ego obscurus: si Seriphius: aut tu si Atheniensis: clarus esses.

The story comes from Cicero, *De sen.* iii, 8, where, as in Plato, *Republic* i, 329e, it is told this way:

> non eum sua, sed patriae gloria splendorem assecutum: "nec hercule," inquit, "si ego Seriphius essem, nec tu, si Atheniensis, clarus umquam fuisses.

> "Your reputation is due not to your but your country's glory." "True, indeed," Themistocles replied, "then I could not have been famous, had I been a Seriphian; nor could you have had any renown, had you been an Athenian."

Seriphos (Serfo), an island of the Cyclades group in the Aegean, is frequently referred to as a symbol of smallness and insignificance. Cf., e.g., Juvenal, *Sat.* x, 170.

17   1492: quod hominem eum non mutum animal
      1581: quod hominem eum & non mutum animal

18   1492: mentio
      1581: merito
19   1492: dicam similiter
      1581: dicam simul
20   1492: incontanter asserere
      1581: incunctanter asserere
21   Reason paraphrases Plutarch, as discussed in Lactantius, *Div. inst.* iii, 19, *PL*
      6, cc. 412–414:

> Non dissimile Platonis illud est, quod *aiebat, se gratias agere naturae: primum,
> quod homo* natus esset potius, quam *mutum animal*; deinde, *quod mas* potius,
> quam *foemina*; *quod Graecus, quam Barbarus*; postremo, *quod Atheniensis, et
> quod temporibus Socratis.* Dici non potest, quantam mentibus caecitatem,
> quantosque pariat errores ignoratio veritatis. Ego plane contenderim, *numquam*
> quidquam *dictum* esse in rebus humanis *delirius.* Quasi vero *si* aut *Barbarus,*
> aut *mulier,* aut *asinus* denique *natus esset,* idem ipse *Plato esset,* ac non ipsum
> illud, quod natum fuisset. Sed videlicet *Pythagorae credidit,* qui ut vetaret ho-
> mines animalibus vesci, dixit, animas *de corporibus in* aliorum animalium *cor-
> pora* commeare: quod et vanum et impossibile est. Vanum, quia necesse non
> fuit veteres animas in nova corpora inducere, cum idem artifex, qui primas
> aliquando fecerat, potuerit semper novas facere. Impossibile, quia rectae ra-
> tionis anima tam immutare naturam status sui non potest, quam ignis aut
> deorsum niti, aut in transversum, fluminis modo, flammam suam fundere. Ex-
> istimavit igitur homo sapiens, potuisse fieri, ut anima, quae tunc erat in
> Platone, in aliquod mutum animal includeretur, essetque humano sensu
> praedita, ut intelligeret ac doleret incongruenti se corpore oneratam. Quanto
> sanius faceret, si gratias agere se diceret, quod *ingeniosus,* quod docilis natus
> esset, quod in iis opibus, ut liberaliter *erudiretur.* Nam quod Athenis natus est,
> quid in eo beneficii fuit? An non plurimi extiterunt in aliis civitatibus excellenti
> ingenio atque doctrina viri, qui meliores singuli, quam omnes Athenienses fu-
> erunt? Quanta hominum millia fuisse credamus, qui et Athenis nati, et
> temporibus Socratis, *indocti* tamen, ac stulti fuerunt? Non enim aut parietes,
> aut locus in quo quisque est effusus ex utero conciliat homini sapientiam. Quid
> vero attinuit Socrates ingenia discentibus potuit commodare? Non venit in
> mentem Platoni *Alcibiadem* quoque *et Critiam* eiusdem Socratis assiduos
> auditores fuisse; quorum alter *hostis patriae* acerrimus fuit, alter *crudelissimus*
> omnium *tyrannorum.*

Not altogether different is Plato's statement that he gave thanks to Nature for
having been born, first of all, a human rather than a mute beast; next, male
rather than female; a Greek, not a Barbarian; and, last, an Athenian in the age
of Socrates. One cannot tell how much ignorance of the truth contributes to
the blindness of minds, and how many errors it creates. I simply maintain that
nothing more foolish has ever been said about a man's circumstances. As if,
indeed, what has been born a Barbarian, or a woman, or an ass, would as such
be Plato and not whatever Nature brought forth. But, evidently, he believed
Pythagoras, who forbade people to eat meat, saying this could result in the

eating of human souls that had migrated into the bodies of animals—which is both absurd and impossible. Absurd, because there is no need for souls to be introduced into new bodies, since the Creator, who made them, can of course make new ones. Impossible, because if we think straight, the soul clearly cannot radically alter its natural state, like fire burning downward, or have its flames lick horizontally like a flowing stream. However, our wise man apparently thought it possible for the soul that just had been Plato's to be imprisoned in a dumb beast, yet still be possessed by human intelligence that discerned and deplored being burdened with an incompatible body. How much more rational it would have been for him to say that he rendered thanks to have been born highly gifted and capable of learning, into a family wealthy enough to have him superbly educated! That he was born in Athens—what boon was that? As if men of shining intellect and expertise did not exist in other cities—each of them superior to all Athenians put together! How many thousands born in Athens in the age of Socrates, must have been uneducated and stupid. Neither the surroundings nor the precise spot where some one issued forth from the womb produce wisdom in a man. What, in fact, did it matter that a Socrates could minister to the minds of students? It did not occur to Plato that among the eager pupils listening to the same Socrates were Alcibiades and Critias—one, a savage enemy of his own city, the other one of the most vicious tyrants ever.

22   1492: quibuslibet uiris
1581: quibusdam uiris

23   This may be aimed at Ovid, *Metam.* xv, 158–175; Pythagoras saying:

> Morte carent animae semperque priore relicta
> sede novis domibus vivunt habitantque receptae:
> ipse ego (nam memini) Troiani tempore belli
> Panthoides Euphorbus eram, cui pectore quondam
> haesit in adverso gravis hasta minoris Atridae;
> cognovi clipeum, laevae gestamina nostrae,
> nuper Abanteis templo Iunonis in Argis!
> Omnia mutantur, nihil interit: errat et illinc
> huc venit, hinc illuc, et quoslibet occupat artus
> spiritus eque feris humana in corpora transit
> inque feras noster, nec tempore deperit ullo,
> utque novis facilis signatur cera figuris
> nec manet ut fuerat nec formas servat easdem,
> sed tamen ipsa eadem est, animam sic semper eandem
> esse, sed in varias doceo migrare figuras.
> Ergo, ne pietas sit victa cupidine ventris,
> parcite, vaticinor, cognatas caede nefanda
> exturbare animas, nec sanguine sanguis alatur!

Our souls are deathless, and ever, when they have left their former seat, do they live in new abodes and dwell in the bodies that have received them. I myself (for I well remember it) at the time of the Trojan war was Euphorbus, son of Panthoüs, in whose breast once hung the heavy spear of Menelaus. Recently, in Juno's temple in Argos, Abas' city, I recognized the shield which I once wore on my left arm! All things are changing; nothing dies. The spirit wanders, comes now here, now there, and occupies whatever frame it pleases. From beasts it passes into human bodies, and from our bodies into beasts, but never perishes. And, as the pliant wax is stamped with new designs, does not remain as it was before nor keep the same form long, but is still the selfsame wax, so do I teach that the soul is ever the same, though it passes into ever-changing bodies. Therefore, lest your piety be overcome by appetite, I warn you as a seer, do not drive out by impious slaughter what may be kindred souls, and let not life be fed on life.

LCL, Miller, p. 377. On the migration of souls, Plato, e.g., *Phaedrus* 249b, *Phaedo* 81e, *Republic* x, 618a–620d, *Timaeus* 91d–92b, Chalcidius, chaps. 195–199, and *Tim.* 42a 7, Waszinck (1969), pp. 217–220; and Herodotus ii, 123. On related Socratic notions, Jaeger (1943), ii, pp. 38–41. On the Neoplatonic views, Augustine, *De civ. Dei* x, 30:

Si post Platonem aliquid emendare existimatur indignum, cur ipse Porphyrius nonnulla et non parva emendavit? Nam Platonem animas hominum post mortem revolvi usque ad corpora bestiarum scripsisse certissimum est. Hanc sententiam Porphyrii doctor tenuit et Plotinus; Porphyrio tamen iure displicuit. In hominum sane non sua quae dimiserant, sed alia nova corpora redire humanas animas arbitratus est. Puduit scilicet illud credere, ne mater fortasse filium in mulam revoluta vectaret; et non puduit hoc credere ubi revoluta mater in puellam filio forsitan nuberet. Quanto creditur honestius quod sancti et veraces angeli docuerunt, quod prophetae Dei spiritu acti locuti sunt, quod ipse quem venturum Salvatorem praemissi nuntii praedixerunt, quod missi apostoli qui orbem terrarum evangelio repleverunt—quanto, inquam, honestius creditur reverti totiens ad diversa! Verum tamen, ut dixi, ex magna parte correctus est in hac opinione Porphyrius, ut saltem in solos homines humanas animas praecipitari posse sentiret, beluinos autem carceres evertere minime dubitaret.

If it is thought to be disgraceful to improve upon anything that Plato said, why did Porphyry himself improve upon several of his doctrines, and important ones at that? For nothing is more certain than that Plato said in writing that after death the souls of men return to earth in a cycle and pass even into the bodies of animals. This theory was held by Plotinus also (*Enneads* iii, 4, 2, iv, 3, 12), the teacher of Porphyry, but Porphyry was right to reject it. He held that human souls return to earth and enter human bodies, not indeed those they had discarded, but new and different ones. He was ashamed, apparently, to adopt the Platonic theory, for fear that a mother, returning to earth in the form of a mule, might perhaps carry her son on her back. Yet he was not ashamed to believe in a doctrine by which a mother, returning in the form of a girl, might perhaps marry her son. How much more respectable is the belief, in accord with what holy and truthful angels have taught men, with what the prophets, moved by the spirit of God, announced, with the words of the Saviour himself, whose coming was foretold by messengers sent in advance, and with the preaching of the apostles whom he sent forth and who covered the whole earth with the gospel—how much more respectable it is, I say, to believe that souls return once to their own bodies than to believe that they return so many times to all sorts of bodies! However, as I said, Porphyry has to a great extent corrected the error of this doctrine, insofar at least as he held that human souls can only be cast down into human bodies, and did not have the slightest hesitation in abolishing incarceration of souls in the bodies of monstrous beasts.

LCL, Wiesen, pp. 393, 395. Related, *De civ. Dei* xii, 14; Jerome, *Ep.* 84, 3, 4, and 6, 3; *In Rufin.* 39–40; *Fam.* x, 3, 8–9; and *De sui ipsius* (1581: 1048 = H. Nachod in Cassirer [1948], p. 92), citing Lactantius, *Div. inst.* iii, 18. Note also *De ocio* (1581: 307). On the whole issue, Sarton, i (1952), pp. 201–203, 249, 309; and J. Choron in Wiener (1973), i, pp. 638–639, 643, 646.

24   I.t.: Flaccus
25   1492: quem imitationi inaccessibilem
     1581: quem imitatione prorsus inaccessibilem
26   The Pindar reference is to Horace, *Carm.* iv, 2, 1–4:

> Pindarum quisquis studet aemulari,
> Iule, ceratis ope Daedalea
> nititur pinnis vitreo daturus
> nomina ponto.

> Whosoever strives, Iulus, to rival Pindar,
> relies on wings fastened with wax by Daedalean craft,
> and is doomed to give his name
> to some crystal sea.

LCL, Bennett, p. 287. Petrarch read about Liber Pater in many sources (e.g., Horace, *Ep.* ii, 1, 5), but seems to base the Theban association on Macrobius, *Saturn.* i, 18 and 19. The kings of Macedonia believed that they were descended from Hercules (Q. Curtius Rufus, iv, 2, 3). Father Liber and Hercules played an important role in the story of Alexander; cf., e.g., Q. Curtius Rufus, viii, 5, 8–24.

27   Cicero, *De orat.* iii, 34, 139:

> Thebanum Epaminondam, haud scio an summum virum unum omnis Graeciae.

> Epaminondas of Thebes, perhaps the most outstanding man in all of Greece.

28   Cf. Cicero, *De orat.* iii, 34, 139:

> Quid Critias? quid Alcibiades? Civibus quidem suis non boni sed certe docti atque eloquentes nonnec Socraticis erant disputationibus eruditi?

What of Critias? and Alcibiades? These though not benefactors of their fellow-citizens were undoubtedly learned and eloquent; and did they not owe their training to the discussions of Socrates?

LCL, Rackham, p. 109. On Alcibiades and Critias, Justin, Book v, especially, 9, 1, and 9, 15.

29 *Fam.* x, 3, 17:

> credo ut intelligi detur nullum hic adminiculum literarum, nullum opus ingenii, sed totum Dei munus esse . . .

> I think it is granted to me to understand that there is no help in literature or in our intellects, but all is the work of God . . .

Bishop (1966), p. 93. —Reason alludes to Augustine's doctrine of the inner master, which appeared first in his *De beata vita* iv, 35, and the *Soliloquies* i, 1, 1, and is fully developed in *De magistro* (*PL* 32, cc. 1194 et seq.; Gilson [1960], chap. v; Mazzeo [1964], chap. 1, esp. pp. 16–23; R. McKeon in Crane [1952], pp. 266–267). Teachers do not teach us their own ideas. They help us to see a common truth and to recognize it as such:

> Who then is the real master? Is it the teacher . . . The real master is that Truth which belongs neither to teacher nor student but is common to both and present in both.

Gilson (1960), p. 74. The truth is God's and God is *magister internus*—the inner master. We learn from Him, Christ, the teacher within (*De magistro* xi, 8; *Eph.* 3, 16–17), not from the teacher without:

> utinam autem vera dicantur, eum docere solum, qui se intus habitare, cum foris loqueretur, admonuit.

> In order to know the truth of what is spoken, I must be taught by him who dwells within and gives me counsel about words spoken externally . . .

De magistro xiv, 46; *PL* 32, c. 1220; Burleigh (1953), p. 101. Note Gerosa (1966), pp. 351–354; *Fam.* xvii, 1, 3–4; and the references below, *DR* i, 45, 11–12, ii, 40, 12–13, ii, 96, 37–42. Cf. also *intus in anima, DR* i, 11, note 10.

30 Cf. above, *DR* i, 12, 79–80.
31 On Xanthippe and Myrto, below, *DR* ii, 19, note 10.
32 I.t.: Flaccus
33 Horace, *Ep.* ii, 2, 68–69:

> . . . . . . cubat hic in colle Quirini,
> hic extremo in Aventino. visendus uterque:

LCL, Fairclough, p. 429.

34 Peter Peregrinus to Siger of Fauçaucourt, August 8, 1269:

> vii. *How Iron Touched by a Lodestone Turns Towards the Poles of the World*

It is well known to all who have made the experiment, that when an elongated piece of iron has touched a lodestone and is then fastened to a light block of wood or to a straw and made float on water, one end will turn to the star which has been called the Sailor's star because it is near the pole; the truth is, however, that it does not point to the star but to the pole itself . . .

Grant (1974), p. 371. Note Machaut, *Remede de Fortune* 298: *Com l'aymant le fer attrait*—just as a magnet attracts iron (Wimsatt & Kibler [1988], p. 184).

35   Twyne, f. 18r, omits the reference to public baths.

36   I.t.: Flaccus

37   Horace, *Ep.* i, 7, 48–49:

. . . Fore nimium distare Carinas
iam grandis natu queritur . . .

LCL, Fairclough, p. 299.

38   1492: He parue in oppido
1581: Hae paruo in oppido

39   1492: Nec miror
1581: Nec minor

40   Reason mentions the topic of *ubi sunt*—where are they? Cf. Valerius Maximus, v, 6, Ext. 4, as discussed in *Fam.* xvii, 3, 46–47; Boethius, *Cons. phil.* ii, M 7, 15–22; Hugh of St. Victor, *De vanitate mundi*, *PL* 176, c. 712; and Dante, *Div. Comm.*, Purg. xxii, 97 *et seq.*, Note Johannes von Tepl, *Ackerm.* xvii, 17–23, Walshe (1951), p. 20: *Wo sint sie hin* . . . ? Petrarch complains, *my sweet friends, where are they now,* in *Fam.* viii, 7, 20. Also *Sen.* x, 2 (Wilkins [1958], p. 222, and Wilkins [1961], p. 174); *Secretum* iii, *Prose* (1955), p. 208; *De ocio*, ibid., pp. 596–598, Thompson (1971), pp. 153–154; and *Trionfi*, Tr. mort. i, 82–84. On *ubi sunt*, Patch (1927), p. 72; Huizinga (1931), chap. 11; Gilson (1932), pp. 9–11; De Bruyne (1946), ii, p. 195; Von den Steinen (1965), i, p. 105; Rico (1974), p. 429, n. 597, with additional literature; Dronke (1977), p. 69; and Mann (1984), pp. 35, 64, 82. On Cola di Rienzo's *dove suono quelli buoni Romani* . . . , Gibbon (1789), chap. 70, Bury, vii (1914), p. 270.

41   1492: Sed ubi nam tales? uiri non tuto
1581: Sed ubi nam tales uiri? Non tuto

16 ❖ A PROMINENT, OLD FAMILY

1   Boethius, *Cons. phil.* iii, P 6, 20–21:

Iam uero quam sit inane quam futtile nobilitatis nomen, quis non uideat? Quae si ad claritudinem refertur, aliena est. Videtur namque esse nobilitas quaedam de meritis ueniens laus parentum. Quod si claritudinem praedicatio facit, illi sint clari necesse est qui praedicantur. Quare splendidum te, si tuam non habes, aliena claritudo non efficit. Quod si quid est in nobilitate bonum, id esse arbitror solum, ut inposita nobilibus necessitudo uideatur ne a maiorum uirtute degeneret.

Moreover, everyone knows that to be called noble is a stupid and worthless thing. If it has anything to do with fame, the fame belongs to others; for nobility appears to be a kind of praise which is really merited by parents. If praise makes a person famous, then those who receive praise are famous; therefore, the praise of others (in this case, of your parents) will not make you famous if you have no fame of your own. In my opinion, therefore, if there is anything to be said for nobility, it lies only in the necessity imposed on the nobility to carry on the virtues of their ancestors.

Green (1962), p. 53. Cf. also, Juvenal, *Sat.* viii, esp. 272–273; and Seneca, *Ep.* 44, 1. Related to Boethius, *Roman de la Rose* 18607–18896, Dahlberg (1971), pp. 308–312; Dante, *Conv.* iv, esp. xx, 5 and 7; and Chaucer, *Canterbury Tales*, Wife of Bath's Tale 1109–1162. See below, *DR* ii, note 15.

2 The example of the unworthy son of Scipio Africanus Maior opens the chapter on *Qui a parentibus claris degeneraverunt*—Those Who Disgraced Illustrious Parents—in Valerius Maximus, iii, 5. Reason takes time to list ten examples in *DR* ii, 24, 45–52. *Fam* xxiii, 12, 28–37, xxiv, 6, 4, discuss the subject *quod perraro summi viri filius summus evaserit*—that only seldom a great son is born to a great father. In his copy of the *Historia Augusta* (Paris, B. N. f. lat. 5816), Petrarch annotated a similar list exemplifying *neminem prope magnorum virorum optimum et utilem filium reliquisse*—that practically no great man has left the world a son of real excellence or value (*Hist. Aug.*, Sev. 20, 5 through 21, 8, LCL, Magie, pp. 420–423):

> Adde hic illud Homericum: pauci certe filii similes patri sunt, plures peiores, pauci autem patre meliores

> Add to this these Homeric words: Only very few sons are like their father. Many are worse, but few are better than the father.

(Nolhac [1907], ii, p. 55, n. 7. On the topic, also Dante, *Div. Comm.*, Parad. viii, 82–148.) Petrarch considered his own son, Giovanni Petrarca (ab. 1337–1361), a failure. On Petrarch's relations with his son, Wilkins (1961); Cochin (1892), pp. 59–66; Cochin (1901), pp. xlii–xlvi; and Foresti (1977), chaps. 33 and 47.

3 Cf. *Met.* iii, 27: *fabula quod populo fuerim digitoque notatus.* Compare *Rime* i, 9–11:

> al popol tutto
> favola fui gran tempo, onde sovente

di me medesmo meco mi vergogno; . . .

To the whole people like a tale I seem,
so that I feel ashamed of my own name.

Armi (1946), p. 3. Cf. Horace, *Epod*. xi, 7–8; and Ovid, *Amores* iii, 1, 21. To
be *in fabula*—in everyone's mouth—is a popular phrase also in medieval
texts: e.g., *Carmina Burana*, Huc usque, Schmeller (1847), p. 171; Hilka
(1941), p. 209; Raby (1934), ii, p. 275: *ego sum in fabula;* and the Petrarchan
references (Mann [1984], p. 87), *Fam*. x, 3, 21, xix, 3, 16, *Sen*. xii, 1 (1581:
902): *& si fabulam peregi*, SN 1, Piur (1925), p. 166, 17–21, Zacour (1973), p.
34, *Secretum* iii, Prose (1955), p. 182, and *De vita sol*. i, Prose (1955), p. 310:
ut bene aciam vite fabulam pulcro fine concludat. —On *digitoque notatus*, below, *DR* i, 29, note 6.

4   SN 4, Piur (1925), pp. 179–180:

> Certe Romanus erat ille qui scripsit: *Omnia orta occidunt, et aucta senescunt.*
> Senescent ergo hec omnia si durent: et si cuiusque rei finis est senectus sua,
> utique omnia senescent, nisi iam forte senuerint; quando et que stant, cunta
> occident, et occasum, si non preuenerit, saltem comitabitur senectus. Ita nulla
> est exceptio: seu durent seu non durent, orta omnia serius aut ocius tandem
> occident et senescent. Voluet motu continuo rotam suam *instabilis Fortuna* et
> de gente in gentem *uolubilia* regna uersabit. Faciet illa, cum uolet, reges ex
> seruis. seruos ex regibus, et in urbem Romam et in orbem Romanum suam
> *ineluctabilem* potentiam exercebit.

> Furthermore, it was a Roman who said "everything that is born must die; all
> things that grow, grow old" [Sallust, *Jug*. ii, 3]. In time, therefore, all things
> grow old. Indeed, if the end of anything is its old age, then everything not
> already senile is certainly becoming so: for everything upright eventually falls
> and the fall is either preceded or at least accompanied by old age. There is no
> exception; whether they last long or not, all growing things sooner or later
> decline and waste away [e.g., *Fam*. vi, 3, 11, xvii, 3, 25–27, as in *DR* ii, 83, note
> 19, and 42–43]. Inconstant Fortune [cf. Pacuvius in *Ad Herenn*. ii, 23, 36] will
> turn her wheel ceaselessly, and will toss transient kingdoms from one people
> to another [Ps. 104, 13, as above, *DR* i, 14, note 8]. In her wilfullness she will
> fashion kings out of slaves and slaves out of kings. She will wield her irresist-
> ible power [Virgil, *Aeneid* viii, 334] over the city of Rome and the Roman world
> [cf. *Fam*. xi, 16, 5].

Zacour (1973), p. 51. The Sallust quotation recurs in *Fam*. vi, 3, 11, ix, 13, 3,
and xvii, 3, 42. Cf. also *Var*. 32, Fracassetti, iii (1863), p. 383: *omnes senes-
cerent qui nascuntur*—all who have been born grow old; and *Collatio* 23:
Longa etas magnos animos debilitat; vivendo senescunt omnia—a long life
weakens great souls (echoing Lucan, viii, 27–28, quoted in *De sui ipsius,*
below); anything that lives grows old. —The topic of senescence was trans-

mitted from late Antiquity (e.g., Aulus Gellius, iii, 10, 11; and Pliny, *Nat hist.* ii, 45, 118: *mores hominum senuere*—age has overtaken the characters of mankind [LCL, Rackham, p. 259]) and was reinforced by the Christian view of history (Von den Steinen [1959], pp. 19–20). Augustine related the six days of creation, the six ages of the world, the six periods of human life, and the world empires, of which Rome is the last in the world's age (Curtius [1953], pp. 27–28; Ladner [1959], chap. v, esp. sect. 6; Mazzotta [1979], pp. 26–31, 39–40; note also Trompf [1979], pp. 200–220, on age theory from later Antiquity to early Renaissance). And the course of events seemed to bear out these assumptions. The hopeless phrase of the Merovingian age, *mundus senescit*—the world is getting old (Thompson [1942], i, p. 165; Focillon [1969], pp. 11, 13; Von den Steinen [1965], i, p. 173)—regained considerable significance in Petrarch's troubled century:

> senescunt solito citius. Nec id forsan usquequaque verum est; sed, quod incuntanter affirmem, solito citius canescunt, sive id latens causa, sive curarum multitudo efficit. Profecto enim nostri maiores melioribus, nos pluribus curis involvimur; nichil est autem quod magis precipitet iuvente florem, quam curarum anxietas et labor animi.

> One does age more quickly than usual. It may be that that is not true generally; but I affirm without hesitation that one does indeed acquire white hair more quickly than usual, whether the cause lies in an earlier aging or in the large number of worries that one has today. There is little doubt that where our ancestors were involved in more useful cares we are involved in too many cares. And there is nothing which causes the flower of youth to wither more rapidly than the anxiety of cares and a troubled mind.

Fam. vi, 3, 33–34; Bernardo (1975), p. 303. Petrarch extended the topic to himself in *De sui ipsius* of 1367:

> . . . & heu amice, quid non mali affert vita longior? Cui unquam tam firma prosperitas fuit, ut non quandoque variaverit, & quasi vivendo senuerit? Senescunt homines, senescunt fortunae, senescunt famae hominum, senescunt denique humana omnia, quodque aliquando non credidi, ad extremum animi senescunt, quamvis immortales, verumque fit illud Cordubensis:

> > . . . longius aevum
> > destruit ingentes animos.

> Non quod animi senium, mors sequatur, sed discessus a corpore, resolutioque illa, quam cernimus, & quae, vulgo mors dicitur, & est mors corporis profecto, non animi. Senuit, ecce, refrixit animus meus. Nunc experior senex, quod iuvenis inexpertus & pastorium canens dixi:

> > . . . Quid vivere longum
> fert homini?

Quo enim ante hos non multo annos haec tulissem animo? quibus nisibus obstitissem? . . . Certe ego, quam praesagiens quid mihi testaret, nunquam sine compassione quadam Laberii historiam legi, qui cum vitam omnem honesta militia exegisset, sexagenarius ad extremum Iulii Caesaris blanditiis ac precibus (quae de ore principum armare prodeunt) productus in scaenam de Romano equite factus est Mimus, quam iniuriam ipse quidem non tacitus tulit, imo multis, interque alia his quaestus est verbis:

> Ego bis tricenis annis actis sine nota
> eques Romanus lare egressus meo
> domum revertar Mimus. Nimirum hoc die
> uno plus vixi mihi quam vivendum fuit.

Alas, my friend, is there an evil that does not happen to a man who lives too long? Who has ever enjoyed a prosperity so permanent that it did not at some time suffer a change and become old, so to speak, by sheer living? Men grow old, so does fortune, so does man's fame: every human thing grows old, and— there was a time when I did not believe it—finally even souls grow old, though they are immortal, and the Cordovan's words become true:

> Too long a life undoes vast souls.

[Lucan, viii, 27–28.] This does not mean that the old age of the soul is followed by death. What actually follows is its separation from the body and that dissolution we observe, which is commonly called death and actually is the death of the body and not of the soul. But, look, my soul has become old and cold. As an old man I now experience what I sang in my pastoral poem when I was an inexperienced youth:

> But little long life avails a man.

[*Buc. carm.*, ix, 37–38; Bergin (1974), p. 133.] In what mood should I have borne this but a few years ago? How should I have opposed it with all my strength? . . . . . . It must certainly have been a foreboding of what I still had before me that never did I read without compassion the story of Laberius. This man lived all his life in honest knighthood. When he was sixty years old, he was at last put on the stage, persuaded by Julius Caesar's flatteries and requests, such as come forth in full armor from the mouth of a prince, and was thus changed from the status of a Roman knight to that of a mimic actor. He himself did not suffer this disgrace in silence. He deplored it in many words, among others in the following:

> Thus I lived thirty years without reproach as a
> Roman knight, and as a Roman knight I left my
> house today, to come back an actor. Certainly
> I have lived one day longer than I ought to have lived.

[Macrobius, *Saturn.* ii, 7, 3; Aulus Gellius, viii, 15.]

(1581: 1040–1041); H. Nachod in Cassirer (1948), pp. 67–68, adjusted. On *mundus senescens*—the aging world—note also *Fam.* i, 9, 10, xvii, 3, 42, xxi, 12, 1; *Sen.* xii, 1 (1581: 898–899); *Contra med.* ii, Ricci (1950), 347–355; and *Africa* ii, 344–345. On senescence in Dante, Mazzotta (1979), pp. 26–27, 39–41. On the Epicurean notion of "Nature, aging," Lucretius, ii, 1150–1174, v, 826–827; and Columella, i, Pref., 2–3. The topic had wide currency in post-Petrarchan texts, e.g., Leon Battista Alberti, as quoted in Alsop (1982), pp. 327–328.

5   Reason seems to echo Dante, *Div. Comm.*, Parad. xvi, 1–9:

> O poca nostra nobiltà di sangue,
>   se glorïar di te la gente fai
>   qua giù dove l'affetto nostro langue,
> mirabil cosa non mi sarà mai:
>   ché là dove appetito non si torce,
>   dico nel cielo, io me ne gloriai.
> Ben se' tu manto che tosto raccorce:
>   sì che, se non s'appon di dì in die,
>   lo tempo va dintorno con le force.

> O our petty nobility of blood! if you
> make folk glory in you here below where
> our affections languish, it will nevermore
> be a marvel to me, since there where appetite
> is not warped, I mean in Heaven, I myself
> gloried in you. Truly you are a mantle
> that soon shrinks, so that if naught be added
> from day to day, time goes round about you
> with its shears.

Singleton (1975), p. 175. On *le vostre cose tutte hanno lor morte,/sì come voi*— your affairs all have their death, even as have you (Dante, ibid., 79–80), note 8, below. On the glory of nations, also Dante, *Conv.* iv and Canz. iii; and *Mon.* ii, 3, 4. Note also Boccaccio, *L'Amorosa visione* xxx–xxxvii; and Bergin (1981), pp. 156–157.

6   Ps. 35, 10: *quoniam apud te est fons vitae . . .* —For with thee is the fountain of life. The *fons aquae vitae*—fountain of the water of life—is based upon the river in the middle of Paradise (Gen. 2, 9–10), which came to be interpreted as a symbol of Godhead—the "river of water of life, clear as crystal proceeding from the throne of God and of the Lamb" (Apoc. 22, 1; cf. ibid. 7, 17, and 21, 6; on this, Panofsky [1953], i, p. 216, discussing the fountain of life in Hubert van Eyck's Ghent altarpiece). The fountain of life is an old topic (cf. Panofsky [1939], figs. 79, 110, and p. 154; and, on the Carolingian Godescalc Gospels, Mâle [1978], p. 44; Von den Steinen [1965], i, pp. 196–197, 288–289, and pl. 266), which, Panofsky observes, still flourished or even revived in fourteenth- and fifteenth-century art (idem [1953], i, p. 216). Related is the

paradisiac triune fountain in the *Roman de la Rose* (20369–20404, 20465–20578), the contrary of the perilous fountain of Narcissus, that Amant sees in Deduit's garden. On this, Tuve (1966), pp. 277, 329; and Fleming (1969), pp. 224–225. On the whole topic, Underwood (1950), pp. 41–138, esp. 80 f.; Patch (1950), esp. pp. 120, 137, 200–202; and Ladner (1979), pp. 236, 240, and the literature cited there. Cf. *Fam.* iv, 7, 12, vi, 3, 23, xvi, 2, 5; *Sen.* iii, 1 (1581: 771), v, 4 (1581: 801), xiii, 2 (1581: 917); and *Rime* 231, 12–14:

> D'un vivo fonte ogni poder s'accoglie:
> ma tu come 'l consenti, o somno Padre,
> che del tuo caro dono altri ne spoglie?

> A single living source each act fulfills,
> But how can you allow, O supreme Father,
> that others dare your dear gift to destroy?

Armi (1946), p. 333. Cf. also Boccaccio, *De casib.* (1520), f. lv.

7   Plato, *Theaetetus* 174e. Cf. above, *DR* i, 14, note 7. Note also Juvenal, vii, 197–198; and the commentary in John of Salisbury, *Policrat.* iii, 8, v, 4, *PL* 199, cc. 488–491, 545–546. Cf. SN 4, note 4, above; and *DR* i, 14, 30–33. —Medieval men

> were familiar from everyday experience with a hierarchical society which they would have recognized in the following paradigm. Supreme authority was vested in the king or emperor. He was surrounded by his vassals, the dukes, marquesses, earls, counts and barons of the realm. Below them on the social scale came the knights, followed by the professional classes and the richer merchants. Then came tradesmen, craftsmen and yeomen, and, finally, peasants, labourers and feudal serfs.

Boyde (1981), p. 223.

8   Cf. Dante, *Div. Comm.*, Par. xvi, 79–87:

> Le vostre cose tutte hanno lor morte,
>   sì come voi; ma celasi in alcuna
>   che dura molto, e le vite son corte;
> E come 'l volger del ciel de la luna
>   cuopre e discuopre i liti sanza posa,
>   così fa di Fiorenza la Fortuna:
> per che non dee parer mirabil cosa
>   ciò ch'io dirò de li alti Fiorentini
>   onde è la fama nel tempo nascosa.

> Your affairs all have their death, even as
> have you; but it is concealed in some things
> that last long, whereas lives are short.
> And as the revolution of the heaven of the moon
> covers and uncovers the shores without pause,

> so Fortune does with Florence; wherefore it
> should appear no wondrous thing which I shall
> tell of the great Florentines whose fame
> is hidden by time.

Singleton (1975), p. 181. On this, Mazzotta (1979), pp. 128–130.

9   On believing others rather than oneself, above, *DR* i, 11, note 15. On examples, *DR* i, Pref., note 52.

10 Aulus Nunnius, slain 100 B.C., an adversary of Marius, was the rival of Lucius Apuleius Saturninus, who usurped the office of tribune of the commons but was subdued with the aid of Marius (Livy, *Perioch.* 69). Clodius Pulcher, as tribune of the commons, sent Cicero into exile in 58 B.C. (Livy, *Perioch.* 103).

11 *Raro excellentis viri filius excellens fuit.* —Compare *Fam.* xxiii, 12, 28, note 2, above.

17 ❖ BORN RICH

1   On this, Patch (1927), pp. 106–107. Note also the image in *DR* ii, 76, 14.

2   Cf. above, *DR* i, 16, 30–32, and note 2.

3   Horace, *Carm.* ii, 10, 9–12:

> saepius ventis agitatur ingens
> pinus et celsae graviore casu
> decidunt turres feriuntque summos
>   fulgura montis.

LCL, Bennett, p. 131. Cited also *Secretum* ii, *Prose* (1955), p. 114; in Petrarch's Paris oration (Barbeu du Rocher [1854], p. 219); and below, *DR* i, 96, 71–73. Cf. also *Africa* vi, 877–879 (1581: 55). Similar, Seneca, *Agam.* 96; Lucretius, vi, 420; and Ovid, *Rem. am.* 369–370. Note Jerome, *Ep.* 60, 16, LCL, Wright, p. 300.

4   Cf. Seneca, *Ep.* 19, 9:

> Volo tibi hoc loco referre dictum Maecenatis vera in ipso culmine elocuti: "Ipsa enim altitudo attonat summa." Si quaeris, in quo libro dixerit; in eo, qui Prometheus inscribitur. Hoc voluit dicere, attonita habet summa. Est ergo tanti ulla potentia, ut sit tibi tam ebrius sermo? Ingeniosus ille vir fuit, magnum exemplum Romanae eloquentiae daturus, nisi illum enervasset felicitas, immo castrasset. Hic te exitus manet, nisi iam contrahes vela, nisi, quod ille sero voluit, terram leges.

> At this point I should like to quote a saying of Maecenas, who spoke the truth when he stood on the very summit: "There's thunder even on the loftiest

peaks." If you ask me in what book these words are found, they occur in the volume entitled *Prometheus*. He simply meant to say that the highest position is full of terrors as of thunder. But is any power worth so high a price that a man like you would ever, in order to obtain it, adopt a style so debauched as that? Maecenas was indeed a man of parts, who would have left a great pattern for Roman oratory to follow, had his good fortune not made him effeminate— nay, had it not emasculated him! An end like his awaits you also, unless you forthwith shorten sail and—as Maecenas was not willing to do until it was too late—hug the shore!

LCL, Gummere, pp. 129, 131.

5   Twyne, f. 21r:

> that it is not subiect both to trouble, and care, and sorow, and envie, and griefe, and in the ende obnoxious to death.

6   The topic of the ups and downs of Fortune (above, *DR* i, 1, note 10) persisted over the centuries. Cf. Pascal, *Pensées* ii:

> The great and the humble have the same misfortunes, the same griefs, the same passions; but the one is at the top of the wheel, and the other near the centre, and so less disturbed by the same revolutions.

Trotter (1941), no. 180.

7   Cf. the proverb

> quidquid agis, prudenter agas, et respice finem.

> Whatever you do, do it wisely, and be mindful of the end.

The related topic, *ad finem vitae respice*, goes back to Herodotus' story about Solon, one of the Seven Sages of Greece (above, *DR* i, 12, 75–77). Cf. *Rer. mem. libri* iii, 62, 1–5:

> Athicum Solonem predicare solitum ferunt expectandum novissimum vite diem ut quis beatus iure vocaretur. Omnes nempe dum vivimus, quocunque gradu positi, subiacemus imperio ac ludibriis fortune, a quibus perraro quidem immunes, a periculo autem ac minis nunquam tuti sumus: in quantalibet igitur rerum affluentia, de futuro semper incerti, dici non possumus felices. Quod verbum altius intelligitur ab hiis qui ex altissimo dignitatis ac potentie solio, ubi firmiter stare videbantur, repente corruerunt. Id cum in multis sepe, tum clarissime in Creso Lidorum rege, cui hoc dictum Solone tradit Herodotus, apparuit. Hunc enim potentissimum sue etatis Solon ut ad longe vite finem respiceret admonuit; quod ille tunc fortune fidens despexit, nec prius intellexit quam a Ciro Persarum rege brevi post victus ac vinctus flammisque traditus est, mediaque iam ex morte Solonem vere vatem exclamavit. Quod admirans Cirus differri tantisper supplicium imperavit, dum quid ille Solonem vociferaretur agnosceret; et adiuvit repentinus imber imperium flammasque compescuit. Re autem intellecta fortune vim reputans et statum hostis miseratus,

vitam sibi, sed sine regno et, ut quidam adiciunt, sine libertate, restituit. Recte igitur dici potest quod de mortali felicitate sola mors iudicat.

They say Solon of Athens used to warn people that they must wait for the very last day of someone's life before being justified to call him happy—since, obviously, everyone, no matter what his position, is subject to the power and whims of Fortune as long as he lives. Very seldom only people seem to be immune to Fortune, and no one is ever safe from her threats. No matter how great the affluence of wealth, we remain uncertain about what is yet to come and, therefore, cannot be counted to be happy. This is particularly evident in the case of those who are suddenly thrust from the highest seats of dignity and power, in which they seemed firmly established. This has happened to many, but the most celebrated instance was that of Croesus, King of the Lydians, who, as Herodotus reports [i, 32–33], was the one to whom Solon addressed his warning to mark the end of a long life [Ausonius, *Lud. sept. sap.* 55–58], which advice Croesus disdained, because he did not know beforehand that shortly thereafter he, vanquished and fettered, would be sentenced to the stake by Cyrus, King of the Persians, and faced with death, would acknowledge Solon as a truthful seer. Surprised, Cyrus ordered a halt to the execution to find out why Croesus had shouted Solon's name, and a sudden rain shower further restrained the sentence and the flames. When he had learned the circumstances, Cyrus pondered the powers of Fortune, took pity on the plight of his enemy, and granted him his life, though not his kingdom, nor, as some add, his freedom. Thus it is correct to say that death alone adjudges the happiness of mortals.

On the Croesus story, Herodotus, i, 32–33; 86–91; Aristotle, *Eth. Nic.* i, 10, 1100 a 10, Barnes (1984), ii, p. 1738; Ausonius, *Lud. sept. sap.* 55–58, 73–130; Justin, i, 7, 3–10; Cicero, *De fin.* ii, 27, 87, iii, 22, 76; Juvenal, x, 274–275; *Fam.* viii, 1, 8; and *Trionfi*, Tr. fame 46–48. On *ad finem vite respicere*, none be counted happy till his death—Aristotle, *Eth. Nic.* i, 10; Ovid, *Metam.* iii, 135–137; Valerius Maximus, vii, 2, Ext. 2; Eccli. 11, 30, as below, *DR* i, 108, note 13; Jerome, *Ep.* 54, 6, LCL, Wright, p. 238, and *De ocio*, Rotondi, p. 64; and *Rime* 56, 12–14. On *mark the end* (Ovid, *Heroides* ii, 85), e.g., *Fam.* iii, 7, 4, vii, 18, 9, xiv, 1, 42; *Sen.* xvii, 2, as below, *DR* i, 46, note 21; *Met.* i, 6, 198–199, *Rime* (1951), p. 738; and below, *DR* i, 18, 121–123, i, 103, 12–13.

8 Petrarch refers often to Fortune, all-powerful in her kingdom, the mistress of humankind (Virgil, *Aeneid* viii, 334; Cicero, *Tusc. disp.* v, 9, 25; Sallust, *Catil.* viii, 1; etc.)—e.g., *Fam.* i, 1, 24, iii, 16, 12, iv, 12, 15 and 30, viii, 1, 38, xviii, 16, 7; *Var.* 7; SN 4, as above, *DR* i, 16, note 4. On this, Heitmann (1958), pp. 25–39.

9 On *prosperitatis insolentiam*, Heitmann (1958), p. 153, n. 17.

10 1492: in ergastulis. &c.
 1581: in ergastulis.

18 ✧ SUMPTUOUS FARE

1   1492: Hispanum
     1581: Hispaniam
2   Throughout the late antique Latin literature, Manius Curius Dentatus, Gaius
     Fabricius Luscinus, and Tiberius Coruncanius "of old" (Macrobius, *Saturn.* i,
     5, 1) stand for honesty and patriotism, simple language, clean, frugal living,
     dedication to the soil, and hard work. Reason's remarks are aware of Valerius
     Maximus, iv, chaps. 2, 3, where the examples of L. Quinctius Cincinnatus, C.
     Atilius Serranus, and M. Porcius Cato Censorius may be found (iv, 4, 7; 4, 5;
     3, 11). Reason appears to cite the example of Cato after Pliny, *Nat. hist.* xiv,
     14, 91:

> Idem Cato cum *in Hispaniam navigaret, unde* cum triumpho *rediit, non aliud*
> vinum bibit *quam remiges*

> Moreover Cato, *when sailing on his expedition to Spain, whence he returned* with
> a triumph (over the Celtiberi, 195 B.C.), drank *no other wine than what was
> drunk by the crew of his galley* . . .

LCL, Rackham, p. 247. Yet note Valerius Maximus, iv, 3, 11; Frontinus, *Strat.*
iv, 3, 1; and John of Salisbury, *Policrat.* v, 7, *PL* 199, c. 557. Cf. *Fam.* vii, 3, 1,
xiii, 4, 12, xvi, 3, 3; *De vita sol.* ii, *Prose* (1955), p. 546; and *Rer. mem. libri* iii,
51 and 83.

3   Petrarch tells the story of the two greatest anchorites of the desert (*Sen.* xii, 1,
     xvii, 2 [1581: 900, 964]) in *De vita sol.* ii, *Prose* (1955), p. 414:

> Ut tot iam spiritalibus bellis victor, tot invisibilium hostium exercitibus tri-
> umphatis, cum ad nonagesimum vite annum pervenisset et, nullo uspiam ap-
> parente hominum, se iam solum heremicolam cogitaret, multo vetustiorem
> atque remotiorem solitudinis incolam alterius, Paulum Thebeum, querere ad-
> monitus revelatione nocturna, paruit: quesivit, invenit, horrificis in itinere
> primum monstris inventis. Ut congressis tandem et post longum silentium
> collocutis, ad ripam fontis exigui et veteris umbram palme, secretissima in
> spelunca, missus e celo panis unus duobus Cristi fortissimis veteranis, multo
> ieiunio exhaustis, abunde suffecerit.

> How when he reached his ninetieth year, victorious in so many spiritual bat-
> tles, with so many hosts of invisible enemies overpowered, and thought that he
> was the only one who lived in that desert, no human being having anywhere
> shown himself, it was manifested to him by a revelation at night that he should
> seek out Paul the Theban, who had been living much longer in an even remoter
> region of the solitude, how he looked for him and found him, not without

encountering dreadful monsters on the way; how at last when they met and broke their long silence in the retirement of the cave near the bank of a little spring beneath the shade of an aged palm, a single loaf sent down from the sky sufficed amply to still the hunger of these two valiant veterans in the service of Christ, worn out as they were with much fasting.

Zeitlin (1924), p. 192. Cf. Athanasius-Evagrius, *Vita Antonii*, *PL* 73; Jerome, *Vita Pauli*, *PL* 23; and Jacobus de Voragine, *Legenda aurea* xv (January 10, Graesse [1890], pp. 94–95). The scene is represented on a capital sculpture in Ste. Marie-Madeleine at Vézelay (Mâle [1978], pp. 239–240). On the antithetic *hinc* and *illinc*—here and there—e.g., Cicero, *In Catil.* ii, 11, 25; Isidore, *Etym.* ii, 21, 5; Fontaine (1959), ii, pp. 697–698; and Lausberg (1960), i, p. 391. On such *loci*—places—Yates (1966), chap. iv, esp. pp. 63–64, 93–94; and above, *DR* i, 8, note 12.

4   Gaius Julius Caesar Octavianus (63 B.C.–A.D. 14) assumed the title Augustus, bestowed upon him by the Roman senate, January 16, 27 B.C. On this, Gibbon (1789), chap. 3, Bury, i (1909), p. 77.

5   Suetonius, ii, Aug. 76, 1:

> *Cibi*—nam ne haec quidem omiserim—*minimi* erat atque *vulgaris fere. Secundarium panem et pisciculos minutos et caseum bibulum* manu pressum et ficos virides biferas maxime appetebat; vescebaturque et ante cenam quocumque tempore et loco, quo stomachus desiderasset.

> He was a light eater (for I would not omit even this detail) and as a rule ate plain food. He particularly liked coarse bread, small fishes, handmade moist cheese, and green figs of the second crop; and he would eat before dinner, wherever and whenever he felt hungry.

LCL, Rolfe, p. 241. Referred to *Sen.* xv, 3 (1581: 934). Also quoted in John of Salisbury, *Policrat.* v, 7, *PL* 199, c. 557.

6   Cf., e.g., Statius, *Silvae* iv, 6, 3–16:

> . . . rapuit me cena benigni
> Vindicis. Haec imos animi perlapsa recessus
> inconsumpta manet. Neque enim ludibria ventris
> hausimus aut epulas diverso a sole petitas
> vinaque perpetuis aevo certantia fastis.
> A miseri! quos nosse iuvat, quid Phasidis ales
> distet ab hiberna Rhodopes grue, quis magis anser
> exta ferat, cur Tuscus aper generosior Umbro,
> lubrica qua recubent conchylia mollius alga:
> nobis verus amor medioque Helicone petitus
> sermo hilaresque ioci brumalem absumere noctem
> suaserunt mollemque oculis expellere somnum,
> donec ab Elysiis prospexit sedibus alter
> Castor et hesternas risit Tithonia mensas.

> . . . kind Vindex took me off to dine.
> That feast sank deep into the recesses of my soul,
> and remains unconsumed. For it was no wanton dainties
> of the belly that we devoured, no sweetmeats sought
> under distant suns, no wines whose ages rival our continuous Annals.
> Unhappy they whose delight is to know how the bird of Phasis
> differs from a crane of wintry Rhodope, what kind of goose
> has the largest liver, why a Tuscan boar is richer than an Umbrian,
> on what seaweed the slippery shell-fish most comfortably recline:
> as for us, real affection and discourse fetched from the heart
> of Helicon and merry jests persuaded us to sit out a winter's night
> and to banish soft sleep from our eyes, until the other Twin
> looked forth from Elysium, and Tithonia laughed at yesterday's banquet.

The twins Castor and Pollux were allowed to live on alternate days; Tithonia is the Dawn. LCL, Mozley, p. 245, and note a. On dining in Antiquity, Hale (1968), chap. 2, esp. p. 56; and Sandys (1929), pars. 248–250.

7   Ovid, *Fasti* vi, 173–176:

> Piscis adhuc illi populo sine fraude natabat,
> ostreaque in conchis tuta fuere suis.
> Nec Latium norat, quam praebet Ionia dives,
> nec quae Pygmaeo sanguine gaudet, avem.

LCL, Frazer, p. 331.

> 1492: Piscis adhuc illis populis sine fraude natabat.
> Ostraeaque in conchis tuta fuere suis.
> Nec latium norat quam praebet Ionia diues.
> Nec quae pigmaeo sanguine gaudet auis.

> 1581: Piscis adhuc illis populis sine fraude natabat,
> Nec Latium norat, quam praebet Ionia diues.
> Ostreaque in conchis tuta fuere suis.
> Nec quae pygmeo sanguine gaudet auis.

Cf. also, Ovid, *Metam.* vi, 90.

8   On this, *Sen.* xii, 1 (1581: 901–902).

9   Cf. below, *DR* i, 21, 6, and note 1.

10   Suetonius, ii, Aug., 77:

> *Vini quoque* natura *parcissimus* erat. Non amplius ter bibere eum solitum super cenam in castris apud Mutinam, Cornelius Nepos tradit. Postea quotiens largis-sime se invitaret, senos sextantes non excessit, aut si excessisset, reiciebat. Et maxime delectatus est Raetico neque temere interdiu bibit. Pro potione sumebat *perfusum aqua frigida panem aut cucumeris frustrum vel lactuculae thyrsum aut recens aridumve pomum suci vinosioris.*

He was by nature most sparing also in his use of wine. Cornelius Nepos writes that in camp before Mutina [Modena] it was his habit to drink not more than three times at dinner. Afterwards, when he indulged most freely he never exceeded a pint; or if he did, he used to throw it up. He liked Raetina wine best, but rarely drank before dinner. Instead he would take a bit of bread soaked in cold water, a slice of cucumber, a sprig of young lettuce, or an apple with a tart flavour, either fresh or dried.

LCL, Rolfe, p. 243.

11   Pliny, *Nat. hist.* xiv, 7, 58:

Nec alienum fuerit commemorare hoc in loco quod Androcydes sapientia clarus ad Alexandrum Magnum scripsit intemperantiam eius cohibens: '*Vinum poturus, rex, memento bibere te sanguinem terrae. Cicuta homini venenum est, cicutae vinum.*' *Quibus praeceptis ille si obtemperavisset, profecto amicos in temulentia non interemisset.*

And it will not be out of place to recall here what the famous philosopher Androcydes wrote to Alexander the Great in an attempt to restrain his intemperance: 'When you are about to drink *wine*, O King, remember that you are *drinking the earth's blood*. Hemlock is poison to a human being and *wine is poison to hemlock.*' If Alexander had obeyed this advice, doubtless he would not have killed his friends (Clitus and Callisthenes?) in his drunken fits.

LCL, Rackham, p. 225. On Clitus, Q. Curtius, viii, 1, 52, and 2, 5; and *De vir. ill.* xv, Alex., 17–23. On Callisthenes, Q. Curtius, viii, 8, 19–23. Cf. Fox (1980), pp. 293–295, 299–307. For examples of the baneful effects of drunkenness see *Sen.* xii, 1 (1581: 902).

12   Suetonius, i, Jul. Caes., 53.

13   *De vita sol.* i, *Prose* (1955), p. 382:

Qui illud insania exultantes dicere soliti sunt: nam quid si somnum, si concubitum, si cibum potumque subtraxeris acturi sumus? Aut quenam vita futura est, vite muneribus et officiis spoliata? Ut penitus pre se ferant et impudissime fateantur, ad nil se aliud vivere quam ad ea, que comunia brutis animantibus sunt nobiscum. Quasi vero non perditum illud tempus, quo brevissimam hanc vitam cum somno et voluptate partimur, in melioribus curis, et vel in contemplatione Dei, vel in cognitione rerum, vel in exercitio virtutum possit expendi.

Exulting in their own madness, they are in a habit of saying, "If you take away sleep and carnal pleasure and food and drink, what are we going to do? And what will life be when it is stripped of life's gifts and employments?" So completely do they expose their natures and acknowledge without the least sense of shame that they live only for those things which we have in common with brute beasts, as if that lost time, in which we share this brief space of life with sleep and pleasure, could not be spent in better thoughts, in the contemplation of God, or the study of nature, or the practice of virtue.

Zeitlin (1924), p. 169. Cf. also *Fam.* xxiv, 8, 3.

14 Twyne, f. 23r, omits *professor voluptatis.* —On Epicurus, *Sen.* xv, 3 (1581:
    934). Cf. Augustine, *De civ. Dei* xix, 1; and Boethius, *Cons. phil.* iii, P 2,
    46–51.
15 Cf. Cicero, *Tusc. disp.* v, 34, 99:

> Adde siccitatem, quae consequitur hanc continentiam in victu, adde integri-
> tatem valetudinis.

> Add dryness, which follows upon restraint in diet, add unimpaired health.

LCL, King, p. 524, adds here: "The four elements were earth, air, fire, and
water, whose mixture and cardinal properties dryness, warmth, coldness, and
moistness form the body and its constituent parts. Dry bodies were healthiest
and strongest." On this, Aristotle, e.g., *Metaph.* iii, 4, 1000b, Barnes (1984),
ii, p. 1580; Ovid, *Metam.* i, 1–75; Chalcidius, *Comm. Tim.* 120, Waszink
(1962), p. 100 = Hugh of St. Victor, *Didasc.* i, 1, Taylor (1962), pp. 46–47.
Note Augustine, *De trin.* x, 10, 14; Isidore, *Lib. num.* v, 23, *PL* 83, c. 183,
Fontaine (1959), ii, pp. 656–657; and Leibbrand (1953), pp. 45, 109–110,
172–174. On the four elements in Dante, Toynbee (1968), art. "Corpi sem-
plici"; and Boyde (1981), chap. 2. Cf. *DR* i, 11, note 19, and ii, Pref., note 84.
16 Cicero, ibid. v, 34, 100: *confer sudantes, ructantes.* LCL, King, p. 525.
17 Eccli. 37, 32–34:

> Noli avidus esse in omni epulatione,
> et non te effundas super omnem escam;
> in multis enim escis erit infirmitas
> et aviditas appropinquabit usque ad choleram.
> Propter crapulam multi obierunt:
> qui autem abstinens est adiiciet vitam.

18 Twyne, f. 23v, translates *Horse.*

19 ❖ FEASTS

1   Horace, *Ep.* ii, 2, 61–63:

> tres mihi convivae prope dissentire videntur,
> poscentes vario multum diversa palato.
> quid dem? quid non dem?

LCL, Fairclough, p. 429.

2   I.t.: Flaccus

3   1492: seu quid facias:
     1581: sed quid facias:

4   *ille illotis vasis aquam tepidam.* Twyne, f. 24r, translates: "This seruant brought warme water to the table with unwashed handes."

5   *triumphus:* "In the days of ancient Rome a general returning after a great victory might be given the honor of a triumph—an elaborate procession, including captives, that ended in a ceremony on the Capitoline" (Wilkins [1961], p. 22, note also R. Chevallier in Dumur [1965], pp. 316–317)—hence any spectacular parade mostly of riders and horse-drawn floats in celebration of a cause or idea. Cf., e.g., Pliny, *Nat. hist.* xxxvii, 6, 14, on Pompey's triumph, as below, *DR* i, 37, note 21. Petrarch conceived the idea of poetic triumphs. His *Trionfi*, six Italian poems offering pictorial visions of love, chastity, death, fame, time, and eternity, begun in the 1340s, "constituted the most triumphant poem of the early Renaissance: for a hundred years and more they outshone both the Divine Comedy and Petrarch's own sonnets and canzoni." (Wilkins [1962], p. v.)

6   Twyne, f. 24r: "the trumpets also and shalomes sounde foorth togeather."

7   Cicero, *De off.* ii, 18, 64:

> est enim ut mihi videbitur valde decorum patere domos hominum illustrium hospitibus illustribus.

LCL, Miller, p. 237.

8   Lactantius, *Div. inst.* vi, 12, *PL* 6, cc. 677–678:

> "Recte," inquit Cicero, "a Theophrasto est laudata hospitalitas. Est enim (ut mihi quidem videtur) valde decorum, patere domos hominum illustrium hospitibus illustribus." Eodem modo rursus erravit, quo tum, cum idoneis esse diceret largiendum. Non enim iusti et sapientis viri domus illustribus debet patere, sed humilibus et abiectis . . . At ille in recipiendis illustribus nihil spectavit aliud, nisi utilitatem; nec dissimulavit homo ingeniosus, quid ex eo commodi speraret. Ait enim, qui id faciat, potentem apud exteros futurum per gratiam principum, quos sibi hospitii et amicitiae iure constrinxerit. O quam multis argumentis Ciceronis inconstantia, si id agerem, coargui posset!

> "Hospitality," says Cicero, "also is a theme of Theophrastus's praise [*Characters, De divitiis*], and rightly so. For, as it seems to me at least, it is most proper that the homes of distinguished men should be open to distinguished guests." [*De off.* ii, 18, 64; LCL, Miller, p. 237.] He errs equally so when he says one ought to be generous only with the worthy poor [ibid. ii, 15, 54]. The house of a just and wise man should be open not to distinguished people, but to the lowly and the downtrodden . . . For receiving the illustrious means nothing else but currying favor. Nor does a clever man deny that he expects to profit thereby: Who does this, he says, is destined to become powerful, because he is

being favored by the princes he has obligated to himself by the laws of hospitality and friendship! O with how many instances could I expose Cicero's duplicity, if I cared to.

9   Cicero, *De off.* i, 15, 49:

hoc maxime officium est, ut quisque maxime opis indigeat ita ei potissimum opitulari; quod contra fit a plerisque; a quo enim plurimum sperant, etiamsi ille his non eget, tamen ei potissimum inserviunt.

LCL, Miller, p. 53.

10   Juvenal, v, 157–158:

. . .   . . .   nam quae comoedia mimus
Quis melior plorante gula?

LCL, Ramsay, p. 81.

11   Cicero, *Tusc. disp.* v, 38, 111:

docto homine et erudito, cui vivere est cogitare.

LCL, King, p. 537.

12   Rom. 13, 13. Cf. Letter to Posterity, *Sen.* xviii, 1; and *Prose* (1955), pp. 2, 4:

Non [michi], ut ista cura esset, lautarum facultas epularum: ego autem tenui victu et cibis vulgaribus vitam egi letius, quam cum exquisitissimis dapibus omnes Apicii successores. Convivia que dicuntur—cum sint comessationes modestie et bonis moribus inimice—semper michi displicuerunt. Laboriosum et inutile ratus sum ad hunc finem vocare alios, nec minus ab aliis vocari; convivere autem cum amicis adeo iucundum, ut eorum superventu nil gratius habuerim, nec unquam volens sine sotio cibum sumpserim.

I certainly do not long to be able to give gorgeous banquets. I have, on the contrary, led a happier existence with plain living and ordinary fare than all the followers of Apicius, with their elaborate dainties. So-called *convivia*, which are but vulgar bouts, sinning against sobriety and good manners, have always been repugnant to me. I have ever felt that it was irksome and profitless to invite others to such affairs, and not less to be bidden to them myself. On the other hand, the pleasure of dining with one's friends is so great that nothing has ever given me more delight than their unexpected arrival, not have I ever willingly sat down to table without a companion.

Robinson in Robinson-Rolfe (1914), p. 61. On Apicius, *nepotum omnium altissimus gurges*—the most gluttonous gorger of all spendthrifts—Pliny, *Nat. hist.* ix, 66, x, 68; LCL, Rackham, p. 377; Juvenal, iv, 23, xi, 2; Martial, ii, 69, 3, ii, 89, 5, iii, 2, 1; Jerome, *Ep.* 33, 3, Wiesen (1964), p. 24; and Harvey (1974), art. Apicius.

13   Twyne, f. 25r, italicizes this sentence as a quotation. I think it is Petrarch's.

14   Cf. above, *DR* i, 18, 65; and *Hist. Aug.*, Verus, esp. iv and v.

15   Juvenal, iii, 86–91, 100–108:

Quid quod *adulandi gens prudentissima* laudat
sermonem indocti, faciem deformis amici,
et longum invalidi collum cervicibus aequat
Herculis Antaeum procul a tellure tenentis,
miratur vocem angustam, qua deterius nec
ille sonat quo mordetur gallina marito? . . . . . .

natio comoeda est. Rides, maiore cachinno
concutitur; flet, si lacrimas conspexit amici,
nec dolet; igniculum brumae si tempore poscas,
accipit endromidem; si dixeris 'aestuo,' sudat.
Non sumus ergo pares: melior, qui semper et omni
nocte dieque potest aliena sumere vultum
a facie, iactare manus, laudare paratus,
si bene ructavit, si rectum minxit amicus,
si trulla inverso crepitum dedit aurea fundo.

What of this again, that these *people are experts in flattery*, and will commend the talk of an illiterate, or the beauty of a deformed friend, and compare the scraggy neck of some weakling to the brawny throat of Hercules when holding up Antaeus high above the earth; or go into ecstasies over a squeaky voice not more melodious than that of a cock when he pecks his spouse the hen? . . . . . . they are a *nation of play-actors*. If you smile, your Greek will split his sides with laughter; if he sees his friend drop a tear, he weeps, though without grieving; if you call for a bit of fire in winter-time, he puts on his cloak; if you say 'I am hot,' he breaks into a sweat. Thus we are not upon a level, he and I; he has always the best of it, being ready at any moment, by night or by day, to take his expression from another man's face, to throw up his hands and applaud if his friend gives a good belch or piddles straight, or if his golden basin make a gurgle when turned upside down.

(Hercules slew Antaeus by raising him from the ground, till when he was invincible.) LCL, Ramsay, pp. 39, 41. Renaissance commentators such as Mancinelli and Badius dwelt with relish on this passage and the *incontinentium epule*—feasts of the incontinent.

16 I.t.: Flaccus. —Horace, *Carm.* i, 35, 26–27:

. . . . . . diffugiunt cadis,
cum faece siccatis amici.

Cf., e.g., *Sen.* v, 2 (1581: 795):

Omitto enim hanc hominum fecem, uulgus, cuius dicta atque sententiae irrideri merentur, potius quam reprehendi.

I say nothing of the dregs of men, the base mob, whose words and opinions deserve only our laughter, rather than our reproof.

Bishop (1966), p. 245.

17   The theme recurs in *La Celestina* vii, 1, Marciales (1985), ii, p. 124; Simpson (1955), p. 79.

18   Reason's juxtaposition *vulgus/docti*—the crowd/the educated (nearly identical, *Fam.* xiv, 2, 7, xxi, 9, 13; and *DR* ii, 117, 22) invokes related dichotomous distinctions echoing Stoic views (*DR* ii, 34, note 3), such as *vulgus/pauci*—the crowd/the few—*Secretum* i, *Prose* (1955), p. 34; *multi/pauci*—the many/the few—*Fam.* i, 6, 9, xiv, 2, 7, xxi, 13, 1, related *Fam.* ii, 4, 13–14, and *DR* ii, 117, 56–57; multi/rari—the many/the very few—*DR* ii, 114, 57–58; or, *populus* vs. *bonos*—the people vs. the good—below, *DR* ii, 67, 14. Note also the passages in Boethius, *Cons. phil.*, as discussed in Gruber (1978), p. 104, 7; and the related notion of, often desirable, rarity, such as *unus ex paucis, Fam.* xiv, 1, 42, xxiii, 18, 6, *Sen.* xii, 1 (1581: 897), and *DR* ii, 83, 27, ii, 102, 22, ii, 114, 49–70; *unus ex paucissimis, Sen.* xiii, 2; *unus tu tantis ex millibus,* v, 2 (1581: 916, 793); *unus ex millibus, DR* i, 1, 49; and *learned men are scarce,* above, *DR* i, Pref., 35–39, and note 14, and *DR* i, 12 *passim.*

20 ❖ FINE APPAREL

1   Marius in Sallust, *Jug.* lxxxv, 40:

> munditias mulieribus, laborem viris convenire.

LCL, Rolfe, p. 321. Also quoted in *Fam.* iii, 10, 5. Note the echo in *Fam.* xxi, 9, 11.

2   Above, *DR* i, 18, 36–40.

3   Suetonius, ii, Aug., 73:

> Veste non temere alia quam domestica usus est, ab sorore et uxore et filia neptibusque confecta.

4   Cf. Isidore, *Etym.* ix, 2, 40.

5   Pliny, *Nat. hist.* ix, 60–65; Isidore, *Etym.* xii, 6, 50, xv, 1, 27; etc.

6   I.t.: Gaius

7   Referring to Suetonius, iv, Caligula, 52.

8   On the topic *ars—natura*, the instructive overview in Lausberg (1960), i, pp. 25–33; De Bruyne (1946), i, p. 313, ii, pp. 116–119, 253, 266–267, 381–385, iii, pp. 114, 212, 316; Von den Steinen (1965), i, pp. 100–112, 128–129, 190–211; and Von den Steinen (1959), pp. 92–96. Note also Quintilian, *Inst. orat.* ii, 19; Matthew of Vendôme, *Ars* i, 56, 1–2, ii, 5, Galyon (1980), pp. 43, 64; and the discussion in the *Roman de la Rose* 16005–16148, Dahlberg (1971), pp. 271–273.

9   *quin autem magis conspectam efficiunt: aut suspectam.*
10   On Petrarch's and his brother Gherardo's youthful concern with their attire, *Fam.* x, 3; and Wilkins (1961), p. 8.

21 ❖ LEISURE AND REST

1   On the Augustinian *frui* and *uti*, above, *DR* i, 10, note 19.
2   Sleep as the brother of death: Virgil, *Aeneid* vi, 278, and Homer, *Iliad* xiv, 231; as the image of death: Cicero, *Tusc. disp.* i, 38, 91–92, as in *DR* ii, 117, note 14, Homer, *Odyssey* xiii, 80, and Virgil, *Aeneid* vi, 522 = Macrobius, *Saturn.* v, 3, 12, and Pliny, *Nat. hist.* vii, 50, 167. On this, *Rer. mem. libri* iv. 34, 5. Note also *Fam.* xix, 16, 20: *et somnum morti et lectulum busto simillimum duco*—I regard sleep as a kind of death, my bed as a tomb (Bishop [1966], p. 164); and *Fam.* xxii, 7, 5: *languido mortique simillimo sopore*—sluggish sleep so similar to death. The notion was proverbial, e.g., *Dicta Catonis*:

> mortis imago iuvat somnus, mors ipsa timetur.

> Death's image, sleep, refreshes; death itself, frightens.

LCL, Duff, p. 625, 19. Also *Fiori e vita di filosafi* . . . xxviii, Secundus, *La prosa del duecento* (1959), p. 531:

> Che è sonno?
> Sonno è imagine de la morte, riposo de le fatiche, talento de l'infermi, desiderio de' miseri.

> Che è la morte?
> La morte èe sonno eternale, paura dei ricchi, desiderio de' poveri, avenimento da non cessare, ladrone delli uomini, cacciatrice di vita, risolvimento di tutti.

3   Cf. Bartholomaeus Anglicus, *De propr. rer.* vi, 24 (Trevisa, p. 333).
4   Job 7, 14:

> terrebis me per somnia,
> et per visiones horrore concuties.

> Thou wilt frighten me with dreams
> and terrify me with visions.

5 I.t.: Vacia

6 On Servilius Vatia *in sua rure* (= Cicero, *Tusc. disp.* v, 35, 102), *De vita sol.* i, *Prose* (1955), p. 376:

> sic Servilii Vatie solitudo ridicula est, qui non procul inde Neapolitano in litore prope Campanie Cumas latens senuit, otio famosus inutili, et intra villule sue septum non tam habitans quam sepultus. Et quam multos esse credimus ubique Servilios? sed hic ante alios occurrit, quem irrisor nobilis notum fecit et prestitit ne inferre coetaneis nostris veritatis iniuriam exemplique molestiam cogeremur.

> Ridiculous is the solitude of Servilius Vatia, who grew old in obscurity not far from that island on the Neopolitan shore near Cumae in Campania [i.e., Capri] famous for his wasted opportunity, buried rather than living within the walls of his country house. I suppose there are a great many people like Servilius everywhere, but he occurs first to the mind because a noble writer [Seneca, *Ep.* 55] has made him known by his mockery and delivered him over to us that we may be free from the necessity of inflicting upon our contemporaries the injury of a truthful exposure and the annoyance of serving as an awful example.

Zeitlin (1924), p. 165. Note also *Fam.* xv, 4, 3.

Scipio, fighting in Africa, could be Q. Metellus Pius (Caesar, *De bello Africo*), who commanded Pompey's center at Pharsalus. Another possibility is Scipio Africanus Maior, whose habit it was *et in otio de negotiis cogitare*—to be occupied with public business even in his leisure hours (Cicero, *De off.* iii, 1, 1; inverted in *Fam.* xvii, 10, 28). Thus Scipio

> numquam se minus otiosus esse quam cum otiosus,
> nec minus solum quam cum solus esset

> was never less at leisure than in his leisure,
> and never less lonely than when alone

(Cicero, ibid., Zeitlin [1924], p. 314) and cherished leisure and solitude amidst the din of the camp and the blast of trumpets (*Rer. mem. libri* i, 2; *De vita sol.* ii, *Prose* [1955], pp. 432, 552, 554, 588). —During the Civil War, M. Porcius Cato (Uticensis) crossed the Libyan desert (Dante, *Div. Comm.*, Inf. xiv). Lucan (ix, 379–410) has him address his troops prior to this:

> "O quibus una salus placuit mea signa secutis
> Indomita cervice mori, conponite mentes
> Ad magnum virtutis opus summosque labores.
> Vadimus in campos steriles exustaque mundi,
> Qua nimius Titan et rarae in fontibus undae,
> Siccaque letiferis squalent serpentibus arva.
> Durum iter ad leges patriaeque ruentis amorem.
> Per mediam Libyen veniant atque invia temptent,
> Si quibus in nullo positum est evadere voto,

Si quibus ire sat est. Neque enim mihi fallere quemquam
Est animus tectoque metu perducere volgus.
Hi mihi sint comites, quos ipsa pericula ducent,
Qui me teste pati vel quae tristissima pulchrum
Romanumque putant. At qui sponsore salutis
Miles eget capiturque animae dulcedine, vadat
Ad dominum meliora via. Dum primus harenas
Ingrediar primusque gradus in pulvere ponam,
Me calor aetherius feriat, mihi plena veneno
Occurrat serpens, fatoque pericula vestra
Praetemptate meo. Sitiat, quicumque bibentem
Viderit, aut umbras nemorum quicumque petentem,
Aestuet, aut equitem peditum praecedere turmas,
Deficiat: si quo fuerit discrimine notum,
Dux an miles eam. Serpens, sitis, ardor harenae
Dulcia virtuti; gaudet patientia duris;
Laetius est, quotiens magno sibi constat, honestum.
Sola potest Libye turba praestare malorum,
Ut deceat fugisse viros." Sic ille paventes
Incendit virtute animos et amore laborum . . .

"Men who have chosen this one path of safety—to follow my standard to the
death with spirits unsubdued, prepare your minds for a high feat of valour and
for utmost hardships. We march towards barren plains and the furnace of the
world, where the sun's heat is excessive and water is seldom found in the
springs, and where the parched fields are foul with venomous serpents. Hard is
the path to freedom, and hard to win the love of our country in her fall. Let
those march through the heart of Africa, seeking a path where there is none,
who do not regard escape as a thing to be at all desired, and are content merely
to march on. For I do not intend to deceive any man, nor to draw the army on
by concealing the danger. I seek as my companions men who are attracted by
the risks themselves, men who think it glorious and worthy of a Roman to
endure even the worst, with me to watch them. But if any man craves a
guarantee of safety and is tempted by the sweetness of life, let him take an
easier path and go to a master. Foremost I shall tread the desert, and foremost
set foot upon the sand; let the heat of the sky then beat upon me and the
poisonous serpent stand in my path; and test your perils beforehand by what
befalls me. If any man see me drinking, or seeking the shade of trees, or riding
in front of the marching troops, then let him feel thirst and heat and weari-
ness—if there is any distinction to mark whether I am the general or a soldier
in the ranks. Serpents, thirst, burning sand—all are welcomed by the brave;
endurance finds pleasure in hardship; virtue rejoices when it pays dear for its
existence. Africa alone, with all her plagues, can bring it about, that to have
fled (at Pharsalus) is no disgrace to the brave." Thus he fired their frightened
hearts with courage and love of hardship . . .

LCL, Duff, pp. 533, 535.

The adventure of M. Atilius Regulus during the First Punic war (256 B.C.) is recorded in a fragment of Livy, xviii, preserved in Valerius Maximus, i, 8, ext. 19:

> Serpentis quoque a T. Liuio curiose pariter ac facunde relatae fiat mentio. Is enim ait in Africa apud Bagradam flumen tantae magnitudinis anguem fuisse ut Atilii Reguli exercitum usu amnis prohiberet; multisque militibus ingenti ore correptis, compluribus caudae oluminibus elisis, cum telorum iactu perforari nequiret, ad ultimum ballistarum tormentis undique petitam silicum crebris et ponderosis uerberibus procubuisse, omnibusque et cohortibus et legionibus ipsa Carthagine uisam terribiliorem. Atque etiam cruore suo gurgitibus imbutis, corporisque iacentis pestifero afflatu uicina regione polluta, Romana inde summouisse castra. Dicit etiam beluae corium centum uiginti pedum in urbem missum.

> Let me mention also the serpent decribed by Titus Livius no less exactly than eloquently. For Livy says that in Africa at the Bagradas River, there was a snake of such size that it kept the army of Atilius Regulus from using the river. It caught many of the soldiers in its huge jaws, and crushed large numbers of them in the coils of its tail. Hurled missiles could not penetrate its skin, but at last when it was attacked on all sides with missiles from the catapults, it succumbed to the continuous heavy blows of the stones. Both legions and auxiliary troops without exception regarded it as more to be feared than Carthage itself. Even after death the pools were stained with its blood, and the area round about was defiled with the poisonous stench of the exposed body, till it drove the Roman camp away from there. Livy also says that the monster's skin, measuring one hundred and twenty feet, was sent to Rome.

LCL, Schlesinger, p. 179. Pliny records the event in *Nat. hist.* viii, 14, 37. Aulus Gellius, vii, 3, retells the story based on the *Historiae* by Tubero. Cf. also *Fam.* iii, 10, 5.

7   On *materia*, cf. Cicero, e.g., *De inv.* i, 7; *De orat.* i, 49, ii, 238; *Ad Quintum fratrem* ii, 1, 1; and *Top.* 58. On Aristotle's four "causes," Randall (1960), pp. 123–127; and Boyde (1981), pp. 52–53. On *materia* = ὕλην, Augustine, *Contra Faustum* xx, 14, PL 42, c. 379; Isidore, *Etym.* xiii, 3, 1, xix, 19, 4; and Fontaine (1959), ii, pp. 653–654.

8   Similar: *Fam.* ii, 4, 19, ix, 13, 18, x, 1, 12–13, xxi, 9, 7–11; *Sen.* vii, 1 (1581: 825); and below, *DR* ii, 56, 2, ii, 117, 224–229.

9   *bene si non curis mordacibus . . . male autem si non honesti studii cura cuiuspiam sopor abrumpitur.*

10 A reference to the Doloneia, Book x of Homer's *Iliad*? Or to a recurring *sententia*, such as Book ii, 24–25 = 61–62:

> He should not sleep night long who is a man burdened with counsels and responsibility for a people and cares so numerous.

(Lattimore [1951], pp 76–77), which Petrarch annotated *Audite hoc reges somno dediti ac ventri*—hear this you rulers who are given to sleep and gorging (Nolhac [1907], ii, p. 181; Koerting [1878], p. 477). Note also *Fam.* x, 3, 45. On perpetual vigilance as one of the attributes of kingship, Kantorowicz (1957a), pp. 133–134, 142–143.

11   Suetonius, ii, Aug. 78.

12   Aristotle, *Eth. Nic.* i, 13, 1102 b, 4–11:

> . . . for this part or faculty seems to function most in sleep, while goodness and badness are least manifest in sleep (whence comes the saying that the happy are not better off than the wretched for half their lives; and this happens . naturally enough, since sleep is an inactivity of the soul in that respect in which it is called good or bad), unless perhaps to a small extent some of the movements actually penetrate, and in this respect the dreams of good men are better than those of ordinary people.

Barnes (1984), p. 1741. Petrarch's text was the *translatio vetus* by Robert Grosseteste, Paris, B. N. f. lat. 6458.

13   1492: Iure igitur: ut pars illa pro uiribus evitanda: quae solam inter homines differentiam somniorum linquit sic sectanda contraria est nil difficultatis allatura uolentibus.

1581: Iure igitur ut pars illa pro uiribus evitanda, quae solam inter homines, differentiam linquit: sic sectanda contraria est, nihil difficultatibus allatura uolentibus.

Twyne, f. 28r: Wherefore, as that part is diligently to be eschewed, whiche leaueth so small a difference of dreames onely betweene men and beastes: so is the the contrary to be pursued, whiche offereth no hardnesse to them that are willing.

14   Cf. *Fam.* xx, 4, 27–28:

> alioquin si omnia quibus male utuntur homines, mala essent, quid omnio uspiam non malum? Non corporei sensus, non ingenium, non opes, et hec quibus pascimur alimenta. Ipsa Dei misericordia et patientia abutuntur multi; et sepe quorum natura optima est, nostri perversitate usus est pessimus.

> Otherwise, if everything man puts to evil use would be evil, then what, indeed, would not be evil? Not our bodily senses, not our intellect, not possessions, not the food and drink that nourish us. Even God's patience and mercy are abused by many, and only too often our perverseness exploits things of the very best kind for the worst ends.

Note also *Contra eum*; and *Sen.* iii, 9 (1581: 1074, 799):

> naturae donum hominum perversitate confundi . . .

> to taint Nature's gift with the perverseness of mankind.

Cf. *desiring what is harmful*, below, *DR* i, 89, 11–13, and note 2. On Augustine's notion of "use" and "abuse," Huppé (1959), pp. 6–7; and below, *DR* ii, 74, note 1.

15   . . . *& familiarum patres vigilant, ac nocte consurgunt, quod ad sanitatem atque oeconomiam, & philosophiam utile, ait Aristoteles:* Cf. Pseudo-Aristotle, *Economics* i, 6, 1345a, 12–17, Barnes (1984), ii, p. 2133:

> And since it is good for the formation of character and useful in the interests of economy, masters ought to rise earlier than their slaves and retire to rest later . . . . . . There are occasions when a master should rise while it is still night; for this helps to make a man healthy and wealthy and wise.

As far as I know, this is the only reference to the *Economics* in Petrarch's writings. On the *translatio vetus* of this text and its revision in 1295, known as the *Recensio Durandi,* cf. Weiss (1977), pp. 61, 91; and Kretzmann (1982), p. 64. Note also Susemihl (1887) and Hauréau (1881). Thus far, it has not been established that the work was in Petrarch's library. More research needs to be done on this, and on Petrarch's use of the maxim (e.g., Whiting [1968], R 143).

16   Horace, *Ep.* i, 2, 32–33:

> ut iugulent hominem, surgunt de nocte latrones:
> ut te ipsum serves, non expergisceris?

LCL, Fairclough, p. 265. 1581 italicizes only the first line; Twyne, f. 28r, both. 1492 gives the text correctly with *ut,* which is left out in 1581.

17   See above, note 12. Cf. also Seneca, *Ep.* 99, 11; Pliny, *Nat. hist.* vii, 50, 167, xxxvi, 1, 3, as below, *DR* i, 30, note 8.

18   Jerome, *Ep.* 22, 37:

> Noctibus bis terque surgendum, revolvenda de scripturis, quae memoriter tenemus.

19   1492: Denique his studiis fatigati oculi alterno sopore recreandi: & breui quiete recreati alterno exertitio fatigandi erunt: ne totis noctibus dormiendo: culcitrae incumbendo: sepulta cadauera uideamini: motu crebro atque honesto uos uiuos: & uirtuti deditos comprobate. &c.

      1581: Denique his studiis fatigati, oculi alterno sopore recreandi erunt, ne totis noctibus dormiendo, culcitrae incumbendo, sepulta cadauera uideamini, motu crebro, atque honesto uos uiuos, & uirtuti deditos comprobate.

22 ❖ PLEASANT ODORS

1   Dialogues 22–28 deal with pleasures.

2   Reason may refer to Aristotle, *Eth. Nic.* (Book vii?). Twyne, f. 29r, translates: If ever thou hast applyed thy mynde to the readyng of Heathen writers.

3   Reason refers to the *notae* of the ancient method of memorizing through
visualizing written marks on a tablet or page. Cf. Martianus Capella, v, 539,
Dick (1925), p. 269:

> . . . ut scribamus ipsi quae facile volumus retinere; deinde ut, si longiora
> fuerint, quae sunt ediscenda, divisa per partes facilius inhaerescant; tum ap-
> ponere notas rebus singulis oportebit in his, quae volumus maxime retinere;
> nec voce magna legenda sunt, sed murmure potius meditanda; et nocte magis
> quam interdiu maturius excitari memoriam manifestum est, cum et late silen-
> tium iuvat, nec foras a sensibus avocatur intentio.

> . . . we should write down the things we wish easily to retain. Also, when the
> material to be remembered is rather lengthy, it sticks to the mind more readily
> if divided into sections. In that case it is useful to place *notae* against the
> specific items we wish to retain most. These should not be read out loud, but
> reflected upon with hardly a murmur. And, obviously, it is better to exercise
> the memory not during the day, but at night, when we are aided by silence
> everywhere, and our attention is not distracted by other sense impressions.

Cf. Yates (1966), p. 51. Note Quintilian, *Inst. orat.* xi, 2, 23–26.

4   On moderation, above, *DR* i, 2, note 25.

5   Terence, *Andria* i, 61. Cf. above, *DR* i, 5, note 1.

6   Pliny, *Nat. hist.* vii, 2, 25:

> Ad extremos fines Indiae ab oriente circa fontem Gangis Astomorum gentem
> sine ore, corpore toto hirtam, vestiri frondium lanugine, halitu tantum
> viventem et odore quem naribus trahant; nullum illis cibum nullumque potum,
> radicum tantum florumque varios odores et silvestrium malorum, quae secum
> portant longiore itinere ne desit olfactus; graviore paulo odore haut difficulter
> exanimari.

> At the extreme boundary of India to the East, near the source of the Ganges,
> . . . the Astomi tribe, that has no mouth and a body hairy all over; they dress
> in cottonwool and live only on the air they breathe and the scent they inhale
> through their nostrils; they have no food or drink except the different odours of
> the roots and flowers and wild apples, which they carry with them on their
> longer journeys so as not to lack a supply of scent; . . . they can easily be
> killed by a rather stronger odour than usual.

LCL, Rackham, p. 523. This passage directly precedes one (vii, 2, 26) referred
to below, *DR* ii, Pref., 54–55, and note 13.

7   Cf. Catullus 68, 144: *Fragrantem Assyrio venit odore domum;* Tibullus i, 3:
Non soror, Assyrios cineri quae dedat odores; and Propertius, ii, 19: *Afflabunt
tibi non Arabum de gramine odores, / sed quos ipse suis fecit Amor manibus.*
Petrarch read in this Solinus (46, 1):

> Nam ibi copias Darii fudit, ipsumque subegit expugnatisque eius castris in

reliquo apparatu regis repperit scrinium unguentis refertum, unde primum Romana luxuria fecit ingressum ad odores peregrinos.

Now here [at Arbela, the Assyrian headquarters of Darius III in 331 B.C.], the forces of Darius were wiped out, he was defeated, and in his conquered quarters, among his regal treasures, a chest was found, full of ointments—which introduced Rome to the scent of strange perfumes for the first time.

The corresponding passage in Pliny, *Nat. hist.* xiii, 3, reads:

unguentum Persarum gentis esse debet; illi madent eo et accersita commendatione inluvie natum virus extingunt. Primum, quod equidem inveniam, castris Darii regis expugnatis in reliquo eius apparatu Alexander cepit scrinium unguentorum. Postea voluptas eius a nostris quoque inter lautissima atque etiam honestissima vitae bona admissa est, honosque et ad defunctos pertinere coepit . . .

Perfume ought by right to be accredited to the Persian race: they soak themselves in it, and quench the odor produced from dirt by its adventitious attraction. The first case that I am able to discover was when a chest of perfumes was captured by Alexander among the rest of the property of King Darius when his camp was taken. Afterwards the pleasure of perfume was also admitted by our fellow countrymen as well as among the most elegant and also most honorable enjoyments of life, and even began to be an appropriate tribute to the dead . . .

LCL, Rackham, p. 99. On the victor vanquished, *Fam.* xi, 16, 23; and *DR* i, 37, 135–138, i, 42, 80–86, i, 53, 35–40, i, 100, 14–20, ii, 9, 110–112, ii, 32, 26–28, *DR* i, 106, notes 4 and 6.

8   Pliny, *Nat. hist.* xiii, 5:

Quando id primum ad Romanos penetravit non facile dixerim. Certum est Antiocho rege Asiaque devictis urbis anno DLXV P. Licinium Crassum L. Iulium Caesarem censores edixisse ne quis venderet unguenta exotica: sic enim appelavere.

I could not readily say when the use of unguents first made its way to Rome. It is certain that in 188 B.C. after the defeat of Seleucid King Antiochus (III) and Asia (i.e., "Syria"), the censors Publius Licinius Crassus and Lucius Julius Caesar issued a proclamation forbidding any sale of "foreign essences"—that being the regular name for them.

LCL, Rackham, p. 113. Pliny's story is repeated by Polydore Vergil, *De rerum inventoribus* i, 18.

9   Cf. Cicero, *Ep. ad Att.* ii, 1, 1:

ut mulieres ideo bene olere, quia nihil olebant, videbantur.

just as women were thought to have the best scent, who used no scent.

LCL, Winstedt, p. 101.

10   Suetonius, viii, Vesp. 8, 3:

>   Ac ne quam occasionem corrigendi disciplinam praetermitteret, adulescen-
>   tulum fragrantem unguento, cum sibi pro impetrata praefectura gratias ageret,
>   nutu aspernatus, voce etiam gravissima increpuit: "Maluissem alium oboluisses
>   [1492, 1581: oboleuisses]," litterasque revocavit.

>   To let slip no opportunity of improving military discipline, when a young man
>   reeking with perfumes came to thank him for a commission which had been
>   given him, Vespasian drew back his head in disgust, adding the stern repri-
>   mand: "I would rather you had smelt of garlic"; and revoked the appointment.

LCL, Rolfe, p. 301.

11   Reason recounts Pliny, *Nat. hist.* xiii, 5:

>   L. Plotium, L. Planci bis consulis censorisque fratrem, proscriptum a triumviris
>   in Salernitana latebra unguenti odore proditum constat, quo dedecore tota
>   absoluta proscriptio est; quis enim non merito iudicet perisse tales?

>   It is a well-known fact that Lucius Plotius, the brother of Lucius Plancus who
>   was twice consul and censor, when proscribed by the Triumvirs was given
>   away in his hiding-place at Salerno by the scent of the unguent he had been
>   using—a disgrace that acquitted the entire proscription of guilt, for who would
>   not consider that people of that sort deserved to die?

LCL, Rackham, p. 113.

12   Cf. above, *DR* i, 20, note 8.

13   Florus, i, 22, 12.

14   Luc. 7, 37–38:

>   Et ecce mulier, quae erat in civitate peccatrix, ut cognovit quod accubuisset in
>   domo pharisaei, attulit alabastrum unguenti; et stans retro secus pedes eius,
>   lacrymis coepit rigare pedes eius, et capillis capitis sui tergebat, et osculabatur
>   pedes eius et unguento ungebat.

>   And behold a woman that was in the city, a sinner, when she knew that he
>   [Jesus] sat at meat in the Pharisee's house, brought an alabaster box of oint-
>   ment; and standing behind at his feet, she began to wash his feet, with tears,
>   and wiped them with the hairs of her head, and kissed his feet, and anointed
>   them with the ointment.

15   Prov. 27, 9: *Unguento et variis odoribus delectatur cor.* This describes also the
reaction of Stupeus in *Buc. carm.* iii, 12–14.

16   Augustine, *Conf.* x, 32, *PL* 32, c. 799:

>   De illecebra odorum non satago nimis. Cum absunt, non requiro; cum adsunt,
>   non respuo, paratus etiam eis semper carere.

Oates (1948), i, p. 171.

23 ❖ SWEET MUSIC

1　Published separately, Rawski (1971), in slightly different form and with more inclusive commentary, some of which is used here, with permission. —As far as Reason's contributions to the subject are concerned, it is instructive to read the remarks on music by Petrarch's younger contemporary Nicole Oresme (c. 1323–1382; Grant [1966], pp. 3–10; Sarton [1975], iii, pp. 1486–1497) in his *De configurationibus* ii, 23 and 24, Clagett (1968), pp. 304–335, 478–479. (Oresme, one of the greatest men of science of his time, for long, was credited with the first French translation of the *DR*, produced actually by Jean Daudin upon the orders of Charles V. Cf. Fowler [1916], p. 18.)

2　Cf. Eccl. 7, 3–7; *Fam.* xxii, 8, 6; and *DR* i, 27, 50–53, i, 77, 53–56, i, 85, 75–79, ii, 113, 3–5. Note Jacobus de Voragine, *Legenda aurea* xi, 3, Graesse (1890), p. 68:

> Haec est vera mutatio dextre excelsi, dum cantus moeroris vertitur in canticum laudis

> This is truly a turn of things wrought by the hand of the Almighty, when the chants of mourning are changed into songs of praise.

3　*Cantibus sonisque permulceor* echoes Augustine's *et multa canere ac sonare* (*De musica* i, 4, 6) and Isidore's definition *musica est peritia modulationis sono cantuque consistens* (*Etym.* iii, 15, 1). Isidore elaborates: *Cantus est inflexio vocis, nam sonus directus est; praecedit autem sonus cantum* (*Etym.* iii, 19, 8)—music is the skill of rhythmic motion using sound and song; song being the melodious use of the voice, but sound denoting straightforward sonority, hence superordinate to song. Cf. Fontaine (1959), i, pp. 418–420.

4　Petrarch applies to Herodotus this Ciceronian epithet also in the *Triumph of Fame* iii, 58. In his copy of Ausonius, *Ludus septem sapientium*, Petrarch noted under the miniature of the last of the seven sages: *Hic est Periander, ille amicus Arionis fidicinis, cuius fabulam scripsit Herodotus*—This is Periander, the friend of the musician Arion, whose story was written by Herodotus (Nolhac [1907], i, p. 208).

5　Reason refers to Herodotus, i, 23–24, but tells the Arion story after Aulus Gellius, xvi, 19 (= *Gesta Romanorum* 148, Oesterley [1872], p. 506). Petrarch may have been aware of Pliny's endorsement of the credibility of the incident, *Nat. hist.* ix, 8, 28, and of the reference in Augustine, *De civ. Dei* i, 14. In *Fam.* iii, 22, 6, written in 1346, Petrarch refers to

> Arionem quendam tergo huius piscis insidentem per tumidos fluctus mari

evasisse historica seu potius fabulosa narratio est. Vectorem ipsum fidibus canentem faciunt, quo navigationi facilior fides sit, mulcente auras musica et navigium sublevante. Visum est enim fabulam non admitti, nisi color mendacio quaereretur: gubernaculum, malus, vela, remi deerant: pro his omnibus unius musicae suavitas subrogata est.

And there is a historical or rather a fabulous story about a certain Arion who seated on the back of this fish rides about the crashing waves of the sea. And it is said that this unusual passenger sings to the lyre, the instrument making the voyage easier, the music charming the ears and lifting the unusual vessel over the surface of the water. Such a story, it appears, could not be accepted except as fable, for instead of rudder, mast, sail, and oars there was only the sweetness of music.

Bernardo (1975), p. 170.

6   George Gascoigne, *The Grief of Joye* (1576), Cunliffe, ii (1914), pp. 511–557, iv: The varieties of Activityes 14, lines 1–2:

> Alas alas, who sooner dothe deceave,
> Then doe the *Cirenes* wth theire sugred songes?

The remarks on the passages dealing with music in this poem in Hollander (1961), pp. 108–110, should be read with awareness of the fact that Gascoigne's lines are largely based on the present dialogue. On the Sirens, below, *DR* i, 62, note 2. Cf. also, *DR* ii, 97, 22–24; and *Sen.* xv, 3 (1581: 934): *quasi a Sirenum cantibus.*

7   Cf. above, *DR* i, 9, 82–87; and *DR* ii, 97, 35, ii 103, 28–30.

8   On the soothing fowler, Augustine, *De magistro* x, 32, *PL* 32, c. 1213. Closely related to our text (and Gascoigne's elaboration, ibid., iv, 13, lines 3–5) is one of the *Dicta Catonis* (i, 27):

> Noli homines blando nimium sermone probare:
> fistula dulce canit, volucrem dum decipit auceps.

> Approve not men who wheedling nothings say:
> Fowlers pipe sweetly to delude their prey.

LCL, Duff, p. 601. Cited in John of Salisbury, *Policrat.* iii, 10, *PL* 199, c. 497. On this, Nolhac (1907), ii, p. 110, n. 2. On *mulcendo fallere*, also *Contra medicum* iii, 35, Ricci (1950), p. 59. Note Schapiro (1979), pp. 177–195, esp. nn. 124, 126, 136.

9   Gascoigne, *The Grief of Joye* (1576), iv, 18, 1–5:

> The Serpent tickleth whome she list to sting/
> The Surgeon stroketh whome he meanes to strike,/
> The fowler whistleth whome he fayne would wryng,
> The *Polipus* (with colling) drawes in dike,
> The dazled wyghts whome she (to drowne) doth like/

On polyps drowning humans, Pliny, *Nat. hist.* ix, 48, 91. The mood of the text suggests Ambrose, *Hexaemeron* v, 8, 21, *PL* 14, c. 229.

10   Suetonius, viii, Domitian, 11.

11   Prov. 14, 13:

> Risus dolore miscebitur,
> et *extrema gaudii luctus occupat.*

Note also Boethius, *Cons. phil.* iii, P 7, 7; John of Salisbury, *Policrat.* iii, 8, *PL* 199, c. 489; Boccaccio, *Decameron*, i, Intr., Singleton (1982), p. 7, v, 1, Singleton (1974), 61v A, 24–27, Singleton (1982), p. 374; Chaucer, *Cant. Tales*, Nun's Priest's Tale 3205, Man of Law's Tale 422–427; Whiting (1968), J58–J61; and the generalization in Johannes von Tepl, *Ackerm.* xii, 24–29, xxii, 22–24, Walshe (1951), pp. 13, 27. Cf. *DR* i, Pref., note 5, ii, 113, 3–5; *Rime* 71, 87, *Rime* (1951), p. 104; *Secretum* i, *Prose* (1955), p. 60; and *Sen.* xv, 3 (1581: 935):

> neque audiunt Dauid. Adhuc (inquit) escae eorum erant in ore ipsorum, & ira Dei ascendit super eos, neque illud uulgatum: *Extrema gaudii luctus occupat.* Et quid tibi uis? His atque aliis, sed obseruatione in primis humanarum rerum quotidie magis assentior Graio uati, qui quando huc loquendo peruentum erat, praetereundus non fuit. Is ergo Odysseae libro xviii. Nil (inquit) miserius terra nutrit homine.

Neither do they listen to David, who said:

> As yet their meat was in their mouth
> and the wrath of God came upon them

[Ps. 77, 30–31]; nor to the well-known line that

> mourning taketh hold of the end of joy

[Prov. 14, 13]. What else do you want? I agree with these thoughts and others, but foremost among them, I approve more and more every day the remark about the condition of man by the Greek seer, who did not ignore the issue when he said in Book xviii of his *Odyssey*: The earth does not foster anything more miserable than man [*Odyssey* xviii, 130–131, Lattimore (1977), p. 273].

Cf. *Posteritati*, *Sen.* xviii, 1, *Prose* (1955), p. 18; and below, *DR* ii, 111, 13–14. —The second quotation is from Prov. 16, 18:

> Contritionem praecedit superbia,
> et *ante ruinam exaltatur spiritus.*

Cf. *Africa* vi, Death of Mago, 889 *et seq.*; and *DR* i, 5, 45, i, 107, note 8.

12   Cf. Gascoigne, note 28, below. The topic of the mournful song of the dying

swan is traced in Rawski (1971), p. 311, n. 17. Note also *Fam.* xviii, 6, 2; *Buc. carm.* x, 308–310; and below, *DR* ii, 119, 72–75, and note 17.

13 This sentence is repeated *ad summam* below, *DR* i, 90, 49. Cf. also *DR* i, 29, 39–47, i, 83, 18–23. On cases of people who died of joy, *DR* i, 29, note 9, i, 83, note 2; Livy, xxii, 7, 13; Aulus Gellius, iii, 15; Valerius Maximus, ix, 12, 2, and Ext. 5; and Pliny, *Nat. hist.* vii, 52, 180; 32, 119—as pointed out by Petrarch in *Var.* 32, Fracassetti, iii (1863), p. 390:

> Quid dicemus de illis matribus, quas Romana narrat historia, post insignem cladem quae ad Trasimenum, ut Livius tradit, cui potius fidem do, et quem Valerius sequitur, vel Cannis, ut Plinio placet, est accepta, nunciatis filiorum mortibus, attonitas flevisse: utramque autem post aliquantulum temporis, alteram scilicet moestam domi sedentem praeter spem conspecto filio, dum in occursum eius assurgit, exanimem corruisse, alteram percunctandi studio anxiam, extraque muros urbis egressam porta Flaminia, qua fusae redibant legiones, obvio repente filio, dum irruit in amplexus expirasse?

> What shall we say about those mothers, who, Roman history tells us, cried bitterly when told of the death of their sons—after the terrible debacle at Lake Trasimene [217 B.C.], as Livy records, whom I trust above all others and whom Valerius Maximus follows, or after Cannae [216 B.C.], if we accept Pliny's statement: later on, one who sat sadly at home, no sooner beheld her son against all expectation and rose to meet him, as she fell down bereft of life; the other one, who, anxious to find out, had gone outside the walls of the city by the Flaminian gate, where the shattered legions were returning, on suddenly seeing her son safe and sound, expired as she rushed to embrace him.

Note also Heitmann (1958), p. 175, n. 124. On contemporary medical views regarding extreme joy, Olson (1982), chap. 2, esp. p. 44.

14 *Cantu ac tibiis delector* corresponds with Joy's opening statement, *cantus delector ac fidibus*. *Fides* and *tibiae* are juxtaposed in Ciceronian texts, such as *De orat.* iii, 197, and many later sources (e.g., Quintilian, *Inst. orat.* xi, 3; and Martianus Capella, *De nuptiis* ii, 117, ix, 923). The usage reflects the ancient distinction between the dignified music of the kithara and the more impassioned strains of the aulos, which appears also in the Scriptures:

> et ablata est voluptas a Jacob, et defecit ibi tibia et cithara.

> and joy was taken away from Jacob, and the pipe and harp ceased there.

I Mach. 3, 45.

15 Statius, *Thebaid* vi, 118–122:

> Iamque pari cumulo geminas hanc tristibus umbris.
> ast illam superis aequus labor auxerat aras,
> cum signum luctus cornu grave mugit adunco
> *tibia, cui teneros suetum producere manes*
> lege Phrygum maesta.

> Two altars now of equal height had they with like toil erected,
> one to the doleful shades, the other to the gods above,
> when the low braying of the pipe with curved horn
> gave signal for lament, the pipe that by Phrygia's mournful use
> was wont to escort the youthful dead.

LCL, Mozley, p. 69. Verses 120 and 121 are quoted in Boethius, *De inst. mus.* i, Friedlein (1867), p. 186, 23–24.

16 Cf. above, *passim,* e.g., *DR* i, 1, i, 4, 18, and i, 6, 13.

17 Cf. W. C. Printz (1690), p. 174:

> Und *Franciscus Petrarcha de Remediis prosperae fortunae* spricht: Es ist ohne Zweifel die Music in denen wohlgearteten Gemuethern der Menschen ueber alle Massen maechtig: aber die Wuerckung /mehr/ als man glauben kan/ mancherley.

On the effects of music, also *Buc. carm.* iv, esp. 44–49, on *cithare solatio.*

18 Augustine, *Conf.* ix, 6, 14, *PL* 32, c. 769. Cf. also ibid. ix, 7, 17, and x, 33, 59.

19 Augustine, *Conf.* x, 33, 50, *PL* 32, c. 800.

20 Augustine, *Conf.* ix, 7, 15, *PL* 32, c. 770.

21 Augustine, *Conf.* x, 33, 49–50, *PL* 32, cc. 799–800. Cf. Wagner (1911), i, pp. 31–33; and the list of documentary data in Apel (1958), pp. 38–42. —The whole passage recurs in altered sequence in Gascoigne's poetic translation, *The Grief of Joye* (1576), iv, 16 and 17:

> For *Ambrose* first the use thereof requires,
> Yn everie churche, and all the world abowt/
> But *Athenase,* forbadd the same throughowt/
> Att last came *Austine,* like a dreamyng Dadd,
> And dyed in doubt, yf it were good or badd/
> Yt is a trewth, and cannott be denyed,
> That *Musicke* styrres. some mynds to godly thought./
> Yt is as trew, and hathe byn often tryed,
> That *Musicke* styrres, moe mynds to be but nought/

22 Cicero, *Tusc. disp.* i, 2, 4, note 23, below. Reason refers to Cicero but follows the order of exposition in Isidore, *Etym.* iii, 16: (2) *eratque tam turpe Musicam nescire quam litteras:* followed by (3) *in conviviis vero lyra vel cithara circumferebatur.*

23 Petrarch, *Rer. mem. libri* i, 1, 7. Cf. Cicero, *Tusc. disp.* i, 2, 4:

> Summam eruditionem Graeci sitam censebant in nervorum vocumque cantibus: igitur et Epaminondas princeps meo iudicio Graeciae *fidibus praeclare cecinisse* dicitur Themistoclesque aliquot ante annos, cum *in epulis recusaret lyram, est habitus indoctior.* Ergo in Graecia musici floruerunt discebantque id omnes nec qui nesciebat satis excultus doctrina putabatur.

The Greeks held that the proof of the highest education was found in instrumental and vocal music: thus it is that Epaminondas, to my mind the leading man in Greek history, was, we are told, an accomplished singer to the accompaniment of the harp, whilst Themistocles, to go back many years previously, was held to show a lack of culture in refusing to play the lyre at banquets. Musicians accordingly flourished in Greece; everyone would learn music, and the man who was unacquainted with the art was not regarded as completely educated.

LCL, King, p. 7.

24 Petrarch, *Rer. mem. libri* i, 1, 9; *Fam.* xvii, 8, 5; *Sen.* i, 5 (1581: 744). The story comes from Plato, Euthydemus 272 c, Hamilton-Cairns (1961), p. 387, and is referred to by Cicero, *Ep. fam.* ix, 22, 3, and *De sen.* viii, 26; and by Quintilian, *Inst. orat.* i, 10, 14. Reason's terminology points to Valerius Maximus, viii, 7, ext. 8:

> Socratem etiam constat aetate prouectum *fidibus* tractandis *operam dare* coepisse satius iudicantem eius artis usum sero quam nunquam percipere . . .

> Even Socrates, as everyone knows, began to practice playing the harp at advanced age, because he thought it was better to learn the art late than never.

25 Reason tells the Alcibiades story (Plutarch, *Alcib.* ii, 4–5) after Aulus Gellius, xv, 17, 1–2:

> Alcibiades Atheniensis, cum apud *avunculum Periclem* puer artibus ac disciplinis liberalibus erudietur et arcessi Pericles Antigenidam tibicinem iussisset, ut eum canere tibiis, quod *honestissimum* tum videbatur, doceret, traditas sibi tibias, cum ad os adhibuisset *inflassetque*, pudefactus oris *deformitate* abiecit *infregitque*. Ea res cum percrebuisset, omnium tum Atheniensium consensu disciplina tibiis canendi desita est.

> Alcibiades the Athenian in his boyhood was being trained in the liberal arts and sciences at the home of his uncle, Pericles; and Pericles had ordered Antigenides, a player on pipes, to be sent for, to teach the boy to play on that instrument, which was then considered a great accomplishment. But when the pipes were handed to him and he had put them to his lips and blown, disgusted with the ugly distortion of his face, he threw them away and broke them in two. When this matter was noised abroad, by the universal consent of the Athenians of that time the art of playing the pipes was given up.

LCL, Rolfe, p. 101.

26 I.t.: Gaius. Suetonius, iv, Caligula, 11 and 54.

27 Suetonius, vi, Nero, 20, 1 *et passim*.

28 Suetonius, ibid., 49, 1. Suetonius has *qualis artifex pereo*—what an artist the world is losing (LCL, Rolfe, p. 177; cf. also John of Salisbury, *Policrat.* viii, 19, *PL* 199, c. 790); Reason substitutes *musicus*, which Gascoigne translates into English (*The Grief of Joye* [1576], iv, 23–24):

And wonderfull, it is that *Neroes* mynde
Which all the world (and more) coulde not suffize
Was never seene, so playnly to be pynde,
As *Musicke* set, the same before owre eyes/
Soe greate a kyng, to dye in hastie wyse,
Ytt greeved hym nott: but that so sweete a synger,
Should dye so sone: that sorrowe seemde a stynger./
And lyke the Swanne, he soong before his deathe/

29   *Venit tamen aurium voluptas: qua caste ac sobrie delectari humanitas quedam.*
On *aurium voluptas*—pleasure of the ear (= *DR* ii, 97, 63; *Sen.* xi, 5 [1581:
885])—cf. Lactantius, *Div. inst.* vi, 21, *PL* 6, c. 713; and Augustine, *Conf.* x,
33, 49, *PL* 32, cc. 799–800. *Humanitas quedam* may echo the Boethian *nihil
est enim tam proprium humanitatis* (cf. Cicero, *De orat.* i, 8, 32) *quam remitti
dulcibus modis, adstringi contrariis* (*De inst. mus.* i, 1, Friedlein, p. 179, 23–
25; cf. Macrobius, *Comm. somn. Scip.* ii, 3, 7).

30   Augustine, *Enarr. in Ps.* 32, 8, 3, *PL* 36, c. 283:

> Quid est in iubilatione canere? Intelligere, verbis explicare non posse quod
> canitur corde . . . Jubilum sonus quidam est significans cor parturire quod
> dicere non potest. Et quem decet ista iubilatio nisi ineffabilem Deum? Inef-
> fabilis enim est, quem fari non potes: et si cum fari non potes, et tacere non
> debes, quid restat nisi ut iubiles; ut gaudeat cor sine verbis, et immensa la-
> titudo gaudiorum metas non habeat syllabarum?

> What does it mean to sing *in iubilatione?* What the heart sings cannot be
> readily grasped and put into words. The sound of the *jubilus* indicates what the
> heart desires to bring forth, what cannot be said. And whom befits this jubila-
> tion if not inexpressible God. Inexpressible He is, because language fails you,
> and if language fails you, but you must not remain silent, what is there left save
> to jubilate—when the heart delights without words, and the immense vastness
> of its joys cannot be reduced to syllables?

Note also idem in Ps. 99, *PL* 37, c. 1272, as in Wagner (1911), i, pp. 37–38;
Apel (1958), p. 267; and Nicole Oresme, *Livre du ciel* ii, 18, esp. 126a–126d,
Menut (1968), pp. 480–485. —On *here and there,* above, *DR* i, 18, note 3.

31   Reference is made to Plato, *Tim.* 28–30 = Chalcidius, *Comm. Tim.* 73; *Repub-
lic* x, 617; Aristotle, *De coelo* ii, 9; and Cicero, *De re publica* vi, 18 =
Macrobius, *Comm.* ii, 1, 8. On this, Mâle (1978), pp. 316–319; J. Haar in
Wiener (1973), iv, pp. 38–42; Rawski (1971), pp. 315–316; Spitzer (1963);
and Allers (1944), pp. 375–376. Note also John of Salisbury, *Policrat.* i, 6;
Roman de la Rose 16939–16954, Dahlberg (1971), pp. 284–285; and Nicole
Oresme, *De commens.* iii, Grant (1971), pp. 297–305, and *Livre du ciel* ii, 18,
124d–126d, Menut (1968), pp. 477–485.

32   The *harmonia coelestis* cannot be heard by humans: Aristotle, *De coelo* ii, 9;
Cicero, *De re publ.* vi, 18, 18–19; Macrobius, *Comm.* ii, 4, 14–15; Boethius,

De inst. mus. i, 2, Friedlein (1867, p. 187, 24–25; and Nicole Oresme, *De commens.* iii, Grant (1971), pp. 302, 232–304, 261, and *Livre du ciel* ii, 18, esp. 126c, Menut (1968), pp. 482–483. Petrarch refers to *coelestis harmonia* in *Sen.* xi, 5 (to Guglielmo Maramaldo, Padua, November 9, 1368; 1581: 885); and, in 1364, in *Misc.* 18, to a monastic choir, which

> tam dulciter canit, tam suaviter psallit, tamque divinis cantibus solemnia celebrat, ut celestem videatur armoniam imitari.

> sang so pleasantly, chanted so sweetly, and rendered the sacred melodies so solemnly, that it sounded like celestial harmony itself.

Speculum 37 (1962), p. 241.

33 On the music of the angels *alter ad alterum, una voce, sine fine*, see Hammerstein (1962), pp. 44–47; and Hammerstein (1974), pp. 15–16.

34 1492: pertinere. &c.
    1581: pertinere.
    Plato, *Republic* iv, 424 b–c:

> To put it briefly, then, said I, it is to this that the overseers of our state must cleave and be watchful against its insensible corruption. They must throughout be watchful against innovations in music and gymnastics counter to the established order, and to the best of their power guard against them, fearing when anyone says that that song is most regarded among men "which hovers newest on the singer's lips" (Homer, *Odyssey* i, 351), lest haply it be supposed that the poet means not new songs but a new way of song and is commending this. But we must not praise that sort of thing nor conceive it to be the poet's meaning. For a change to a new type of music is something to beware of as a hazard of all our fortunes. For the modes of music are never disturbed without unsettling of the most fundamental political and social conventions, as Damon affirms and as I am convinced.

Hamilton-Cairns (1961), pp. 665–666; but consider also ibid. iii, 398 c through 403 c, pp. 643–648—either text suggesting that Petrarch's knowledge of the *Republic* did extend further than the well-known reference to *Republic* iii, 398 a in *Contra med.* iii, 270–275, which is based on Cicero, *Tusc. disp.* ii, 11, 27, and Augustine, *De civ. Dei* viii, 13 (Ricci [1950], p. 66; Weiss [1977], p. 182). Petrarch returns to the subject in *De vita sol.* i, *Prose* (1955), p. 388; and in *Sen.* xiv, 1 (1581: 384), where he cites at length Cicero, *De leg.* iii (14, 31–32, LCL, Keyes, pp. 494–497), as *consentaneus atque conveniens locus*—a pertinent and suitable text—on the fact that the *mores* of the rulers are imitated by the citizenry, hence

> mali mores principum, non eis tandem, sed omnibus sunt damnosi.

> the immoral conduct of princes is not only ruinous for them, but for everyone in their realm.

On Cicero's views, as opposed to Plato's, Wille (1967), ix, 127. Cf. also Boethius, *De inst. mus.* i, 1, Friedlein (1867), p. 181, 20; Strunk (1950), pp. 80–81; and the summary of Boethius, Book i, in Wille (1967), pp. 656–678.

24 ❖ DANCING

1   Cf. above, *DR* i, 23, 40–44, and note 18.
2   1492: te choream ducere: uel cernere: neque tibicinem audire
      1581: te choream cernere, neque tibicinem audire

Reason refers to a choral dance, such as Deduit's carol described in the *Roman de la Rose* (Dahlberg [1971], 727–776, and note on p. 362; on this, Fleming [1969], pp. 82–85). On choral dances and their typology, Sachs (1937), pp. 142–171 *et passim*.

3   An allusion to ii Reg. 6, 14–23:

> Et David saltabat totis viribus ante Dominum; porro David erat accinctus ephod lineo.
> Et David et omnis domus Israel ducebant arcam testamenti Domini in jubilo et in clangore buccinae.
> Cumque intrasset arca Domini in civitatem David, Michol, filia Saul, prospiciens per fenestram, vidit regem David subsilientem atque saltantem coram Domino, et despexit eum in corde suo. . . . . . .
>
> Reversusque est David ut benediceret domui suae. Et egressa Michol, filia Saul, in occursum David, ait: Quam gloriosus fuit hodie rex Israel, discooperiens se ante ancillas servorum suorum, et nudatus est quasi si nudetur unus de scurris! Dixitque David ad Michol: Ante Dominum, qui elegit me potius quam patrem tuum et quam omnem domum ejus, et praecepit mihi ut esse dux super populum Domini in Israel,
> et ludam et vilior fiam plus quam factus sum; et ero humilis in oculis meis, et cum ancillis de quibus locuta es, gloriosior apparebo.
> Igitur Michol, filiae Saul, non est natus filius usque in diem mortis suae.

> And David danced with all his might before the Lord: and David was girded with a linen ephod.
> And David and all the house of Israel brought the ark of the covenant of the Lord with joyful shouting, and with sound of trumpet.
> And when the ark of the Lord was come into the city of David, Michol the

daughter of Saul, looking out through a window, saw king David leaping and dancing before the Lord: and she despised him in her heart. . . . . . .

And David returned to bless his own house: and Michol the daughter of Saul coming out to meet David, said: How glorious was the king of Israel to day, uncovering himself before the handmaids of his servants, and was naked, as if one of the buffoons should be naked.

And David said to Michol: Before the Lord who chose me rather than thy father, and than all his house, and commanded me to be ruler over the people of the Lord in Israel,

I will both play and make myself meaner than I have done: and I will be little in my own eyes: and with the handmaids, of whom thou speakest, I shall appear more glorious.

Therefore Michol the daughter of Saul had no child to the day of her death.

Dante places the dancing, "naked" David among his l'imagini de tante umilitadi (Div. Comm., Purg. x, 64–69, 98):

. . .   . . . l'umile salmista,
e più e men che re era in quel caso.

. . .   . . . the humble Psalmist,
and on that occasion he was both more and less than king.

Singleton (1973), p. 103. On this, ibid., Commentary, pp. 206–210; Mazzotta (1979), chap. 6; and Steger (1961), pp. 25–26, 76–77, without any consideration of contemporary exegetic commentary such as Gregory, Moral. v, 27, 46, 77, as quoted in Singleton (1973), Commentary, pp. 207–208. —In the Roman de la Rose xi, 21021–21059, Pygmalion sings, plays his instruments, and dances before the ivory image he made. Cf. Fleming (1969), pp. 228–237; and Robertson (1962), pp. 99–103, 157–158. On pandura, the Egyptian lute, which Isidore, Etym. iii, 21, 8, incorrectly identifies as a wind instrument, Wille (1967), pp. 216–217, 642, 713.

4   These are not Cicero's motus animi, but the motus loculares. The source passage is probably Plato, Tim. 34a, Hamilton-Cairns (1961), p. 1164; and Waszink (1962), p. 26 et seq. On this, Chalcidius (Waszink, ibid., 186, p. 165 = Macrobius, Comm. i, 6, 91) comments as follows:

Etenim loculares motus septem sunt, opinor: duo quidem juxta longitudinem, id est ante et post, duo item alii per latitudinem, in dextram et sinistram, duoque alii juxta profunditatem, sursum et deorsum, et ultimus supra memoratae circumactioni similis, qui fixo circumuolat cardine.

I believe that there are seven motions in space, namely, two according to linear sequence, i.e., before and after; further, two according to lateral position, right and left; and two in vertical direction, above and below. The last one of the seven, mentioned above, is rotation circling around a fixed point.

Reason appears to be aware of the further explanation in Macrobius, *Saturn.* vii, 9, 3–4.

> septem . . . corporei motus sunt. Aut enim accedit priorsum aut retrorsum recedit, aut in dexteram laevamve devertitur, aut sursum promovet aut deorsum, aut orbiculatim rotetur. Ex his septem motibus unus tantum in divinis corporibus invenitur, sphaeralem dico, quo movetur caelum, quo sidera, quo cetera moventur elementa. Terrenis animalibus illi sex praecipue familiares sunt, sed non nunquam adhibetur et septimus. Sed sex illi ut directi, ita et innoxii; septimus id est qui gyros efficit, crebro conversu turbat et umoribus capitis involvit spiramentum quod animam cerebro quasi omnes corporis sensus gubernanti ministrat.

> The body . . . is capable of making seven movements: it can go forward or backward; turn to the right or to the left; move upward and downward, or rotate in a circle. Of these seven movements only one is found in the heavenly bodies—the rotating movement, which is the movement of the sky, the stars, and the rest of the elements. Creatures that live on the earth are best acquainted with the first six, although they occasionally make use of the seventh as well; and those six, being movements in a straight line, have no ill effects. But the seventh, the circular movement, with its repeated turnings, confuses—and involves in the humors of the head—the spirit that supplies the vital principle to the brain which is the director, so to speak, of all the bodily senses.

Davies (1969), p. 479. Cf. also Martianus Capella, vii, 736. On the perpetual cycle of days, months, and years as a model of eternity, Plato, *Tim.* 37d–39d; and Chalcidius, 178, pp. 162–164. Cf. Stock (1972), p. 160.

5   As a punishment for attempting violence upon Juno, the king of the Lapithae, Ixion, in the underworld, was bound to a fiery wheel which rolled without cease. When Orpheus descended into Tartarus in search of his Eurydice, he "temporarily suspended the tortures of the damned" (Graves [1955], 28.d., i, p. 112). Cf. Ovid, *Metam.* x, 40–44:

> Talia dicentem nervosque ad verba moventem
> exsangues flebant animae; nec Tantalus undam
> captavit refugam, stupuitque Ixionis orbis,
> nec carpsere iecur volucres, urnisque vacarunt
> Belides, inque tuo sedisti, Sisyphe, saxo.

> As (Orpheus) spoke thus, accompanying his words with the
> music of his lyre, the bloodless spirits wept; Tantalus
> did not catch at the fleeing wave; Ixion's wheel stopped
> in wonder; the vultures did not pluck at (Tityus') liver;
> the Belides rested from their urns, and thou, O Sisyphus, didst
> sit upon thy stone.

LCL, Miller, p. 67. Cf. *Fam.* xiii, 4, 5. Boethius, *Cons. phil.* iii, M 12, retells the story based on Seneca, *Hercules furens*. On this, Lerer (1985), pp. 154–165. On Ixion's wheel as the wheel of Fortune, Walter Map, as above, *DR* i, Pref., note 44; and Friedman (1970), p. 206.

6   Ps. 11, 9:

in circuitu impii ambulant.

7   Seneca, *Dial.* ix, De tranqu. 17, 8–9.
8   Seneca, ibid., 17, 4:

Scipio triumphale illud et militare corpus movet ad numeros, non molliter se infringens, ut nunc mos est etiam incessu ipso ultra muliebrem molliciem fluentibus, sed ut antiqui illi viri solebant inter lusum ac festa tempora virilem in modum tripudiare, non facturi detrimentum, etiamsi ab hostibus suis spectarentur.

LCL, Basore, pp. 279, 281. George Gascoigne, *The Grief of Joye,* 1576, Song iv, 29–36, summarizes our text:

What shoulde I coūpt, oure tossings and oure turnes,
Owre frysks, oure flyngs, and all owr motions made/
Butt fewell geven unto the fyre whiche burnes,
Within owr brests; whose flame can never fade?
For when Dame nature yn mans mynde did wade/
And sawe *fonde fancye* occupye the place,
She *fury* sent, to byd that Dame a base./

And thence proceede, the movings wch we make,
As forward, backward, lefte hande turne, and right/
Upwards, and downewards, tyll owre hartes do quake/
And last of all, (to shew owre selves owtright)
A turne on toe, must grace owre giddy spright,
Untyll sometymes, we stoomble in the same,
And fall downeright, to geve the gazers game./

Dancyng delights, are like a whyrlyng wheele,
Which turnethe mylls, or suche lyke frames abowt/
Yt takes no rest, as they doe restless reele/
Yt weares it selfe, as they doe owt of doubt/
And (yf my Muse be bolld to tell trewth mought)
Thes tryppers strive, to throwe theire braynes awaye,
As wheels voyde water to the Daм̃es decaye./

But dyd yt hurte theire owne myndes and no moe,
The losse were light, and easie to be borne/
The gazers eyes, are ofte mysguyded soe,
As makes a hornepype to begett a horne/
The mery night begetts a madder morne/
For he that (over night) did (syngle) trace,

Can (shortely after) dance a dooble pace./

The Matrones mynde leaves of her coomly looke,
The mayde must mynce, and strive to streyne her feete,/
The bryde her selfe, forgetts her marriage booke,
And learnes that daye, some lessons muche unmeete/
She learnes sometymes, to dance and turne in streete,
When her brydegroome, had rather have her home,
For bett nor worse, She shoulde (from hym) so rome./

Were I commaunded, to defyne in fewe,
What daucyng is, and what consysts therein
I should be bolde, my logycke thus to shew/
Daucyng is first, a pors[u]yvaut for Synne,
To tempt the best, that ever yet hathe bene/
A clenly clooke, to cover (often tymes)
The slye pretence, of many subtyle crymes./

Yn dauce the hande, hathè libertye to touche,
The eye to gaze, the arme for to embrace,
Whiche (otherwhere) might gyve great cause of gruch/
The exercyse, acquytts a blushing face,
And lends muche leave, wth much more tyme & place/
The darksome nyght, sharpe enemye to shame,
By candles light, betrayethe many a dame./

But wherefore stand I thus upon this text?
Whoso can dauce as *Scipio* seemd to doe,
Not wantonly, nor as his witts were vext,
Nor mynsing fyne, like such as meane to woe,
But withe suche grace, as love and malyce to,
Might bothe comend, and be afeard to blame,
I saie dance so, and dance in Christ his name./

9   Seneca, ibid., 17, 8:

Non numquam et usque ad ebrietatem veniendum.

LCL, Basore, p. 283.

10   I.t.: Tranquillus. Suetonius, i, Caesar, 53:

vini parcissimum ne inimici quidem negaverunt.

LCL, Rolfe, p. 73.

11   Above, *DR* i, 18, 24–26.

12   Seneca, *De tranqu.* 17, 9:

facilius efficiet, quisquis obiecit ei, crimen honestum quam turpem Catonem.

LCL, Basore, p. 283.

13   Horace, *Carm.* i, 37, 1:

nunc est bibendum, nunc pede libero
pulsanda tellus.

LCL, Bennett, p. 99. On the old notions of relaxation and recreation, Suchomski (1975), esp. pp. 30–35; and Olson (1982).

25 ❖ PLAYING BALL

1   In 335 B.C., Aristotle opened a school of philosophy in Athens which "came to be known as the Peripatetic school from his habit of walking up and down (περιπατεῖν), while conversing with his pupils in the paths of the Lyceum" (Harvey [1974], p. 44). Cf. Augustine, *De civ. Dei* viii, 12; Isidore, *Etym.* viii, 6, 13; and Fontaine (1959), ii, pp. 720–721.
2   Reported in Valerius Maximus, viii, 8, 2. This passage is versified in the early-twelfth-century *De memorabilibus* viii, 8, by Raoul de la Tourte (Raby [1934], ii, p. 25), and referred to in John of Salisbury, *Policrat.* viii, 12, *PL* 199, c. 761; and Suchomski (1975), pp. 51, 271, n. 164. —On Dionysius I of Syracuse playing ball, Cicero, *Tusc. disp.* v, 20, 60.
3   Suetonius ii, Aug. 83:

> Exercitationes campestres equorum et armorum statim post civilia bella omisit et ad pilam primo folliculumque transiit, mox nihil aliud quam vectabatur et deambulabat, ita ut in extremis spatiis subsultim decurreret segestria vel lodicula involutus.

> Immediately after the civil war he gave up exercise with horses and arms in the Campus Martius, at first turning to pass-ball and balloon-ball, but soon confining himself to riding and taking a walk, ending the latter by running and leaping, wrapped in a mantle or a blanket.

LCL, Rolfe, p. 249.
4   *Hist. Aug., Mar. Aur. Antonin.,* iv, 9:

> pila lusit adprime.

LCL, Magie, p. 143. On Petrarch's copy of the *Historia Augusta,* Vat. lat. 899, Nolhac (1907), ii, pp. 50–59; Hohl (1916); and the noteworthy introduction by D. Magie in his LCL edition, pp. xxv–xxviii.

26 ❖ DICE AND BOARDGAMES

1   The Latin title of this dialogue is *De ludo aleae et calculorum. Alea* denotes a game of hazard or chance. In Antiquity and, apparently also during the Middle Ages, games of dice were usually played on a board (*tabula*), with a cup, called *tower (pyrgus, turricula, fritillus,* etc.). Two kinds of dice were used, *tesserae,* with six sides, marked i to vi, and the larger *tali,* rounded on two sides and marked i (*unio*), iii (*trinio*), iv (*quaternio*), and vi (*senio*). The highest throw was called *Venus;* the worst, or lowest, throw, *dog (canis* or *canicula*). —*Calculus* is a piece or token used in gaming, such as a draughtsman or chessman. On this, Isidore, *Etym.* xviii, 59–68. Cf. Ovid, *Ars amat.* ii, 203–209:

> Seu ludet, numerosque manu iactabit eburnos,
>   Tu male iactato, tu male iacta dato:
> Seu iacies talos, victam ne poena sequatur,
>   Damnosi facito stent tibi saepe canes:
> Sive latrocinii sub imagine calculus ibit
>   Fac pereat vitreo miles ab hoste tuus.

If she be gaming, and throwing with her hand the ivory dice [*numeri* indicating both *tesserae* and *tali*], do you throw amiss and move your throws amiss; or if it is the large dice you are throwing, let no forfeit follow if she lose; see that the ruinous dogs often fall to you; or if the piece be marching under the semblance of a robber's band [when playing the *ludus latrunculorum,* note 5, below], let your warrior fall before his glassy foe.

LCL, Mozley, p. 81. Cf. also, ibid., iii, 353–366. On the whole subject, Pauly-Wissowa, *RE,* art. Lusoria tabula; and R. G. Austin, *Roman Boardgames.* The old literature is summarized in Johann Albert Fabricius' forgotten, but still useful, *Bibliographia antiquaria* (1716), chap. xxii.

2   On Scaevola, Valerius Maximus, viii, 8, 2, as above *DR* i, 25, note 2. On Augustus, Suetonius, ii, Aug. 70, 2:

> et deinde bello Siciliensi epigramma vulgatum est:

> Postquam bis classe victus naves perdidit,
> Aliquando ut vincat, ludit assidue aleam.

Later during the Sicilian war, this epigram was current:

> After he has twice been beaten at sea and lost his ships,
> he plays at dice all the time in the hope of winning a victory.

LCL, Rolfe, p. 233, Cf. also ibid., ii, 71.

3   Twyne, f. 35r: *for al things are not worthy to be praised which are praysed.*

4   The *ludus latrunculorum* (Ovid, *Ars amat.* ii, 203–209; cf. note 1, above) was

> a game of skill of the ancient Romans played on a board with men (*latrones, latrunculi,* raiders) moving like the men and kings of modern checkers. A piece was captured and removed from the board when it stood between two opposing pieces. . . . Sometimes, as in the Arabic *seegà,* dice were used to determine the moves.

Leach (1950), ii, pp. 605–606. Nevertheless, Fabricius (1716), p. 638, identifies the *ludus latrunculorum* as "Dam-Spiel." On this, Leibniz's "Annotatio de quibusdam Ludis . . . differentiaque Scachii & Latrunculorum . . . ," *Miscellanea Soc. Reg. Berol.* i (1710), 4, p. *22 et seq.* Cf. Seneca, *Ep.* 106, 11:

> latrunculis ludimus. In supervacuis subtilitas teritur; non faciunt bonos ista, sed doctos.

> What a game of pawns! We dull our fine edge by such superfluous pursuits; these things make men clever, but not good.

LCL, Gummere, pp. 221–223. Cf. also Varro, *De lingua latina* x, 22.

5   Pliny, *Nat. hist.* viii, 80, 215:

> mira sollertia . . . Mucianus et latrunculis lusisse, fictas cera nuces visu distinguere, luna cava tristes esse quibus in eo genere cauda sit, novam exultatione adorari:

> They are marvellously cunning . . . according to Mucianus the tailed species have even been known to play at draughts, are able to distinguish at a glance sham nuts made of wax, and are depressed by the moon waning and worship the new moon with delight.

LCL, Rackham, p. 151.

6   Horace, *Sat.* i, 8, 26–28:

> *scalpere* terram
> *unguibus* et pullam divellere mordicus aquam
> coeperunt;

> then they began to dig up the earth with their nails,
> and to tear a black lamb to pieces with their teeth.

LCL, Fairclough, p. 99.

7   The key passages for this text are Aulus Gellius, xviii, 13, 1–4, and 2, 1–6;

and ibid., vii, 13, 1–4. Reason refers clearly to the "game" described in ibid., xviii, 13:

> Saturnalibus Athenis alea quadam festiva et honesta lusitabimus huiuscemodi: ubi conveneramus conplusculi eiusdem studii homines ad lavandi tempus, captiones quae "sophismata" appellantur mente agitabimus easque, quasi talos aut tesserulas, in medium vice sua quisque iaciebamus. Captionis solutae aut parum intellectae praemium poenave erat nummus unus sestertius. Hoc aere conlecto, quasi manuario, cenula curabatur omnibus qui eum lusum luseramus. Erat autem captiones ad hoc fere exemplum, tametsi Latina oratione non satis scite ac paene etiam inlepide exponuntur: "Quod nix est, hoc grando non est; nix autem alba est: grando igitur alba non est." Item aliud non dissimile: "Quod homo est, non est hoc equus. Homo autem animal est: equus igitur animal non est." Dicere ergo debebat qui ad sophisma diluendum ac refellendum ritu aleatorio vocatus erat, in qua parte quoque in verbo captio foret, quid dari concedique non oporteret; nisi dixerat, nummo singulo multabatur. Ea multa cenam iuvabat.

> At Athens during the Saturnalia we engaged in a pleasant and improving diversion of this kind: when a number of us who were interested in the same study had met at the time of the bath, we discussed the catch questions which are called "sophisms," and each one of us cast them before the company in turn, like knucklebones or dice [note 1, above]. The prize for solving a problem, or the penalty for failing to understand it, was a single sestertius. From the money thus collected, as if it had been won at dice, a little dinner was provided for all of us who had taken part in the game. Now the sophisms were somewhat as follows, although they cannot be expressed very elegantly in Latin or even without clumsiness: "What snow is, that hail is not; but snow is white, therefore hail is not white." A somewhat similar one is: "What man is, that a horse is not; man is an animal, therefore a horse is not an animal." The one who was called upon by the throw of the dice to solve and refute the sophism was expected to tell in what part of the proposition and in what word the fallacy consisted, and what ought not to be granted and conceded; if he did not succeed he was fined one sestertius. The fine contributed to the dinner.

LCL, Rolfe, p. 341. Yet note Macrobius, *Saturn.* vii; John of Salisbury, *Policrat.* viii, esp. chaps. 8, 10; and the thoughtful discussion in Suchomski (1975), pp. 46–53.

8   Horace, *Ep.* i, 14, 36:

> nec *lusisse pudet,* sed non incidere ludum,

> It is not shameful to have played, but not to have stopped playing.

1492: non pudeat. &c.
1581: non pudeat.

27 ❖ LUCK IN GAMBLING

1   *De ludo taxillorum prospero.* —According to Cicero, *Orator* 45, 153, *taxillus* is the "inelegant" root form of *talus*—die; it is a diminutive of *talus*. In later Latin, *taxillus* indicates a small wooden piece or token, and the *lusoriae tesserae*—dice used for gambling. *Tabulae lusoriae*—gaming boards were widely used (e.g., Juvenal, *Sat.* i, 90; and Polydore Vergil, ii, 13), hence the expression *gaming at tables* (Twyne, f. 35v). On Trecento practices, Rickert (1948), pp. 201–202.

2   Cf. above, *DR* i, 8, 56. On despair, the worst of all evils (*Secretum* ii, *Prose* [1955], p. 70; *De ocio,* Rotondi, p. 25; *Fam.* ii, 3, 25; *DR* ii, 118, 23, ii, 126, 73), the affliction of Cain and Judas (*Fam.* xvi, 4, 17–20), cf. *Fam.* ii, 3, 25, viii, 1, 18, xxi, 9, 20; and *DR* i, 8, 56, i, 36, 86, i, 69, 25, ii, 93, 2–6, ii, 98, 3. Note Trinkaus (1970), i, pp. 28–41; Wenzel (1967), esp. pp. 79, 82, 95; Snyder (1965); and Bloomfield (1952), pp. 103–104.

3   Similar: *DR* i, 110, 73–75, ii, 13, 8, and ii, 127, 26–30. Cf. *Carmina Burana* xix, Utar contra vitia 10, Schmeller (1847), p. 20:

> Nummus in hac curia
> non est qui non vacet:
> crux placet, rotunditas
> placet, totum placet:
> et cum ita placeat,
> et Romanis placet,
> ubi nummus loquitur,
> et lex omnis tacet.

> At the Curia coins
> are not what is lacking:
> the cross pleases, roundness
> pleases, it all pleases:
> And since it seems so pleasant,
> it pleases them also in Rome,
> where coins do the talking,
> and all just laws remain silent.

Many gold coins of the period showed a cross, hence the German name *Kreuzer* for coins of small denomination. Cf., e.g., Braudel (1979), p. 467; and Grupp, iv (1924), p. 213, v (1925), p. 127.

4   The key passage for this colloquial phrase is probably Terence, *Phormio* 950–951:

> nolo volo; volo nolo rursum; cape, cedo;
> quod dictum indictumst; quod modo ratum erat inritumst.

> I won't, I will; I will, I won't again; take, give back;
> what was said unsaid, what was settled upset.

LCL, Sargeaunt, p. 107. Note Cicero, *De natura deorum* i, 17. Cf. *Secretum* iii, *Prose* (1955), p. 154; *Fam.* x, 5, 18; *Sen.* xvii, 3, *Griseldis* (1581: 542); etc.; also the emblematic use of *Velis nolisve* on Camillo Agrippa's medal, Saxl (1957), i, pp. 68–69, ii, pl. 41d; and Rom., 7, 19, above, *Dram. pers.*, note 2.

5   Cf. above, *DR* i, 23, notes 2 and 11.

6   1492: delectari queat ludi nomen habente nequitiae: atque impietatis foedissimae.

   1581: delectari queat ludi nomine abundante nequitia, atque impietate foedissima?

7   Cf. below, *DR* ii, 9, note 7.

8   1492: non amor erga homines: non erga deum reuerentia:

   1581: nec amor erga homines, non erga Deum reuerentia, (ignoring the elegant anastrophic *commutatio*).

9   On blaspheming gamblers, Tubach (1969), nos. 1949 and 2240.

10   In *De vita sol.* i, *Prose* (1955), p. 320, Petrarch describes *Cretensium imprecatio*—the curse of the Cretans—quoting Valerius Maximus, vii, 2, ext. 18:

> illi hostibus suis optant ut mala consuetudine delectantur,

> They wish their enemies may find delight in depraved habits.

11   I.t.: Naso

12   Reason echoes Ovid, *Ars amat.* iii, 501–504

> Pertinet ad faciem rabidos compescere mores:
>   Candida pax homines, trux decet ira feras.
> Ora tument ira: nigrescunt sanguine venae:
>   Lumina Gorgoneo saevius igne micant.

> Fair peace is becoming to men, fierce anger to beasts. The face becomes swollen with passion; the veins grow black with blood, the eyes flash more savagely than Gorgon fire.

LCL, Mozley, p. 155. The advice on gambling occurs ibid. iii, 367–380; it suggests to abstain from anger, not from gaming:

> Mille facesse iocos; turpe est nescire puellam
>   Ludere: ludendo saepe paratur amor.
> Sed minimus labor est sapienter iactibus uti:
>   Maius opus mores composuisse suos.
> Tum sumus incauti, studioque aperimur in ipso,
>   Nudaque per lusus pectora nostra patent:

Ira subit, deforme malum, lucrique cupido,
    Iurgiaque et rixae sollicitusque dolor:
Crimina dicuntur, resonat clamoribus aether,
    Invocat iratos et sibi quisque deos:
Nulla fides, tabulaeque novae per vota petuntur;
    Et lacrimis vidi saepe madere genas.
Iuppiter a vobis tam turpia crimina pellat,
    In quibus est ulli cura placere viro.

Make up a thousand games; it is unseemly for a girl to know not how to play; by play love is often won. But the smallest task is to use your throws wisely: more important is it to control one's own behaviour. Then are we incautious and reveal ourselves in our very zest, and in our games our hearts show clear to see; anger steals in, an unsightly evil, and desire for gain, and brawls and quarrels and distressful grief; reproaches are hurled; the air resounds with cries, and each calls angry gods to his aid: none trusts his neighbour, and amid vows new tables are demanded; oft have I seen cheeks wet with tears. May Jupiter keep such foul reproach far from you, who seek to win a man's favour.

LCL, Mozley, p. 145.

13   Joy seems to allude to the laconic *veni, vidi, vici*—I came, I saw, I conquered, with which Julius Caesar announced to his friend Amintius his victory at Zela in Asia Minor, over Pharnaces, son of Mithridates, who had aided Pompey (47 B.C.). Petrarch knew Plutarch's story (*Life of Caesar* 50) through Suetonius, i, Jul. Caes. 37.

14   *Omnes huiusmodi ludi magistros, nudos esse, atque inopes, et egenos.*

1492: egenos. &c.
1581: egenos.

Based on this dialogue, George Gascoigne, *The Grief of Joye*, 1576, Song iv, 41–42:

For yf we coūpt, those pleasures worthy price,
Whiche (in them selves) do purchase privy payne
Then might we prayse (as well) bothe cards and dyse,
Whiche lyve by losse, and few (god knowes) yᵗ, gayne/
Thexample not unlyke: for bothe be vayne,
That one playes pownds, and lacketh pence at length,
That other streynes, and styll decreasethe strength./

To see soṁe one, sitt scratching of his hedde
(Yea teare his bearde sometymes), when he hathe lost,
Another chafing, tyll his cheekes be redd,
And bothe waxe warme to co[ū]tervayle theire cost/
To see the cardes and dyse abowt howse tost/

Tyll anger vex bothe father, kỹne, and brother:
Ys it not madnes? sure it is none other./

Cunliffe, ii (1910), p. 556.

28 ❖ ENTERTAINERS

1   1492: De histrionibus
    1581: De histrionum iocis

The term *histrio* was used for tragic and comic actors and for performers in
pantomime. In later times, *artifex* indicated a serious actor (cf. *DR* i, 23, 71,
and note 28), and *histrio* continued to be used for entertainers of any kind.
On this, cf. Glare (1983), arts. *artifex* and *histrio;* Hartnoll (1951), art.
"Rome," p. 676; and Suchomski (1975), pp. 26–28, 58–59, on medieval
usage.

2   Livy, vii, 2; Valerius Maximus, ii, 4, 4, Polydore Vergil, iii, chap. 13.

3   Valerius Maximus, viii, 7, 7, and 10, 2; Macrobius, *Saturn.* iii, 14, 11–12; *Rer.*
    mem. libri i, 22. On Aesopus' wastrel son—Horace, *Sat.* ii, 3, 239–242; Valer-
    ius Maximus, ix, 1, 2; and Macrobius, *Saturn.* iii, 14, 14.

4   Cicero, *De orat.* i, 28, 129:

    in artificio perquam tenui et levi.

    in an extremely mean and trivial craft.

    LCL, Sutton-Rackham, p. 91.

5   Horace, *Ep.* ii, 1, 76–82:

    Indignor quicquam reprehendi, non quia crasse
    compositum illepideve putetur, sed quia nuper,
    nec veniam antiquis, sed honorem et praemia posci.
    Recte necne crocum floresque perambulet Attae
    fabula si dubitem, clament periisse pudorem
    cuncti paene patres, ea cum reprehendere coner,
    quae gravis Aesopus, quae doctus Roscius egit

    I am impatient that any work is censured, not because it is thought to be
    coarse or inelegant in style, but because it is modern, and that what is claimed

for the ancients should be, not indulgence, but honour and rewards. If I were to question whether a play of Atta's keeps its legs or not amidst the saffron and flowers, nearly all our elders would cry out that modesty is dead, when I attempt to blame what stately Aesopus and learned Roscius once acted.

LCL, Fairclough, p. 403. Cicero, *De orat.* i, 61, etc.; also Valerius Maximus, viii, 10, 2 and viii, 7, 7. —Quintus Roscius Gallus (d. 62 B.C.) and Claudius Aesopus were two famous Roman actors and friends of Cicero. Cf. *Rer. mem. libri* i, 21 and 22.

6   Reason may have reference to Cicero's extant oration *Pro Roscio comoedo* or to passages such as *De orat.* i, 28, 129–130 and 58, 251–253; or *De divin.* i, 36, 79, ii, 31, 66.

7   I.e., the symbol of equestrian rank. Cf. Pliny, *Nat. hist.* xxxiii, 7, 29–30.

8   The *denarius* was a Roman silver coin of about 70 g, roughly equivalent to the Greek *drachma.* The same name was also used for a gold coin worth 25 silver *denarii.* Cf. Varro, *De ling. lat.* ix, 85.

9   Pliny, *Nat. hist.* vii, 39, 128–129; Macrobius, *Saturn.* iii, 14, 13–14; John of Salisbury, *Policrat.* viii, 12, *PL* 199, c. 759b–d; *Rer. mem. libri* i, 21; and *Contra medicum* ii, 47–53, Ricci (1950), p. 40:

> Habent suum secula nostra portentum: mechanicus etiam libros arat. Quis non Roscio deinceps artis histrionice librum donet? Erat et ille mechanicus, sed insignis, ingenioque promeritus non modo maximorum ducum gratiam, sed ipsius quoque familiaritatem atque amicitiam Ciceronis. Mulcebat ille oculos: mechanicus noster aures vulnerat; agebat ille quod placeret omnibus: hic quod nulli.

> Our age has its own monstrous sight. Now even a mechanic is plowing with his pen [cf. Curtius (1953), pp. 313–314]. Who would not henceforth forgive Roscius a book on stage acting? He too was a mechanic, but a distinguished one, whose talent earned him not only the favor of the greatest princes, but, indeed, close friendship with Cicero. He delighted the eyes—our mechanic hurts the ears; his acting pleased everybody—this one's nobody.

10   Cf. above, *DR* i, 19, 113–126.

29 ❖ WRESTLING

1   Dialogues 29–35 deal with courtly pursuits and concerns.

2   Reason discusses the sport of wrestling as practiced in Antiquity. She does

not seem to differentiate between wrestling and the *pancratium,* a rough-and-tumble fight combining wrestling and boxing. On this, Marrou (1956), pp. 122–123. For a blow-by-blow description of such a contest, see Statius, *Thebaid* vi, 729–825; of a wrestling match, ibid., 826–910. Propertius gives a less detailed account of nude Spartan girls participating in these sports, *Elegies* iii, 14.

It is worth noting that Reason expects Joy—and the reader—to be familiar with the antique practices and does not offer descriptive materials, such as Statius, with which Petrarch was thoroughly familiar and which may have been of great interest to the warrior Azzo, who did not know such kinds of fighting. Reason's task seems to be to whet the reader's appetite for further information.

3   Cf. above, *DR* i, 25, 4–10.

4   I.e., Augustine's *exercitatio animae*—exercising the mind—and its disciplines, the practice of which permits one to rise *per corporalia ad incorporalia*—from corporeal to incorporeal matters. On this, below, *DR* i, 44, note 18.

5   Reason refers to the seven *artes mechanicae*—mechanical arts—as below, *DR* ii, Pref. note 79. Cf. also *De vita sol.* i, *Prose* (1955), p. 358, on the inventors of the arts.

6   Cicero *De re publ.* vi, 24, 26:

> Nec enim tu is es, quem forma ista declarat, sed mens cuiusque is est quisque, non ea figura, quae digito demonstrari potest.

LCL, Keyes, p. 279. Cf. Macrobius, *Comm.* ii, 12, 1; John of Salisbury, *Metalog.* iii, 7, *PL* 199, c. 906. On to "point out/being pointed to with the finger," Horace, *Carm.* iv, 3, 22:

> quod monstror digito praetereuntium
> Romanae fidicen lyrae.

> that I am pointed out by the finger of those passing by
> as the minstrel of the Roman lyre.

LCL, Bennett, p. 293; and Persius, i, 28 (quoted in *Fam.* x, 3, 16):

> at pulchrum est digito monstrari et dicier 'hic est.'

> O but it is a fine thing to have a finger pointed at one, and to hear people say, 'That's the man.'

LCL, Ramsay, p. 319; Martial, ix, 97, 3–4; and the echoes below, *DR* i, 117, 26–29, ii, 35, 12–14. Note *Sen.* viii, 2 (1581: 832). The phrase—which was also used in a pejorative sense (e.g., Ovid, *Amores* iii, 1, 19, and 6, 77; and Jerome, *Ep.* 22, Ad Eustochium, 27, and *Ep.* 38, 5)—occurs not infrequently in medieval texts, e.g., *Carm. Bur.*, Huc usque, Schmeller (1847), p. 171; Hilka (1941), p. 209; and Raby (1934), ii, p. 275:

> semper pulsant cubito
> me designant digito
> ac si mirum fecerim.

> They elbowed each other
> and pointed to me
> with their fingers,
> as if I were some marvel.

Stock (1971), p. 61. —On Persius' *hic est,* Martial, v, 13, 3; Juvenal, i, 161; Cicero, *Tusc. disp.* v, 36, 103; and Pliny the Younger, *Ep.* ix, 23, 4.

7   On life as palaestra, e.g., *Sen.* xi, 11; and *De vita sol.* ii, as in *DR* ii, 119, note 12.

8   1492: more Dyagore. Non enim caelum ascensurus es:
1581: Morere Diagora. Nunc enim in coelum ascensurus es

The panhellenic games of Antiquity

> were gradually increased from a foot-race of a single course of about 200 yards to include first a double course, than a long race, then the pentathlon, then boxing. From 680 B.C. chariot racing was added.

Harvey (1974), p. 176.

9   Reason tells the Diagoras story according to Cicero, *Tusc. Disp.* i, 46, 111:

> Hanc sententiam significare videtur Laconi illa vox, qui, cum Rhodius Diagoras, Olympionices nobilis, *uno die duo suos filios* victores Olympiae vidisset, accessit ad senem et gratulatus; *Morere, Diagora;* inquit: *non enim in caelum ascensurus es.* Magna haec et nimium fortasse Graeci putant vel tum potius putabant, isque, qui hoc Diagorae dixit, permagnum existimans tris Olympionicas una e domo prodire cunctari illum diutius in vita fortunae objectum inutile putabat ipsi.

> This seems to be the meaning of the well-known utterance of a Lacedaemonian who, when Diagoras of Rhodes, a famous Olympian victor, had seen his two sons victorious in one day at Olympia, approached the old man and, congratulating him, said: "Die, Diagoras, for you will not have to ascend to heaven any more." Such achievements the Greeks think glorious—too much so perhaps— or rather thought so in that day, and he, who spoke in this way to Diagoras, considered it very glorious for three Olympian victors to come from one home, and judged it inexpedient for the father to linger longer in life exposed to the buffets of fortune.

LCL, King, pp. 133–135, cf. also *Fam.* xi, 5, 1. J. E. King, in his LCL edition of the Tusculans, draws attention to Pindar's phrase, *Pythia* x, 22: ὁ χάλκεος

οὐρανὸς οὔ ποτ' ἀμβατὸς αὐτῷ—the brazen heaven, he cannot ever scale—
which is echoed by the old Lacedaemonian. The man who has seen such
glory has "reached the height of human felicity and cannot hope for more"
(ibid., p. 132, n. 2).

Petrarch knew also the story Gellius tells about Diagoras, *Noct. Att.* iii, 15,
3, according to which he died amidst joy, when his three sons placed on his
head the victor's crowns they had earned at Olympia on the same day.
Pindar's Olympian Ode vii, engraved in golden letters in the temple of Athene
at Lindos in Rhodes, was dedicated to Diagoras of Rhodes who was Olympic
champion 464 B.C. "Statues of Diagoras, his three sons, and two grandsons,
all Olympic victors, stood in a group at Olympia." Harvey (1974), p. 329. Cf.
also *Fam.* viii, 1, 8; and *DR* i, 23, 28.

10   I.e., πλάτος—*latitudo;* πλατύς—*latus, amplus*—wide, broad (Buck [1949],
12.6).

11   Cf. *Rer. mem. libri* i, 25, 3, possibly based on Diogenes Laertius, iii, 4. On
Diogenes Laertius and Latin translations of his text in the Middle Ages, Sabbadini (1905), p. 219; and idem (1914), pp. 262–263. On Petrarch's Augustinian friend in Avignon, Dionigi da Borgo San Sepolcro (Wilkins [1961], pp.
10, 32), and Diogenes Laertius, Sabbadini (1914), p. 41.

12   Cf. *DR* i, 5. Milo is reported to have executed this feat at Olympia, 532 B.C.
See also Quintilian, *Inst. orat.* i, 9, 5.

13   *sibi fidentibus.* Cf. Horace, *Ep.* i, 19, 22–23:

> . .   . .   qui sibi fidet,
> dux reget examen. . .   .   . .

> . .   . .   Who trusts himself
> will lead and rule the swarm. . .   . . .

LCL, Fairclough, p. 383.

14   I.t.: Crispus. Sallust, *Catil.* 54, 6:

> Non divitiis cum divite neque factione cum factioso, sed cum strenuo virtute,
> cum modesto pudore, cum innocente abstinentia certabat.

LCL, Rolfe, p. 113.

15   Livy, xxviii, 43, 6:

> Maximo cuique id accidere animo certum habeo ut se non cum praesentibus
> modo, sed cum omnis aevi claris viris comparent.

LCL, Moore, p. 179. Petrarch's text reads *comparet* with most older editions.
Cf. the echo in Wordsworth, "The Prelude," 393–395:

> . .   . .   There is
> one great society alone on earth;
> The noble Living and the noble Dead.

On Scipio in the *DR,* Bernardo (1962), pp. 95–98.

16   *caestus*—boxing strap filled with lead. Cf. Virgil, *Aeneid* v, 378–379:

> quaeritur huic alius; nec quisquam ex agmine tanto
> audet audire virum manibusque inducere caestus.

> For him a match is sought; but none from all that throng
> durst face him or draw the gloves on to his hands.

LCL, Fairclough, p. 471; or Statius, *Thebaid* vi, 729–730; 732–734:

> . . . infestos tollite caestus
> comminus . . . .
> . . . ac cum nigrante plumbo
> tegmina cruda boum non mollior ipse lacertis
> induitur . . .

> wield ye the terrible *caestus* in close conflict;
> . . . . binding on his arms the
> raw ox-hide black with lumps of lead,
> himself no softer.

LCL, Mozley, p. 115. On this, Cicero, *Tusc. disp.* ii, 17, 40; 23, 56; 24 57.

17   Seneca, *Ep.* 11, 8–10:

Accipe, et quidem utilem ac salutarem, quam te affigere animo volo: 'Aliquis vir bonus nobis diligendus est ac semper ante oculos habendus, ut sic tamquam illo spectante vivamus et omnia tamquam illo vidente faciamus.' Hoc, mi Lucili, Epicurus praecepit. Custodem nobis et paedagogum dedit, nec inmerito. Magna pars peccatorum tollitur, si peccaturis testis adsistit, Aliquem habeat animus, quem vereatur, cuius auctoritate etiam secretum suum sanctius faciat. O felicem illum, qui non praesens tantum, sed etiam cogitatus emendat! O felicem, qui sic aliquem vereri potest, ut ad memoriam quoque eius se conponat atque ordinet! Qui sic aliquem vereri potest, cito erit verendus. Elige itaque Catonem. Si hic tibi videtur nimis rigidus, elige remissioris animi virum Laelium. Elige eum, cuius tibi placuit et vita et oratio et ipse animum ante se ferens vultus; illum tibi semper ostende vel custodem vel exemplum. Opus est, inquam, aliquo, ad quem mores nostri se ipsi exigant; nisi ad regulam prava non corriges.

Hear and take to heart this useful and wholesome motto: 'Cherish some man of high character, and keep him ever before your eyes, living as if he were watching you, and ordering all your actions as if he beheld them.' Such, my dear Lucilius, is the counsel of Epicurus (Frag. 210, Usener); he has quite properly given us a guardian and an attendant [cited in *De vita sol.* ii, *Prose* (1955), p. 350]. We can get rid of most sins, if we have a witness who stands near us when we are likely to go wrong. The soul should have someone whom it can respect—one by whose authority it may make even its inner shrine more hallowed. Happy is the man who can make others better, not merely when he is in their company, but even when he is in their thoughts! And happy also is he who can so revere a man as to calm and regulate himself by calling him to mind! One who can so revere another, will soon be himself worthy of reverence. Choose therefore a Cato; or, if Cato seems too severe a model, choose some Laelius, a gentler spirit. Choose a master whose life, conversation, and soul-expressing face have satisfied you; picture him always to yourself as your protector or your pattern. For we must indeed have someone according to whom we may regulate our characters; you can never straighten that which is crooked unless you use a ruler.

LCL, Gummere, pp. 63, 65. Cf. also, Seneca, *Ep.* 6, 6; 25, 5, as below, *DR* ii, 53, note 10; *Dial.* v, *De ira* iii, 22, 1; Pohlenz, i (1959), pp. 157–158, 319. —The ancient topic of *imitatio* extended to both *res*—subject—and *verba*— words (Seneca's *vita et oratio*):

> The imitation of models was one of the basic methods recommended by writers on rhetoric for developing a good style. More than that, much writing on ethics by rhetoricians like Cicero—and much of Petrarch's own moral doctrine—recommended the imitation of exemplars of virtue. A chief purpose of the study of history as Petrarch and his followers conceived it was to encourage the imitation of great men.

Seigel (1968), p. 50; cf. Aristotle, *Poet.* 4, 1448b, 6, and Livy, i, Praef., 10–12. The imitation of virtue (cf. *Fam.* xii, 2, 34: *pulcra emulatio est que de virtute suscipitur*—beautiful is the rivalry that involves virtue; and Cicero, *Tusc. disp.* iv, 17: *imitatio virtutis aemulatio dicitur*—the imitation of virtue is called rivalry), like imitation of content and form in literature, art and music, does not detract from the achievement that is being imitated. In this vein Petrarch wrote to Homer, *Fam.* xxiv, 12, 15–18:

> Iam vero de imitatione quid dicam? Debuisti presagire, dum tam alte alis animi te sublatum cerneres, nunquam tibi defuturos imitatores; gaudendum vero talem te cui multi similes fieri velint sed non multi possint. Quidni autem gaudeas tu, primi semper certus loci, cum ego, ultimus hominum, gaudeam, nec gaudere sat est, glorier quoque, tanti me nunc fieri, ut sit aliquis, si tamen est aliquis, qui imitari optet ac fingere? illud magis gavisurus tales imitatores fore qui superent; atque illum non Apollinem tuum sed meum verum ingenii Deum precor, ut siquis me imitatione dignum duxerit, nisu facili quem sequitur consequatur ac transeat. Ego mecum bene gloriose feliciter agi credam, si ex amicis—nemo enim nisi amet imitabitur—multos michi pares, aliquantoque felicius si superiores aspexero, quique ex imitatoribus sint victores. Si enim genitor carnis filium se maiorem cupit, quid optare debeat pater ingenii? Tu qui maiorem victoremque non metuis, imitatores equanimis fer.

> What, then, am I to say about imitation? When you realized you were soaring so high on the wings of your mind, you should have anticipated that you would never lack imitators. It must be gratifying that many want to be like you, but only very few are able to do so. Why, then, are you not joyful, since

you will always be assured first place? Even I, the least of all men, enjoy and, as if joy were not enough, glory in the fact that I have become esteemed enough so that some—if there be some—would care to imitate me and to write the way I write. I would enjoy it even more if these imitators were good enough to surpass me, and I pray, not to your Apollo, but to the true God, Who granted me talent, that anyone who thinks I am worth imitating may follow me with ease and catch up and overtake me. I shall consider I have worked gloriously well and fruitfully when I discover among my friends many who are my equals—I call them friends because no one imitates what he does not love! I will be all the more happy if some turn out to be superior and, having started as imitators, become conquerors, because, just as a father hopes his son will be greater than himself, should not the father of one's intellect, as it were, do likewise? [Cf. *Sen.* v, 2(1581: 794): *nemo pius pater neget* . . .] You, who do not have to fear a conqueror greater than you, can afford to treat your imitators with kindness.

Cf. *Fam.* i, 8, 2–5, vi, 4, esp. 8–13, xxi, 15, 12, xxii, 2, 16–21, 27, xxiii, 19, 11–13 (Rawski [1967], pp. 79–80; Spitzer [1959], Sect. vi, 3, esp. pp. 927–928; Martellotti [1983], pp. 480–481, 501–503; Mann [1984], pp. 18–20); *Sen.* v, 2 (1581: 793–796, esp. 794–795), xvi, 9 (1581: 962); *Buc. carm.* iv, 38–39; *Rer. mem. libri* iii, 42, 4, iii, 77, 12; *DR* ii, 57, 62–67, ii, 114, 43–56, ii, 119, 128–131; and, on deterrent models, *DR* i, 96, 194–197. On imitating the wrong models in life, *De vita sol.* i, *Prose* (1955), pp. 384–388; and *DR* i, 119, 21–25. Related, Juvenal, xiv; and Chaucer, *Canterbury Tales,* Physician's Tale, 93–102. On the whole topic, Gmelin (1932); R. McKeon in Crane (1952), pp. 147–231; Curtius (1953), p. 467; Preminger (1965), art. "Imitation"; and Gombrich (1966), pp. 122–128. On *imitatio Dei,* Javelet (1967). On personifications of imitation, Janson (1952), chap. x. On the related topic of *exempla,* above, *Dramatis personae,* note 18; and *DR* i, Pref., note 52. On *aemulatio, DR* i, Pref., note 34, and i, 44, note 3.

18   On this, George Gascoigne, *The Grief of Joye,* 1576, Song iv, 43–44:

> . . . .
> Wrastlyng is thought, meete for a martiall guest,
> And therefore seemes, defended from the blames,
> Which grow wth griefe in other Joyfull games/
>
> Yet hee thatt marks what I have sayed before,
> Of leaping, roõnyng, vaultyng, and suche lyke
> The same of this maie well be sayed and more,
> For here of two, that one must lye in dyke/
> And yf therewithe he doe his fall dyslyke,
> From wrastlyng trycks, they fall to warlyke blowes,
> Suche earnest oft, in deepest dalliaunce growes/

Cunliffe, ii (1910), p. 556.

30 ❖ SPECTACLES

1   *etiam qui humano generi spectaculum facti erant.* Compare i Cor. 4, 9:

> quia spectaculum facti sumus mundo, et angelis, et hominibus

We are made a spectacle to the world, and to the angels, and to men.

—Only the ancient Roman theater is being discussed. On survival of knowledge about the theater of Antiquity in the Middle Ages, Norton-Smith (1974), pp. 162–164; Young (1933), i, pp. 1–2. —Petrarch himself was not impervious to the spectacles of his day—cf., e.g., his description of the Venetian celebrations marking Luchino del Verme's victory in Sicily, *Sen.* iv, 3, to Pietro da Muglio of Bologna, Venice, August 10, 1364 (1581: 783):

> Et si magnificentia regnum suum tenuit, ne inde modesta ac sobrietas exularent, sed in sua illam urbe, & in sua festiuitate regnantem regerent, frenarentque. Multos quidem festos dies, uario apparatu celebritas haec deduxit, duobus tandem tota res ludis clauditur. Quibus ego nunc propria nomina Latina non habeo, dicam tamen ut intelligas. Alter nempe discursus, alter concursus, ut arbitror dici potest. In altero enim recto calle decurrunt singuli, in altero singuli singulis hinc inde concurrunt, uterque ludus equester, sed inermis primus, nisi quod hastis, & clypeis decurrentes, sericis exuuiis uento effusis, quandam bellici actus imaginem repraesentant? At secundus armatus, & duelli species quaedam, itaque in illo quidem elegantiae plurimum, periculi minimum, in hoc autem artificio par discrimen: unde non sat proprie hastiludium Galli uocant, quod nomen primo magis conuenit, illo enim uere luditur, hoc certatur. Caeterum in utroque, quod narrari alteri uix me credulum praebuissem, sed nunc oculis meis credo, magna & mira prorsus industria, non ut mundo persuasum est nauticae atque aequoreae, sed militaris ac Martiae gentis eminuit. Ea equitandi, tractandorumque ars armorum, ea demum aestus, & laborum patientia, quae quibusuis acerrimis terrae bellatoribus satis esset: uterque ludus in platea illa, cui nescio an terrarum orbis parem habeat, ante ipsam marmoream atque auream templi faciem exhibitus, & priori quidem ludo, nemo externus interfuit, quatuor & uiginti nobiles adolescentes, forma, habitu & aetate conspicui, hanc sibi partem laetitiae delegere, accersito Ferraria Thoma Bambasio, qui ut posteris breuiter notus fiat, siquid ego apud illos, aut notitiae sum habiturus, aut fidei, talis est hodie in uniuersa Venetia, qualis quondam Romae Roscius, mihi uero tam charus, tamque familiaris, quam Tullio ille fuit, etsi ut in altera quidem harum amicitiarum parte portio ingens, sic in altera multa infit imparitas. Caeterum huius ductu, & consilio, ludus hic actus, & pactus tanto est ordine, ut non homines currere, sed uolare angelos iudicares. Mirum spectaculum tot ephoebos, ostro atque auro uestitos cernere,

tot Aeripedes ac fulgentes phaleris equos, sic regentes frenis, sic urgentes stimulis, ut uix terram pedibus tangere uiderentur. Atque ita sui ducis edictum praesentibus animis obseruantes, ut hoc ad terminum propinquante, ille claustris erumperet, ille autem se cursui praepararet, qui alternatione hac, & summa omnium paritate, in circulos re digesta, unus, isque perpetuus cursus erat, dum unius finis principium esset alterius, & desinente ultimo, rursum primus inciperet, ita ut cum multi tota luce currerent, sero unum diceres concurrisse. Et uicissim nunc hastarum fragmina coelo uolitantia, nunc uento crepitantia cerneres, signa purpurea, nec dictu facile, nec credibile est auditu, quae nam ibi in dies hominum frequentia. Nullus sexus, nulla aetas, nullus status defuit. Iam Dux ipse, cum immenso procerum comitatu, frontem templi supra uestibulum occuparat, unde marmoreo e suggestu essent, cuncta sub pedibus, locus est, ubi quatuor illi aenei & aurati equi stant, antiqui operis ac praeclari, quisquis ille fuit artificis, ex alto pene uiuis adimentes, ac pedibus obstrepentes, neve aestiuus sol, pronus ad uesperam, aut castore offenderet, aut fulgore diuersi coloris auleis usquequaque pendentibus prouisum erat.

Everything breathed joy, courtesy, concord, love. Such a lofty mood pervaded the city that modesty and sobriety, far from disappearing, ruled everywhere and prevented excesses in the celebrations . . . These continued in various forms through many festive days, and concluded with two great functions. I don't know the Latin names for them, so I shall describe them. The first could be called a race; the second a contest, or joust. In the first the contestants dash down a straight course; in the second they dash against each other. In both the participants are mounted; in the first the riders do not clash but give a warlike note by brandishing spear and shield and carrying fluttering silk banners. The second is a sort of duel in armor. In the first reigns the utmost elegance, with a minimum of peril. The second is a mock conflict; the French call it, not very properly, "jeu de lance"; this would better fit the first game, for in that they play, and in the second they fight. In both I realized something I should hardly have accepted on others' testimony, but I must credit my own eyes: this people possesses a rare eminence, not only, as everyone is aware, in nautical and seafaring skills but in military exercises. They display the arts of horsemanship and of weapon-handling, *élan* and endurance, enough to rank them with the fiercest fighters on earth. Both performances were held in that great square, which I doubt has any match in this world, in front of the marble and gold façade of the temple [the Basilica of St. Mark]. No outsider took part in the first contest. Twenty-four noble youths, handsome and splendidly clad, were chosen for this part of the ceremony. And Tommaso Bombasi was summoned from Ferrara. Let me record for the benefit of our sons—if my words are to persist at all among them—that he has the same standing in the Venetian state as the actor Roscius had in Rome, and he is as close a friend of mine as Roscius was to Cicero (although this comparison of persons is far from exact). Anyway, under his direction the performance was staged so skillfully that you would have said the riders were flying angels. It was a marvellous sight to see all these gallant youths, dressed in purple and gold, checking and spurring their fleet-footed steeds adorned with glittering trappings so that they seemed hardly to touch the ground. They followed their captain's orders so exactly that at the moment one reached the goal another sprang from the mark, and another made ready for his race. With this alternation of uniform riders there was a constant race. One man's finish was another man's starting point; when one stopped another began; so that, though many coursed in full view, you would have said at the end that just one man had ridden the whole way. Now you would see the spear-points flash through the air, now the purple banners fluttering in the breeze. The size of the multitude is hard to reckon and hard to believe; both sexes and every age and station were represented. The Doge himself with a great band of the leading men occupied the loggia above the church vestibule; at their feet, below this marble tribune, the crowd was massed. This is where the four gilded bronze hourses stand, the work of some ancient unknown but illustrious sculptor [below, *DR* i, 40, note 10]. On their high place they look almost alive, whinnying and stamping. To avoid the heat and dazzle of the descending summer sun, the loggia was everywhere protected with varicolored awnings.

Bishop (1966), pp. 236–237. —In 1370 Petrarch bequeathed his *luteum bonum*—his good lute—to Tommaso Bombasi of Ferrara,

> ut eum sonet, non pro vanitate seculi fugacis, sed ad laudem Dei eterni,

> that he may play it, not for the vainglory of this fleeting world, but in praise of God everlasting.

Mommsen (1957), pp. 82–83.

2 Suetonius ii, Aug. 44, 3:

> Solis virginibus Vestalibus *locum in theatro* separatim et contra praetoris tribunal dedit.

> Only the Vestal virgins were assigned a place to themselves, opposite the praetor's tribunal.

LCL, Rolfe, p. 197.

3 1492: quantaque insaniae proxima ducum cura:
  1581: quantaque insaniae cura

4 *paria gladiatorum*—cf. Seneca, *Ep.* 7, 3; Cicero, *Opt. gen. or.* vi, 17.

5 On this, Cicero, *Ep. fam.* vii, 1.

6 Reason seems to describe Corinthian capitals decorated with two ranks of acanthus leaves, or the Roman composite type, which combines the Corinthian leaves with volutes as used in Ionic capitals.

7 The theater built in Rome by M. Aemilius Scaurus, when he was *aedile* in 58 B.C. Pliny, *Nat. hist.* xxxvi, 2, 5–7:

> . . . M. Scauri, cuius nescio an aedilitas maxime prostraverit mores maiusque sit Sullae malum tanta privigni potentia quam proscriptio tot milium. In aedilitate hic sua *fecit opus maximum omnium quae umquam fuere humana manu*

facta, non temporaria mora, verum etiam aeternitatis destinatione. Theatrum hoc fuit; scaena ei triplex in altitudinem CCCLX columnarum . . . Ima pars scaenae e marmore fuit, media e vitro, inaudito etiam postea genere luxuriae, summa e tabulis inauratis; columnae . . . im<u>ae</u> duodequadragenum pedum. Signa aer<u>ea</u> <u>inter</u> columnas, . . . fuerunt iii numero; cavea ipsa cepit hominum lxxx, cum Pompeiani <u>theatri</u> totiens multiplicata urbe tantoque maiore populo sufficiat large xxxx sedere. Relicus apparatus tantus Attalica veste, tabulis pictis, cetero choragio fuit ut, in Tusculanam villam reportatis quae superflu<u>ebant</u> cotidiani usus deliciis, incensa villa ab iratis servis concremaretur HS ⌐ccc⌐.

. . . Marcus Scaurus, whose aedileship may perhaps have done more than anything to undermine morality and whose powerful ascendancy may have been a more mischievous achievement on the part of his stepfather Sulla than the killing by proscription of so many thousands of people. As aedile he *constructed the greatest of all the works ever made by man, a work that surpassed not merely those erected for a limited period but even those intended to last for ever.* This was his theatre, which had a stage arranged in three storeys with 360 columns; . . . The lowest storey of the stage was of marble, and the middle one of glass (an extravagance unparalleled even in later times), while the top storey was made of gilded planks. The columns of the lowest storey were . . . each 38 feet high. The bronze statues in the spaces between the columns numbered 3000 . . . As for the auditorium, it accommodated 80,000; and yet that of Pompey's theatre amply meets all requirements with seats for 40,000 even though the city is so many times larger and the population so much more numerous than it was at that time. The rest of the equipment, with dresses of cloth of gold, scene paintings, and other properties was on so lavish a scale that when the surplus knick-knacks that could be put to ordinary use were taken to Scaurus' villa at Tusculum and the villa itself set on fire and burnt down by indignant servants, the loss was estimated at 30,000,000 sesterces.

LCL, Eichholz, pp. 89–91.

8   Cf. Pliny, *Nat. hist.* xxxvi, 1, 1–3:

. . . . montes natura sibi fecerat ut quasdam compages telluris visceribus densandis, simul ad fluminum impetus domandos fluctusque fragendos ac minime quietas partes coercendas durissima sui materia. Caedimus hos trahimusque nulla alia quam deliciarum causa, quos transcendisse quoque mirum fuit. In portento prope maiores habuere Alpis ab Hannibale exsuperatas et postea a Cimbris: nunc ipsae caeduntur in mille genera marmorum. Promunturia aperiuntur mari, et rerum natura agitur in planum; evehimus ea quae separandis gentibus pro terminis constituta erant, navesque marmorum causa fiunt, ac per fluctus, saevissimam rerum naturae partem, huc illuc portantur iuga, maiore etiamnum venia quam cum frigidos potus vas petitur in nubila caeloque proximae rupes cavantur, ut bibatur glacie. Secum quisque cogitet, et quae pretia horum audiat, quas vehi trahique moles videat, et quam sine iis multorum sit beatior vita. Ista facere, immo verius pati mortales quos ob usus quasve ad voluptates alias nisi ut inter maculas lapidum iaceant, ceu vero non tenebris noctium, dimidia parte vitae cuiusque, gaudia haec auferentibus!

Mountains, however, were made by Nature for herself to serve as a kind of framework for holding firmly together the inner parts of the earth, and at the same time to enable her to subdue the violence of rivers, to break the force of heavy seas and so to curb her most restless elements with the hardest material of which she is made. We quarry these mountains and haul them away for a mere whim; and yet there was a time when it seemed remarkable even to have succeeded in crossing them. Our forefathers considered the scaling of the Alps by Hannibal and later by the Cimbri to be almost unnatural. Now these self-same Alps are quarried into marble of a thousand varieties. Headlands are laid open to the sea, and nature is flattened. We remove the barriers created to serve as the boundaries of nations, and ships are built specially for marble. And so, over the waves of the sea, Nature's wildest element, mountain ranges are transported to and fro, and even then with greater justification than we can find for climbing to the clouds in search of vessels to keep our drinks cool, and for hollowing out rocks that almost reach the heavens, so that we may drink from ice (that is, from rock-crystal). When we hear of the prices paid for these vessels, when we see the masses of marble that are being conveyed or hauled, we should each of us reflect, and at the same time think how much more happily many people live without them. That men should do such things, or rather endure them, for no purpose or pleasure except to lie amid spotted marbles, just as if these delights were not taken from us by the darkness of night, which is half our life's span!

LCL, Eichholz, pp. 3, 5. Note also, ibid, xxxiii, 1.

9   Cf. Florus, *Epit.* i, 1, 10:

Erat unius aetatis populus virorum. Itaque matrimonia a finitimis petita, quia non inpetrabantur, manu capta sunt. Simulatis quippe ludis equestribus virgines, quae ad spectaculum venerant, praedae fuere: et haec statim causa bellorum.

But a population consisting solely of men could only last for a single lifetime; wives were therefore demanded from the neighbouring peoples and, when they were refused, were seized by force. For, a pretence being made of holding horse-races, the maidens who had come to look on were carried off. This immediately gave rise to wars.

LCL, Forster, p. 11.

10   *adulterio glorientur*—cf. Seneca, *Ep.* 28, 10: *Quidam vitiis gloriantur*—some boast of their faults (LCL, Gummere, p. 203); and above, *DR* i, 27, 46. Petrarch knew the Seneca passage; cf. *Sen.* ii, 1, *Prose* (1955), p. 1052.

11   The last two paragraphs echo Ovid, *Ars amat.* i, 89–134:

Sed tu praecipue curvis venare theatris:
Haec loca sunt voto fertiliora tuo.

Illic invenies quod ames, quod ludere possis,
  Quodque semel tangas, quodque tenere velis.
Ut redit itque frequens longum formica per agmen,
  Granifero solitum cum vehit ore cibum,
Aut ut apes saltusque suos et olentia nactae
  Pascua per flores et thyma summa volant,
Sic ruit in celebres cultissima femina ludos:
  Copia iudicium saepe morata meum est.
Spectatum veniunt, veniunt spectentur ut ipsae:
  Ille locus casti damna pudoris habet.
Primus sollicitos fecisti, Romule, ludos,
  Cum iuvit viduos rapta Sabina viros.
Tunc neque marmoreo pendebant vela theatro,
  Nec fuerant liquido pulpita rubra croco;
Illic quas tulerant nemorosa Palatia, frondes
  Simpliciter positae, scaena sine arte fuit;
In gradibus sedit populus de caespite factis,
  Qualibet hirsutas fronde tegente comas.
Respiciunt, oculisque notant sibi quisque puellam
  Quam velit, et tacito pectore multa movent.
Dumque, rudem praebente modum tibicine Tusco,
  Ludius aequatam ter pede pulsat humum,
In medio plausu (plausus tunc arte carebant)
  Rex populo praedae signa petita dedit.
Protinus exiliunt, animum clamore fatentes,
  Virginibus cupidas iniciuntque manus.
Ut fugiunt aquilas, timidissima turba, columbae,
  Utque fugit visos agna novella lupos:
Sic illae timuere viros sine more ruentes;
  Constitit in nulla qui fuit ante color.
Nam timor unus erat, faciens non una timoris:
  Pars laniat crines, pars sine mente sedet;
Altera maesta silet, frustra vocat altera matrem:
  Haec queritur, stupet haec; haec manet, illa fugit;
Ducuntur raptae, genialis praeda, puellae,
  Et potuit multas ipse decere timor.
Siqua repugnarat nimium comitemque negabat,
  Sublatam cupido vir tulit ipse sinu,
Atque ita "quid teneros lacrimis corrumpis ocellos?
  Quod matri pater est, hoc tibi" dixit "ero."
Romule, militibus scisti dare commoda solus:
  Haec mihi si dederis commoda, miles ero.
Scilicet ex illo sollemnia more theatra
  Nunc quoque formosis insidiosa manent.

But specially do your hunting in the round theatres: more bountifully do these repay your vows. There will you find an object for passion or for dalliance, something to taste but once, or to keep, if so you wish. As crowded ants pass and repass in a long train, bearing in grain-burdened mouth their wonted food, or as bees, having gained their dells and fragrant pastures, flit o'er the blossoms and hover o'er the thyme: so hasten the smartest women to the crowded games; many a time have their numbers made my judgment falter. They come to see, they come that they may be seen: to chastity that place is fatal. Thou first, Romulus, didst disturb the games, when the rape of Sabine women consoled the widowed men. No awnings then hung o'er a marble theatre, nor was the plaform ruddy with crocus-spray; there, artlessly arranged, were garlands which the leafy Palatine had borne; the stage was unadorned; the people sat on steps of turf, any chance leaves covering their unkempt hair. They look about them, and each notes with his glance the woman he desires, and they brood much in their secret hearts. And while to the Tuscan flute-player's rude strains the dancer struck thrice with his foot the levelled floor, in the midst of the applause (the applause then was rough and rude) the king gave to the people the expected sign of rape. Straightway they leap forth, by their shouts betraying their eagerness, and lay lustful hand upon the maidens. As doves, most timorous of birds, flee from the eagles, and the weanling lamb when it spies the wolf, so feared they the men rushing wildly on them; in none remained her former colour. For their fear was one, but not one was the appearance of their fear: some tear their hair, some sit crazed; one is silent in dismay, one calls in vain upon her mother; this one bewails, that one is struck dumb; this one remains, that one flees. The captured women are led off, spoil for the marriage-couch, and to many their very fear had power to lend grace. If any struggled overmuch and resisted her mate, upborne on his eager breast he carried her off himself, saying: "Why do you spoil those tender eyes with tears? What your sire was to your mother that will I be to you." Ah, Romulus, thou only didst know how to bestow bounty on thy warriors; so thou but bestow such bounty upon me, I will be a warrior. And, mark you, in accord with that tradition our theatres now too are fraught with danger to the fair.

LCL, Mozley, pp. 19, 21. On the *spectacula* of late Antiquity and the Church, Suchomski (1975), esp. pp. 26–28.

12   Gaius Curio was killed 49 B.C., fighting against Juba in Africa.

13   Pliny, *Nat. hist.* xxxvi, 24, 116–120:

C. Curio, *qui bello civili in Caesarianibus partibus* obiit, funebri patris munere cum opibus apparatuque non posset superare Scaurum . . . . . . *ingenio* ergo utendum suo Curioni et aliquid excogitandum fuit. . . . . . Theatra iuxta duo fecit amplissima ligno, cardinum singulorum versatili suspensa libramento, in quibus utrisque antemeridiano ludorum spectaculo edito inter sese aversis, ne invicem obstreperent scaenae, repente circumactis—ut constat, post primos dies etiam sedentibus aliquis—cornibus in se coeuntibus faciebat amphitheatrum gladiatorumque proelia edebat, ipsum magis auctoratum populum Romanum circumferens. Quid enim miretur quisque in hoc primum, inventorem an inventum, artificem an auctorem, ausum aliquem hoc excogitare an suscipere an iubere? Super omnia erit populi sedere ausi furor tam infida instabilique sede. En hic est ille *terrarum victor* et totius domitor orbis, qui gentes, regna diribet, iura exteris mittit, deorum quaedam immortalium generi humano portio, in machina pendens et *ad periculum suum plaudens!* Quae vilitas animarum ista aut quae querela de Cannis! Quantum mali potuit accidere!

Gaius Curio, who died during the Civil War while fighting on Caesar's side, could not hope, in the entertainment which he provided in honour of his father's funeral, to outstrip Scaurus in the matter of costly embellishments. . . . . . . Curio, therefore, had to use his wits and devise some ingenious scheme. . . . . . . He built close to each other two very large wooden theatres, each poised and balanced on a revolving pivot. During the forenoon, a performance of a play was given in both of them and they faced in opposite directions so that the two casts should not drown each other's words. Then all of a sudden the theatres revolved (and it is agreed that after the first few days they did so with some of the spectators actually remaining in their seats), their corners met, and thus Curio provided an amphitheatre in which he produced fights between gladiators, though they were less in chancery than the Roman people itself as it was whirled around by Curio. Truly, what should first astonish one in this, the inventor or the invention, the designer or the sponsor, the fact that a man dared to plan the work, or to undertake it, or to commission it? What will prove to be more amazing than anything is the madness of a people that was bold enough to take its place in such treacherous, rickety seats. Here we have a nation that has conquered the earth, that has subdued the whole world, that distributes tribes and kingdoms, that despatches its dictates to foreign peoples, that is heaven's representative, so to speak, among mankind, swaying on a contraption and applauding its own danger! What a contempt for life this showed! What force now have our complaints of the lives lost at Cannae! What a disaster it could have been!

LCL, Eichholz, p. 93.

14 A.D. 27. —Suetonius, iii, Tiberius, 40:

. . . propter cladem, qua apud Fidenas *supra viginti hominum milia* gladiatorio munere *amphitheatri ruina* perierant.

. . . because of the disaster at Fidenae, where more than twenty thousand spectators had perished through the collapse of the amphitheater during a gladiatorial show.

LCL, Rolfe, p. 351. Also, Tacitus, *Ann.* iv, 62, 63.

15 On bridling the mind, cf. *Fam.* viii, 7, 10; *Sen.* xiii, 14 (1581: 926); *Rime* 73, 25–26; 97, 6; 141, 7; 240, 6; *Secretum, Prose* (1955), pp. 46, 60, 86, 122, 124, 134; *De vita sol.* i, *Prose* (1955), p. 288; *DR* i, Pref. 149–151, i, 6, 37, i, 9, 60; etc. Note Chaucer, *Troilus, passim,* and the comment in Rowland (1971), pp. 135–136. The image evokes Cicero, *De off.* i, 26, 90, and, based on this, *Rer. mem. libri* iii, 32; *Fam.* xvii, 3, 19–20, as below, *DR* i, 38, note 10; and *DR* i, Pref., note 41.

16   Cf. *castrum humani corporis,* as discussed in Cornelius (1930), pp. 18, 53–54; and Saville (1972), pp. 24–27. On the ecclesiastical opposition to the theater and related entertainments, Suchomski (1975), chap. 1, esp. pp. 23–30, 46–53, 58–60.

17   Horace, *Ars poet.* 180–182:

> segnius irritant animos demissa per aurem
> quam quae sunt oculis subiecta fidelibus et quae
> ipse sibi tradit spectator:

> Less vividly is the mind stirred by what finds entrance
> through the ears than by what is brought before the trusty
> eyes, and what the spectator can see for himself.

LCL, Fairclough, p. 465. Related, Cicero, *Ep. fam.* vii, 30, 1; and Seneca, *Ep.* 6, 5. Note *Fam.* xxiii, 10, 5: *vivacius in anima est quod per oculos, quam quod per aures introiit*—more lasting in one's mind is what enters through the eyes rather than through the ears. —On eyes and ears as windows of the mind, below, *DR* ii, 96, and ii, 97, note 1.

18   Cf. below, *DR* i, 89, note 2.

31   ❖   A GOOD HORSE

1   Contrary to Aristotle, *Hist. anim.* iv, 10, 536b, 25–30. The medieval bestiaries do not mention sleeplessness as a trait of the horse, but ascribe to lions the peculiarity *cum dormierint, vigilant oculi*—to keep their eyes open when they sleep. Isidore, *Etym.* xii, 2, 5 = Hrabanus Maurus, *De univ.* viii, 1, *PL* 111, c. 217; White (1954), p. 8; etc.

2   *bis equum male facere: quamvis hinc humile, hinc superbum sit.*

3   1492: duris stringi fasciis nodosque fune uinciri: freno frenari: ferro calciari pertusa clauis ungula: ferro urgeri: ferratum ferre uictorem turpem carcerem: ac graue seruitium pati possit:

   1581: duris stringi fasciis nodosque fune uinciri, freno frenari, ferro calcitrari pertusa clauis ungula ferro urgeri, ferratum ferre uectorem, turpem carcerem, ac graue seruitium pati possit.

4   Pliny, *Nat. hist.* viii, 64, 154:

> Eidem Alexandro et equi magna raritas contigit. Bucephalan eum vocarunt sive
> ab aspectu torvo sive ab insigni taurini capitis armo inpressi. xvi talentis ferunt

ex Philonici Pharsalii grege emptum etiam tum puero capto eius decore. Neminem hic alium quam Alexandrum regio instratu ornatus recepit in sedem, alias passim recipiens. Idem in proeliis memoratae cuiusdam perhibetur operae, Thebarum oppugnatione vulneratus in alium transire Alexandrum non passus; multa praeterea eiusdem modi, propter quae rex defuncto ei duxit exequias urbemque tumulo circumdedit nomine eius.

Alexander also had a good fortune to own a great rarity in horseflesh. They called the animal Bucephalus, either because of its fierce appearance or from the mark of a bull's head branded on its shoulder. It is said that it was bought for sixteen talents (ca. £4000 gold) from the herd of Philonicus of Pharsalus while Alexander was still a boy, as he was taken by its beauty. This horse when adorned with the royal saddle would not allow itself to be mounted by anybody except Alexander, though on other occasions it allowed anybody to mount. It is also celebrated for a memorable feat in battle, not having allowed Alexander during the attack on Thebes to change to another mount when it had been wounded; and a number of occurrences of the same kind are also reported, on account of which when it died the king headed its funeral procession, and built a city round its tomb which he named after it (Bucephala).

LCL, Rackham, p. 109. Cf. also Quintus Curtius, ix, 3, 23.

5   Julius Caesar.

6   Pliny, *Nat. hist.* viii, 64, 155:

Nec Caesaris dictatoris quemquam alium recepisse dorso equus traditur, idemque similis humanis pedes priores habuisse, hac effigie locatus ante Veneris Genetricis aedem. Fecit et divus Augustus equo tumulum, de quo Germanici Caesaris carmen est.

Also the horse that belonged to Caesar the Dictator is said to have refused to let anyone else mount it; and it is also recorded that its fore feet were like those of a man (i.e., with toes not united into a hoof: if true, a throwback to the prehistoric horse), as it is represented in the statue that stands in front of the Temple of Venus Genetrix (in Rome). The late lamented Augustus also made a funeral mound for a horse, which is the subject of a poem by Germanicus Caesar.

LCL, Rackham, p. 109.

7   Lucius Verus Antoninus, A.D. 130–169, reigned with Marcus Aurelius, A.D. 161–169. Both 1492 and 1581 have Antonius Verus.

8   Reason refers to Verus' racehorse *Volucer*—Flyer. The story comes from *Hist. Aug.,* Verus, vi, 3–5:

Nam et Volucri equo Prasino *aureum simulacrum* fecerat, quod secum portabat. Cui quidem passas uvas et nucleos in vicem hordei in praesepe ponebat, quem sagis fuco tinctis coopertum in Tiberianam ad se adduci iubebat, *cui mortuo* sepulchrum *in Vaticano* fecit.

For he had a golden statue made of the "Green" horse Volucer, and this he always carried around with him; indeed he was wont to put raisins and nuts instead of barley in this horse's manger and to order him brought to him, in the House of Tiberius covered with a blanket dyed with purple, and he built him a tomb, when he died, on the Vatican Hill.

LCL, Magie, p. 219.

9   Probably a reference to a passage in Virgil, *Aeneid* vi, such as 652–655:

> stant terra defixae hastae, passimque soluti
> per campum pascuntur equi; quae gratia currum
> armorumque fuit vivis, quae cura nitentis
> pascere equos, eadem sequitur tellure repostos.

Their lances stand fixed in the ground, and their steeds, unyoked, browse freely over the plain. The selfsame pride in chariot and arms that was theirs in life, the selfsame care in keeping sleek steeds, attends them when hidden beneath the earth.

Aeneas sees this in

> locos laetos et amoena virecta
> Fortunatorum Nemorum sedesque beatas.

> a land of joy, the green plesaunces
> and happy seats of the Blissful Groves.

LCL, Fairclough, p. 551. Reason's emphasis is on Virgil's heroes being described as lovers of horses, even after death. Twyne translates, f. 43r:

> The Poet thinkyng on this, and suche lyke thinges, maketh the soules of such men to be delighted with horses in hell.

10   For a later proverbial use of this observation, cf. Rowland (1973), pp. 107–108.

11   The warlike Mars is a horsegod. On his two horses, Homer, *Iliad* xv, 119; on the races connected with his cult, Harvey (1974), p. 261. On Thessaly, first in horsemanship, e.g., Virgil, *Georg.* iii, 113–119; and Pliny, *Nat. hist.* vii, 56, 202, still echoed in Polydore Vergil, *De rer. inv.* ii, 12.

12   Reason may foremost have in mind Thessaly during the Persian wars, and Caesar's victory over Pompey at Pharsalus, 48 B.C. (Dante, *Div. Comm.*, Par. vi, 64–66).

13   Virgil, *Georg.* iii, 72–283.

14   Ps. 75, 7:

> Ab increpatione tua, Deus Jacob,
> dormitaverunt qui ascenderunt equos.

Cf. the elaborate reference in the Parson's Tale to *Zach.* 10, 5:

Also the synne of aornement or of apparaille is in thynges that apertenen to ridynge, as in to manye delicat horses that been hoolden for delit, that been so faire, fatte, and costlewe;/ and also in many a vicious knave that is sustened by cause of hem; and in to curious harneys, as in sadeles, in crouperes, peystrels, and bridles covered with precious clothyng, and rich barres and plates of gold and silver./ For which God seith by Zakarie the prophete, "I wol confounde the rideres of swiche horses."/

Chaucer, *Canterbury Tales,* The Parson's Tale, 432–434, Robinson (1933), p. 286. —George Gascoigne (*The Grief of Joye,* 1576, Song iv, 45–46) treated the subject of *Rydinge* as follows:

> But ryding is, of nobles muche desired,
> And what can be brought in agaynst the same?
> Alas alas, my Muze must needes be tyred,
> To recken griefe in every kynde of game/
> But trust me (*Queene*) I am not yet so lame,
> But that I can in ryding finde some fault,
> As earst I dyd in them which leape and vault./

> For sett asyde, the danger of a fall,
> (Which so maye chañce, that (woulde wee ride or no,)
> Agaynst owre wylles, at last wee must or shall,
> When withe a broken legg wee cannott goe)
> I can rehearce yett many myschieves mo,
> And sundry greeves, thatt &c. &c.

> *Left unperfect for feare of Horsmen/*

Cunliffe, ii (1910), p. 557. The *Queene* referred to is Queen Elizabeth, daughter by Anne Boleyn of Henry VIII.

32 ❖ HUNTING AND HAWKING

1   Hugh of St. Victor, *Didasc.* ii, 25:

> Venatio dividitur in ferinam, aucupium et piscaturam. Ferina multis modis exercetur, retibus, pedicis, laqueis, praecipitiis, arcu, iaculis, cuspide, indagine, pennarum odore, canibus, accipitribus. Aucupium fit laqueis, pedicis, retibus, arcu, visco, hamo. Piscatura fit sagenis, retibus, gurgustiis, hamis, iaculis.

Hunting is divided into gaming, fowling, and fishing. Gaming is done in many

ways—with nets, foot-traps, snares, pits, thë bow, javelins, the spear, encir-
cling the game, or smoking it out, or pursuing it with dogs and hawks. Fowling
is done by snares, traps, nets, the bow, birdlime, the hook. Fishing is done by
drag-nets, lines, hooks, and spears.

Taylor (1962), p. 77.

2   I.t.: Flaccus. Horace, *Ars poet.* 162–165:

> *gaudet equis canibusque et aprici gramine Campi,*
> *cereus in vitium flecti, monitoribus asper,*
> *utilium tardus provisor, prodigus aeris,*
> *sublimis cupidusque et amata relinquere pernix.*

LCL, Fairclough, p. 465. Cf. John of Salisbury, *Policrat.* viii, 24, *PL* 199, c.
817.

3   On hawk and falcon, Goldstaub (1892), pp. 388–394. Note Hrabanus
Maurus, *De universo* viii, 6, *PL* 111, c. 253; Alain de Lille, *Distinct. dict. theol.*,
art. herodius, *PL* 210, c. 810; and Brunetto Latini, *Li Livres dou Tresor* i, 149.
On the falcon in Dante's *Commedia,* Boyde (1981), p. 121.

4   *Hist. Aug.* Hadrian, xx, 12–13:

> equos et canes sic amavit ut iis sepulchra constitueret. Oppidum Hadria-
> notheras in quodam loco, quod illic et feliciter esset venatus et ursam occidis-
> set aliquando, constituit.

> His horses and dogs he loved so much that he provided burial-places for them,
> and in one locality he founded a town called Hadrianotherae, because once he
> had hunted successfully there and killed a bear.

LCL, Magie, p. 65.

5   Marcellinus is M. Marcellus, the son of Octavia, nephew and adopted son of
emperor Augustus, and heir apparent, who died in 23 B.C., aged 20 (Virgil,
Aeneid vi, 860–886; Propertius, iii, 18). The grief of his mother and Augustus
is described in Ovid, *Consol. ad Liv.* 65–72,441–442; and Seneca, *Dial.* vi, 2,
3–4. Suetonius, *Vergil* 32, relates that Octavia *defecisse fertur atque aegre
focilata est*—is said to have fainted and to have been revived with difficulty
(LCL, Rolfe, p. 475) when Virgil read to Augustus from the *Aeneid* vi, 882–
883:

> heu! miserande puer, si qua fata aspera rumpas,
> tu Marcellus eris!

> Ah! child of pity, if haply thou couldst burst the harsh bonds of fate, thou shalt
> be Marcellus!

LCL, Fairclough, p. 569. —I cannot find an ironic passage on bird catching in
Virgil or a specific source relating such an incident. Cf. also Reason's serious
remarks about Marcellinus, below, *DR* i, 114, 74–82.

6   This may be Louis IX, Saint Louis, or Charles I of Anjou, King of Naples. Yet
     Joinville's history (*Historiens* . . . [1952], pp. 207–372) just implies Louis,
     the perfect knight and humane Christian, without reference to hunting. It is
     interesting that Reason does not mention Frederick II, whose *De arte venandi*
     cum avibus—Art of Hunting with Birds (Haskins [1927], pp. 299–326), was
     the mainstay of the French contemporary literature on the subject
     (Kantorowicz [1957b], pp. 359–363). On the love of hunting among the
     Normans, Gibbon (1789), chap. 56; in medieval France, Gautier (1883), pp.
     149–150. On hunting with falcons, ibid., pp. 174–184.

                          33 ✤ MANY SERVANTS

1   Matth. 10, 36 (quoted in Augustine, *De civ. Dei* xix, 5):

          et inimici hominis, domestici eius.

          And a man's enemies shall be they of his own household.

     Note also *Ps. poen.* v, 6: *utrobique hostes domesticos inveni;* and *DR* ii, 2, 39.
2   1492: opulentissimae Persarum: aut Lidorum regiae crederet
     1581: opulentissimae Persarum, aut Lydorum regiae cedere
3   Cf. John of Salisbury, *Policrat.* iv, 4, *PL* 199, c. 519:

          Plato, ut ferunt historiae gentium, cum vidisset Dionisium Siciliae tirannum
          corporis sui septum custodibus: Quod tantum, inquit, malum fecisti, ut a tam
          multis necesse habeas custodiri?

          The history books relate that Plato, when he saw the seven bodyguards sur-
          rounding Dionysius, the tyrant of Sicily, said, "What enormous crime did you
          commit that so many are required to watch you?"

4   Reason's discourse rings the changes on the characteristic complaints associ-
     ated with the age-old topic of *the trickery and arrogance of servants.* Cf., e.g.,
     Walter Map, *De nugis cur.* i, 10, which expounds the trials and tribulations of
     a small household that

          certe . . . unum habet servum et plures dominos; quia qui preest servit omni-
          bus, quibus servitur domini videntur.

          in truth . . . has one servant and many masters. The head serves everyone;
          those by whom he is served are to be reckoned as masters.

James et al. (1983), p. 25. On Petrarch's own difficulties with his servants, *Fam.* xxii, 12; Wilkins (1958), p. 198; and Wilkins (1961), pp. 167, 187. Cf. also *Buc. carm.* xi, 102; and below, *DR* ii, 29, note 6.

34 ❖ GREAT HOUSES

1   I.t.: Tullianum illud. —Cicero, *De off.* i, 39, 139:

> Ornanda enim est dignitas domo, non ex domo tota quaerenda, nec domo dominus, sed domino domus honestanda est.

LCL, Miller, pp. 141, 143.
2   Cf. Livy, i, 31, 8, i, 40, 7, i, 59, 11–12, ii, 1, 3.
3   1492: gloriare. &c.
    1581: gloriare

On this, above, *DR* i, 2, note 22.

35 ❖ STOUT CASTLES

1   Valerius Maximus, iii, Ext. 8:

> Eiusdem uir urbis atque animi hospiti suo *patriae muros* excelsos latosque *ostendenti* dixit, 'si mulieribus istos comparastis, *recte, si uiris, turpiter.*'

> The same Spartan said to his host and friend, who *showed* him the high, thick *walls of his town:* "If you prepared these against women, *well and good; if against men, it is shameful.*"

2   On P. Valerius Publicola, 509 B.C., Livy, ii, 7, 5–12:

> Consuli deinde qui superfuerat, ut sunt mutabiles volgi animi, ex favore non invidia modo sed suspicio etiam cum atroci crimine orta. Regnum eum adfectare fama ferebat, quia nec collegam subrogaverat in locum Bruti et aedificabat in summa Velia: ibi alto atque munito loco arcem inexpugnabilem fieri. Haec dicta volgo creditaque cum indignitate angerent consulis animum, vocato ad concilium populo submissis fascibus in contionem escendit. Gratum id mul-

titudini spectaculum fuit, submissa sibi esse imperii insignia confessionemque factam populi quam consulis maiestatem vimque maiorem esse. Ibi audire iussis consul laudare fortunam collegae, quod liberata patria, in summo honore, pro re publica dimicans, matura gloria necdum se vertente in invidiam, mortem occubuisset: se superstitem gloriae suae ad crimen atque invidiam superesse, ex liberatore patriae ad Aquilios se Vitelliosque recidisse. "Numquamne ergo," inquit, "ulla adeo vobis spectata virtus erit, ut suspicione violari nequeat? Ego me, illum acerrimum regum hostem, ipsum cupiditatis regni crimen subiturum timerem? Ego si in ipsa arce Capitolioque habitarem, metui me˙ crederem posse a civibus meis? Tam levi momento mea apud vos fama pendet? Adeone est fundata leviter fides ut ubi sim quam qui sim magis referat? Non obstabunt P. Valeri aedes libertati vestrae, Quirites; tuta erit vobis Velia. Deferam non in planum modo aedes, sed colli etiam subiciam, ut vos supra suspectum me civem habitetis; in Velia aedificent quibus melius quam P. Valerio creditur libertas." Delata confestim materia omnis infra Veliam et, ubi nunc Vicae Potae est, domus in infimo clivo aedificata.

Soon after this the surviving consul, so fickle are the affections of the mob, became unpopular; not only did the people dislike him, but they actually suspected him and made cruel charges against him. It was noised about that he was aspiring to the power of a king, since he had not caused a colleague to be elected in the place of Brutus, and was building a house on the highest part of the Velia, an elevated position of natural strength, men said, which he was converting into an impregnable citadel. The frequency of these remarks and the general acceptance they met with, shamefully unjust as they were, distressed the consul. He summoned the people to a council, and with lowered fasces mounted the speaker's platform. It was a welcome spectacle to the multitude when they beheld the emblems of authority there abased before them, in acknowledgment that the people's majesty and power were superior to the consul's. Then, bidding them to attend, the consul extolled the good fortune of his colleague, who, after his country had thrown off the yoke, had held the highest office in her gift, and, fighting for the state, at the height of a reputation as yet untarnished by envy, had met his death. He had himself outlived his glory, and survived to face accusations and ill-will. From being the saviour of his country he had sunk to the level of the Aquilii and Vitellii. "Will there never be worth and merit, then," he exclaimed, "so established in your minds that suspicion cannot wrong it? Could I possibly have feared that I, well known as the bitterest enemy of kings, should myself incur the charge of seeking kingly power? Could I have believed that, though I dwelt in the very Citadel and on the Capitol itself, I could be feared by my fellow-citizens? Can so trivial a cause ruin my reputation with you? Does your confidence rest on so slight a foundation that it makes more difference where I am than who I am? There shall be no menace in the house of Publius Valerius to your liberties, Quirites; your Velia shall be safe. I will not only bring my house down on to level ground, but will even place it under a hill, that you may live above me, the citizen whom you suspect. Let those build on the Velia who can better be trusted with men's liberty than can Publius Valerius!" Immediately the materials were all brought down below the Velia, and the house was erected where the temple of Vica Pota is now, at the bottom of the slope.

LCL, Foster, pp. 241, 243. Cf. also Valerius Maximus, iv, 1, 1; and Ps. Aurelius Victor, Pichlmayr (1911), *De vir. ill.* xv. Petrarch often mentions Publicola: e.g., *Africa* i (Bergin, 790); *Trionfi,* Tr. Fame i, 43–45, *Rime* (1951), p. 565; and *Fam.* vi, 2, 8, vi, 3, 40, x, 1, 16, xi, 16, 21, xv, 9, 26.

3   Cicero, *Ad Att.* i, 16, 7:

> Nunc est exspectatio comitiorum; in quae omnibus invitis trudit noster Magnus Auli filium atque in eo neque auctoritate neque gratia pugnat, sed quibus Philippus omnia castella *expugnari posse dicebat, in quae* modo *asellus onustus auro posset ascendere.*

> Now everyone is looking forward to the elections. Our "great" Pompey is pushing Aulus' son amidst general disapproval: and the means he is using are neither authority nor influence, but those which Philip said would storm any fort to which an ass laden with money could climb.

LCL, Winstedt, p. 61. Also quoted in *Fam.* xx, 1, 24. For a late echo, cf. *La Celestina* iii, 1, Marciales (1985), ii, p. 67; Simpson (1955), p. 41; and Deyermond (1966), p. 59.

4   M. Furius Camillus relieved the Tarpeian citadel from the onslaught of the Gauls 390 B.C.; Fabius Maximus Cunctator relieved Tarentum 209 B.C.

5   On the loss of Locri, 205 B.C., Livy, xxix, 6–9. Lucius Mummius razed Corinth 146 B.C.

6   Reason alludes to the war between the Colonna faction and Pope Boniface VIII (Dante, e.g., *Div. Comm.* Inf. xxvii, 85–105). Boniface assumed the papacy in 1294, after Celestine V's *gran rifiuto* (*Inf.,* iii, 59–60, xix, 52–57). On this, Singleton (1970), *Commentary,* pp. 47–52, 334–336; Toynbee (1968), arts. Bonifazio[1], Celestino V; and Padoan (1961). The Ghibellin Colonnas, led by their two cardinals, Jacopo and Pietro, opposed Boniface.

> In the true fashion of the wild Roman nobles their resentments led to a young lay Colonna, Stephen, later sung by Petrarch [i.e. Stefano Colonna the Elder], raiding a great papal treasure as it was being brought to Rome (1297). Boniface in a towering rage deprived the Colonna cardinals. They restored the treasure, but declared Celestine's abdication invalid and appealed to a General Council. Interdict, confiscation, and a crusade, the last degradation of the Holy War, were the Pope's answer. By September 1298 he was victorious. Palestrina, the Colonna stronghold, surrendered under false expectations and was razed to the ground.

C. W. Previté-Orton [1952], ii, p. 771. This is probably the *lunga promessa con l'attender corto*—long promise with short keeping, Dante, *Inf.* xxvii, 110. Cf. Singleton (1970), pp. 474–492; and Toynbee (1968), art. Colonnesi. If Reason's *some seventy years ago* is accurate, this passage of the dialogue would have to be dated about 1368, some two years after the date of completion of the *DR* as indicated in the Fossadolce explicit. —Petrarch enjoyed the patronage and friendship of the Colonna family since early youth. *Sen.* x, 2; Wilkins (1961), p. 4, and chaps. iv, vi *et passim.* He was no stranger to the Colonna stronghold in Palestrina. *Fam.* v, 2, 5, to Giovanni Cardinal Colonna, Oct. 7, 1343.

7   On the bridle of self-control, above, *DR* i, Pref., 149–151, i, 30, note 15.

8   In Livy xxxvii, 53, 16, King Eumenes observes:

> *Quod miserrimum est in bello, obsidionem* passus sum, Pergami inclusus cum discrimine ultimo simul vitae regnique.

> The most wretched fate in war, siege, I suffered, shut up in Pergamum, to the extreme peril at once of life and throne.

LCL, Sage, p. 449.

9   This is Stefano Colonna the Elder, head of the Colonna family until the time of his death in or before 1350.

> Persecution and exile displayed to the nations his abilities in peace and war; in his distress he was an object, not of pity but of reverence; the aspect of danger provoked him to avow his name and country; and when he was asked, "Where is now your fortress?" he laid his hand on his heart, and answered, "Here."

Gibbon (1789), chap. 69, Bury, vii (1914), p. 262. Petrarch recalled that at his coronation as poet laureate in 1341:

> Hinc Stephanus, quo fata virum iam tempore nostro
> Majorem, non Roma tulit, me laudibus amplis
> Accumulat . . .

> Stefano, whom the fates, and not Rome, destined to be the great man of our age, bestowed on me his ample praise . . .

Met. ii, 1, 54–56; Wilkins (1951), p. 64. In 1343 Petrarch described the elder Stefano:

> Deus bone, que maiestas hominis, que vox, que frons, que facies, quis habitus, que in illa etate vis animi, quod corporis robur! Iulium Caesarem aut Africanum spectare michi visus sum, nisi quia utroque multum iste longevior; et tamen idem prorsus aspectu qui ante septennium erat, dum eum Rome iterum dimisi, vel qui ante annos duodecim, dum eum apud Avinionem Rodani primum vidi. Mirum et pene incredibile: vir unus, Roma senescente, non senescit!

> Dear God, what human majesty, what a voice, what a presence, what a face, what a stature—what mental power for his age, what a physique! It was like beholding Julius Caesar or the Africanus, except that he is older than either of them. Yet he seemed to have the same appearance he had seven years ago when I left him in Rome, or when I had seen him for the first time twelve years

ago in Avignon at the Rhone. It was amazing and almost incredible that while Rome grows old, this man alone does not seem to have aged!

Fam. v, 3, 6, November 29, 1343. These lines are devoted to Stefano in the *Triumph of Fame* ii, 162–163:

> . . . il mio gran Colonnese,
> magnanimo, gentil, constante e largo

> . . . my great Colonna,
> Constant and generous, and of noble heart.

Wilkins (1962), p. 85. On this, Wilkins (1961), pp. 118–119. Cf. also *Met.* ii, 15. In Petrarch's *Rime,* Sonnet 10 remembers Stefano:

> Gloriosa columna in cui s'appoggia
> nostra speranza, e 'l gran nome latino,
> ch'ancor non torse del vero camino
> l'ira di Giove per ventosa pioggia;

> qui non palazzi, non teatro o loggia,
> ma 'n lor vece un abete, un faggio, un pino
> tra l'erba verde, e 'l bel monte vicino,
> onde si scende poetando e poggia,

> levan di terra al ciel nostr'intelletto;
> e 'l rosigniuol che dolcemente all'ombra
> tutte le notti si lamenta e piagne,

> d'amorosi penseri il cor ne 'ngombra:
> ma tanto ben sol tronchi, e fai imperfetto
> tu che da noi, signor mio, ti scompagne.

> O glorious Column against which does lean
> Our highest hope and the great Latin name,
> Which has not yet been twisted from the mean
> Path by Jupiter's windy rain and flame!

> Here not palaces, theatre or sill,
> But in their stead a fir, a beech, a pine,
> Between the green grass and the neighbour hill
> Whence we descend and make songs and recline,

> Lift up our mind from the earth to the skies;
> Also the nightingale that in the shade
> Sweetly will weep every night and mourn,

> Entangles all our heart in loving ties.
> But so much good you break and make forlorn
> Because away from us, my lord, you strayed.

Rime (1951), p. 12, and the annotations given there; *Armi* (1946), p. 11. Another reference to *una gran marmorea colonna,* the armorial device of the Colonna family (Gregorovius [1872], i, pp. 1049–1050, ii, pp. 95–96), occurs in *Rime* 53, 71–73, *Rime* (1951), p. 79. —In *Sen.* x, 2 (1581: 871) Petrarch referred to

> ex cineribus ueterum renatus Phoenix, unicus senex ille gloriosissimus Stephanus Columnensis.

> a Phoenix reborn from the ashes of the Ancients, that unique, most illustrious old man, Stefano Colonna.

On Stefano, cf. Fedele (1940). On the phoenix, below, *DR* i, 64, note 7. The phoenix image is probably based on Seneca, *Ep.* 42, 1. It recurs in *Sen.* iii, 1, and x, 4 (1581: 771, 878). —When, in 1372, cardinal Philippe de Cabassoles had the occasion to commend Petrarch to Pope Gregory XI, he referred to him as *vere Phoenix unicus . . . in terris*—truly a unique phoenix in this world (*Sen.* xii, 13 [1581: 925]; Wilkins [1959], pp. 224–225).

10   1492: Timidi: & ignaui
     1581: tumidi, & ignaui

11   Reason ignores the fact that among those seeking refuge in fortified strongholds were such popes as Gregory VII (Canossa, A.D. 1077—though "hardly mentioned by contemporaries," Langer [1940], p. 208), or, for that matter, Boniface VIII (Anagni, September 7, 1303; Barber [1978], pp. 23–25; Toynbee [1968], art. Bonifacio[1]), whom Reason, of course, may class among the scoundrels. Edward Gibbon (1789, chap. 69, Bury, vii [1914], p. 253) notes that this pope's

> memory is stained with the glaring vices of avarice and pride; nor has the courage of a martyr promoted this ecclesiastical champion to the honours of a saint: a magnanimous sinner (say the chronicles of the time), who entered like a fox, reigned like a lion, and died like a dog.

36 ❖ PRECIOUS FURNITURE

1   Dialogues 36–42 deal with precious things and possessions.
2   Cf. *Sen.* xiv, 1 (1581: 380):

Virtutum thesauros, et praeclaram famae suppellectilem concupisce, quibus nec tineae, nec fures, officiant, nec rubigo.

Covet the treasures of virtue, the precious furniture of honest fame, that neither moth, nor thieves, nor rust can hurt.

This clearly echoes Matth. 6, 19–20:

Nolite thesaurizare vobis thesauros in terra, ubi aerugo, et tinea demolitur, et ubi fures effodiunt, et furantur. Thesaurizate autem vobis thesauros in caelo, ubi neque aerugo, neque tinea demolitur, et ubi fures non effodiunt, nec furantur.

Lay not up to yourselves treasures on earth; where the rust and moth consume, and where thieves break through and steal. But lay up to yourselves treasures in heaven: where neither the rust nor moth doth consume, and where thieves do not break through, nor steal.

37 ❖ PRECIOUS STONES AND PEARLS

1   Cf. *De sui ipsius,* and *Secretum* ii, as below, *DR* ii, Pref., note 14.
2   *aureus*—a gold piece of various weights, first struck by the Romans during the Second Punic War. 1 aureus = 100 sesterces. Cf. Pliny, *Nat. hist.* xxxii, 13, 47.
3   Form in Aristotle's sense:

The intelligible structure, characters constituting a substance or a species of substances, as distinguished from the matter in which these characters are embodied.

Runes (1960), art. Form. In a reference, similarly general in nature, Dante, *Quest. de aqua* i, 4, cites Aristotle's *Categories* 8, 10a (cf. also Dante, *Convivio* ii, 13, 17). On substance, matter, and form, Aristotle, ibid. 2, 2a, and 8; *Phys.* i, 7, 190b, 1–4, i, 9, 192a; and *Metaph.* v, 8, viii, 2 and 3. Cf. also Scotus Erigena, *De div. nat.* i, 56–57, *PL* 122, cc. 498–501. On the topic in Dante's works, Toynbee (1968), arts. Aristotile, forma, materia. Note also the rewarding discussion of form and becoming in Gilson (1957), pp. 106–113.
4   I.e., exile and death. This is a Ciceronian topic. Cf. Cicero, *Tusc. disp.* v, 37, 106:

. . . . . . quod extimescendum sit? Exsilium, credo, quod in maximis malis ducitur.

. . . . . . what is there to be dreaded? Exile, I suppose, which is reckoned among the greatest evils.

and ibid. i, 4, 9:

A.: Malum mihi videtur esse mors.
M.: Iisne, qui mortui sunt, an iis, quibus moriendum est?
A.: Utrisque.
M.: Est miserum igitur, quoniam malum.
A.: Certe.
M.: Ergo, et ii, quibus evenit iam ut morerentur, et ii, quibus eventurum est, miseri.
A.: Mihi ita videtur.

A.: To my thinking death is an evil.
M.: To the dead or to those who have to die?
A.: To both.
M.: As it is an evil it is therefore wretchedness.
A.: Certainly.
M.: Then those whose lot it has already been to die and those whose lot it is to be are wretched.
A.: I think so.

LCL, King, pp. 533; 11, 13.

5 Reason's question is a rhetorical device inviting attention: the case of Nonius is *not* "well known" in the old literature.

6 I.e., 2,000,000 sesterces as given by Pliny, note 8, below.

7 Pliny, *Nat. hist.* viii, 47, 109:

Easdem partes sibi ipsi Pontici amputant fibri periculo urguente, ob hoc se peti gnari: castoreum id vocant medici.

The beavers of the Black Sea region practice self-amputation of the same organ [i.e., the testicles], when beset by danger, as they know that they are hunted for the sake of its secretion, the medical name for which is beaver-oil.

LCL, Rackham, p. 79. White (1954), p. 29, notes that the medicine *castoreum* "was situated not in the testicles, but in a different gland. The testicles of a beaver are internal and cannot be bitten off."

8 Pliny, *Nat. hist.* xxxvii, 21, 81–82:

insignit etiam apud nos historia, siquidem exstat hodieque huius generis gemma, propter quam ab Antonio proscriptus est Nonius senator . . . . . . Ille proscriptus fugiens hunc e fortunis omnibus anulum abstulit secum. Certum est sestertio vicies tum aestimatum, sed mira Antoni feritas atque luxuria propter gemmam proscribentis, nec minus Noni contumacia proscriptionem suam amantis, cum etiam ferae abrosa parte corporis, propter quam periclitari se sciant, et relicta redimere se credantur.

Even among us history makes it [i.e., the opal] famous, since there still exists even to-day a precious stone of this variety which caused Antony to outlaw a senator Nonius . . . . . . This Nonius, when outlawed, fled, taking with him this ring alone of all his many possessions. There is no doubt that at that time the value of the ring was 2,000,000 sesterces; but how amazing was Antony's savagery and extravagant caprice in outlawing a man for the sake of a gem-stone, and, equally, how extraordinary was the obstinacy of Nonius in clinging to his 'doom,' when even wild creatures [i.e., beavers] are believed to buy their safety by biting off the member which, as they know, endangers their lives, and leaving it behind for their pursuers!

LCL, Eichholz, p. 229.

9   Cf. Augustine, *Conf.* x, 34, 53, *PL* 32, c. 801:

Quam innumerabilia, variis artibus et opificiis, in vestibus, calceamentis, vasis, et cuiuscemodi fabricationibus picturis etiam, diversisque figmentis, atque his usum necessarium atque moderatum et piam significationem longe trans-gredientibus, addiderunt homines ad illecebras oculorum; foras sequentes quod faciunt, intus relinquentes a quo facti sunt, et exterminantes quod facti sunt! At ego, Deus meus, et decus meum, etiam hinc dico tibi hymnum, et sacrificio laudem sacrificatori meo; quoniam pulchra traiecta per animas in manus ar-tificiosas, ab illa pulchritudine veniunt, quae super animas est, cui suspirat anima mea die ac nocte. Sed pulchritudinum exteriorum operatores et sectatores inde trahunt approbandi modum, non autem inde trahunt utendi modum. Et ibi est, et non vident eum, ut non eant longius, et fortitudinem suam ad te custodiant, nec eam spargant in deliciosas lassitudines. Ego autem haec loquens atque discernens etiam istis pulchris gressum innecto; sed tu evellis, Domine, evellis tu, quoniam misericordia tua ante oculos meos est.

What numberless things, made by various arts and manufactures, both in our apparel, shoes, vessels, and every kind of work, in pictures, too, and sundry images, and these going far beyond necessary and moderate use and holy signification, have men added for the enthralment of the eyes; following out-wardly what they make, forsaking inwardly Him by Whom they were made, and destroying that which they themselves were made! But I, O my God and my Joy, do hence also sing a hymn unto Thee, and offer a sacrifice of praise to Thee Who dost sacrifice for me, because those beautiful patterns, which through the medium of men's souls are conveyed into their artistic hands, emanate from that Beauty which is above our souls, which my soul sigheth after day and night. But as for the makers and followers of those outward beauties, they from thence derive the way of approving them, but not of using them. And though they see Him not, yet is He there, that they might not go astray, but keep their strength for Thee (Ps. 58, 10), and not dissipate it upon delicious lassitudes. And I, though I both say and perceive this, impede my course with such beauties, but Thou dost rescue me, O Lord, Thou doest rescue me; for Thy loving kindness is before mine eyes (Ps. 25, 3).

J. G. Pilkington in Oates (1948), i, pp. 173–174. The lower things of beauty appeal to the *amor inferioris pulchritudinis,* which pollutes the mind (Augustine, *De musica* vi, 12, 41).

> . . . the word of God may be called the form of everything that exists since, in virtue of His perfect likeness to the Father, He confers on everything its being, unity, beauty, and truth [*De vera rel.* 36, 66, *PL* 34, cc. 151–153]. Thus, the Augustinian universe derives its metaphysical structure from a complex participation in the nature of divine being . . . God is being and consequently the Good. By expressing Himself in Himself He is the One, Beauty and Truth, the universal source of every participated perfection.

Gilson (1960), p. 214. Cf. also Scotus Erigena, *Super hier. coel.* 3, *PL* 122, c. 138: *visibiles quidem formas invisibilis pulchritudinis imaginationes arbitrans*—all visible forms are the reflections of the invisible beauty, which is purely intelligible. Similarly, idem, *De div. nat.* v, 3, *PL* 122, cc. 865–866. On this, Gilson (1955), pp. 120–121; De Bruyne (1946), iii, chaps. v, 4, vi, 5 and 6, and p. 204; and Panofsky (1946), pp. 18–21. On God as *omnis boni fons,* below, *DR* i, 86, note 6.

10 In his LCL edition of Pliny, *Nat. hist.* xxxvi–xxxvii, D. E. Eichholz explains that *adamas* "is left untranslated because the term refers to other stones besides diamonds" (p. 206). "Pliny's *carbunculi* include rubies, red garnet (pyrope and almandine), and possibly red spinel" (p. 238).

11 Pliny, *Nat. hist.* xxxvii, 15, 55:

> Maximum in rebus humanis, non solum inter gemmae, pretium habet adamas, diu non nisi regibus et iis admodum paucis cognitus.

> The most highly valued of human possessions, let alone gemstones, is the 'adamas,' which for long was known only to kings, and to very few of them.

LCL, Eichholz, p. 207.

12 Pliny, ibid., xxxvii, 16, 62.

13 Pliny, ibid., xxxvii, 41, 125.

14 The modern name is Saint Bertrand des Comminges.

15 About 78 B.C. Cf. also note 21, below.

16 On the *puer-senex*—boy and old man—topic of late Antiquity referring to a youth

> ante annos animumque gerens curamque virilem.

> with a man's mind and a spirit beyond his years.

(Virgil, *Aeneid* ix, 311, LCL, Fairclough, p. 133), Burrow (1986), pp. 95–102, 105–106, 111–116, 120–123, 137–141, 189, Curtius (1953), pp. 98–101,

381, 427, and Ghellinck (1948); and the story of Tages, *puerili specie* . . .
sed senili . . . *prudentia*—who had the appearance of a boy but the wisdom
of a seer—Cicero, *De div.* ii, 23, 50, LCL, Falconer, p. 429; and *Rer. mem.*
libri iv, 77, 2. Note Seneca, *Dial.* vi, Ad Marciam 23, 3–5; Boethius, *Cons.*
phil. ii, P 3, 22–24; the rhetorical descriptions in Matthew of Vendôme, *Ars* i,
52, 44–50, Galyon (1980), p. 39; and Petrarch's remarks in *Fam.* xii, 2, 9; *De*
vita sol. ii, *Prose* (1955), pp. 570, 572, 1052–1064, *Sen.* ii, 1, xiii, 2, xvii, 3
(1581: 754–755, 917, 542), and *Sen.* xvi, 4 (1581: 954):

> [Iacobus de Columna], qui etate tunc iuuenis, sed morum grauitate & mortis
> uicinitate senex . . .

> [Giacomo Colonna], who, as to age, was still a youth, but, as to gravity of
> deportment and the proximity of his death, was an old man . . .

17   Florus, i, 41; Hadas (1956), pp. 64–66.
18   The triumph of 61 B.C. Cf. Pliny, *Nat. hist.* vii, 98, xxxvii, 12–16. On tri-
     umphs, above, *DR* i, 19, note 5.
19   Pliny lists Gaius Caligula and Nero.
20   Pliny, below, note 21, refers to what seems to be a sundial or a water clock
     (the term *horologium* indicates any kind of time keeping device). He says
     nothing about moving parts. Does Reason think of a mechanical clock (first
     constructed in the thirteenth century, and mentioned in Dante, *Div. Comm.*,
     Par. xxiv, 13–18)? Petrarch was familiar with such devices, including the
     planetarium, as he called the mechanical masterpiece made by his friend
     Giovanni de' Dondi, "designed to indicate the motions of the planets accord-
     ing to the Ptolemaic theory, that is, of the sun, the moon, and the five planets
     then known, in addition to the mean and sidereal times." Bedini (1966), p.
     14. Cf. *Testament,* Mommsen (1957), pp. 33–35, 84–85, item 22; *Var.* 44,
     Fracassetti, iii (1863), p. 419; *Sen.* xii, 1 and 2, xiii, 15 and 16; Landes (1983),
     pp. 6–11, and chaps. 3, 4; Alsop (1982), pp. 307–311; J. Bronowski in
     Gingerich (1975), pp. 173–175; Sarton (1975), iii, pp. 1676–1677; Singer, iii
     (1957), pp. 601–604; and the older literature listed in Bedini (1966), pp.
     63–66.
21   Pliny, *Nat. hist.* xxxvii, 6, 12–16:

> Ergo tertio triumpho, quem de piratis, Asia, Ponto gentibusque et regibus in vii
> volumine operis huius indicatis M. Pisone M. Messala cos. pr. k. Octobres
> natali suo egit, transtulit alveum cum tesseris lusorium e gemmis duabus latum
> pedes tres, longum pedes quattuor—ne quis effetas res dubitet nulla gem-
> marum magnitudine hodie prope ad hanc amplitudinem accedente, in eo fuit
> luna aurea pondo xxx—lectos triclinares aureos tres, vasa ex auro et gemmis
> abacorum novem, signa aurea tria Minervae, Martis, Apollinis, coronas ex mar-
> garitis xxxiii, montem aureum quadratum cum cervis et leonibus et pomis
> omnis generis circumdata vite aurea, musaeum ex margaritis, in cuius fastigio

horologium. Erat et imago Cn. Pompei e margaritis, illa relicino honore grata, illius probi oris venerandique per cunctas gentes, illa, inquam, ex margaritis, illa, severitate victa et veriore luxuriae triumpho! Numquam profecto inter illos viros durasset cognomen Magni, si prima victoria sic triumphasset! E margaritis, Magne, tam prodiga re et feminis reperta, quas genere te fas non sit, fieri tuos voltus? Sic te pretiosum videri? Non ergo illa tua similior est imago quam Pyrenaei iugis imposuisti? Grave profecto, foedum probrum erat, ni verius saevum irae deorum ostentum id credi oporteret clareque intellegi posset iam tum illud caput orientis opibus sine reliquo corpore ostentatum.

Thus, Pompey's third triumph was held on his own birthday, September 29th of the year in which Marcus Piso and Marcus Messala were consuls, to celebrate his conquest of the pirates, Asia, Pontus and all the peoples and kings mentioned in the seventh volume of this work [vii, 98]. In this triumph, then, there was carried in the procession a gaming-board complete with a set of pieces, the board being made of two precious minerals and measuring three feet broad and four feet long. And in case anyone should doubt that our natural resources have become exhausted seeing that to-day no gems even approach such a size, there rested on this board a golden moon weighing 30 pounds. There were also displayed three gold dining couches; enough gold vessels inlaid with gems to fill nine display stands; three gold figures of Minerva, Mars and Apollo respectively; thirty-three pearl crowns; a square mountain of gold with deer, lions and every variety of fruit on it and a golden vine entwined around it; and a grotto of pearls, on the top of which there was a sundial. Furthermore, there was Pompey's portrait rendered in pearls, that portrait so pleasing with the handsome growth of hair swept back from the forehead, the portrait of that noble head revered throughout the world—that portrait, I say, that portrait was rendered in pearls. Here it was austerity that was defeated and extravagance that more truly celebrated its triumph. Never, I think, would his surname 'the Great' have survived among the stalwarts of that age had he celebrated his first triumph in this fashion! To think that it is of pearls, Great Pompey, those wasteful things meant only for women, of pearls, which you yourself cannot and must not wear, that your portrait is made! To think that this is how you make yourself seem valuable! Is not then the trophy that you placed upon the summit of the Pyrenees a better likeness of yourself? This, to be sure, would have been a gross and foul disgrace were it not rather to be deemed a cruel omen of Heaven's wrath. That head, so ominously manifested without its body in oriental splendour, bore a meaning which even then could not be mistaken.

LCL, Eichholz, pp. 173, 175. On pomp and circumstance in Petrarch's time, *Sen.* iv, 3 (1581: 782); and above, *DR* i, 30, note 1.

22   I.e., Pompey's defeat by Caesar at Pharsalus, Agusut 9, 48 B.C.; and his death in Egypt at the hands of the deserter Septimius in the same year. Florus, ii, 13; Hadas (1956), pp. 77–78.

23   On *ibi*—*hic*—here—there—cf. above, *DR* i, 18, note 3.

24   Florus, i, 40, 30.
25   Pliny, *Nat. hist.* xxxiii, 148–149:

> At eadem Asia donata multo etiam gravius adflixit mores, inutiliorque victoria illa hereditas Attalo rege mortuo fuit. Tum enim haec emendi Romae in auctionibus regiis verecundia exempta est urbis anno DCXXII, mediis LVII annis erudita civitate amare etiam, non solum admirari, opulentiam externam . . .

> But receiving Asia also as a gift dealt a much more serious blow to our morals, and the bequest of it that came to us on the death of King Attalus was more disadvantageous than the victory of Scipio. For on that occasion all scruples entirely disappeared in regard to buying these articles at the auctions of the king's effects at Rome—the date was the 622nd year of the city [132 B.C.], and in the interval of 57 years our community had learnt not merely to admire but also to covet foreign opulence . . .

LCL, Rackham, p. 111. On the corrupting influence of the East, above, *DR* i, 22, 29–37; and ibid., note 7.

26   Pliny, ibid., xxxvii, 3, 6:

> qui cum Romanis bellum gessit.

27   Pliny, ibid. xxxvii, 54, 139.
28   Solinus, 5, 25, Mommsen (1895), 53, 14:

> Unde anulus Pyrrhi regis, qui adversus Romanos bella gessit, non ignobilis famae fuit, cuius gemma achates erat, in quo novem Musae cum insignibus suis singulae et Apollo tenens citharam videbantur, *non impressis figuris sed ingenitis.*

> The ring of King Pyrrhus, who warred with the Romans, was not unworthy of its fame. That stone was an *achates*—agate in which could be seen the nine Muses, each with her implement, and Apollo holding his lyre, *not engraved, but naturally imprinted.*

29   Florus, i, 13, as quoted below, *DR* ii, 32, note 6.
30   Pliny, *Nat. hist.* xxxvii, 2, 3–5:

> His initiis coepit auctoritas in tantum amorem elata ut Polycrati Samio, insularum ac litorum tyranno, felicitatis suae, quam nimiam fatebatur etiam ipse qui felix erat, satis piamenti in unius gemmae voluntario damno videretur, si cum Fortunae volubilitate paria fecisset, planeque ab invidia eius abunde se redimi putaret, si hoc unum doluisset, adsiduo gaudio lassus. Ergo provectus navigio in altum anulum mersit. At illum piscis, eximia magnitudine regi natus, escae vice raptum, ut faceret ostentum, in culina domino rursus Fortunae insidiantis manu reddidit. Sardonychem eam gemmam fuisse constat, ostenduntque Romae, si credimus, in Concordiae delubro cornu aureo Augustae dono inclusam et novissimum prope locum praelatis multis optinentem

Hence arose the esteem in which gemstones are held; and this soared into such a passion that to Polycrates of Samos, the overlord of islands and coasts, the voluntary sacrifice of a single gemstone seemed a sufficient atonement for his prosperity, which even he himself, the happy recipient, owned to be excessive. Thereby he hoped to settle his account with the fickleness of Fortune. Clearly he supposed that he would be fully indemnified against her ill-will if he, who was weary of unremitting happiness, suffered this one unhappy experience. Accordingly, he put out in a boat and threw the ring into deep water. The ring, however, was seized as bait by a huge fish, fit for a king, which restored the ring as an evil omen to its owner in his own kitchen, thanks to Fortune's treacherous intervention. The gem, it is agreed, was a sardonyx and is displayed in Rome (if we can believe that this is the original stone) in the temple of Concord, set in a golden horn. It was presented by the empress and is ranked almost last in a collection containing many gems that are valued more highly.

LCL, Eichholz, pp. 165, 167. According to Herodotus iii, 41, the gemstone was an emerald.

31   I.e., September 19, 1356, at Maupertuis, in the battle of Poitiers. Note *Buc. carm.* xii, esp. 151–160. On this, Wilkins (1958), p. 157.

32   The friend was Galeazzo (II) Visconti, who, in 1361, dispatched Petrarch, accompanied by four military officers and one professor of jurisprudence, to Paris, to congratulate John the Good upon his liberation from captivity in England and safe return to France. The delegation brought

> as gifts from Galeazzo to the King, two rings: one that had been torn from the King's hand at the battle of Maupertuis and had eventually been recovered by Galeazzo, and a fine ruby ring of Galeazzo's own.

Wilkins (1961), pp. 173 *et passim*. On this mission, Barbeu du Rocher (1854); Hortis (1874), pp. 205–217; and Delachenal (1909), ii, pp. 270–272. Cf. *Fam.* xxii, 13, xxii, 14, xxiii, 2; *Sen.* x, 2, xvii, 2, *Prose* (1955), pp. 1108–1110, Bishop (1966), p. 270; and *Prose* (1955), p. 1148, and n. 2.

33   Pliny, *Nat. hist.* xxxvii, 40, 124:

> quae quidem scripsisse eos non sine contemptu et inrisu generis humani.

LCL, Eichholz, p. 267.

34   Yet note Thomas Aquinas, *Summa contra gent.* iii, 92 (citing Aristotle, *Magna mor.* ii, 8–9, 1206b–1207b) on the hidden powers of stones and plants (Pegis [1945], ii, pp. 176–177); and Panofsky (1960), p. 88.

35   Pliny, ibid., xxxvii, 76, 198:

> Nos contra rationem deprendendi falsas demonstrabimus, quando etiam luxuriam adversus fraudes muniri deceat.

LCL, Eichholz, p. 327.

38 ❖ PRECIOUS CUPS

1   Virgil, *Georg.* ii, 505–506:

> hic petit excidiis urbem miserosque penatis
> ut gemma bibat et Serrano dormiat ostro.

LCL, Fairclough, p. 151. 1492 omits line 506. —On Petrarch's golden wine bowl, a gift of emperor Charles IV, *Fam.* xxiii, 8, 1–3.

2   The *calix argenteus diuino cultui satis* is probably the silver chalice of the Last Supper (cf. i Cor. 10, 16) in the legend of the Holy Grail. On this, Ten Brink, i (1899), pp. 201–203; Voretzsch (1925), pp. 316–321; and Holmes (1948), pp. 284–290. Robert de Boron's romance of the story of the Grail is available in English in Goodrich (1964), chap. ix. Note also Sir Thomas Malory (1983), and the documentation in idem, ii, p. 843, "Sank(e)greal."

3   Juvenal, x, 25–27:

> . . . . . . sed nulla aconita bibuntur
> fictilibus, tunc illa time, cum pocula sumes
> gemmata . . .

LCL, Ramsay, p. 195.

4   Pliny, *Nat. hist.* xxxvii, 75, 197:

> nulla fraus vitae lucrosior.

LCL, Eichholz, p. 327.

5   Pliny, ibid. 40, 124.

6   1492: Saepe ira iocos parit.
    1581: saepe ita iocos parit,

7   1492: amniciosior: laetiorque sit ebrietas.
    1581: ambitiosior, letiorque sit ebrietas.

8   1492: & certior causa:
    1581: & certior causa est,

9   Reference is probably to Seneca, as above, *DR* i, 24, 97.

10 *Fam.* xvii, 3, 19–20:

> Africani verbum est a Panetio relatum, a Cicerone autem *Officiorum* libris insertum: "ut equi propter crebras contentiones preliorum ferocitate exultantes domitoribus tradi soleant ut his facilioribus possint uti, sic homines secundis rebus effrenatos sibique presidentes, tanquam in girum rationis et doctrine duci oportere, ut perspicerent rerum humanarum imbecillitatem varietatemque fortune." Quod quid est aliud dictu quam quod ait Psalmista, sed aliis verbis et brevius: "Ut sciant gentes quoniam homines sunt"? Multos quidem cogit humane conditionis oblivisci nimia felicitas.

Cicero inserted into *De officiis* [i, 26, 90, LCL, Miller, p. 93] the words of Africanus, as related by Panaetius: "As, when horses have become mettlesome and unmanageable on account of their frequent participation in battles, their owners put them in the hands of trainers to make them more tractable; so men who through prosperity have become restive and over self-confident ought to be put into the training ring, so to speak, of reason and learning, that they may be brought to comprehend the frailty of human affairs and the fickleness of fortune." And how varies that other saying, uttered by the Psalmist, save for its use of different words and being shorter: "that the nations* may know themselves to be but men" [Ps. 9, 21; *Douay has *Gentiles*]? Yet excessive good fortune causes many to forget their human condition.

Cf. below, *DR* i, 58, note 11.

11   On *necessaria,* cf. Hugh of St. Victor in De Bruyne (1946), ii, pp. 381–382; on *necessitas,* below, *DR* ii, 7, note 16, ii, 15, note 7.

12   Isidore, *Etym.* x, 9:

Avidus dictus ab avendo; avere enim cupere est. Hinc et avarus. Nam quid est avarum esse? progredi ultra quam sufficit. Avarus ex eo dictus, quod sit avidus auri . . .

Avidus—covetous—comes from *avendo*—craving—because *avere*—to crave—means *cupere*—to long for. And so also *avarus*—eagerly desirous. What does *avarum esse* mean? To strive beyond what is sufficient. The expression *avarus* derives from *avidus auri*—covetous of gold . . .

On Petrarch's note to this passage in his Isidore ms., Billanovich (1981), p. 187. For a derivation *avarus<avidus aeris,* cf. Gellius, x, 5. Similarly, Augustine, *De lib. arb.* iii, 48, *PL* 32, c. 1294.

13   Cf. Augustine, *De civ. Dei* xi, 13–15, esp.:

suo recusans esse subditus creatori et sua per superbiam velut privata potestate laetatus, ac per hoc falsus et fallax.

[the devil] refused to be second to his creator, and so was proud that he exulted in his power as if it were something of his own, and in so doing he was deceived and a deceiver.

LCL, Wiesen, p. 481. Cf. above, *DR* i, 10, 17–20.

14   On pride, "the root of all evils," cf. below, *DR* ii, 105, note 1.

15   Pliny, *Nat. hist.* xxxvii, 9, 23.

16   Pliny, ibid., 10, 29:

Fragmenta sarciri nullo modo queunt. Mire his ad similitudinem accessere vitrea, sed prodigii modo, ut suum pretium auxerint, crystalli non deminuerint.

Once it has been broken, rock-crystal cannot be mended by any method whatsoever. Glass-ware has now come to resemble rock-crystal in a remarkable manner, but the effect has been to flout the laws of Nature and actually to increase the value of the former without diminishing that of the latter.

LCL, Eichholz, p. 185.

17   In A.D. 68.

18   Suetonius, vi, Nero, 47, 1:

> Nuntiata interim etiam ceterorum exercituum defectione litteras prandenti sibi redditas concerpsit, mensam subvertit, duos scyphos gratissimi usus, quos Homerios a caelatura carminum Homeri vocabat, solo inlisit . . .

> When meanwhile word came that the other armies had revolted, he tore to pieces the dispatches which were handed to him as he was dining, tipped over the table, and dashed to the ground two favourite drinking cups, which he called "Homeric," because they were carved with scenes from Homer's poems.

LCL, Rolfe, p. 173.

19   This is Pliny's story (*Nat. hist.* xxxvii, 10, 29):

> Nero amissarum rerum nuntio accepto duos calices crystallinos in suprema ira fregit inlisos. Haec fuit ultio saeculum suum punientis, ne quis alius iis biberet.

> Nero, on receiving a message that all was lost, broke two crystal cups in a final outburst of rage by dashing them to the ground. This was the vengeance of one who wished to punish his whole generation, to make it impossible for any other man to drink from these cups.

LCL, Eichholz, p. 185.

20   Myrrhine vessels were made from fluorspar or agate. Cf. Pliny, *Nat. hist.* xxxvii, 8, 21–22.

21   Pliny, ibid. xxxvii, 7, 18–20:

> Eadem victoria primum in urbem myrrhina invexit, primusque Pompeius capides et pocula ex eo triumpho Capitolino Iovi dicavit. Quae protinus ad hominum usum transiere, abacis etiam escariisque vasis expetitis; et crescit in dies eius luxuria. Myrrhino LXX HS empto, capaci plane ad sextarios tres calice, potavit . . . anus consularis, ob amorem adroso margine eius, ut tamen iniuria illa pretium augeret; neque est hodie myrrhini alterius praestantior indicatura. Idem in reliquis generis eius quantum voraverit, licet aestimare ex multitudine, quae tanta fuit ut auferente liberis eius Nerone exposita occuparent theatrum peculiare trans Tiberim in hortis, quod a populo impleri canente se, dum Pompeiano proludit, etiam Neroni satis erat. Vidi tunc adnumerari unius scyphi fracti membra, quae in dolorem, credo, saeculi invidiamque Fortunae tamquam Alexandri Magni corpus in conditorio servari, ut ostentarentur, placebat. T. Petronius consularis moriturus invidia Neronis, ut mensam eius exheredaret, trullam myrrhinam HS CCC emptam fregit; sed Nero, ut par erat principem, vicit omnes HS ⌈X⌉ capidem unam parando. Memoranda res tanti imperatorem patremque patriae bibisse!

> It was the same victory that brought myrrhine ware for the first time to Rome.

Pompey was the first to dedicate myrrhine bowls and cups, which he set aside from the spoils of his triumphs for Jupiter of the Capitol. Such vessels immediately passed into ordinary use, and there was a demand even for display stands and tableware. Lavish expenditure on this fashion is increasing every day. . . . , an ex-consul, drank from a myrrhine cup for which he had given 70,000 sesterces, although it held just three pints. He was so fond of it that he would gnaw its rim; and yet the damage he thus caused only enhanced its value, and there is no other piece of myrrhine ware even to-day that has a higher price set upon it. The amount of money squandered by this same man upon the other aticles of this material in his possession can be gauged from their number, which was so great that, when Nero took them away from the man's children and displayed them, they filled the private theatre in his garden aross the Tiber, a theatre which was large enough to satisfy even Nero's desire to sing before a full house at the time when he was rehearsing for his appearance in Pompey's theatre. It was at this time that I saw the pieces of a single broken cup included in the exhibition. It was decided that these, like the body of Alexander, should be preserved in a kind of catafalque for display, presumably as a sign of the sorrows of the age and the ill-will of Fortune. When the ex-consul Titus Petronius was facing death, he broke, to spite Nero, a myrrhine dipper that had cost him 300,000 sesterces, thereby depriving the Emperor's dining-room table of this legacy. Nero, however, as was proper for an emperor, outdid everyone by paying 1,000,000 sesterces for a single bowl. That one who was acclaimed as a victorious general and as Father of his Country should have paid so much in order to drink is a detail that we must formally record.

LCL, Eichholz, pp. 177, 179.

22   The European hazel, *corylus avellana pontica*. Cf. Pliny, *Nat. hist.* xv, 24, 88–89. Did Petrarch see such cups of hazelwood when he visited Paris in 1361 to congratulate John of France on behalf of Galeazzo Visconti?

23   1492: uenis & notis
     1581: aduenis, & notis

24   1492: murinorum iactantia uicta sua sit
     1581: murrhinorum iactantia uita sit

25   Cf. Suetonius vi, Nero, 35.

26   Pliny, *Nat. hist.* xxxvii, 12, 47:

Domitius Nero in ceteris vitae suae portentis capillos quoque Poppaeae coniugis suae in hoc nomen adoptaverat quodam etiam carmine sucinos appellando, quoniam nullis vitiis desunt pretiosa nomina; ex eo tertius quidam hic colos coepit expeti matronis.

Among the other portentous events of his career is the fact that Domitius Nero bestowed this name on the hair of his wife Poppaea, even going so far as to call it in one of his poems 'sucini,' or 'amber-coloured,' for no defect lacks a term that represents it as an asset. From that time, respectable women began to aspire to this as a third possible colour for their hair.

LCL, Eichholz, pp. 201, 203.

39 ❖ CUT GEMS

1   On gem collecting in the Middle Ages, Alsop (1982), pp. 302–303, and the literature cited there. On the reemergence of connoisseurship and art collecting in Trecento Italy, Baxandall (1971); Panofsky (1960), chap. 1; Alsop, ibid., chap. x.

2   Pliny (note 3, below) does not omit the name Dioscurides. Petrarch's manuscript Pliny (Paris, B.N., f. lat. 6802, Nolhac [1907], ii, pp. 70–78), has a *lacuna* in the text. Petrarch got the name from Suetonius, ii, Aug., 50.

3   Pliny, Nat. hist. xxxvii, 4, 8–10:

> Ismeniae aetate . . . apparet scalpi etiam smaragdos solitos. Confirmat hanc eandem opinionem edictum Alexandri Magni, quo vetuit in hac gemma ab alio se scalpi quam ab Pyrgotele, non dubie clarissimo artis eius. Post eum Apollonides et Cronius in gloria fuere quique divi Augusti imaginem simillime expressit, qua postea principes signant, Dioscurides. . . . . . . Divus Augustus inter initia sphinge signavit. Duas in matris anulis eas indiscretae similitudinis invenerant. Altera per bella civilia absente ipso signavere amici epistulas et edicta quae ratio temporum nomine eius reddi postulabat, non inficeto lepore accipientium, aenigmata adferre eam sphingem. Quippe etiam Maecenatis rana per collationes pecuniarum in magno terrore erat. Augustus postea ad devitanda convicia sphingis Alexandri Magni imagine signavit.

> In the time of Ismenias . . . it seems evident that it had become customary to engrave even 'smaragdi.' This impression is supported, moreover, by an edict of Alexander the Great forbidding his likeness to be engraved on this stone by anyone except Pyrgoteles, who was undoubtedly the most brilliant artist in this field. Next to him in fame have been Apollonides, Cronius, and the man who made the excellent likeness of Augustus of Revered Memory which his successors have used as their seal, namely Dioscurides. . . . . . . Augustus of Revered Memory at the beginning of his career used a signet engraved with a sphinx, having found among his mother's rings two such signets which were so alike as to be indistinguishable. During the Civil Wars, one of these was used by his personal advisers, whenever he himself was absent, for signing any letters and proclamations which the circumstances required to be despatched in his name. The recipients used to make a neat joke saying 'the Sphinx brings its problems.' Of course, the frog signet belonging to Maecenas was also greatly feared because of the contributions of money that it demanded. In later years Augustus, wishing to avoid insulting comments about the sphinx, signed his documents with a likeness of Alexander the Great.

LCL, Eicholz, pp. 169, 171. Note Horace, *Ep.* ii, 1, 237–241; and Q. Curtius, i, LCL, Rolfe p. 6.

4   *natura—ars:* Reason's phraseology reflects the medieval notion of the Three
Works, described by M. D. Chenu as

> religious metaphysics which defined man as artisan (*homo artifex*) in relation
> to God's creative work (*opus Creatoris*) and the work of nature (*opus naturae*).
> The relationship to God's creative work conferred a religious significance upon
> human productive activity; the relationship to the work of nature provided
> such activity with its earthly standard of the truth. The threefold distinction
> was drawn from the commentary of Chalcidius upon the *Timaeus*; "All things
> that exist are the work of God, or the work of nature, or the work of a human
> artisan imitating nature"—*omnia enim quae sunt vel dei opera sunt vel naturae
> vel naturam imitantis hominis artificis.* (Chalcidius, 23, Waszink [1962], p. 73.)

Chenu (1957), pp. 40–44. On this, Hugh of St. Victor, *Didasc.* i, 9, Taylor
(1961), pp. 55–56. Cf. also Gilson (1957), pp. 119–121; and above, *DR* i, 20,
note 8.

5   Cf. above, *DR* 1, 37, 56–61, and note 9.

6   Cf. below, *DR* i, 89, note 2—Reason's talk about things that are *not necessary, but superfluous,* such as spacious houses, precious furniture, gems, and
pearls, invoke the rigorous notions of the monastic domain addressed in *De
ocio*, echoing Bernard of Clairvaux (De Bruyne [1946], ii, chap, iv, 1; and
Panofsky [1946], pp. 13–15). On the supreme *artifex*—craftsman (e.g., *Secretum* iii, *Prose* [1955], p. 148)—as compared to the human craftsman, Augustine, *Conf.* xi, 13; idem, *De vera rel.* xxxvi, 67; Boethius, *Cons. phil.* iv, P 6,
25–51; and Anselm of Canterbury (*Monolog.* cc. 10–11, Proslog. c.2). For
Abelard on Priscian's architect and related Platonic notions, as discussed in
Stock (1983), pp. 339–340, 345, 347, 379, 398; Alain de Lille, *De planctu
nat.* Q. v, *PL* 210, c. 453; Thomas Aquinas, *Summa theol.* i, Q 45, 6, resp.;
Javelet (1967), i, pp. 103–104, ii, p. 46, n. 61, pp. 70–73, nn. 9–11, pp. 115–
117, n. 131, pp. 290–291, n. 122; De Bruyne, ibid., ii, pp. 255–259; Curtius
(1953), chap. 21; Von Simson (1956), chap. 2; and Stock (1972), pp. 240–
242, 247, 253–256, 268–269. —Dante, *Div. Comm.,* Par. xix, 40–42, refers to

>   . . . Colui de volse il sesto
> a lo stremo del mondo, e dentro adesso
> distinse tanto occulto e manifesto . . .
>
> He that turned His compass round
> the limit of the world, and within it
> marked out so much both hidden and revealed . . .

Singleton (1975), p. 211. Note also Inferno xi, 100 (below, *DR* i, 56, note 4);
and *Mon.* i, 3, 2, ii, 2, 3. On this, Singleton (1970), Commentary, pp. 179–
180; and Boyde (1981), pp. 232–238. The poet of the *Carmina Burana* sang
exuberantly:

> Artifex qui condidit
> hominem ex luto,
> et linivit oculos
> ceci sacro sputo,
> salvet vestras animas
> crimine soluto,
> pax vobis omnibus! . . .

> The craftsman, who created
> man from clay,
> and healed blind eyes
> with sacred spittle [Ioan. 9, 6],
> He saves your souls,
> absolves you from your crime—
> may peace be with you all! . . .

Schmeller (1847), 197, 1. Cf. also below, *DR* i, 40, note 7.

40 ❖ PAINTINGS

1   For a rewarding interpretation of this and the following dialogue as "the longest discussion of art one has from the humanist Trecento," see Baxandall (1971), pp. 51–66, 140–143, where the two dialogues are given in the Latin text of the *Opera* (1581) and Twyne's translation of 1579. On Petrarch's relationship to art, Baxandall, ibid., esp. p. 51, n. 1, p. 52, n. 2; Krautheimer (1956/1982), chap. 19; G. Contini in Bernardo (1980), pp. 115–131; Panofsky (1960), pp. 10–13; Wilkins (1978), pp. 197–200; Wilkins (1961), pp. 23, 27, 130, 160, 223; Mommsen (1952); and Chiovenda (1933).

2   *sine fine miramini* seems to echo the *sine fine* of the regal acclamation and its liturgical corollary in the preface of the mass. Cf. *Missale Romanum* . . . , Praef.; Jungmann (1949), ii, pp. 155–156; and Hammerstein (1962), pp. 25, 31, 47. Cf. above *DR* i, 23, 80–81.

3   1492: ualde
      1581: uide

4   Cf. *Fam.* iv, 1, 27–29, describing a climb to the peak of Mont Ventoux (April 26, 1336; Wilkins [1961], pp. 12–13), where Petrarch, following the example of Augustine and Anthony (*Conf.* viii, 12; *Fam.* iv, 1, 30–31) opened at random his book—Augustine's *Confessions*—and read:

"Et eunt homines admirari alta montium et ingentes fluctus maris et latissimos lapsus fluminum et occeani ambitum et giros siderum, et relinquunt se ipsos." Obstupui, fateor; audiendique avidum fratrem rogans ne michi molestus esset, librum clausi, iratus michimet quod nunc etiam terrestria mirarer, qui iampridem ab ipsis gentium philosophis discere debuissem "nichil preter animum esse mirabile, cui magno nichil est magnum," Tunc vero montem satis vidisse contentus, in me ipsum interiores oculos reflexi, et ex illa hora non fuit qui me loquentem audiret donec ad ima pervenimus . . .

"And men go about wondering at mountain heights and the mighty waves of the sea and broad flowing streams and the circuit of the ocean and the wheeling of the stars: and to themselves they give no heed" [Augustine, *Conf.* x, 8, 15; Wilkins, ibid., p. 13]. I was stunned, asked my brother, who was eager to hear more, not to bother me, and closed the book—angry with myself that I was still admiring earthly things, although I should have learned long ago from the pagan philosophers that "nothing is worthy of admiration except the mind, compared to which, if it be great, nothing else is great" [Seneca, *Ep.* 8, 5; identified in Levi (1937), p. 86]. Then, satisfied that I had seen enough of the mountain, I turned my inner eyes upon myself, and from then on, no one heard me speak until we had reached the foot of the mountain.

On this, Kristeller (1956), pp. 264–265; Billanovich (1947), pp. 193–198; Billanovich (1966); Bishop (1963), chap. 8; Baron (1968), pp. 17–20; Seung (1976), pp. 50–53, 104–109, 114–115; and Mann (1984), chap. 1, and pp. 89–91.

5   Cf. above, *DR* i, 37, 59–61, and note 9.
6   Cf. Boethius, *Cons. phil.* i, M 2, 24–27:

> Nunc iacet effeto lumine mentis
> Et pressus grauibus colla catenis
> Decliuemque gerens pondere uultum
> Cogitur, heu, stolidam cernere terram.

> Now he lies here, bound down by heavy chains,
> the light of his mind gone out;
> his head is bowed down and he is forced
> to stare at the dull earth.

Green (1962), p. 6, Gruber (1978), pp. 86–88; and *De vita sol.* i, *Prose* (1955), p. 384:

Ita pars magna mortalium, seu volens seu coacta, beluarum moribus procurva in terram corpori obsequens, animi negligens, sine virtutis illecebra, sine ulla notitia suimet spiritum trahit inglorium atque anxium; quamvis enim natura melior interdum pungat ac vellicet et admoneat sui, obstant tamen impedimenta que dixi.

Thus the majority of mortals, whether willingly or because they are forced [cf., e.g., *DR* ii, 10, 77, ii, 33, 12], bent to the earth [*Fam.* x, 3, 27; *Sen.* x, 1, as below, *DR* i, 90, note 16] like beasts, obedient to their body, unmindful of their soul, without the blessings of virtue, without any awareness of it, drag along their spirit [*DR* ii, 90, note 39], inglorious and full of anxiety—and though, now and then, their better nature pricks and taunts them, and draws attention to its urgings, the obstacles I talked about remain.

Reason inveighs against man abandoning his erect, heavenward stance and with it his complete superiority in God's creation. Cf. Ovid, *Metam.* i, 84–88:

> pronaque cum spectent animalia cetera terram,
> os homini sublime dedit caelumque videre
> iussit et erectos ad sidera tollere vultus:

> And, though all other animals are prone [Sallust, *Cat.* i, 1], and fix
> their gaze upon the earth, he gave to man an uplifted face
> bade him stand erect and turn his eyes to heaven.

LCL, Miller, p. 9; quoted below, *DR* ii, 93, 150–152 (cf. Gruber [1978], pp. 406–407). —On the ancient *homo erectus* topic, Plato, *Tim.* 90 a-d; Aristotle, *De part. an.* 656a, 12–14, 686a, 26–28; Cicero, *Tusc. disp.* i, 28, 69, *De nat. deor.* ii, 56, 140, and *De leg.* i, 9, 26; Seneca, *Dial.* viii, De otio, 5, 4, xii, Ad Helviam, 8, 5, *Ep.* 94, 56, and 92, 30; Juvenal, xv, 142–147; Lactantius, *Div. inst.* ii, 1 and 18, iii, 9, vii, 5 and 9, *PL* 6, cc. 257–258, 343, 372, 750, 765–766, *De opif. Dei* viii and x, *PL* 7, cc. 34 (as below, *DR* ii, 93, note 46), 42, 45 (*rigidus*), 47, and Jansen (1952), p. 81; Augustine, *De trin.* xii, 1–2; *De civ. Dei* xiii, 14 as below, *DR* ii, 93, note 24, xxii, 24 (LCL, Levine, p. 331), and Ladner (1959), pp. 188–189; Macrobius, *Comm.* i, 14, 8–10; Prudentius, *Cathem.* x, 25–32, and Von den Steinen (1965), i, p. 110; Boethius, *Cons. phil.* i, P 3, 1–3, iii, P 8, 17–19, as in *DR*, i, 2, note 8, iii, M 8, 18, iv, P 2, 71–73, iv, M 7, 29–30, v, M 5, 10–15, and Lerer (1985), esp. pp. 176, 179, 195, 227–228; Isidore, *Etym.* xi, 1, 5, and Fontaine (1959), ii, pp. 678–680; Anselm, *Proslog.* i, *PL* 158, c. 225; Bernardus Silvestris, *Cosmogr.* ii, 10, Wetherbee (1973), p. 113, and n. 10, and Von den Steinen (1959), p. 277; Bernard of Clairvaux, *Super Cantica* 24, as discussed in Stock (1983), pp. 439–440; Huch of St. Victor, *Didasc.* i, 1, Taylor (1961), p. 176, n. 3; Alain de Lille, *Ars praedic.* vii, *PL* 210, c. 126; Also Ladner (1965), pp. 86–87, n. 54; Javelet (1967), i, pp. 59, 61, 233–234, ii, p. 31, n. 250, p. 35, n. 276, pp. 204–205, nn. 513–520; Thomas Aquinas, *Summa theol.* i, Q 91, a 3; Nicole Oresme, *De commens.*, Proem., 21–27, and iii, 266–269, Grant (1971), pp. 172–175, 304–305; Bartholomaeus Anglicus, *De propr. rer.* ii, i (after Lactantius-Isidore), v, 12 (after Aristotle); Johannes von Tepl, *Ackerm. aus Boehmen* xxv, Walshe (1951), pp. 30–32, and Bernt-Burdach (1917), pp. 314–323. Note *Roman de la Rose* 18999–19054, Dehlberg (1971), p. 314; Dante, *Div. Comm.*, Inf. xiv, 111, and Mazzotta (1979), p. 25. Cf. below, *DR* i, 54, 9–11, i, 86, note 3, i,

Homo erectus. God Creates Adam. Before 1100. Santiago di Compostela. Photo MAS.

90, 64–67; ii, 93, 63–64; and, e.g., *Fam.* xx, 1, 6, xxiii, 5, 1, or xxiii, 9, 3; and *Ps. poen.* iv, 15, *Rime* (1951), p. 840.

7   *On opifex ille*—the great craftsman; Chalcidius, *Comm. Tim. passim*, e.g. Waszink (1962), 41 a 7–13; 200, c. 139, 5–10; pp. 35 and 179; also, De Bruyne (1946), vol. ii, pp. 256–258; Curtius (1953), chap. 21; De Lubac, vol. ii, 2 (1964), chap. vii; Javelet (1967), vol. ii, pp. 81–82, n. 36; p. 87, n. 60; p. 280, n. 16. Related, above, *DR* i, 39, note 6.

8   1492: ad alta disponitis
1581: ad alta despicitis

Related, *Sen.* i, 7 (1581: 748), citing Ps. 35, 10: *in lumine tue uidebimus lumen.* —*sol et luna*—sun and moon (Von den Steinen [1959], p. 13)—represent the cosmos and its sorrow in scenes of the Crucifixion (cf., e.g., the miniature in the 11th-century Uta Manuscript, Munich, lat. 13601, f. 3v, Von den Steinen, ibid., pl. 4/5, and p. 361; note *De ocio* i [1581: 305]. They are also the attibute of the Virgin Mary as "a woman clothed with the sun, and the moon under her feet." Apoc. 12, 1; cf. *Rime* 366, 1–3. On ignoring the connection to the highest things, Job 31, 26–28, as below, *DR* i, 86, note 7.

9   William Durand, *Rationale div. off.* (as quoted in Holt [1947], p. 67) on "carved images which project from the walls." On the epideictic topic of lifelikeness, Baxandall (1971), pp. 51–78; Panofsky (1960), chap. i, iii, and iv; and Alsop (1982), pp. 286–292, 308–309.

10   On talent and artistic craftsmanship, *Fam.* vi, 2, 13; *Itin. Syr.* (1581: 560, on Giotto; cf. also *Fam.* v, 17, 6). On lifelike images, *Sen.* iv, 3 (1581: 783, as above, *DR* i, 30, note 1), referring to the bronze horses of St. Mark's in Venice (Norwich [1982], p. 140, and pl. 15; Alsop [1982], pp. 143–144; Gibbon [1789], chap. 60, Bury vi [1912], p 429); and the remarkable description of the twelfth-century polychrome stucco relief of St. Ambrose that Petrarch saw in Sant' Ambrogio near his house in Milan (now in the Museum Sant' Ambrogio), *Fam.* xvi, 11, 12–13:

> . . . imaginemque eius summis parietibus extantem, quam illi viro simillimam fama fert, sepe venerabundus in saxo pene vivam spirantemque suspicio. Id michi non leve precium adventus; dici enim non potest quanta frontis autoritas, quanta maiestas supercilii, quanta tranquillitas oculorum; vox sola defuerit vivum ut cernas Ambrosium.

> I often gaze reverently at his image, set high in the wall and said to be a close likeness of the man: it seems almost to be living and breathing. It is enough in itself to repay me for having come here. Words fail me to describe the authority of his countenance, the majesty of his expression, the tranquillity of his eyes: if he could only speak you would behold the living Ambrose.

Wilkins (1961), p. 131, adjusted: On this Wilkins (1958), pp. 16–18; and Baxandall (1971), p. 51. The topic recurs in the two "portrait sonnets," *Rime*

Cosmic Crucifixion. Ca. 1020. Uta Codex, Regensburg. Munich, Staatsbibl., lat. B 601, f. 3v. Bildarchiv Foto Marburg im Kunstgeschichtlichen Institut der Philipps Universitaet, Marburg, X101.583.

Roman Bronze Horses. Venice, St. Mark's. Alinari/Art Resource.

77 and 78, that Petrarch wrote in the spring of 1336 in appreciation of
Simone Martini's painting of Laura (Wilkins [1961], p. 12; Wilkins [1978], pp.
198–199; Billanovich [1981], pp. 95–96):

> Per mirar Policleto a prova fiso,
> con gli altri ch'ebber fama di quell'arte,
> mill'anni, non vedrian la minor parte
> della beltà che m'ave il cor conquiso;
>
> ma certo il mio Simon fu in paradiso,
> onde questa gentil Donna si parte;
> ivi la vide e la ritrasse in carte,
> per far fede qua giù del suo bel viso.
>
> L'opra fu ben di quelle che nel cielo
> si ponno imaginar, non qui tra noi,
> ove le membra fanno a l'alma velo;
>
> cortesia fe', né la potea far poi
> che fu disceso a provar caldo e gelo,
> e del mortal sentiron gli occhi suoi.

Tondo of Saint Ambrose. 12th c., according to Wilkins (1958), p. 17. Milan, Museo Sant Ambrogio. Alinari/Art Resource.

If Polycletus put it to a test,
With all the other masters of his art,
A thousand years, they would not see the best
Part of that beauty which conquered my heart.

But certainly Simon saw paradise
wherein this gentle lady had her place;
There he saw her and portrayed in such guise
This is the witness here of her fair face.

The work is one of those that in the sky
Can be conceived, and not in our sheepfold
Where the flesh throws a shadow on the soul.

Courtesy is the work; nor could he try
It when he was exposed to heat and cold,
And when his eyes aimed at a mortal goal.

Armi (1946), p. 131.

Quando giunse a Simon l'alto concetto
ch'a mio nome gli pose in man lo stile,
s'avesse dato a l'opera gentile
colla figura voce ed intelletto,

di sospir molti mi sgombrava il petto
che ciò ch'altri à più caro a me fan vile,
però che 'n vista ella si mostra umile

promettendomi pace ne l'aspetto.

Ma poi ch'i' vengo a ragionar con lei,
benignamente assai par che m'ascolte:
se risponder savesse a' dette miei!

Pigmalion, quanto lodar ti dei
de l'imagine tua, se mille volte
n'avesti quel ch'i' sol una vorrei!

When Simon was inspired by the elect
Idea that to his hand the brush consigned,
If he had given to the fair object
With a figure and a voice too and a mind,

He would have freed my heart of many sighs,
That depreciate for me what others love;
Because she looks as humble as a dove
And she promises comfort with her eyes.

And when I come and try to speak to her
She seems to listen with benignity;
If she could only answer to my prayer!

Pygmalion, how happy you must be
With your image, who thousand times have had
From her what only once would make me glad!

Armi (1946), p. 131. Cf. also Dante, *Div. Comm.*, Purg. xi, 26–33. On the expert judgment of sensitive connoisseurs, *Testament* 12, Mommsen (1957), pp. 21–25, 78–81; *Sen.* xv, 3 (1581: 935); Dante, *Div. Comm.*, Purg. xi, 79–108, on illuminators, Cimabue, and Giotto; Boccaccio, *Decam.* vi, 5, on Giotto (Panofsky [1960], pp. 12–13; Krautheimer [1956/1982], p. 296; Alsop [1982], pp. 287–289); and Giovanni Dondi (Panofsky, ibid., pp. 208–209, as below, *DR* i, 41, note 2). On humanists on painting, Baxandall (1971), chap. ii.

11   Reason alludes to Pliny, *Nat. hist.* xxxv, 7, 20:

laeva is manu pinxit, quod de nullo ante memoratur. Parvis gloriabatur tabellis extinctus nuper in longa senecta Titedius Labeo praetorius, etiam proconsulatu provinciae Narbonensis functus, sed ea re inrisa etiam contumeliae erat.

[Turpilius] painted with his left hand, a thing recorded of no preceding artist. Titedius Labeo, a man of praetorian rank who had actually held the office of Proconsul of the Province of Narbonne, and who died lately in extreme old age, used to be proud of his miniatures, but this was laughed at and actually damaged his reputation.

LCL, Rackham, p. 275.

12 Cf. Pliny, ibid. xxv, 7, 34–37.

13 Pliny, ibid., 36, 77:

> Pamphili cognatio et proelium ad Phliuntem ac victoria Atheniensium, item Ulixes in rate. Ipse Macedo natione, sed . . . primus in pictura omnibus litteris eruditus, praecipue arithmetica et geometria, sine quibus negabat artem perfici posse, docuit neminem talento minoris—annuis Ҳ D—quam mercedem at Apelles et Melanthius dedere ei. Huius auctoritate effectum est Sicyone primum, deinde in tota Graecia, ut pueri ingenui omissam ante graphicen [hoc est picturam] in buxo, docerentur recipereturque ars ea in primum gradum liberalium. Semper quidem honos ei fuit, ut ingenui eam exercerent, mox ut honesti, perpetuo interdicto ne servitia docerentur. Ideo neque in hac neque in toreutice ullius, qui servierit, opera celebrantur.

> To Pamphilus belong Family Group, and a Battle at Philus and a Victory of the Athenians, and also Odysseus on his Raft. He was himself a Macedonian by birth, but [was brought up at Sicyon, and] was the first painter highly educated in all branches of learning, especially arithmetic and geometry, without the aid of which he maintained art could not attain perfection. He took no pupils at a lower fee than a talent, at the rate of 500 drachmae per annum, and this was paid him by both Apelles and Melanthius. It was brought about by his influence, first at Sicyon and then in the whole of Greece as well, that children of free birth were given lessons in drawing on boxwood, which had not been included hitherto, and that this art was accepted into the front rank of the liberal sciences. And it has always consistently had the honour of being practised by people of free birth, and later on by persons of station, it having always been forbidden that slaves should be instructed in it. Hence it is that neither in painting nor in art of statuary are there any famous works that were executed by any person who was a slave.

LCL, Rackham, pp. 317, 319. There is no evidence that Petrarch's age knew any classical paintings (Baxandall [1971], p. 59; below, DR i, 41, 7–8).

14 On brevity, cf. above, DR i, Pref., note 21.

15 *vulgus . . . consuetudinum genitrix*. On *consuetudo*—general habit inculcated upon everyone by parents, relatives, friends, associates, and circumstances—the κατήχησις τῶν πολλῶν of the Stoa (SVF, iii, 229a–232; Pohlenz, i [1959], p. 124)—deception which we drank in *cum lacte nutricis*—with our nurse's milk (Cicero, *Tusc. disp.* ii, 1, 3; LCL, King, p. 227)—and which continues through our lifetime—*Fam.* ii, 2, 14 and 20, viii, 3, 18, xi, 12, 6, xii, 3, 4; *Sen.* v, 2 (1581: 793), referring to *consuetudo* as *second nature*; and below, DR i, 69, 123–126, and note 17, ii, 10, 16–19, ii, 41, 41, ii, 58, 63–64. See also DR i, 11, note 18. —On Augustine's *consuetudo*, based on the usage of juridical rhetoric, which distinguished routinely between *ius*—law *secundum naturam*—according to Nature—or *secundum consuetudinem*—according to established custom—and that based upon *lex*—the statutes (Cicero, *De*

inv. ii, 22, 65)—cf. R.A. Markus in Armstrong (1967), p. 387. Note also Isidore, *Etym.* ii, 10, 6, ii, 10, 2–3 = v, 3–4; Fontaine (1959), i, pp. 259–261; Lausberg (1960), i, p. 81. —Reason's *as I have said* refers to *DR* i, 30, 26.

16   On *deus artifex*, above, *DR* i, 39, note 6.

41 ❖ STATUES

1   See above, *DR* i, 40, note 1.

2   Cf. Giovanni Dondi's letter (Venice, Bibl. di. San Marco, ms. lat. cl. xiv, 223, 5 and 58; Essling [1902], p. 45, Baxandall [1971], p. 52, n. 3; and as quoted and translated in Panofsky [1960], pp. 208–210:

> Hec profecto sunt magnorum argumento virorum. Talibus similia ob similes causas hoc nostro evo non fiunt et quare putas nisi quia desunt tam hi qui illa agant quibus talia premia debeantur, quam hi qui sic agentibus, si forent, faverent quo talia largirentur.

> De artificiis ingeniorum veterum quamquam pauca supersint, si que tamen manent alicubi, ab his qui ea in re sentiunt cupide queruntur et videntur magnique penduntur. Et si illis hodierna contuleris, non latebit auctores eorum fuisse ex natura ingenio potiores et Artis magisterio doctiores. Edificia dico vetera et statuas sculpturasque cum aliis modi hujus quorum quedam cum diligenter observant hujus temporis artifices obstupescunt. Novi ego marmorarium quemdam famosum illius facultatis artificem inter eos quos tum haberet Ytalia, presertim in artifitio figurarum; hunc pluries audivi statuas atque sculpturas quas Rome prospexerat tanta cum admiratione atque veneratione morantem, ut id referens poni quodamodo extra se ex rei miraculo videretur. Aiebant enim se quinque cum sociis transeuntem inde ubi alique hujusmodi cernerentur ymagines, intuendo fuisse detentum stupore artificii et societatis oblitum substitisse tam diu donec comites per quingentos passus et amplius preterirent; et cum multa de illarum figurarum bonitate narraret et auctores laudaret ultraque modum comendaret ingenia, ad extremum hoc solebat addicere, ut verbo utar suo, nisi illis ymaginibus spiritus vite deesset, meliores illas esse quam vivas, ac si diceret a tantorum artificum ingeniis non modo imitatam fuisse naturam verum etiam superatam.

> These [viz., the triumphal arches, columns, etc., described in the preceding sentences] verily bear witness to great men; similar monuments, [erected] for

similar reasons, are not produced in our own age, and this, indubitably, because of the absence not only of those whose actions would deserve such tributes but also of those who, provided that there were such as had acted accordingly, would be in favor of their being so lavishly honored.

Few of the works of art produced by the ancient geniuses have been preserved; but those which have survived somewhere are eagerly looked for and inspected by sensitive persons and command high prices. And if you compare to them what is produced nowadays, it will be evident that their authors were superior in natural genius and more knowing in the application of their art. When carefully observing ancient buildings, statues, reliefs, and the like, the artists of our time are amazed. I knew a sculptor in marble famous in his craft among those living in Italy, particularly as far as figures are concerned; him I have often heard hold forth upon the statues and reliefs which he had seen in Rome with such admiration and reverence that, in merely relating it, he seemed to get beside himself with enthusiasm. Once (so I was told), when in the company of five friends he passed by a place where images of this kind could be seen, he stayed behind and looked at them, enraptured by their artistry; and he kept standing there, forgetful of his companions, until they had proceeded five hundred paces or more. After having talked a good deal about the excellence of those figures and having praised their authors and their authors' genius beyond all measure, he used to conclude, to quote his own words, with the statement that, if those images did not lack the breath of life, they would be superior to living beings—as though he meant to say that nature had not so much been imitated as vanquished by the genius of those great artists.

On this, Krautheimer (1956/1982), pp. 295–298; Baxandall (1971), pp. 52–53; and Alsop (1982), pp. 307–311. On Dondi, Mommsen (1957), pp. 33–35; and above, *DR* i, 37, note 20. Panofsky's observation regarding Dondi's text that "the word *sculptura* is consistently used in contradistinction to *statura*" (ibid., p. 209, n. 1) holds true also for our text.

3   Cf. Pliny, *Nat. hist.* xxxv, 5, 15–16, and 36, 67–68.

4   Pliny, *ibid.*, vii, 37, 125:

> idem hic imperator edixit ne quis ipsum alius quam Apelles pingeret, quam Pyrgoteles scalperet, quam Lysippus ex aere duceret . . .

> This ruler also issued an edict that only Apelles could paint him, only Pyrgoteles engrave his likeness, and only Lysippus cast him in bronze . . .

LCL, Rackham, p. 591. Cf. *Rime* 232, as below, *DR* ii, 107, note 15. Pliny's use of *scalpere* in *Nat. hist.* xxxvii, 4, 8–10, as above, *DR* i, 39, note 3 also suggests "engraving."

5   *illustrious of the second order*, i.e., the second *ordo* of the three ranks: *senatorius*, *equestris*, and *plebeius*. On Augustus, Vespasian, etc., Pliny, *Nat. hist.* xxxvi, 4, 27–29.

6   1492: Non fit de nihilo magnum nomen magnum esse uel uideri oportet de
      quo serio magni tractant
      1581: Non fit de nihilo magnum, esse uel uideri oportet, de quo serio magni
      tractant
7   Pliny, *Nat. hist.* xxxv, 43, 151, and 44, 153:

> Contexuisse his et plasticen conveniat. Eiusdem opere terrae fingere ex argilla
> similitudines Butades Sicyonius figulus primus invenit Corinthi filiae opera,
> quae capta amore iuvenis, abeunte illo peregre, umbram ex facie eius ad
> lucernam in pariete lineis circumscripsit, quibus pater eius inpressa argilla
> typum fecit et cum ceteris fictilibus induratum igni proposuit, eumque
> servatum in Nymphaeo, donec Mummius Corinthum everterit, tradunt. . . .
> . . . Hominis autem imaginem gypso e facie ipsa primus omnium expressit
> ceraque in eam formam gypsi infusa emendare instituit Lysistratus Sicyonius,
> frater Lysippi, de quo diximus. Hic et similitudines reddere instituit; ante eum
> quam pulcherrimas facere studebant. Idem et de signis effigies exprimere in-
> venit, crevitque res in tantum, ut nulla signa statuaeve sine argilla fierent. Quo
> apparet antiquiorem hanc fuisse scientiam quam fundendi aeris.

> It may be suitable to append to these remarks something about the plastic art.
> It was through the service of that same earth that modelling portraits from clay
> was first invented by Butades, a potter of Sicyon, at Corinth. He did this owing
> to his daughter, who was in love with a young man; and she, when he was
> going abroad, drew in outline on the wall the shadow of his face thrown by a
> lamp. Her father pressed clay on this and made a relief, which he hardened by
> exposure to fire with the rest of his pottery; and it is said that this likeness was
> preserved in the Shrine of the Nymphs until the destruction of Corinth by
> Mummius [146 B.C..]. . . .   . . . The first person who modelled a likeness in
> plaster of a human being from the living face itself, and established the method
> of pouring wax into this plaster mould and then making final corrections on
> the wax cast, was Lysistratus of Sicyon, the brother of Lysippus of whom we
> have spoken. Indeed he introduced the practice of giving likenesses, the object
> aimed at previously having been to make as handsome a face as possible. The
> same artist also invented taking casts from statues, and this method advanced
> to such an extent that no figures or statues were made without a clay model.
> This shows that the knowledge of modelling in clay was older than that of
> casting bronze.

LCL, Rackham, pp. 371, 373, 375. Cf. also Pliny, ibid. xxxv, 2, 6.
8   1492: quae cognatis licet artibus cunctis amicior: sic uirtuti: aut certe minus
      inimica modestiae imprimis: & frugalitati:
      1581: quae cognatis licet artibus, cunctis amicitior sit, uirtuti, aut certe mi-
      nus inimica modestie in primis & frugalitati.

On *frugality and moderation,* above, *DR* i, 41, 38, and i, Pref., note 27. Note
Fam. i, 8, 9: *Adsit ergo cuntis in rebus modestia*—therefore let moderation be
exercised in everything.

9   Pliny, *Nat. hist.* xxxv, 45, 157:

> . . . Vulcam Veis accitum, cui locaret Tarquinius Priscus Iovis effigiem in
> Capitolio dicandam; fictilem eum fuisse et ideo miniari solitum; fictiles in fas-
> tigio templi eius quadrigas, . . . ab hoc eodem factum Herculem, qui hodieque
> materiae nomen in urbe retinet. Hae enim tum effigies deorum erant lautis-
> simae, nec paenitet nos illorum, qui tales eos coluere; aurum enim et argentum
> ne diis quidem conficiebant.

> [Varro states] . . . that Vulca was summoned from Veii to receive the contract
> from Tarquinius Priscus for a statue of Jupiter to be consecrated in the Capitol,
> and that this Jupiter was made of clay and consequently was regularly painted
> with cinnabar; and that the four-horse chariots . . . . . . on the pediment of
> the temple were modelled in clay; and that the figure of Hercules, which even
> to-day retains in the city the name of the material it is made of [*Hercules
> Fictilis*—Hercules in Clay], was the work of the same artist. For these were the
> most splendid images of gods at that time; and we are not ashamed of those
> ancestors of ours for worshipping them in that material. For they used not
> formerly to work up silver and gold even for the gods.

LCL, Rackham, p. 377.

10   Daniel 3, 1–6:

> Nabuchodonosor rex fecit statuam auream, altitudine cubitorum sexaginta, la-
> titudine cubitorum sex, et statuit eam in campo Dura, provinciae Babylonis.
> Itaque Nabuchodonosor rex misit ad congregandos satrapas, magistratus, et
> judices, duces, et tyrannos, et praefectos, omnesque principes regionum, ut
> convenirent ad dedicationem statuae quam erexerat Nebuchodonosor rex.
> Tunc congregati sunt satrapae, magistratus, et judices, duces, et tyranni, et
> optimates qui erant in potestatibus constituti, et universi principes regionum,
> ut convenirent ad dedicationem statuae quam erexerat Nabuchodonosor rex.
> Stabant autem in conspectu statuae quam posuerat Nabuchodonosor rex; et
> praeco clamabat valenter: Vobis dicitur populis, tribubus, et linguis: In hora
> qua audieritis sonitum tubae, et fistulae, et citharae, sambucae, et psalterii, et
> symphoniae, et universi generis musicorum, cadentes adorate statuam auream
> quam constituit Nabuchodonosor rex. Si quis autem non prostratus adoraverit,
> eadem hora mittetur in fornacem ignis ardentis.

> King Nabuchodonosor made a statue of gold, of sixty cubits high, and six
> cubits broad, and he set it up in the plain of Dura of the province of Babylon.
> Then Nabuchodonosor the king sent to call together the nobles, the magis-
> trates, and the judges, the captains, the rulers, and governors, and all the chief
> men of the provinces, to come to the dedication of the statue which king
> Nabuchodonosor had set up. Then the nobles, the magistrates, and the judges,
> the captains, and rulers, and the great men that were placed in authority, and
> all the princes of the provinces, were gathered together to come to the dedica-
> tion of the statue, which king Nabuchodonosor had set up. And they stood
> before the statue which king Nabuchodonosor had set up. Then a herald cried

with a strong voice: To you it is commanded, O nations, tribes and languages: That in the hour that you shall hear the sound of the trumpet, and of the flute, and of the harp, of the sackbut, and of the psaltery, and of the symphony, and of all kind of music; ye fall down and adore the golden statue which king Nabuchodonosor hath set up. But if any man shall not fall down and adore, he shall the same hour be cast into a furnace of burning fire.

11   Pliny, *Nat. hist.* xxxvii, 32, 108:

Ex hac primum inportatam Berenicae reginae, quae fuit mater sequentis Ptolemaei, ab Philone praefecto; regi mire placuisse et inde factam statuam Arsinoae Ptolemaei uxori quatturo cubitorum, sacratam in delubro quod Arsinoeum cognominabatur.

[Juba records] that the stone was first brought from here as a gift for Queen Berenice, the mother of Ptolemy the Second, by his governor Philo; and that, because the king greatly admired it, a statue 4 cubits high was later made of peridot in honour of this Ptolemy's wife, Arsinoë, and consecrated in the shrine which was named after her the Arsinoëum.

LCL, Eichholz, p. 253.

12   On matter and art, Baxandall (1971), pp. 61–62; Baxandall (1972), pp. 14–17; and Alsop (1982), p. 342.

13   Twyne, f. 59v: the Embassadours that were slayne by the king of the Vetii. Cf. Livy, i, 15, iv, 17; and Cicero, *Philipp.* ix, 2, 4.

14   Livy, xxxviii, 56.

15   Augustine, *Conf.* viii, 2, 3, *PL* 32, c.750:

[Victorinus] . . . ille doctissimus senex, et omnium liberalium doctrinarum peritissimus, quippe philosophorum tam multa legerat, et dijudicaverat, et diluciidaverat; doctor tot nobilium senatorum, qui etiam ob insigne praeclari magisterii, quod cives hujus mundi eximium putant, statuam in Romano foro meruerat et acceperat.

[Victorinus] . . . this learned old man, highly skilled in all the liberal sciences, who had read, criticized, and explained so many works of the philosophers; the teacher of so many noble senators, who also, as a mark of his excellent discharge of his duties, had (which men of this world seem to esteem a great honor) both merited and obtained a statue in the Roman Forum.

J. G. Pilkington in Oates (1948), i, p. 112. This passage is cited in *De sui ipsius*, *Prose* (1955), p. 762. On Marius Victorinus, Cayré, i (1936), pp. 331–332.

16   1492: Sentio autem ut tua haec omnis delectatio plena sit ingenii materiaeque nobilitas iuncta perficiet

   1581: Sentio autem, ut tua delectatio plena sit ingenii, materiaeque nobilitas iuncta perficiet

Twyne: but I perceyve how this thy delight is ful of wisdome, and ioyned
with the most noble matter (f. 59v.)

17 Twyne, f. 59v, substitutes:

To take delight also in the images and statues of godly and vertuous men, the
beholding of which may stirre us up to have remembrance of their maners &
lives, is reasonable, & may profite us in imitating ye same.

On artistic expression "designed to lead the mind through exercise to spiritual understanding," Robertson (1963), pp. 58–61. On exercising the mind,
below, *DR* i, 44, note 18.

18 I Ioan. 5, 21:

custodite vos a simulacris.

19 On Protogenes, Pliny, *Nat. hist.* xxxv, 36, 101–106; Apelles, ibid., 36, 79–97;
Polycletus, xxxiv, 19, 49 and 55; and Phidias, xxxiv, 19, 54, xxxvi, 4, 15–19.
Note Baxandall (1971), pp. 39–40 *et passim*; Alsop (1982), pp. 184, 188–
189, 206–207, 266–267, 290–291. On God the maker, above, *DR* i, 40,
notes 7 and 15.

42 ❖ CORINTHIAN VESSELS

1 1492: et seipsum
1581: seipsum

Cf. above, *DR* i, 40, 12–14.

2 On *deus artifex*, *DR* i, 39, note 6. On contempt of earthly things, *Fam.* iv, 1,
27–29, as above, *DR* i, 40, note 4, i, 1, 82–84.

3 In 146 B.C.

4 Florus, i, 32, 6–7:

Tum ab incolis deserta civitas direpta primum, deinde tuba praecinente deleta
est. Quid signorum, quid vestium quidve tabularum raptum incensumque atque proiectum est! Quantas opes et abstulerit et cremaverit, hinc scias, quod
quidquid Corinthii aeris toto orbe laudatur incendio superfuisse comperimus.
Nam et aeris notam pretiosiorem ipsa opulentissimae urbis fecit iniuria, quia
incendio permixtis plurimis statuis atque simulacris aeris auri argentique venae
in commune fluxerunt.

The city, deserted by its inhabitants, was first plundered and then destroyed at
a signal given by trumpets. What a vast quantity of statues, garments and

pictures was carried off, burnt, and thrown away! How great was the wealth which was plundered or burnt may be judged from the fact that we are told that all the Corinthian bronzework, which enjoys so high a repute throughout the world, was a survival from the conflagration. For the damage inflicted on this rich city in itself caused a higher value to be placed upon Corinthian bronze, because, by the melting together of countless statues and images by the flames, brass, gold and silver ore were fused into one common mass.

LCL, Forster, p. 143.

5   Cf. Suetonius ii, Aug. 27, 1.

6   Suetonius, ibid., 70, 2:

Notatus est et ut pretiosae supellectilis Corinthiorumque praecupidus . . . Nam et proscriptionis tempore ad statuam eius ascriptum est:
          Pater argentarius, ego Corinthiarius,
cum existimaretur quosdam propter vasa Corinthia inter proscriptos curasse referendos.

He was criticized too as over fond of costly furniture and Corinthian bronzes . . . Indeed, as early as the time of the proscriptions there was written on his statue—
          In silver once my father dealt, now in Corinthians I,
since it was believed that he caused some men to be entered in the list of the proscribed because of their Corinthian vases.

LCL, Rolfe, p. 233. Cf. *Sen.* xv, 3 (1581: 935).

7   Reason refers to the proscription of Gaius Verres in 43 B.C.
     Cf. Pliny, *Nat. hist.* xxxiv, 3, 6–7:

Ex illa autem antiqua gloria Corinthium maxime laudatur. Hoc casus miscuit Corintho, cum caperetur, incensa, mireque circa id multorum adfectatio furuit, quippe cum tradatur non alia de causa Verrem, quem M. Cicero damnaverat, proscriptum cum eo ab Antonio, quoniam Corinthiis cessurum se ei negavisset. Ac mihi maior pars eorum simulare eam scientiam videtur ad segregandos sese a ceteris magis quam intellegere aliquid subtilius; et hoc paucis docebo. Corinthus capta est olympiadis CLVIII anno tertio, nostrae urbis DCVIII, cum ante haec saecula fictores nobiles esse desissent, quorum isti omnia signa hodie Corinthia appellant. Qua propter ad coarguendos eos ponemus artificum aetates; nam urbis nostrae annos ex supra dicta comparatione olympiadum colligere facile erit. Sunt ergo vasa tantum Corinthia, quae isti elegantiores modo ad esculenta transferunt, modo in lucernas aut trulleos nullo munditiarum dispectu. Eius aeris tria genera: candidum argento nitore quam proxime accedens, in quo illa mixtura praevaluit; alterum, in quo auri fulva natura; tertium, in quo aequalis omnium temperies fuit. Praeter haec est cuius ratio non potest reddi, quamquam hominis manu est, at fortuna temperatur in simulacris signisque illud suo colore pretiosum ad iocineris imaginem vergens, quod ideo hepatizon appellant, procul a Corinthio, longe tamen ante Aegineticum atque Deliacum, quae diu optinuere principatum.

Of the bronze which was renowned in early days, the Corinthian is the most highly praised. This is a compound that was produced by accident, when Corinth was burned at the time of its capture; and there has been a wonderful mania among many people for possessing this metal—in fact it is recorded that Verres, whose conviction Marcus Cicero had procured [70 B.C.], was, together with Cicero, proscribed by Antony for no other reason than because he had refused to give up to Antony some pieces of Corinthian ware; and to me the majority of these collectors seem only to make a pretence of being connoisseurs, so as to separate themselves from the multitude, rather than to have any exceptionally refined insight in this matter; and this I will briefly show. Corinth was taken in the third year of the 158th Olympiad, which was the 608th year of our city [146 B.C.], when for ages there had no longer been any famous artists in metalwork; yet these persons designate all the specimens of their work as Corinthian bronzes. In order therefore to refute them we will state the periods to which these artists belong; of course it will be easy to turn the Olympiads into the years since the foundation of our city by referring to the two corresponding dates given above. The only genuine Corinthian vessels are then those which your connoisseurs sometimes convert into dishes for food and sometimes into lamps or even washing basins, without nice regard for decency. There are three kinds of this sort of bronze: a white variety, coming very near to silver in brilliance, in which the alloy of silver predominates; a second kind, in which the yellow quality of gold predominates, and a third kind, in which all the metals were blended in equal proportions. Besides these there is another mixture the formula for which cannot be given, although it is man's handiwork; but the bronze valued in portrait statues and others for its peculiar colour, approaching the appearance of liver and consequently called by a Greek name 'hepatizon' meaning 'liverish,' is a blend produced by luck; it is far behind the Corinthian blend, yet a long way in front of the bronze of Aegina and that of Delos which long held the first rank.

LCL, Rackham, pp. 131, 133.

8   Seneca, *Ep.* 31, 11:

Animus, sed hic rectus, bonus, magnus. . . . Hic animus tam in equitem Romanum quam in libertinum, quam in servum potest cadere. Quid est enim eques Romanus aut libertinus aut servus? Nomina ex ambitione aut ex iniuria nata. Subsilire in caelum ex angulo licet. Exurge modo

> et te quoque dignum
Finge deo.

Finges autem non auro vel argento; non potest ex hac materia imago deo exprimi similis; cogita illos, cum propitii essent, fictiles fuisse.

It is the soul—but the soul that is upright, good, and great. . . . A soul like this may descend into a Roman knight just as well as into a freedman's son or a slave. For what is a Roman knight, or a freedman's son, or a slave? They are mere titles, born of ambition or of wrong. One may leap to heaven from the very slums. Only rise

> And mould thyself to kinship with thy God (Virgil, *Aeneid* viii, 364–365).
> This moulding will not be done in gold and silver; an image that is to be in the
> likeness of God cannot be fashioned of such materials; remember that the
> gods, when they were kind unto men, were moulded in clay.

LCL, Gunmere, p. 229. Cf. also Seneca, ibid., 90.

9   This seems to be a reference to Valerius Maximus, iv, 3, 7, and 4, 8; but no
excuse is given.

10 Seneca, *Ep.* 95, 72–73:

> . . . Tuberonis ligneos lectos, cum in publicum sternerent, haedinasque pro
> stragulis pelles et ante ipsius Iovis cellam adposita conviviis vasa fictilia. Quid
> aliud paupertatem in Capitolio consecrare? Ut nullum aliud factum eius
> habeam, quo illum Catonibus inseram, hoc parum credimus? Censura fuit illa,
> non cena. O quam ignorant homines cupidi gloriae, quid illa sit aut
> quemadmodum petenda! Illo die populus Romanus multorum supellectilem
> spectavit, unius miratus est. Omnium illorum aurum argentumque fractum est
> et milliens conflatum, at omnibus saeculis Tuberonis fictilia durabunt.

> or the wooden couches of Tubero, spread at a public feast, goatskins instead of
> tapestry, and vessels of earthenware set out for the banquet before the very
> shrine of Jupiter! What else was this except *consecrating poverty on the Capitol*?
> Though I know no other deed of his for which to rank him with the Catos, is
> this one not enough? It was a censorship, not a banquet. How lamentably do
> those who covet glory fail to understand what glory is, or in what way it
> should be sought! On that day the Roman populace viewed the furniture of
> many men; it marvelled only at that of one! The gold and silver of all the others
> has been broken up and melted down times without number; but Tubero's
> earthenware will endure throughout eternity.

LCL, Gummere, pp. 103, 105, and note *a*. Cf. also Seneca, *Ep.* 98, 13.

11 Cf. note 10, above.

12 1492: Caius

1581: Galienus

On extravagant silverware, Pliny, *Nat. hist.* xxxiii, 49–53.

13 Cf. Krautheimer (1956/1982), p. 61, and note 35.

14 190–189 B.C. Livy, xxxvii *passim*; Pliny, *Nat. hist.* xxxiii, 53.

15 Above, *DR* i, 37, 97–103.

16 Pliny, *Nat. hist.* xxxv, 8, 24:

> Tabulis autem externis auctoritatem Romae publice fecit primus omnium L.
> Mummius, cui cognomen Achiaci victoria dedit. Namque cum in praeda
> vendenda rex Attalus ✕ ⌐vi⌐ emisset tabulam Aristidis, Liberum patrem, pre-
> tium miratus suspicatusque aliquid in ea virtutis, quod ipse nesciret, revocavit
> tabulam, Attalo multum querente, et in Cereris delubro posuit, quam primam
> arbitror picturam externam Romae publicatam.

The high esteem attached officially to foreign paintings at Rome originated from Lucius Mummius who from his victory received the surname of Achaicus. At the sale of booty captured King Attalus bought for 600,000 denarii a picture of Father Liber or Dionysus by Aristides, but the price surprised Mummius, who suspecting there must be some merit in the picture of which he was himself unaware had the picture called back, in spite of Attalus's strong protests, and placed it in the Shrine of Ceres: the first instance, I believe, of a foreign picture becoming state-property at Rome.

LCL, Rackham, pp. 277, 279, and note *a*. In *Nat. hist.* vii, 38, 126, Pliny referred to Attalus' bidding 100 talents for a picture by Aristides.

17   Cf. above, *DR* i, 22, note 7.

18   1492: Samia
      1581: Famia

Pliny, *Nat. hist.* xxxv, 46, 160:

Samia etiam nunc in esculentis laudantur.

Among table services Samian pottery is still spoken highly of.

LCL, Rackham, p. 379. Note *Fam.* xxiii, 17, 6:

Licet enim inter vasa aurea miserum esse, inter fictilia felicem, neque ad bene vivendum aut argilla auro vilior aut samos est inferior quam Chorintus.

It is possible to be wretched amidst golden vessels, and happy amidst earthen ones, for to live well, potter's clay is not meaner than gold, nor Samos lower than Corinth.

19   I Thess. 4, 4–5:

ut sciat unusquisque vestrum vas suum possidere in
sanctificatione et honore, non in passione desiderii . . .

That everyone of you should know how to possess his
vessel in sanctification and honour:
Not in the passion of lust . . .

43 ❖ MANY BOOKS

1   Dialogues 1, 43–46, have been published in Rawski (1967). As they appear here, the dialogues are based on this previous text, but are presented in

accordance with the editorial practices of the present edition. Some of the notes of the 1967 edition are reprinted here. —Dialogues 43–49 deal with personal accomplishments.

2   *Fam.* vi, 1, 22:

> Animadverti olim tale aliquid in principibus dominisque terrarum, qui omni studio libros querunt petunt rapiunt mercantur, non literarum amore quas ignorant, sed avaritia inducti, nec animi sed thalami querentes ornatum, nec scientiam sed nomen, neque librorum sententias sed pretia cogitantes. Verum his colorata excusatio, licet falsa, non deerit; dicent enim sobolem se ac posteros cogitare; et verbo quidem nondum natis aut quod vite genus eligant prorsus incertis, vere autem avaritie proprie atque ignorantie ingens bibliotheca congeritur.

> I have often noted something similar among the princes and lords of the world who with great fervor seek books, beg them, steal then, buy them, not because of a love of letters, of which they are ignorant, but induced by greed, seeking splendor not for their mind but for their chamber. They do not crave knowledge but a reputation, and consider not the teachings of the books but their price. Nevertheless, they do not lack a colorful though admittedly false excuse. They claim that they think of their children and of the future generation, and point to those as yet unborn, whose kind of life is still uncertain. In truth, however, they amass an immense library because of their own greed and ignorance.

Cf. also *Fam.* iii, 18; Wilkins (1958b), pp. 46–48; and Rawski (1967), pp. 129–130.

3   Seneca, *Ep.* 2, 2–4:

> . . . ne ista lectio auctorum multorum et omnis generis voluminum habeat aliquid vagum et instabile. Certis ingeniis inmorari et innutriri oportet, si velis aliquid trahere, quod in animo fideliter sedeat. . . . . . . Non prodest cibus nec corpori accedit, qui statim sumptus emittitur; nihil aeque sanitatem impedit quam remediorum crebra mutatio; non venit vulnus ad cicatricem, in quo medicamenta temptantur; non convalescit planta, quae saepe transfertur. Nihil tam utile est, ut in transitu prosit. Distringit librorum multitudo. Itaque cum legere non possis, quantum habueris, satis est habere, quantum legas. "Sed modo," inquis, "hunc librum evolvere volo, modo illum." Fastidientis stomachi est multa degustare; quae ubi varia sunt et diversa, inquinant, non alunt. Probatos itaque semper lege, et si quando ad alios deverti libuerit, ad priores redi.

> . . . lest this reading of many authors and books of every sort may tend to make you discursive and unsteady. You must linger among a limited number of masterthinkers, and digest their works, if you would derive ideas which shall win firm hold in your mind. . . . . . . Food does no good and is not assimilated into the body if it leaves the stomach as soon as it is eaten; nothing

hinders a cure so much as a frequent change of medicine; no wound will heal when one salve is tried after another; a plant which is often moved can never grow strong. There is nothing so efficacious that it can be helpful while it is being shifted about. And in reading of many books is distraction. Accordingly, since you cannot read all the books which you may possess, it is enough to possess only as many books as you can read. "But," you reply, "I wish to dip first into one book and then into another." I tell you that it is the sign of an over-nice appetite to toy with many dishes; for when they are manifold and varied, they cloy but do no nourish. So you should always read standard authors; and when you crave a change, fall back upon those whom you read before.

LCL, Gummere, pp. 7, 9. Cf. Augustine, *De beata vita* ii, 13–14; Boethius, *Contra Eut.*, Pref., 33–36; and Petrarch's remarks to Boccaccio, *Sen.* i, 5 (1581: 744), Rawski (1967), pp. 130–131. The alimentary metaphor (Curtius [1953], pp. 134–136) recurs in Geoffrey of Vinsauf, *Poetria nova* (Leyser [1721], p. 877, lines 264–275).

4   Cf. above, *DR* i, Pref., 246–247, and note 64. Cf. Augustine, *De lib. arb.* ii, 16, 24; and the passages cited in Ladner (1959), p. 218, n. 18.
5   Terence, *Andria*, i, 1, 61. Cf. above, *DR* i, 5, note 1.
6   Seneca, *Dial.* ix, *De tranqu.* ix, 5:

Quadraginta milia librorum Alexandriae arserunt; pulcherrimum regiae opulentiae monimentum alius laudaverit, sicut T. Livius, qui elegantiae regum curaeque egregium id opus ait fuisse. Non fuit elegantia illud aut cura, sed studiosa luxuria, immo ne studiosa quidem, quoniam non in studium sed in spectaculum comparaverant, sicut plerisque ignaris etiam puerilium litterarum libri non studiorum instrumenta sed cenationum ornamenta sunt. Paretur itaque librorum quantum satis sit, nihil in apparatum. "Honestius," inquis, "hoc se impensae quam in Corinthia pictasque tabulas effuderint." Vitiosum est ubique, quod nimium est.

Forty thousand books were burned at Alexandria; let someone else praise this library as the most noble monument to the wealth of kings, as did Titus Livius, who says that it was the most distinguished achievement of the good taste and solicitude of kings. There was no "good taste" or "solicitude" about it, but only learned luxury—nay, not even "learned," since they had collected the books, not for the sake of learning, but to make a show, just as many who lack even a child's knowledge of letters use books, not as the tools of learning, but as decorations for the diningroom. Therefore, let just as many books be acquired as are enough, but none for mere show. "It is more respectable," you say, "to squander money on these than on Corinthian bronzes and on pictures." But excess in anything becomes a fault.

LCL, Basore, pp. 247, 249. Seneca's remarks constitute the oldest surviving reference to the burning of the Alexandrian library during Caesar's attack in 47 B.C. Livy's narrative—Book 112 of the *Belli civilis libri*—is lost.

7   *Fam.* xx, 4, 28:

> Bonae equidem leges sunt mundoque non tantum utiles sed necessariae.

> Laws are certainly good, and not only useful but necessary in this world.

8   On the translation of the Hebrew Pentateuch into Greek under Ptolemy II, cf. Augustine, *De civ. Dei* xviii, 42–43.

9   *Hist. aug.*, Gordians, 18:

> In studiis gravissimae opinionis fuit . . . Sereno Sammonico, qui patris eius amicissimus, sibi autem praeceptor fuit, nimis acceptus et carus usque adeo ut omnes libros Sereni Sammonici patris sui, qui censebantur ad sexaginta et duo milia, Gordiano minori moriens ille relinqueret. Quod eum ad caelum tulit, si quidem tantae bibliothecae copia et splendore donatus in faman hominum litterarum decore pervenit.

> [Gordian II] took his studies very seriously. . . . Serenus Sammonicus, a great friend of his father's, was his tutor, and a very beloved and agreeable one he was; in fact, when he died, he left the younger Gordian all the books that had belonged to his father, Serenus Sammonicus, and these were estimated at sixty-two thousand. And this raised him to the seventh heaven, for being now possessed of a library of such magnitude and excellence, thanks to the power of letters he became famous among men.

LCL, Magie, pp. 411, 413. Note the reference in *Fam.* iii, 18, 13.

10 Cf. Horace, *Sat.* i, 1, 68–69:

> Tantalus a labris sitiens fugientia captat
> flumina—

> Tantalus, thirsty soul, catches at the streams
> that fly from his lips—

LCL, Fairclough, p. 9. The Tantalus topic occurs in Innocent III, *De miseria cond. hum.* of 1195:

> Tantalus sitit in undis, et avarus eget in opibus. Cui tantum est quod habet quantum est quod non habet, quia nunquam utitur adquisitis, sed semper inhiat adquirendis.

> Tantalus is thirsty among the waves, and the avaricious man is needy among his riches. To him what he has is as great as what he has not, because he never uses the things acquired, but always gapes at the things to be acquired.

Lewis (1978), ii, 14, p. 160. George Gascoigne translated the passage in his *The Droomme of Doomes day* (1576; Cunliffe, ii, [1910], p. 242).

11 Replying to Lombardo della Seta's dialogue (LAP 71) of March 1369, Petrarch noted in *Sen.* xv, 3 (1581: 935):

Iam uero, quod quaerenti quis'nam tibi cocus esset? Ignem respondisti, & id quoque perproprie, fuit apud maiores nostros cocus seruorum omnium uilissimus, nunc familiae princeps est.

But when your questioner asked who is your cook, you answered, "the fire"—and very properly so! Our forefathers considered the cook the meanest of all servants, now he is the ruler of the family. [Livy, xxxix, 6,9].

Cf. *Fam.* xiii, 4 (Vaucluse, June 10, 1352; to the Apostolic Secretary, Francesco Calvo), 22–24:

[viri] qui munditias supervacuas mulieribus linquentes, honestis ac virilibus delectentur; quibus non sordeat vel ad umbram arboris vel ad ripam fluminis dormire; qui leti possint bonam diei partem in herbosis collibus expendere, prandium ad vesperam differre, cenam oblivisci, noctem—si res tulerit—insomnem inter literas cum delectatione traducere, nec minus antra rorantia quam thalamos ebeno atque ebore vestitos, nec minus floreum cespitem quam cubile purpureum amare; qui ingenuam diligant paupertatem, divitias non tam oderint quam contemnant; quos nec terreat aurum nec suspendat; qui pictas tabulas ac statuas et vasa chorintia et coas gemmas ostrumque sidonium non ut possidentium ornamentum sed ut nature decus aut artificum aspiciant eodemque animo illis utantur et careant; qui quod olim apud maiores nostros, optimos illos quidem vereque viros, fuerat, vilissimum mancipium coquum putent; qui gulam ac ventrem ceu contumaces et inertes servos longo ieiunio domare audeant, durum et inelaboratum atque ex omni fruge compositum panem sibi familiarem fecerint, neque haustum puri gurgitis horreant neque victum agrestem, terre matris munera sponte nascentia, herbas atque arborum baccas et dulcia poma fastidiant, possintque sine animantium interitu suam aliquando vitam agere; qui ad auxilium fessi ac languentis stomaci non copiam mollesque delitias sed abstinentiam et famem et exercitium implorent; postremo qui corpori non servire sed leges dare atque imperare didicerint. Horum ego me numeris ascribere non ausim; nitor tamen et aliquantulum profecisse videor . . .

[men], who leave empty niceties to the women, and enjoy attending to important things that befit a man; who do not feel demeaned by sleeping outdoors in the shade of a tree or at the river's bank; who are glad to be able to spend part of the day amidst grassy hills, to put off lunch until evening, to forget about dinner, and to pass the night, whenever possible, wakefully relishing their books—men, who like roaring gorges no less than bedrooms adorned with ebony and ivory, the flowery heath no less than the couch of purple silk; who choose noble poverty, who do not so much hate riches as despise them; who are not awed or tantalized by gold; who consider paintings, and statues, and Corinthian vessels [the sequence of *DR* i, 40, 41, 42], and Coan gems, and Sidonian purple [Horace, *Ep.* i, 10, 26], not as a prestigious badge of ownership, but a gift of nature or of artistry, and remain unconcerned about having or not having them—men, who, as did our forebears, who were the best, and

real men, regarded the cook the vilest of their servants; who dare to tame their gullets and bellies by long fasting like insolent and worthless slaves; get used to hard, unleavened bread made from any kind of cereal; nor fear to drink from a pure mountain stream, or disdain coarse foods, the gifts of the earth that grow wild, herbs, fruit on the trees, and sweet apples, willing to lead their lives without killing animals; who seek to aid their weak and listless stomachs, not by huge amounts of soft morsels, but with abstinence, hunger and exercise—in short, men who have learned not to serve their bodily needs, but to control and rule them. I do not dare to count myself among such men. But I do try and sometimes seem to measure up a little.

On this, Wilkins (1955), p. 128. Note also *De ocio, Prose* (1955), p. 598.

12   The pun—the rhetorical figure of *paronomasia*—occurs in *Sen.* x, 2, *Prose* (1955), p. 1118:

> non queror ergo mutata tempora, nec causas quero.

> therefore I do not complain that times have chanaged, nor do I search for the causes.

13   *If Cicero or Livy were to return today* invokes Juvenal, vii, 139–140, as cited below, *DR* i, 46, 104–107. On this, Nolhac (1907), ii, p. 70. On the general incompetence of scribes, Rawski (1967), pp. 117–118, n. 21.

14   Aurelius Victor, *Epit.* 41, 8; Pichlmayr (1911), pp. 166–167:

> [*Licinius*] . . . infestus litteris, quas per inscitiam immodicam virus ac pestem publicam nominabat . . .

> [*Licinius*] . . . hostile to letters, which in his enormous ignorance he called *a poison and a social disease.*

Petrarch used the Licinius example also in *Fam.* vii, 15 (March 13, 1348, to Luchino Visconti), 49–51: Licinius Caesar,

> . . . qui rusticane vir originis ita literis oderat, ut eas "virus ac pestem publicam" appellaret; vox non quidem imperatore digna, sed rustico.

> a man of rustic origin who so hated learning that he called it *a poison and a social disease*—words of a yokel, unworthy of an emperor.

15   Horace, *Epod.* iv, 6:

> Fortuna non mutat genus.

Interpreted in emblem form as late as Otho van Veen's *Qu. Horat. Flacci Emblemata* (Brussels, 1607), Pickering (1970), p. 200, n. 2, and pl. 5b.

16   *Fam.* i, 7, 12:

> mechanicorum est lucra captare; honestarum artium generosior finis est.

It is for the mechanical trades to strive for lucre; the higher arts have a more generous end in view.

Robinson & Rolfe (1914), p. 221.

17   Eusebius, *De vita Constantini* iv, 36. Eusebius was to produce fifty copies of the necessarsy sacred texts, on fine parchment, in easy-to-read script and of convenient format, executed by scribes competent in the art of writing.

18   Horace, *Ep.* i, 18, 109–110:

> Sit bona librorum et provise frugi in annum
> copia, ne fluitem dubie spe pendulus hore.

> May I have a goodly supply of books and of food to last
> the year; nor may I waver to and fro with the hopes of
> each uncertain hour.

(LCL, Fairclough, p. 377), as quoted *Secretum* ii, *Prose* (1955), p. 84. The *bona copia librorum* appears also in *De vita sol.* ii, ibid., p. 560, and in *Sen.* xvi, 1 (1581: 948); Bishop (1966), p. 296.

19   Seneca, *Ep.* 27, 5–8. Petrarch retold Seneca's story in *Rer. mem. libri.* ii, 49:

> Sabinus quidam nomine dives ineptissimus a Seneca refertur, qui etate sue fuit, hebes quanquam et obliviosus, glorie tamen avidissimus, quam ex literarum notitia procurabat. Itaque magnis preciis servos comparavit, quorum alter hunc, alter illum poetam familiariter ac memoriter nosset, hoc scilicet expeditum iter ad eam quam petebat gloriam ratus, ceu servi ut peculium sic et literas domino quererent. Hac tali *familia* instructus, convivas suos questiunculis exagitabat: servi *ad pedes* aderant et de quacunque re sermo esset obortus, accommodatos materie versus insursurrabant; quos ille gloriabundus dum pronuntiare vellet, *in medio* labebatur. In hunc ergo Satellius Quadratus, ut ipsius hoc narrantis verbis utar, *stultorum divitum arrasor et arrisor et derisor,* ita iocatus est: cum enim ille iactaret *centenis milibus servos sibi singulos* constitisse: "Minori pretio" inquit Quadratus, "*totidem scrinia emisses.*" Idem Sabinum *ut luctaretur* orabat, cumque ille admirans diceret: "*Quomodo* luctabor homo eger ac fragilis et vix vivere valens?" "*Noli* queso" *inquit* Quadratus. "hoc *dicere*: aspice quot servos habes robustissimos." Merito has nugas audiebat demens qui ex alienis bonis gloriam speraret.

> Seneca refers to a crazy rich man, named Sabinus, who lived at his time. He was stupid and forgetful, but extremely eager to be admired for his knowledge of literature. Thus, at enormous expense, he collected slaves, one of whom was familiar with this poet and knew him by heart, another with that—and so paved the way to the glory he desired, for he thought that knowledge of letters, like slaves and other property, all belonged to who owned them. Having procured this retinue, he began to harass his guests with questions. And on any subject that was talked about, the slaves, at the foot of his couch, whispered appropriate verses in his ears, which he might repeat triumphantly, but, often, he broke down in the middle of his sentence. With him, Satellius Quadratus,

who in the words of our storyteller was a feeder on addlepated millionaires, a fawner, and a flouter of them, joked this way. When Sabinus boasted that each slave had cost him one hundred thousand sesterces, Quadratus said: "You might have bought as many bookcases for a smaller sum." He also advised Sabinus to take wrestling lessons. "How can I possibly wrestle—sickly, thin, and barely alive as I am?" "Don't say that," replied Quadratus, "just think how many brawny slaves you have!" Anyone mad enough to hope for glory to be afforded him by the efforts of others deserves to have to listen to this shaggy tale.

20   Reason's antithetic paraphrase may echo Ovid, *Metam.* iii, 466:

> quod cupio mecum est: inopem me copia fecit.

What I desire, I have; the very abundance of my riches beggars me.

LCL, Miller, p. 157. *copia-inopia*—abundance-scarcity—is often used in Petrarchan texts—as antithetic homeoteleuton, line 13, above, *DR* i, 44, 35–36, and *Fam.* vi, 5, 6; as oxymoron in *Fam.* xvii, 1, 2, xix, 17, 3–4, *Sen.* viii, 3, ix, 2 (1581: 835, 866, as in *DR* ii, 79, note 12, and *Sen.* xi, 11 (1581; 703, as in *DR* ii, 119, note 12).

21   Seneca, *Ep.* 45, 1:

> Librorum istic inopiam esse quereris. Non refert, quam multos, sed quam bonos habeas; lectio certa prodest, varia delectat. Qui, quo destinavit, pervenire vult, unam sequatur viam, non per multas vagetur. Non ire istuc, sed errare est.

You complain that in your part of the world there is a scant supply of books. But it is quaility, rather than quantity, that matters; a limited list of reading benefits; a varied assortment serves only for delight. He who would arrive at the appointed end must follow a single road and not wander through many ways. What you suggest is not travelling; it is mere tramping.

LCL, Gummere, p. 291.

22   The reference is probably to Saint Jerome and his Latin translation of the Bible.

23   The German translator of the *DR* depicted this *indolent miser* ·with earthy eloquence

> Es hat mancher Geitzwurm viel daheym / da sich viel andere an behelffen möchten / So thustu auch / sitzest ob den Büchern wie ein Hund an der Krippen / der frißt das Heu nicht / und läßt es auch die Ochsen nicht fressen.

1620 edition, p. 70b.

Portions of this dialogue are based on Seneca, *Dial.* ix, De tranqu. an., as follows:

Seneca,		DR
De tranqu. an.		i, 43
5; 7	Books used for show and decoration	1–9; 143–155
6	Excess in anything becomes a fault	23–56
5	The forty thousands books of Ptolemy Philadelphus	28–35
4; 6	Owners of countless books looking at the outside of volumes	47–56; 116–120
4	Many books, a burden to students	129–141

Seneca's discussion of the use of books is summarized in Hadas (1954), p. 25.

44 ❖ FAME AS A WRITER

1 Cf. above, *DR* i, 43, note 1. Dialogues 43–49 form a group on personal accomplishments—from having many books to preferment by the king.

2 Juvenal, vii, 50–52:

> nam si discedas, laqueo tenet ambitiosi
> consuetudo mali, tenet insanabile multos
> scribendi cacoethes et aegro in corde senescit.

For if you would give it up, the evil habit holds you in its noose, and the incurable itch to write possesses you and stays forever in your ailing mind.

(On this text, G. G. Ramsay in *Juvenal and Persius*, LCL, p. 140, n. 2.) Petrarch quoted the passage in *Rer. mem. libri* ii, 93, 12, and referred to it again in *Fam.* xiii, 7, 7 (to Pierre d'Auvergne, November, 1352):

Quid igitur dicam? ita ne verum est ut, sicut ceterarum rerum, sic scribendi *cacoethes insanabile*, quod ait Satyricus; quod ego addo, contagiosus etiam morbus sit? Quam multos enim putas me, qui tecum loquor, morbi huius contagiis infecisse? solebant in memoria nostra rari esse qui hoc scriberent; nunc nemo non scribit; rari aliud scribunt.

What then? Is it true, as the Satirist says, that the itch to write, like other kinds of itch, is incurable? and, as I must add, that it is contagious? How many men do you suppose I have infected with this disease, I who am writing to you? You and I can remember the time when those who wrote things of this sort were few: now there is no one who does not write, and there are but few who write things of any other sort.

Wilkins (1958b), p. 147. Cf. also *Contra med.* ii, Ricci (1950), 461–462.

3   Reason distinguishes between *aemulari*—to be competitive (in various ways)—and *imitari*—to equal (an example: the intent and the doing). Cf. above, *DR* i, 24, 66–69. Note *Sen.* v, 2 (1581: 794):

sine riuali amor, sine aemulo uirtus torpet.

Love whithers without rivalry, virtue without contest.

Also, *Fam.* xxiii, 19, 13, as in Rawski (1967), pp. 79–80; *DR* i, Pref., note 34; and i, 29, note 17.

4   Eccl. 12, 12:

Faciendi plures libros nullus est finis.

Also quoted in *Contra med.* ii, Ricci (1950), 34.

5   This is the *ordo rerum*—the cosmic hierarchy as fixed within the grand order of creation. God commands us to observe the natural order and forbids us to disturb it. Augustine, *Contra Faustum* xxii, 27, *PL* 42, c. 418, *De lib. arb.* i, 6, 15; Boethius, *Cons, phil.* iv, P 6, 90–101, 189–195; above, *DR* i, 11, note 1, i, P 4, 14–18, iii M2, iii, P 12, 20–24, iv, P 5, 22–24. Among the frequent references to this order in Petrarch's works are *Secretum* ii, *Prose* (1955), p. 112, iii, ibid., p. 148; *De vita sol.* i, *Prose* (1955), p. 340; and *Sen.* v, 2 (1581: 793). On *ordo* concepts in medieval thought, C.A. Patrides in Wiener (1973), ii, pp. 438–441; Hillgarth (1971), pp. 13–14; Chenu (1968), p. 81, n. 60; Von den Steinen (1965), i, pp. 172–175; Robertson (1962), pp. 6–9, 200 *et passim*; Steinbuechel (1935), pp. 65–131; and above, *DR* i, 16, note 7. On the notion of order in Augustine, R.A. Markus in Armstrong (1967), chap. 25; and Gilson (1960), pp. 127–132.

6   Cicero, *Tusc. disp.* i, 3, 6:

Fieri autem potest ut recte quis sentiat et id, quod sentit, polite eloqui non possit; sed mandare quemquam litteris cogitationes suas, qui eas nec disponere nec illustrare possit nec delectatione aliqua adlicere lectorem, hominis est intemperanter abutentis et otio et litteris.

LCL, King, p. 9. Petrarch quoted the same passage *Rer. mem libri* iii, 93, 11; and in his coronation oration of 1341 (Wilkins [1955], p. 308).

7   Reason refers to Saint John and Apoc. 14, 13:

Et audiui uoce, de caelo, dicentem mihi: Scribe:

And I heard a voice from heaven saying unto me, Write.

Cf. also, Apoc. 19, 9; 21, 5. In a different context (*Rime* 93, 1–2:

> Più volte Amor m'avea già detto: Scrivi,
> scrivi quel che vedesti in lettre d'oro,

> Love had already often told me: —Write,
> Write what you saw in clear letters of gold,

Armi [1946], p. 149), Petrarch paraphrased Ovid (*Heroides* iv, 13–14:

> Ille mihi primo dubitanti scribere dixit:
> "scribe! . . . "

> 'Twas [Love] who spoke to me when first I doubted if to write or no:
> "Write! . . . "

LCL, Showerman, p. 45). On this, Billanovich (1981), p. 323. —On *drying puddles*, *Secretum* ii, *Prose* (1955), p. 72; and Alain de Lille, *Anticlaud.*, Pref., PL 210, c. 487. The well of *truth* is Ioan. 4, 13–14:

> Omnis qui bibit ex aqua hac, sitiet iterum; qui autem biberit ex aqua quam ego dabo ei, non sitiet in aeternum; sed aqua, quam ego dabo ei, fiet in eo fons aquae salientis in vitam aeternam.

> Whosoever drinketh of this water, shall thirst again; but he that shall drink of the water that I will give him shall not thirst forever: But the water that I will give him shall become in him a fountain of water, springing up into life everlasting.

Cf. *De sui ipsius*, Rawski (1967), p. 148, n. 7; and *Secretum* ii, *Prose* (1955), p. 72.

8   *Sen.* v, 2, to Boccaccio, August 28, 1364 (1581: 796):

> In hoc tempus incidimus amice, in hac uiuimus, iamque senescimus aetate, interque hos iudices, quod saepe quaeri soleo, & indignari, quos scientiae uacuos, ac uirtutis falsa sui implet opinio. Quibus libros ueterum perdidisse non sufficit, nisi ingeniis, ac cineribus dicerent, & ignorantia sua laeti, quasi quod nesciunt, nihil sit, pingui ac tumido lasciuiunt intellectu, nouos uulgo auctores, & exoticas inuehunt disciplinas.

> These are the days, my friend, upon which we have come, this is the period in which we live and age, and these the critics, as I have noted often with sorrow and disgust, men without knowledge and virtue, but filled with self-esteem. Not content with the loss of the books of the ancients, they malign their genius and their ashes. They rejoice in their own ignorance as if that which they did not know were not worth knowing. They indulge freely their doltish, swelled-up minds and assail us with newfangled authors and exotic teachings.

Note also *Fam.* i, 12; *Sen.* iv, 5, xii, 1 (1581: 785, 899); and *De sui ipsius*, Rawski (1967), p. 148, n. 8. *Fam.* xxiv, 6, Petrarch's letter to the ancient

Roman scholar Marcus Varro, refers to *this barren and foul age given to studying and writing about so many things which had better remain unknown*, but neglecting the noble authors of Antiquity. Cosenza (1910), pp. 68–75. Cf. also below, *DR* ii, 117, 63–73.

9   Cicero, *Tusc. disp.* i, 3, 6:

> Itaque suos libros ipsi legunt cum suis, nec quisquam attingit praeter eos, qui eandem scribendi licentiam, sibi permitti volunt.

LCL, King, p. 9. Quoted also in *Rer. mem. libri* iii, 93, 12. On this, Rawski (1967), p. 150, n. 11.

10   i Cor. 8, 1: *Scientia inflat* . . . Cf. *Contra med.* ii, Ricci (1950), 629–635; *De sui ipsius, Prose* (1955), pp. 714–718; *Fam.* i, 3, 8; and below, *DR* ii, 8, 42–45.

11   Cf. *Secretum* i, *Prose* (1955), p. 32:

> Et profecto si illas philosophorum veras saluberrimasque sententias . . . memorie commendasses; si . . . et lectionem tot voluminum ad vite tue regulam, non ad ventosum vulgi plausum et inanem iactantiam traduxisses, tam insulsa et tam rudia ista non diceres.

> If you had remembered those true and salutary sayings of the philosphers . . . and turned that which you read in all these books into a rule of life rather than into empty ostentation to gain the windy plaudits of the throng, you would not say such absurd, stupid things.

Cf. Rico (1974), pp. 58, 134.

12   Reason refers to the mechanical arts, above, *DR* i, 29, note 5.

13   *Fam.* xxiv, 6, 9, to Marcus Varro, November 1, 1350:

> Tu vero solare animum, et laboris egregii fructum ex conscienta percipiens, mortalia periisse ne doleas; sciebas peritura dum scriberes: mortali enim ingenio nichil efficitur immortale.

> Treasure the moral comfort deriving from thy uncommon labors, and grieve not that mortal things have perished. Even while writing thou must have known that thy work was destined to perish; for nothing immortal can be written by mortal man.

Cosenza (1910), p. 73. Cf. also *Met.* ii, 18, 30–38 (1581, iii: 103).

14   Petrarch tried to do just that in *Rer. mem. libri* i, 15: Cicero; i, 14: Varro; i, 18: Livy; i, 19: Pliny. *Fam.* xxiv, 4, lists the lost and fragmentary works of Cicero, *Fam.* xii, 8, to Lapo da Castiglionchio, April 1, 1352, those works Petrarch was acquainted with. *Fam.* xxiv, 8, repeats the statistics on Livy. On this, Nolhac (1907) ii, pp. 16–17; Cosenza (1910), pp. 21–42, 100–111, and, on Varro, pp. 69–83; and Billanovich (1981), esp. chaps. iv–viii.

15   Isidore, *Etym.* vi, 7, 1–3: *Qui multa scripserunt*—Of Those Who Wrote Much:

Marcus Terentius Varro apud Latinos innumerabiles libros scripsit. Apud Graecos quoque Chalcenterus miris attolitur laudibus, quod tantos libros ediderit quantos quisque nostrum alienos scribere propria manu vix possit. De nostris quoque apud Graecos Origenes in scripturarum labore tam Graecos quam Patinos operum suorum numero superavit. Denique Hieronymus sex milia librorum eius legisse fatetur. Horum tamen omnium studia Augustinus ingenio vel scientia sui vicit. Nam tanta scripsit ut diebus ac noctibus non solum scribere libros eius quisquam, sed nec legere quidem occurrat.

Among the Latins Marcus Terentius Varro wrote innumerable books [Augustine, *De civ. Dei* vi, 2; *Fam.* xviii, 3, 6]. Among the Greeks, also, Chalcenterus is accorded extravagant praise, because he composed so many books that, today, one could hardly copy them all by hand. Among the Greek authors of later times Origenes surpassed the ancient Greeks and Romans in the number of his works. Jerome, in fact, stated that he had read six thousand of Origen's books. But Augustine mastered them all with his intellect and knowledge. And he wrote so much that it occurs to no one to spend his days and nights to copy, nay, even to read his works.

On this, Fontaine (1959), ii, pp. 728, 757, 794. Cf. Hugh of St. Victor, *Didasc.* iv, 14, Taylor (1961), p. 115; Jacobus de Voragine, *Leg. aurea* ii, 496, Graesse (1890), p. 560; Fazio degli Uberti, *Il dittamondo* i, 9, 49–54, v, 19, 7–9, Corsi (1952), i, pp. 113, 390; Boccaccio, *Geneal. deor.* xiv, 22. Isidore's figure of six thousand comes from an estimate by Epiphanius (*Adv. Haereses* 64, 63, *PG* 41, c. 1177), reported by Jerome, *PL* 23, c. 495. On the Origen tradition, De Lubac, i, 1 (1959), chap. iv.

16   Reason may have in mind Cicero, some of whose works "have (unless I am mistaken) perished in this generation, and I know not whether they will ever be recovered" (*Fam.* xxiv, 4, 12, Cosenza [1910], p. 26); Livy, of whom we know that he wrote "one hundred and forty-two books on Roman affairs . . . . . . and of that entire number there are now extant scarcely thirty" (*Fam.* xxiv, 8, 2, Cosenza [1910], p. 100); and Varro, the zealous scholar, who today is "of no profit to us, or, at best, of only small profit . . . All thy works are lost to us today" (*Fam.* xxiv, 6, 2, Cosenza [1910], p. 69).

17   The topic of exercising the mind is Augustinian. *De magistro* viii, 21, *PL* 32, c. 1207:

Dabis igitur veniam, si praeludo tecum non ludendi gratia, sed exercendi vires et mentis aciem, quibus regionis illius, ubi beata vita est, calorem ac lucem non modo sustinere, verum etiam amare possimus.

You will pardon me, therefore, if I play with you to begin with, not for the sake of playing, but in order to exercise and sharpen your mental powers so that we may be able not merely to endure the heat and light of the region where lies the blessed life, but also to love them.

Burleigh (1953), p. 85. Similar, *De doct. Christ.* iii, 8, 12, iv, 6, 9, and 8, 22.

On the concept of *exercitatio animi*, Marrou (1938), ii, chap. 6, esp. pp. 308, 486–489; and Robertson (1963), pp. 60–62. On Petrarch's familiarity with the concept, cf. *Fam.* vi, 4, 1–5; *Contra med.* iii, Ricci (1950), 400–411; Wilkins (1951), p. 39; and *DR* i, 29, 6–8, i, 41, 87–89, ii, 2, 16–17, etc.

18   Cf. above, note 2.

19   *De vita solitaria* i, *Prose* (1955), pp. 356, 358:

> . . . et lectioni dare operam et scripture, et alternum laborem alterno solatio lenire, legere quod scripserunt primi, scribere quod legant ultimi, et beneficii literarum a maioribus accepti, qua in illos non possumus, in posteros saltem gratum ac memorem animum habere, in eos quoque qua possumus non in-gratum, sed nomina illorum vel ignota vulgare, vel obsolefacta renovare, vel senio obruta eruere et ad pronepotum populos veneranda transmittere; illos sub pectore, illos ut dulce aliquid in ore gestare, denique modis omnibus amando, memorando, celebrando, si non parem, certe debitam meritis referre gratiam.

> . . . to devote oneself to reading and to writing, finding in turn exertion and repose in each; to read what those who lived before us wrote; to write what will be read by those to come; to make, at least, the later generations appreci-ate the writings of the ancients, this gift for which we cannot thank them any more—and yet not to remain wholly ungrateful, but spread their names if they are little known, receive them if they are forgotten, dig them out when they are buried in oblivion and hand them to our grandchildren to be revered; to carry them in the heart and as something sweet in the mouth [Apoc. 10, 9] and, by loving, remembering, and celebrating them in every way, henceforth, to show them our gratitude, although it is not equal to their greatness.

Note also *Met.* i, 6, as above, *DR* i, Pref., note 15.

20   Juvenal, vii, 27–35:

> Frange miser calamum vigilataque praelia dele,
> qui facis in parva sublimia carmina cella,
> ut dignus venias hederis, et imagine macra.
> Spes nulla ulterior; didicit nam dives avarus
> tantum admirari, tantum laudare disertos,
> ut pueri Iunonis avem. Sed defluit aetas
> et pelagi patiens et cassidis atque ligonis.
> Taedia tunc subeunt animos, tunc seque suamque
> Terpsichoren odit facunda et nuda senectus.

> Break your pen, poor wretch; destroy the battles that have robbed you of your sleep—you that are inditing lofty strains in a tiny garret, that you may come forth worthy of a scraggy bust wreathed with ivy! No hope have you beyond that; your rich miser has now learnt only to admire, only to commend the eloquent, just as boys admire the bird of Juno. Meantime the years flow by that could have endured the sea, the helmet, or the spade; the soul becomes wea-

ried, and an eloquent but penniless old age curses itself and its own
Terpsichore!

LCL, Ramsay, pp. 139, 141. Petrarch used this quotation in his coronation
oration (Wilkins [1955], p. 303). Cf. also Boccaccio, *Geneal. deor.* Pref. (Osgood [1930], p. 9) and ibid. xiv, 4, 47–51 (Reedy [1978], p. 20; and Osgood
[1930], p. 23). On writing as a waste of time, *Secretum* iii, *Prose* (1955),
p. 194:

Augustinus: . . . Quid tamen tam grande facturum esse te iudicas?

Franciscus: Preclarum nempe rarumque opus et egregium.

Augustinus: Nolo nimis obluctari: preclarum opus, concedatur; at quanto
preclarioris impedimentum si cognosceres, quod cupis horreres. Hoc enim dicere ausim: vel in primis animum tuum ab omnibus melioribus curis abstrahit.
Adde quod hoc ipsum preclarum neque late patet, nec in longum porrigitur,
locorumque ac temporum angustiis coartatur.

Augustinus: . . . what considerable work do you expect to achieve?

Franciscus: Oh, certainly, one of great excellence, quite out of the common and
likely to attract attention.

Augustinus: I have no wish to seem contradictory: let us suppose it may be a
work of great excellence. But if you knew of what greater excellence still is the
work which this will hinder, you would abhor what you now desire. For I will
go so far as to assert that this work of yours is, to begin with, taking off your
attention from cares of a nobler kind; and, greatly excellent as you think it, has
no wide scope nor long future before it, circumscribed as it must be by time
and space.

Draper (1911), p. 171.

21   Virgil *Aeneid* v, 59–60:

> poscamus ventos, atque haec me sacra quotannis
> urbe velit posita templis sibi ferre dicatis.

> Let us pray for the winds and may he grant that year
> by year when my city is founded I may offer these rites
> in temples consecrated to him!

LCL, Fairclough, p. 451, quoted by Petrarch in *De ocio* (1581: 320); cf.
Lactantius, *Div. inst.* i, 15, *PL* 6, c. 195.
    The figure of the wind indicating the transient and momentary finds a
close parallel in medieval scriptural interpretation. Referring to Job 30, 22
and 15, Alain de Lille explains that the wind represents prosperity in this
transitory life and transitory matters in general. Thus we must view the glory

that this life can bestow as if high up, instable, without solid support, riding the wind that raises us to the height of success only to dash us down precipitously into adversity. *(Dist. dict. theol., PL* 210, c. 995; *Glossa ordinaria,* Job, *PL* 113, c. 835.)

45 ❖ THE MASTER'S DEGREE

1   See above, *DR* i, 44, note 1.
2   In Petrarch's time the *magisterium* i.e., the degree of *magister*, indicated completion of the academic requirements for admission to the teaching profession. The faculty members of a university were referred to as *magistri*—masters. In general usage, the term applied to teachers on all levels: *ille qui docet in scholis, dicitur magister*—he who teaches in schools is called master (Thomas Aquinas, *In Phys.* vii, 8 g, *In Sent. P. Lomb.* iv, 17, 4; Chenu [1964], pp. 20–22; Powicke [1936], i, pp. 19–20). The term implied mastery of a subject and competence in scholarly pursuits. The Middle Ages envisioned the house of intellect within the grand design of creation (above, *DR* i, 44, note 5) as a many-storied structure, inhabited by masters on all its levels, which ascend in gradual order to the pinnacle of learning, Truth itself; *Christus magister.* "Neither be ye called masters; for one is your master, Christ" (Matth. 23, 10). Cf. *Glossa ordinaria, PL* 114, c. 158; among frequent Petrarchan references, *Fam.* xvii, 1, esp. 3 and 36, *De ocio* ii (1581: 318), and *De sui ipsius, Prose* (1955), p. 734, H. Nachod in Cassirer (1948), p. 95; and Gilson (1960), chap. V, secs. 1 and 2. On *aeternus preceptor,* below, *DR* ii, 40, 32–34.
3   *DR* i, 80, 13–22, mentions Virgil, Horace, Cicero, and also Plato, his master Socrates notwithstanding, as having attained excellence without a master. *DR* ii, 40, adds Epicurus, Augustine, Bernard, and Adam and Eve.
4   Cf. above, *DR* i, 15, note 29.
5   *Believing others rather than themselves*—cf. above, *DR* i, 11, note 15.
6   *DR* i, 11, 4–5: *It is madness for one who knows to rejoice in something false.*
7   Richard de Bury, *Philobiblon* ix:

> . . . clerici celebres his diebus. Ambitione siquidem in aetate tenera laborantes, ac praesumptionis pennas Icarias inexpertis lacertis fragiliter coaptantes, pileum magistralem immaturi praeripiunt, fiuntque pueruli facultatum plurium professores immeriti, quas nequaquam pedetentim pertran-

seunt, sed ad instar caprearum saltuatim ascendunt; cumque parum de grandi torrente gustaverint, arbitrantur se totum funditus sorbuisse, vix faucibus humectatis; et quia in primis rudimentis tempore congruo non fundantur, super debile fundamentum opus aedificant ruinosum. Iamque provectos pudet addiscere, quae tenellos decuerat didicisse, et sic profecto coguntur perpetuo luere quod ad fasces indebitos praepropere salierunt.

. . . the clerks who are famous in these days . . . Afflicted with ambition in their tender years, and slightly fastening to their untried arms the Icarian wings of presumption, they prematurely snatch the master's cap; and mere boys become unworthy professors of the several faculties, through which they do not make their way step by step, but like goats ascend by leaps and bounds; and having slightly tasted of the mighty stream, they think that they have drunk it dry, though their throats are hardly moistened. And because they are not grounded in the first rudiments at the fitting time, they build a tottering edifice on an unstable foundation, and now that they have grown up, they are ashamed to learn what they ought to have learned while young, and thus they are compelled to suffer forever for too hastily jumping at dignities they have not deserved.

Thomas (1960), pp. 103, 105. Cf. above, *DR* i, 12, 90–98.

46 ❖ ACADEMIC TITLES

1   See above, *DR* i, 44, note 1.
2   Petrarch, *Rime* 142, 35–36:

> mostranmi altro sentier di gire al cielo
> e di far frutto, non pur fior e frondi.

> Show me another path to climb to heaven
> And to bear fruit, not only flowers and leaves.

Armi (1946), p. 235. One of the many passages using the metaphor of leaves and fruit (*Fam.* xxiv, 4, 8, and the references in Rawski [1967]), pp. 165–167), is Alain de Lille, *Anticlaud.* vii, 6, 21–24, *PL* 210, c. 555, 394:

> Vel si forte fluat sermo sub flumine verbi,
> Fluminet uberior sententia, copia fructus

> Excuset folii silvam, paleasque vagantes
> Ubertas granis redimat, sensusque loquelam.

Or if perchance the discourse flows on with a flood of words, more fully yet should flow the meaning, so that the abundance of fruit may excuse the forest of leaves, the profusion of grain make up for the flying chaff and meaning for words.

On grain and flying chaff, Jerome, *In Is.*, *PL* 24, c. 651, used as preface to the book of Isaiah in the Vulgate. Petrarch knew the *Anticlaudianus*. In the invective *Contra eum*, he criticized it as *little less tiresome than the* Architrenius (Wilkins [1959], p. 239; cf. Nolhac [1907], ii, pp. 226–227; on John de Hanville's *Architrenius*, Raby [1934], ii, pp. 100–102), but included in *Rime* 138, 76–79, the description of the Isle of Fortune, *Anticlaud.*, *PL* 210, cc. 557–558 (Patch [1927], pp. 126–127). —As late as 1690, Cotton Mather used the image of blossom and fruit in the preface to his *Companion for Communicants* (A 3).

3   *Fam.* iv, 15, 19:

> Uni ingenio satis est unius studii gloriam mereri; qui multarum titulis artium superbiunt, aut divini homini sunt aut impudentes aut insani. Quis uspiam aut Grecorum aut nostrorum id presumpsisse memoratur? novus mos, nova temeritas. Gloriosas inscriptiones pre se ferunt, "propter quas" ut ait Plinius, "vadimonium deseri possit; at cum intraveris, dii deeque! quam nichil in medio invenies!"

> For one mind it is enough to have merited glory in one field of knowledge. Those who pride themselves with titles in many of the arts are either divine, or without shame, or mad. Who among the Greeks or us Romans is remembered as having been so presumptuous? New is the custom; new its affront! These men carry before them glorious titles, so intriguing, Pliny says, that "they might tempt a man to forfeit his bail. But when you get inside them, dear God, what a void you will find there" [*Nat. hist.*, Praef. 24].

4   The entire passage dealing with the degree in theology is omitted in Twyne's translation. The text continues directly: "I have deserved to be a Maister of Philosophie" (f. 67v).

5   Cf. above, *DR* i, 12, 90–92. On the Aristotelian controversy and the "second Averroism" in Italy, Gilson (1955), pp. 521–527; and Toffanin (1964), ii, pp. 124–131. On Petrarch's antipathy to Aristotle and Averroës, *Sen.* v, 2 (1581: 795–796); and Rawski (1967), pp. 168–170, n. 4.

6   *De vita sol.* ii, *Prose* (1955), p. 524:

> Philosophos autem dico, non istos quos, qui cathedrarios primum dixit, ille michi proprium rei nomen imposuisse visus est. In cathedris enim philosophantur in actionibus insaniunt, precipiunt aliis preceptisque suis primi obstant primi legibus a se latis derogant, et signiferos se professi primi ordines

deserunt primi virtutis imperio rebellant. Non hos igitur dico, sed illos veros, qui semper pauci, nunc nescio an penitus nulli sint, qui quod profitentur exhibeant amorem studiumque sapientie.

When I speak of philosophers, I do not refer to those properly named, it seems to me, by the one who first called them *cathedrarios* [—classroom philosophers (Seneca, *Dial* x, De brev. vitae 1)], for they are philosophers only *ex cathedra*. In their actions they are demented. They teach, but are the first to act counter to their own teachings, the first to disregard the rules they have laid down, and having proclaimed themselves standard bearers, they are the first to desert the ranks, the first to rebel against the commands of virtue. I, therefore, do not speak of these, but of those true philosophers who, always scarce and at present hardly to be found at all, show the love and the desire for wisdom that they profess.

On the ancient interpretation of the Greek compound term "philosophy" as love of wisdom (*Sen.* xv, 6 [1581: 734]), which was well known in Petrarch's time, see Rawski (1967), pp. 171–172; and below, *DR* ii, 117, note 17.

7   This is Augustine's version of Job 28, 28, *De trin.* xii, 14, 22, xiv, 1, and *Conf.* v, 5, etc.; see above, *DR* i, 13, note 12. If Petrarch quoted from *De trin.* xii, he quoted from a chapter which is directly related to the concept of wisdom developed by Reason in the present dialogue. Similar: *Sen.* xiii, 5, xv, 6 (1581: 920, 734); *Contra med.* ii, Ricci (1950), 600, quoting Augustine, *De civ. Dei* viii, 1; and *De sui ipsius*, *Prose* (1955), pp. 746, 748.

8   Twyne, f. 67v: Your Philosophers standyng in contempt and ignorance of this opinion, fell unto brabblying and bare Logike.

9   Ps. 2, 4:

> Qui habitat in caelis irridebit eos
> et Dominus subsannabit eos.

> He that dwelleth in heaven shall laugh at them:
> and the Lord shall deride them.

On Petrarch's *dialectici*, Foster (1984), pp. 151–155, 160–161, 201–202, n. 16; Rawski (1967), pp. 168–170; and Wilkins (1978), pp. 193–194. Also Kristeller (1980), pp. 117–118; and Toffanin, ii (1964), pp. 124–134.

10   Cf. Cicero, *De nat. deor.* i, 8, 18, as quoted in *De sui ipsius*, *Prose* (1955), pp. 722, 724:

> et facetissima illa Ciceronis irrisio temerarie disputantium, nullaque de re dubitantium, tanquam, "modo deorum ex concilio descendentes," quid ibi agatur oculis suis asperxerint auribusque perceperint.

And there are very clever remarks Cicero made to ridicule frivolous disputants who are heedlessly arguing and arguing about nothing, "as if they just came from the council of the gods" and had seen with their eyes what was going on there, and heard it with their ears.

H. Nachod in Cassirer (1948), p. 77.

11   The text of Rom. 11, 34 reads:

> Quis enim cognovit sensum Domini? aut quis consiliarius eius fuit?

> For who hath know the mind of the Lord? Or who hath been his counsellor?

Also quoted in *Fam.* iv, 12, 27. On Petrarchan citation habits, Rawski (1967), p. 175, n. 8.

12   Twyne, f. 67v., has *Saint Ierome.*

13   Ambrose, *De exc. frat. Satyri* ii, De fide resurrectionis, *PL* 16, c. 1398:

> De solis cursu coelique ratione philosophi disputant, et sunt qui putant his esse credendum, cum quid loquatur ignorent.

Petrarch refers to Ambrose's work in *Fam.* iv, 10 (to Pellegrino Caloiro, 1341), 3; *Fam.* xiii, 1 (to Gui de Boulogne, May 14, 1352), 13; and twice in *Sen.* i, 5 (to Boccaccio, May 28, 1362). In *Sen.* iii, 1 (to Boccaccio, September 7, 1363), the quotation appears in the same form as in our text (1581: 770). On Petrarch's Ambrose manuscript (Paris, B.N. *f. lat.* 1757) which contains *eiusdem de obitu Satyri fratris sui,* Nolhac (1907), ii, pp. 203–206.

14   *melior sane tutiorque confessio quam professio est*—cf. *De ocio* i (Rotondi, pp. 24–25): *Infinitam Dei misericordiam* fateor, *sed eius* profiteor *me non capacem* . . .

15   Cf. Augustine, *Conf.* v, 5, 8, *PL* 32, c. 709:

> Sed tamen quis quaerebat Manichaeum nescio quem etiam ista scribere, sine quorum peritia pietas disci poterat? Dixisti enim homini, *Ecce pietas et sapientia*; quam ille ignorare posset, etiam si ista perfecte nosset: ista vero quia non noverat, impudentissime audens docere, prorsus illam nosse non posset. Vanitas est enim mundana ista etiam nota profiteri, pietas autem tibi confiteri.

> But yet who was it that ordered Manichaeus to write on these things likewise, skill in which was not necessary to piety? For Thou hast told man to behold piety and wisdom [Job 28, 28; above *DR* i, 13, note 3], of which he might be in ignorance although having a complete knowledge of these other things; but since, knowing not these things, he yet most impudently dared to teach them, it is clear that he had no acquaintance with piety. For even when we have a knowledge of these worldly matters, it is folly to make profession of them; but confession to Thee is piety.

J.G. Pilkington in Oates (1948), i, pp. 61–62. On virtue and knowledge, *DR* ii, 41 and ii, 100.

16   On the ancient definition *wisdom is the knowledge of things both human and divine*, Augustine, *De trin.* xiv, 1, 3, *PL* 42, c. 1037; Cassiodorus, *Inst.* ii, 3, 5;

Isidore, *Etym*. ii, 24, 9; and the sources collected in Fontaine (1959), ii, pp. 604–610.

17 Cf. above, *DR* i, 12, 53–60.

18 Reason refers to the Capitoline contests of imperial Rome, and to the crown, "the due reward of Caesars and of poets . . . made of the leaves of the laurel" (Wilkins [1955], p. 309), which Petrarch, accepting an inaccurate tradition, confused with the crown of oak leaves granted to the winners of the competition in poetry. Petrarch's own coronation took place on April 8, 1341, in Rome, in the audience hall of the Senatorial Palace on the Capitoline. In the oration delivered on this great occasion, Petrarch hoped *that, if God wills, I may renew in the now aged Republic a beauteous custom of its flourishing youth.* (Wilkins) [1955], p. 304). For a detailed account of the coronation and its historical background, see Wilkins' admirable study "The Coronation of Petrarch" (1951), pp. 9–69, in which thirty-one important references in Petrarchan texts, among them our passage, as number 29, are listed and discussed. Cf. also Rawski (1967), pp. 178–179, n. 15.

19 Petrarch, *De vita sol.* ii, *Prose* (1955), pp. 524, 526, directly continuing the text given in note 6 above:

> Rursum et poetas intelligo, non hos quibus contexere versus sit satis, et, ut ait Flaccus,
>
> > versus inopes rerum nugasque canoras,
>
> quibus usque ad fastidium abundamus; sed eos qui, siquid Ciceroni credimus, fuerunt semper ipsis quoque philosophis rariores; poetas, inquam, veros, quibus *ingenium sit*, ut Flaccus idem ait,
>
> > mens divinior atque os
> > magna sonaturum,
>
> et quibus ex merito huius *honor nominis* debeatur.

By poets I understand not those content with joining lines—

> verses void of thought, and sonorous trifles

[Horace, *Ars poet.* 322, LCL, Fairclough, p. 477]—and with whom we now abound to the point of disgust [*Sen.* xii, 2 (1581: 904)]—but those who, if we believe Cicero, are even scarcer than philosophers [*De orat.* i, 3, 11; *Contra med.* iii, Ricci (1950), 321–326; Boccaccio, *Gen. deor.* xiv, 7, Reedy (1978), 5–7], true poets, I say, who have gifts inborn,

> a mind divine and tongue
> of noble utterance,

and thus deserve the honor of that name [paraphrasing Horace, *Sat.* i, 4, 43–44, LCL, Fairclough, p. 53].

Cf. Rawski (1967), and the literature cited there.

20   Petrarch wrote in the Letter to Posterity, *Sen.* xviii, 1, *Prose* (1955), p. 16:

> Veni tandem; et quamlibet indignus, ... summo cum gaudio Romanorum, qui illi solemnitati interesse potuerunt, lauream poeticam adhuc scolasticus rudis adeptus sum . . . Hec michi laurea scientie nichil, plurimum vero quesivit invidie.

> I went to Rome, and however unworthy . . . I, a raw pupil heretofore, received the poet's laurel to the great delight of those Romans who were able to attend the ceremony. . . . This laurel brought me no knowledge whatsoever, but a great deal of envy.

Similarly, *Sen.* xvii, 2, to Boccaccio, April 28, 1373, *Prose* (1955), p. 1152:

> Laurea autem illa michi immaturo evi fateor atque animi, immaturis quidem texta frondibus, obtigit; quam si fuissem maturior non optassem. Amant enim ut senes utilia, sic iuvenes speciosa, nec respiciunt finem. Et quid putas? Nil prorsus scientie, nil eloquentie illa michi, invidie autem infinitum attulit et quietem abstulit; sic inanis glorie et iuvenilis audacie penas dedi.

> I admit that I was immature in age and mind when I received immature laurel leaves. I would not have desired them, had I been more mature. Just as old men love useful things, so youth loves splendor, *heedless of consequences* [cf. above, *DR* i, 17, note 7]. And, as you may imagine, the laurel gave to me neither knowledge nor eloquence, but endless jealousy, and took away my peace. I paid the penalty for inane glory and juvenile swagger.

On the topic of the empty token dangerous in battle, Rawski (1967), pp. 183–184.

21   Cf. above, *DR* i, 9.

22   Martianus Capella, *De nupt.* v, 508, Dick (1925), p. 250: *copiose ornateque dicere.* Cf. De Bruyne (1946), i, p. 238.

23   The entire passage is Ciceronian. The *notable rareness of orators* comes from *De orat.* i, 3, 11, note 19, above. The topic recurs frequently, e.g., *DR* i, 9, 25–29, and notes 5–6, ii, 102, 20–28; and *Sen.* xii, 2 (1581: 905). The "most arrogant" assertion that orators should be able to speak on any matter is shown to be Ciceronian in *De sui ipsius* (1581: 1058):

> . . . Gorgias Leontinus Rhetor vetustissimus, non modo aliquid, sed sciri omnia posse credit, non a Philosopho tantum, sed ab Oratore: nempe, qui, ut ait Cicero, omnibus de rebus Oratorem optime posse dicere existimavit, quod certe ipse non potuit, non posset autem optime de rebus omnibus dicere, nisi optime omnes noscet. Idem sensit Hermagoras, qui non modo Rhetoricam, sed Philosophiam omnem, rerumque omnium notitiam tribuit Oratori. Magna me-

diocris ingenii fiducia[,] & longe omnibus fidentior[.] Hippias scire se omnia profiteri ausus, ut non modo de liberalibus studiis, deque universa Philosophia, sed de merchanicis quoque plenam sibi gloriam usurparet: dicerem divinum hominem, nisi insanum crederem.

. . . Georgias of Leontini, the very ancient rhetor, believed that not just knowing something, but knowing everything, was possible, not only for a philosopher, but for the orator. As, in fact, Cicero tells us, *that an orator could speak of all matters in the best manner imaginable* [*De inv.* i, 5, 7], though he himself certainly could not. However, he would have been unable to speak of all matters in the best manner, unless he knew them in that manner. This was also what Hermagoras felt when he said that the orator must master not only rhetoric but the whole of philosophy and all knowledge of everything [*De inv.* i, 6, 8]. Great confidence indeed for a mediocre genius! By far the most confident of all was Hippias, who dared to declare that he knew everything, thus usurping the full glory not only of the liberal studies and all philosphy, but even of the mechanic arts [*De orat.* iii, 32, 127]. This man I should call divine, if I did not believe he was mad.

H. Nachod in Cassirer (1948), p. 126. Cf. also Cicero, *De amic.* iv, 17; and *Fam.* xix, 11, iv, 15.

24 Cf. *Fam.* iv, 15, 19, note 3, above. —On *seethe and puff to the summit*, Rawski (1967), pp. 187–188, n. 26.

25 Seneca Rhetor, *Controv.* iii, Praef. 11:

Magna et varia res est eloquentia, neque adhuc ulli sic indulsit ut tota contingeret; satis felix est qui in aliquam eius partem receptus est.

LCL, Winterbottom, p. 385. Petrarch knew Martial's reference (i, 61, 7–12) to *duos Senecas*—the two Senecas (*Buc. carm.* x, 332–341; *Fam.* xxiv, 5, 17; *DR* ii, 125, 75; Martellotti [1983], chap. 24)—but did not derive from it the separate identities of Seneca the rhetorician and, his son, Seneca the philosopher. Cf. Nolhac (1907), ii, p. 117; Billanovich (1981), pp. 104–105; and Trimpi (1983), pp. 335–336, n. 9.

26 On Petrarch's animosity against run-of-the-mill physicians and lawyers, cf., e.g., Fort (1883), pp. 305, 398, 420–423; Wilkins (1961), pp. 7, 113–114, 123, 124, 165, 169–172, 198–199, 224–228, 230; and Rawski (1967), pp. 192–195, nn. 30, 31.

27 Juvenal, vii, 135–136:

. . . . purpura vendit
causidicum, vendunt amethystina; . . .

LCL, Ramsay, p. 149. Cf. John of Salisbury, *Policrat.* viii, 14, *PL* 199, c. 769.

28 Juvenal, vii, 139–140:

[ut redeant veteres] Ciceroni nemo ducentos
nunc dederit nummos, nisi fulserit anulus ingens.

LCL, Ramsay, p. 149. Petrarch quotes the old text in which, line 139, Juvenal's *fidimus eloquio*—Trust in eloquence, indeed?—is replaced by *ut redeant veteres*. On this, Rawski (1967), p. 194, n. 31.

29 Cf. above, *DR* i, 12, note 11.

30 In the *Secretum*, glory is one of the *adamantine chains* (= *SN* 9, 2, Piur [1925], p. 236, Zacour [1973], p. 118, which hold Franciscus in bondage. Cf. Wilkins (1978), pp. 231–234; and *Secretum* iii, *Prose* (1955), pp. 130, 188–194. On this, Rico (1974), pp. 400–415.

31 Cf. above, *DR* i, 11, 2–9 *et passim*; *Secretum* iii, *Prose* (1955), p. 132; and Rawski (1967), pp.197–198, n. 35. Note also *Fam.* xvii, 3, 48, as above, *DR* i, Pref., note 6.

32 1492: id essent: &c.
    1581: id essent.

47 ❖ PUBLIC OFFICE

1 In the old empire

> Judaea and Noricum and Raetia were ruled by 'procuratores.' This title, which of old was applied to the agents of citizens, with full power to represent them, was chiefly applied to the financial agents of the emperor.

Sandys (1929), sec. 396. The imperial chief treasury was administered by a *procurator*. Pontius Pilate was *procurator* of Judaea. The title *procurator* for the fiscal agent of the emperor survived to the times of Prince von Metternich. Cf. *Ital.*: procuratore; and *Germ.*: Prokurist. Lamer (1933), art. procuratores.

2 Cf., e.g., *Fam.* ix, 5, 39.

3 1492: unum tribunal incorruptum
    1581: unum tribunal corruptum

4 1492: falso corio iudicis
    1581: falsi corio iudicis

5 1492: Ea in sella quisquis iudicum sedet: ubi si iniuste iudicabitur: nec pecunia nec gratia: nec falsi testes: nec indignae preces nec inanes minae: nec diserti proderunt patroni.

6 Reason uses the word *consul* in Varro's sense that

consul nominatus qui consuleret populum et senatum, nisi illinc potius unde
Accius ait in Bruto:

> Qui recte consulat, consul fiat.

The consul was so named as the one who should *consulere* 'ask the advice of'
people and senate, unless rather from this fact whence Accius takes it when
he says in the *Brutus* [*Trag. Rom. Frag.* 39 Ribbeck; R.O.L. ii, 564–565
Warmington]:

> Let him who counsels right, become the Consul.

De ling. Lat. v, 14, 80. LCL, Kent, pp. 77, 79. On Petrarch's knowledge of
Varro, Nolhac (1907), *passim*, esp. ii, pp. 110–115. It is improbable that he
knew this passage.

7   I.t.: Flaccus. Horace, *Ep.* i, 1, 76:

> belua multorum es capitum.

> You are a many-headed monster-thing.

LCL, Fairclough, p. 257. Cf. Plato, *Republic* ix, 12, 538c.

8   Reason's punning wordplay *vile-vilicus* is based on Juvenal, iv, 75–77:

> . . .   .   primus clamante Liburno
> "currite iam sedit," rapta properabat abolla
> Pegasus, attonitae positus modo vilicus urbi.

> . . .   .   First to answer the Liburnian's call
> "Haste, haste! he is seated!" was Pegasus,
> hastily catching up his cloak—he that had newly been
> appointed as bailiff over the astonished city.

LCL, Ramsay, p. 63. In an old note, Johannes Britannicus, *Juvenal* (1522), f.
46v, points out that Pegasus was a lawyer who held the appointment of
praefectus urbi—chief civil official of Rome. Juvenal calls him *vilicus urbi*—
Rome having been so decimated by Emperor Domitian's cruelty that it appeared like a village rather than a metropolis.

9   Cf. *Sen.* xv, 12, to Giovanni Malpaghini, Arquà, before the end of 1370?
(1581: 942):

> Gratulor quoque, quod urbem Roman uideris, ex omnibus erroribus tuis,
> orbem totum licet ambias, simile nil uidebis. Vidisti mundi caput, squalidum
> fateor, & impexum, quod ne hostes quidem negent, qui se nunc etiam Roma-
> nos Imperatores, Romanosque Pontificies dici optant, & his titulis gloriantur,
> cum omnia sint potius, quam Romani. Hoc ergo per teipsum cogita, & sic
> habe, non te Roman uidisse, sed montes ubi Roma fuit.

> I congratulate you also on seeing the city of Rome, since in your wanderings
> you might have circled the earth without ever seeing anything like it. You saw

Rome, filthy and disheveled, I admit, but the capital of the world, which is not denied even by her enemies, who nowadays choose to call themselves Roman emperors and Roman pontiffs, and glory in these titles, although they are more likely to be anything but Romans. Reflect upon this by yourself, and you will find that you did not see Rome, but only hills upon which Rome once stood.

Rawski (1967), pp. 87–88.

48 ❖ MILITARY SERVICE

1   I.e., the Roman sword belt (Sandys [1929], § 731; Davenport [1948], i, p. 86; Singer, ii, [1956], p. 704) as sign of military authority and responsibility (cf., e.g., Niermeyer [1976], art. *cingulum*). On this, John of Salisbury, *Policrat.* vi, *passim*; Gautier (1883), pp. 16–19.

2   I.t.: Flaccus. —Horace, *Ep.* i, 2, 65–68:

> . . . . . . venaticus, ex quo
> tempore cervinam pellem latravit in aula,
> *militat in silvis catulus.*

> . . . . . . the hound that is to hunt
> does service in the woods from the time that it
> first barked at a deer-skin in the yard.

LCL, Fairclough, p. 267.

3   Job 7, 1:

> Militia est vita hominis super terram;
> et sicut dies mercenarii, dies eius.

> The life of man upon earth is a warfare,
> and his days are like the days of a hireling.

Cf. *DR.* i, Pref., note 6, ii, Pref.; and *Fam.* i, 1, 26, xvi, 6, 2, xxi, 9, 7, etc. Note also Seneca, e.g., *Ep.* 96, 5:

> Atqui vivere, Lucili, militare est.

> And yet life, Lucilius, is really a battle.

LCL, Gummere, p. 107. On this John of Salisbury, *Policrat.* ii, 27, iii, 8, *PL*

199, c. 471, 488–489; Johannes von Tepl, *Ackerm.*, Bernt & Burdach (1917), Anmerkungen, pp. 214–217; Lewis (1938), esp. pp. 59–60, 63–64, 72–73; and Pohlenz, ii, (1955), p. 157: *vivere militare est*. This topic survives in the Office of the Roman Catholic Church (most recently, *Liturgy of the Hours*, Ord. Time, Week iv, Tuesday, Morning Prayer).

4   Cf. above, *DR* i, 11, note 10.

5   *pectus et caput ferreum* implies both a man whose breast and head are clad in iron (armor) and one with an unfeeling heart and a doltish mind. —On the heavily armed horseman, the man-at-arms, Contamine (1984), pp. 126–127.

6   Cf. above, *DR* i, 46, note 30.

7   1492: aures tuas
     1581: ad res tuas

8   The command is Julius Caesar's, Lucan, v, 362–364:

> Et tu, quo solo stabunt iam robore castra,
> Tiro rudis, specta poenas et disce ferire,
> Disce mori. . . .

> And you raw recruits, who alone will form the
> backbone of the army in the future, watch their
> execution, and learn how to slay and to be slain.

LCL, Duff, p. 265. For an interesting echo of Lucan's lines in a decree by Merovingian King Childebert II (A.D. 595), cf. McCall (1979), p. 47.

9   Reason refers to *praemia militiae*, Juvenal, xvi, 1–2 (LCL, Ramsay, p. 303). The *licentia peccandi*—in *Juvenal* (1522), f. 160v, Badius Ascensius speaks of *licentia nocendi*—may include the *other profits and perquisites of the service* listed ibid., 35–60. The whole passage may be ironic. *Silent under the threat of arms* is Cicero, *Pro T. Annio Milone* 11.

10   1492, 1581, and Twyne read *bellum*—war—which, considering the whole passage, makes little sense. I have taken the liberty of substituting *balteus*—swordbelt (Juvenal, xvi, 48)—for *bellum*.

11   On contemporary military attire and equipment, cf., e.g., Seward (1978), pp. 51–55; and Contamine (1984), chap. 5. On *golden spurs* as insignia of the Christian knight (Gautier) [1883], esp. pp. 198, 293), *Fam.* xxiii, 11.

12   Independent professionals of warfare and their Free Companies of mercenaries (*Fam.* xviii, 16, 17–18, xix, 9, 10, xxii, 14, xxiii, 1), which replaced the town militias, were only too familiar to the fourteenth-century reader (Contamine [1984], chap. 4; McNeill [1982], pp. 72–75; Mallett [1974], pp. 3–51). Sir John Hawkwood (Condottiere Giovanni Acuto), one of the most flamboyant captains (Contamine, ibid., pp. 158–159), stated bluntly:

> Do you not know that I live by war and that peace would be my undoing?

(Seward [1978], p. 15.) On *militares viri* and *bellorum duces*, among whom belonged Azzo de Correggio, *Sen.* v, 2; and the great letter, *Sen.* iv, 1, to the commander Luchino dal Verme (1581: 795, 386–392).

13   On triumphs, above, *DR* i, 19, note 5.

14   *vulgo fabulam*—above, *DR* i, 16, note 2.

15   1492: tibi nihil: &c.

1581: tibi nihil.

49 ❖ ROYAL FAVOR

1   1492: timorque animi

1581: tumorque animi

On *tumor animi*, Cicero, *Tusc. disp.* iv, 29, 63:

> . . . vetat Chrysippus ad recentes quasi tumores animi remedium adhibere.

> . . . the remedy of which Chrysippus [*SVF* iii, 484; Pohlenz (1959), p. 151, (1955), pp. 82, 155] forbids the application to fresh ferments as it were of the soul.

(LCL, King, p. 401); and ibid. iii, 12, 26, as below, *DR* ii, 95, note 8; ibid. iii, 31, 76; Seneca, *Thyestes* iii, 519; Lactantius, *Div. inst.* v, 23, *PL* 6, c. 625: . . . *animo insolenter elato tumet*; and Augustine, *Conf.* vii, 7, 11, *PL* 32, c. 740:

> . . . quia *humiliasti tanquam vulneratum, superbum*; et tumore meo separabar abs te, et nimis inflata facies claudebat oculos meos.

> . . . for Thou humblest the proud like one that is wounded (Ps. 88, 11), and through my own swelling was I separated from Thee; yea, my too much swollen face closed up mine eyes.

J. G. Pilkington in Oates (1948), i, p. 99. Note Boethius, *Cons. phil.* i, P 5, 42. Singleton (1973), *Commentary* p. 240, n. 119, cites this passage in connection with Dante, *Div. Comm.*, Purg. xi, 118–119:

> E io a lui: "Tuo vero dir m'incora
> bona umiltà, e gran tumor m'appiani . . . "

> And I to him, "Your true words fill my heart
> with good humility and abate in me a great swelling . . . "

Singleton (1973), p. 117. —Cf. *DR* i, Pref., 112–114, i, 66, 11–12, ii, 41, 23, and ii, 116, 17. Related, *Sen.* ii, 1 (1581: 754); *De vir. ill.* xv, Alex., 30; and *Met.* i, 7, 198. Note also *DR* i, 12, note 31 and i, 13, note 9.

2   Sallust, *Cat.* vii, 2:

> Nam regibus boni quam mali suspectiores sunt semperque
> aliena virtus formidulosa est.

LCL, Rolfe, p. 13. CF. *Sen.* v, 2 (1581: 795).

3   Above, *DR* i, 32.

4   Cf. Seneca, *Dial.* v, De ira iii, 17, 1:

> . . . Haec barbaris regibus feritas in ira fuit, quos nulla eruditio, nullus litter-
> arum cultus imbuerat.

> . . . Such was the ferocity of barbarian kings when in anger—men who had
> no contact with learning or the culture of letters.

LCL, Basore, p. 299. Cf. above, *DR* i, 43, 89–100.

5   Lysimachus, one of Alexander's generals and closest friends, was said to have been thrown to a lion by Alexander. This is accepted by Pliny, *Nat. hist.* viii, 21, 54; Seneca, *De ira* iii, 17, 2; *De clem.* i, 25, 1; and Justin xv, 3. But Quintus Curtius, viii, 14–17, records the story as follows:

> . . . . cum leo magnitudinis rarae ipsum regem invasurus incurreret, forte
> Lysimachus, qui postea regnavit, proximus Alexandro venabulum obicere ferae
> coeperat; quo rex repulso et abire iusso, adiecit tam a semet uno quam a
> Lysimacho leonem interfici posse. Lysimachus enim quondam, cum venarentur
> in Syria, occiderat quidem eximiae magnitudinis feram solus, sed laevo humero
> usque ad ossa lacerato, ad ultimum periculi pervenerat. . . . . . . Fabulam
> quae obiectum leoni a rege Lysimachum temere vulgavit ab eo casu quem
> supra diximus ortam esse crediderim.

> . . . . . . when a lion of extraordinary size rushed to attack the king himself,
> it happened that Lysimachus, who was afterwards a king, being beside Alexan-
> der, began to oppose his hunting-spear to the animal; but the king pushed him
> aside and ordered him to retire, adding that a lion could be killed by himself
> alone as well as by Lysimachus. And in fact Lysimachus, once when they were
> hunting in Syria, had indeed alone killed a lion of remarkable size, but had had
> his left shoulder torn to the bone and thus had come into great peril of his life.
> . . . . . . I am inclined to believe that the story which without evidence
> spread the report that Lysimachus was exposed by the king to the attack of a
> lion arose from the incident which we have just mentioned.

LCL, Rolfe, p. 237. —Lucius Aelius Seianus held *great, unlooked for, and comprehensive* offices of the highest kind under Emperor Tiberius:

> Quo die illum senatus deduxerat, populus in frustra divisit; in quem quicquid

congeri poterat di hominesque contulerant, ex eo nihil superfuit, quod carnifex traheret!

Yet on the day on which the senate played the escort [A.D. 31], the people tore him to pieces! Of the man who had had heaped upon him all that gods and men were able to bestow nothing was left for the executioner to drag to the river!

Seneca, *Dial.* ix, *De tranqu. an.*, 11, 11, LCL, Basore, p. 261. On Seianus, Suetonius, iii, Tiberius, *passim*. Shakespeare's name appears in the cast list of Ben Jonson's play *Sejanus His Fall*, 1603 (Schoenbaum [1970], p. 37; Schoenbaum [1975], p. 150).

6   On the wiles of the fowler, above, *DR* i, 23, 17–18, and note 8.

7   1492: sic periculis emitur. Periculum multis unum magis maximum
     1581: sic periculis emi periculum unum magnis maximum

8   1492: quod sic esse uita Regum probat
     1581: quod sic esse uita reprobat

9   In the Latin text of *DR* i, 49, Joy's ten statements exhibit a distinctive pattern:

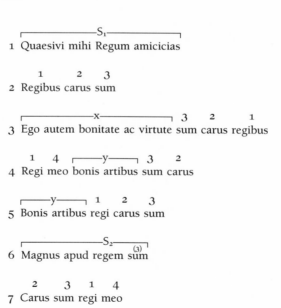

1 Quaesivi mihi Regum amicicias

2 Regibus carus sum

3 Ego autem bonitate ac virtute sum carus regibus

4 Regi meo bonis artibus sum carus

5 Bonis artibus regi carus sum

6 Magnus apud regem sum

7 Carus sum regi meo

8 Meo sum carus regi

9 Spero me Regi meo carum

┌────────────────────────S₃────────────────────────┐
10 Amiciciam regis mei multis periculis; ac sudore promerui

50 ❖ MANY FRIENDS

1   Dialogues 50–56 are on friendship and material wealth.
2   Cicero, *De amic.* iv, 15:

> . . . quod ex omnibus saeculis vix tria aut quattuor nominantur paria
> amicorum . . .

> . . . because in the whole range of history only three or four pairs of friends
> are mentioned . . .

LCL, Falconer, p. 125. W.A. Falconer speculates that these are Theseus and
Pirithous; Achilles and Patroclus; Orestes and Pylades; and, perhaps, Damon
and Pythias (cf. Cicero, *De off.* iii, 10, 45; *De fin.* ii, 24, 79). Note Spenser,
Faerie Queene iv, 10, 27.

3   Lucan, vii, 727:

> foelix se nescit amari.

Also quoted in *Fam.* xiv, 1, 34.

4   1492: Amicus certus in re certa cernitur
     1581: Amicus certus, in re incerta cernitur

Cicero, *De amic.* xvii, 64:

Quamquam Ennius recte:

> Amicus certus in re incerta cernitur;

tamen haec duo levitatis et infirmitatis plerosque convincunt, aut si in bonis
rebus contemnunt aut in malis deserunt.

Ennius, however, is right when he says:

> When Fortune's fickle the faithful friend is found;

yet it is on these two charges that most men are convicted of fickleness: they either hold a friend of little value when their own affairs are prosperous, or they abandon him when his are adverse.

LCL, Falconer, p. 175. Cf. Also Publilius Syrus, *Sent* 41:

amicum an nomen habeas aperit calamitas,

Misfortune reveals whether you have a friend or only one in name.

LCL, Duff, p. 19. —The Ennius maxim recurs in *La Celestina* vii, 1, Marciales (1985), ii, p. 124, Simpson (1955), p. 79, where it is immediately followed by [*en las adversidades* . . .] what may be an echo of *DR* i, 51, 42; and [*Entonces se allega* . . .] a sentence from *DR* i, 19, 126.

5 On moderation, cf. above, *DR* i, 2, note 25.
6 Probably a reference to Livy. On Livy's conception of Rome, e.g., Mazzolani (1976), pp. 87–139.
7 *aut equidem imperfectae: ut philosophis placet.* This may recall Seneca's reference to *viri imperfecti*—imperfect men—e.g., *Ep.* 92, 29, and 94, 52. The context is clearly Aristotle, *Eth. Nic.*, Book viii.
8 *ad vulgares amicicias descendis.* Compare Cicero, *De amic.* xxi, 76:

iam enim a sapientium familiaritatibus ad volgaris amicitias oratio nostra delabitur.

for now our discussion descends from the intimacies of the wise to friendships of the ordinary kind.

LCL, Falconer, p. 185. Similar, ibid. vi, 22.
9 Aristotle, *Eth. Nic.* viii, 3, 1156 a, b:

There are therefore three kinds of friendship, equal in number to the things that are lovable; for with respect to each there is a mutual and recognized love, and those who love each other wish well to each other in that respect in which they love one another. Now those who love each other for their utility do not love each other for themselves but in virtue of some good which they get from each other. So too with those who love for the sake of pleasure; it is not for their character that men love ready-witted people, but because they find them pleasant. Therefore those who love for the sake of utility love for the sake of what is good for themselves, and those who love for the sake of pleasure do so for the sake of what is pleasant to themselves, and not insofar as the other is the person loved but insofar as he is useful or pleasant . . .   . . . Perfect friendship is the friendship of men who are good, and alike in excellence; for these wish well alike to each other *qua* good, and they are good in themselves. Now those who wish well to their friends for their sake are most truly friends; for they do this by reason of their own nature and not incidentally; therefore their friendship lasts as long as they are good—*and excellence is an enduring thing. And each is good without qualification and to his friend,* for the good are both good without qualification and useful to each other. So too they are pleasant; for the good are pleasant both without qualification and to each other, since to each his own activities and others like them are pleasurable, and the actions of the good are the same or like. *And such a friendship is as might be expected* [*firm and stable*].

W. D. Ross and J. O. Urmson in Barnes (1984), ii, pp. 1826–1827. On the stability of virtue, also *Fam.* xx, 3, 3; *Sen.* xiv, 1 (1581: 380), as above, *DR* i, 36, note 2; and *DR* ii, 13, 33, ii, 83, 265–275 *et passim.*

10   1492: Estque haec Ecatonis Graeci philosophi amatorium notissimum
      1581: Estque haec Hecatonis Graeci philosophi, amatorum notissimum
11   Seneca, *Ep.* 9, 6:

> Hecaton ait: Ego tibi monstrabo amatorium sine medicamento, sine herba, sine ullius veneficae carmine: si vis amari, ama.

> Hecato says: "I can show you a philtre, compounded without drugs, herbs, or any poisoner's incantation: 'If you would be loved, love.' "

LCL, Gummere, p. 45. Cf. *Roman de la Rose* 4803–4836, as below, *DR* i, 110, note 10.

12   Cf. above, *DR* i, 19, 126–127. The topic returns in *La Celestina* viii, 3, Marciales (1985), ii, p. 148; and Simpson (1955), p. 96.
13   Cf. Aristotle, as note 9, above; and Cicero, *De amic.* iv, 18, xviii, 65.
14   Cicero, *De amic.* xxiv, 90:

> Scitum est enim illud Catonis, ut multa: melius de quibusdam acerbos inimicos mereri, quam eos amicos, qui dulces videantur; illos verum saepe dicere, hos numquam.

> For there is shrewdness in that well-known saying of Cato, as there was in much that he said: "Some men are better served by their bitter-tongued enemies than by their sweet-smiling friends; because the former often tell the truth, the latter, never."

LCL, Falconer, p. 199.

51 ❖ UNKNOWN FRIENDS

1   *De vir. ill.* xxi, Scipio 2, 15; γii, 74–75:

> . . . qui semper primus in equitatu Carthaginensium fuisset, ex illa hora concupisceret amicitiam Romanorum.

[Masinissa] . . . who always was the first in the Carthagenian cavalry, from this moment on was desirous of the friendship of the Romans.

Similar, *Fam.* ix, 11, 4–5; and xviii, 2, 2. Cf. also Livy, xxviii, 35, 5–9; and Valerius Maximus, v, 2, ext. 4.

2   *De vir. ill.* xxi, Scipio, 12, 41–44:

Illic vero, ... magnificum illud inter multa magnificentissimus exul vidit; virtutis enim admiratio, que suos cives non moverat, predonum aciem contraxit, qui quasi ad visendum deum aliquem congregati venerant. Hos Africanus ad nocendum venisse ratus, quod accolarum paucitas credibile faciebat, presidium suorum in superiore domus parte constituit. Id ubi animadverterunt qui longe alio proposito veniebant, abiectis armis relictisque militibus, duces ipsi cum paucis accesserunt propius atque alta voce 'Minime insidiatores' inquiunt 'sed miratores huc venimus, virique huius aspectum pro inextimabili munere flagitamus; neu illi sit molestum nostris se parumper oculis intuendum dare'. Quod audiens Scipio apertis eos foribus excipi imperat. Illi autem introgressi et, tanquam sanctissimi cuiuspiam templi aram, postes primum ianue limenque ipsum venerati, inde certatim ad contingendam victricem illam hostium servatricem patrie dexteram concurrunt. Quam multis osculis fatigatam vix ad ultimum relinquentes, muneribus qualia diis offerri mos tunc erat ipso domus in vestibulo depositis, leti gloriantesque, quod tanti viri vultum conspexissent, et pleni admirationis abiere; sic sepe omnibus homo est carior venerabiliorque quam suis.

Here, however, ... the eminent exile witnessed in a most remarkable incident the appreciation of virtue, which had failed to move his countrymen, but brought together a horde of robbers, so that they came, all together, as if to see a godlike creature. Scipio thought that they intended to do harm, which the lack of appreciation he had experienced previously made probable indeed, and positioned a detachment of his men in the upper story of the house. As soon as the robbers, who had come from afar with wholly different intentions, noticed this they laid down their weapons, the chieftains dismissed their escorts and approached with but a few men insisting with a loud voice: "We have come not as bushwhackers, but as admirers of a man whose face to see we consider an inestimable privilege. Nor do we wish to impose on him, only gaze at him for a short while." When Scipio heard this he ordered his men to open the gate and meet the robbers, who entered, first paid homage to the gateposts and the threshold, and then proceeded to vie eagerly to touch that right hand which had defeated the enemy and preserved the fatherland. Finally they let it go, nearly worn out by their many kisses, and having placed such gifts as it was then the custom to offer to the gods in the entrance hall of the house, left in admiration, pleased and full of praise that they had seen the face of such a great man. Thus, often, a man is dearer and more worthy of respect to strangers than he is to his own people.

Based on Valerius Maximus, ii, 10, 2. Cf. also *Africa* ii, 702–709, and v, 977–992.

3   Claudian, *De bello Gild.*, 385:

> . . . . minuit praesentia famam.

Cf. the echo *et magnis semper nominibus inimica praesentia* in *Fam.* ii, 14, 2; and *Fam.* i, 2, 5:

> Delicatissima res est iugis conversatio: minimis offenditur, et fame semper inimica presentia est, multumque admirationi hominum familiaritas detrahit frequensque convictus.

> Close association is a most delicate matter. It is affected by the smallest incidents—and one's presence is invariably inimical to his fame. Familiarity and frequent contact with a man detract a great deal from the admiration accorded him by those around him.

Fam. i, 2, 27, returns to the subject quoting Livy, xxxv, 10, 5–6; cf. below, *DR* ii, 38, note 6. —The Claudian line is cited and reversed in Boccaccio's panegyric remarks about Petrarch, *Geneal. deor.* xiv, 19, Reedy (1978), pp. 80–81; and Osgood (1930), pp. 91–92. Note Jerome, *Ep.* 60, 10, LCL, Wright, p. 282.

4   Terence, *Andria*, 67–68:

> . . . . . . namque hoc tempore
> obsequium amicos, veritas odium parit.

> . . . . . . Nowadays it's complaisance that makes
> friends and truthfulness is the mother of unpopularity.

LCL, Sargeaunt, p. 11. Also quoted *Fam.* xv, 12, 2; and xxiv, 4, 1; and alluded to, *Fam.* xvi, 8, 6.

5   1492: desinant: &c.
1581: desinant:

52 ❖ A FAITHFUL FRIEND

1   1492: Saepe in experiendo uestrum errat acumen
1581: Saepe experiendo uestrum errat acumen

Cf. Cicero, *Tusc. disp.* i, 6, 12:

Ubi est acumen tuum?

Where have your wits gone?

LCL, King, p. 15.

2   Cf. above, *DR* i, 50, 58–60, and 95.

3   The Latin phraseology includes children and siblings of both sexes. But the nomenclature, as used throughout the *DR*, refers to males only. Reason may be paraphrasing Cicero, *De off.* i, 17, 57:

> Cari sunt parentes, cari liberi, propinqui, familiares.

> Parents are dear; dear are children, relatives, friends.

LCL, Miller, pp. 59, 61.

4   On Saturn and Jupiter, Graves (1955), i, 7. The Bithynian king Prusias II, who ruled 183–149 B.C., was succeeded by his son, Nicomedes II, who reigned to 115 B.C. Ptolemy IV, Philopater (= loving his father) ruled Egypt 221–203 B.C. On Prusias' death, Livy, Perioch. 50; and Boccaccio, *De casib.* (Hall [1962]), f. 53r–53v. On the parricide of Ptolemy, ibid. f. 49v. On the Oresteia, Harvey (1974), p. 297. On Nero and Agrippina, Suetonius vi, Nero, 24; and Boccaccio, ibid. f. 83v. On Antipater, son of Cassander and his mother, Thessalonice, Justin, xvi, 1, 1.

5   I.e., Ptolemy II, Philadelphus (= lover of his sister), 285–246 B.C. He adopted the practice of the ancient Pharaos and married his sister, Arsinoë II (276 B.C.).

6   I.t.: Maleus

7   On Theseus and Hippolytus, Graves (1955), i, 101; and Seneca's tragedy *Hippolytus*. Philip V of Macedonia (d. 179 B.C.) suspected that his son Demetrius was dealing with the hostile Romans and ordered him put to death (Livy, xxxix, 53; cf. *Fam.* ix, 5, 48). Ptolemy II killed the two sons of Arsinoë (Boccaccio, *De casib.*, f. 43v–44v). Herod the Great of Judea (d. 4 B.C.) executed three sons, first, Aristobulus and Alexander by Mariamne, and, later, Antipater, son of his first wife (cf. Macrobius, *Saturn.* ii, 4, 11), when he found out that Antipater's intrigues had caused him to execute Aristobulus and Alexander. Crispus was put to death at Pola, Istria, in A.D. 326, upon the orders of his father, Constantine (Aurelius Victor, *Epit.* 41, 11–12; Gibbon [1789], chap. 18; Lietzmann [1952], p. 181). Boccaccio, *De Casib.* iii, Aphri quidam queruli, f. 32r, refers to Carthalo, *patris iussu cruci adfixus*—crucified upon the order of his father—based on Justin xviii, 7, 1–15.

8   Cf. Graves (1955), ii, 156; Harvey (1974), pp. 263–264; and Euripides, *Medea*, 1271–1307, Oates (1938), i, pp. 752–753. Petrarch may have known Seneca's tragedy *Medea*; cf. *Fam.* iii, 2; and SN 6, Zacour (1973), pp. 62–63, and n. 3.

9   Phraates IV, King of Parthia, 37–2 B.C., killed his father, Orodes I, who had

been victorious over Crassus at Carrhae (53 B.C.; cf. below, *DR* ii, 132, 36–39, and note 7). Cf. Justin, xlii, 4, 14 through 5, 3.

10   According to Heitmann (1957, p. 21), reference is made to Edward III, who replaced his father, Edward II, on the throne of England in 1327 (Previté-Orton [1952], pp. 888–889), and to the contest between Peter the Cruel, King of Leon and Castile (1349–1369), and his half-brother, Don Henry of Trastamara, who killed him near Montiel, March 28, 1369 (Previté-Orton [1952], p. 906).

11   Agamemnon was treacherously slain by his wife, Clytemnestra, and her lover, Aegisthus. Cf. Graves (1955), ii, 162. t.; and Seneca's tragedy *Agamemnon*. Deiphobus was married to Helen of Troy when she thrust a dagger into his back (Graves, ibid., 166. f.). Claudius was husband to the adulterous Messalina (executed A.D. 48) and, subsequently, to Agrippina, who poisoned him (Suetonius, v, Claudius, *passim*). The younger Scipio Africanus (185–129 B.C.), grandson by adoption to Scipio Africanus the Elder, and victor in the Third Punic War, was married to Sempronia, sister of the Gracchi, whose social reforms Scipio opposed. Sempronia was suspected of having poisoned him. Livy, Perioch. 59. The examples of Agamemnon, Claudius, and Scipio appear also in *Fam.* xxii, 12, to Albertino da Cannobio, Milan, October 26, 1360, 16–17.

12   On Octavia, wife of her adopted brother, Nero, Suetonius, vi, Nero, 35; and pseudo-Seneca, *Octavia* (cf. *Fam.* i, 1, 43, xii, 2, 6, xxiv, 5, 15–19; and Cosenza [1910], pp. 49–51, 56–66). On Arsinoë, wife of her natural brother, Ptolemy II, Philadelphus, notes 5 and 7, above. —Lists displaying Petrarch's erudition occur in the *DR*, as well as in his other works, e.g., the *Trionfi*, and *Buc. carm.*, Eclogue x (Bergin [1974], pp. 236–247; Martellotti [1968]; Grant [1965], pp. 96–97; Mann [1984], pp. 96–97). They point to a tendency in medieval literature that may have taken its cue from enumerative characteristics associated with the *locus amoenus* in medieval rhetoric (Curtius [1953], pp. 195–200)—a tendency to dwell in great detail on certain points of interest and offer copious materials for consideration and study by the attuned reader. On such lists and catalogues, Lewis (1964), pp. 198–200; Bryan & Dempster (1958), pp. 550–559; and Curtius (1953), pp. 92–93.

13   Eccli. 27, 21–23:

> . . . sicut qui dimittit avem de manu sua
> sic dereliquisti proximum tuum, et non eum capies.
> Non illum sequaris quoniam longe abest;
> effugit enim quasi caprea de laqueo, quoniam vulnerata est anima eius:
> ultra eum non poteris colligare.

On Petrarch's efforts to restore broken friendships, Wilkins (1961), pp. 116–117, 161.

53 ❖ WEALTH

1   On the "new" *joy of possessing,* Duby (1981), pp. 252–254; and Braudel, i (1981), chaps. 3, 4, ii (1982), chaps. 4, 5.

2   1492: Ham si nescis plures multo sunt qui habentur: quam qui habent: multoque crebriores: quos propheticus sermo notat: Viros diuitiarum quam diuitias uirorum

      1581: nam si nescis plures multo sunt qui habentur, quam qui habent, multoque crebriores, quos propheticus sermo notat. Viri diuitiarum, quam diuitiae uirorum

viri divitiarum is Ps. 75, 6, note 3, below. I cannot identify a *propheticus sermo* on the subject other than that, unless a passage such as Seneca, *Ep.* 119, 11–12 (as below, *DR* i, 85, note 1), or *Dial.* vii, 22, 5, is so designated by Reason. Heitmann (1958), p. 187, n. 211, points to Ambrose, *Nab.* 15, 63, *PL* 14, c. 787:

> Bene viros divitiarum appellavit, non divitias virorum; ut ostendere eos non possessores divitiarum esse sed a suis divitiis possideri.

> The psalmist says correctly 'the men of riches' and not 'the riches of men' [Ps. 75, 6, cited below], so as to show that they are not the possessors of their riches, but are being possessed by them.

Similarly, *Glossa ordinaria, PL* 113, cc. 963–964.

3   1492: in manibus suis. &c.
      1581: in manibus suis.

Ps. 75, 6:

> Dormierunt somnum suum,
> et nihil invenerunt omnes *viri divitiarum* in manibus suis.

54 ❖ DISCOVERING GOLD

1   No inclusive account of mining practices and techniques before the sixteenth century seems to exist. Singer, ii (1956), pp. 11–24, is based on Agricola's *De re metallica* of 1556.

2 On the *homo erectus* topic, cf. above, *DR* i, 40, note 6.

3 *Nero Caesar suprema illa suo nocte terribili et misera, sed sibi debita.* Cf.
   above, *DR* i, 23, 67–68: *Nero, . . . quod nocte illa que sibi vite ultima: mundo
   autem respirandi vel modicum prima fuit.*

4 Suetonius, vi, Nero, 48, 3:

   > Ibi hortante eodem Phaonte, ut interim in specum egestae harenae concederet,
   > *negavit se vivum sub terram iturum, ac parumper commoratus,* dum clandestinus
   > ad villam introitus pararetur, aquam ex subiecta lacuna poturus manu hausit et
   > "Haec est," inquit, "Neronis decocta."

   > Here the aforesaid Phaon urged him to hide for a time in a pit, from which
   > sand had been dug, but *he declared that he would not go under ground while still
   > alive,* and after waiting for a while until a secret entrance into the villa could be
   > made, he scooped up in his hand some water to drink from a pool close by,
   > saying: "This is Nero's distilled water." [Cf. Pliny, *Nat. hist.* xxxi, 40.]

   LCL, Rolfe, p. 177.

5 I.t.: Naso

6 Ovid, *Metam.* i, 138–140:

   > . . .   .   itum est in viscera terrae
   > quasque recondiderat Stygiisque admoverat umbris,
   > effodiuntur opes, inritamenta malorum.

   LCL, Miller, p. 13.

7 On tracking and hunting, and the hare as game and symbol, Rowland (1971),
   chap. 6; and idem (1973), pp. 88–93.

8 Cf. the summary of Theophrastus, *Liber aureolus de nuptiis* (Jerome, *Adv. Jov.*
   i, 47, *PL* 23, c. 276) in John of Salisbury, *Policrat:* viii, 11, *PL* 199, c. 750:

   > Difficile custoditur quod plures amant.

   > It is difficult to guard what many love.

   Note also Innocent III, *De miseria cond. hum.* i, 16, 44–46, Lewis (1978), p.
   121; and the related maxim attributed to Hermes Trismegistus (*DR* i, 13,
   notes 14, 15) in Johannes von Tepl, *Ackerm.* xx, 36–39, Walshe (1951), p. 25,
   with the commentary in Bernt & Burdach (1917), pp. 293–296.

9 The text is not clear. Pliny, *Nat. hist.* iii, 20, 138:

   > [Italia] *metallorum omnium fertilitate nullis cedit terris;* sed *interdictum id vetere
   > consulto patrum Italiae* parci iubentium.

   > [Italy] is inferior to no country in abundance of mineral products of every kind;
   > but mining is prohibited by an old resolution of the Senate forbidding the
   > exploitation of Italy.

   LCL, Rackham, p. 103.

10   Cf. above, *DR* i, 23, 2–3, 23–25.
11   Cf. the crass answer to such a question asked by the friar, in the Summoner's
       Prologue of Chaucer's *Canterbury Tales* iii (D), 1665–1708.
12   1492: inuenisti. &c.
       1581: inuenisti.

55 ❖ DISCOVERING TREASURE

1   *Fam.* vii, 3, 2:

> Michi quidem, ut eram—memini enim—occurrebat illud Annei: "Vitate
> quecunque vulgo placent, que tribuit casus; ad omne fortuitum bonum suspiti-
> osi et pavidi subsistite: et fera et piscis spe aliqua oblectante decipitur; munera
> ista fortune que putatis, insidie sunt."

As I stood there, I remember recalling these words of Seneca:

> Avoid whatever pleases the throng: avoid the gifts of Chance! Halt before
> every good which Chance brings to you, in a spirit of doubt and fear; for it
> is the dumb animals and fish that are deceived by tempting hopes. Do you
> call these things the gifts of Fortune? They are snares.

[Seneca, *Ep.* 8, 3; LCL, Gummere, p. 39.]

On soothing entrapment, also above, *DR* i, 23, 16–20.
2   Cf. above, *DR* i, 51, 50–53.

56 ❖ USURY

1   Ps. 48, 19:

> confitebitur tibi cum beneficeris ei.

2   Ps. 72, 7:

>   Prodiit quasi ex adipe iniquitas eorum.

3   1492: et deiecti animi tamquam inhertis indicium:
     1581: & delecti animi, tamquam inertis indicium?

4   "The very worst art" reflects the contemporary view of usury as a violation
     of both man's art and God's Nature. Cf. Thomas Aquinas, *Summa theol.* ii, 2,
     Q 78, a. 1 ad 3; Dante, *Div. Comm.*, Inferno xi, 97–111:

>   "Filosofia," mi disse, "a chi la 'ntende,
>   nota, non pure in una sola parte,
>   come natura lo suo corso prende
>   dal divino 'ntelletto e da sua arte;
>   e se tu ben la tua Fisica note,
>   tu troverai, non dopo molto carte
>   che l'arte vostra quella, quanto pote,
>   segue, come 'l maestro fa 'l discente;
>   sì che vostr' arte a Dio quasi è nepote.
>   Da queste due, se tu ti rechi a mente
>   lo Genesì dal principio, convene
>   prender sua vita e avanzar la gente;
>   e perché l'usuriere altra via tene,
>   per sé natura e per la sua seguace
>   dispregia, poi ch'in altro pon la spene."

>   "Philosophy makes plain by many reasons,"
>   he answered me, "to those who heed her teachings,
>   how all of Nature, —her laws, her fruits, her seasons,—
>   springs from the Ultimate Intellect and Its art:
>   and if you read your *Physics* [Aristotle, *Phys.*,
>   e.g., ii, 2, 194a] with due care,
>   you will note, not many pages from the start,
>   that Art strives after her by imitation,
>   as the disciple imitates the master;
>   Art, as it were, is the Grandchild of Creation.
>   By this, recalling the Old Testament
>   near the beginning of Genesis [e.g., 3, 17], you will see
>   that in the will of Providence, man was meant
>   to labor and to prosper. But usurers,
>   by seeking their increase in other ways,
>   scorn Nature in herself and her followers."

Ciardi (1977), pp. 56–57. On the idea of usury and its scriptural ramifi-
cations, Nelson (1969), pp. 3–18; and Berenson (1983), pp. 248–250,
338–339.

5   Cf. above, *DR* i, 53, 18.

6   1492: foeneratores
      1581: foederatores

7   Reason refers to the flowering of the great banking houses in Trecento Italy
      (Olschki [1949], chap. ix; Schevill [1936], chap. xiv. e.g., pp. 218–220),
      which engaged in large-scale financial transactions (for the church, secular
      rulers and governments, wholesale import-export) as well as routine loans of
      the kind available also from the lowly money changers and usurers (Grupp, v
      [1925], chaps. 113, 124; McCall [1979], pp. 280–282). Dante's *usurai*, the
      gente mesta seated among the violent in Round 3 of Circle VII of Hell (*Div.
      Comm.*, Inf. xvii, 34–75), all are *from distinguished Florentine and Paduan
      families* (Singleton [1970], *Commentary*, p. 300, n. 52). Included is Rinaldo
      degli Scrovegni, whose son, Enrico, built the Scrovegni chapel in Padua's S.
      Maria dell' Arena (1305), with its frescoes by Giotto (Toynbee [1968], p.
      543); cf. Bernath (1916), pp. 239–244. Another prominent Treviso money-
      lender and collector of classical texts and artifacts was Petrarch's contempo-
      rary Oliviero Forzetta (1300–1373). On him, L. Gargan in Bolgar (1971),
      chap. 7; and Alsop (1982), chap. 10. On early capitalism in Europe, J. Strie-
      der in Goetz (1932), pp. 3–26; Steinbuechel (1935), part v; Coulter (1938),
      chap. 27; Braudel, ii (1982), pp. 559–565. Note also the relevant titles in the
      bibliographic section of Nelson (1969).

8   On this, e.g., Petrus Cantor (late twelfth century), *Verbum abbreviatum*, PL
      205, cc. 144–147, 255; Nelson (1969), pp. 10–13.

9   Cicero, *De off.* ii, 25, 89:

> Ex quo genere comparationis illud est Catonis senis: a quo cum quaereretur,
> quid maxime in re familiari expediret, respondit: "Bene pascere"; quid secun-
> dum: "Satis bene pascere"; quid tertium: "Male pascere"; quid quartum:
> "Arare"; et cum ille, qui quaesierat, dixisset: "Quid faenari?", tum Cato: "Quid
> hominem," inquit, "occidere?"

> To this class of comparisons belongs that famous saying of old Cato's: when he
> was asked what was the most profitable feature of an estate, he replied: "Rais-
> ing cattle successfully." What next to that? "Raising cattle with fair success."
> And next? "Raising cattle with but slight success." And fourth? "Raising
> crops." And when his questioner said, "How about money-lending?" Cato
> replied: "How about murder?"

LCL, Miller pp. 266–267.

10   1492: semper inops: &c.
      1581: semper inops.

Twyne, f. 79v.:

> Then shalt thou always be a wretch, alwaies covetous, always poore, and in
> the ende goo to the Dyvel.

57 ❖ FERTILE LAND

1   Dialogues 57–64 deal with the subjects of *res rustica*—farming—in the traditional sequence established in the antique literature (e.g., Varro's *Three Books De re rustica*): *agri cultura*—fields and gardens—Dialogues 57, 58; *res pecuaria*—livestock—Dialogue 59 and, on more exotic animals, 60, 61; and *villatica pastio*—birds, poultry, bees—Dialogue 62 and, fish, 63, aviaries, 64. —Regarding the text of this dialogue, note the parallels in *Buc. carm.*, Eclogue ix.

2   *si & sobrietatem & modestiam fertilitas non excludet*: Cf. Tit. 2, 12:

> erudiens nos, ut abnegantes impietatem et saecularia desideria, sobrie, et iuste, et pie vivamus in hoc saeculo . . .

> Instructing us that, denying ungodliness and wordly desires, we should live soberly, and justly, and godly in this world.

3   Cf. above, *DR* i, 53, 20–26.
4   Virgil, *Georg.* ii, 473–474:

> . . . . . . externa per illos
> Iustitia excedens terris vestigia fecit.

5   Cf. below, *DR* ii, Pref., note 79.
6   Cf. Isidore, *Etym.* xvii, 1; and Fontaine (1959), ii, pp. 713–714.
7   This is Pliny, *Nat. hist.* vii, 27, 100, as above, *DR* i, 7, note 6. In *De vir. ill.* xxii, Cato, 5, *Fam.* xix, 18, 20, and *DR* i, 7, 19–20, the correct sequence of Pliny's text is maintained. Does Reason quote from memory *triplex Catonis laus*—the threefold praise of Cato? Cf. Nolhac (1907), i, p. 243, and ii, pp. 109–110.
8   Pliny, *Nat. hist.* xiv, 5, 44, note 11, below.
9   Cf. *drinking like Cato and dancing like Scipio*, above, *DR* i, 24, 112–119.
10   Cf. above, *DR* i, 51, 6–16.
11   Pliny, *Nat. hist.* xiv, 5, 44:

> Catonum ille primus, triumpho et censura super cetera insignis, magis tamen etiamnum claritate litterarum *praeceptisque* omnium rerum expetendarum datis generi Romano, inter prima vero agrum colendi, ille aevi confessione optimus ac *sine aemulo agricola*, pauca attigit vitium genera, quarundam ex his iam etiam nominibus abolitis . . .

> The elder Cato, who was exceptionally celebrated for his triumph [194 B.C. for his victories in Spain] and his censorship [184 B.C.], though yet more for his

literary distinction and for the *precepts* that he has given to the Roman nation
upon every matter of utility, and in particular as to agriculture—a man who by
the admission of his contemporaries was a supremely competent and *unrivalled agriculturalist*—has dealt with only a few varieties of the vine, including
some even the names of which are now extinct . . .

LCL, Rackham, pp. 215, 217. —In Cicero, *De sen.* xv, 51 through xvi, 55,
Cato speaks about the pleasures of agriculture and his book *De re rustica* (or
De agri cultura):

> Venio nunc ad voluptates agricolarum, quibus ego incredibiliter delector, quae
> nec ulla impediuntur senectute et mihi ad sapientis vitam proxime videntur
> accedere. Habent enim rationem cum terra, quae numquam recusat imperium
> nec umquam sine usura reddit quod accepit, sed alias minore plerumque
> maiore cum faenore; quamquam me quidem non fructus modo, sed etiam ip-
> sius terrae vis ac natura delectat . . . . . . Quid ego vitium ortus satus incre-
> menta commemorem? Satiari delectatione non possum, ut meae senectutis
> requietem oblectamentumque noscatis. Omitto enim vim ipsam omnium quae
> generantur e terra, quae ex fici tantulo grano aut ex acini vinaceo aut ex
> ceterarum frugum aut stirpium minutissimis seminibus tantos truncos
> ramosque procreet; malleoli plantae sarmenta viviradices propagines nonne
> efficiunt ut quamvis cum admiratione delectent? . . . . . . Cuius quidem non
> utilitas me solum, ut ante dixi, sed etiam cultura et natura ipsa delectat . . .
> . . . Quid ego irrigationes, quid fossiones agri repastinationesque proferam,
> quibus fit multo terra fecundior? Quid de utilitate loquar stercorandi? Dixi in eo
> libro, quem de rebus rusticis scripsi. De qua doctus Hesiodus ne verbum
> quidem fecit cum de cultura agri scriberet. At Homerus, qui multis ut mihi
> videtur, ante saeculis fuit, Laerten lenientem desiderium, quod capiebat e filio,
> colentem agrum et eum stercorantem facit. Nec vero segetibus solum et pratis
> et vineis et arbustis res rusticae laetae sunt, sed hortis etiam et pomariis, tum
> pecudum pastu, apium examinibus, florum omnium varietate. Nec consitiones
> modo delectant, sed etiam insitiones, quibus nihil invenit agri cultura soller-
> tius. Possum persequi permulta oblectamenta rerum rusticarum, sed ea ipsa
> quae dixi sentio fuisse longiora.

> I come now to the pleasures of agriculture in which I find incredible delight;
> they are not one whit checked by old age, and are, it seems to me, in the
> highest degree suited to the life of the wise man. For these pleasures have an
> account in the bank of Mother Earth who never protests a draft, but always
> returns the principal with interest added, at a rate sometimes low, but usually
> at a high per cent. And yet what I enjoy is not the fruit alone, but I also enjoy
> the soil itself, its nature and its power. . . . . . . Why should I mention the
> origin, cultivation, and growth of the vine? But, that you may know what
> affords the recreation and delight of my old age, I will say that vine-culture
> gives me a joy of which I cannot get too much. For I pass over the inherent
> force of all those things which are generated from the earth—a force that, from
> the tiny fig-seed, or grape-stone, or from the smallest seeds of other fruits and

plants, can produce such mighty trunks and boughs. Are not the results obtained from mallet-shoots, sprouts, cuttings, divisions, and layers enough to afford wonder and delight to any man? . . .   . . .   Indeed it is not only the utility of the vine, as I said before, that gives me joy, but I find joy also in its culture and very nature; . . . Why need I allude to the irrigation, ditching, and frequent hoeing of the soil, whereby its productiveness is so much enhanced? Why need I discuss the advantage of manuring, already dealt with in my book on agriculture? This is a matter about which the learned Hesiod, though he wrote on agriculture, has not one word to say. But Homer, who, I believe, lived many generations earlier, represents Laertes as soothing his sorrow at the absence of his son [Odysseus] in cultivating his farm and in manuring it, too. Nor does the farmer find joy only in his cornfields, meadows, vineyards, and woodlands, but also in his garden and orchard, in the rearing of his cattle, in his swarms of bees, and in the infinite variety of flowers. And not only does planting delight him, but grafting also, than which there is nothing in husbandry that is more ingenious. I might enlarge upon all the many charms of country life, but I realize that I have already said too much.

LCL, Falconer, pp. 63–67. Cicero's Cato enumerates the joys of farming in the traditional sequence agriculture, livestock, bees, etc., note 1, above. On Cato the husbandman, *Sen.* xii, 1 (1581: 900).

12   The most outstanding example being Virgil's *Georgics*. On the antique literature of agriculture, *Sen.* xii, 1 (1581: 900); *Contra medicum* iv, Ricci (1950), 268–269; and Barbeu de Richer (1854), p. 215. Cf. Varro, *De re rustica* i, 1; the relevant chapters in Polydore Virgil, *De rer. inv.* iii; and Sandys (1929), chap. v, 7. On Petrarch's copies of Varro, Nolhac (1907), ii, pp. 214–215; of Palladius (in ms. Vat. lat. 2193), Nolhac, ibid., ii, pp. 98–101 and pp. 109–110, where our text is cited. Note Sabbadini (1905), p. 22; and idem, (1914), pp. 126–127.

13   At Vaucluse, Petrarch had

two gardens, of which he tells with delight: one a shaded place close to the point where the Sorgue gushes forth from the base of the rockbound mountainside, the other, cultivated and vineclad, on an island in the river. Near his house was a rock formation that made a cool shelter in hot weather: he speaks of it as a place conducive to study. He spent mornings on the hills, noontides in his rock shelter, and afternoons in the fields or in his upper garden, where poetic inspiration often came to him.

(Wilkins [1961], pp. 106–107.) On this and Petrarch's agricultural notes in his Palladius, Nolhac (1907), ii, Exc. 2. Note also below, *DR* ii, 93, note 38.

14   Petrarch refers frequently to Nature as *parens optima* (John of Salisbury, *Metalog.* iv, 17, *PL* 199, c. 926; *parens omnium*: Cicero, *Tusc. disp.* i, 49, 118); *parens prudentissima* (*DR* i, 60, 31; related, *Sen.* xv, 3 [1581: 934]; *mater optima* (*DR* ii, 83, 298); *blanda parens et benigna* (*DR* ii, 93, 139–140); *dux et*

genitrix optima (*Fam.* xii, 3, 13); etc. Note also *DR* ii, 2, 47, ii, 90, 112, ii, 93, 118, and ii, 119, 127.

15   Cato, *De re rust.* i, 6:

> Scito idem agrum quod hominem, *quamvis quaestuosus* siet, *si sumptuosus* erit, relinqui non multum.

> But remember it is the same with land as with a human being—it may make large profits, yet if it involves large expense, not much will be left over.

Petrarch owned Palladius and, probably, Varro (on the latter, *Fam.* ix, 4, 5 = Varro, *De re rust.* ii, 7, 9; *Sen.* ii, 1 [1581: 752]; compare *Fam.* xxi, 11, 8 = Varro, ibid., ii, 3, 7), note 12 above. We do not know whether he owned Cato's text, samples of which he encountered in many authors, e.g., Cicero, Aulus Gellius (x, 26, 8 = Cato, i, 3), Macrobius (*Saturn.* vi, 4, 16 = Cato, xxi, 2; *Saturn.* vii, 6, 13 = Cato, vii, 3), and, above all, Pliny. The present reference occurs in Pliny, *Nat. hist.* xviii, 6, 28:

> Itaque Cato de bono domino melius emi, nec temere contemnendam alienam disciplinam, agroque ut homini, quamvis quaestuosus sit, si tamen et sumptuosus, non multum superesse.

> For this reason Cato says that it is better to purchase from a good landlord, and that the lessons to be learnt from others should not be despised, and that it is the same with land as with a human being—it may make large profits, yet if it also involves large expenses, not much balance is left over.

LCL, Rackham, pp. 207, 209.

16   1492: impugnabis
       1581: impinguabis
17   l.t.: Flaccus
18   Horace, *Carm.* ii, 14, 22–24:

> . . . . . . harum, quas colis, arborum
> te praeter invisas cupressos
> ulla brevem dominum sequetur.

LCL, Bennett, p. 145. The ancients put cypress twigs into the coffins of the dead *ut odorem cadaverum, dum urerentur, opprimerent iucunditate odoris sui*—to overcome with the sweetness of their odor the stench of the corpses while they burned (Isidore, *Etym.* xvii, 7, 34 = Hrabamus Maurus, *De univ.* xix, 6, *PL* III, c. 517; Fabricius [1716], pp. 657–658). Cf. Shakespeare, *Twelfth Night* ii, 4, 52: *In sad cypress let me be laid.* Reason ignores here another meaning the Middle Ages attached to the cypress:

> Cypressus namque Christum vel Ecclesiam significat; unde est illud: *Sicut cedrus exaltata sum in Libano, et sicut cypressus in montibus Hermon.* Item cypressus prophetas vel patriarchas vel doctores sanctos figurat; unde in Can-

tico canticorum sponsa dicit: *Tigna domorum nostrorum cedrina, laquearia nostra cypressina*. Tigna et laquearia doctores sunt in sancta Ecclesia propter munimen et decorem: cedrina et cypressina, propter eximias virtutes eorum et odorem bonae vitae.

For the cypress signifies Christ or the Church. Hence this: *I was exalted like a cedar in Libanus, and as a cypress tree on mount Sion* [Eccli. 24, 17]. The cypress represents also the prophets and patriarchs, and the blessed doctors. Therefore, in the Canticle of Canticles, the spouse says: *The beams of our houses are of cedar, our rafters of cypress trees* [Cant. 1, 16]. The beams and rafters are the doctors of holy Church because of their support of the Church and their distinction: they are of cedar and cypress trees because of the extreme virtue of the doctors and the sweet presentiment of the blessed life.

Hrabanus Maurus, ibid.., cc. 517–518. Note also Alain de Lille, *Eluc. in Cant. Cant., PL* 210, c. 64.

58 ✤ GREEN PLACES

1   Cicero charged Catiline, C. Verres, P. Clodius Pulcher, Piso Caesoninus, and Mark Antony with heinous crimes. In his texts, bristling with devices of rhetorical invective, are passages that render each one of these personages a possible candidate for Reason's remarks, which, most likely, are aimed at Verres (*In Verr.* iii, 76, 176; cf. *Fam.* xx, 1, 10) or Antony (*Philip.* ii).

2   *ille senex hircinus, loca ipsa seposita quibus probris infecerit:* an allusion to the suicide of Mallonia, who vigorously refused to submit to Tiberius—and its consequences, Suetonius, iii, Tib., 45:

Unde nota in Atellanico exhodio proximis ludis adsensu maximo excepta percrebruit, "hircum vetulum capreis naturam ligurire."

Hence a stigma put upon him [Tiberius] at the next plays in an Atellan farce was received with great applause and became current, that "the old goat was licking the [genitals of the] does."

LCL, Rolfe, p. 357.

3   Suetonius, ibid., 43, 44. Cf. *Fam.* xx, 1, 8–9.
4   Cf. above, *DR* i, 51, 6–16, and note 2.
5   Compare *Rer. mem. libri* iv, 24, 3:

> . . . non enim exterius sed introrsus et in ipso animo vera felicitas sita est.

> . . . because true happiness dwells not without, but inward, within your very heart.

Related: *DR* i, 121, 28–29, ii, 6, 17–19; and *Sen.* viii, 6 (1581: 839). Note also above, *DR* i, 40 note 4. On the topic *intus in anima,* above, *DR* i, 11, note 10.

6   Cf. Isidore, *Etym.,* xvii, 6, 3: *arbor.*

7   1492: quid pronunciem uidero
     1581: quid pronunciem uideto

8   A play on the word *locus*—place—which indicates both a place on the earth or a logical ground for description, argument, etc.

9   Quintus Curtius, vii, 2, 22–27:

> Deversoria regionis illius magnos recessus habent amoenosque nemoribus manu consitis; ea praecipua regum satraparumque voluptas erat. Spatiabatur in nemore Parmenion, medius inter duces quibus erat imperatum litteris regis ut occiderent. Agendae autem rei constituerant tempus, cum Parmenio a Polydamante litteras traditas legere coepisset. Polydamas procul veniens, ut a Parmenione conspectus est, vultu laetitiae speciem praeferente, ad complectendum eum cucurrit, mutuaque salutatione facta, Polydamas epistulam a rege scriptam ei tradidit. Parmenio vinculum epistulae solvens, quidnam rex ageret requirebat. Ille ex ipsis litteris cogniturum esse respondit. Quibus Parmenio lectis: "Rex," inquit, "expeditionem parat in Arachosios. Strenuum hominem et numquam cessantem! Sed tempus saluti tuae, tanta iam parta gloria, parcere." Alteram deinde epistulam Philotae nomine scriptam laetus, quod ex vultu notari poterat, legebat; tum eius latus gladio haurit Cleander, deinde iugulum ferit, ceteri exanimum quoque confodiunt.

> The residences in that region have extensive, charming, and secluded parks with groves artificially planted; these were the special delight of both kings and satraps. Parmenion was walking about in a grove, surrounded by his officers, who had been ordered by the king's letter to kill him. And they arranged to do the deed at the time when Parmenion had begun to read the letters delivered by Polydamas. As Polydamas came near and was seen by Parmenion to have an expression presenting the appearance of joy, he ran to embrace him, and after they had exchanged greetings, Polydamas handed him the letter written to him by the king. Parmenion, as he loosed the fastening of the letter, asked what the king was doing. Polydamas replied that he would learn from the letter itself. Parmenion, after reading the letter, said: "The king is preparing an expedition against the Arachosii. An active man, who never rests! But it is time for him to show consideration for his own welfare, after having already gained so much glory." Afterwards he was reading the second letter, written in the name of Philotas, with pleasure, as could be seen from his expression; then Cleander plunged his sword into his side and struck him again in the throat, and the others stabbed him even after he was lifeless.

LCL, Rolfe, pp. 137, 139. Cf. Nolhac (1907), ii, p. 94, n. 3.

10   Among the many sources for Cicero's death in 43 B.C. are Florus, *Epit.* ii, 16, 5; Seneca Rhetor, *Suas,* vi, 17, 7; Appian iv, 1–51; *Res gestae* 7; Julius Obsequens 69; etc. The most likely source for our text, however, is Valerius Maximus, v, 3, 4:

> . . . M. Cicero C. Popilium Laenatem Picenae regionis rogatu M. Caeli non minore cura quam eloquentia defendit eumque causa admodum dubia fluctuantem saluum ad penates suos remisit. Hic Popilius postea nec re nec uerbo a Cicerone laesus ultro M. Antonium rogauit ut ad illum proscriptum persequendum et iugulandum mitteretur, impetratisque detestabilis ministerii partibus gaudio exultans Caietam cucurrit et uirum, mitto quod amplissimae dignitatis, certe salubritate studio praestantis officii priuatim sibi uenerandum, iugulum praebere iussit ac protinus caput Romanae eloquentiae et pacis clarissimam dexteram per summum et securum otium amputauit eaque sarcina tamquam opimis spoliis alacer in urbem reuersus est: neque enim scelestum portanti onus succurrit illud se caput ferre, quod pro capite eius quondam peroraerat. Inualidae ad hoc monstrum suggillandum litterae, quoniam qui talem Ciceronis casum satis digne deplorare possit, alius Cicero non extat.

> . . . Marcus Cicero defended one Gaius Popilius Laenas from the Picene district with no less care than eloquence when he was cross-examined by Marcus Caelius Rufus, and returned him safe and sound to his home, although his case and testimony were highly doubtful. This Popilius, thereafter, never having been hurt by Cicero in deed or word, spontaneously asked Marc Antony to send him to pursue and kill Cicero, who had been proscribed. Having secured assignment to the detestable mission, he hurried, bursting with joy, to Caieta and ordered a man, whose great dignity it is needless to stress and whose earnest efforts in office he should have personally admired, to be murdered. And on the spot he cut off the head of Roman eloquence and that most noble right hand of peace engaged in thoughtful and courageous intellectual pursuits—and returned eagerly to Rome with his load as if it were sumptuous booty. Nor did it occur to him, as he carried his abominable burden, that he held the head which once had pleaded for his head. To revile this monster, letters are not enough. And there is no second Cicero to deplore fittingly this end of Cicero.

11   Consideration of the human condition protects man in prosperity and adversity. Cf., e.g., *Fam.* viii, 7, 23–26; xvii, 3, 27–28; *Secretum* i and ii, *Prose* (1955), pp. 28, 92; *De ocio* i (1581: 306); and *Sen.* viii, 1 (1581: 830), quoting Job 14, 1, xv, 3 (1581: 935), quoting Pliny, *Nat. hist.* vii, 1 (Nolhac [1907], ii, p. 73; and below, *DR* ii, 31, note 5), the *Asclepius* (above, *DR* i, 13, note 14), Ps. 77, 30, Prov. 14, 13, and Homer, *Odyssey* xviii, 131, quoted in *DR* ii, 111, 14. Note also *DR* i, 38, 70, and note 10, ii, 17, 11–13; *De vita sol.* i, as below, *DR* ii, 13, note 25; and Augustine, *De civ. Dei* xix, 4, xxii, 22.

59 ❖ LIVESTOCK

1   *Gaudeo gregibus et armentis.* On this, Isidore, *Etym.* xii, 1, 8:

> Discretio est autem inter armenta et greges:
> nam armenta equorum et boum sunt, greges vero
> caprarum et ovium.

> Distinction must be made between *armenta*—herds—and
> *greges*—flocks: for herds consist of horses and cattle,
> but flocks of goats and sheep.

2   On *desiring what is harmful*, DR i, 89, note 2.

3   Cf. below, *DR* ii, 104, note 11.

4   Regarding this puzzling statement, Nolhac (1907, i, p. 165, n. 1) notes *mais je n'ai retrouvé le texte de Catulle auquel Pétrarque veut faire allusion.* —The specificity of the reference to *Catullus Veronensis* in our text makes a misreading for "Tibullus" (e.g., i, 1 and 5, or ii, 3) improbable. Ullman (1955, pp. 199–200) suggests that Petrarch actually had in mind *Culex* 58–122, "on the blessings of the shepherd's life," and, for once, made an error.

5   1492: illusor rudis
     1581: illusor ludis

6   I.t.: Maro. Cf., e.g., Lucretius, vi, 1138; and Virgil, *Georg.* iii, 478. However, the source of this reference could well be Macrobius, *Saturn.* vi, 2, 7–14:

> Ipsius vero pestilentiae, quae est in tertio Georgicorum, color totus et linia-
> menta paene omnia tracta sunt de descriptione pestilentiae quae est in sexto
> Lucretii. Nam Vergiliana incipit:
>> hic quondam morbo caeli miseranda coorta est
>> tempestas, totoque auctumni incanduit aestu
>> et genus omne neci pecudum dedit, omne ferarum.
> Lucretii vero sic incipit:
>> haec ratio quondam morborum et mortifer aestus
>> finibus in Cecropis funestos reddidit agros
>> vastavitque vias, exhausit civibus urbem.
> Sed quatenus totum locum utriusque ponere satis longum est, excerpam aliqua
> ex quibus similitudo geminae descriptionis appareat.

> Vergilius ait:
>> tum vero ardentes oculi atque attractus ab alto
>> spiritus, interdum gemitu gravis, imaque longo
>> ilia singultu tendunt, it naribus ater
>> sanguis et oppressas fauces premit aspera lingua.

Lucretius ait:
> principio caput incensum fervore gerebant
> et duplices oculos suffusa luce rubentes.
> Sudabant etiam fauces intrinsecus artae
> sanguine, et ulceribus vocis via saepta coibat,
> atque animi interpres manabat lingua cruore,
> debilitata malis, motu gravis, aspera tactu.

Vergilius ait:
> haec ante exitium primis dant signa diebus,
> et quae darent signa supra retulit idem:
> . . . . demissae aures incertus ibidem
> sudor et ille quidem morituris frigidus, aret
> pellis et attactu tractandi dura resistit.

Lucretius ait:
> multaque praeterea mortis tunc signa dabantur:
> perturbati animi, mens in maerore metuque,
> triste supercilium, furiosus vultus et acer,
> sollicitae porro plenaeque sonoribus aures,
> creber spiritus aut ingens raroque coortus,
> sudorisque madens per collum splendidus umor,
> tenuia sputa, minuta, croci contacta colore
> salsaque per fauces raucas vix edita tussis.

Vergilius ait:
> profuit inserto latices infundere cornu
> Lenaeos: ea visa salus morientibus una.
> Mox erat hoc ipsum exitio . . .

Lucretius ait:
> nec ratio remedi communis certa dabatur.
> Nam quod alis dederat vitalis aeris auras
> volvere in ore licere et caeli templa tueri,
> hoc aliis erat exitio letumque parabat.

Vergilius ait:
> praeterea nec mutari iam pabula refert,
> quaesitaeque nocent artes, cessere magistri.

Lucretius ait:
> nec requies erat ulla mali: defessa iacebant
> corpora, mussabat tacito medicina timore.

Vergilius ait:
> ipsis est aer avibus non aequus et illae
> praecipites alta vitam sub nube relinquunt.

Lucretius ait:
> nec tamen omnino temere illis sedibus ulla
> comparebat avis nec tristia saecla ferarum

exsuperant silvis, languebant pleraque morbo
et moriebantur . . .
nonne vobis videntur membra huius descriptionis ex uno fonte manasse?

The general "color," and almost all the details, of a description of a plague in
the third *Georgic* are taken from the description of the plague in the sixth Book
of Lucretius. Thus Vergil begins:

> In this country once from the tainted air a woeful season came and glowed
> with the full heat of autumn. All the race of cattle it gave over to death
> and all the race of wild creatures
>
> *Georgics* 3, 478

and this is how Lucretius begins his description:

> Such a cause of disease and a deadly wave of heat once brought death to
> the fields, in the land of Cecrops, made the streets a desert and emptied
> the town of its citizens.
>
> vi, 1138

Since it would be long and tedious enough to quote the whole passage from
each poet, I shall cite extracts, to show how closely the two resemble one
another.

Vergil:

> Then their eyes burn with heat, the breathing is deep-drawn, at times
> heavy with a groan, and their flanks below heave with long-drawn sobs;
> black blood flows from their nostrils and a rough tongue cleaves to a
> choked throat.
>
> *Georgics* 3, 505

Lucretius:

> First they would feel their heads burning with heat and both eyes be
> bright and bloodshot. Their throats, too, within would choke and sweat
> with blood, and the passage of the voice be clogged and closed with
> ulcers; the tongue, the mind's interpreter, would ooze with gore, enfee-
> bled by pain, heavy to move, and rough to touch.
>
> vi, 1145

Vergil:

> These are the signs they give of approaching death in the first days
>
> *Georgics* 3, 503

(they were described thus in the preceding lines):

> The ears droop and on them breaks forth a fitful sweating, and that too, as
> death draws near, grows cold; the skin is dry and hard and resists the
> touch.
>
> *Georgics* 3, 500

Lucretius:

> And many signs of death besides would then be given: the spirits and
> mind perturbed by depression and fear, a clouded brow, a delirious, fierce
> expression; the ears troubled, too, and filled with noises; the breathing
> rapid, or deep and intermittent; the damp sweat oozing and shining on the

neck; the spittle thin and scant, stained with a yellow tinge, and a salty
cough forced with difficulty through the hoarse throat.

vi, 1182

Vergil:

> It was helpful to insert a horn and pour in draughts of wine (Pliny, *Nat.
> hist.* xxiii, 23, 44); this seemed to be the one cure for the dying; but
> presently this very aid was fatal.

Georgics 3, 509

Lucretius:

> No sure form of cure was found for all; for what had given to some the
> power to draw in through the mouth the life-giving breath of air and to
> gaze on the expanse of heaven, this to others was fatal and brought
> death.

vi, 1226

Vergil:

> Moreover, change of pasture no longer avails; the remedies they sought
> work harm; the masters of the art of healing retire baffled

Georgics 3, 548

Lucretius:

> No respite was there from the evil; their bodies would lie exhausted; the
> healing art muttered in voiceless fear.

vi, 1178

Vergil:

> To the very birds the air was unkind, and headlong they fall and leave
> their life in the clouds on high.

Georgics 3, 546

Lucretius:

> Yet hardly at all was any bird seen in those places; nor does the grim race
> of wild beasts survive in the woods; most would languish under the
> plague and die.

vi, 1219

You will agree, will you not, that the details in Vergil's description have come
from a single source?

Davies (1969), pp. 399–401. On Petrarch and Lucretius, Koerting (1878), p.
487, and n. 2 (which should read *DR* i, 59); Nolhac (1907), i, p. 160, n. 1;
and Gasparotto (1967–1968). Note also *Buc. carm.*, Eclogues vii, ix; and the
reference to Lucretius, below, *DR* ii, 90, 231–235.

7 Job 1, 13–15:

> Cum autem quadam die filii et filiae ejus comederant et biberent vinum in
> domo fratris sui primogeniti, nuntius venit ad Job, qui diceret: Boves arabant,
> et asinae pascebantur juxta eos; et irruerunt Sabaei, tuleruntque omnia, et
> pueros percusserunt gladio; et evasi ego solus, ut nuntiarem tibi.

> Now upon a certain day when his sons and daughters were eating and
> drinking wine in the house of their eldest brother,

There came a messenger to Job, and said: The oxen were ploughing, and the asses feeding beside them,

And the Sabeans rushed in, and took all away, and slew the servants with the sword, and I alone have escaped to tell thee.

Who abounded in livestock is a reference to Job 1, 1–3.

60 ❖ ELEPHANTS AND CAMELS

1   On Pyrrhus, cf. Florus, i, 13, ii, 13 (Juba); on Hannibal, Livy xxx, 33.

2   On this, Pliny, *Nat. hist.* viii, 6, 16.

3   Livy xxx, 37, 3:

> perfugas fugitivosque et captivos omnes redderent Romanis, et naves rostratas praeter decem triremes traderent elephantosque quos haberent domitos, neque domarent alios;

> They were to deliver all deserters and runaway slaves and captives to the Romans, and to surrender their war-ships except ten triremes, and the trained elephants in their possession, and not train others.

LCL, Moore, pp. 505, 507.

4   Frederick II (1194–1250), who collected rare animals (Salimbene [Coulter 1972)], p. 42).

5   Probably Sultan Orkhani (1326–1359) or, before him, El Melik Al Kamil, who sent exotic animals to Frederick's zoological garden in Sicily (Kantorowicz [1957b], pp. 358–359).

6   *De viris ill.* xvii, Hannibal, 26. Cf. Nepos, xxiii, Hannibal 3–4; and Livy, xxii, 2, 1–2, and 10–11.

7   As reported in Pliny, *Nat. hist.* viii, 1, 1, 13, 34.

8   Job 1, 3:

> Et fuit possessio ejus septem millia ovium, et tria millia camelorum, quingenta quoque juga boum, et quingentae asinae, ac familia multa nimis.

> And his possession was seven thousand sheep and three thousand camels, and five hundred yoke of oxen, and five hundred she asses, and a family exceeding great.

61 ❖ MONKEYS AND OTHER AMUSING ANIMALS

1   On this dialogue and its use by Rabelais, Janson (1952), pp. 202–203, 227, n. 18.

2   Cf. Cicero, *Ad Att.* vi, 1, 25.

3   Cicero, *De div.* ii, 32, 69:

> Simiae vero Dodonaeae improbitatem historiis Graecis mandatam esse demiror. Quid minus mirum quam illam monstruosissimam bestiam urnam evertisse, sortes dissupavisse? Et negant historici Lacedaemoniis ullum ostentum hoc tristius accidisse!

> I am indeed astonished that Greek historians should have recorded the mischievous pranks of the Dodonean ape. For what is less strange than for this hideous beast to have turned over the vase and scattered the lots? And yet the historians declare that no portent more direful than this ever befell the Spartans!

The scene at Dodona before the battle of Leuctra, 371 B.C., where the Thebans under Epaminondas defeated the Spartans, is described in *De div.* i, 34, 76:

> Maximum vero illud portentum isdem Spartiatis fuit, quod, cum oraculum ab Iove Dodonaeo petivissent de victoria sciscitantes legatique vas illud in quo inerant sortes collocavissent, simia, quam rex Molossorum in deliciis habebat, et sortes ipsas et cetera, quae erant ad sortem parata, disturbavit et aliud alio dissipavit. Tum ea, quae praeposita erat oraculo, sacerdos dixisse dicitur de salute Lacedaemoniis esse non de victoria cogitandum.

> But the most significant warning received by the Spartans was this: they sent to consult the oracle of Jupiter at Dodona as to the chances of victory. After their messengers had duly set up the vessel in which were the lots, an ape, kept by the king of Molossia for his amusement, disarranged the lots and everything else used in consulting the oracle, and scattered them in all directions. Then, so we are told, the priestess who had charge of the oracle said that the Spartans must think of safety and not of victory.

LCL, Falconer, pp. 449, 307. The story is retold in *Rer. mem. libri* iv, 100.

4   On *simia quam similis, turpissima bestia, nobis!* (Cicero, *De nat. deor.* i, 35, 97), cf. Janson (1952), pp. 14, 23, n. 9; and McDermott (1938), pp. 38, 150.

62 ❖ PEACOCKS, FOWL, HENS, BEES, AND PIGEONS

1   1492: Ex illorum caudis argi oculos
     1581: Ex illorum caudis argioculis

     1492: tegularum pestis
     1581: regularum pestis

The *eyes of Argus* refers to the story of Io, who was ravished by Zeus. When confronted by Hera, Zeus turned Io into a white cow, "which Hera claimed as hers and handed over for safekeeping to Argus Panoptes"—Argus of the hundred eyes (Ovid, *Metam.* i, 625). Zeus sent Hermes to bring Io back. Hermes put Argus to sleep by playing the flute, killed him, and freed Io. "Hera, having placed Argus's eyes in the tail of a peacock, as a constant reminder of his foul murder, set a gadfly to sting Io and chase her all over the world." (Graves [1955], i, 56.a.) Ovid tells the story, *Metam.* i, 568–779. Reasons's remarks relate to i, 722–724, and ii, 531–533.

The reference to the peacock's feet is an allusion to the medieval bestiary. According to Bartholomaeus Anglicus (*De Prop. rer.* xii, 32; Trevisa, p. 638), the peacock

> wondred on þe fairenesse of his feþeres and areriþ hem vp as it were a cercle aboute his heed, and þanne he lookeþ to his feet and seeþ þe foulnesse of his feet and is as þey he were aschamed, and letiþ his feþires falle sodeyneliche and alle þe tayle donward as þogh he took none hede of þe fairnesse of his feþeris.

Similarly, Brunetto Latini, *Li livres dou tresor* i, 169: Des paons (Goldstaub [1892], pp. 43–44, 341–344; White [1954], p. 149). The peacock's plumage, feet, and harsh voice figure in *Piers Plowman* (B), passus xii. On this, Klingender (1971), pp. 370–371; and Robertson & Huppé (1951), pp. 154–155.

2   Circe advised Ulysses (Odysseus) to plug his men's ears with beeswax while he alone, tied to the mast of his ship, listened to the irresistible song of the Sirens. Graves (1955), ii, 170.q and r. Cf. Homer, *Od.* xii, 39–54; Ovid, *Metam.* v, 552–562; Hyginus, *Fab.* 125 and 141; Fulgentius, *Mitol.* ii, 8; and *Gesta Rom.* 237, app. 41. On the topic, well known in medievel times, Hammerstein (1974), chap. v, 7; Toynbee (1968), art. Sirene; Wille (1967), pp. 390, 541–542, 557–558, 702; and, Meyer-Baer (1970), pp. 234–239. Cf. *Fam.* xxiii, 2, 32. The song of the sirens is mentioned above, *DR* i, 23, 11.

3   l.t.: Naso

4   Ovid; *Fasti* vi, 177: *et praeter pennas nihil in pavone placebat.* LCL, Frazer, p. 331.

5   Augustine, *De civ. Dei* xxi, 4:

> Quis enim nisi Deus creator omnium dedit carni pavonis mortui ne putesceret? Quod cum auditu incredibile videretur, evenit ut apud Carthaginem nobis cocta apponeretur haec avis, de cuius pectore pulparum quantum visum est decerptum servari iussimus. Quod post dierum tantum spatium quanto alia caro quaecumque cocta putesceret prolatum atque oblatum nihil nostrum offendit olfactum. Itemque repositum post dies amplius quam triginta idem quod erat inventum est, idemque post annum, nisi quod aliquantum corpulentiae siccioris et contractioris fuit.

> For who if not God, the creator of all things, has granted to the flesh of the dead peacock immunity from decay? Although when I heard this it seemed incredible, it happened that at Carthage a roast peacock was served to me. I ordered as much meat as seemed good to be taken from its breast and kept. After a period of days in which any other roast meat would go bad, it was brought out and served without having the least offensive odor. It was put back again and after more than thirty days it was found as before, and again after a year it was the same except that its texture was somewhat more dry and shrunken.

LCL, Green, pp. 15, 17. Cf. also Martial, xiii, 70, as cited in Isidore, *Etym.* xii, 7, 48.

6   Pliny, *Nat. hist.* x, 23, 46; Varro, *De re rust.* iii, 6; Macrobius, *Saturn.* iii, 13, 1. On Q. Hortensius Hortalus (114–50 B.C.), Cicero, *Brutus* 63, 228–229 *et passim.*

7   Aulus Gellius, i, 5, 2–3:

> Ad eundem modum Q. Hortensius omnibus ferme oratoribus aetatis suae, nisi M. Tullio, clarior, quod multa munditia et circumspecte compositeque indutus et amictus esset manusque eius inter agendum forent argutae admodum et gestuosae, maledictis compellationibusque probris iactatus est multaque in eum, quasi in histrionem, in ipsis causis atque iudiciis dicta sunt. Sed cum L. Torquatus, subagresti homo ingenio et infestivo, gravius acerbiusque apud consilium iudicum, cum de causa Sullae quaereretur, non iam histrionem eum esse diceret, sed gesticulariam Dionysiamque eum notissimae saltatriculae nomine appellaret, tum voce molli atque demissa Hortensius "Dionysia," inquit, "Dionysia malo equidem esse quam quod tu, Torquate, ἄμουσος, ἀναφρόδιτος, ἀπροσδιόνυσος."

> In like manner Quintus Hortensius, quite the most renowned orator of his time with the exception of Marcus Tullius [Cicero], because he dressed with extreme foppishness, arranged the folds of his toga with great care and exactness, and in speaking used his hands to excess in lively gestures, was assailed with gibes and shameful charges; and many taunts were hurled at him, even while he was

pleading in court, for appearing like an actor. But when Sulla was on trial, and Lucius Torquatus, a man of somewhat boorish and uncouth nature, with great violence and bitterness did not stop with calling Hortensius an actor in the presence of the assembled jurors, but said he was a posturer and a Dionysia—which was the name of a notorious dancing-girl—then Hortensius replied in a soft and gentle tone: I would rather be a Dionysia, Torquatus, yes, a Dionysia, than like you, a stranger to the Muses, to Venus and to Dionysus.''

LCL, Rolfe, p. 29.

8   Cf. Valerius Maximus, viii, 3, 3: *Hortensiana eloquentia*—Hortensian eloquence.

9   I.e., the queens, which were regarded as male kings throughout Antiquity and the Middle Ages. Sandys (1929), p. 631; Wilson (1971), p. 94.

10   Cf. Virgil, *Georg.* iv *passim*, esp. 21–23; 67–87. Clang of bronze: Pliny, *Nat. hist.* xi, 22, 68; dust being thrown, ibid., 18, 58.

11   Virgil, *Georg.* iv, 189–190:

> Post ubi iam thalamis se composuere, siletur
> in noctem, fessosque sopor suus occupat artus.

Anon, when they have laid them to rest in their chambers, silence reigns into the night, and well-earned sleep seizes their weary limbs.

LCL, Fairclough, p. 209.

12   *columbaria*: cf. Sandys (1929), p. 57.

13   1492: En magni gaudii materia. &c.
     1581: en magni gaudii materia

On Reason's *simulatio* and the verbal irony of inversion, Lausberg (1960), pp. 442, 447; Green (1979), chap. 6, esp. pp. 199–208.

63 ❖ FISHPONDS

1   1492: extruxisse
     1581: destruxisse

2   Eccl. 2, 6:

> et extruxi mihi piscinas aquarum,
> ut irrigarem silvam lignorum germinantium,

> And I made me [fish] ponds of water,
> to water therewith the wood of the young trees.

In the Douay version, this chapter in the book in which "Solomon, as an excellent *preacher*, setteth forth the vanity of the things of this world: to withdraw the hearts and affections of men from such empty toys," is entitled *The vanity of pleasures, riches, and wordly labours.*

3   Eccl. 2, 11:

> Cumque me convertissem ad universa opera quae fecerant manus meae, et ad labores in quibus frustra sudaveram, vidi in omnibus vanitatem et afflictionem animi.

> And when I turned myself to all the works which my hands had wrought, and to the labours wherein I had laboured in vain, I saw in all things vanity, and vexation of the mind.

4   1492: aquae etiam tentantur
    1581: atque etiam tentantur

5   Suetonius, i, Jul. Caes. 44, 2–3:

> siccare Pomptinas paludes; emittere Fucinum lacum; . . . perfodere Isthmum; . . .

> to drain the Pomptine marshes; to let out the water from Lake Fucinus; . . . to cut a canal through the Isthmus; . . .

LCL, Rolfe, p. 61. On Caesar's Tiber project, Sandys (1929), sec. 44.

6   Cf. Pliny, *Nat. hist.* ix, 79, 168.

7   Pliny, ibid., 80, as in note 12, below.

8   *uterque cognomen, seu illud agnomen a pisce sortitus.* In later Latin, *cognomen* designates the family name, *agnomen*, a predicative surname, *quod ab aliquo eventu imponitur, ut 'Africanus'*—which derives from some circumstance, such as *Africanus*. Priscian, *Inst. gramm.* ii, 24 (578 P).

9   Pliny discusses the spiny-finned *sparus auratus* in *Nat. hist.* xxxii, 43 and 135; *muraena helena, lampetra planeri*, etc., ibid., 12–14, and 57. On this, Macrobius, *Saturn.* iii, 15, 1.

10 Scipio Africanus Maior, the victor over Hannibal, and Aemilius Paulus, who defeated the Macedonians under Perses at Pydna, 168 B.C. Cf. Florus, i, 22; 28.

11 *quantitate curas hominum pene pares qualitate vero longe impares.*

12 Pliny, *Nat. hist.* ix, 80, 170:

> Eadem aetate prior Licinius Murena reliquorum piscium vivaria invenit, cuius deinde exemplum nobilitas secuta est Philippi, Hortensi. Lucullus exciso etiam monte iuxta Neapolim maiore impendio quam villam exaedificaverat euripum

et maria admisit, qua de causa Magnus Pompeius Xerxen togatum eum appel-
labat. ⌐XL⌐ HS e piscina ea defuncto illo veniere pisces.

In the same period the elder Licinius Murena invented fishponds for all the
other sorts of fish, and his example was subsequently followed by the celebrated record of Philip and Hortensius. Lucullus built a channel that cost more
than a country house, by actually cutting through a mountain near Naples and
letting in the sea; this was why Pompey the Great used to call him 'Xerxes in
Roman dress.' After his decease the fish from this pond sold for 4,000,000
sesterces.

The translator of this passage points out that Xerxes made a channel for his
fleet through Mount Athos. LCL, Rackham, pp. 278–279. On this, Herodotus,
vii, 22 et seq.; Sallust, *Cat.* xiii, 1; and Jerome, *Ep.* 60, 18, LCL, Wright, p.
306. On Philip, Hortensius, and Lucullus, cf. also Macrobius, *Saturn.* iii, 15,
6; and Cicero, *Ad Att.* i, 19, 6, and 20, 3. Note Horace, *Carm.* iii, 1, 33–34, as
below, *DR* i, 96, note 31.

13   Pliny, ibid., 81, 171:

Murenarum vivarium privatim excogitavit ante alios C. Hirrius, qui cenis tri-
umphalibus Caesaris dictatoris sex milia numero murenarum mutua appendit;
nam permutare quidem pretio noluit aliave merce.

The first person to devise a separate pond for lampreys was Gaius Hirrius, who
added to the triumphal banquets of Caesar (46 and 45 B.C.) lampreys to the
number of 6000—as a loan, because he would not exchange them for money
or for any other commodity.

Cf. Varro, *De re rust.* iii, 17, 3; and Macrobius, *Saturn.* iii, 15, 10.

14   Cf. above, *DR* i, 62, 19–22.

15   Pliny, *Nat. hist.* ix, 81, 172:

Invasit dein singulorum piscium amor. Apud Baulos in parte Baiana piscinam
habuit Hortensius orator in qua murenam adeo dilexit ut exanimatam flesse
credatur.

Subsequently affection for individual fish came into fashion. At Baculo in the
Baiae district the pleader Hortensius had a fishpond containing a lamprey
which he fell so deeply in love with that he is believed to have wept when it
expired.

LCL, Rackham, p. 279. Reason says Hortensius *luxerit*—mourned, went into
mourning. This may echo Macrobius, *Saturn.* iii, 15, 3, the story of Lucius
Crassus who went into formal mourning when his beloved eel died.

16   Cf. above, *DR* i, 62, 19–22.

17   I.e., Hannibal's victory at Cannae, 216 B.C. On this, *De vir. ill.* xvii, Hanibal,
36–42. Cf. Livy, xxii, 46, 8–9; and Florus, i, 22, 15–20.

18   Pliny, as cited in note 15, above, continued:

> In eadem villa Antonia Drusi murenae quam diligebat inaures addidit, cuius propter famam nonnulli Baulos videre concupiverunt.

> At the same country house Drusus's wife Antonia adorned her favourite lamprey with earrings, and its reputation made some people extremely eager to visit Baculo.

LCL, Rackham, p. 279.

19   Pliny, ibid., 82, 173, and 79, 169. In the LCL edition (p. 276), Rackham suggests that the two bridges may have been the Sublician and the Palatine.

64 ❖ AVIARIES AND TALKING BIRDS

1   Cf. Pliny, *Nat. hist.* x, 72, 141: *animalia coercere quibus rerum natura caelum adsignaverat*—imprisoning living creatures to which the nature of things assigned the open sky.

2   According to Pliny, *Nat. hist.* x, 72, 141,

> Aviaria primus instituit inclusis omnium generum avibus M. Laenius Strabo Brundisi equestris ordinis.

> Aviaries with cages containing all kinds of birds were first set up by Marcus Laenius Strabo of the Order of Knighthood at Brindisi.

LCL, Rackham, p. 383. This may be the second "erroneous" reference to Pliny's text in the *DR*, the first being *DR* i, 39, 11–13. However, as late as 1499, Polydore Vergil, *De rer. inv.* iii, 5, refers to M. *Laelius Strabo Brundusii equestris ordinis*. On the wise Laelius, Cicero, *De amic.* ii, 6–7, as above, *DR* i, 12, 75, and note 15.

3   Juvenal, i, 142–143:

> poena tamen praesens, cum tu deponis amictus
> turgidus et crudum pavonem in balnea portas.

LCL, Ramsay, p. 15.

4   Macrobius, *Saturn.* ii, 4, 29–30:

> Sublimis Actiaca victoria revertebatur. Occurrit ei inter gratulantes corvum tenens, quem instituerat haec dicere: *ave Caesar victor imperator.* Miratus Cae-

sar officiosam avem viginti milibus nummum emit. Socius opificis, ad quem nihil ex illa liberalitate pervenerat, adfirmavit Caesari habere illum et alium corvum, quem ut adferre cogeretur rogavit. Adlatus verba quae didicerat expressit: *ave victor imperator Antoni*. Nihil exasperatus satis duxit iubere illum dividere donativum cum contubernali. Salutatus similiter a psittaco, emi eum iussit. Idem miratus in pica hanc quoque redemit. Exemplum sutorem pauperem sollicitavit ut corvum institueret ad parem salutationem, qui impendio exhaustus saepe ad avem non respondentem dicere solebat: *opera et impensa periit*. Aliquando tamen corvus coepit dicere dictatam salutationem. Hac audita dum transit Augustus respondit: *satis domi salutatorum talium habeo*. Superfuit corvo memoria, ut et illa quibus dominum querentem solebat audire subtexteret: *opera et impensa periit*. Ad quod Caesar risit emique avem iussit quanti nullam adhuc emerat.

Among those who welcomed him on his return in state from his victory at Actium was a man with a raven which he had taught to say: "Greetings to Caesar, our victorious commander." Augustus was charmed by this compliment and gave the man twenty thousand sesterces for the bird. But the bird's trainer had a partner, and, when none of this large sum of money had come his way, he told the Emperor that the man had another raven and suggested that he should be made to produce it as well. The bird was produced and repeated the words which it had been taught to say: they were: "Greetings to Antony, our victorious commander." Augustus, however, instead of being at all angry, simply told the first man to share the money with his mate. He was greeted in a similar way by a parrot, and he ordered that bird to be bought, and a magpie too, which he fancied for the same trick. These examples encouraged a poor cobbler to try to train a raven to repeat a like form of greeting, but the bird remained dumb, and the man, ruined by the cost incurred, used often to say to it: "Nothing to show for the trouble and expense." One day, however, the raven began to repeat its lesson, and Augustus as he was passing heard the greeting. "I get enough of such greetings at home," he replied. But the bird also recalled the words of his master's customary lament and added: "Nothing to show for the trouble and expense." This made the Emperor laugh, and he ordered the bird to be bought, giving more for it than he had given for any of the others.

Davies (1969), pp. 174–175.

5   Cf. above, *DR* i, 52, 50–52, and note 11.

6   Pliny, *Nat. hist.* x, 60, 121–123:

Tiberio principe ex fetu supra Castorum aedem genito pullus in adpositam sutrinam devolavit, etiam religione commendatus officinae domino. Is mature sermoni adsuefactus, omnibus matutinis evolans in rostra in forum versus Tiberium, dein Germanicum et Drusum Caesares nominatim, mox transeuntem populum Romanum salutabat, postea ad tabernam remeans, plurium annorum adsiduo officio mirus. Hunc sive aemulatione vicinitatis manceps proximae sutrinae sive iracundia subita, ut voluit videri, excrementis aspersa calceis macula, exanimavit tanta plebei consternatione ut primo pulsus ex ea regione, mox et interemptus sit, funusque aliti innumeris celebratum exequiis, constratum lectum super Aethiopum duorum umeros praecedente tibicine et coronis omnium generum ad rogum usque qui constructus dextra viae Appiae ad secundum lapidem in campo Rediculi appellato fuit. Adeo satis iusta causa populo Romano visa est exequiarum ingenium avis ac supplicii de cive Romano in ea urbe in qua multorum principum nemo deduxerat funus, Scipionis vero Aemiliani post Carthaginem Numantiamque deletas ab eo nemo vindicaverat mortem.

When Tiberius was emperor, a young raven from a brood hatched on the top of the Temple of Castor and Pollux flew down to a cobbler's shop in the vicinity, being also commended to the master of the establishment by religion. It soon picked up the habit of talking, and every morning used to fly off to the platform that faces the forum and salute Tiberius and then Germanicus and Drusus Caesar by name, and next the Roman public passing by, afterwards returning to the shop; and it became remarkable by several years' constant performance of this function. This bird the tenant of the next cobbler's shop killed, whether because of his neighbour's competition or in a sudden outburst of anger, as he tried to make out, because some dirt had fallen on his stock of shoes from its droppings; this caused such a disturbance among the public that the man was first driven out of the district and later actually made away with, and the bird's funeral was celebrated with a vast crowd of followers, the draped bier being carried on the shoulders of two Ethiopians and in front of it going in procession a flute-player and all kinds of wreaths right to the pyre, which had been erected on the right hand side of the Appian Road at the second milestone [where Hannibal had turned back from marching on Rome] on the ground called Rediculus's Plain. So adequate a justification did the Roman nation consider a bird's cleverness to be for a funeral procession and for the punishment of a Roman citizen, in the city in which many leading men had no obsequies at all, while the death [129 B.C.] of Scipio Aemilianus after he had destroyed Carthage [146 B.C.] and Numantia [133 B.C.] had not been avenged by a single person.

LCL, Rackham, pp. 371, 373. Petrarch believed Pliny was born in Verona, although he was a native of Como (cf. *Rer. mem. libri* i, 19, 1; *Fam.* xii, 5, 7, xxiv, 8, 6; *Met.* ii, 10, 67–68; 15, 128; *Trionfi*, Tr. fame iii, 42; and *Itin. Syr.* 61). Nolhac (1907), ii, p. 69, n. 2, speculates that Petrarch may have been misled by Pliny's referring to Catullus of Verona (see above, *DR* i, 59, 18) as *concerraneum meum*—my boon companion. An old variant (Jahn-Mayhoff), *conterraneum meum*, indicates "my countryman," "my fellow citizen." Cf. Pliny, *Nat. hist.*, pref. 1.

7   Cf. the punishment of Vanni Fucci of Pistoia (Toynbee [1968], art. Fucci) in Dante, *Div. Comm.*, Inf. xxiv, 97–120:

> Ed ecco a un ch'era da nostra proda,
> s'avventò un serpente che 'l trafisse

là dove 'l collo a le spalle s'annonda.
Né o sì tosto mai né i si scrisse,
  com' el s'accese e arse, e cener tutto
  convenne che cascando divenisse;
e poi che·fu a terra sì distrutto,
  la polver si raccolse per sé stessa
  e 'n quel medesmo ritornò di butto.
Così per li gran savi si confessa
  che la fenice more e poi rinasce,
  quando al cinquecentesimo anno appressa;
erba né biado in sua vita non pasce,
  ma sol d'incenso lagrime e d'amomo,
  e nardo e mirra son l'ultime fasce.
E qual è quel che cade, e non sa como,
  per forza di demon ch'a terra il tira,
  o d'altra oppilazion che lega l 'omo,
quando si leva, che 'ntorno si mira
  tutto smarrito de la grande angoscia
  ch'elli ha sofferta, e guardando sospira:
tal era 'l peccator levato poscia.
  Oh potenza di Dio, quant' è severa,
  che cotai colpi per vendetta croscia!

One of the damned came racing round a boulder,
  and as he passed us, a great snake shot up
  and bit him where the neck joins with the shoulder.
No mortal pen—however fast it flash
  over the page—could write down o or i
  as quickly as he flamed and fell in ash;
and when he was dissolved into a heap
  upon the ground, the dust rose of itself
  and immediately resumed its former shape.
Precisely so, philosophers declare,
  the Phoenix dies and then is born again
  when it approaches its five hundreth year.
It lives on tears of balsam and of incense;
  in all its life it eats no herb or grain,
  and nard an precious myrrh sweeten its cerements.
And as a person fallen in a fit,
  possessed by a Demon or some seizure
  that fetters him without his knowing it,
struggles up to his feet and blinks his eyes
  (still stupefied by the great agony
  he has just passed), and, looking round him, sighs—
such was the sinner when at last he rose.
  O Power of God! How dreadful is Thy will
  which in its vengeance rains such fearful blows.

Ciardi (1977), pp. 126–127. On the phoenix (Ovid, *Metam.* xv, 391–407; Seneca, *Ep.* 42) and its golden collar, Pliny, *Nat. hist.* x, 2, 3–5; Solinus, 33, 11–14; *De ave Phoenice*, attributed to Lactantius, *PL* 7, cc. 277–284, and LCL, *Minor Latin Poets*; Claudian, *Phoenix* (LCL, xxvii = Birt, 44), and *De cons. Stilich.* ii, (LCL, xxii), 414–420; Ambrose, *Hexaem.* v, 23; Isidore, *Etym.* xii, 7, 22; *Roman de la Rose* 15976–16004, Dahlberg (1971), p. 271; Brunetto Latini, *Tresor* i, 162; Goldstaub (1892), pp. 407–413; Hubaux & Leroy (1939); White (1954), pp. 125–128; Kantorowicz (1957a), pp. 388–395; F. N. Blake in *The Phoenix* (1964), pp. 8–16, and the literature cited there; Toynbee (1968), art. Fenice; F. Chiappelli in Scaglione (1975), p. 113. Note *De sui ipsius* (1581: 1038), H. Nachod in Cassirer (1948), p. 57; and *Contra eum* (1581: 1080). —For the parrot, I have been unable to find a golden collar instead of the red one widely attested in the medieval bestiary. Cf. Isidore, *Etym.* xii, 7, 24; Goldstaub (1892), pp. 420–422; and White (1954), p. 112. Note *Fam.* iv, 14, 19, as below, *DR* ii, 29, note 13.

8   Martial, xiv, 73:

> Psittacus a vobis aliorum nomina discam;
> hoc didici per me dicere 'Caesar have.'

LCL, Ker, p. 465. Cited by Isidore, *Etym.* xii, 7, 24 (= Hrabanus Maurus, *De univ.* viii, *PL* 111, c. 246). See note 10, below.

9   Cf. above, *DR* i, 9, 39 *et passim*.

10   Cf. Martial, iii, 95, 1–2, and xiv, 76:

> Pica loquax certa dominum te voce saluto:
> si me non videas, esse negabis avem.

LCL, Ker, p. 467. This too is quoted by Isidore, *Etym.* xii, 7, 46 (= Hrabanus Maurus, *De univ.* viii, *PL* 111, c. 247). There is no direct evidence that Petrarch knew the collection of epigrams by Martial. On this, Nolhac (1907), i, p. 209; Sabbadini (1905), pp. 29, 216–217; and Sabbadini (1914), pp. 227, 235, on Boccaccio; Billanovich (1947), pp. 263–266; and Martellotti (1983), chap. 24. On parrot and magpie as a medieval topic, Mazzoni (1959).

11   Pliny, *Nat. hist.* x, 59, 118:

> Minor nobilitas, quia non ex longinquo venit, sed expressior loquacitas certo generi picarum est. Adamant verba quae loquantur nec discunt tantum sed diligunt, meditantesque intra semet cura atque cogitatione intentionem non occultant. Constat emori victas difficultate verbi ac, nisi subinde eadem audiant, memoria falli, quaerentesque mirum in modum hilarari si interim audierint id verbum.

> A certain kind of magpie is less celebrated, because it does not come from a distance, but it talks more articulately. These birds get fond of uttering particular words, and not only learn them but love them, and secretly ponder them

with careful reflexion, not concealing their engrossment. It is an established fact that if the difficulty of a word beats them this causes their death, and that their memory fails them unless they hear the same word repeatedly, and when they are at a loss for a word they cheer up wonderfully if in the meantime they hear it spoken.

LCL, Rackham, p. 369.

12   Valerius Maximus, ix, 12, Ext. 3:

Non uulgaris etiam Homeri mortis causa fertur, qui in *Io* insula, quia quae-stionem a piscatoribus positam soluere non potuisset, dolore absumptus creditur.

Also the cause of Homer's death is said to have been an uncommon one. He is believed to have died on the island of *Ios*, overcome by grief about being unable to solve a puzzle question, put to him by the local fishermen.

In his letter to Homer, *Fam.* xxiv, 12, 13, written on October 9, 1360, in reply to *epystolam magnam multaque continentem sub Homeri poete missam nomine et apud Inferos datam*—a great letter containing much, sent under the poet Homer's name and written in the Underworld—Petrarch notes:

Quamvis enim etiam apud nostros illa mortis fama vulgata sit atque ipse ego alibi famam sequens idem scripserim, sed nota ambiguitatis adhibita.

Among us, as well, this story of your death is widespread and I myself wrote about it elsewhere, following the common version, but adding a note of caution.

If this refers to our text passage, which seems to answer exactly Petrarch's description, it is fairly certain that the present dialogue was written before October 1360. On this, Cosenza (1910), pp. 190–192. The letter to Homer is translated into English in Cosenza, pp. 148–204, and Bernardo (1985), pp. 342–350, and carefully discussed in Wilkins (1958), pp. 213–217.

13   Cf. Pliny, *Nat. hist.* x, 59, 119.

14   *Picarum species et fama insignis et ingenio*—omitted in Twyne, f. 88r.

15   Pliny, *Nat. hist.* x, 59, 120:

Agrippina Claudii Caesaris turdum habuit, quod numquam ante, imitantem sermones hominum. Cum haec proderem, habebant et Caesares iuvenes sturnum, item luscinias, Graeco ac Latino sermone dociles, praeterea medi-tantes assidue et in diem nova loquentes, loquentes, longiore etiam contextu.

Claudius Caesar's consort Agrippina had a thrush that mimicked what people said, which was unprecendented. At the time when I was recording these cases, the young princes [Britannicus, Claudius's son, and Nero, his stepson] had a starling and also nightingales that were actually trained to talk Greek and Latin, and moreoever practiced diligently and spoke new phrases every day, in still longer sentences.

LCL, Rackham, p. 369.

16 For Petrarch, this is Verona; cf. note 6, above. Is this a reference to an event experienced by Azzo da Correggio, who was closely connected with the city under the Scaligeri? Cf. above, *DR* i, Pref., note 48. Did Azzo own a parrot? Cf. text below.

17 On *avaritia* as lust for gold and money, above, *DR* i, 38, note 12; and Cicero, *Tusc. disp.* iv, 11, 26.

18 1492: siue illud in fidem recepimus
    1581: siue illud in finem recepimus

19 I.e., A.D. 47.

20 The whole passage seems to be a somewhat ambigious paraphrase of Pliny, *Nat. hist.* x, 2, 5:

> Cornelius Valerianus phoenicem devolavisse in Aegyptum tradit Q. Plautio Sexto Papinio coss.; allatus est et in urbem Claudii principis censura anno urbis DCCC et in comitio propositus, quod actis testatum est, sed quem falsum esse nemo dubitaret

> Cornelius Valerianus reports that a phoenix flew down into Egypt in the consulship of Quintus Plautius and Sextus Papinius [A.D. 36]; it was even brought to Rome in the Censorship of the Emperor Claudius, A.U.C. 800, and displayed in the Comitium, a fact attested by the Records, although nobody would doubt that this phoenix was a fabrication.

LCL, Rackham, p. 295. Cf. Aurelius Victor, *Caes.* iv, 14; and *Epit.* iv, 9.

21 On the oxymoron and *joking in earnest*, Colie (1966), pp. xiii, 5, 26–27, 100–101, 110–111, etc.; Highet (1950), pp. 305–307; idem (1962), pp. 36–37, 233–237; Green (1979), pp. 184–187, also, pp. 21–28. Related, John of Salisbury, *Policrat.* viii, 11, *PL* 199, c. 753:

> Fortasse falso interdum finguntur plurima, nihil tamen impedit "ridentem dicere verum," et fabulosis narrationibus, quas philosophia non rejicit, exprimere quid obesse possit in moribus.

> Now and then, most things may be misrepresented. Yet nothing keeps us from telling the truth through jest—showing in tall tales (which philosophy does not reject) what might be injurious in our habits.

In LAP 71 (below, *DR* i, 65, note 1), Lombardo della Seta refers to stating the truth jokingly.

22 Prov. 1, 22:

> Usquequo, parvuli, diligitis infantiam.

Prov. 1, 23:

> Convertimini ad correptionem meam.

23   Cf. Matth. 15, 14:

> Sinite illos: caeci sunt et duces caecorum.

> Let them alone: they are blind, and leaders of the blind.

24   Cf. Matth. 13, 31–32:

> Aliam parabolam proposuit eis, dicens: Simile est regnum caelorum grano sina-
> pis, quod accipiens homo seminavit in agro suo. Quod minimum quidem est
> omnibus seminibus; cum autem creverit, majus est omnibus oleribus, et fit
> arbor, ita ut volucres caeli veniant, et habitent in ramis ejus.

> Another parable he proposed unto them, saying: The kingdom of heaven is like
> a grain of mustard seed, which a man took and sowed in his field. Which is the
> least indeed of all seeds: but when it is grown up, it is greater than all herbs,
> and becometh a tree, so that the birds of the air come, and dwell in the
> branches thereof.

—and Alain de Lille's commentary, *Dist. dict. theol.*, PL 210, c. 1009:

> [Dominus] ipse est granum sinapis qui in horti sepultura plantatus arbor magna
> surrexit. Granum fuit cum moreretur, arbor cum resurgeret; hujus arboris rami
> sunt praedicatores, in cujus ramis volucres coeli requiescunt, quia sanctae
> animae, quae quasi quibusdam virtutum pennis aeternorum cogitatione se sub-
> levant, ex eorum dictis et consolationibus ab hujus vitae fatigatione suspirant.

> The Lord Himself is the grain of mustard seed, which when buried in the
> garden where it is planted, rises as a great tree. He was a grain when He died,
> but a tree when He rose again, a tree whose branches are the preachers; in
> whose branches rest the birds of heaven, which are the pious souls uplifted, as
> it were, by the wings of meditation, considering the eternal virtues, and re-
> lieved from the weariness of this life by their priestly words of comfort.

Similarly, *Glossa ordinaria*, PL 114, cc. 132–133. Also Hrabanus Maurus, *De
univ.* xxii, 6, PL 111, cc. 241–242, and the story of Saint Francis preaching to
the birds, which sing the praises of their Creator; Jacobus de Voragine, *Leg.
aurea* 149, October 4, Graesse (1890), p. 670; Ryan & Ripperger (1941), pp.
605–606; and Thomas a Celano (1906), xxi, 58, p. 61: *Fratres mei, volucres
. . .* The related scriptural passage is Matth. 6, 25–26, *Glossa ordinaria*, PL
114, c. 106. On this, Burdach (1926), ii, pp. 275–276, 351–356.
   The flight of birds, upwards, overcoming terrestrial gravity, symbolized
exultation, soaring of the mind. Boyde (1981), pp. 121–123. Cf. also related
topics, such as *assurgere; in altum niti;* and *exercitatio animae,* e.g., *DR* i,
Pref., note 7; i, 2, 29–33, and note 12, i, 12, note 30, i, 29, note 4, i, 44,
note 18.

25   1492: profer &c.
      1581: profer.

65 ❖ A PROMINENT MARRIAGE

1   Dialogues 65–85 ostensibly address now *whatever is fit for a man to be joyful about*, namely, topics pertaining to him and his loved ones—love and marriage, children, in-laws, grandchildren, nephews and nieces, parents and siblings, etc.

DR i, 65, is the first of a number of dialogues in which Reason appears sharply critical of women. Later commentators have interpreted this antifeminism as indicative of Petrarch's personal attitude. Koerting (1878, p. 555) speaks of *Weiber—und Ehehass* in the *DR*. Yet Reason, in effect, dispenses age-old views, widely known and accepted in the fourteenth century. Androcentric tendencies are reflected in the literature of Antiquity (e.g., Hesiod, *Theog.* 570–612; Euripides, *Medea* 421; Aristotle, *Polit.* 1259a, 39, and *De gen. anim.* 737a, 28; 775a, 15; Plutarch, *Praecepta coniugalia;* Seneca, *De matrim.*, Fragm. 45–88; and Juvenal, vi); the Scriptures (e.g., the story of Adam and Eve, Gen. 3; Eccli. 42, 12–14; i Tim. 2, 11–15; and Eph. 5, 24); and the Fathers (e.g., Tertullian, *De exh. cast.*, *De cultu fem.*, etc.; and Jerome, *Adv. Iovin.* i). Augustine and Thomas Aquinas link these views with the contemporary concepts of natural order (*DR* i, 44, note 5). Augustine, *De civ. Dei* xix, 14:

> Hinc itaque etiam pax domestica oritur, id est ordinata imperandi oboediendique concordia cohabitantium. Imperant enim qui consulunt, sicut vir uxori, parentes filiis, domini servis. Oboediunt autem quibus consulitur, sicut mulieres maritis, filii parentibus, serve dominis. Sed in domo iusti viventis ex fide et adhuc ab illa caelesti civitate peregrinantis etiam qui imperant serviunt eis quibus videntur imperare. Neque enim dominandi cupiditate imperant, sed officio consulendi, ned principandi superbia, sed providendi misericordia.

> So at this point begins domestic peace, the ordered agreement among those who dwell together, concerning command and obedience. For those who are concerned for others give commands, the husband to his wife, the parents to their children, the masters to their servants; while those who are objects of concern obey; for example, the women obey their husbands, the children their parents, the servants their masters. But in the home of the just man who lives

by faith and who is still a pilgrim in exile from the celestial city, even those who give commands serve those whom they seem to command. For they command not through lust for rule but through dutiful concern for others, not with pride in exercising princely rule but with mercy in providing for others.

LCL, Greene, pp. 185, 187. Thomas Aquinas, *Summa theol.* i, Q. 92, a. 1 and 2:

> Dicendum quod, per respectum ad naturam particularem, femina est aliquid deficiens et occasionatum. Quia virtus activa quae est in semine maris, intendit producere sibi simile perfectum secundum masculinum sexum; sed quod femina generetur, hoc est propter virtutis activae debilitatem, vel propter aliquam materiae indispositionem, vel etiam propter aliquam transmutationem ab extrinseco, puta a ventis australibus, qui sunt humidi, ut dicitur in lib. iv *De gen. anim.* (cap. ii). Sed, per comparationem ad naturam universalem, femina non est aliquid occasionatum, sed est de intentione naturae, ad opus generationis ordinata. . . . Dicendum quod duplex est subiectio. Una, servilis: secundum quam praesidens utitur subiecto ad suiipsius utilitatem; et talis subiectio introducta est post peccatum. Est autem alia subiectio oeconomica, vel civilis: secundum quam praesidens utitur subiectis ad eorum bonum; et ista subiectio fuisset etiam ante peccatum. Defuisset enim bonum ordinis in humana multitudine, si quidam per alios sapientiores gubernati non fuissent. Et sic ex tali subiectione naturaliter femina subiecta est viro: quia naturaliter in homine magis abundat discretio rationis.

> As regards the individual nature, woman is defective and misbegotten, for the active power in the male seed tends to the production of a perfect likeness according to the masculine sex; while the production of woman comes from defect in the active power, or from some material indisposition, or even from some external influence, such as that of a south wind, which is moist, as the Philosopher observes (Aristotle, *De gen. anim.* 766b, 33). On the other hand, as regards universal human nature, woman is not misbegotten, but is included in nature's intention as directed to the work of generation. . . . Subjection is twofold. One is servile, by virtue of which a superior makes use of a subject for his own benefit; and this kind of subjection began after sin. There is another kind of subjection, which is called economic or civil, whereby the superior makes use of his subjects for their own benefit and good; and this kind of subjection existed even before sin. For the good of order would have been wanting in the human family if some were not governed by others wiser than themselves. So by such a kind of subjection woman is naturally subject to man, because in man the discernment of reason predominates.

Pegis (1945), i, pp. 880–881. Misogyny runs through the books of penance (Ziegler [1956]; cf. also Innocent III, *De miseria cond. hum.* i, 16, Lewis [1978], pp. 118–123), and the popular literature, e.g., in the *Roman de la Rose* (16323–16700, and other passages), in Machaut's poetry (Calin [1974], pp. 44–45, 110–117, 185–186), and in Chaucer's *Canterbury Tales*, Monk's Tale (2015–2094).

Reason's discourse represents the accepted view (as summarized in *Fiori e vita di filosafi* xxviii, Secundus, *La Prosa del duecento* [1959], p. 530), but does so, perhaps, more sharply, in keeping with her antidotal function to counter with opposites (compare, e.g., *DR* ii, 18, with ii, 21, and ii, 50, 49–56)—although exaltation and debasement of women, both, are conventional topics in the courtly literature of the period. On the popular topic *an vir sapiens ducat uxorem*—Ought a wise man to take a wife?—*Fam.* xxii, 1; Curtius (1953), p. 155; and Johannes von Tepl, *Ackerm.*, Bernt & Burdach (1917), pp. 293–296. Note also Dist. iv, 3, in Walter Map, *De nug. cur.*, *Dissuasio Valerii ad Ruffinum philosophum ne uxorem ducat* (James et al. [1983], pp. 289–311), a tract against marriage which Boccaccio copied into his collection of misogynic texts in the *Zibaldone laurenziano* (Cassell [1975], pp. xx–xxi); and John of Salisbury, *Policrat.* viii, chap. 11, *PL* 199, cc. 748 756. On contact with women as undesirable for lovers of peace and quiet, *De vita sol.* ii, *Prose* (1955), pp. 432, 434. On contemporary attitudes toward women and the antifeminist literature, Bergin (1981), esp. chaps. 11, 15; Cassell (1975), pp. xviii–xxi; M. Daly in Wiener (1973), iv, pp. 523–530; Coulter (1938), chap. 45; and Wiesen (1964), chap. 4. On the expression of these attitudes in art, Kraus (1967), chap. 3; and Mâle (1978), pp. 238, 372–376.

Of related interest is the literary controversy (1401–1403) surrounding the thirteenth-century *Roman de la Rose*, with Christine de Pizan, the French royal secretaries Jean de Montreuil and Gontier Col, Col's brother Pierre, who was a canon at Notre Dame, and the theologian and chancellor of the University of Paris, Jean Gerson, as principals—a debate which initially concerned the merits of Jean de Meun's part of the great poem but turned into heated invective regarding the reputation and virtue of women and, ultimately, sexual love and lechery as such. On this, Hicks (1977); Willard (1984), chap. 4; and Huizinga (1931), esp. pp. 151–168.

About March 1, 1369, Petrarch received a letter from Lombardo della Seta, a close friend whom he was to remember in his testament (Mommsen [1957], pp. 27–28; on Lombardo, Wilkins [1958], p. 87, Lorenzo Ghiberti, *Third Commentary*, Holt [1947], pp. 92–93, and Alsop [1982], *passim*). The letter (LAP 71, *Fervet animus*), written perhaps at Lombardo's country place at Sarmeola, illustrates the manner in which this and related topics were apparently routinely discussed. Its *iocosa et abscissa brevitas*—amusing cut-and-dry brevity—moved Petrarch to laughter, its *liberata veritas*—uninhibited truth—to admiration, and elicited a spirited reply (*Sen.* xv, 3, 1581: 933–937) "approving the positions taken by Lombardo in his dialogue" (Wilkins [1959], p. 164). LAP 71 (published in Fracassetti, iii [1863], pp. 506–513, where it is erroneously attributed to Petrarch, and, with significant revisions, in Ferante [1933–34] and Petrarch's reply are fully discussed in Wilkins (1959), pp. 161–164.

2   On this, cf. above, *DR* i, 2, *passim*.

3   Cf. Juvenal, x, 297–298, as below, *DR* i, 66, note 4.

4   Juvenal, vi, 167–168:

> malo Venusinam quam te, Cornelia, mater
> Gracchorum . . .

LCL, Ramsay, p. 97. Cf. also Prov. 21, 19:

> Melius est habitare in terra deserta
> quam cum muliere rixosa et iracunda.

> It is better to dwell in a wilderness,
> than with a quarrelsome and passionate woman.

Also quoted in Chaucer, *Canterbury Tales*, Melibee vii, 1087, Robinson (1933), p. 205.

5   1492: caros pellere
      1581: charos perdere

6   1492: sola scilicet mors excludat
      1581: sola scilicet mores excludat

7   Cf. Valerius Maximus, ii, 1, 4. On *repudium* as the formal declaration of intention to dismiss a spouse or betrothed, *Digesta* (Libri pandectarum) 50, 16, *passim*. Cf. Sohm (1931), pp. 15–19, 524–525.

8   Reason, in good legal style, differentiates between *repudium*—the declaration of divorce—and *divortium*—the dissolution of marriage or betrothal. Cf. *D* 24, 22, 1 and 3, 39; and note 7, above. Cicero uses exclusively the term *divortium*, e.g., *Ad Att.* xii, 52, 2. On *divortium* in medieval canon law, which did not permit divorce in the modern sense, Berman (1983), pp. 228–229.

9   *quae me ardenter amat.* Twyne, f. 89v: I have a wife, whom I love ardently.

10   *caste, pie, sobrie.* Cf. caste, sobrie, modeste, above, *DR* i, 2, 78.

11   Juvenal, vi, 268–269:

> Semper habet lites alternaque iurgia lectus
> in quo nupta iacet; minimum dormitur in illo.

> The bed that holds a wife is never free from wrangling
> and mutual bickerings; no sleep is to be got there!

LCL, Ramsay, p. 105. Cf. *De vita sol.* ii, *Prose* (1955), pp. 432, 434. Note also, Boccaccio, *Decameron* x, 10, Griselda, Singleton (1982), p. 790.

12   The Danaids were the fifty daughters of King Danaus of Lybia, who married the fifty sons of his twin brother, Aegyptus. Ordered by their father to kill their husbands during their wedding night, all but Hypermnestra did so. Graves (1955), i, 60.

13   Cf. above, *DR* i, 52, note 11.

14   King Alboin of the Lombards was assassinated May 25 or June 28, 572 A.D., in

Verona, located on the Adige river. (Hodgkins [1895], v, pp. 168, 181.) Paul the Deacon tells the story in his *Historia Langobardorum* ii, 28–29. Reason alludes to chap. 28:

> After this king had ruled in Italy three years and six months, he was slain by the treachery of his wife, and the cause of his murder was this: While he sat in merriment at a banquet at Verona longer than was proper, with the cup which he had made of the head of his father-in-law, King Cunimund, he ordered it to be given to the queen [Rosemund] to drink wine, and he invited her to drink merrily with her father. Lest this should seem impossible to any one, I speak the truth in Christ. I saw King Ratchis holding this cup in his hand on a certain festal day to show it to his guests. Then Rosemund, when she heard the thing, conceived in her heart deep anguish she could not restrain, and straightway she burned to revenge the death of her father by the murder of her husband, and presently she formed a plan with Helmechis who was the king's squire (*scilpor*)—that is, his armor-bearer—and his foster brother, to kill the king, and he persuaded the queen that she ought to admit to this plot Peredeo, who was a very strong man. As Peredeo would not give his consent to the queen when she advised so great a crime, she put herself at night in the bed of her dressing-maid with whom Peredeo was accustomed to have intercourse, and then Peredeo, coming in ignorance, lay with the queen. And when the wicked act was already accomplished and she asked him whom he thought her to be, and he named the name of his mistress that he thought she was, the queen added: "It is in no way as you think, but I am Rosemund," she says, "and surely now you have perpetrated such a deed, Peredeo, that either you must kill Alboin or he will slay you with his sword." Then he learned the evil thing he had done, and he who had been unwilling of his own accord, assented, when forced in such a way, to murder the king. Then Rosemund, while Alboin had given himself up to a noon-day sleep, ordered that there should be a great silence in the palace, and taking away all other arms, she bound his sword tightly to the head of the bed so it could not be taken away or unsheathed, and according to the advice of Peredeo, she, more cruel than any beast, let in Helmechis the murderer. Alboin suddenly aroused from sleep perceived the evil which threatened and reached his hand quickly for his sword, which, being tightly tied, he could not draw, yet he seized a foot-stool and defended himself with it for some time. But unfortunately alas! this most warlike and very brave man being helpless against his enemy, was slain as if he were one of no account, and he who was most famous in war through the overthrow of so many enemies, perished by the scheme of one little woman.

Foulke (1907; 1974), pp. 81–83. The entire story is retold in Boccaccio's *De casibus* ix, "De Rosimunda Langobardorum regina" (ed. Hall [1962], f. 100r–[101]r), where Helmechis appears under the name of Amechild.

15 *Roman de la Rose* 8687:

> By Saint Denis! Worthy women, as Valerius bears witness, are fewer than phoenixes. No man can love one but what she will pierce his heart with great

fears and cares and other bitter misfortunes. Fewer than phoenixes? By my head, a more honest comparison would say fewer than white crows, however beautiful their bodies may be. . . .

Dahlberg (1971), p. 159, and note on p. 387. *White crow / black crow* points to the talking raven or crow that once was white, Cicero, *Ad fam.* vii, 28, 2; Ovid, *Metam.* ii, 534–632; Juvenal, vii, 202. On the Asclepius story, Graves (1955), i, 50. The remark invokes also Juvenal, vi, 165, quoted in John of Salisbury, *Policrat.* viii, 11, *PL* 199, c. 753, calling a charming, rich, fertile wife of noble birth and caste,

> rara avis in terris nigroque simillima cycno.

> as rare a bird upon the earth as a black swan.

This line stands in Juvenals's satire two lines above 167–168, quoted in our text, lines 19–20, above. Note also Whiting (1968), S 931. On *rara avis*, Persius, i, 46; Jerome, *Adv. Iovin.*, i, 47, after Seneca, *De matrim.*, Fragm. xiii); and *Contra Pelag.* ii, 11. Cf. also Wiesen (1964), p. 10, n. 44, p. 151, n. 135. The topic returns in John of Salisbury, *Policrat.* i, 6, *PL* 199, c. 403; Alain de Lille, *Ars praedic.* xxv, *PL* 210, c. 162; and Boccaccio, *Il Corbaccio* (1975), pp. 33–34.

66 ✤ A BEAUTIFUL WIFE

1   Above, *DR* i, 54, 27–30, and note 8. Related, *DR* i, 65, 11–13.
2   *parietate gaudere imparietatem ac dissimilitudinem aspernari* is an old topic. Here it may well refer to Augustine's notion that

> et tanto est pulchrius corpus, quanto similioribus inter se partibus suis constat.

> the more the parts of a body resemble one another, the more beautiful the body.

De Gen. ad litt. 16, 59, *PL* 34, c. 243. "In general, then, it is order, harmony, proportion, i.e., the unity produced by likeness, that causes beauty" (Gilson [1960], p. 213). Cf. Augustine, *De trin.* vi, 10, 11, *PL* 42, c. 931. In *De quant. an.*, *PL* 32, cc. 1042–1043, Augustine demonstrates to his friend Evodius the fundamental concept of harmonious congruence *in a circuitous manner:*

Augustinus: Postestne fieri, ut in figura, quae tribus rectis paribus, lineis facta sit, impares anguli sint; an non potest?
Evodius: Nullo prorsus modo.

A: Quid? si rectis lineis tributus, sed imparibus figura constet, possunt etiam in ista pares esse anguli, an aliud intelligis?
E: Omnino non possunt.
A: Recte dicis: sed dic, quaeso, quaenam tibi figura melior videatur et pulchrior? eane quae paribus, an quae imparibus lineis constat?
E: Quis dubitet eam esse meliorem in qua aequalitas praevalet?
A: Ergo inaequalitati aequalitatem praeponis?
E: Nescio utrum quispiam non praeponat. . . . . . .
A: Quid ergo? istam quae quatuor recti paribus lineis confit, consesne posse etiam ita fieri ut non anguli omnes in ea pares sint, an non putas?

E: Video posse.
A: Quonam modo?
E: Si duo contractiores duo apertiores sint.
A: Videsne etiam quemadmodum et ambo contractiores, et ambo apertiores sibi contrarii sint?
E: Ac verissime atque apertissime.
A: Servatam igitur et hic, quanta servari potuit, cernis aequalitatem: cernis enim profecto fieri non posse, ut cum quatuor paribus lineis figura perficitur, non aut omnes, aut certe vel bini anguli pares sint; quaeque tamen paria sunt, sibi ex contrario respondere.
E: Cerno, et firmissime teneo.
A: Nihilne te movet etiam in his rebus tanta et tam inconcussa quaedam justitia?
E: Quonam modo?
A: Quia nihil, ut arbitror, dicimus esse justitiam nisi aequitatem: aequitas autem ab aequalitate quadam videtur appellata. Sed quae in hac virtute aequitas, nisi ut sua cuique tribuantur? Porro sua cuique, nisi quadam distinctione tribui non possunt. An aliter putas?
E: Manifestum est, et prorsus assentior.
A: Quid? distinctionem arbitrarisne esse ullam, si omnia paria sint, ut nihil omnino inter se differant?
E: Nullo modo.
A: Ergo justitia servari non potest, nisi in rebus in quibus servatur, sit quaedam, ut ita dicam, imparilitas et dissimilitudo.

E: Intelligo.

A: Cum igitur fateamur istas figuras, de quibus agimus, inter se esse dissimiles, illam scilicet quae tribus, et hanc quae quatuor angulis constat, cum ambae paribus lineis fiant; nonne videtur tibi quaedam retenta justitia, ut illa quae habere non potest parilitatem contrariorum, inconcussam teneat angulorum aequalitatem: in haec vero qua tanta est contrariorum congruentia, illa lex angulorum admittat nonnullam inaequalitatem? Hoc ergo cum me multum moveret, quaerendum abs te visum est, quonam modo ista veritate, aequitate, aequalitate delectarere.

E: Jam cerno quid dicas, et non mediocriter admiror.

A: Age nunc, quia inaequalitati aequalitatem jure praeponis, nec quisquam omnino est, ut opinor, humano sensu praeditus, cui non id videatur; quaeramus, si placet, figuram in qua summa aequalitas inveniri queat: quaecumque enim erit, ea caeteris sine dubitatione praeferetur.

Augustine: In a figure whose three sides are equal, are the angles necessarily equal also?

Evodius: They must be equal.

A: Now suppose that the three sides of the figure are unequal, is there any possibility of the angles being equal?

E: None whatever.

A: Correct. Now, another question. Which figure has the more beautiful and striking proportions—the one whose sides are equal or unequal?

E: Undoubtedly the one that excels in equality is more perfect.

A: So you prefer equality to the lack of it.

E: Certainly, like everyone else. . . . .

A: Another point. Can a figure of four equal lines be made in such a way that the angles are not all equal?

E: I think it is possible.

A: How?

E: By widening two angles and closing up the other two.

A: Do you notice that the wider angles face each other and the same is true of the smaller ones?

E: That is absolutely true.

A: You notice that here, too, equality obtains as far as possible. Once you make a figure of four equal lines, either all four angles are exactly equal or at least are equal in pairs, and the pairs are opposite to each other.

E: I notice that and hold it as correct.

A: Does it not strike you that these figures in their own way reveal unmistakably a kind of unfailing justice?

E: What do you mean?

A: Because we say, I believe, that justice is equity, and equity seems to be derived from equality. Now, the virtue of equity certainly requires that each man be given what is his. This 'to each his own' implies a definite distinction of persons. Do you not think so?

E: That is evident and I agree entirely.

A: Do you think there is any distinction, if all things are equal without any difference whatever between them?

E: None whatever.

A: Therefore justice cannot be maintained unless there is some inequality, if I may use the word, in the things in which [justice] is maintained, and some likeness.

E: I understand.

A: Since, therefore, we admit dissimilarity between those figures under discussion, for, although both are composed of equal sides, yet one has three and the other four angles—do you not perceive a certain closeness to justice in this: that the figure which cannot admit equality of opposite parts maintains invariably an equality of angles, while in the other figure, which has complete equality of opposites the law of angles permits inequality up to a point? Since I was excited over this fact, I cannot help but put the question to you whether this truth, this equity, this equality, would be a source of delight to you.

E: I see now what you mean and I am indeed filled with wonder.

A: Another point. You have good reason to prefer equality to inequality; in fact, I think there is no human being who would not make the same choice. Well, then, let us look for the figure, if you will, that has the greatest equality. For, whatever it be, we shall certainly prefer it to all others.

J. J. MacMahon in *Saint Augustine* (1974), pp. 73–76. On this, also Aristotle, *Metaph.* 1078a, 32, and *Poet.* 1450b, 34; and Boethius, *Quomodo substantiae* ix, 49–50:

Omnis diuersitas discors, similitudo uero appetenda est; et quod appetit aliud, tale ipsum esse naturaliter ostenditur quale est illud hoc ipsum quod appetit.

Diversity repels; likeness attracts. That which seeks something outside itself is demonstrably of the same nature as that which it seeks.

LCL, Stewart & Rand, p. 43. For the theological interpretation of *similitudo*, cf. Anselm of Canterbury, *Monolog.* xxxi. For the views of Bonaventure, De Bruyne (1946), iii, chap. vi. On the subject, Robertson (1962), chap. ii, 3.

3   On *tumor animi*, above, DR i, 49, note 1. On the arrogance of married women, Terence, *Phormio* 342; Ambrose, *De Nab.*, CSEL xxxii, 480–481; and Jerome, e.g., *Ep.* 22, 16.

4   Juvenal, x, 297–298:

> . . .   . . . rara est adeo concordia formae
> atque pudicitiae.

LCL, Ramsay, p. 215.

67 ❖ A FERTILE AND FAIR-SPOKEN WIFE

1   Terence, *Adelphoë*, 867–868:

> duxi uxorem: quam ibi miseriam vidi! nati filii:
> alia cura

LCL, Sargeaunt, p. 309. 1492 and 1581 insert *non* after *quam*.

2   Juvenal, vi, 448–450:

> non habeat matrona, tibi quae iuncta recumbit,
> dicendi genus aut curvum sermone relato
> torqueat enthymema, nec historias sciat omnes.

LCL, Ramsay, p. 121. Enthymema—a rhetorical form of proof; cf. above, *DR* i, 9, note 12.

3   Juvenal, ibid., 456:

> soloecismum licet fecisse marito.

LCL, Ramsay, p. 121.

68 ❖ A HUGE DOWRY

1   1492: Et optima tyrannide:
     1581: Et opima tyrannide,

2   Petrarch, *Rer. mem. libri* iii, 69, 4, 30:

> Ex legibus autem quas civibus suis sanxit hec memoratu digna narrantur. . . .

Virgines indotatas nubere, ne dotis respectus aut eis insolentiam adderet, aut viris et in uxorem electione verum iudicium et in matrimoniis regendis virilem preriperet libertatem.

From the laws which [Lycurgus of Sparta] decreed for his citizens [Tacitus, *Ann.* iii, 26, 4] the following is being recalled as noteworthy [cf. Justin, *Epit.* iii, 2, 5–12; iii, 1–9]: . . . . . . Virgins are to be married without dowry, lest the dowry encourage their insolence or deprive the men of good judgment when selecting a wife and of a husband's authority as head of the household to attend to family affairs.

Justin's summary is also the basis for John of Salisbury, *Policrat.* iv, 3, *PL* 199, c. 517.

3   Valerius Maximus, vii, 2, Ext. 9:

Unicae filiae pater Themistoclen consulebat utrum eam pauperi, sed ornato, an locupleti parum probato conlocaret. Cui is "malo" inquit "uirum pecunia quam pecuniam uiro indigentem." Quo dicto stultum monuit ut generum potius quam diuitias generi legeret.

The father of an only daughter consulted Themistocles whether he should give her in marriage to a poor man held in high regard or to one who had plenty, yet was not esteemed. Themistocles said to him: "I prefer a man without money to money without a man"—which saying should have reminded the dumb father that he had better choose a son-in-law, not the riches of a son-in-law.

4   *esurire cum paupercula humili, quam cum insolenti divite litigare.* Twyne, f. 92r: and to be hungrie with a poore wenche that is humble, then to lyve in brawlyng with a ryche and insolent Peacocke?

5   I.e., Emperor Marcus Aurelius Antoninus, A.D. 121–180.

6   *Hist. Aug.*, Marcus Antoninus xix, 8–9:

. . . si quidem Faustinam satis constet apud Caietam condiciones sibi et nauticas et gladiatorias elegisse. De qua cum diceretur Antonino Marco ut eam repudiaret, si non occideret, dixisse fertur "si uxorem dimittimus, reddamus et dotem." Dos autem quid habebatur? Imperium, quod ille ab socero volente Hadriano adoptatus acceperat.

. . . since it is generally known that Faustina, while at Caieta, used to choose out lovers from among the sailors and gladiators. When Marcus Antoninus was told about this, that he might divorce, if not kill her, he is reported to have said: "If we send our wife away, we must also return her dowry." And what was her dowry? The Empire, which, after he had been adopted at the wish of Hadrian, he had inherited (from his father-in-law Pius).

LCL, Magie, pp. 179, 181. Cf. also *Trionfi*, Tr. cup. i, 100–102; and *Rime* (1951), p. 484:

> Vedi 'l buon Marco d'ogni laude degno,
> pien di filosofia la lingua e 'l petto,
> ma pur Faustina 'l fa qui star a segno.

> See the good Marcus, worthy of all praise
> His tongue and heart full of philosophy—
> And yet Faustina bends him to her will.

Wilkins (1962), p. 9. On the legal aspects, note Sohm (1931), § 84.

7   "Heliopolitan habits" may refer to the city in Egypt which was the seat of government when the Ptolemies came to power or, possibly, to Baalbek, also called Heliopolis (Macrobius, *Saturn.* i, 23, 10). Either case would involve incestuous marriage among siblings, which kept the dowry in the family. Cf. above, *DR* i, 52, notes 5, 7, on Ptolemy II, Philadelphus, and Arsinoë; and Tacitus, *Ann.* ii, 3, on Tigranes III, who married his sister Erato and named her co-regent.

The "Punic way," probably, alludes to Hannibal's espousing a prostitute in the town of Salpi during his Capuan sojourn after the victory at Cannae, 216 B.C. (Pliny, *Nat. hist.* iii, 11, 103; Seneca, *Ep.* 51, 5–6), which Petrarch excoriated in his *De viris ill.* xvii, 45–46:

> Inter Capue quidem Campanieque delitias militare robur illud elanguit et martius ardor ille defervuit, ut non minus vere quam proprie a Marco Marcello dictum sit: "fuisse Capuam Cannas Hannibali". Neque vero tantummodo ille malo ac labori innutritus exercitus circumfusis illecebris enervatus et suarum oblitus est artium, sed dux ipse, quod attento viri rigore fabulosum videri posset nisi a claris proditum esset auctoribus, apud Salapiam Apulie oppidum—o humanum animum inconstantem et passionibus semper obnoxium!—magno nec honesto quidem nec se digno amore correptus est, et bellis indomitum meretricula blanda perdomuit Ticinique et Trebie et Transimeni et Cannarum et Carthaginis et glorie et sui ipsius fecit immemorem.

> Amidst the delights of Capua and the Campania that warlike vigor grew faint, the martial zeal cooled down, and the remark by Marcus Marcellus that *Capua was Hannibal's Cannae* is no less true than it is appropriate [Livy, xxiii, 45, 2–4; Florus, i, 22, 21]. Nor was it only the army that, afflicted with these ills, became debauched by the surrounding allurements and oblivious to the arts of war—in the Apulian town of Salpi the commander himself (which, with a man of such renowned hardness would seem wholly inconceivable, ·were it not attested by outstanding writers), this fierce warrior—O wavering human mind forever enslaved by heedless passion—was seized by a great love, indecent, and unworthy of him, and he whom wars had not subdued, was vanquished by a sleezy whore who made him forget the victories at the Ticinus river and the Trebia, Lake Trasimeno, and Cannae [cf. Pliny, *Nat. hist.* vii, 29, 106], and the glory of Carthage and himself.

Cf. also, *Rime* 360, Quell' antiquo, 91–92; and *Trionfi*, Tr. cup. iii, 25–27, *Rime* (1951), pp. 463, 495.

69 ❖ LOVE AFFAIRS

1 *Prose* (1955), pp. 618–632 (dialogue numbered erroneously i, 49).
2 The passage is paraphrased in *La Celestina* x, 3, Marciales (1985), ii, p. 182; and Simpson (1955), p. 118. Reason uses *oxymoron*, one of the stock rhetorical figures in the description of love. Compare *Roman de la Rose* 4293–4334:

> Love is hateful peace and loving hate. It is disloyal loyalty and loyal disloyalty, fear that is completely confident and despairing hope. It is reason gone mad and reasonable madness, the sweet danger of drowning, a heavy burden easily handled. It is the treacherous Charybdis, repellent but attractive. It is a healthful languor and diseased health, a hunger satiated in the midst of abundance, a sufficiency always covetous. It is the thirst that is always drunk, a drunkenness intoxicated by its own thirst. False delight, joyous sorrow, enraged happiness, sweet ill, malicious sweetness, and a foul-smelling sweet perfume, love is a sin touched by pardon but a pardon stained by sin. It is suffering which is too joyous, a piteous cruelty, a movement without any certainty, a state of rest both too fixed and too movable. It is a spineless force, a strong weakness that moves all by its efforts. It is foolish sense, wise folly, a prosperity both sad and pleasant. It is the laugh filled with tears and weeping, and the repose always occupied by labor. Sweet hell and heaven of sorrow, it is the prison which solaces captivity. It is the springtime full of cold winter, the moth that refuses nothing but consumes everything from purple robes to homespun, for lovers are found beneath coarse clothing as well as in fine.

Dahlberg (1971), pp. 94–95. Cf. also the *Canticus Troili* in Chaucer's *Troilus and Criseyde* i, 400–420, and its Petrarchan source, *Rime* 132, *Rime* (1951), p. 194 (Wilkins [1951], chap. 19):

> S'amor non è, che dunque è quel ch'io sento?
> ma s'egli è amor, per Dio, che cosa e quale?
> se bona, ond'è l'effetto aspro mortale?
> se ria, ond'è sì dolce ogni tormento?

> S'a mia voglia ardo, ond'è 'l pianto e lamento?
> s'a mal mio grado, il lamentar che vale?
> O viva morte, o dilettoso male,
> come puoi tanto in me, s'io nol consento?

> E s'io 'l consento, a gran torto mi doglio.
> Fra sì contrari venti in frale barca
> mi trovo in alto mar senza governo:

sì lieve di saver, d'error sì carca,
ch'i' medesmo non so quel ch'io mi voglio,
e tremo a mezza state, ardendo il verno.

If not love, then what is it that I feel?
If it is love, good God, what kind of thing?
If good, why does the effect smite and sting,
If bad, why does the torment sweetly steal?

If I burn at my will, why do I cry?
If in spite of myself, what is the use?
O living death, o delightful abuse,
How can you conquer me if I deny?

And if I yield, my heart must quietly break.
Among such warring winds in a frail boat
Without a helm on the high seas I float,

So light in wisdom, so full of mistake,
That what I want I myself cannot learn,
And freeze in summer and in winter burn.

Armi (1946), p. 217. Cf. also *Rime* 134. Related, e.g., *amara dulcedo*, *Fam.* ii, 9, 2, ix, 1, 1; *Sen.* iii, 1, viii, 5, xi, 11, xiii, 2; (1581: 766, 839, 703, 917); *Var.* 19 and 32, as based on Horace, *Carm.* ii, 26–27, Fracassetti, iii (1863), pp. 345–346, 392; *Rer. mem. libri* iii, 96, 17, as below, *DR* ii, 93, note 4, and Billanovich in his edition, p. 186, n. 96, and *DR* i, 70, 7; *phalerata felicitas*, *Fam.* iv, 17, 3; *frivola laetitia*, *Fam.* v, 17, 13; and *mestum gaudium* (= Whiting [1968], L 513), *Sen.* xi, 11, ibid. Note also *Sen.* viii, 3 (1581: 835); *Var.* 29, Fracassetti, ibid., pp. 376–377; Alain de Lille, *De planctu nat.*, PL 210, cc. 455–456; and above, *DR* i, 1, note 10, i, 14, note 8, i, 43, note 20, i, 64, note 21, i, 66, 39, and i, 70, 7.

3   On "love is blind, lovers are blind," echoing Plato, *Laws* v, 731e, according to Rossi & Bosco (Ediz. naz., xii, p. 256, xiii, p. 121); and *Fam.* vii, 14, 2, xi, 11, 1, xvii, 9, 1, xix, 11, 1 and 9, and xxii, 7, 11. Note Ovid, *credula res amor est*—a credulous thing is love—*Metam.* vii, 826; and *Heroides* vi, 21. Cf. *Var.* 29, Fracassetti, iii (1863), p. 377.

4   A paraphrase of Ovid, *Rem. am.* 13–14:

Siquis amat quod amare iuvat, *feliciter ardet:*
Gaudeat, et vento naviget ille suo.

If any lover has delight in his love, blest is his passion:
let him rejoice and sail on, with favouring wind.

LCL, Mozley, p. 179.

5   Virgil, *Ecl.* viii, 108:

> qui amant, ipsi somnia fingunt.

LCL, Fairclough, p. 65. Quoted in *Fam.* vii, 12, 6–7, xii, 5, 4; and *Secretum* iii, *Prose* (1955), p. 142, Rico (1974), p. 289, n. 137. Related, *Africa* v, 680:

> Somnia sunt que fingis amans, et falleris amens.

> Dreams you dream when in love, and, out of mind, deceive yourself.

On *amans/amens* (Terence, *Andria* i, 218), see below, DR ii, 97, note 15.

6   Cf. Lewis (1964), pp. 198–203.

7   Suetonius, i, Jul. Caes., 52, 1–2:

> Dilexit et reginas . . . sed maxime Cleopatram, cum qua et convivia in primam lucem saepe protraxit et eadem nave thalamego paene Aethiopia tenus Aegyptum penetravit, nisi exercitus sequi recusasset, quam denique accitam in urbem non nisi maximis honoribus praemiisque auctam remisit filiumque natum appellare nomine suo passus est. Quem quidem nonnulli Graecorum similem quoque Caesari et forma et incessu tradiderunt. M. Antonius adgnotum etiam ab eo senatui adfirmavit, idque scire C. Matium et C. Oppium reliquosque Caesaris amicos; quorum Gaius Oppius, quasi plane defensione ac patrocinio res egeret, librum edidit, non esse Caesaris filium, quem Cleopatra dicat.

> [Caesar] had love affairs with queens too . . . above all with Cleopatra, with whom he often feasted until daybreak, and he would have gone through Egypt with her in her state-barge almost to Aethiopia, had not his soldiers refused to follow him. Finally he called her to Rome and did not let her leave until he had ladened her with high honors and rich gifts, and he allowed her to give his name to the child which she bore. In fact, according to certain Greek writers, this child was very like Caesar in looks and carriage. Mark Antony declared to the senate that Caesar had really acknowledged the boy, and that Gaius Matius, Gaius Oppius, and other friends of Caesar knew this. Of these Gaius Oppius, as if admitting that the situation required apology and defence, published a book, to prove that the child whom Cleopatra fathered on Caesar was not his.

LCL, Rolfe, p. 71. On Hannibal, cf. above, *DR* i, 68, note 7. Note *Trionfi*, Tr. cup. i, 88–93, and iii, 25–27, *Rime* (1951), pp. 484, 495.

8   Reason's allusive list of ancient stories of great love is essentially Ovidian. On Jupiter, e.g., *Metam.* ii, 847–875, v, 327, and vi, 103–122. On Mars and Venus caught in Hephaestus-Vulcan's hunting net, *Metam.* iv, 171–189; *Roman de la Rose* 13823–13874, and 18061–18089, Dahlberg (1971), pp. 237–238, 300–301; and Graves (1955), i, 18.b. (Tr. cup. i, 151–153). On Hercules and Omphale, Graves, ibid., ii, 136. Musaeus' story of Hero and Leander is outlined in Virgil, *Georg.* iii, 258–263. Note also Ovid, *Heroides* 19 (Tr. cup.

iii, 421). On Byblis, Ovid, *Metam.* ix, 454–665; *Ars am.* i, 283–284; Procris, *Metam.* vii, 694–865; *Ars amat.* iii, 687–746, Graves, ibid., i, 89; Tr. cup. iii, 73–78; Pyramus and Thisbe, *Metam.* iv, 55–166; *Rem. am.* 19 (Tr. cup. iii, 19–20); Iphis, *Metam.* xiv, 699–769; *Rem. am.* 18 (Tr. cup. ii, 152–153). On Petrarch's sources for Homer's *Iliad*, Nolhac (1907), ii, p. 131. On other medieval sources connected with the story of Troy, Harvey (1974), art. Trojan War.

9   1492: amo
    1581: amor

10   This is the Aristotelian *virtus in medio*. Cf. above, *DR* i, 5, note 2.

11   1492: *Gaudium*: Ergo malum est amare: hoc ego fateor: malo nihil melius inuenio.
    Ratio: Credo Hercle: ut est animus sed tua opinio rem mutat.
    1581: *Gaudium*: Ergo malum est amare.
    Ratio: Hoc est fateor.
    Gaudium: Malo hoc nihil melius inuenio.
    Ratio: Credo, hercle, ut est animus, sed tua rerum opinio nutat.

Based on the maxim *opinio rem non mutat* (*DR* i, 11, 2, and note 1) and Pier Giorgio Ricci's reading (*Prose* [1955], p. 622), I have emended the 1492 text to read *rem* non *mutat*. Twyne, f. 93v., translated a text kindred to 1581:

> *Ioy:* Then it is euyl to loue.
> *Reason:* That I confesse.
> *Ioy:* But I fynde nothyng better then this euyl.
> *Reason:* I thynke wel, as thy iudgement now standeth, but thyne opinion concernyng matters, is affectionate and blinded.

12   *Tu quid ames videris*—echoing Augustine, e.g., *Enarr. in Ps.* 31, 2, 5, *PL* 36, c. 260. —Stoic philosophy defined ἀδιάφορα—indifferents—as having no direct connection with good and evil (*SVF* i, 191–196, 559–562, iii, 117–168; Pohlenz, i [1959], pp. 121–123, ii [1955], pp. 69–70). Reason's example recalls Augustine's commentary in *De civ. Dei* xiv, 3–9 (Gilson [1960], pp. 135–136) on Virgil, *Aeneid* vi, 730–734, which Petrarch's *Augustinus* in *Secretum* i (*Prose* [1955], p. 64, as above, *Dramatis personae*, note 11) interprets in a strikingly different manner (Heitmann [1960], esp. pp. 38–43; Rico [1974], pp. 107–110; Foster [1984], pp. 170–171). Reason's terminology is Ciceronian, *De fin.* iii, 16, 53:

> Quoniam autem omne quod est bonum primum locum tenere dicimus, necesse est nec bonum esse nec malum hoc quod praepositum vel praecipuum nominamus; idque ita definimus, quod sit indifferens cum aestimatione mediocri; quòd enim illi ἀδιάφορον dicunt, id mihi ita occurrit ut indifferens dicerem.

> But since we assign to all that is good the top place, it follows that what we call preferred or special is neither good nor evil. Accordingly we define it as being

indifferent, of a middling quality—since it occurred to me to translate as *indifferent* what the stoics term ἀδιάφορον.

The entire exchange, lines 69–81, suggests Seneca's argument in *Ep.* 82, 9–14:

> Zenon noster hac collectione utitur: "nullum malum gloriosum est; mors autem gloriosa est; mors ergo non est malum." . . . Nam et ipse interrogationem contrariam opposuit ex eo natam, quod mortem inter indifferentia ponimus, quae ἀδιάφορα Graeci vocant. "Nihil," inquit, "indifferens gloriosum est; mors autem gloriosum est; ergo mors non est indifferens." Haec interrogatio vides ubi obrepat: mors non est gloriosa, sed fortiter mori gloriosum est. Et cum dicis: "indifferens nihil gloriosum est," concedo tibi ita, ut dicam nihil gloriosum esse nisi circa indifferentia. Tamquam indifferentia esse dico, id est nec bona nec mala, morbum, dolorem, paupertatem, exilium, mortem. Nihil horum per se gloriosum est, nihil tamen sine his. Laudatur enim non paupertas, sed ille, quem paupertas non summittit nec incurvat. Laudatur non exilium, sed ille qui in exilium ivit tanquam misisset. Laudatur non dolor, sed ille, quem nihil coegit dolor. Nemo mortem laudat, sed eum, cuius mors ante abstulit animum quam conturbavit. Omnia ista per se non sunt honesta nec gloriosa, sed quicquid ex illis virtus adiit tractavitque, honestum et gloriosum facit; illa in medio posita sunt; interest, utrum malitia illis an virtus manum admoverit. . . . aut malitia aut virtus dat boni vel mali nomen. Massa per se nec calida nec frigida est; in fornacem coniecta concaluit, in aquam demissa refrixit. Mors honesta est per illud, quod honestum est, id est virtus et animus extrema contemnens.

> Our master Zeno [the founder of the Stoa] uses a syllogism like this: "No evil is glorious; but death is glorious; therefore death is no evil." . . . and he proposed a counter-syllogism, based upon the proposition that we regard death as *indifferent*—one of the things which the Greeks call ἀδιάφορα. "Nothing," he says, "that is indifferent can be glorious; death is glorious; therefore death is not indifferent." You comprehend the tricky fallacy which is contained in this syllogism: mere death is, in fact, not glorious; but a brave death is glorious. And when you say: "Nothing that is indifferent is glorious," I grant you this much, and declare that nothing is glorious except as it deals with indifferent things. I classify as *indifferent*—that is, neither good nor evil—sickness, pain, poverty, exile, death. None of these things is intrinsically glorious; but nothing can be glorious apart from them. For it is not poverty that we praise, it is the man whom poverty cannot humble or bend. Nor is it exile that we praise, it is the man who withdraws into exile in the spirit in which he would have sent another into exile. It is not pain that we praise, it is the man whom pain has not coerced. One praises not death, but the man whose soul death takes away before it can confound it. All these things are in themselves neither honourable nor glorious; but any one of them that virtue has visited and touched is made honorable and glorious by virtue; they merely lie in between (i.e., are *indifferent*), and the decisive question is only whether wickedness or virtue has laid hold upon them . . . . . . it is the wickedness or the virtue that bestows the name of good and evil. An object is not by its own essence either hot or cold; it

is heated when thrown into a furnace, and chilled when dropped into water. Death is honourable when related to that which is honourable; by this I mean virtue and a soul that despises the worst hardships.

LCL, Gummere, pp. 245, 247, 249. Note also Seneca, *Ep.* 31, 4; Gellius, ii, 7, 20, ix, 5, 5; Boethius, *Cons. phil.* iv, P 7; and John of Salisbury, *Policrat.* viii, 11, *PL* 199, c. 755. Cf. *Fam.* xx, 8, 20, and xxi, 9, 13; *Sen.* ii, 2 (1581: 757); and below, *DR* ii, 117, 163. Note also *Sen.* v, 2 (1581: 795): *Siquidem actus idem, pro intentione agentis, nunc laudabilis, nunc infamis est*—for an identical act can be either laudable or blamable according to the motives of the actor (Bishop [1966], p. 244).

13   ii Cor. 4, 18:

> . . . non contemplantibus nobis quae videntur, sed quae non videntur; quae enim videntur temporalia sunt, quae autem non videntur aeterna sunt.

Also quoted *Sen.* xvi, 8; *De ocio* (1581: 960, 297); and below, *DR* ii, 96, 39.

14   Cf. *Secretum* iii, *Prose* (1955), p. 154:

> Nichil est quod eque oblivionem Dei contemptum ve pariat atque amor rerum temporalium; iste precipue, quem proprio quodam nomine Amorem, et (quod sacrilegium omne transcendit) Deum etiam vocant, ut scilicet humanis furoribus excusatio celestis accedat fiatque divino instinctu scelus immane licentius.

> Nothing so much leads a man to forget or despise God as the love of things temporal, and most of all this passion that we call love; and to which, by the greatest of all desecrations, we even gave the name of God, without doubt only that we may throw a heavenly veil over our human follies and make a pretext of divine inspiration when we want to commit an enormous transgression.

Draper (1911), pp. 131–132. Note also Seneca, *Phaedra*, 195–196, and *Octavia*, 557–558; and Cicero, *Tusc. disp.* iv, 32, 69, as cited in *Prose* (1955), p. 154, n. 1, and *Fam.* ix, 4, 7, as in Rico (1974), p. 315, n. 217.

15   Cf., e.g., Ovid, *Ars amat.* iii, 26:

> conveniunt cumbae vela minora meae.

> Smaller sails become my bark.

LCL, Mozley, p. 121.

16   Cf. *Secretum* iii, *Prose* (1955), p. 132:

> [*Augustinus:*] Oh miser! an tibi philosophica illa vox excidit: tum consumatum fore miseriarum cumulum, cum opinionibus falsis persuasio funesta subcrescit ita fieri oportere?

> [*Augustinus:*] Ah, unhappy man, have you forgotten quite this axiom of philosophy, that the climax of all evils is when a man, rooted in some false opinion, by degrees grows fatally persuaded that such and such a course is right?

Draper (1911), p. 110. On this, Rico (1974), pp. 252–254. Heitmann (1958), p. 161, n. 28, points to Seneca, *Ep.* 39, 6:

> Serviunt itaque voluptatibus, non fruuntur, et mala sua, quod malorum ultimum est, et amant. Tunc autem est consummata infelicitas, ubi turpia non solum delectant, sed etiam placent, et desinit esse remedio locus, ubi quae fuerant vitia, mores sunt.

> And so they are the slaves of their pleasures instead of enjoying them; they even love their own ills—and that is the worst ill of all! Then it is that the height of unhappiness is reached, when men are not only attracted, but even pleased, by shameful things, and when there is no longer any room for a cure, now that those things which once were vices have become habits.

LCL, Gummere, p. 263.

17   On *consuetudo in naturam versa,* cf. below, *DR* ii, 41, 41, and ii, 58, 62; *Fam.* iii, 2, 4, viii, 3, 18, xi, 12, 6, and xii, 3, 4; *Sen.* v, 2 (1581: 793); and *Rime* 81, 2, and 264, 99–108, *Rime* (1951), pp. 341–342:

> ché mortal cosa amar con tanta fede
> quanto a Dio sol per debito convensi,
> più si disdice a chi più pregio brama.
> E questo ad alta voce anco richiama
> la ragione sviata dietro ai sensi:
> ma perch'ell'oda e pensi
> tornare, il mal costume oltre la spigne
> et agli occhi depigne
> quella che sol per farmi morir nacque,
> perch'a me troppo et a se stessa piacque.

> To love a mortal thing beyond the mean,
> With a faith that to God only pertains,
> Is less becoming when praise we desire.
> And this does with loud voice also require
> That reason cease to bear the senses' chains;
> But although it does mean
> To return, the bad custom drives it on,
> And paints to it like sun
> One who was born only to make me die,
> Because she pleased to mine and to her eye.

Armi (1946), p. 375. See also above, *DR* i, 40, note 15.

18   *homines doctissimi* = Cicero, *Tusc. disp.* iv, 33, 71; cf. note 20, below.

19   The reference to Sappho as *puella*—a girl—which recurs in *Fam.* xxi, 8, 6, and *Buc. carm.* x, 89, suggests Horace, *Carm.* iv, 9, 11–12:

> Vivuntque commissi calores
> Aeoliae fidibus puellae.

> Still breathes the love of the Aeolian maid [i.e., Sappho],
> and lives her passion confided to the lyre.

LCL, Bennett, p. 319.

20   Cicero, *Tusc. Disp.* iv, 33, 71:

> Quid denique homines doctissimi et summi poetae de se ipsis et carminibus
> edunt et cantibus? Fortis vir in sua re publica cognitus quae de iuvenum amore
> scribit Alcaeus! Nam Anacreontis quidem tota poesis est amatoria.

> What disclosures lastly do men of the highest culture and poets of supreme
> merit make about their own life in their poems and songs? What things Al-
> caeus, a man of bravery and of note in his country, writes about the love of
> youths! Of Anacreon I say nothing, for his work is all love-poetry.

LCL, King, pp. 409, 411.

21   With identical sequence, *Trionfi*, Tr. cup. iv, 19–24; *Rime* (1951), p. 502:

> Virgilio vidi, e parmi ch'egli avesse
> compagni d'alto ingegno e da trastullo,
> di quei che volentier già il mondo lesse:
>   l'uno era Ovidio, e l'altro era Catullo,
> l'altro Properzio, che d'amor cantaro
> fervidamente, e l'altro era Tibullo.

> And I saw Virgil; and it seemed to me
> He had companions whom the olden world
> Had gladly read, for wisdom and delight:
>   Ovid was there, and with him were Catullus,
> Propertius, and Tibullus, and they all
> Were fervid singers of the power of Love.

Wilkins (1962), p. 28. Related, *Secretum* iii, *Prose* (1955), p. 162, on remedies
for love.

22   *vitae duces philosophos.* Compare Cicero, *Tusc. disp.* iv, 33, 70:

> ad magistros virtutis, philosophos.

> to the teachers of virtue, the philosophers.

LCL, King, p. 409. Note also below, *DR* ii, 117, 58–63, and note 17.

23   This is Cicero, ibid., iv, 33, 72: *Stoici vero et sapientem amaturum esse dicunt.*

24   Above, *DR* i, 46, 16–20, and note 7.

25   Cicero, *Tusc. disp.* iv, 33, 72: *Stoici . . . amorem ipsum conatum amicitiae
faciendae ex pulcritudinis specie definiunt.*

26   All texts consulted have *anum*—old woman—for Cicero's *senem*—old man:

> Quis est enim iste amor amicitiae? Cur neque deformem adolescentem quis-
> quam amat neque formosum senem?

LCL, King, p. 409.

27   Reason paraphrases Cicero, ibid., 72:

> Qui si quis est in rerum natura sine sollicitudine, sine desiderio, sine cura, sine suspirio, sit sane; vacat enim omni libidine; haec autem de libidine oratio est.

> And if in the actual world there is an instance of love free from disquietude, from longing, from anxiety, from sighing, then so be it! if you will; for such love has no element of lust; but our discourse is about lust.

28   On *tumultus*—tumult, panic—cf. Horace, *Carm.* ii, 16, 10: *tumultus mentis*—tumult of the soul. *angor*—the feeling of anxiety—is one of the disorders listed under *aegritudo*—distress—Cicero, *Tusc. disp.* iv, 7, 16; 8, 18; 12, 27; etc.

29   Cf. Cicero, ibid. iv, 33, 70.

30   Cf. *Fam.* xviii, 2, 11; and *Rer. mem. libri* i, 25, 10:

> Itaque iure optimo, non Greci tantum, sed Marcus Cicero et omnes doctiores Latinorum uno ore vel Platonem philosophorum principem appellant, vel, qui minus, hunc vel illum glorie sibi tribuunt collegam: alii Plotinum ut Macrobius, alii Xenophontem ut Agellius. Ita de collega fortassis aliqua, de Platone nulla questio est.

> More so than the Greeks, but with utter justification, Marcus Cicero and all the leading Latin scholars, like one man, name Plato the prince of philosophers and, with less agreement, assign him a comrade in this glory, some Plotinus, as Macrobius does [*Comm.* i, 8, 5; cf. *De vita sol.* ii, 12, *Prose* (1955), p. 526], some Xenophon, as Gellius [xiv, 3, 11]. There does remain some question as to the merit of these colleagues, but none about the merit of Plato.

De sui ipsius, Prose (1955), p. 750, is more specific:

> . . . et philosophiae principem Platonem. —Et quis—inquient—principatum hunc Platoni tribuit?— Ut pro me respondeam, non ego, sed veritas, ut aiunt, etsi non apprehensa, visa tamen illi, propiusque adita, quam ceteris. Dehinc magni tribuunt auctores, Cicero primum et Virgilius, non hic quidem nominando, sed sequendo. Plinius preterea et Plotinus, Apuleius, Macrobius, Porphirius, Censorinus, Iosephus, et ex nostris Ambrosius, Augustinus, et Ieronimus, multique alii. Quod facile probaretur, nisi omnibus notum esset.

> . . . and the prince of philosophy, Plato [*Fam.* iv, 15, 8, xvii, 8, 5, xviii, 2, 11]. And who, they will say, has assigned this principate to Plato? I answer, not I, but truth, as is said—that truth which he saw and to which he came nearer than all the others, though he did not comprehend it. Moreover, there are many authorities who assign this highest rank to him: first of all Cicero and Virgil—who does not mention his name, it is true, but was a follower of his— then Pliny and Plotinus, Apuleius and Macrobius, Porphyry and Censorinus, Josephus, and among our Christian authors Ambrose, Augustine, and Jerome,

and many others still. This could easily be proved if it were not known to everybody.

Nachod in Cassirer (1948), pp. 107–108. The editorial apparatus in Nachod and *Prose* (1955) identifies the works referred to by Petrarch. The following list of relevant passages is based on this apparatus, but somewhat modified: Cicero, *De fin.* v, 3, 7; *Tusc. disp.* i, 10, 22; *Acad.*—The Virgil (*Aeneid* vi) reference is Augustine, *De civ. Dei* x, 30, 22–26. Pliny, *Nat. hist.* vii, 30, 110 and 31, 1; Plotinus, *Enneads* iii, 5, 1, as referred to in Augustine, ibid. ix, 10, and *Contra acad.* i, 3, 18; and Macrobius, *Comm.*, i, 8, 5. Apuleius, *De Platone et eius dogmate*; on this, Nolhac (1970), ii, pp. 102, 99, n. 2; and Gerosa (1966), p. 249—cf. Augustine, *De civ. Dei* viii, 12, 14 and 19. Macrobius, *Comm.* ii, 15, 18–26. On Porphyry, Augustine, ibid. vii, 25, x, 9–11; and Gerosa, ibid.—Censorinus, *De die natali* 14, 12, Hultsch, p. 27. Josephus Flavius, *Contra Apionem*, Jewish Antiqu. ix, *CSEL* 37, p. 124; on this, Nolhac, ibid., ii, pp. 153–156. Ambrose, *De Abraham* ii, 7, 37, *PL* 14, c. 495; Augustine, *De civ. Dei*, e.g., viii, 4–9, Gerosa, ibid., pp. 248–254; Jerome, *Contra Pelagianos* i, 14, iii, 7, *PL* 23, cc. 603 et seq; on this, Nolhac, ibid., ii, pp. 142–143, 145–148. On Plato, "had he seen Christ," *Prose* (1955), p. 760 = Nachod, p. 115; note also *Rer. mem. libri* i, 25, 18–24.

God of philosophers points to Ciceronian passages such as *De orat.* i, 11, 49; *Ad Att.* iv, 16, 3 (cf. *Fam.* iv, 15, 8); *De nat. deor.* ii, 12, 32; *De leg.* iii, 1, 16; and *De sen.* xiii, 44, where Plato's quip about sensual pleasure being κακὸν δέλεαρ = *esca malorum*—the bait of sin (*Timaeus* 69D)—is called "divine." This is discussed in *Rer. mem. libri* iii, 72. In *Secretum* ii, *Prose* (1955), p. 100, Franciscus refers to Plato's statements as "holy." On this, Rico (1974), pp. 184–185. Note also Augustine, *De civ. Dei* ii, 11 and 14; and *Contra med.* iv, 347–350, Ricci (1950), p. 91.

31   *Secretum* ii, *Prose*, p. 102:

> *Augustinus*: Unum semper ante oculos habeto Platonis superiorem illam haud spernendam esse sententiam: ab agnitione divinitatis nil magis quam appetitus carnales et inflammatam obstare libidinem.

> *Augustine*: Keep ever in mind that saying of Plato we were speaking of just now, "Nothing so much hinders the knowledge of the Divine as lust and the burning desire of carnal passion."

Draper (1911), p. 81.

32   Cited by Nolhac (1907), ii, p. 144, n. 2. Petrarch, who did not know Greek but claimed to possess *aliquot*—several—Platonic texts (Nolhac, ibid., p. 134; *De sui ipsius*, *Prose* [1955], p. 756), may have been acquainted with Henricus Aristippus' translation of the *Meno*. He owned Chalcidius-Timaeus (Paris, B.N., f. lat. 6280) and a Latin translation of the *Phaedo*—the *Hecatonis liber* of the *Rer. mem. libri* ii, 29—also by Henricus Aristippus (Minio-Paluello

[1949]). On this, Weiss (1949), pp. 33–34; Gerosa (1966), pp. 250–251; and Gentile (1936), pp. 5–66. On Petrarch's knowledge of Plato, Nolhac (1907), ii, chap. viii; Weiss (1977), chap. xii.

The Platonic dialogues in which main portions are devoted to sex, and homosexuality in particular, are the *Symposium*, the *Phaedrus*, and, less so, the *Republic* (e.g., 402D–403C; 468B–C) and the *Laws* (636A–D; 835B–842A). Cf. Levinson (1953), *passim*, esp. chaps. 4 and 5. Reason's censure of Platonic love, a perennial argument which has been renewed in our times by a number of writers, among them Chapman (1931) and Popper (1950), may conceivably be based on some of these texts. However, much closer at hand in Petrarch's bibliographic scheme of things, hence more probable, is the *epigramma erotico* attributed to Plato by Aulus Gellius and Macrobius, and, again in the words of Ricci, "accompagnato da un' elegante parafrasi in versi latini" (*Prose* [1955], p. 628, n. 3). Petrarch had Gellius and Macrobius in his library (Nolhac [1907], ii, p. 240), and he knew the Plato story as recorded by Macrobius. On February 9, 1373, Petrarch wrote *Sen.* xv, 11, to Benvenuto da Imola. In the letter, he commented on the distich, or rather its explicit Latin paraphrase, essentially along the same lines as Reason does in the dialogue (1581: 942):

> Neque rursus id mirari conuenit, magnos nonnunquam uiros, non ridiculo tantum, sed obscoeno etiam usos stylo, qualia sunt in Saturnalibus illa Platonica, quae mallem tantus philosophus tacuisset, fert interdum error, quidam interdum feruor animi, quo non decet, et quanquam res malae sint, stylus tamen est bonus, et ars irrepraehensibilis, si ad foeliciorem materiam conuertatur.

> On the other hand, we must not admire some great men for sometimes having written what was not so much ridiculous as obscene. The Platonic lines in the *Saturnalia* are of this nature and I wish the great philosopher had kept quiet. Sometimes it is the perversion, sometimes that passionate fervor of his imagination, which embarrasses, yet, although the subject matter is evil, the style nevertheless is good, and the poetic craftsmanship impeccable—had it only been lavished on a more wholesome theme.

Macrobius, *Saturn.* ii, 2, 15–17, follows closely Gellius, xix, 11.

> Post hunc Horus quoque, 'adfero ad vos,' inquit, 'δίστιχον Platonis, quo ille adulescens luserit cum tragoediis quoque eadem aetate praeluderet:

> τὴν ψυχὴν Ἀγάθωνα φιλῶν ἐπὶ χείλεσιν ἔσχον·
> ἦλθε γὰρ ἡ τλήμων ὡς διαβησομένη'.

(*Anthologia Graeca* v, 78.)

> Orta ex his laetitia et omnibus in censorium risum remissis ac retractantibus quae a singulis antiquae festivitatis sapore prolata sunt, Symmachus ait, 'hos Platonis versiculos, quorum magis venustatem an brevitatem mireris incertum

est, legisse memini in Latinum tanto latius versos quanto solet nostra quam
Graecorum lingua brevior et angustior aestimari; et ut opinor haec verba sunt:

> Dùm sémiúlco sáviò
> meum puellum savior
> dulcemque florem spiritus
> duco ex aperto tramite,
> animula aegra et saucia
> cucurrit ad labias mihi
> rictumque in oris pervium
> et labra pueri mollia
> rimata itineri transitus
> ut transilire nititur.
> Tum si morae quid plusculae
> fuisset in coetu osculi,
> amoris igne percita
> transisset et me linqueret,
> et mira prorsum res foret
> ut ad me fierem mortuus,
> ad puerulum intus viverem.

(Willis, *Saturnalia*, pp. 138–140.)

And [Disarius] was followed by Horus. My contribution, he said, is a couplet
which the famous Plato amused himself by composing in his youth, at the time
when he used also to practice writing tragedies. It runs as follows:

> My soul was on my lips as I was kissing Agathon.
> Poor soul! She came hoping to cross over to him.

These anecdotes gave rise to merriment, and there was polite laughter as all
the company discussed the tales, with their flavor of a bygone gaiety, which
each had told. Then Symmachus said: As for those verses of Plato's it is hard to
say which is the more remarkable, the charm or the conciseness of expression.
I remember having read a Latin version—it is of course longer than the original, since the resources of our language are usually held to be smaller and
more restricted than those of the Greek tongue—and this, I think, is how it
goes:

> While with parted lips I was kissing my love and drawing
> his sweet fragrant breath from his open mouth, my poor,
> my love-sick, wounded soul rushed to my lips as it strove
> to find a way to pass between my open mouth and my love's
> soft lips. Then, had the kiss been, even for a little while,
> prolonged, my soul, smitten with love's fire, would have
> passed through and left me; and (a marvel this!) I should be
> dead—but alive within my love.

Davies (1969), pp. 164–165. It is interesting to note Petrarch's enthusiasm for these quasi-Ausonian, run-on iambic dimeters, which hardly compare to the Ambrosian meter of Christian-Latin poetry (Raby [1953], pp. 35–36 *et passim*)

33   I.t.: Flaccus. Horace, *Sat.* i, 2, 109–110:

> hiscine versiculis speras tibi posse dolores
> atque aestus curasque gravis e pectore pelli?

LCL, Fairclough, p. 27.

34   I.t.: Naso

35   Reference is made to Ovid's *Remedia amoris*—The Remedies of Love; and to Cicero, *Tusc. disp.*, Book iv.

36   Cf., e.g., Celsus, *De medicina* iv, 10, 4.

37   Cf. above, *DR* i, 16, 32, and note 3. Petrarch often uses the phrase or part of it, e.g., *De vita sol.* ii, 12, *Prose* (1955), p. 526. Cf. above, *DR* i, 11, note 18.

38   Cicero, *Tusc. disp.* iv, 35, 76:

> est etiam illud, quod in omni perturbatione dicitur, demonstrandum, nullam esse nisi inopinabilem, nisi iudicio susceptam, nisi voluntariam. Etenim si naturalis amor esset, et amarent omnes et semper amarent et idem amarent, neque alium pudor, alium cogitatio, alium satietas deterreret.

LCL, King, p. 415.

39   Aristotle, *Polit.* v, 11, 1314a, 4–5; Barnes (1984), p. 2086:

> Moreover, the bad are useful for bad purposes; 'nail knocks out nail,' as the proverb says.

Cf. Cicero, ibid. iv, 35, 75; and Ovid, *Rem. am.* 462, as cited in *Secretum* iii, *Prose* (1955), p. 162. Note Jerome, *Ep.* 125, 14, LCL, Wright, p. 421.

40   Cf. *Trionfi*, Tr. cup. iii, 62–66; and *Rime* (1951), p. 497:

> Vedi Assuero il suo amor in qual modo
> va medicando, a ciò che 'n pace il porte:
>   da l' un si scioglie, e lega a l'altro nodo;
> cotal ha questa malizia rimedio
> come d'asse si trae chiodo con chiodo.

> See how Ahasuerus seeks to cure
> His love, that he may find some quietness:
>   One knot he severs, and another ties,
> Finding a remedy for his distress
> E'en as one nail may drive another out.

Wilkins (1962), p. 22. Assuerus (Josephus, *Jewish Antiquities* xi, 2; i Esdr. 4, 6 Esth., esp. ii, 1–16; and Jerome, *Ep.* 125, 14, LCL, Wright, p. 420) is identified with Artaxerxes in the Septuagint, by Josephus, and by other commenta-

tors. The Douay version of the Old Testament notes that Assuerus "is also
. . . named Artaxerxes, by a name common to almost all the kings of Persia."
—On the similar discussion of remedies of love in *Secretum* iii, *Prose* (1955),
pp. 160–188, Rico (1974), pp. 326–329, where in n. 256 the Latin of our
lines 187–233 is reproduced as parallel text. On Petrarch and Josephus
Flavius, Nolhac (1907), ii, pp. 154–156; Sabbadini (1905), esp. p. 28; Sabbadini (1914), esp. p. 264; Ussani (1943–44); and Ullman (1955), p. 181.

41 1492: ualitudo & forma elegans: opes: ocium: Iuuenta:
1581: ualetudo, & forma elegans, ocium, iuuenta.

42 On therapy by contraries, Hippocrates, *Breaths* i, 33–34. Cf. above, *DR* i, 11,
note 19. On old age, the critic of youth, above, *DR* i, 1, 44–46. On bitter
remedies, *Dramatis personae*, note 19.

70 ❖ CHILDREN

1 *angores* (cf. above, *DR* i, 69, note 28). Note Cicero, *Tusc. disp.* iv, 12, 27:

> estque aliud iracundum esse, aliud iratum, ut differt *anxietas* ab *angore*; neque
> enim omnes anxii qui aguntur aliquando nec qui anxii semper aguntur . . .

> and it is one thing to be irascible, another thing to be angry, just as an *anxious
> temper* is different from *feeling anxiety;* for not all men who are at times anx-
> ious are of an anxious temper, nor are those who have an anxious temper
> always feeling anxious . . .

LCL, King, p. 355.

2 1492: Nec timere: nec sperare: nec uota facere noueras
1581: Nec timere, nec sperare, nec nota facere nouerat

3 1492: O matres miserae ait Oratius
1581: O matres miseri ait Horatius

> I cannot find this in Horace. The passage is clearly Statius, *Thebaid* vii, 503,
> where Jocasta says: *a miserae matres!* I have, therefore, taken the liberty of
> changing the text's *Oratius* to *Statius*. (*Thebaid* vii, 478, is quoted in *Fam.*
> xvii, 4, 1. Note also the anaphoric echo in *Sen.* xii, 1 [1581: 901]: *Nisi miseras
> tot alpinas gentes . . . Miseros patres . . . Miseras matronas . . . Miseros
> Gallorum antiquissimos . . . Miseros ad extremum . . . populos orientis.*)

4 Reason refers to the bitter grief of Nestor, *che tanto seppe e tanto visse*—who

knew so much and lived so long (*Trionfi*, Tr. fame ii, 19; Wilkins [1962], p. 79)—about the death at Troy of his son Antilochus, who, trying to save his father's life, "had been killed before his very eyes" by Memnon, the son of Tithonus and Eos, goddess of Dawn (Schwab [1946], p. 512; Graves [1955], ii, 164.e). To these references to Nestor are to be added *DR* ii, 2, 22, ii, 120, 10, and *Fam.* iii, 10, 14, vi, 3, 13, xxiii, 5, 13; Nolhac (1907), ii, 177; and Weiss (1977), p. 173. On Petrarch's Homeric sources, Weiss (1977), esp. chaps. xi, xii. I have been unable to identify Petrarch's immediate source.

5   1492: Foelicitas anxia: sollicitum gaudium: & saepe moestum: foelicitas misera.

1581: Foelicitas anxia, sollicitum gaudium, & saepe moestum gaudium, foelicitas misera.

Cf. line 7, above, and *DR* i, 69, note 2.

6   1492: quod filios habuerunt &c.

1581: quod filios habuerunt.

71 ❖ A FINE YOUNG SON

1   1492: *G*: Infans est mihi bonae spei.
            R: Quid si sit nullius rei. Caduca . . .
    1581: *G*: Infans est.
            R: Caduca . . .

2   1492: sic fere nil amarius
    1581: sic sere nil amarius

3   A paraphrase or corrupt reading of Statius, *Theb.* v, 613–615:

> heu ubi siderei vultus? ubi verba ligatis
> imperfecta sonis risusque et murmura soli
> intellecta mihi?

> Alas, where is that star-bright face? Where are thy
> half-formed words and tongue-tied utterances, those smiles
> and mutterings that I alone could understand?

LCL, Mozley, pp. 47, 49.

4   On *mediocritas*—the Aristotelian notion of μεσότης—above, *DR* i, 2, note 25.

5   I.t.: Verus. *Hist. Aug.*, Hadrian, 23, 11–14:

> adoptavit ergo Ceionium Commodum Verum invitis omnibus cumque Helium
> Verum Caesarem appellavit. . . . quem cum minus sanum videret, saepissime
> dictitavit: "In caducum parietem nos inclinavimus et perdidimus quater milies
> sestertium, quod populo et militibus pro adoptione Commodi dedimus."

> Accordingly, despite the opposition of all, he adopted Ceionius Commodus
> Verus and called him Aelius Verus Caesar. . . . And when he saw that the man
> was diseased, he used often to say: "We have leaned against a tottering wall
> and have wasted the four hundred million sesterces which we gave to the
> populace and the soldiers on the adoption of Commodus."

LCL, Magie, pp. 71, 73. —L. Ceionius Commodus was, not a boy, but the
son-in-law of C. Avidius Nigrinus. He was praetor in A.D. 130 and consul in
136, the year of his adoption. He died January 1, A.D. 138. On Petrarch's
marginalia on Aelius Verus in his copy of the *Historia Augusta* (Paris, B.N., lat
5816, f. 7), Nolhac (1907), ii, p. 54.

6   Virgil, *Aeneid* vi, 869–870:

> ostendent terris hunc tantum fata, nec ultra
> esse sinent.

LCL, Fairclough, p. 569.

72 ❖ BEAUTIFUL CHILDREN

1   Cf. above, *DR* i, 2.
2   Cf. above, *DR* i, 66, 14–16.
3   1492: quidam illesi in finem: inter multorum odia senuere
    1581: quidam illaesi inter multorum odia senuere
4   On Joseph and the wife of Potiphar, Gen. 39. On Hippolytus, son of Theseus,
    who rejected the advances of his stepmother, Phaedra, was falsely accused by
    her, torn to pieces by horses, and miraculously restored to life by Aescula-
    pius, e.g., Ovid, *Metam.* xv, 497–546. Cf. Graves (1955), i, 101. *Fam.* ix, 5,
    47, xviii, 7, 3, *Contra med.* iii, Ricci (1950), 752–754; *Trionfi*, Tr. cup. i, 109–
    117; above, *DR* i, 52, 29–32. Boccaccio, *De casib.*, Hall (1962), f. 7r. On
    Bellerophon and Anteia, Homer, *Iliad* vi, 156–202. Cf. Graves, ibid., 75. For
    other references to Bellerophon, cf. *Fam.* iii, 21, 5; *Secretum* iii, *Prose* (1955),

p. 156, citing Homer, *Iliad* vi, 201–202, after Cicero, *Tusc. disp.* iii, 26, 63; and *Sen.* iii, 1, xi, 5 (1581: 772, 885), the latter referring to Petrarch as *alterum pene Bellerophon*—almost another Bellerophon—as in *Rime* 35 and 129, 2–3, *Rime* (1951), pp. 51, 189. On this, Weiss (1977), p. 184.

5   Here, as in *DR* i, 2, Twyne's text (ff. 97v and 4r) refers to Spurina as female.

6   On Thamar, ii Reg. 13; *Trionfi*, Tr. cup. iii, 46–48. Penelope, e.g., Ovid, *Heroides* i. Cf. Graves (1955), ii, 171. *Fam.* ii, 15, 2, xxi, 12, 1; *Trionfi*, Tr. cup. iii, 22–24, and Tr. pud. 130–135. Lucrece, Livy i, 56–59; Florus, i, 1, 10–11, and 3, 9. Cf. *De viris ill.* v, 1; *Fam.* vi, 2, 7, xviii, 7, 3, xxi, 8, 24, etc; *Rime* 260, *In tale stella*, 9–10; ibid. 262, *Cara la vita*, 9–11; ibid. 360, *Quell' antiquo*, 100; and *Trionfi*, Tr. pud. 130–135. Also Cicero, *De re publ.* ii, 25, and *De fin.* ii, 20, 66; Valerius Maximus, vi, 1, 1; and Boccaccio, *De casib.*, Hall (1962), f. 24v. —On the ages of the world, *DR* i, 16, note 4.

7   *Rostra*: a stage or platform for speakers in the Forum in Rome, from which the assembled people were addressed. Cf., e.g., Cicero, *De off.* iii, 20, 80; and Livy, xxx, 17.

8   *Fam.* xiii, 8 (to Francesco Nelli, Summer 1352), 3:

> postremo nullius usquam mulieris nisi villice mee faciem, quam si videas, soli-tudinem lybicam aut ethiopicam putes te videre, aridam penitus et vere solis ab ardoribus adustam faciem, cui nichil viroris nichil suci inest; faciem qualem si Tyndaris habuisset, Troia nunc etiam staret; si Lucretia et Virginia, nec regno Tarquinius pulsus esset nec Appius vitam in carcere finivisset.

> and no woman's face, except that of my overseer's wife. And if you see that face you would think that you were looking at a Libyan or an Ethiopian desert: a face, dried and burned by the sun, in which there is no vestige of any vital freshness, a face such that if Helen, the daughter of Tyndareus, had had it, Troy would still be standing; and if Lucretia or Virginia had had it, Tarquin would not have been driven from the kingdom, and Appius would not have ended his life in prison.

Wilkins (1958b), pp. 119–120. Cf. also *Fam.* vi, 2, 9; *Trionfi*, Tr. pud. 130–135; and *Rime* (1951), p. 567, 79–81. For the story, see Livy, iii, 44–59; Florus, i, 17, 24; and Boccaccio, *De casib.*, Hall (1962), ff. 28r–29r.

9   1492: quare effectus formae bonos quos inueneris renuncia: ut cum contrariis comparentur.
     1581: Quare effectus formae bonos quos inueheris, renuncia, ut cum contrariis comparentur.

10   On Messalina, wife of Emperor Claudius (above, *DR* i, 52, note 11), Juvenal, vi, 115–132:

> respice rivales divorum, Claudius audi
> quae tulerit. Dormire virum cum senserat uxor,
> ausa Palatino tegetem praeferre cubili,
> sumere nocturnos meretrix Augusta cucullos

linquebat comite ancilla non amplius una.
Sed nigrum flavo crinem abscondente galero
intravit calidum veteri centone lupanar
et cellam vacuam atque suam; tunc nuda papillis
prostitit auratis titulum mentita Lyciscae
ostenditque tuum, generose Britannice, ventrem.
Excepit blanda intrantis atque aera poposcit;
mox lenone suas iam dimittente puellas
tristis abit, et quod potuit tamen ultima cellam
clausit, adhuc ardens rigidae tentigine volvae,
et lassata viris necdum satiata recessit,
obscurisque genis turpis fumoque lucernae
foeda lupanaris tulit ad pulvinar odorem.

Then look at those who rival the Gods, and hear what Claudius endured. As soon as his wife perceived that her husband was asleep, this august harlot was shameless enough to prefer a common mat to the imperial couch. Assuming a night-cowl, and attended by a single maid, she issued forth; then, having concealed her raven locks under a light-colored peruque, she took her place in a brothel reeking with long-used coverlets. Entering an empty cell reserved for herself, she there took her stand, under the feigned name of Lycisca, her nipples bare and gilded, and exposed to view the womb that bore thee, O nobly-born Britannicus! Here she graciously received all comers, asking from each his fee; and when at length the keeper dismissed his girls, she remained to the very last before closing her cell, and with passion still raging hot within her went sorrowfully away. Then exhausted by men but unsatisfied, with soiled cheeks, and begrimed with the smoke of lamps, she took back to the imperial pillow all the odours of the stews.

LCL, Ramsay, p. 93.

11   1492: adulterio autem nihil praeter exiguam laeti morulam quaesierit
1581: adulterio autem nihil exiguam laeti morulam quaesierit.

Cf. *Fam.* x, 5, 14:

voluptas blanda sed brevis, dulce principium amari exitus.

alluring pleasure, but only for a short while, a sweet beginning with a bitter end.

12   Portions of the entire dialogue but, in particular, lines 27–45 are clearly based on Juvenal, x, 289–345.

13   On the three heroes and seducers of mythology, Graves (1955), ii, §§ 148–157 (Jason), i, §§ 95–104 (Theseus), and i, §§ 159–166 (Paris). Cf. also *Fam.* x, 5, 14; and *Trionfi*, Tr. cup. i, 116, 128–132, 136–140.

14   This is either the text of Petrarch's Latin source for Homer, *Iliad* xxiv, 258–259:

and Hektor, who was a god among men, for he did not seem like
one who was child of a mortal man, but of a god. . . .

Lattimore (1951), p. 482; or a paraphrase current in Petrarch's time. Dante
adapted it to Beatrice in his *Vita nuova* ii, 8:

> che certo di lei si poeta dire quella parola
> del poeta Omero: "Ella non parea figliuola
> d'uomo mortale, ma di deo."

Opere (1921), p. 4. In *Conv.* iv, 20, 4, and *Mon.* ii, 3, 9, Dante acknowledges
that the Homer quotation comes from Aristotle, *Eth. Nic.* vii, 1, a Latin version of which was also in Petrarch's library. On Petrarch and Homer, Weiss
(1977), chaps. 11, 12; and Nolhac (1907), ii, esp. pp. 156–188. On our passage, ibid., pp. 168–169; and Koerting (1878), p. 478.

73 ❖ A STERLING SON

1   On *fortitudo*—courage—above, *DR* i, Pref., note 53.
2   I think Creon's son referred to is Menoeceus/Megareus (Oates [1938], i, p.
    460, n. 3), who killed himself before the gates of Thebes in accordance with
    Teiresias' prophecy (Statius, *Theb.* x; Lactantius, *Div. inst.* iii, 12, *PL* 6, c. 381;
    Graves [1955], ii, 106.j.). Petrarch cites the Seven Against Thebes in *DR* i, 84.
    —The death of Pallas is described in Virgil, *Aeneid* x, esp. 474–500. Cf. also
    Trionfi, Tr. cup. i, 106–108.
3   Homer, *Iliad* xxii, 37–40, 79–85:

> The old man stretching his hands out called pitifully to him:
> 'Hektor, beloved child, do not wait the attack of this man
> alone, away from the others. You might encounter your destiny
> beaten down by Peleion, since he is far stronger than you are.'
>
> . . . .
>   . . . his mother in tears was mourning
> and laid the fold of her bosom bare and with one hand held out
> a breast, and wept her tears for him and called to him in winged words:
> 'Hektor, my child, look upon these and obey, and take pity
> on me, if ever I gave you the breast to quiet your sorrow.
> Remember all these things, dear child, and from inside the wall
> beat off this grim man. Do not go out as champion against him.'

Lattimore (1951), pp. 436–437; Nolhac (1907), ii, p. 169. —Reason refers to three speeches by Priam, Hekabe, and Andromache (Lattimore, ibid., and p. 448) in the climactic Book xxii of the *Iliad*, which describes the death of Hector at the hands of Achilles.

4   This seems to be the text of Petrarch's Latin source for *Iliad* vi, 406–408; Lattimore (1951), p. 164. Cf. Nolhac, as above, note 3; and Koerting (1878), p. 478.

5   Statius, *Achill*. i, 37–38:

> iam pelago terrisque meus quaereretur Achilles.
> Et volet ipse sequi.

LCL, Mozley, p. 511.

6   *Dumque illum frustra iam ferventis belli motibus ereptum: & imbellem tranquilli senis in regiam invectum virgineis latebris occultaret*

Twyne, f. 99r: Whilst in vain she tooke hym, being feeble, out of the garboyle of the hotte warres, and carrying hym into the pallace of the calme olde man, hyd hym up in her virgins secrete closets.

On Thetis, the mother of Achilles, Graves (1955), ii, 160.j.

7   1492: sed praecipue mors declarat
    1581: sed praecipue mos declarat

8   *nihil imbecillius homine: nilque superbius* —Cf. Homer, *Odyssey* xviii, 130, as below, *DR* ii, 111, note 5; Seneca, *Dial*. vi, Ad Marc., 11, 3–5; and Boethius, *Cons. phil*. ii, P 6, 18–21. Note *monstrum est superbus homuncio*, below, *DR* ii, 111, 43–44.

74 ❖ A VIRTUOUS DAUGHTER

1   Cf. above, *DR* i, 54, 30–34, i, 65, 11–13, i, 66, 3, etc.

2   Virgil, *Aeneid* iv, 569–570:

> . . .   . . . varium et mutabile semper
> femina.

LCL, Fairclough, p. 435. Related, Seneca, *De rem. fort*. xvi, 4, Haase, iii (1886), p. 456.

3   I.t.: Maro

75 ❖ A WONDERFUL SON-IN-LAW

1   On Agrippa, Suetonius, ii, Aug. On Marcus Aurelius, *Hist. Aug.*, M. Aurel. Antoninus, esp. v, vi, vii.
2   I.e., from Hadrian's death, July 10, A.D. 138, to that of Antoninus Pius, March 7, A.D. 161. Cf. *Hist. Aug.*, ibid., vi, 1; Anton. Pius, xii, 4.
3   Suetonius v, Claudius; ibid. vi, Nero, esp. v, 26–27, vi, 7–8, and 33.
4   On Julius Caesar and his son-in-law Pompey, Harvey (1974), art. Caesar; and Hadas (1956), pp. 73–79.
5   Above, *DR* i, 65, 76–77, and note 12.
6   Orosius, *Historiarum adversus paganos libri vii*, *PL* 31, cc. 663–1174; CSEL, ed. Zangemeister (1882), vii, 24–25:

> In the one thousand and thirty-ninth year after the founding of the City, Carus of Narbo took up the power as the thirty-second emperor and held it for two years [A.D. 282–283]. When he had made his sons, Carinus and Numerian, colleagues in his rule [A.D. 283–285, 283–284, respectively], and after he had captured two very famous cities, Coche and Ctesiphon, in a war against the Parthians, in a camp upon the Tigris he was struck by lightning and killed. Numerian, who had been with his father, was treacherously killed, while re-treating, by his father-in-law [Arrius] Aper. In the one thousand and forty-first year after the founding of the City, Diocletian was chosen as the thirty-third emperor by the army and was emperor for 20 years [A.D. 284–305], and as soon as he had full power he immediately, with his own hand, killed Aper, the murderer of Numerian.

R. Deferrari (1964), p. 320. Cf. Hadas (1956), p. 174.

Stilicho, the Vandal general who defeated Alaric at Pollentia, April 6, A.D. 402, was married to Serena, niece and adopted daughter of Theodosius I. He was executed upon the orders of Emperor of the West, Honorius, his son-in-law, on August 23, A.D. 408. Petrarch refers to Stilicho and his poetic biographer, Claudian, in a fragmentary appendage to the *Triumphus fame* of 1371 (*Rime* [1951], p. 575, 67–69) and in *Fam.* vi, 3, 35. Contrary to Reason's assessment of Stilicho, which echoes Jerome, *Ep.* 123, 17, and Orosius, vii, 38, Gibbon remarked in his *Decline and Fall of the Roman Empire* (chap. xxx):

> The services of Stilicho are great and manifest, his crimes, as they are vaguely stated in the language of flattery and hatred, are obscure, at least, and improb-able. . . .   . . . The pride and power of Stilicho constituted his real guilt.

Bury, iii (1909), pp. 296–297.

76 ❖ A SECOND MARRIAGE

1   Twyne, f. 100v., omits this sentence. Suetonius, viii, Vespasian, 3:

> Ex hac liberos tulit Titum et Domitianum et Domitillam. Uxori ac filiae super-
> stes fuit atque utramque adhuc privatus amisit. Post uxoris excessum
> Caenidem, Antoniae libertam et a manu, dilectam quondam sibi revocavit in
> contubernium habuitque etiam imperator paene iustae uxoris loco.

> By her [Flavia Domitilla] he had three children, Titus, Domitian, and Domitilla.
> He outlived his wife and daughter; in fact lost them both before he became
> emperor. After the death of his wife he resumed his relations with Caenis,
> freedwoman and amanuensis of Antonia, and formerly his mistress; and even
> after he became emperor he treated her almost as a lawful wife.

LCL, Rolfe, p. 287.

The extramarital arrangement of the elder Stefano Colonna (Billanovich
[1981], p. 204) is also acknowledged in an autograph note in Petrarch's copy
of the *Historia Augusta* (Paris, B.N., lat. 5816, f. 15v; Nolhac [1907], ii, p. 56).
The topic of *ne sit ancillae tibi amor pudori*—let not affection for thy hand-
maiden put thee to the blush (Horace, Carm. ii, 4, 1, LCL, Bennett, p. 117)—
occurs in *Rime* 360, 93–94, where, Nolhac points out, a reference to a lowly
love affair by

il più chiaro
un altro e di vertute e di fortuna

(*Rime* [1951], p. 463), which is commonly associated with Scipio Africanus
and a slave girl, may constitute a double entendre aimed at Stefano Colonna
(Nolhac· [1907], ii, p. 56, n.2). On the elder Stefano, cf. *Fam.* viii, 1; and
above, *DR* i, 35, and note 9. On Reason's ironic *litotes*—understatement—
Lausberg (1960), pp. 304–305; and Green (1979), pp. 189–194.

2   I Cor. 7, 8–9:

> Dico autem non nuptis, et viduis: Bonum
> est illis si sic permaneant, sicut et ego.
> Quod si non se continent, nubant;
> melius est enim nubere quam uri.

> But I say to the unmarried, and to the widows:
> It is good for them if they so continue, even as I.
> But if they do not contain themselves, let them marry.
> For it is better to marry than to be burnt.

Cf. Jerome, *Ep.* 77, 3, LCL, Wright, p. 314, and Wiesen (1964), pp. 115–116; and Innocent III, *De miseria cond. hum.* i, 16, Lewis (1978), p. 119.

3   Cf. below, *DR* ii, 21, 49–52. On this, Wiesen (1964), chap. iv: Women and Marriage. On the topic *virile: prudence and steadfastness* in later literature, note, e.g., Boccaccio, *Corbaccio*, Cassell (1975), pp. 33–34; Christine de Pizan, *Livre des Trois Vertus* (1405) iii, 4, Willard (1984), pp. 48, 151.

4   1492: actum
     1581: auctum

5   1492: uulnerat &c.
     1581: uulnerat.

77 ❖ THE MARRIAGE OF ONE'S CHILDREN

1   1492: provide
     1581: proinde

2   Above, *DR* i, 75, 1–4.

3   *fons curarum*—wellspring of worries. Cf. above, *DR* i, 70, 9.

4   Cf. above, *DR* i, 65, 13–24, and 66, 11–12.

5   *Illum sibi salvis vobis interdictum videns quid nunc animo volvat: et quid oret: haud difficilis coniectura est.*

     Twyne, f. 101v.: For in case she perceyve herselfe (by meanes of your lyfe) debarred thereof, what she imagineth then in her mynde, and what she wysheth, it were an harde matter to coniecture.

6   1492: Egyptus
     1581: Aegisthus

7   A reference to the Danaids. Cf. above, *DR* i, 65, note 12.

8   1492: & secundae sortis impatientia
     1581: & secundi fortis impatientia.

9   Florus, i, 1, 7, 1–3:

     Postremus fuit omnium regum Tarquinius, cui cognomen Superbo ex moribus datum. Hic regnum avitum, quod a Servio tenebatur, rapere maluit quam expectare, missisque in eum percussoribus scelere partam potestatem non melius egit quam adquisiverat. Nec abhorrebat moribus uxor Tullia, quae, ut virum regem salutaret, supra cruentum patrem vecta carpento consternatos equos exegit.

The last of all the kings [of Rome] was that Tarquinius to whom the name Superbus was given on account of his character. He preferred to seize rather than to wait for the kingdom of his grandfather which was held by Servius [Tullius], and, having sent assassins to murder him, administered the power thus won by crime no more righteously than he had acquired it. His wife Tullia was of like character, and, driving in her chariot to hail her husband as king, forced her affrighted horses over the bloodstained corpse of her father [534 B.C.].

LCL, Forster, p. 23. Cf. Livy, i, 47–48, and 59, 10; Valerius Maximus, ix, 11, 1; and *Fam.* vi, 2, 6.

78 ❖ GRANDCHILDREN, NEPHEWS AND NIECES

1   Num. 1, 45–46:

> Fueruntque omnis numerus filiorum Israel per domos et familias suas a vigesimo anno et supra, qui poterant ad bella procedere,
> sexcenta tria millia virorum quingenti quinquaginta.

> And the whole number of the children of Israel
> by their houses and families, from twenty years old
> and upward, that were able to go to war,
> Were six hundred and three thousand five hundred and fifty men.

2   Cf. above, *DR* i, 11, note 22.

3   1492: uarii: subiti: et inopini hominum casus
     1581: uarii, subditi, et inopi hominum casus

4   On Lucan, cf. Suetonius, *Lucanus*, and *Persius*; and Juvenal, vii, 79–80. On Jugurtha, Florus, i, 36; Sallust, *Jug.*; and Juvenal, vi, 169. The uppermost example of Libyan treachery probably refers to the Second Punic War and the treason of Syphax. Cf. *Africa*, esp., v; and *De viris ill.*, Scipio, vi, 47 et seq.

5   Both 1492 and 1581 read Pseusippus for Speusippus (Cicero, *De orat.* iii, 18, 67),

> the son of Plato's sister who, after Plato's death, together with Xenocrates, succeeded him in his school which was called the Academy, for which reason they were called Academics.

Augustine, *De civ. Dei* viii, 12, LCL, Wiesen, p. 57. Cf. Dante, *Conv.* iv, 6, 14:

> E questi furono Academici chiamati, si come fue Platone
> e Speusippo suo nepote: chiamati per luogo così dove Plato
> studiava, cioè Academia.

Opere (1921), p. 257; John of Salisbury, *Policrat.* vii, 6, *PL* 199, c. 648.
On Alcibiades, cf. Nepos, vii; and *Trionfi*, Tr. fame, ii, 25–27, *Rime* (1951), p. 537. On Junius Brutus, first consul of the Romans, Livy, i, 60, 1–3; Florus, i, 2–3. Also Valerius Maximus, vii, 2; *Fam.* vi, 2, 7; and *De vir. ill.* v.

6   Cf. Horace, *Ep.* ii, 1, 50–55; Gellius, *passim.* On Ennius, also *Africa* ix, 1–328. Pacuvius was the nephew of Ennius (Pliny, *Nat. hist.* xxxv, 7, 19). On both, Harvey (1974), arts. Ennius, Pacuvius.

7   *Hist. Aug.*, Severus Alexander, ix, 1–2:

> si pietatem, quid Pio sanctius? si doctrinam, quid Marco prudentius? si in-
> nocentiam, quid Vero simplicius? si fortitudinem, quid Bassanio fortius? nam
> Commodi meminisse nolo, qui hoc ipso deterior fuit quod cum illis moribus
> Antonini nomen obtinuit.

> If you think of righteousness, who was more holy than Pius? If of learning, who
> more wise than Marcus? If of innocence, who more honest than Verus? If of
> bravery, who more brave than Bassanius? For on Commodus I have no wish to
> dwell, who was the more depraved for this very reason, that with those evil
> ways of his he still held the name of Antoninus.

LCL, Magie, p. 193. Cf. also ibid., Commodus and Hadas (1956), pp. 137–140.

8   On Romulus and Remus, Numitor, Ancus Martius, and Numa, Livy, i, *passim;* Florus, i, 1; and Hadas (1956), pp. 2–11. For the modern reader, the story of Astyages and Cyrus, which Petrarch knew from Justin's abridgment of Trogus (i, 4–6), Valerius Maximus (e.g., i, 7, 5), etc., is best available in Herodotus i, 107–130, Godolphin (1942), i, pp. 48–58. Boccaccio retells it briefly in *De casib.*, Hall (1962), f. 20r.

79 ❖ ADOPTED CHILDREN AND STEPCHILDREN

1   On Nerva, who adopted Trajan, cf. *Hist. Aug.*, Hadrian, ii, 5. On Trajan's adoption of Hadrian (A.D. 117), ibid., iv, 6–10. On Agrippa, Suetonius, ii,

Aug., 65. Augustus' *own words* could be his addition to the official adoption formula for Tiberius: *hoc rei publicae causa facio*—This I do for reasons of state—reported by Velleius Paterculus (ii, 104, 1, LCL, Shipley, p. 265). On the last will of Augustus, Suetonius, ii, Aug., 101; and *Res gestae divi Augusti*, Shipley, pp. 332–333. Cf. Hadas (1956), pp. 102–103.

2   Above, *DR* i, 78, 35–37.

3   Sallust, Jugurtha ix, 3 through x, 8:

> Igitur rex . . . statimque eum adoptavit et testamento pariter cum filiis heredem instituit. Sed ipse paucos post annos morbo atque aetate confectus cum sibi finem vitae adesse intellegeret, coram amicis et cognatis itemque Adherbale et Hiempsale filiis dicitur huiuscemodi verba cum Iugurtha habuisse. "Parvom ego, Iugurtha, te amisso patre sine spe sine opibus in regnum meum accepi, existumans non minus me tibi, quam si genuissem, ob beneficia carum fore. Neque ea res falsum me habuit. . . . Nunc, quoniam mihi natura finem vitae facit, per hanc dexteram, per regni fidem moneo obtestorque te, uti hos, qui tibi genere propinqui, beneficio meo fratres sunt, caros habeas neu malis alienos adiungere quam sanguine coniunctos retinere. . . . Equidem ego vobis regnum trado firmum, si boni eritis, sin mali, imbecillum. Nam concordia parvae res crescunt, discordia maxumae dilabuntur. Ceterum ante hos te, Iugurtha, qui aetate et sapientia prior es, ne aliter quid eveniat providere decet. Nam in omni certamine qui opulentior est, etiam si accipit iniuriam, tamen, quia plus potest, facere videtur. Vos autem, Adherbal et Hiempsal, colite, observate talem hunc virum, imitamini virtutem et enitimini *ne ego meliores liberos* sumpsisse *videar quam genuisse.*"

> Then the king . . . adopted [Jugurtha] at once and in his will named him joint heir with his sons. But a few years later and upon his own motion the king, then enfeebled by years and illness and realizing that the end of his life was near, is said to have talked with Jugurtha in the presence of his friends and kinfolk, including his sons Adherbal and Hiempsal, in some such terms as the following. "When you were a small boy, Jugurtha, an orphan without prospects or means, I took you into the royal household, believing that because of my kindness you would love me as if you were my own child. And I was not mistaken. . . . Now, since nature is bringing my life to its close, I conjure and implore you by this right hand, by the loyalty due to the kingdom, hold dear these youths who are your kinsmen by birth and through my favour are your brothers; and do not desire to make new friends among strangers in preference to keeping the love of those who are bound to you by ties of blood. . . . I deliver to you three a realm that is strong if you prove virtuous, but weak if you do ill; for harmony makes small states great, while discord undermines the mightiest empires. As for the rest, it devolves upon you, Jugurtha, rather than upon these children, since you are older and wiser than they, to see to it that my hopes are not disappointed. For in all strife the stronger, even though he suffer wrong, is looked upon as the aggressor because of his superior power. As for you, Adherbal and Hiempsal, love and respect this great man, emulate his virtues, and strive to show that I did not adopt better children than I begat."

LCL, Rolfe, pp. 147, 149, 151.

4   Twyne, ff. 103r–103v, translates *privignus* as son-in-law, and *vitricus* as father-in-law.

5   On Drusus, the son of Tiberius Claudius Nero and Livia, hence stepson of Augustus, Suetonius, ii, Aug., 101. On Claudius and Nero, ibid., v, Claudius, 27, 2, and above, *DR* i, 75, note 3.

80 ❖ AN EXCELLENT TEACHER

1   Cf. above, *DR* i, 2, note 26.
2   The topic is dealt with at length in *DR* i, 16. Cf. also *DR* i, 11, 40–41, and 48, 20–23.
3   Below, *DR* i, 81.
4   Cf. above, *DR* i, 15, 99–108.
5   Reason's remark is probably aimed at Virgil's text proper. Petrarch knew the Virgil biography by Aelius Donatus (Vat. lat. 1575; Sabbadini [1905] p. 217; Nolhac [1907], i, pp. 124–125) and may have been aware of the passage which mentions that Virgil *a Scirone audivit quidem praecepta Epicura*— learned from Siron some of the ideas of Epicure (Fabricius [1773], i, p. 349). On the various redactions of this biography, Sabbadini (1914), p. 219; and idem (1906), pp. 193–198.

    Horace, *Ep.* ii, 1, 69–71, does mention the grammarian Orbilius as the teacher:

> non equidem insector delendave carmina Livi
> esse reor, memini quae *plagosum* mihi parvo
> Orbilium dictare . . .

> Mark you! I am not crying down the poems of Livius—
> I would not doom to destruction verses which I remember
> Orbilius of the rod dictated to me as a boy . . .

LCL, Fairclough, p. 403; cited *Fam.* xii, 3, 18. On Lucius Orbilius, *cruel by nature*, and his Horatian nickname, Suetonius, *De gramm.* ix; and Jerome, *Adv. Rufin.* i, 30.

6   Cicero, *De div.* i, 3, 5:

> Cratippus quoque familiaris noster, quem ego
> parem summis Peripateticis iudico . . .

> and my intimate friend Cratippus, whom I
> consider the peer of the greatest of the Peripatetics . . .

LCL, Falconer, p. 229. On the education of Cicero's only son, e.g., Cicero, *De off.* i, 1, 1:

> Quamquam te, Marce fili, annum iam audientem Cratippum, idque Athenis, abundare oportet praeceptis institutisque philosophiae propter summam et doctoris auctoritatem et urbis, quorum alter te scientia augere potest, altera exemplis . . .

> My dear son Marcus, you have now been studying a full year under Cratippus, and that too in Athens, and you should be fully equipped with the practical precepts and the principles of philosophy; so much at least one might expect from the pre-eminence not only of your teacher but also of the city; the former is able to enrich you with learning, the latter to supply you with models.

LCL, Miller, p. 3. Note Pliny, *Nat. hist.* xiv, 28, 147; and the discussion in *Fam.* xxiii, 12, 29–36.

7   Cf. above, *DR* i, 15, 59–61, etc.
8   *quorum alter libris eminus, alter verbis cominus in eum incubuerat.*
9   Reason seems to think of *pathētikos nous*—passive intellect—and *poiētikos nous*—active intellect—in Aristotle's notion of the agent intellect which illuminates the passive object, i.e., effects the intelligible and "makes us know, just as light makes us see" (Randall [1960], pp. 99–100). Cf. Aristotle, *De anima* iii, 2, and 4–5; and Gilson (1956), chap. 6, esp. pp. 209–210.
10   But note below, *DR* i, 119, esp. 21.

81 ❖ A REMARKABLE PUPIL

1   Juvenal, vii, 240–241:

> . . . tot puerorum
> observare manus oculosque in fine trementis.

LCL, Ramsay, p. 157.

2   1492: in praeceptores
     1581: praeceptores
3   "Epistola Plutarchi instruentis Traianum" in the *Institutio Traiani*, a late Latin compilation ascribed to Plutarch:

Tuae itaque virtuti congratulor, et fortunae meae, si tamen recte gesseris, quem probe meruisti. Alioquin te periculis, et me detrahentium linguis subiectum iri non dubito, cum et ignaviam imperatorum Roma non ferat, et sermo publicus delicta discipulorum refundere soleat in praeceptores. Sic *Seneca* Neronis sui merito detrahentium carpitur linguis, adolescentium suorum temeritas in *Quintilianum* refunditur, et *Socrates* in pupillum suum fuisse clementior criminatur.

Therefore I congratulate you upon your excellence and myself upon my good fortune, provided you will continue the righteous conduct which has made you so richly deserving. Otherwise, without the slightest doubt, you will be exposed to dangers and I to critical remarks by the detractors, since Rome does not tolerate worthless emperors and *public gossip is wont to ascribe the crimes of the pupils to their teachers*. Thus *Seneca* is justly censured by the slurs of the critics of his pupil Nero [cf. *Fam.* xxiv, 5], *Quintilian* blamed for the rashness of his young students, and *Socrates* denounced for having been too soft on his ward.

(Plutarch, *Moralia* [Gregorius N. Bernardakis], *Institutio Traiani* ii, 7–16, vol. vii, p. 183.) Quintilian's young students were the grandsons of Emperor Domitian's sister, Domitilla (*Fam.* xxiv, 7, 10). The ward of Socrates is either Alcibiades or Critias (cf. above, DR i, 15, 101–103).
    Petrarch quoted the *Epistola Traiani* in his letter to Quintilian, *Fam.* xxiv, 7, 10:

> ut statim post Plutarchus ad Traianum scribit, *tuorum adulescentium temeritas in te refunditur;*

As somewhat later Plutarch wrote to Trajan, you were blamed for the rashness of your young students;

and again in *Fam.* xi, 5 (to the Florentines, 1351), 4:

> ut Traianum principem Plutarchus alloquitur *et virtuti vestre gratulor et fortune mee.*

as Plutarch told prince Trajan, I congratulate you upon your excellence and myself upon my good fortune.

Fam. xviii, 16, to the Doge Andrea Dandolo (Milan, May 28, 1354), 30, notes:

> . . . ut a Plutarcho philosopho aliquid sumam, tuque sis hodie Traianus meus.

> . . . that I have taken something from the philosopher Plutarch and you should be today my Trajan.

Petrarch may have owned a copy of the *Institutio Traiani*. On this, Nolhac (1907), ii, pp. 122–128; Cosenza (1910), pp. 55–56, n. 3, pp. 98–99, n. 10; and Hortis (1879), pp. 30–31. The texts Petrarch used were also available in John of Salisbury's *Policraticus*, Book v of which deals with the *Institutio* (PL

199, c. 539; on John himself being the author of the *Institutio* and the subse-
quent debate, Wilks [1984], esp. pp. 32–33, 194–196, 203–206, and
Kantorowicz [1957a], p. 94, n. 20; on Petrarch's quotations from the *Institutio*,
Momigliano [1955]; note also Weiss [1977], chap. xiv, and Billanovich [1981], p.
138, n. 1). Petrarch's acquaintance with John of Salisbury's work is indicated in
Fam. ix, 5, to Ugolino dei Rossi, Bishop of Parma (December 28, 1351), 28:

> Sed hoc Hadriani quarti dictum minus vulgatum est, quod inter philosophicas
> nugas legi.

> Less widely known is this statement of [Pope] Adrian IV [1154–1159], which I
> have read in the philosophical *nugae*—trifles.

The *Policraticus* is subtitled *sive de nugis curialium et vestigiis philosophorum*—Or Trifles of Courtiers and Footsteps of the Philosophers. The passage referred to is *Policrat.* viii, 23, PL 199, c. 814. Another passage (vii, 6,
ibid., c. 647), is quoted in *Fam.* v, 1, 3, and xv, 7, 10. Heitmann (1957, p. 22)
fails to consider these circumstances when he refers only to Quintilian's note
"che l'imperatore Domiziano gli ha affidato l'educazione dei suoi nepoti,"
and derives from this December 1350—the date of Petrarch's finding an
incomplete copy of Quintilian in Lapo da Castiglionchio's library (Wilkins
[1961], p. 94)—as a *terminus post quem* for the dating of the *DR*.

Petrarch's acquaintance with the *Policraticus* serves to underscore the
need for a careful, close reading of Petrarchan texts, such as the well-known
passage in *Sen.* iv, 5 (1581: 788; Nolhac [1907], i, pp. 135–139), in which
Petrarch discusses the historical impossibility of the meeting in Virgil's
Aeneid of Dido and Aeneas, born three hundred years apart, and the conster-
nation he created among the *literati* of his day when he first pointed this out.
He acknowledges the supporting remarks to this effect in Macrobius (*Saturn.*
v, 17, 5–6); Virgil commentaries (Servius, *Ad Aen.* iv, 459); Augustine, *Conf.*
(i, 13, 22, PL 32, c. 671); and Justin-Trogus, xviii (4–6) but fails to mention
John of Salisbury, *Policrat.* viii, 14, PL 199, c. 768. This may be simply an
oversight. Yet Petrarch establishes his own priority with an assiduous, and
possibly ironic, circumspection that may indicate his awareness of the great
Chartrian bishop, who anticipated his statement—some two hundred years
earlier, and did so outside Italy—when he writes:

> . . . ego enim primus imo solus, hac aetate, & his locis mendacium hoc
> discussi.

> . . . But I am the one and only person in this age and in these parts who has
> exposed this lie.

Cf. also *Africa* iii, Bergin, 524–536. On this, Hollander (1977), pp. 171–173.
On the influence of John of Salisbury on medieval Italian jurists, W. Ullmann
(1944); and idem (1978).

4   On the *chimera*, a "fire-breething she-monster with lion's head, goat's body, and serpent's tail," which Bellerophon slew, Graves (1955), i, 75. Note also the gloss to Virgil, *Aeneid* vi, 288 in *Comm. Enn.*, Jones (1977), p. 72.

5   1492: puer mihi creditus me ueretur
    1581: pueri mihi creditus me uetur

6   Is this a reference to a fresco painting that fades when the wall upon which it is painted is not free from dampness, i.e., not finished? Cf. Anthony (1951), p. 64.

7   Virgilius Wellendorffer, *Heptalogium* (Leipzig, Melchior Lotter, 1502), f. 96r, quotes the preceding two sentences in support of the notion *nihil igitur est faciendum dicendum repugnante minerva*—that nothing can be accomplished by teaching when Minerva objects. Cf. Rawski (1967), p. 154, n. 17. On the topic *ars-natura*, cf. above, *DR* i, 20, note 8; i, 39, note 4.

8   *intra esse.* Cf. Gerosa (1966), p. 353; and above, *DR* i, 11, note 10. In *Fam.* xii, 3, to the Florentine schoolteacher Zanobi da Strada (Avignon, April 1, 1352 (Wilkins [1955], pp. 115, 171), Petrarch relates and supports the opinion of Niccolò Acciaiuoli (Wilkins [1961], pp. 111, 114) that Zanobi should leave teaching kids to those *qui maiora non possunt*—who can do nothing greater; instead, *surge, circumspice teque ipsum nosse incipe et quam viribus assume materiam*—rise up, look around you, begin to know yourself, and take on a subject equal to your strength (Horace, *Ars poet.* 38–39, as below *DR* ii, 117, note 21).

82 ❖ A GOOD FATHER

1   1492: caro lateri
    1581: charo latere

83 ❖ A MOST LOVING MOTHER

1   I.e., Lago Trasimeno or Lago di Perugia, the scene of Hannibal's victory over the Romans. Livy, xxii, 4–7; Florus, i, 22, 13; *De vir. ill.* xvii, 30–35.

2   *De vir. ill.* xvii, 35:

due matres uno die, filiis totidem quos occisos audierant preter spem repertis, repentino gaudio exanimate sunt.

On the same day two mothers expired because of too much joy, when their sons, who, they had heard, were killed, unexpectedly returned to them.

On dying of joy, *DR* i, 23, 28, and note 13, i, 29, 39–47, and note 9, and below, i, 90, 36–49.

84 ❖ DEAR BROTHERS AND SISTERS

1   Ovid, *Metam.* i, 145.

> . . .   . . .   fratrum quoque gratia rara est.

Cf. above, *DR* i, 52, 48.

2   I.e., Atreus and Thyestes (Graves [1955], ii, 111); Eteocles and Polyneices (ibid., 106); Romulus and Remus (e.g., Livy, i, 3; and Hadas [1956], pp. 2–6).
3   I.e., Cain and Abel, Gen. 4.
4   1581 omits the name Phraates.
5   Above, *DR* i, 52, 38–43.
6   Justin, xlii, 4, 13 through 5, 12. Cf. Horace, *Carm.* ii, 2, 17.
7   Pliny, *Nat. hist.* xxxiii, 19, 59–60:

> sed quia rerum uni nihil igne deperit, tuto etiam in incendiis rogisque. Quin immo quo saepius arsit, proficit ad bonitatem, aurique experimentum ignis est, ut simili colore rubeat ignescatque et ipsum; obrussam vocant. Primum autem bonitatis argumentum quam difficillime accendi. Praeterea mirum prunae vi- olentissimi ligni indomitum palea citissime ardescere atque, ut purgetur, cum plumbo coqui.

> but because gold is the only thing that loses no substance by the action of fire, but even in conflagrations and on funeral pyres receives no damage. Indeed as a matter of fact it improves in quality the more often it is fired, and fire serves as a test of its goodness, making it assume a similar red hue and itself becomes the colour of fire; this process is called assaying. The first proof of quality in gold is however its being affected by fire with extreme difficulty; beside that, it is remarkable that though invincible to live coal made of the hardest wood it is very quickly made red hot by a fire of chaff, and that for the purpose of purifying it it is roasted with lead.

LCL, Rackham, pp. 47, 49. Cf. also Job 23, 10; Sap. 3, 6; Zach. 13, 9; i Petr. 1, 7; and Whiting (1968), S 298.

8   *divini omnis humanique iuris* [cf. *Fam.* x, 3, 36]: *dum expleri studet immemor.* Cf. the standard definition of *iurisprudentia* as *divinarum humanarumque rerum notitia iusti atque iniusti scientia*—the knowledge of things divine and human and the science of what is just and what is unjust (Dig. 1, 1, 10, § 2 = Inst. i, 1, 1; Sohm [1931], pp. 11–15, 89–108)—a definition which Petrarch may well have remembered from the days of his legal studies at Montpellier and Bologna. Wilkins (1961), pp. 4–8.

85 ❖ A GOOD LORD

1   Cf. Seneca, *Ep.* 119, 11–12:

> At excaecant populum et in se convertunt opes, si numerati multum ex aliqua domo effertur, si multum auri tecto quoque eius inlinitur, si familia aut corporibus electa aut spectabilis cultu est. Omnium istorum felicitas in publicum spectat; ille, quem nos et populo et fortunae subduximus, beatus introsum est. Nam quod ad illos pertinet, apud quos falso divitiarum nomen invasit occupata paupertas, sic divitias habent, quomodo habere dicimur febrem, cum illa nos habeat. E contrario dicere solemus: febris illum tenet. Eodem modo dicendum est: divitiae illum tenent.

> Wealth, however, blinds and attracts the mob, when they see a large bulk of ready money brought out of a man's house, or even his walls crusted with abundance of gold, or a retinue that is chosen for beauty of physique, or for attractiveness of attire. The prosperity of all these men looks to public opinion; but the ideal man, whom we have snatched from the control of the people and of Fortune, is happy inwardly. For as far as those persons are concerned in whose minds poverty which is never satisfied has wrongly stolen the title of riches—these individuals have riches just as we say that we "have a fever," when really the fever has *us*. Conversely, we are accustomed to say: "A fever grips him." And in the same way we should say: "Riches grip him."

LCL, Gummere, p. 377. Cf. also *DR* i, 114, 104, ii, 13, 7–8, ii, 18, 9, and ii, 79, 67.

2   In the invective *Contra quendam* (1355), Petrarch claimed to *have a good lord* in his defense against Cardinal Jean de Caraman,

> who had been speaking ill of him in Avignon, disparaging his writings, and calling him a companion and friend of tyrants. . . . Answering the charge that he is consorting with tyrants, he maintains that the young Visconti are not tyrants, and that he lives and moves in perfect freedom . . .

Wilkins (1961), pp. 147–148. On Petrarch's stay in Milan under Archbishop Giovanni Visconti, 1353–1361, Wilkins (1961), chaps. xx–xxiv; and idem (1958a), pp. 8–15 *et passim*. On the Visconti, note Baron (1955), pp. 12–21; and idem (1966), pp. 14–28.

3   E.g., Ex. 20, 2.

4   Suetonius ii, Augustus, 53, 1:

> *Domini appellationem ut maledictum et oprobrium semper exhorruit.* Cum spectante eo ludos pronuntiatum esset in mimo:
> "O dominum aequum et bonum!"
> et universi quasi de ipso dictum exsultantes comprobassent, et statim manu vultuque indecoras adulationes repressit et insequenti die *gravissimo corripuit edicto*; dominumque se posthac appellari ne a liberis quidem aut nepotibus suis vel serio vel ioco passus est atque eius modi blanditias etiam inter ipsos prohibuit.

> [Augustus] *always shrank from the title of Lord as reproachful and insulting.* When the words
> "O just and gracious Lord!"
> were uttered in a farce at which he was a spectator and all the people sprang to their feet and applauded as if they were said of him, he at once checked their unseemly flattery by look and gesture, and on the following day *sharply reproved them in an edict.* After that he would not suffer himself to be called Sire even by his children or his grandchildren either in jest or earnest, and he forbade them to use such flattering terms even among themselves.

Ibid. iii, Tiberius, 27:

> Dominus appellatus a quodam denuntiavit, ne se amplius contumeliae causa nominaret.

> Being once called *Lord,* [Tiberius] warned the speaker not to address him again in an insulting fashion.

LCL, Rolfe, pp. 207, 209, 335. Rolfe notes:

> *Dominus,* 'master,' in the time of the Republic indicated the relation between master and slaves. . . . it was first adopted by Caligula and Domitian. From the time of Trajan it was usual in the sense of 'Lord' or 'Sire.'

Suetonius, LCL, i, p. 206, note *a.*

5   *I.e.,* Severus Alexander (A.D. 222–235). Cf. Hadas (1956), pp. 155–161.

6   *Hist. Aug.,* Severus Alexander, iv, 1:

> Dominum se appelari vetuit. Epistulas ad se quasi *ad privatum* scribi iussit servato tantum nomine imperatoris.

> He forbade men to call him *Lord*, and he gave orders that people should write to him *as they would to a commoner*, retaining only the title *imperator*.

LCL, Magie, p. 185. On this, *Sen.* xiv, 1 (1581: 383).

7   This unflattering characterization (possibly harkening back to Augustine, *De civ. Dei* v, 24: *Sed felices eos dicimus, si iuste imperant* . . . *et se homines esse meminerunt*—But we call [emperors] happy if they rule justly . . . [and] remember that they are men; LCL, Green, p. 263) seems to fit rather closely Azzo da Correggio—Koerting's

> raenkevolle und ergeizige Usurpator . . . welcher, soweit es sich ersehen laesst, in seinem politischen Handeln einzig von dem crassesten Egoismus sich leiten liess und jegliche Moral verhoehnte

(Koerting [1878], pp. 188, 101)—to whom the DR is dedicated and whose private circumstances are described in positive terms in *DR* i, Pref. Note also *Fam.* vii, 15, 5.

8   *rex* = *tyrannus*: Virgil, *Aeneid* vii, 266:

> pars mihi pacis erit dextram tetigisse tyranni.

LCL, Fairclough, p. 21. Also quoted in John of Salisbury, *Policrat.* viii, 17, *PL* 199, c. 778.

9   The Justinian Code (i, 14, 4) stated:

> Digna vox maiestate regnantis legibus alligatum se principem profiteri: adeo de auctoritate iuris nostra pendet auctoritas. Et re vera maius imperio est submittere legibus principatum.

> It is a word worthy of the majesty of the ruler that the Prince professes himself bound to the Law: so much does our authority depend upon the authority of the Law. And truly, greater than the imperium is the submission of the principate to the laws.

Kantorowicz (1957a), p. 104. Note also Dante, *Mon.* iii, 10, 10. On the prince as *imago aequitatis*—the very image of Equity—as well as *servus aequitatis*—servant of Equity—John of Salisbury, *Policrat.* iv, 2, *PL* 199, cc. 514–515. Cf. also the notion of the king as *pater et filius iustitiae*—the father and the son of Justice—in Frederick II, *Liber augustalis* (Cervone [1773]; Powell [1971]), Title xxxi. On this, Kantorowicz (1957a), chap. iv, "Law-centered Kingship." On the medieval concept of communal order and government, Ullmann (1977), esp. chaps. i, ii; Von den Steinen (1965), i, pp. 175–179; and Steinbuechel (1935), esp. part iv, 4.

10   Reason alludes to Isidore's often quoted etymological derivation *ex causa*— by intended effect:

reges a [regendo et] recte agendo.

rulers from [ruling and] acting according to the rule.

Etym. i, 29, 3. Cf. *Sen.* v, 2 (1581: 795): . . . *ut regant, unde & regis oritur nomen* . . . Isidore elaborates *Etym.* ix, 3, 4:

> Reges a regendo vocati. Sicut enim sacerdos a sacrificando, ita et rex a regendo. Non autem regit, qui non corrigit. Recte igitur faciendo regis nomen tenetur, peccando amittitur. Unde et apud veteres tale erat proverbium: 'Rex eris, si recte facias: si non facias, non eris.'

> *Reges*—kings are so called because they rule. Just like *sacerdos*—priest—derives from *sacrificando*—sacrificing—so does *rex*—king—from *regendo*—ruling. But he does not rule who does not correct. Hence the title *rex* is held by doing the correct thing and lost by committing transgression. Thus this proverb of the ancients: "You will be king, if you act correctly. If you do not, you will not."

On this, Von den Steinen (1959), pp. 76–77, 370; and Ullmann (1977), chap. ii. —Cf. also *Fam.* iv, 2, 8–10:

> Illum ego vere regem dixerim, qui non subditos modo, sed se ipsum regit ac frenat; qui exercet in passiones suas imperium, que sunt animo rebelles, illum, si cesserit, oppressure. Ut nulla est quidem clarior victoria quam se ipsum vincere, sic nullum regnum altius quam se ipsum regere. Quomodo ille michi rex erit, in quem regnat ambitio? quomodo invictus quem sternit adversitas? quomodo serenus quem meror obnubilat? quomodo magnanimus quem minimarum etiam rerum pavor exanimat? et ut fulgida virtutum nomina taceamus, quis michi liberum dicet eum qui cupidinum variarum iugo premitur multiplici? Infra omnia ista descendam: qua fronte hominem dicimus, quem scimus ex homine nichil preter nudam effigiem retinere, beluarum moribus deformem et sevorum animantium feritate terribilem? Mira ergo, licet publica, dementia regem eum dicere, qui nec rex nec liber et sepe ne homo quidem sit.

> Him I call truly a king who governs and curbs not only his subjects, but himself; who takes command of the passions that rebel against the mind and would overwhelm him if he yielded. Just as there is no victory more glorious than to overcome oneself, so is there no kingship more exalted than controlling oneself. How could he be a king governing me, who himself is governed by ambition? How can he be invincible who caves in in adversity? How can he be serene whom grief enshrouds? How can he be magnanimous whom the smallest things frighten out of his wits? And, not to mention the shining names of the virtues, who shows me as free a man weighed down by the yoke of all sorts of desires? Let me stoop below all this, and question the nerve to call someone a man who, we all know, preserves nothing but the empty tokens of a man— behaving in the manner of a monstrous animal, terrifying, like a raging beast in his ferociousness. And so, with amazing, though generally accepted, folly, we call "king" him who is not a ruler, not a freeman, and often not even human.

The topic is briefly mentioned in Boccaccio, *Decameron* vii, 10, Singleton (1974), 81r A:

> Manifestissima cosa e che ogni gusto re primo servatore dee essere delle leggi facte da lui, et se altro ne fa servo degno di punitione et non re si dee giudicare, nel quale peccato et riprensione ad me che vostro re sono quasi costrecto cader conviene.

> It is a very manifest thing that every just king should be the first to observe the laws made by him, and if he do otherwise, he must be adjudged a slave deserving of punishment and not a king, into which offense and under which reproach I, who am your king, am in a manner constrained to fall.

Singleton (1982), p. 546.

11   Cf. i Petr. 2, 11–25. Note the verse by Sextus Amarcius (Raby [1934], i, p. 401; Manitius, ii [1923], p. 569), as quoted in Kantorowicz (1957a), p. 54, n. 26:

> Reges ergo boni venerandi et sunt imitandi,
> Perversi non sunt imitandi, sed venerandi.

> Thus good kings should be revered and imitated,
> And wicked ones not imitated, but revered.

To the contrary, John of Salisbury, *Policrat.* viii, 17, *PL* 199, c. 778. On the distinction between the power of kingship, which derives from God, and the king's mortal person, John of Salisbury, ibid. iv, 1. Cf. *PL* 199, c. 514:

> Neque enim potentis est, cum vult saevire in subditos, sed divinae dispensationis, pro beneplacito suo punire, vel exercere subjectos. Unde et in persecutiones Hunnorum, Attila interrogatus a religioso cuiusdam civitatis episcopo, quis esset; cum respondisset: "Ego sum Attila flagellum Dei," veneratus in eo, ut scribitur, divinam maiestatem episcopus: "Bene," inquit, "venerit minister Dei"; et illud: "Benedictus qui venit in nomine Domini," ingeminans, reseratis ecclesiae foribus persecutorem admisit, per quem et assecutus est martyrii palmam. Flagellum enim Domini excludere non audebat, sciens quia dilectus filius flagellatur, et nec ipsius flagelli esse nisi a Domino potestatem.

> The power does not belong to the despot who wants to savagely tyrannize those under him, but depends upon God's permission to punish or discipline his subjects as he pleases. Thus when, during the assault of the Huns, Attila [king of the Huns, c. A.D. 433–453] was asked by the bishop of a religious community who he was, he replied: "I am Attila, the scourge of God" [Dante, *Div. Comm.*, Inf. xii, 134]. The bishop, in accordance with the Scripture, revered the divine majesty in him and said: "The servant of God is welcome," and then, reciting the *Benedictus qui venit in nomine Domini*—Blessed be he that cometh in the name of the Lord [Ps. 117, 26; Gradual for the Mass at Dawn of the Nativity of Our Lord; Offertory for the Mass of Saturday in Easter

Week]—unlocked the gates of the church and admitted the avenger, who let him earn the palm of martyrdom. The bishop did not dare to shut out the scourge of God, knowing that His beloved son [Matth. 3, 17; ii Petr. 1, 17] had been scourged, and that Attila could not be a scourge unless empowered by Almighty God.

On this, Kantorowicz (1957a), pp. 54–55, 454–455. A less realistic version of the story appears in Jacobus de Voragine, *Legenda aurea* (for July 31; Graesse [1890], p. 449, Ryan & Ripperger [1941], pp. 397–398), where it is ascribed to Saint Lupus, Bishop of Troyes, whose suffering obedience is rewarded by God. Miraculously blinded, the invading Huns pass through the city from one gate to the other without harming anyone. —Note also SN 4: *Et profecto quicquid ab homine bene agitur, divinum opus est*, as below, DR i, 89, note 4.

12   *unde optimum quidam semper prospero caruisse diffiniunt.* Possibly echoing a popular maxim. Note Guillaume de Blois, *Alda*, 31–50 (Cohen [1931], i, pp. 131, 133), esp. 31–32 and 47–48:

> Accidit . . . solum modo prosperitatis,
>   Hoc homini quod nil prosperitatis habet . . .
> Prosperitas igitur est prosperitate carere,
>   Nam venit ex sola prosperitate dolor.

> Prosperous only is the man who never prospers. . . .
> Thus true prosperity is being without prosperity,
>   since all it brings is sorrow.

On this, Suchomski (1975), esp. p. 126.

13   Cf. the Diagoras story, above, *DR* i, 29, 29–46, and note 9. On praying for death at the height of good fortune, Seneca, *Dial.* vi, Ad Marc. 22, 1.

86 ✥ CLEAR AIR

1   Dialogues 86–92 deal with gratifying conditions and experiences.

2   Cf. *DR* i, 54, 9–11, and i, 90, 64–67.

3   An ironic reference alluding in sense and choice of words to the topic of *erigere mentem*—lifting up the mind. Cf., e.g., Anselm, *Proslogion*, Pref., *PL* 158, c. 224: *erigere mentem suam ad contemplationem*—to lift his mind to the contemplation of God (Deane [1962], p. 2). On this, Javelet (1967), i, pp. 391–393, ii, pp. 297–298, nn. 181, 188; and Ladner (1965), pp. 39, 94–95, n. 69. Related topics, *homo erectus*, above, *DR* i, 40, note 6, and *assurgere*, as in *Secretum* i, *DR* i, Pref., note 7; and *DR* i, 12, note 30; ii, 1, 39–40, and ii, 48, 85–86. Note Augustine, *Enarr. in Ps.* 145, 5:

Ab exterioribus ad interiora, ab inferioribus ad superiora.

From outward things to those within, from lowly things to those on high.

4   I failed to locate the specific source for Reason's statement. The notion and related topics occur frequently in the astro-geographic and the medical literatures of Antiquity from Xenophanes of Colophon, who divided the earth into climatic zones (ca. 540 B.C.), and Hippocrates (e.g., *Airs, Waters, Places*) to Strabo and Pliny (d. A.D. 79).

5   1492: *Gaudium*: Aer hic lucidus me delectat.
          Ratio: Delectari . . .
      1581: *Gaudium*: Aer hic lucidus me delectari . . .

without indication of the beginning of Reason's response.

6   An allusion to the hymn of St. Ambrose, *Aeterne rerum conditor* (*Anal hymn.* 50, 11; Raby [1953], pp. 34–35)—the hymn of Lauds i on Sundays between January 14 and Septuagesima of the Roman Breviary. —On earthly delights and the heavenly Maker, cf. above, *DR* i, 37, 59–61, and note 9; and *DR* i, 40, 16–19, and note 5. On God as *fons omnis boni*, e.g., above, *DR* i, 37, 56–61, i, 39, 17–29, and i, 40, 16–20.

7   Job 31, 26–28:

> Si vidi solem cum fulgeret,
> et lunam incedentem clare,
> et laetatum est in abscondito cor meum,
> et osculatus sum manum meam ore meo:
> quae est iniquitas maxima,
> et negatio contra Deum altissimum.

8   The key passages here may be Cicero, *Tusc. disp.* i, 28, 68–70; and *De nat. deor.* ii, 20–22, and 62, 155.

9   Cf. the remedy for love, *DR* i, 69, 197–198.

10   *si qualitate rerum non potest, saltem varietate satiatur.* Pseudo-Augustine? Cf. Quintilian ix, 3, 5: *ut novitate aurem excitant, ita copia satiant.*

87 ❖ SMOOTH SAILING

1   Virgil, *Aeneid* v, 848–849:

> mene salis placidi voltum fluctusque quietos
> ignorare iubes? mene huic confidere monstro?

> Me dost thou bid shut my eyes to the sea's calm face
> and peaceful waves? Me put faith in this monster?

LCL, Fairclough, p. 503. Quoted in *Secretum* i, *Prose* (1955), p. 60; and *Fam.* viii, 1, 10. *Fam.* v, 5, to Giovanni Cardinal Colonna, describes a "storm without equal" that Petrarch experienced November 24–25, 1343, in Naples.

> The storm raged throughout the day—Petrarch himself was in danger at one time—but ceased suddenly at nightfall (it had wrought havoc not only at Naples but to the north and south as well: most of Amalfi slid into the sea). Petrarch resolved never again to venture on the sea—and he never did.

Wilkins (1961), p. 42. On Petrarch's sea voyages since childhood, ibid., pp. 3, 6, 10, 26, 39–40.

88 ❖ BEING SAFELY IN PORT

1   In 1492 sequence and numbering of the next four dialogues is as follows:

> No dialogue numbered 88.
> 89. De carceris exitu
> 90. De tranquillo statu
> 90. (*sic!*) De uotiua portus apprehensione
> 91. De potentia

I follow 1581 and Twyne, ordering as

> 88. De uotiua . . .
> 89. De carceris . . .
> 90. De tranquillo . . .
> 91. De potentia

2   *Fam.* v, 5, 21:

> Scio quid adversus hec a doctioribus disputetur: ubique par perciulum, etsi in mari clarius apparet.

> I know what more learned men have to say against this: that danger is the same everywhere, although it is more obvious on the sea.

3   I.e., probably Ulysses, who *maria lustravit ac terras*—roamed seas and

land—*erroribus suis clarus*—famous for his wanderings. *Fam.* ix, 13, 24–25. Cf. also *Fam.* i, 1, 21–22 and; xiii, 4, 10.

4   Statius, *Theb.* vii, 718–722:

> Alcathoum . . . , cui circum stagna Carysti
> et domus et coniunx et amantes litora nati.
> Vixerat ille diu *pauper scrutator aquarum,*
> decepit tellus, *moriens hiemesque notosque*
> *laudat et experti meliora pericula ponti.*

> Alcathous, to whom by the meres of Carystus was
> home and wife and his children who loved its shores.
> Long had he lived a poor searcher of the waters:
> earth played him false, and dying he praises the storms and winds,
> and the more welcome dangers of the familiar sea.

LCL, Mozley, pp. 185, 187.

5   *quibus ea pars rerum scatet*

6   On earthquakes, Pliny, *Nat. hist.* ii, 81–96.

7   A reference to *the vast and portentous earthquake* of 91 B.C., Pliny, *Nat. hist.* ii, 85, 199. Note also Pliny's observation that *the city of Rome has never shaken without this being a premonition of something about to happen,* ibid. ii, 86, 200, quoted in *Fam.* xi, 7, 7.

8   Severe earthquakes shook Rome, all of Italy, and the Alps in January 1348, when Petrarch was in Verona and, again, in September 1349, when he was in the vicinity of Parma. *Fam.* xi, 7 to Socrates (Ludwig van Kempen), Piacenza, June 11, 1351 (4), refers to this tremor which damaged churches and buildings:

> Roma ipsa insolito tremore concussa est tam graviter ut ab eadem urbe condita, supra duo annorum milia, tale ibi nichil acciderit.

> Rome itself was terribly jolted by a tremor of unusual severity. Nothing like it ever happened since the city's founding over two thousand years ago.

On this, also *Fam.* xv, 9, 23; Billanovich in *Rer. mem. lib.,* p. cii, n. 2; and Wilkins (1961), pp. 74, 84. On the Naples quake of 1343, *Fam.* v, 5, 7; and *DR* i, 87, note 1. The earthquake which devestated the banks of the Rhine destroyed Basel, October 18, 1356. Years later, Petrarch recalled these quakes in *Sen.* x, 2, a long autobiographical letter to Guido Sette, Archbishop of Genoa, Venice, 1367, *Prose* (1955), pp. 1122–1124 (below, *DR* ii, 91, note 10); and in an interpolation in his *De ocio,* Rotondi, p. 52. Cf. Wilkins (1959), pp. 129–131; idem (1961), pp. 154, 159; and Heitmann (1957), pp. 22–23.

9   Cf. above, *DR* i, 66, note 2.

89 ❖ RELEASE FROM PRISON

1   *sed non omnia: quae delectant prosunt: saepe nociva sunt dulcia: & amara salubria* —On Reason's frequent use of *dulcia/amara* (*DR* i, Pref., note 56, i, 69, note 2, i, 90, note 5), cf. Augustine, *Conf.* x, 14, 21 and 22, *PL* 32, c. 788:

> . . . laetitia vero atque tristitia quasi cibus dulcis et amarus: . . .
> . . . laetitiae dulcedo vel amaritudo moestitiae . . .

> . . . joy and sadness like sweet and bitter food . . .
> . . . the sweetness of joy or the bitterness of sorrow . . .

J. G. Pilkington in Oates (1948), i, pp. 157, 158. Note also Is. 5, 20:

> Vae qui dicitis malum bonum,
> et bonum malum;
> ponentes tenebras lucem,
> et lucem tenebras;
> ponentes amarum in dulce,
> et dulce in amarum!

> Woe to you that call evil good,
> and good evil;
> that put darkness for light,
> and light for darkness:
> that put bitter for sweet,
> and sweet for bitter.

For a late echo of the topic, cf. Richard Burton, *Anatomy of Melancholy* I, i, 1, 5, Dell (1948), pp. 125–126.

2   On *desiring what is harmful,* based on Ovid, *Am.* iii, 4, 17 (Curtius [1953], pp. 58–59), e.g., *Fam.* xiii, 4, 7:

> Felicitati contraria sunt hec que felicia vulgus vocat . . .

> Contrary to happiness is what the vulgar crowd calls happy . . .

Cf. *Fam.* iv, 12, 28, xx, 4, 28, xxi, 9, 13; *Sen.* xiii, 14, xvii, 2 (1581: 928, 964); *Buc. carm.* ix, 39; *Rime* 72, 67–71, Rime (1951), p. 107; and *DR* i, 30, 128, i, 33, 73–76, i, 39, 28–29, i, 59, 9–12, i, 109, 48–51, 80–81, i, 112, 22–25, i, 116, 37–39; ii, 10, 17–19; ii, 13, 65–68, ii, 73, 56–57; ii, 79, 91–92. Cf. also *consuetudo,* above, *DR* i, 11, note 17; *what is good you make evil, DR* i, 21, 66, and note 14; and below, ii, 90, note 16. Note the echo in *Der Ackermann aus Boehmen* xvi, 1–2, Walshe (1951), p. 17.

3 Cola di Rienzo (1313–1354), the self styled *Nicolaus Severus et Clemens, liber-ator Urbis, zelator Italiae, amator Orbis et Tribunus Augustus,* which Gibbon (chap. 70, Bury, vii [1914], p. 279) translates as *Nicholas, Severe and Merciful; Deliverer of Rome; Defender of Italy; Friend of Mankind, and of Liberty, Peace, and Justice; Tribune August,* abdicated December 15, 1347. Cf. Wilkins (1961), p. 73; Burdach & Piur (1928), pp. 70–75; and Voigt (1880), i, p. 59. Note Wright (1975), pp. 47–48.

4 Released from his Avignon prison in 1352, Cola returned to Rome and, under the auspices of Pope Innocent VI and Cardinal Albornoz, was made senator. He was killed by an angry mob early in October 1354 (Wright [1975], pp. 146–153; Gregorovius [1872], ii, pp. 363–385). Two years earlier, when he was still imprisoned, Petrarch wrote to the people of the City of Rome in SN 4, Piur (1925), pp. 183–184:

> Septem enim mensium non amplius spatio frena reipublice tenuit, ut uix ab origine mundi maius aliquid attentatum rear, et si successisset ut ceperat, diuinum potius quam humanum opus esse uideretur. Et profecto quicquid ab homine bene agitur, diuinum opus est. Huic ergo, quem uestre glorie, non ambitioni proprie desudasse notum est, fauor haud dubius debetur. De euentu Fortuna culpanda est. Si quis autem tepor feruenti principio interuenit, humane uarietati atque imbecillitati ueniam date; et, dum licet, uendicate ciuem ues-trum ab iniuria, qui Grecos a Macedonum, Siculos a Carthaginensium, Campa-nos a Samnitum, Tuscos a Gallorum iniuriis non sine graui uestro periculo uendicastis.

> He held the reins of government for no more than seven months (May–Decem-ber 1347), and in such a way, I believe, that hardly anything greater than this has been tried since the beginning of time. If he had brought to completion what he had begun, it would have seemed a divine rather than a human achievement. Indeed, whatever is well done by man is a divine achievement. To him, therefore, who as we know exerted himself for your glory rather than his own ambition, you surely owe much. Fortune must be held responsible for what happened afterwards. If any slackening followed the initial enthusiasm, blame the foolish waywardness of men, and liberate while you still can your fellow-citizen from injustice, just as, despite the great danger, you freed the Greeks from the injustices of the Macedonians, the Sicilians from the Carthaginians, the Campanians from the Samnites, the Etruscans from the Gauls.

Zacour (1973), pp. 56–57. But Petrarch was primarily interested in the rees-tablishment of the empire in Italy and the restoration of Rome to its old dignity (*Var.* 38, 40, 42, 48; *Fam.* vii, 1; SN 2, 3 and 4; *Buc. carm.* v), and ceased to support Cola when he failed (*Fam.* vii, 5, vii, 7, xiii, 6, 5–28). *Fam.* xviii, 1, to Emperor Charles IV (Milan, November 23, 1353), offers this cool assessment of the commoner, Cola, in an effort to stress the infinitely greater effectiveness imperial power would have in the revitalization process—*the*

road being straight and easy, but lacking one capable of taking it (Fam. xviii,
1, 15):

> Nudiustertius caput extulit quidam e plebe humili, non romanus rex, non con-
> sul, non patritius, et vix bene cognitus romanus civis, nullis titulis suorum,
> nullis maiorum imaginibus, denique nullis ad id tempus virtutibus suis clarus,
> qui *vindicem* se romane *libertatis* assereret: obscuri hominis clara professio.
> . . . . iam rediisse iustitia et pax et harum comites, alma
> fides, tranquilla securitas, ad postremum aurei seculi vestigia videbantur. Ille
> tamen in ipso rerum flore peraruit. Noli sibi culpam dare nec alteri; non con-
> demno hominem, non absolvo; non sum iudex; quid opiner scio. Et sumpserat
> ille titulum tribuni, quod inter romuleas dignitates humillimum nomen fuit. Si
> tantum ergo tribunitium potuit, quid cesareum nomen posset?

> Yesterday's ruler of Rome was of humble parentage, not a Roman king, not a
> consul, not a patrician, but an ordinary Roman citizen, hardly known, without
> titles, without ancestry, and without prior distinction, who pronounced himself
> defender of Roman liberty [said of Brutus by Livy, ii, 1, 8; on Cola di Rienzo as
> a third Brutus, *Var.* 38, and *Contra eum,* 1581: 1181]: a noble declaration by an
> obscure man. . . .   . . . soon justice and peace returned, and their compan-
> ions, fruitful confidence, tranquil security, and, at length, the vestiges of a
> golden age could be seen. Yet amidst all this flourishing he withered. I do not
> wish to blame him or anybody else for this. I do not condemn the man, I do not
> absolve him, I am not a judge. But I know what I believe. He assumed the title
> of tribune, which designated the lowest magistrates among Romuleian digni-
> taries [Livy, ii, 33]. If a mere tribune could accomplish that much, what is there
> that could not be accomplished by an emperor?

(*Fam.* xviii, 1, 17–19; on this, Voigt, i [1880], pp. 66–67.) On Petrarch and
Cola di Rienzo, Wilkins (1961), chap. xii; idem (1978), pp. 188–190; Piur
(1925), esp. pp. 165–184, 191–193, 325–331, 342–347; Robinson (1914), pp.
335–359; Burdach & Piur (1912–1928); the documentation in Cosenza
(1913); Baron (1955), pp. 95–96; idem (1966), pp. 102–104, 119–120;
Zacour (1973), pp. 35–37; Mann (1984), pp. 26–39; and Krautheimer
(1980), p. 228. Note Gibbon (1787–1789), chap. 70; Gregorovius (1872), xi,
5, 2–6, 4; and Wright (1975).

5   On equanimity, e.g., *Fam.* ii, 7, 3, ii, 9, 7, echoing Seneca, *Ep.* 66, 6, *Fam.* vi,
3, 69, viii, 1, 33, viii, 7, 7, xiv, 1, 43, xvi, 6, 13 (*eodem vultu*—cf. Seneca,
Dial. vii, 19, as above *DR* i, 10, note 1); *Sen.* ii, 2, xvii, 2 (1581: 758, 964);
Africa iv, 83, vii, 435;, and *DR* ii, 68, 76, and note 17, ii, 75, 68–70, ii, 114,
esp. 298–299, ii, 118, 92–93, ii, 120, 62–65. On *in omni fortuna eosdem
animos habere*—to keep unchanged in any kind of fortune (Livy, xxxvii, 45,
12)—*Fam.* xiv, 5, 15–16; *Contra eum* xiv, Cocchia (1920), p. 171, *Prose*
(1955), p. 790; Venice oration, 1354, Hortis (1874), p. 833; and on this,
Wilkins (1958), chap. vi. —Related, *De ocio* (1581: 316); *De vita sol.* i and ii,
Prose (1955), pp. 308, 518; *Var.* 17, Fracassetti, iii (1863), p. 340; and *Sen.* ii,

2, ii, 3, viii, 3, ix, 2 (1581: 757–758, 758–759, 836, 860). Cf. also *DR* ii, 75, 68–70, i, 2, note 23, on *mediocritas,* and i, Pref., note 56, on *paratus ad omnia.* On the entire topic from Aristotle to Petrarch, Heitmann (1958), pp. 61–69.

6   Cf. above, *DR* i, 15, 74–77.

90 ❖ TRANQUILLITY

1   1492: nunc nunc maxime metuendum
     1581: nunc maxime metuendum

2   Similar, *Fam.* vii, 6, 3, xx, 4, 17; *Sen.* ix, 2 (1581: 859); and *DR* i, 17, 27–37, i, 107, 53–63.

3   Cf. above, *DR* i, 14, note 8.

4   Cf. *DR* i, Pref., note 5, and i, 23, 23–25. Also *DR* i, 2, note 11.

5   On this, *Fam.* xiv, 1 (to Cardinal Elie de Talleyrand, Vaucluse, September 22, 1352), 13–14:

> Plurima quidem sunt, optime virorum, que secum fert vita mortalis, a quibus non mediocritas status, non humilitas, non liberat altitudo; sed in his amara multo plura quam dulcia, ut non immerito dici putes in vestibulo vite duo dolia esse, dulce unum sed exiguum, amarum vero alterum sed illud amplissimum, quo pro varietate intellectuum non absurde forsitan trahi posset illud daviticum: "Calix in manu domini vini meri plenus mixto," ut calix dominicus quo in hoc exilio potamur miseri, aliquid velut merum et dulce habeat; plenitudo eius multis amaritudinibus sit admixta. Dulcia quidem, ut dixi, pauca sunt et brevia; breve gaudium brevis delectatio brevis risus breve denique quicquid iuvat; quod expertum se fatebitur quisquis aliquantulum in huius peregrinationis calle processerit. Contra vero fortune prelia quam longeva quam gravia, quot adversitatum species, quam multe et varie affligentium rerum forme, nemo facile dixerit; nemo rem infinitam brevi oratione collegerit.

> There are, however, even for the best of men, things that go with the life of mortals that cannot be overcome by observing the mean, by humility, or by high station—things most of which are bitter rather than sweet—so that you might agree it is not altogether unjust to say there are two casks in the doorway of this life, a small one holding sweet drafts and an enormous one full of bitterness, for which, considering the diversity of views, it is perhaps not meaningless to substitute this line of David's [Ps. 74, 9]:

> For in the hand of the Lord there is a cup
> of strong wine full of mixture—

His cup from which, in this exile, we wretched creatures must drink the tart
and the sweet. Into His fullness [Ps. 23, 1, and 88, 12; Ioan. 1, 16] many bitter
pills are mixed. And, as I have said, sweet things are scant and quite short-
lived. Brief is the joy, brief the delight, brief the laughter, brief, indeed, whatever gratifies. Anyone will admit that this is so, no matter how briefly he has
trodden the road of this journey far away from the heavenly home. Conversely,
no one can easily tell how long, how severe the onslaughts of Fortune will be,
how many forms adversity may assume, how many different kinds of distress-
ing events might occur. No one can deal adequately with an immense phenomenon in a brief statement.

The analogous image of the two casks is based on Homer, *Iliad* xxiv,
527–530:

> There are two urns that stand on the door-sill of Zeus. They are unlike
> for the gifts they bestow: an urn of evils, an urn of blessings.
> If Zeus who delights in thunder mingles these and bestows them
> on man, he shifts, and moves now in evil, again in good fortune.

Lattimore (1951), p. 489. On this, Willcock (1976), p. 271. The image recurs
in Boethius, *Cons. phil.* ii, P 2, 40:

> Nonne adulescentulus δοιοὺς πίθους τὸν μὲν ἕνα κακῶν τὸν δ' ἕτερον ἑάων
> in Iovis limine iacere didicisti?

> You must have learned as a boy that on Jupiter's doorstep there are two
> barrels, one holding good things, the other bad.

Green (1962), p. 24 —Note also Patch (1927), pp. 52–54; *Fam.* viii, 1, 36,
xvii, 3, 9, xxiii, 12, 34; *DR* i, 89, 3–4, and note 1, ii, 88, 81–84, ii, 93, 153–
161, etc.; and Augustine, *De civ. Dei* xxi, 14. —On *sweet/bitter,* above, *DR* i,
89, note 1.

6   Cf. above, *DR* i, 57.
7   *longus labor: usus brevis.* Cp. *Rime* 244, 14; *Rime* (1951), p. 318:

> perché 'l cammin è lungo e 'l tempo è corto.

> Because the way is long, and the time is short.

Armi (1946), p. 348; related, *Fam.* xii, 3, 5. The Hippocratic prototype, *Aph.*
i, 1—

> Ὁ Βίος Βραχύς, ἡ δὲ τέχνη μακρή . . .

> Life is short, the Art is long . . .

(LCL, Jones, p. 99)—was well known in Petrarch's time. Cf. Guy de Chauliac, *Chirurgia magna* i, Ogden (1971), p. 11, 33–34; and Chaucer, *Parl. of Fowls* i, 1. Note Manzalaoui (1962).

8   *DR* i, 29. 39–46, i, 85, 84. Cf. also *Fam.* xi, 5, 1.

9   1492: inter uictorum filiorum amplexus
     1581: inter uiuorum filiorum amplexus

10   Above, *DR* i, 29, note 9.

11   Cf. *DR* i, 23, 28, and note 13, and i, 83, 18–23, and note 2.

12   Cf. *Secretum* i, as above, *DR* i, Pref., note 7.

13   Cf. *DR*. i, 17, 39–41.

14   On delusions and false opinions, e.g., *DR* i, 11, note 1, and i, 46, 116–118.

15   Cf. *DR*. i, 50, 20–21, i, 39, note 6, and i, 2, note 25.

16   For *homo caelestis/homo terrenus* note Prudentius, *Liber cathemerinon* x, 25–32; and the comment in Von den Steinen (1965), i, pp. 109–110. Cf. *Africa* vi, 901–906, *Rime* (1951), p. 688:

> . . . . . . Video nunc quanta paravi,
> ah miser, in cassum, subii quot sponte labores,
> quos licuit transire michi. Moriturus ad astra
> scandere querit homo, sed mors docet omnia quo sint
> nostra loco.

> . . . . . . At last I can perceive
> how long and fruitless have my labors been.
> What countless toils I've faced that I might well
> have put aside! Doomed though he be to die,
> man still aspires to Heaven, but death reveals
> the worth of his endeavor.

Bergin (1977). pp. 140–141, lines 1176–1181. On *casting off one's burden to reach his goal,* *DR* ii, 9, note 29. On the image *curvatus*—bent down, i.e., the mind overburdened by earthly cares—as opposed to *rectitudo*—the righteous mind of man created to stand upright facing his God—cf. *Sen.* x, 1 (1581: 865):

> . . . si curua, & in terram prona est uoluntas tua ut sursum non possit as-picere, si claudi motus, si affectus Paralytici, neque attollere se ualentes, si manus aridae, atque operibus pietatis inualidae, ipse curuos, & claudos, & Paralyticos erexit. Ipse aridos salubri humore restituit.

> . . . if your will is bent down and stooping to the ground [*Fam.* x, 3, 27] so it cannot look up high, if your sympathies are halting, your moods palsied and unable to raise themselves up, if the hands are withered [Matth. 12, 10; Marc. 3, 1, above, *DR* i, 2, 58] and too weak for works of kindness—He Himself straightened those that were bent and lame and palsied [e.g., Act. 8, 8]. He restored to a healthy condition those that had withered limbs.

Cf. Bernard of Clairvaux, *Sermo* 24, as discussed in Stock (1983), pp. 439–

440. Note also *humi acclivis, DR* i, 54, 8. —On aspiring to rise up, *Secretum* i, as above, *DR* i, Pref., note 7; the related *homo erectus* topic, *DR* i, 40, note 6; and Augustine, *Conf.* viii, 5, 10–12, as in *Dramatis personae,* note 2.

17 1492: magna pars mortalium
    1581: magna mortalium

18 On *vite adminicula,* i.e., the Stoic *commoda.* (εὐχρηστήματα in Cicero, *De fin.* iii, 21 69, as below, *DR* ii, 114, note 28), *Fam.* v, 18, 1:

> De statu meo, quem nosse desideras, breviter sic habe: etsi inter vere philosophantes unum sit hominis bonum et non tria, id scilicet quod in animo est bene celitus instituto et possessione generosi habitus insignito, quoniam corporis ac fortune non bona sed commoda quedam ac levia adminicula dici debent; quia tamen credo vello te de omnibus audire, geram morem voluntati tue.

> Regarding my circumstances, since you asked about them, briefly this. Although among true philosophers [i.e, the Stoics] the goods of man are not three [i.e., the Peripatetic notion of goods of mind, body, and Fortune as in Cicero, *Tusc. disp.* v, 30, 85, based on Aristotle, *Eth. Nic.* i, 8, 1099 a–b], but just one, namely, that of a mind, well endowed by Heaven and distinguished by noble habits (since assets of body and Fortune should be regarded not as bona— goods—but as *commoda*—conveniences, as it were, and inconsequential comforts)—I shall, nevertheless, carry out what I think are your wishes, and write about all three of these goods.

Cf. also, *Fam.* iii, 6, 1, xxiii, 12, 13; and *Sen.* xvii, 2 (1581: 964). On this, e.g., Cicero, *De fin.* iii, 16, 52, *De inv.* ii, 18, and *Tusc. disp.* i, 36, 87, ii, 4, 10; and Seneca, *Ep.* 74, 17, ibid. 87, 29 and 36–37, and ibid. 92, 16.

19 Similar, *Secretum* i, *Prose* (1955), pp. 60, 62.

20 On *crisis* and *prognosis* in ancient medicine, Jones in *Hippocrates,* LCL, i (1923), pp. lii–lv, ii (1923), pp. ix–xiii; and Majno (1975), pp. 171, 373–374.

21 1492: libidine sumptus
    1581: libitinae sumptus

22 Cf. above, *DR* i, 5, 45, and note 8, i, 23, 25, and note 11, and i, 107, note 8.

23 Ps. 30, 16:

> in manibus tuis sortes meae.

> My lots are in thy hands.

Cf. below, *DR* ii, 76, 23.

24 'Fortune—rather, God'—cf. *Fam.* xii, 1, 2, xv, 12, 2; and *Sen.* ii, 2 (1581: 758), ii, 5 (1581: 763).

25 Luc. 12, 20:

> Stulte, hac nocte animam tuam repetunt a te;
> quae autem parasti, cuius erunt?

91 ❖ POWER

1   Cf. above, *DR* i, 17, *passim,* and, related, *Fam.* xxii, 1, 8; and *Africa* vii, Bergin (1977), 323–328, 361–376, 417–422. Note also *Contra quendam,* Ricci (1949), 20, citing Juvenal, iii, 38–40.

2   1492: expugnant
      1581: expurgant

3   Cf. below, *DR,* ii, 90, note 15.

92 ❖ GLORY

1   *Prose* (1955), pp. 632–637.

2   *Si temporum: si locorum angustias metiare:* Cf. *Secretum* iii, *Prose* (1955), p. 194: *locorumque ac temporum angustiis coartatur,* as above, *DR* i, 44, note 21. Related, *Africa* ii, 470–471. On this, Cicero, *De re publ.* vi (Somn. Scip.), 16, 16; 19, 20; 20, 22; 23, 25; Macrobius, *Comm.* ii, 10, 3; ii, 11, 4; Boethius, *Cons. phil.* ii, P 7, 23–24; and Rico (1974), pp. 391–392, 401, 406–407.

3   *ut tempus praesens puncto minus:* Cf. Seneca, *Ep.* 49, 3:

   Punctum est quod vivimus et adhuc puncto minus.

   The time which we spend in living is but a point, nay, even less than a point.

   LCL, Gummere, p. 325.

4   Reason refers to the old topic of *vana gloria* in terms of the geocentric world system (*DR* ii, 67, note 15). The key texts here are Cicero, *Tusc. disp.* i, 17, 40, and, more extensively, *De re publ.* vi (Somn. Scip.), 16, and 19–20 (*DR* ii, 68, note 13); and, based on these, Macrobius, *Comm.* i, 16, 6, ii, 9, 6, ii, 10, 3; and Boethius, *Cons. phil.* ii, P 7, Gruber (1978), pp. 212, 215, 6. Petrarch probably knew also Seneca's remarks in his *Dial.* vi, Ad Marciam, 21, 2, and *Nat. quaest.* i, Praef. 8 and 11; and Pliny, *Nat. hist.* ii, 68, 173–175:

   Ita terrae tres partes abstulit caelum. Oceani rapina in incerto est; sed et relicta nobis una portio haud scio an etiam in maiore damno sit, idem siquidem oceanus infusus in multos, ut dicemus, sinus adeo vicino accessu interna maria adlatrat ut centum quindecim milibus passuum Arabicus sinus distet ab Aegyptio mari, Caspius vero CCCLXXV milibus a Pontico, idem interfusus intra per

tot maria quibus Africam Europam Asiam dispescit, quantum terrarum occupat? Conputetur etiamnum mensura tot fluminum, tantarum paludium, ad-
dantur et lacus, stagna, iam elata in caelum ac ardua adspectu quoque iuga,
iam silvae vallesque praeruptae et solitudines et mille e causis deserta; detra-
hantur hae tot portiones terrae, immo vero, ut plures tradidere, *mundi puncto*
(neque enim aliud est terra in universo): haec est materia gloriae nostrae, haec
sedes, hic honores gerimus, hic exercemus imperia, hic opes cupimus, hic
tumultuamur humanum genus, hic instauramus bella etiam civilia mutuisque
caedibus laxiorem facimus terram! Et ut publicos gentium furores transeam,
haec in qua conterminos pellimus furtoque vicini caespitem nostro solo ad-
fodimus, ut qui latissime rura metatus fuerit ultraque famam exegerit adcolas
quota terrarum parte gaudeat, vel cum ad mensuram avaritiae suae propa-
gaverit, quam tandem portionem eius defunctus obtineat!

Thus the sky has stolen three quarters of the earth. The extent of the trespass
of ocean is unascertained; but even the one portion left to us suffers perhaps an
even greater loss, inasmuch as the same ocean, spreading out, as we shall
describe, into a number of bays, advances with its threatening roar so close to
the inner seas that there is only a distance of 115 miles between the Arabian
Gulf and the Egyptian Sea and of 375 between the Caspian and the Black Sea;
and also with its inner channels through so many seas whereby it sunders
Africa, Europe and Asia, it occupies—what area of the land? Calculate moreover the dimensions of all those rivers and vast swamps, add also the lakes and
pools, and next the ridges too that rise into the heaven and are precipitous
even to the eye, next the forests and steep glens, and the deserts and areas for
a thousand reasons left deserted; subtract all these portions from the earth or
rather from *this pin-prick,* as the majority of thinkers have taught, *in the
world*—for in the whole universe the earth is nothing else: and this is the
substance of our glory, this is its habitation, here it is that we fill positions of
power and covet wealth, and throw mankind into an uproar, and launch even
civil wars and slaughter one another to make the land more spacious! And to
pass over the collective insanities of the nations, this is the land in which we
expel the tenants next to us and add a spade-full of turf to our own estate by
stealing from our neighbour's—to the end that he who has marked out his
acres most widely and banished his neighbours beyond all record may rejoice
in owning—how small a fraction of the earth's surface? Or, when he has
stretched his boundaries to the full measure of his avarice, may still retain—
what portion, pray, of his estate when he is dead?

LCL, Rackham, pp. 307, 309. On the Stoic view of the earth, Pohlenz, i
(1959), pp. 219–222. On earth as a mere dot, also Nicole Oresme, Menut
(1968), pp. 336–337. Chaucer, *House of Fame* ii, 898–909, Robinson (1933),
pp. 340–341. —The topic is discussed in some detail in *Secretum* iii, *Prose*
(1955), pp. 199–215, where Franciscus observes (ibid., p. 194):

Intelligo istam veterem et tritam iam inter philosophos fabellam: terram
omnem punti unius exigui instar esse, annum unum infinitis annorum millibus

constare; famam vero hominum nec punctum implere nec annum, ceteraque huius generis, quibus ab amore glorie animos dehortantur.

I know that old, worn fairy tale of the philosophers: that the earth is but a tiny dot; that within the span of but a single year thousands of years may be contained [Plato, *Republic* viii, 546; *Timaeus* 39d; Chalcidius, 118, Waszink (1962), pp. 162–164; Cicero, *De fin.* ii, 31, 102, *De nat. deor.* ii, 20, 51, and *De re publ.* vi, 22, 24; Macrobius, *Comm.* ii, 11, 10–12] that a man's fame cannot fill either that dot or such a year; and other stuff of this sort, by which they try to dissuade the mind from the love of glory.

Augustinus returns to the subject (ibid., pp. 200, 202):

Illud equidem ex ore tuo auditum esse doleo philosophorum in hac re veterem, ut ais, fabellam posse contemni. Ea ne, queso, fabula est, que geometricis demonstrationibus terre totius designat angustias: artamque licet et longiusculam insulam esse confirmat; an ea que asserit ex omni terra quinque distincta—ita vocant—zonis, maximam illam mediamque solis ardoribus, duas autem dextera levaque importunis frigoribus perpetuaque glacie oppressas habitaculum hominibus non prestare; duas reliquas, inter mediam et extremas, incoli? An ea que bipartite huius habitabilis alteram partem obice magni maris inaccessibilem vobis sub pedibus vestris locat, quam utrum homines teneant scis quanta dissensio inter doctissimos homines olim sit. Ego autem quid sentirem absolvi in libris *De civitate Dei* quos te legisse non dubito. Alteram vero vel totam vobis linquit habitabilem, vel, ut quibusdam placet, in duas partes subdividens, unam usibus vestris attribuit, aliam septentrionalis Oceani reflexibus circumcludit atque aditum interdicit. An ea que hanc ipsam vobis habitabilem, quantulacunque sit, freto paludibusque ac silvosis arenosisque et desertis locis imminuit, peneque ad nichilum redigit hoc telluris exiguum, in quo tantopere superbitis? An ea forte que in hoc ad extremum arctato habitaculi vestri situ, diversos vivendi mores, adversosque religionis ritus, dissonas linguas dissimilesque habitus edocet, atque hoc modo propagandi late nominis preripit facultatem? Si hec tibi fabulosa sunt, fabulosa quoque sunt omnia que de te michi promiseram. Nulli enim ferme notiora hec rebar esse quam tibi. Nempe, ut omittam et Ciceronis et Maronis disciplinam ceteraque vel philosophica vel poetica, quibus hac de re instructissimus videbaris, sciebam te nuper in *Africa* tua hanc ipsam sententiam preclaris versibus descripsisse, ubi dixisti:

> . . . . . . angustis arctatus finibus orbis
> insula parva situ est, curvis quam flexibus ambit
> Occeanus.

I was sorry when I heard fall from your lips that phrase about despising what you called the old [fairy-tale] of the philosophers on this matter. Is it, then, a fairy-tale, pray, by figures of geometry, to show how small is all the earth, and to prove it but an island of little length and width [Aristotle, *De caelo* 298a, as cited and discussed in Sarton, i (1952), p. 510; Boethius, *Cons. phil* ii, P 7, 10]? Is it a fairy-tale to divide the earth into five zones, the largest of which, lying in the centre, is burned by the heat of the sun, and the two utmost, to right and left, are a prey to binding frost and eternal snow, which leave not a corner where man can dwell; but those other two, between the middle and two outmost zones, are inhabited by man? Is it a fairy-tale that this habitable part is divided again into two parts, whereof one is placed under your feet, guarded by a vast sea, and the other is left you to inhabit everywhere, or, according to some authorities [Pliny, *Nat. hist.* ii, 67, 167–170; Macrobius, *Comm.* ii, 5, 18, and 9, 5], is again in two parts subdivided, with but one part habitable and the other surrounded by the winding intricacies of the Northern Ocean, preventing all access to it? As to that part under your feet, called the antipodes [Macrobius, *Comm.* ii, 5, 31], you are aware that for a long time the most learned men have been of two opinions whether it is inhabited or not: for myself, I have set forth my opinion in the book called *The City of God* [xvi, 9], which you have doubtless read. Is it also a fairy-tale that your habitable part, already so restricted, is yet further diminished to such an extent by seas, marshes, forests, sands and deserts, that the little corner left you, of which you are so proud, is brought down to almost nothing? And, finally, is it a fairy-tale to point out to you that on this narrow strip, where you dwell, there are divers kinds of life, different religions which oppose one another, different languages and customs [Boethius, *Cons. phil.* ii, P 7, 25], which render it impossible to make the fame of your name go far? But if these things are to you nought but fables, so, to me, all I had promised myself of your future greatness must be a fable also; for I had thought, hitherto, that no man had more knowledge of these things than you yourself. To say nothing of the conceptions of Cicero and Virgil [Cicero, *De re pub.* vi, 20, 21; Virgil *Georg.* i, 233–243; Macrobius, *Comm.* ii, 5, 7] and other systems of knowledge, [philosophical] or poetic [Ovid, *Metam.* ii, 129–132], of which you seemed to have a [perfect grasp], I knew that not long since, in your *Africa,* you had expressed the very same opinions in these pretty lines—

> The Universe itself is but an isle
> Confined in narrow bounds, small, and begirt
> By Ocean's flowing waves.

Africa ii, 361–363. Draper (1911), pp. 177–179. On these *Secretum* passages, Rico (1974), pp. 391–406. Cf. also *Africa* ii (Bergin [1977], 467–515); *De ocio,* Rotondi, p 46; and below, *DR* i, 96, 253–263. On the measurement of the earth in Antiquity, Neugebauer (1975), ii, pp. 646, 650, 652–654, 734–735. On *magnus annus*—the Great Year (Neugebauer, ibid., ii, p. 618)—and the implied idea of eternal recurrence (Plato, *Tim.* 22–23, Hamilton & Cairns [1961], pp. 1157–1158; Seneca, *Dial.* vi, Ad Marciam, xxvi, 6; Augustine, *De civ. Dei* xii, 1; Honorius of Autun, *PL* 172, c. 155; Hugh of St. Victor, *PL* 175, c. 144; John of Salisbury, *Enth.* 989–996, *PL* 199, c. 986; *Roman de la Rose* 16801–16832; and Chaucer, *Parl. of Fowls* 57–70) explicitly condemned A.D. 1277 by Etienne Tempier, Archbishop of Paris, Russell in Fraser (1966), pp.

66–71; Grant (1966), pp. 306–309, 429–431; idem [1971a], pp. 103–124 *et passim;* idem [1974], pp. 48–312; and idem in Kretzmann (1982), chap. 26. Note also Duhem, i (1913), pp. 275–296, ii (1914), pp. 447–453; Thorndike, i, ii (1923), as indexed under *magnus annus;* Eliade (1954), pp. 87–88, 122, 134–136; Capek in Wiener (1973), iv, pp. 390–392; Kantorowicz (1975a), pp. 275–284; and Trompf (1979), esp. pp. 201–202. —Centuries later, Pascal was to observe:

> Let man then contemplate the whole of nature in her full and grand majesty, and turn his vision from the low objects which surround him. Let him gaze on that brilliant light, set like an eternal lamp to illumine the universe; let the earth appear to him a point in comparison with the vast circle described by the sun; and let him wonder at the fact that this vast circle is itself but a very fine point in comparison with that described by the stars in their revolution round the firmament. But if our view be arrested there, let our imagination pass beyond; it will sooner exhaust the power of conception than nature that of supplying material for conception. The whole visible world is only an imperceptible atom in the ample bosom of nature. No idea approaches it. We may enlarge our conceptions beyond all imaginable space; we only produce atoms in comparison with the reality of things. It is an infinite sphere, the centre of which is everywhere, the circumference nowhere. In short, it is the greatest sensible mark of the almighty power of God, that imagination loses itself in that thought.

Pensées (1670), Trotter (1941), p. 22. Cf. also Boyde (1981), pp. 96–99; Colie (1966), chap. 8; and Lovejoy (1936), chap. 4. —In essence, the notion holds for modern scientific results, which

> seem to tell us that we live in a vast universe, consisting almost wholly of space empty of matter and filled with radiation. It only contains a little matter, most of it in violent agitation; also a vanishingly small amount of living matter; and a still smaller amount of living matter endowed with consciousness.

K. R. Popper in Popper & Eccles (1977), p. 149.

5 *aut diluviis: aut aestu nimio: aut peste aliqua: aut coeli inclementia: vel terrarum*—cf. *Africa* ii, 460–461; and *Secretum* iii, Prose (1955), p. 202:

> Non ego te ad opiniones illas veterum revoco, qui crebra terris incendia diluviaque denuntiant, quibus et platonicus *Thimeus* et ciceronianus *Reipublice* sextus liber refertus est.

> I spare to call to your mind those opinions of the men of old, laid up in Plato's *Timaeus* [Chalcidius, 22 C, Waszink (1962), p. 14] and in the sixth book of Cicero's *Republic* [vi, 21, 23 = Macrobius, *Comm.* ii, 10, 4], where it is foretold that floods and conflagrations shall be coming not seldom on the earth.

Draper (1911), p. 179. Note also Augustine, *De civ. Dei* xii, 10, LCL, p. 46. On *world conflagration,* below, *DR* ii, 55, note 11.

6   1492: Plurimum est gloriae
      1581: Primum est gloriae
7   Ovid, *Tristia* iii, 4, 25, echoing Epicurus' maxim *live unknown* (Oates [1940],
      no. 86):

> crede mihi, bene qui latuit, bene vixit . . .

> Let me tell thee, he who hides well his life, lives well . . .

LCL, Wheeler, p. 117. Cf. above, *DR* i, 16, 30; i, 17, 13; i, 46, 57-60. Note
also *Fam.* ix, 5, 18.

8   *pauci quorum famae non noceat: ad plenum nosci.* Twyne, f. 114 v: *fewe whom
      fame woulde not hurt to be fully knowen.*
9   Claudian, *De bello Gildonico,* 385. Cf. above, *DR* i, 51, 18–21.
10   Cf. above, *DR* i, 46, 115–116.
11   Cicero, *Tusc. disp.* i, 45, 109:

> Sed profecto mors tum aequissimo animo oppetitur, cum suis se laudibus vita
> occidens consolari potest. Nemo parum diu vixit, qui *virtutis perfectae* perfecto
> functus est munere. Multa mihi ipsi ad mortem tempestiva fuerunt, quam
> utinam potuissem obire! Nihil enim iam acquirabatur, cumulata erant officia
> vitae, cum fortuna bella restabant. Qua re si ipsa ratio minus perficiet ut mor-
> tem negligere possimus, at vita acta perficiat ut satis superque vixisse
> videamur. Quamquam enim sensus enim sensus aberit, tamen suis et propriis
> bonis laudis et gloriae, quamvis non sentiant, mortui non carent. Etsi enim
> nihil habet in se gloria cur expetatur, *tamen virtutem tamquam umbra sequitur.*

> But assuredly death is encountered with most equanimity when the failing life
> can find solace in the reputation it has won. No one has lived too short a life
> who has discharged the perfect work of *perfect virtue.* In my life there have
> been many occasions when death would have been timely, and would I could
> have found it! for there was no longer anything to be won; life's duties had
> been discharged in full; the war with fortune alone remained. If therefore my
> arguments fail to convince us that we can ignore death, yet let a life completed
> make us think that we have lived sufficiently and more. For though conscious-
> ness may have gone, nevertheless the dead, unconscious though they be, are
> not without their own peculiar blessings of fame and glory. There is, it may be,
> nothing in glory that we should desire it, *but none the less it follows virtue like a
> shadow.*

LCL, King, p. 131. Another key passage is Seneca, *Ep.* 79, 13:

> Gloria umbra virtutis est; etiam invitam comitabitur. Sed quemadmodum um-
> bra aliquando antecedit, aliquando sequitur vel a tergo est, ita gloria aliquando
> ante nos est visendamque se praebet, aliquando in averso est maiorque quo
> serior, ubi invidia secessit.

> Fame is the shadow of virtue; it will attend virtue even against her will. But, as

the shadow sometimes precedes and sometimes follows or even lags behind, so fame sometimes goes before us and shows herself in plain sight, and sometimes is in the rear, and is all the greater in proportion as she is late in coming, when once envy has beaten a retreat.

LCL, Gummere, pp. 207, 209. Petrarch recalled the topic repeatedly; cf. *Fam.* i, 2, 25, xv, 1, 8, xv, 14, 27, xxii, 14, 7, xxiii, 11, 1, xxiv, 10, 34–35; *Sen.* xiv, 1 (1581: 372); *Secretum* iii, *Prose* (1955), p. 204, and Rico (1974), pp. 411–413; and *Africa* ii, 486–500. On fame and posterity also, below, *DR* i, 117–119, ii, 25, ii, 88, and ii, 130. Cf. Bernardo (1962), pp. 54–59, 66–71 *et passim;* and Mann (1984), pp. 84–85.

12   *ante perfectam virtutem*—a Ciceronian expression; see note 11, above.

93 ❖ GENEROSITY

1   Dialogues 93–107 deal with power, high office, and warfare.
2   On this dialogue, cf. Cicero, *De off.* i, 14, 42–17, 58; and Seneca, *De benef.* Note also Tuve (1966), chap. 2.
3   Pothinus (1492, 1581, and Twyne have Photinus) on Pompey, Lucan, viii, 482–535:

> Sed melior suadere malis et nosse tyrannos
> Ausus Pompeium leto damnare Pothinus
> "Ius et fas multos faciunt, Ptolemaee, nocentes;
> Dat poenas laudata fides, cum sustinet," inquit
> "Quos fortuna premit. Fatis accede deisque,
> Et cole felices, miseros fuge. Sidera terra
> Ut distant et flamma mari, sic utile recto.
> Sceptrorum vis tota perit, si pendere iusta
> Incipit, evertitque arces respectus honesti.
> Libertas scelerum est, quae regna invisa tuetur,
> Sublatusque modus gladiis. Facere omnia saeve
> Non inpune licet, nisi cum facis. Exeat aula,
> Qui volt esse pius. Virtus et summa potestas
> Non coeunt; semper metuet, quem saeva pudebunt.
> Non inpune tuos Magnus contempserit annos,
> Qui te nec victos arcere a litore nostro
> Posse putat. Neu nos sceptris privaverit hospes,
> Pignora sunt propiora tibi: Nilumque Pharonque,

Si regnare piget, damnatae redde sorori.
Aegyptum certe Latiis tueamur ab armis.
Quidquid non fuerit Magni, dum bella geruntur,
Nec victoris erit. Toto iam pulsus ab orbe,
Postquam nulla manet rerum fiducia, quaerit,
Cum qua gente cadat. Rapitur civilibus umbris.
Nec soceri tantum arma fugit: fugit ora senatus.
Cuius Thessalicas saturat pars magna volucres,
Et metuit gentes, quas uno in sanguine mixtas
Deseruit, regesque timet, quorum omnia mersit,
Thessaliaeque reus nulla tellure receptus
Sollicitat nostrum, quem nondum perdidit, orbem.
Iustior in Magnum nobis, Ptolemaee, querellae
Causa data est. Quid sepositam semperque quietam
Crimine bellorum maculas Pharon arvaque nostra
Victori suspecta facis? cur sola cadenti
Haec placuit tellus, in quam Pharsalica fata
Conferres poenasque tuas? iam crimen habemus
Purgandum gladio. Quod nobis sceptra senatus
Te suadente dedit, votis tua fovimus arma.
Hoc ferrum, quod fata iubent proferre, paravi
Non tibi, sed victo; feriam tua viscera, Magne,
Malueram soceri: rapimur, quo cuncta feruntur
Tene mihi dubitas an sit violare necesse,
Cum liceat? Quae te nostri fiducia regni
Huc agit, infelix? populum non cernis inermem
Arvaque vix refugo fodientem mollia Nilo?
Metiri sua regna decet viresque fateri.
Tu, Ptolemaee, potes Magni fulcire ruinam,
Sub qua Roma iacet? bustum cineresque movere
Thessalicos audes bellumque in regna vocare?
Ante aciem Emathiam nullis accessimus armis:
Pompei nunc castra placent, quae deserit orbis?
Nunc victoris opes et cognita fata lacessis?
Adversis non desse decet, sed laeta secutos:
Nulla fides umquam miseros elegit amicos."

But there was one, more fit to counsel wicked kings and know their heart, and a Pothinus dared to sign the death-warrant of a Pompey. He said: "Ptolemy, the laws of God and man make many guilty: we praise loyalty, but it pays the price when it supports those whom Fortune crushes. Take the side of destiny and Heaven, and court the prosperous but shun the afflicted. Expediency is as far from the right as the stars from earth or fire from water. The power of kings is utterly destroyed, once they begin to weigh considerations of justice; and regard for virtue levels the strongholds of tyrants. It is boundless wickedness and unlimited slaughter that protect the unpopularity of a sovereign. If all your deeds are cruel, you will suffer for it the moment you cease from cruelty. If a man would be righteous, let him depart from a court. Virtue is incompatible with absolute power. He who is ashamed to commit cruelty must always fear it. Let Magnus suffer for having despised your youth; he thinks you cannot repel even a beaten man from our coast. And, that a stranger may not rob us of the throne, remember that you have others nearer of kin; and, if your crown is uneasy, restore the Nile and Pharos to the sister [Cleopatra] you have condemned. Let us in any case protect Egypt from the arms of Rome. Whatever did not belong to Pompey during the war will not belong to Caesar either. Driven from all the world, with no reliance left upon his fortunes, he seeks a people to share his fall. He is dragged down by the ghosts of those who fell in civil war. It is not merely Caesar's sword that he flies from: he flies also from the face of the senators, of whom so many are now glutting the vultures of Thessaly; he fears the foreign nations, whom he forsook and left weltering in blood together; he dreads the kings, whose all he destroyed; guilty of Pharsalia and rejected by every country, he troubles our realm which he has not yet destroyed. But we, Ptolemy, can complain more justly of Pompey than he of us: why does he stain secluded and peace-loving Pharos with the guilt of war and bring down Caesar's displeasure on our land? Why when falling did he choose this country of all others to bring to it the curse of Pharsalia and the punishment which he alone should pay? Even now we have incurred guilt, which we cannot purge away except by using the sword. On his motion the Senate granted us the sovereignty of Egypt, and therefore we prayed for his victory. The sword, which destiny bids me bring forth, I did not intend for Pompey but for the loser, whichever he might be. I shall pierce your heart with it, Magnus; I had rather have slain Caesar; but we are borne by the current that carries the whole world away. Do you doubt whether I must do you violence? I must, because I may. What reliance upon our kingdom brings him hither, ill-fated man? Does he not see our unwarlike population, scarce able to till the fields softened by the falling Nile? We must take the measure of our kingdom and confess our weakness. Are you, Ptolemy, strong enough to prop the fall of Pompey—that fall beneath which Rome is crushed? Dare you disturb the pyre and ashes of Pharsalia, and summon war to our own realms? Before the battle of Pharsalia we took neither side: do we now adopt Pompey's cause when all the world is forsaking it? Do you now challenge the might and proved success of Caesar? To support the loser in adversity is right, but right only for those who have shared his prosperity; no loyalty ever picked out the wretched as friends.''

LCL, Duff, pp. 473, 475, 477.

I cannot locate a "Sabinus" in Seneca. The Seneca passage which corresponds most closely to Reason's argument is *De benef.* ii, 27,1–2:

Cn. Lentulus augur, divitiarum maximum exemplum, antequam illum libertini pauperem facerent, hic, qui quater milies sestertium suum vidit (proprie dixi; nihil enim amplius quam vidit), ingenii fuit sterilis, tam pusilli quam animi. Cum esset avarissimus, nummos citius emittebat quam verba: tanta illi inopia erat sermonis. Hic cum omnia incrementa sua divo Augusto deberet, ad quem attulerat paupertatem sub onere nobilitatis laborantem, princeps iam civitatis et pecunia et gratia subinde de Augusto solebat queri dicens a studiis se abductum; nihil tantum in se congestum esse, quantum perdidisset relicta eloquentia. At illi inter alia hoc quoque divus Augustus praestiterat, quod illum derisu et labore irrito liberaverat!

Gnaeus Lentulus, the augur, who, before his freedmen reduced him to poverty, was the most conspicuous example of wealth—this man, who saw his four hundred millions (I have spoken with strict accuracy, for he did no more than "see" them!), was destitute of intelligence, as contemptible in intellect as he was in heart. Though he was the greatest miser, it was easier for him to disgorge coins than words—so great his poverty when it came to talking. Though he owed all his advancement to the deified Augustus, to whom he had come with nothing but the poverty that was struggling under the burden of a noble name, yet, when he had now become the chief citizen of the state, both in wealth and influence, he used to make constant complaint, saying that Augustus had enticed him away from his studies; that he had not heaped upon him nearly so much as he had lost by surrendering the practice of eloquence. Yet the deified Augustus, besides loading him with other benefits, had also rescued him from ridicule and vain endeavor!

LCL, Basore, pp. 103, 105.

4   Cf. *Sen.* iii, 1 (1581: 765):

Magna quidem pars quaerelarum humanarum, non iniusta materia, sed stulta est, illud ergo consultius ac rectius, & fateri, & credere, nil hominibus sine iusto licet abdito Dei iuditio euenire, neque fortunam immeritam & incognitam lacerare.

The greater part of human complaints is not due to injustice but to stupidity. Thus it is more appropriate and accurate to state and to believe that nothing happens to man without the just, though admittedly hidden, judgment of God, instead of abusing one's ill fortune as being undeserved and enormous.

The topic is used as an example of rhetorical *vitiosa expositio quae nimium longe repetitur*—defective Proposition tracing things too far back—in *Ad Herenn.* ii, 22, 34:

"Omnium malorum stultitia est mater atque materies. Ea parit immensas cupiditates. Immensae porro cupiditates infinitae, immoderatae sunt. Hae pariunt avaritiam. Avaritia porro hominem ad quodvis maleficium impellit. Ergo avaritia inducti adversarii nostri hoc in se facinus admiserunt."

"Stupidity is the mother and matter of all evils. She gives birth to boundless desires. Furthermore, boundless desires have neither end nor limit. They breed avarice. Avarice, further, drives men to any crime you will. Thus it is avarice which has led our adversaries to take this crime upon themselves."

(Cf. Sallust, *Cat.* 10: "These [the lust for money and the lust for power] were,

I might say, the source [*materies*] of all evils"; and Calpurnius Flaccus, 8: "A man long happy is substance [*materia*] for all disasters.") LCL, Kaplan, pp. 118–119. Note also below, *DR* ii, 34, note 3, and ii, 118, 52–54.

5   1492: opinionumque peruersitas: hinc nimirum pestes animi prodeunt superbia inprimis et cupiditas: quibus nullum obsequium: non contumax . . .

1581: opinionumque peruersitas & cupiditas, quibus nullum obsequium non contumax . . .

On envy, pride and greed, below, *DR* i, 105, 17–18. On stupidity and perverseness of public opinion, above, *DR* i, 11, note 1.

6   Reason refers to Aristotle on μεγαλοψυχία, *Eth. Nic.* iv, 3, 1124b, 9–15:

And he is the sort of man to confer benefits, but he is ashamed of receiving them; for the one is the mark of a superior, the other of an inferior. And he is apt to confer greater benefits in return; for thus the original benefactor besides being paid will incur a debt to him, and will be the gainer by the transaction. They seem also to remember any service they have done, but not those they have received (for he who receives a service is inferior to him who has done it, but the proud man wishes to be superior), and to hear of the former with pleasure, of the latter with displeasure.

W. D. Ross in Barnes (1984), pp. 1774–1775.

7   Seneca, *De benef.* ii, 11, 2:

qui dedit beneficium, taceat, narret, qui accepit.

LCL, Basore, p. 69.

8   1492: Saepe singulis beneficiis: aut nullos: aut singulos amicos obliuiosos: & trepidos hostes: aut tibi multos feceris memores: ac feruentes.

1581: Saepe singulis beneficiis, aut nullos, aut singulos amicos obliuiosos, & trepidos, hostes autem tibi multos feceris memores ac feruentes.

9   Cf., e.g., *Fam.* xxiii, 4, 3. On Scylla and Charybdis, below, *DR* ii, 90, note 7.

10   1492: quos magnitudo status atque hominum necessitas multa largiri cogit.

1581: quos magnitudo hominum necessitas multa largiri cogit.

11   Cf. above, *DR* i, 50, 51–59.

94 ❖ POPULARITY

1   1492: Ne propera

1581: Propera

2   *vita omnis a fine describitur.* Reason used the same words, above, *DR* i, 17, 39.

3   All texts have *Milciades.*

4   Reason lists the *exempla* in the order of Petrarch's *Rerum memorandarum libri: Romana*—Roman—first, followed by *Externa*—foreign ones.

    The Scipios are Publius Cornelius Scipio (Africanus Maior), 234–183 B.C., conqueror of Hannibal (Zama, 202 B.C.), who died in exile; and Publius Cornelius Scipio Aemilianus (Africanus Minor), c. 185–129 B.C., destroyer of Carthage, leader of the conservatives against the Gracchan reforms (below, *DR* i, 95, note 3), said to have been murdered by his wife and mother-in-law. Marcus Furius Camillus, d. c. 365 B.C., Roman hero and conqueror of Veii (c. 396 B.C.), was exiled; P. Rutilius Rufus, consul 105 B.C., and *legatus* in Asia, was condemned and exiled in 92 B.C. Quintus Caecilius Metellus (Numidicus), consul in the Numidian war against Jugurtha, exiled 100 B.C. as a result of efforts by Marius, was poisoned by Q. Varius. —Themistocles, one of the great Athenian statesmen, was ostracized and exiled 472 B.C.; Miltiades, Athenian commander at Marathon, 490 B.C., impeached and fined by Athens 489 B.C. Cimon, son of Miltiades and successor of Themistocles, was ostracized and exiled 461 B.C.; the Athenian statesman Aristides, ostracized 482 B.C. Theseus, mythical king of Athens, was driven from the city by rebellion, took refuge in Scyros, and was murdered there by King Lycomedes. Solon, the founder of the Athenian democracy, experienced civil strife in the wake of his reforms, 589–580 B.C. After the Roman victory, Hannibal, the great Carthaginian general, fled to Syria, then to Crete, and finally to the court of Prusias, king of Bithynia, where he committed suicide to escape extradition. Lycurgus, founder of the Spartan constitution, is said to have been posthumously impeached; his children were imprisoned.

5   *Likeness attracts*—cf. Boethius, *Quomodo subst.* ix, 49, as above, *DR* i, 66, note 2.

6   *aura aestiva* = Horace, *Carm.* i, 22, 18.

7   1492: paria haec si conferantur
    1581: patria hae si conferantur

8   Cf. above, *DR* i, 19, 146–147.

9   1492: Populus me suscipit
    1581: Populus me suspicit

10   *Mirabor si tam inculto cultore fructifices*

11   Desire for fame and glory is discussed in personal terms, *Secretum* iii, *Prose* (1955), pp. 188–192:

    Augustinus: Gloriam hominum et immortalitatem nominis plus debito cupis.
    Franciscus: Fateor plane, neque hunc appetitum ullis remediis frenare queo.
    Aug.: At valde metuendum est, ne optata nimium hec inanis immortalitas vere immortalitatis iter obstruxerit.

Fr.: Timeo equidem hoc unum inter cetera; sed quibus artibus tutus sim a te potissimum expecto, a quo maiorum michi morborum remedia suppeditata sunt.

Aug.: Nullum profecto maiorem tibi morbum inesse noveris, etsi quidam forte fediores sunt. Verum quid esse gloriam reris, quam tantopere expetis? Edixere.

Fr.: Nescio an diffinitionem exigas. At ea cui notior est quam tibi?

Aug.: Tibi vero nomen glorie notum, res ipsa, ut ex actibus colligitur, esse videtur incognita; nunquam enim tam ardenter, si nosses, optares. Certe, sive "illustrem et pervagatam vel in suos cives vel in patriam vel in omne genus hominum meritorum famam" quod uno in loco M. Tullio visum est; sive "frequentem de aliquo famam cum laude" quod alio loco ait idem; utrobique gloriam famam esse reperies. Scis autem quid sit fama?

Fr.: Non occurrit id quidem ad presens et ignota in medium proferre metuo. Ideoque, quod esse verius opinor, siluisse maluerim.

Aug.: Prudenter hoc unum et modeste. Nam in omni sermone, gravi presertim et ambiguo, non tam quid dicatur, quam quid non dicatur attendendum est. Neque enim par ex bene dictis laus et ex male dictis reprehensio est. Scito igitur famam nichil esse aliud quam sermonem de aliquo vulgatum ac sparsum per ora multorum.

Fr.: Laudo seu diffinitionem, seu descriptionem dici mavis.

Aug.: Est igitur flatus quidam atque aura volubilis et, quod egrius feras, flatus est hominum plurimorum. Scio cui loquor; nulli usquam odiosiores esse vulgi mores ac gesta perpendi. Vide nunc quanta iudiciorum perversitas: quorum enim facta condemnas, eorum sermunculis delectaris. Atque utinam delectareris duntaxat, nec in eis tue felicitatis apicem collocasses! Quo enim spectat labor iste perpetuus continueque vigilie ac vehemens impetus studiorum? Respondebis forsitan, ut vite tue profutura condiscas. At vero iam pridem vite simul et morti necessaria didicisti. Era igitur potius quemadmodum in actum illa produceres experiendo tentandum, quam in laboriosa cognitione procedendum, ubi novi semper recessus et inaccesse latebre et inquisitionum nullus est terminus. Adde quod in his, que populo placerent, studiosius elaborasti, his ipsis placere satagens, qui tibi pre omnibus displicebant; hinc poematum, illinc historiarum, denique omnis eloquentie flosculos carpens, quibus aures audientium demulceres.

Fr.: Parce, queso, hoc tacitus audire non possum. Nunquam, ex quo pueritiam excessi, scientiarum flosculis delectatus sum; multa enim adversus literarum laceratores, eleganter a Cicerone dicta notavi, et a Seneca illud in primis: "Viro captare flosculos turpe est, et notissimis se fulcire vocibus ac memoria stare."

Aug.: Nec ego, dum hec dico, vel ignaviam tibi vel memorie angustias obicio; sed quod ex his, que legeras, floridiora in sodalium delitias reservasti, et velut ex ingenti acervo in usus amicorum elegantiora consignasti, quod totum inanis glorie lenocinium est. Et tandem quotidiana occupatione non contentus, que magna licet temporis inpensa nonnisi presentis evi famam promittebat, cogitationesque tuas in longinqua transmittens, famam inter posteros concupisti. Ideoque manum ad maiora iam porrigens, librum historiarum a rege Romulo in Titum Caesarem, opus immensum temporisque et laboris capacissimum, aggressus es. Eoque nondum ad exitum perducto (tantis glorie stimulis urgebaris!) ad Africam poetico quodam navigio transivisti; et nunc in prefatos *Africe* libros sic diligenter incumbis, ut alios non relinquas. Ita totam vitam his duabus curis, ut intercurrentes alias innumeras sileam, prodigus preciosissime irreparabilisque rei, tribuis, deque aliis scribens, tui ipsius obliviceris. Et quidem scis an, utroque inexpleto opere, mors calamum fatigatum e manibus rapiat, atque ita, dum immodice gloriam petens gemino calle festinas, neutro pervenias ad optatum?

Augustinus: Ambition still has too much hold on you. You seek too eagerly the praise of men, and to leave behind you an undying name.

Franciscus: I freely confess it. I cannot beat down that passion in my soul. For it, as yet, I have found no cure.

Aug.: But I greatly fear lest this pursuit of a false immortality of fame may shut for you the way that leads to the true immortality of life.

Fr.: That is one of my fears also, but I await your discovering to me the means to save my life; you, of a truth, will do it, who have furnished me with means for the healing of evils greater still.

Aug.: Think not that any of your ills is greater than this one, though I deny not that some may be more vile. But tell me, I pray you, what in your opinion is this thing called glory, that you so ardently covet?

Fr.: I know not if you ask me for a definition. But if so, who so capable to give one as yourself?

Aug.: The name of glory is well enough known to you; but to the real thing, if one may judge by your actions, you are a stranger. If you had known what it is you would not long for it so eagerly. Suppose you define glory, with Cicero, as being "the illustrious and world-wide renown of good services rendered to one's fellow citizens, to one's country, or to all mankind" [*Pro Marcello* viii, 26]; or as he expresses it elsewhere, "public opinion uttering its voice about a man in words of praise" [*De inv.* ii, 166]. You will notice that in both these cases glory is said to be reputation. Now, do you know what this reputation is?

Fr.: I cannot say any good description of it occurs to me at the moment; and I shrink from putting forward things I do not understand. I think, therefore, the truer and better course is for me to keep silence.

Aug.: You act like a wise and modest man. In every serious question, and especially when the matter is ambiguous, one should pay much less attention to what one will say than to what one will not say, for the credit of having said well is something much less than the discredit of having said ill. Now I submit to you that reputation is nothing but talk about someone, passing from mouth to mouth of many people.

Fr.: I think your definition, or, if you prefer the word, description, is a good one.

Aug.: It is, then, but a breath, a changing wind [cf. Virgil, *Aeneid* vi, 816, as below, *DR* ii, 88, 96, and note 20); and, what will disgust you more, it is the breath of a crowd. I know to whom I am speaking. I have observed that no man more than you abhors the manners and behaviour of the common herd. Now see what perversity is this! You let yourself be charmed with the applause of those whose conduct you abominate; and may Heaven grant you are only charmed, and that you put not in their power your own everlasting welfare! Why and wherefore, I ask, this perpetual toil, these ceaseless vigils, and this intense application to study? You will answer, perhaps, that you seek to find out what is profitable for life. But you have long since learned what is needful for life and for death. What was now required of you was to try and to put in practice what you know, instead of plunging deeper and deeper into laborious inquiries, where new problems are always meeting you, and insoluble mysteries, in which you never reach the end. Add to which the fact that you keep toiling and toiling to satisfy the public; wearying yourself to please the very people who, to you, are the most displeasing; gathering now a flower of poesy, now of history—in a word, employing all your genius of words to tickle the ears of the listening throng.

Fr.: I beg you pardon, but I cannot let that pass without saying a word. Never since I was a boy have I pleased myself with elegant extracts and flowerets of literature. For often I have noted what neat and excellent things Cicero has uttered against butchers of books and especially, also, the phrase of Seneca in which he declares, "it is a disgrace for a man to keep hunting for flowers and prop himself up on familiar quotations, and only stand on what he knows by heart" [Seneca, *Ep.* 33, 7].

Aug.: In saying what I did, I neither accuse you of idleness nor scant memory. What I blame you for is that in your reading you have picked out the more flowery passages for the amusement of your cronies, and, as it were, packed up boxes of pretty things out of a great heap, for the benefit of your friends—which is nothing but pandering to a desire of vainglory; and, moreover, I say that, not being contented with your duty of every day (which in spite of great expense of time, only promised you some celebrity among your contemporaries), you have let your thoughts run on ages of time and given yourself up to dreams of fame among those who come after. And in pursuit of this end, putting your hand to yet greater tasks, you entered on writing a history from the time of King Romulus to that of the Emperor Titus, an enormous undertaking that would swallow up an immensity of time and labour. Then, without waiting till this was finished, goaded by the pricks of your ambition for glory, you sailed off in your poetical barque towards Africa; and now on the aforesaid books of your *Africa* you are hard at work, without relinquishing the other. And in this way you devote your whole life to those two absorbing occupations—for I will not stop to mention countless others that come in also—and throw utterly away what is of most concern and which, when lost, cannot be recovered. You write books on others, but yourself you quite forget. And who knows but what, before either of your works be finished, Death may snatch the pen from your tired hand, and while in your insatiable hunt for glory you hurry on first by one path, then the other, you may find at last that by neither of them have you reached your goal?

Draper (1911), pp. 165–170. The historical work referred to is probably the *De viris illustribus*. On this, Rico (1974), pp. 409–424.

95 ✤ SEIZING A LORDSHIP

1   An interesting background for *DR* i, 95, i, 96, ii, 79, ii, 81, and also i, 85, i, 107, i, 116, and ii, 39, is furnished by *Fam.* xii, 2, and *Sen.* xiv, 1 (printed as *De Republica optime administranda liber* in 1581: 372–386)—both, essays on the education and conduct of princes. *Fam.* xii, 2, to Niccolò Acciaiuoli, Grand Seneschal of the kingdom of Naples, Avignon, Feb. 20, 1352, offers advice on the guidance of Louis of Taranto, the young king of Naples. Its immediate fame is attested by the *Expositio epistolae "Iam tandem,"* Barbato da Sulmona's *long and elaborate commentary* on the letter (Wilkins [1955], pp. 106, 251–252). *Sen.* xiv, 1, was written for Francesco da Carrara the Elder and dated Arquà, November 28 (1373). On this treatise on princely government in general and its requirements for Padua in particular, Wilkins (1959), pp. 252–256; and Baron (1966), pp. 120, 492.

2   1492, 1581, and Twyne read *Elearchus.*

3   Alexander, tyrant of Pherae, was assassinated by his wife 358 B.C. Dionysius II, of Syracuse, was defeated 344 B.C. by Timoleon of Corinth. This resulted in the proverbial phrase *Dionysius Corinthi,* denoting one fallen from great power (cf. below, *DR* ii, 81, 54, and note 12). Phalaris was tyrant of Agrigentum in Sicily during the first half of the sixth century B.C. Hanno is probably the son of Hamilcar, who as a Carthaginian general aspired to be king and was put to death by torture. Clearchus recruited for Cyrus and attempted to seize the tyranny of Byzantium. He was sent in chains to the Persian court by Tissaphernes and executed there 401 B.C. Aristotimus was tyrant of Epirus in the third century B.C. (Justin, xxvi, 1, 4). Nabis was defeated by Quinctius Flaminius and assassinated 192 B.C. Hipparchus, son of Pisistratus, tyrant of Athens, was killed by Harmodius and Aristogiton (514 B.C.), who became revered as champions of liberty in Athens.

4   Spurius Cassius and Spurius Maelius were suspected of aiming at regal power. Cassius was executed 485 B.C.; Maelius, 439 B.C. Marcus Manlius Capitolinus held the Capitol against the invading Gauls 390 B.C.; accused of aspiring to be tyrant, he was thrown from the Tarpeian rock. Catiline attempted to seize power by revolution 65–63 B.C. and was killed near Pistoria 62 B.C. The brothers Tiberius Sempronius Gracchus and Gaius Sempronius Gracchus attempted to solve the economic crisis of Rome's land policy. Tiberius was killed in an election riot 133 B.C.; Gaius by a faithful slave, 121 B.C. Apuleius Saturninus promoted the Gracchan proposals. He was torn to pieces after a revolutionary attempt 100 B.C.

5   I.e., the Roman emperors Gaius Caligula, assassinated A.D. 41; Nero, who

committed suicide A.D. 68; Domitian, murdered A.D. 96; and Commodus, A.D. 192. Bassianus is probably Bassianus Antoninus Caracalla, slain A.D. 217, because Elagabalus, slain A.D. 222, and also named Bassianus, is mentioned separately, below, *DR* i, 96, 81–85. On this, Gibbon, Bury, i (1909), pp. 139, 154.

6   I.e., Pluto, the Greek god of the nether world, who rules over the souls of the dead.

7   Juvenal, x, 112–113:

> ad generum Cereris sine caede ac vulnere pauci,
> descendunt reges et sicca morte tyranni,

LCL, Ramsay, p. 201.

8   Horace, *Ars poet.*, last line, 476:

> non missura cutem, nisi plena cruoris, hirudo.

LCL, Fairclough, p. 489.

9   1492: iisdem atque sacris: iisdem festis diebus: iisdem ludis. & luctibus: 1581: iisdem atque sacris: iisdem ludis & luctibus.

Compare above, *DR* i, 84, 39—46.

10   The story of Dionysius I, of Syracuse and hisi courtier Damocles is told in Cicero, *Tusc. disp.* v, 21, 61–62:

> Nam cum quidam ex eius adsentatoribus, Damocles, commemoraret in sermone copias eius, opes, maiestatem dominatus, rerum abundantiam, magnificentiam aedium regiarum, negaretque umquam beatiorem quemquam fuisse: *Visne igitur,* inquit, *o Damocle, quoniam te haec vita delectat, ipse eam degustare et fortunam experiri meam?* Cum se ille cupere dixisset, collocari iussit hominem in aureo lecto strato pulcherrimo textili stragulo, magnificis operibus picto, abacosque complures ornavit argento auroque caelato; tum ad mensam eximia forma pueros delectos iussit consistere eosque nutum illius intuentes diligenter ministrare. Aderant unguenta, coronae; incendebantur odores; mensae consquisitissimis epulis exstruebantur: fortunatus sibi Damocles videbatur. In hoc medio apparatu fulgentem gladium e lacunari saeta equina aptum demitti iussit, ut impenderet illius beati cervicibus. Itaque nec pulcros illos ministratores aspiciebat nec plenum artis argentum nec manum porrigebat in mensam; iam ipsae defluebant coronae; denique exoravit tyrannum, ut abire liceret, quod iam beatus nollet esse. Satisne videtur declarasse Dionysius nihil esse ei beatum, cui semper aliqui terror impendeat.

> For when one of his flatterers, named Damocles, dilated in conversation upon his troops, his resources, the splendours of his despotism, the magnitude of his treasures, the stateliness of his palaces, and said that no one had ever been happier: "Would you then, Damocles," said he, "as this life of mine seems to you so delightful, like to have a taste of it yourself and make trial of my good fortune?" On his admitting his desire to do so Dionysius had him seated on a

couch of gold covered with beautiful woven tapestries embroidered with magnificent designs, and had several sideboards set out with richly chased gold and silver plate. Next a table was brought and chosen boys of rare beauty were ordered to take their places and wait upon him with eyes fixed attentively upon his motions. There were perfumes, garlands; incense was burnt; the tables were loaded with the choicest banquet: Damocles thought himself a lucky man. In the midst of all this display Dionysius had a gleaming sword, attached to a horse-hair, let down from the ceiling in such a way that it hung over the neck of this happy man. And so he had no eye either for those beautiful attendants, or the richly-wrought plate, nor did he reach out his hand to the table; presently the garlands slipped from their place of their own accord; at length he besought the tyrant to let him go, as by now he was sure he had no wish to be happy. Dionysius seems (does he not?) to have avowed plainly that there was no happiness for the man who was perpetually menaced by some alarm.

LCL, King, pp. 487, 489. Note also Horace, *Carm.* iii, 1, 17–18 = Persius, iii, 40–41; *Hist. Aug.,* Firmus, x, 1–2; Boethius, *Cons. phil.* iii, P5, 15; and John of Salisbury, *Policrat* viii, 23, PL 199, c. 813. Cf. below, *DR* ii, 39, 28–30; and the allusion in *Fam.* xxiv, 5, 9.

11   Macrobius, *Saturn.* ii, 7, 4–5:

in ipsa quoque actione subinde se, qua poterat, ulciscebatur, inducto habitu Syri, qui velut flagris caesus praeripientique se similis exclamabat:
                    porro Quirites libertatem perdimus;
et paulo post adiecit:
          necesse est multos timeat quem multi timent.
quo dicto universitas populi ad solum Caesarem oculos et ora convertit, notantes impotentiam eius hac dicacitate lapidatam.

In the course of his acting too, [Laberius] continually would take his revenge, however he could. Dressed as Syrus, whom he represented as flogged by whips and beating a hasty retreat, he would cry:
          On, Citizens of Rome, we lose our liberty
and shortly afterward came the line:
          Many he needs must fear whom many fear.
And at those last words the audience as one man turned and looked at Caesar, thus indicating that this scathing gibe was an attack on his despotism.

Davies (1969), p. 181. Cited in *Sen.* xiv, 1 (1581: 374). Cf. also John of Salisbury, *Policrat.* viii, 14, PL 199, c. 772, where the sentence is appended to the sayings of Publilius Syrus, although it does not appear in the original list of Publilian sayings, Aulus Gellius, xvii, 14, 4.

12   I.t.: Naso
13   Ovid, *Am.* ii, 2, 10:

quem metuit quisque, perisse cupit.

LCL, Showerman, p. 385.

14   Quoted in Cicero, *De off.* ii, 7, 23:

> Quem metuunt, oderunt; quem quisque odit,
> perisse expetit.

LCL, Miller, p. 191. Cf. also Accius, *Trag.*, 203:

> oderint dum metuant.

> Let them hate if only they fear.

Cicero, ibid., i, 28, 97; Seneca, *Dial.* iii, De ira i, 20, 4; *De clem.* i, 12, 4, ii, 2, 2; Suetonius, iv, Calig., 30, 1; again, in *Fam.* xii, 3, 16; *Contra quendam, Prose* (1955), p. 708. —In *DR* ii, 82, 34–45, the Laberius—Ovid—Ennius sequence recurs, enlarged by an additional quotation from Cicero, *De off.* ii, 7, 24. In *Sen.* xiv, 1 (1581: 374), the sequence of quotes is as follows: Laberius–Cicero, *De off.* ii, 7, 24–Ennius, and the (unidentified) quotation from Accius.

96 ❖ KINGSHIP AND EMPIRE

1   Above, *DR* i, 85.
2   Cf. above, *DR* i, 17, note 7.
3   Cf. John of Salisbury, *Policrat.* iv, 2, PL 199, cc. 514–515; and Kantorowicz (1957a), pp. 94–97. Note also the discussion in Dante, *Mon.* iii, 10, 7–12; and Kantorowicz, ibid., chap. viii.
4   1492: tuas res et teque ipsum
     1581: tuas res et reque ipsum
5   Dante, *Mon.* iii, 12, 4, *Opere* (1921), p. 405:

> . . . aliud est esse hominem et aliud est esse papam; et eodem modo aliud est esse hominem, aliud esse imperatorem, sicut aliud esse hominem, aliud esse patrem et dominum.

> . . . It is one thing to be a man and another to be pope; similarly, it is one thing to be a man, another to be emperor, as it is one thing to be a man and another to be father or lord.

6   *claramque miseriam*—note *Sen.* xi, 11, as below, *DR* ii, 119, note 12: *superba miseria.* Cf. the use of *oxymoron* in the description of love, *DR* i, 69, note 2.

7   I.t.: Alexander

8   *Hist. Aug.,* Severus Alexander, xxxiii, 3:

> nec multum in signa aut ad apparatum regium auri et serici deputabat, dicens *imperium in virtute* esse *non in decore.*

> Nor did he spend much for their standards or for the royal outfit of gold and silk, declaring that the imperial power was based, not on outward show, but on valour.

LCL, Magie, p. 243.

9   *nil non licet regi*—cf. Romulus, iii, 20: *ut regibus omnia licent,* note 47, below. On *quod principi placuit*—what pleases the Prince—and the *lex regna, Dig.* i, 4, 1; Ullmann (1977), pp. 42–44; 133–139; and Kantorowicz (1957a), *passim,* esp. pp. 150–154. Note also Post (1964), chaps. v, x; and Berman (1983), chap. 13.

10   Cf. Terence, *Eun.* ii, 245:

> . . . "quid? tu his rebus credis fieri? *tota erras via.* . . ."

> . . . "What? Do you think that's what does it? You're quite on the wrong road. . . ."

LCL, Sargeaunt, p. 257.

11   On this, note Ullmann (1977), pp. 44–45.

12   1492: multi egent Dura arua ligonibus
      1581: multis egent dura arua legionibus

13   Horace, *Carm.* ii, 10, 9–12, as above, *DR* i, 17, 15–21.

      1492: fulgura montes (Horace)
      1581: fulmina montes

14   On Augustus, Suetonius, ii, Aug. 28. Cf. below, *DR* ii, 78, note 2; Diocletian, Hadas (1956), pp. 175–176, 182–183, and below, *DR* ii, 79, note 6; Marcus Aurelius Antoninus, *Hist. Aug.,* Marc. Aur., v, 4; and Pertinax, ibid., xiii, 1, xxvi, 7–8.

15   On the wheel of Fortune, above, *DR* i, Pref., 157–159, and note 44. Note also *De ocio* (1581: 317): *unde tantus* . . .

16   Varius Avitus Bassianus was the name of Emperor Elagabalus, who, however, is listed in the text, below. Hence the reference is probably to Bassianus Antoninus Caracalla.

17   I.t.: Eliogabalus *and* Alexander

18   All texts read *Maximos quoque & Maximinianos: & Maximos: & Gordianos.* I have taken the liberty to substitute, on frail evidence (below, *DR* i, 97, 42–43), *Maximinos* for the first *Maximos.* On the members of these three groups of imperial names, see note 20, below.

19   On Valerian, *qui fatali quadam necessitate superatus est*—who was vanquished by what seems a destined doom—*Hist. Aug.*, Valerian, vii, LCL, Magie, p. 13.

20   An all but complete list of emperors who were murdered, executed, slain in combat, or died suicides, beginning with Julius Caesar, the founder of Roman imperial sovereignty, who was assassinated March 15, 44 B.C. On Caligula, murdered A.D. 41; Claudius, poisoned by his wife, Agrippina, A.D. 54; Nero (A.D. 54–68); Galba, Otho, and Vitellius (A.D. 68–69), Hadas (1956), pp. 106–117. On Macrinus and Diadumenianus, *Hist. Aug.*, Macr. x. Elagabalus and his cousin Alexander Severus died with their mothers A.D. 222 and 235. The Maximins, father and son, were murdered A.D. 238. The Maximinians include Maximinian (A.D. 286–305) and Galerius, killed A.D. 311. The Maximi are Pupienus, slain A.D. 238; Maximus, executed by Theodosius, A.D. 388; and Maximus Petronius, stoned to death A.D. 455. Gordian I committed suicide; his son, Gordian II, and grandson, Gordian III (A.D. 238–244), were killed, the one slain in battle, the other murdered. Philip and his son died in battle or were massacred A.D. 249. Gallus and his son Volusianus were murdered A.D. 253. Gallienus rejoiced at the news of his father's, Valerian's, capture by King Sapor of Persia (A.D. 260). Aurelian was slain by the military A.D. 274; Probus, A.D. 282. Julian died of wounds suffered in battle with the Persians A.D. 363; Licinius was executed A.D. 324. Constantius I, who is probably referred to here, committed suicide A.D. 306; Valens perished in the flames of a hut, where he lay wounded after the battle of Hadrianople A.D. 378 (cf. Claudian, *De bello Gothico* 610). Valentinian II, the younger brother of Gratian (murdered at Lyons A.D. 383), was strangled A.D. 392; Valentinian III was assassinated A.D. 455 upon the orders of Maximus Petronius (above), whose wife he had violated.

21   On the general concept *princeps*—prince—and its subclass prince-turned-tyrant, cf. Berman (1983), pp. 280–283.

22   I.e., Augustus, Diocletian, Marcus Aurelius, and Pertinax, above, lines 73–79.

23   I.t.: Antonius

24   Nerva was emperor A.D. 96–98. The passage is based on *Hist. Aug.*, Antoninus Pius i, 4–5:

> . . . avus maternus Arrius Antoninus, bis consul, homo sanctus et qui Nervam miseratus esset, quod imperare coepisset.

> . . . his maternal grandfather Arrius Antoninus, twice consul, and a righteous man, who pitied Nerva when he assumed the imperial power.

LCL, Magie, p. 101.

25   On *decorum*, cf. below, *DR* ii, 9, note 7.

26   Suetonius, ii, Aug., 58, 1–2:

> Patris patriae cognomen universi repentino maximoque consensu detulerunt ei: prima plebs legatione Antium missa; dein, quia non recipiebat, ineunti Romae

spectacula frequens et laureata; mox in curia senatus, neque decreto neque adclamatione, sed per Valerium Messalam. Is mandantibus cunctis: "Quod bonum," inquit, "faustumque sit tibi domuique tuae, Caesar Auguste! Sic enim nos perpetuam delicitatem rei p. et laeta huic precari existimamus: senatus te consentiens cum populo R. consalutat patriae patrem." Cui lacrimans respondit Augustus his verbis—ipsa enim, sicut Messalae, posui—: "Compos factus votorum meorum, p. c., quid habeo aliud deos immortales precari, quam ut hunc consensum vestrum ad ultimum finem vitae mihi preferre liceat?"

The whole body of citizens with a sudden unanimous impulse proffered him the title of Father of his Country: first the commons, by a deputation sent to Antium, and then, because he declined it, again at Rome as he entered the theatre, which they attended in throngs, all wearing laurel wreaths; the senate afterwards in the House, not by a decree or by acclamation, but through Valerius Messala. He, speaking for the whole body, said: "Good fortune and divine favour attend thee and thy house, Caesar Augustus; for thus we feel that we are praying for lasting prosperity for our country and happiness for our city. The senate in accord with the people of Rome hails thee Father of thy Country." Then Augustus with tears in his eyes replied as follows (and I have given his exact words, as I did those of Messala): "Having attained my highest hopes, Fathers of the Senate, what more have I to ask of the immortal gods than that I retain this same unanimous approval of yours to the very end of my life."

LCL, Rolfe, p. 215. The title was conferred in 2 B.C., twenty five years after Augustus received the *imperium* and the name Augustus. Cf. also note 5, above.

27 *Hist. Aug.,* Hadrian, xvii, 1:

Quos in privata vita inimicos habuit, imperator tantum neglexit, ita ut uni, quem capitalem habuerat, factus imperator diceret "Evasisti."

Many whom he had regarded as enemies when a private citizen, when emperor he merely ignored; for example, on becoming emperor, he said to one man whom he had regarded as a mortal foe, "You have escaped."

LCL, Magie, p. 53.
28 On kingship and the fisc, Kantorowicz (1957a), esp. pp. 178–192.
29 I.t.: *Gaius*
30 Suetonius, iv, Calig., 19, 1–3:

Novum praeterea atque inauditum genus spectaculi excogitavit. Nam Baiarum medium intervallum ad Puteolanas moles, trium milium et sescentorum fere passuum spatium, ponte coniunxit contractis undique onerariis navibus et ordine duplici ad ancoras conlocatis; superiectoque aggere terreno ac derecto in Appiae viae formam, per hunc pontem ultro citro commeavit biduo continenti, primo die phalerato equo insignisque quercea corona et caetra et gladio aureaque chlamyde, postridie quadrigario habitu curriculoque biiugi famosorum equorum, prae se ferens Dareum puerum ex Parthorum obsidibus, comitante praetorianorum agmine et in essedis cohorte amicorum. Scio plerosque existimasse talem a Gaio pontem excogitatum aemulatione Xerxis, qui non sine admiratione aliquanto angustiorem Hellespontum contabulaverit; alios, ut Germaniam et Britanniam, quibus imminebat, alicuius immensi operis fama territaret. Sed avum meum narrantem puer audiebam, causam operis ab interioribus aulicis proditam, quod Thrasyllus mathematicus anxio de successore Tiberio et in verum nepotem proniori affirmasset non magis Gaium imperaturum quam per Baianum sinum equis discursurum.

Besides this, he devised a novel and unheard of kind of pageant; for he bridged the gap between Baiae and the mole at Puteoli, a distance of about thirty-six hundred paces (over three and a half Roman miles), by bringing together merchant ships from all sides and anchoring them in a double line, after which a mound of earth was heaped upon them and fashioned in the manner of the Appian Way. Over this bridge he rode back and forth for two successive days, the first day on a caparisoned horse, himself resplendent in a crown of oak leaves, a buckler, a sword, and a cloak of cloth of gold; on the second, in the dress of a charioteer in a car drawn by a pair of famous horses, carrying before him a boy named Dareus, one of the hostages from Parthia, and attended by the entire praetorian guard and a company of friends in Gallic chariots. I know that many have supposed that Gaius devised this kind of bridge in rivalry of Xerxes, who excited no little admiration by bridging the much narrower Hellespont; others, that it was to inspire fear in Germany and Britain, on which he had designs, by the fame of some stupendous work. But when I was a boy, I used to hear my grandfather say that the reason for the work, as revealed by the emperor's confidential courtiers, was that Thrasyllus the astrologer had declared to Tiberius, when he was worried about his successor and inclined towards his natural grandson, that Gaius had no more chance of becoming emperor than of riding about over the gulf of Baiae with horses.

LCL, Rolfe, pp. 431, 433.

31   Cf. Sallust, *Catil.* xiii, 1–2:

Nam quid ea memorem, quae nisi eis qui videre nemini credibilia sunt, a privatis compluribus subvorsos montis, maria constrata esse? Quibus mihi videntur ludibrio fuisse divitiae; quippe quas honeste habere licebat, abuti per turpidinem properabant.

Why, pray, should I speak of things which are incredible except to those who have seen them, that a host of private men have levelled mountains and built upon the seas? To such men their riches seem to me to have been but a plaything; for while they might have enjoyed them honourably, they made haste to squander them shamefully.

LCL, Rolfe, p. 23. Rolfe notes that the passage may refer to Xerxes: "Lucullus, called by Pompey '*Xerxes togatus*,' and Pompey himself cut through hills to bring salt water into their fishponds, and villas built out into the sea existed in Sallust's time at Baiae. See Horace, *Carm.* iii, 1, 33–34:

> Contracta pisces aequora sentiunt
> iactis in altum molibus.
>
> [The fishes note the narrowing of the waters
> by piers of rock laid in their depths (LCL, Bennett, p. 171).]

Cf. above, *DR* i, 63, 42, and note 12.

32   Reason's stories are based on Suetonius, iv, Calig., 37, 1–3:

> Nepotatus sumptibus omnium prodigorum ingenia superavit, commentus novum balnearum usum, portentosissima genera ciborum atque cenarum, ut calidis frigidisque unguentis lavaretur, pretiosissima margarita aceto liquefacta sorberet, convivis ex auro panes et obsonia apponeret, aut frugi hominem esse oportere dictitans aut Caesarem. Quin et nummos non mediocris summae e fastigio basilicae Iuliae per aliquot dies sparsit in plebem. Fabricavit et deceris Liburnicas gemmatis puppibus, versicoloribus velis, magna thermarum et porticuum et tricliniorum laxitate magnaque etiam vitium et pomiferarum arborum varietate; quibus discumbens de die inter choros ac symphonias litora Campaniae peragraret. In extructionibus praetoriorum atque villarum omni ratione posthabita nihil tam efficere concupiscebat quam quod posse effici negaretur. Et iactae itaque moles infesto ac profundo mari et excisae rupes durissimi silicis et campi montibus aggere aequati et complanata fossuris montium iuga, incredibili quidem celeritate, cum morae culpa capite lueretur. Ac ne singula enumerem, immensa opes totumque illud Ti. Caesaris vicies ac septies milies sestertium non toto vertente anno absumpsit.

> In reckless extravagance he outdid the prodigals of all times in ingenuity, inventing a new sort of baths and unnatural varieties of food and feasts; for he would bathe in hot or cold perfumed oils, drink pearls of great price dissolved in vinegar, and set before his guests loaves and meats of gold, declaring that a man ought either to be frugal or Caesar. He even scattered large sums of money among the commons from the roof of the basilica Julia for several days in succession. He also built Liburnian galleys with ten banks of oars, with sterns set with gems, particoloured sails, huge spacious baths, colonnades, and banquet halls, and even a great variety of vines and fruit trees; that on board of them he might recline at table from an early hour, and coast along the shores of Campania amid songs and choruses. He built villas and country houses with utter disregard of expense, caring for nothing so much as to do what men said was impossible. So he built moles out into the deep and stormy sea, tunnelled rocks of hardest flint, built up plains to the height of mountains and razed mountains to the level of the plain; all with incredible dispatch, since the penalty for delay was death. To make a long story short, vast sums of money, including the 2,700,000,000 sesterces which Tiberius Caesar had amassed, were squandered by him in less than the revolution of a year.

LCL, Rolfe, pp. 461, 463—On the canal through the Isthmus of Greece, Suetonius, ibid., 21.

33   Suetonius vi, Nero, 31, 1; LCL, Rolfe, p. 135.

34   Suetonius, ibid., 39, 2:

> Roma domus fiet; Veios migrate, Quirites,
> Si non et Veios occupat ista domus.

LCL, Rolfe, p. 159.

35   Suetonius, ibid., 31, 1–2:

> domum a Palatio Esquilias usque fecit, quam primo transitoriam, mox incendio absumptam restitutamque auream nominavit. De cuius spatio atque cultu suf-fecerit haec rettulisse. Vestibulum eius fuit, in quo colossus CXX pedum staret ipsius effigie; tanta laxitas, ut porticus triplices miliarias haberet; item stagnum magis instar, circumsaeptum aedificiis ad urbium speciem; rura insuper arvis atque vinetis et pascuis silvisque varia, cum multitudine omnis generis pecudum ac ferarum. In ceteris partibus cuncta auro lita, distincta gemmis unionumque conchis erant; cenationes laqueatae tabulis eburneis versatilibus, ut flores, fistulatis, ut unguenta desuper spargerentur; praecipua cenationum rotunda, quae perpetuo diebus ac noctibus vice mundi circumageretur; balineae marinis et albulis fluentes aquis. Eius modi domum cum absolutam dedicaret, hactenus comprobavit, ut se diceret quasi hominem tandem habitare coepisse.

> He made a palace extending all the way from the Palatine to the Esquiline, which at first he called the House of Passage, but when it was burned shortly after its completion and rebuilt, the Golden House. Its size and splendour will be sufficiently indicated by the following details. Its vestibule was large enough to contain a colossal statue of the emperor a hundred and twenty feet high; and it was so extensive that it had a triple colonnade (with three parallel rows of columns) a mile long. There was a pond too, like a sea, surrounded with buildings to represent cities, besides tracts of country, varied by tilled fields, vineyards, pastures and woods, with great numbers of wild and domestic ani-mals. In the rest of the house all parts were overlaid with gold and adorned with gems and mother-of-pearl. There were dining-rooms with fretted ceilings of ivory, whose panels could turn and shower down flowers and were fitted with pipes for sprinkling the guests with perfumes. The main banquet hall was circular and constantly revolved day and night, like the heavens. He had baths supplied with sea water and sulphur water. When the edifice was finished in this style and he dedicated it, he deigned to say nothing more in the way of approval than that he was at last beginning to be housed like a human being.

LCL, Rolfe, pp. 135, 137. Cf. also Pliny, *Nat. hist.* xxxvi, 24, 111 and 113. On Nero's Golden House, cf. Boardman (1986), pp. 784–786, and the literature listed p. 805.

36   I.t.: *Tranquillus*

37   Suetonius vi, Nero, 30, 3; and 31, 3:

> *Nullam vestem bis induit.* Quadringenis in punctum sestertiis aleam lusit. *Piscatus est rete aurato et purpura coccoque funibus nexis.* Numquam minus *mille carrucis* fecisse iter traditur, soleis *mularum argenteis,* canusinatis mulionibus, armillata phalerataque Mazacum turba atque cursorum.

> Praeterea incohabat piscinam a Miseno ad Avernum lacum contectam porticibusque conclusam, quo quidquid totis Baiis calidarum aquarum esset converteretur; fossam ab Averno Ostiam usque, ut navibus nec tamen mari iretur, longitudinis per centum sexaginta milia, latitudinis, qua contrariae quinqueremes commearent.

> He never wore the same garment twice. He played at dice for four hundred thousand sesterces a point. He fished with a golden net drawn by cords woven of purple and scarlet threads. It is said that he never made a journey with less than a thousand carriages, his mules shod with silver and their drivers clad in wool of Canusium, attended by a train of Mazaces (Mauretanian horsemen), and courtiers with bracelets and trappings.

> He also began a pool, extending from Misenum to the lake of Avernus, roofed over and enclosed in colonnades, into which he planned to turn all the hot springs in every part of Baiae; a canal from Avernus all the way to Ostia, to enable the journey to be made by ship yet not by sea; its length was to be a hundred and sixty miles and its breadth sufficient to allow ships with five banks of oars to pass each other.

LCL, Rolfe, pp. 135, 137. Cf. also John of Salisbury, *Policrat.* vi, 14, vii, 2; *PL* 199, cc. 610, 639; and "De Nerone Claudio Caesare" in Boccaccio, *De casibus,* Hall (1962), f. 85r.

38   *Hist. Aug., Verus,* v, 1–6:

> Et notissimum eius quidem fertur tale convivium, in quo primum duodecim accubuisse dicitur, cum sit notissimum dictum de numero convivarum "septem convivium, novem vero convicium." Donatos autem pueros decoros qui ministrabant singulis, donatos etiam structores et lances singulis quibusque, donata et viva animalia vel cicurum vel ferarum avium vel quadripedum, quorum cibi adpositi erant, donatos etiam calices singulis per singulas potiones, murrinos et crystallinos Alexandrinos, quotiens bibitum est; data etiam aurea atque argentea pocula et gemmata, coronas quin etiam datas lemniscis aureis interpositis et alieni temporis floribus, data et vasa aurea cum unguentis ad speciem alabastrorum, data et vehicula cum mulabus ac mulionibus cum iuncturis argenteis, ut ita de convivio redirent. Omne autem convivium aestimatum dicitur sexagies centenis milibus sestertiorum. Hoc convivium posteaquam Marcus audivit, ingemuisse dicitur et doluisse publicum fatum. Post convivium lusum est tesseris usque ad lucem.

> One such banquet, indeed, became very notorious. This was the first banquet,

it is said, at which couches were placed for twelve, although there is a very well-known saying about the proper number of those present at a banquet that "seven make a dinner, nine make a din." Furthermore, the comely lads who did the serving were given as presents, one to each guest; carvers and platters, too, were presented to each, and also live animals either tame or wild, winged or quadruped, of whatever kind were the meats that were served, and even goblets of murra [above, *DR* i, 38, 125–141] or of Alexandrine crystal were presented to each man for each drink, as often as they drank. Besides this, he gave golden and silver and even jewelled cups, and garlands, too, entwined with golden ribbons and flowers out of season, golden vases with ointments made in the shape of perfume-boxes, and even carriages, together with mules and muleteers, and trappings of silver, wherewith they might return home from the banquet. The estimated cost of the whole banquet, it is reported, was six million sesterces. And when Marcus heard of this dinner, they say, he groaned and bewailed the fate of the empire. After the banquet, moreover, they diced until dawn.

LCL, Magie, pp. 217, 219.

39   Twyne, f. [122]r: and I knowe that there be some of you that wyll thinke these examples to be longer then neede, and the remedies shorter then promise.

40   Proverbial. E.g., Cicero, *Tusc. disp.* iii, 11, 25, as below, *DR* ii, 93, 22–23, and note 6.

41   Livy, vii, 6, 1–5:

> Eodem anno, seu motu terrae seu qua vi alia, forum medium ferme specu vasto conlapsum in immensam altitudinem dicitur; neque eam voraginem coniectu terrae, cum pro se quisque gereret, expleri potuisse, priusquam deum monitu quaeri coeptum quo plurimum populus Romanus posset; id enim illi loco dicandum vates canebant, si rem publicam Romanam perpetuam esse vellent. Tum M. Curtium, iuvenem bello egregium, castigasse ferunt dubitantes an ullum magis Romanum bonum quam arma virtusque esset, et silentio facto templa deorum immortalium, quae foro imminent, Capitoliumque intuentem et manus nunc in caelum nunc in patentes terrae hiatus ad deos manes porrigentem se devovisse; equo deinde quam poterat maxime exornato insidentem armatum se in specum immisisse, donaque ac fruges super eum a multitudine virorum ac mulierum congestas, lacumque Curtium non ab antiquo illo T. Tati milite Curtio Mettio sed ab hoc appellatum.

> That same year [362 B.C.], whether owing to an earthquake or to some other violent force, it is said that the ground gave way, at about the middle of the Forum, and, sinking to an immeasurable depth, left a prodigious chasm. This gulf could not be filled with the earth which everyone brought and cast into it, until admonished by the gods, they began to inquire what it was that constituted the chief strength of the Roman People; for this the soothsayers declared that they must offer up, as a sacrifice to that spot, if they wished the Roman Republic to endure. Thereupon Marcus Curtius, a young soldier of great prowess, rebuked them, so the story runs, for questioning whether any blessing

were more Roman than arms and valour. A hush ensued, as he turned to the temples of the immortal gods which rise above the Forum, and to the Capitol, and stretching forth his hands, now to heaven, and now to the yawning chasm and to the gods below, devoted himself to death. After which, mounted on a horse caparisoned with all possible splendour, he plunged fully armed into the gulf; and crowds of men and women threw offerings and fruits in after him. It was he, they say, and not Curtius Mettius, the soldier of Titus Tatius in days of old, who gave his name to the Curtian Lake.

LCL, Foster, pp. 373, 375.

42   On *modestia* and Aristotle's ideal of μεσότης, see above, *DR* i, Pref., 98–101, and note 27. Cf. also *DR* i, 2, notes 24, 25, and ii, 99, note 2.

43   *Hist. Aug.*, Hadrian, viii, 3:

> Et in contione et in senatu saepe dixit ita se rem publicam gesturum ut scirent populi rem esse, non propriam.

LCL, Magie, p. 25.

44   Deut. 32, 35: *mea est ultio.*—Note also the remarks on vengeance in *Fam.* xi, 5, 12–13.

45   On *bee kings*, above, *DR* i, 62, 34–36, and note 9.

46   Seneca, *De clem.* i, 19, 2–3:

> Natura enim commenta est regem, quod et ex aliis licet cognoscere et ex apibus; quarum regi amplissimum cubile est medioque ac tutissimo loco; praeterea opere vacat exactor alienorum operum, et amisso rege totum di-labitur, nec umquam plus unum patiuntur melioremque pugna quaerunt; praeterea insignis regi forma nitore. Hoc tamen maxime distinguitur: iracund-issimae ac pro corporis captu pugnacissimae sunt apes et aculeos in volnere relinquunt, rex ipse sine aculeo est; noluit illum natura nec saevum esse nec ultionem magno constaturam petere telumque detraxit et iram eius inermem reliquit. Exemplar hoc magnis regibus ingens . . .

> For Nature herself conceived the idea of a king, as we may recognize from the case of bees and other creatures; the king of the bees has the roomiest cell, placed in the central and safest spot; besides, he does no work, but superin-tends the work of others, and if they lose their king, they all scatter; they never tolerate more than one at a time, and they discover the best one by means of a fight [cf. Virgil, *Georg.* iv, 67–87]; moreover the appearance of the king is striking and different from that of the others both in size and beauty. His greatest mark of distinction, however, lies in this: bees are most easily pro-voked, and, for the size of their bodies, excellent fighters, and where they wound they leave their stings; but the king himself has no sting. Nature did not wish him to be cruel or to seek a revenge that would be so costly, and so she removed his weapon, and left his anger unarmed. Great kings will find herein a mighty precedent . . .

LCL, Basore, pp. 409, 411. Seneca's text is quoted in Alain de Lille, *Ars praedicandi*, PL 210, c. 150.

47   Cf. Chaucer, *Canterbury Tales*, Knight's Tale, 1773-1781:

> . . . . "Fy
> Upon a lord that wol have no mercy,
> But been a leon, bothe in word and dede,
> To hem that been in repentaunce and drede,
> As wel as to a proud despitous man
> That wol mayntene that he first bigan.
> That lord hath litel of discrecioun,
> That in swich cas kan no divisioun
> But weyeth pride and humblesse after oon."

Robinson (1933), p. 40. Note also the proverbial medieval English phrase: *A king should not be a lion in peace nor a hare in war*. Whiting (1968), K 50, which evokes Virgil, *Aeneid* vi, 851–853:

> tu regere imperio populos, Romane, memento
> (hae tibi erunt artes) pacique imponere morem,
> parcere subiectis et debellare superbos.

> Remember thou, O Roman, to rule the nations with thy sway—
> these shall be thine arts—to crown Peace with Law,
> to spare the humbled, and to tame the proud!

LCL, Fairclough, p. 567. The passage is quoted in *Fam.* xii, 2, 31, and xv, 1, 10. However, Reason may allude to the *Leo regnans* fable in Romulus, iii, 20, Hervieux, ii (1894), p. 223:

> [Cum sibi fere regem fecissent fortissimum leonem, voluit ille mores regum bona fama consequi, renuncians prioribus factis, et mutavit consuetudinem: pecus ullum se non ledere, sine sanguine cibum sumere, sanctam et incorruptam iuravit se fidem servare. Postea, ut habere coepit de hac re potentiam], et mutare non posset naturam, coepit aliquos ducere in secretam fallaciam et quaerere si ei os puteret. Illos qui dicebant: Putet, et qui dicebant: Non putet, omnes tamen laniabat, ita ut saturaretur sanguine. Cum multis hoc fecisset, postea symium interrogabat si putorem haberet in ore. Ille quasi synnamomum dixit fragrare, et quasi deorum altaria. Leo erubuit laudatorem, sed, ut deciperet, invitavit fidem et quaesivit fraudem, atque languere se simulavit. Continue venerunt medici. Qui ut venas consideraverunt, pulsum sanum ut viderunt, suaserunt ei sumere cibum aliquem qui levis esset et tolleret fastidium pro digestione, ut regibus omnia licent. Ignota est, inquit, mihi caro simii; vellem illam probare. Ut est locutus, statim necatur beniloquus symius, ut eius carnem cito escam sumeret. (Una enim est poena loquentis et non loquentis.)

> [When they had made the mighty lion king of the beasts, he wanted to follow

royal decorum for a good reputation and, renouncing his past deeds, change his habits: he vowed that he would not hurt any cattle, would eat food that was not bloody, and loyally uphold the sacred trust. Later on, when he had assumed power,] and he found himself unable to change his nature, he began to take aside in private certain of his subjects and to inquire of them guilefully whether or not his breath smelled. Alike for those who said, "It smells" and for those who said, "It does not smell," he slaughtered them all none the less, to glut his appetite for blood. After he had dealt thus with many of them he asked the ape whether he, the king, had a bad smell in his mouth. The ape declared that the king's mouth had the fragrance of cinnamon and that it smelled like the incensed altars of the gods. The lion was ashamed to hurt one who praised him so well, but in order to deceive the ape, he changed his tactics, looked about for another trick, and made believe he was ill. Physicians came immediately and, after examining his veins and seeing that his pulse was normal, they urged him to take some food that was light and that would stimulate his appetite for the benefit of his digestion; for all things are permissible for kings. "I never tasted ape-meat," said the lion; "I should like to try some of that." No sooner had he spoken than the ape of the flattering tongue was killed, in order that the lion might have the benefit of his flesh for food without delay. (The penalty is the same for the one who speaks and for him who does not speak.)

LCL, *Babrius and Phaedrus,* Perry, pp. 323, 325.

48   1492: Habes Augustum: habes et Neronem: & Vitelium quem sequaris
1581: Habes & Neronem, & Vitellium quem sequaris

49   Reason lists in each of the two sets of Roman emperors, one who was an outstanding man, one wholly degenerate and bestial, and one without consequence.

50   On the decay of Rome and its principate, cf. Trompf (1979), pp. 185–200.

51   Paraphrasing Valerius Maximus, vii, 2, ext. 5:

Rex etiam ille subtilis iudicii, quem ferunt traditum sibi diadema prius quam capiti inponeret retentum diu considerasse ac dixisse 'o nobilem magis quam felicem pannum! quem, si quis penitus cognoscat quam multis sollicitudinibus et periculis et miseriis sit refertus, ne humi quidem iacentem tollere uelit.'

Also that king showed shrewd judgment who, it is reported, before putting on his head the crown he had received, paused thoughtfully and said: "O circlet, splendid rather than felicitous! If it were clearly understood how many cares, and dangers, and miseries it brings, no one would as much as pick it up if he found it lying on the ground."

The story is freely retold in *Rer. mem. libri* iii, 94. The king's words are quoted with minor variations from Valerius in *Fam.* ix, 5, 25. John of Salisbury, *Policrat.* viii, *PL* 199, c. 771, cites the text by Valerius Maximus.

52   Cf. above, *DR* i, 92, 3–4, and note 2.

53   Cf. ibid., 3–7, and note 3.

54   Cf. above, *DR* i, 1, note 10.

55 1492: seu uerius punctum (ut dixerim) puncti breuis
    1581: seu uerius, ut sic dixerim puncti breuis
56 Cf. above, *DR* i, 11, 70–71, and note 20.
57 Seneca, *De benef.* v, 25, 2:

> Ti. Caesar inter initia dicenti cuidam: "Meministi—" antequam plures notas familiaritatis veteris proferret: "Nom memini," inquit, "quid fuerim."

> Tiberius Caesar, when a certain man started to say: "You remember—," interrupted him before he could reveal more evidence of an old intimacy with: "I do not remember what I was."

LCL, Basore, p. 359.

97 ❖ A POWERFUL ARMY

1 1492: Exercitum habeo
   1581: Exercitum armatum habeo
2 Seneca, *Ep.* 86, 1:

> In ipsa Scipionis Africani villa iacens haec tibi scribo adoratis manibus eius et ara, quam sepulchrum esse tanti viri suspicor. Animum quidem eius in caelum, ex quo erat, redisse persuadeo mihi, non quia magnos exercitus duxit, hos enim et Cambyses furiosus ac furore feliciter usus habuit, *sed ob egregiam moderationem* pietatemque . . .

> I am resting at the country-house which once belonged to Scipio Africanus himself; and I write to you after doing reverence to his spirit and to an altar which I am inclined to think is the tomb of that great warrior. That his soul has indeed returned to the skies, whence it came, I am convinced, not because he commanded mighty armies—for Cambyses also had mighty armies, and Cambyses was a madman who made successful use of his madness—but because he showed moderation and a sense of duty . . .

LCL, Gummere, p. 311.
3 On this, McNeill (1982), chap. 3; and Seward (1978), chap. 3.
4 Lucan, x, 407: *Nulla fides pietasque viris qui castra secuntur.* LCL Duff, p. 621.
5 On the topic, below, *DR* ii, 31, note 5.

6   *Quem non ille ducem potuit terrere tumultus?* Lucan, v, 300; LCL, Duff, p. 261.
Suetonius, i, Jul. Caes., 69, remarks about the mutiny at Placentia:

> Seditionem per decem annos Gallicis bellis nullam omnino moverunt, civilibus aliquas, sed ut celeriter ad officium redierint, nec tam indulgentia ducis quam auctoritate. Non enim cessit umquam tumultuantibus atque etiam obviam semper iit; et nonam quidem legionem apud Placentiam, quanquam in armis adhuc Pompeius esset, totam cum ignominia missam fecit aegreque post multas et supplicis preces, nec nisi exacta de sontibus poena, restituit.

> They did not mutiny once during the ten years of the Gallic war; in the civil wars they did so now and then, but quickly resumed their duty, not so much owing to any indulgence of their general as to his authority. For he never gave way to them when they were insubordinate, but always boldly faced them, discharging the entire ninth legion in disgrace before Placentia, though Pompey was still in the field, reinstating them unwillingly and only after many abject entreaties, and insisting on punishing the ringleaders.

LCL, Rolfe, p. 91.

7   *Hist. Aug., Sev. Alex.,* 53–54:

> Nam cum Antiochiam venisset, ac milites lavacris muliebribus et deliciis vacarent eique nuntiatum esset, omnes eos comprehendi iussit et in vincula conici. Quod ubi compertum est, mota seditio est a legione, cuius socii erant in vincula coniecti. Tum ille tribunal ascendit vinctisque omnibus ad tribunal adductis, circumstantibus etiam militibus et quidem armatis ita coepit: "Commilitones, si tamen ista vobis quae a vestris facta sunt displicent, disciplina maiorum rem publicam tenet. Quae si dilabitur, et nomen Romanum et imperium amittemus. Neque enim sub nobis ista facienda sunt quae sub impura illa bestia nuper facta sunt. Milites Romani, vestri socii, mei contubernales et commilitones, amant, potant, lavant, et Graecorum more quidem se instituunt. Hoc ego diutius feram? Et non eos capitali dedam supplicio?" Tumultus post hoc ortus est. Atque iterum: "Quin continetis vocem in bello contra hostem, non contra imperatorem vestrum necessariam? Certe campidoctores vestri hanc vos docuerunt contra Sarmatas et Germanos ac Persas emittere, non contra eum, qui acceptam a provincialibus annonam, qui vestem, qui stipendia vobis adtribuit. Continete igitur vocem truculentam et campo ac bellis necessariam, ne vos hodie omnes uno ore atque una voce Quirites dimittam et incertum an Quirites. Non enim digni estis qui vel Romanae plebis sitis, si ius Romanum non agnoscitis." Et cum vehementius fremerent ac ferro quoque minarentur, "Deponite," inquit, "dextras contra hostem erigendas, si fortes sitis, me enim ista non terrent. Si enim unum hominem occideritis, non nobis deerit res publica, non senatus, non populus Romanus, qui me de vobis vindicet." Cum nihilo minus post ista fremerunt, exclamavit, "Quirites, discedite atque arma deponite." Mirando exemplo depositis armis, depositis etiam sagulis militaribus omnes non ad castra, sed ad deversoria varia recesserunt. Tuncque privatim intellectum est quantum eius severitas posset.

After his arrival in Antioch the soldiers began to use their leisure in the women's baths and the other pleasures, but when Alexander learned of it he ordered all who did so to be arrested and thrown into chains. When this was made known, a mutiny was attempted by that legion whose members were put in chains. Thereupon, after bringing all those who had been thrown into chains to the tribunal, he mounted the platform, and, with the soldiers standing about him, and that too in arms, he began as follows: Fellow-soldiers, if, in spite of all, such acts as have been committed by your comrades are to you displeasing, the discipline of our ancestors still governs the state, and if this is weakened, we shall lose the name and the empire of the Romans. For never shall such things be done in my reign which were but recently done under that filthy monster. Soldiers of Rome, your companions, my comrades and fellow-soldiers, are whoring and drinking and bathing and, indeed, conducting themselves in the manner of the Greeks. Shall I tolerate this longer? Shall I not deliver them over to capital punishment?" Thereupon an uproar arose. And again he spoke: "Will you not silence that shouting, needed indeed against the foe in battle but not against your emperor? Of a certainty, your drill-masters have taught you to use this against Sarmatians, and Germans, and Persians, but not against him who gives you rations presented by the men of the provinces, and who gives you clothing and pay. Therefore cease from this fierce shouting, needed only on the battle-field and in war, lest I discharge you all today with one speech and with a single word, calling you 'Citizens.' But I know not whether I should even call you Citizens; for you are not worthy to be members even of the populace of Rome, if you do not observe Rome's laws." And when they clamoured still more loudly and even threatened him with their swords, he continued: "Put down your hands, which, if you are brave men, you should raise against the foe, for such things do not frighten me. For if you slay me, who am but one man, the state and the senate and the Roman people will not lack someone to take vengeance for me upon you." And when they clamoured none the less at this, he shouted: "Citizens, withdraw, and lay down your arms." Then in a most marvellous fashion they laid down their arms and also their military coats, and all withdrew, not to the camp, but to various lodgings. And on that occasion, particularly, it was seen how much could be accomplished by his strictness and discipline.

LCL, Magie, pp. 285, 287. Alexander's "Put down your hands . . ." is quoted in *Fam.* xxiii, 2 (to Charles IV, March 21, 1361), 26.

8 1492: Maximi pater et filius
1581: Maximini pater & filius.

Cf. above, *DR* i, 96, 86, and note 18.

9 After reigning three months, Pertinax was murdered by the praetorians who had made him emperor (A.D. 193). On emperor Maximin and his son, above, *DR* i, 96, note 20; and Hadas (1956), pp. 162–164. Balbinus and Pupienus Maximus were appointed emperors, with the thirteen-year-old Gordian III as Caesar. Both were *murdered by praetorians, who proclaimed Gordian III em-*

peror (A.D. *238–244*); Hadas, ibid. Cf. Gibbon (1789), chap. vii. On Probus, Gratian, and Valentinian II, above, *DR* i, 96, note 20.

10 Horace, *Ep.* i, 1, 76, as above, *DR* i, 47, note 7.

11 Florus, ii, 13, 49:

> nec ulla res magis exitio fuit quam ipsa exercitus magnitudo.

LCL, Forster, p. 283. Pompey was defeated by Caesar at Pharsalus, August 9, 48 B.C.

12 On this, note Boethius, *Cons. phil.* i, P 3; and Gruber (1978), p. 108, 13. Cf. above, *DR* i, 44, 130.—Petrarch disagrees with Reason's statement in *Fam.* xvii, 3, 16, where he ascribes the decisive defeat of the Genoese fleet at Alghero (August 27, 1353; Wilkins [1958], pp. 30–31) to the fact that

> nec iusta acies nec per classis, sed auxiliorum illuvies externorum et plures adversus unam gentes et exercitus inde numerosior, et cum ventis atque hostibus prorsus non equo Marte certatum est.

> neither the lines of battle nor the fleets were fairly matched, in fact, there was a mass of foreign auxiliary forces and troops from several cities, hence a much larger army, all against one—and it was an unequal fight with the winds and the enemies.

98 ❖ A WELL-EQUIPPED NAVY

1 *Classem habeo instructam.* Cf. *Sen.* viii, 7 (1581; 841): . . . *instructas classes.*—On the advances in shipbuilding A.D. 1280–1330, McNeill (1974), pp. 48–51.

2 *I.t.*: Naso

3 Ovid, *Metam.* i, 141–142:

> iamque nocens ferrum ferroque nocentius aurum
>   prodierat . . .

> And now baneful iron had come, and gold more baneful
> than iron.

LCL, Miller, p. 13.

4 At *avenging Caphereus* (Virgil, *Aeneid* xi, 260), on the southern coast of

Euboea, the homeward-bound fleet of the Greeks was wrecked because King Nauplius lit a beacon on the promontory to mislead his enemies (Ovid, *Metam.* xiv, 466–482; *Tristia* i, 1, 83–84; Graves [1955], ii, 169). During the Peloponnesian war (431–404 B.C.), the Spartan navy was defeated by Athens 406 B.C. at Arginusae (Cicero, *De off.* i, 24, 84); the Athenian fleet had been destroyed at Syracuse 413 B.C. (Harvey [1974], art. Peloponnesian War). At the Aegates, three islands west of Sicily, the Carthaginians were vanquished in a naval battle by the Romans under C. Lutatius Catulus 242 B.C. (Cornelius Nepos, xxii, 1). *No greater fight was ever fought at sea* (Florus, i, 18, 33; LCL, Forster, p. 87).

99 ❖ HEAVY WEAPONS

1   An English translation of this dialogue appears in Bergin (1970), pp. 132–133.
2   Cf. above, *DR* i, 96, esp. 108–112; also *DR* i, 95 and 85.
3   1492: Policertes
     1581: Poliorchetes

     I.e., King Demetrius (c. 338–283 B.C.), surnamed Poliorcetes or Expugnator— Besieger of Cities. Cf. Pliny, *Nat. hist.* vii, 38, 126; also Seneca, *Ep.* 9, 18.
4   1492: adriaticos
     1581: Atuaticos
5   Cf. Caesar, *De bello Gallico* ii, 30–32. On this, Billanovich (1960), p. 45.
6   1492: itaque noctu egressi
     1581: itaque egressi
7   Decimus Brutus and Gaius Trebonius conducted the siege of Marseilles, 49 B.C. (Caesar, *De bello civ.* i, 34–58). On Roman siege engines, Sandys (1929), pp. 479–482; A. R. Hall in Singer, ii (1956), chap. 20.
8   The *ballista* shot javelins and large arrows (Koch [1978], p. 52). Yet note Sandys (1929), p. 480, note 2, on the ambiguous use of the term in ancient literature.
9   The mangonel and trébuchet launched stones and other solid objects (Koch, ibid.; Contamine [1984], pp. 103–104, 194–196).
10   Throwing stones is a symptom of insanity in ancient medicine. Cf., e.g., *SVF* iii, 475–478; and Leibbrand (1953), p. 102. Cf. above, *DR* i, 44, 95.
11   "The first reference in literature to gunpowder, which was gradually coming

into use in the fourteenth century." Bergin (1970), p. 133. On this, Sarton (1975), ii, pp. 1036–1040, iii, pp. 722–726; Singer, ii, (1956), pp. 374–382, 726–728; Braudel, i (1979), pp. 385–390; McNeill (1982), esp. pp. 79–87; and Contamine (1984), pp. 137–141.

12   I.t.: *Maro.*—Virgil, *Aeneid* vi, 585–594:

> vidi et crudelis dantem Salmonea poenas,
> dum flammas Iovis et sonitus imitatur Olympi.
> Quattuor hic invectus equis et lampada quassans
> per Graium populos mediaeque per Elidis urbem
> ibat ovans, divumque sibi poscebat honorem
> demens, qui nimbos et *non imitabile fulmen*
> aere et cornipedum pulsu simularet equorum.
> At pater omnipotens densa inter nubila telum
> contorsit, non ille faces nec fumea taedis
> lumina, praecipitemque immani turbine adegit.

> Salmoneus, too, I saw, who paid a cruel penalty while
> aping Jove's fires and the thunders of Olympus. He, borne
> by four horses and brandishing a torch, rode triumphant
> through the Greek peoples and his city in the heart of Elis,
> claiming as his own the homage of deity. Madman! to
> mimic the storm-clouds and inimitable thunder with brass
> and the tramp of horn-footed horses! But the Father
> Almighty amid thick clouds launched his bolt—no firebrands
> he, nor pitch-pines' smoky glare—and drave him headlong
> with furious whirlwind.

LCL, Fairclough, p. 547.

13   When the Roman general Marcellus besieged Syracuse, the difficulty of his task was greatly increased by the resourcefulness of an engineer named Archimedes, who was killed during the sack of the city in 212. According to the legend, Archimedes had invented various machines for defensive purposes, catapults, ingenious hooks, and also concave mirrors by means of which he deflected the sun rays and set the Roman ships on fire. The story is told that a Roman soldier came upon him while he was absorbed in the contemplation of geometric figures drawn up on the earth. Archimedes shouted, "Keep off," and the soldier killed him. The account of the inventions by which he tried to save his native city fired the imagination of people not only during ancient and medieval times but even as late as the eighteenth century, and he was generally thought of as a mechanical wizard.

Sarton, ii, (1959), pp. 69–70. On Archimedes' military technology, Livy, xxiv, 34, 8–15:

> Adversus hunc navalem apparatum Archimedes variae magnitudinis tormenta in muris disposuit. In eas quae procul erant navis saxa ingenti pondere emittebat, propiores levioribus eoque magis crebris petebat telis; postremo, ut sui

The Defenses of Archimedes during the Siege of Syracuse in 212 B.C.
Marius Bettinus, *Apiaria philosophiae mathematicae* (Bologna, 1642).
Cf. Morhof (1747), ii, p. 465.

volnere intacti tela in hostem ingererent, murum ab imo ad summum crebris
cubitalibus fere cavis aperuit, per quae cava pars sagittis, pars scorpionibus
modicis ex occulto petebant hostem. Quae propius subibant naves, quo interiores ictibus tormentorum essent, in eas tollenone super murum eminente fer-
rea manus, firmae catenae inligata, cum iniecta prorae esset gravique
libramento plumbi recelleret ad solum, suspensa prora navem in puppim
statuebat; dein remissa subito velut ex muro cadentem navem cum ingenti
trepidatione nautarum ita undae adfligebat ut, etiamsi recta reciderat aliquan-
tum aquae acciperet. Ita maritima oppugnatio est elusa omnisque spes eo versa
ut totis viribus terra adgrederentur. Sed ea quoque pars eodem omni apparatu
tormentorum instructa erat Hieronis inpensis curaque per multos annos,
Archimedis unica arte. Natura etiam adiuvabat loci, quod saxum, cui inposita
muri fundamenta sunt, magna parte ita proclive est ut non solum missa tor-
mento, sed etiam quae pondere suo provoluta essent, graviter in hostem in-
ciderent. Eadem causa ad subeundum arduum aditum instabilemque ingressum
praebebat.

To meet this naval equipment Archimedes disposed artillery of different sizes
on the walls. Against the ships at a distance he kept discharging stones of great
weight; nearer vessels he would attack with lighter and all the more numerous

missile weapons. Finally, that his own men might discharge their bolts at the enemy without exposure to wounds, he opened the wall from bottom to top with numerous loopholes about a cubit wide [inside], and through these some, without being seen, shot at the enemy with arrows, others from small scorpions [i.e. small catapults; cf. Koch (1978), p. 55]. As for the ships which came closer, in order to be inside the range of his artillery, against these an iron grapnel, fastened to a stout chain, would be thrown on to the bow by means of a swing-beam projecting over the wall. When this swung backward to the ground owing to the shifting of a heavy leaden weight, it would set the ship on its stern, bow in air. Then, suddenly released, it would dash the ship, falling, as it were, from the wall, into the sea, to the great alarm of the sailors, and with the result that, even if she fell upright, she would take considerable water. Thus the assault from the sea was baffled, and all hope shifted to a plan to attack from the land with all their forces. But that side also had been provided with the same complete equipment of artillery, at the expense and the pains of Hiero during many years, by the unrivalled art of Archimedes. The nature of the place also helped, in that the rock on which the foundations of the wall were laid is generally so steep that not only missiles from a machine, but also whatever rolled down of its own weight fell heavily upon the enemy. The same circumstance made approach to the wall difficult and footing unsteady.

LCL, Moore, pp. 285, 287—Reason anticipates strikingly the main topics of Renaissance commentaries on the invention and diabolical character of firearms. On this, Contamine (1984), pp. 138–139.

14   1492: Cum caetera quidem arma inquieti animi: haec & degeneris signa sunt: nec pacificis quidem grata: & bellatoribus inuisa magnanimis.

      1581: cum caetera quidem arma inquieti animi, & degeneris signa sunt, nec pacificis quidem grata, & bellatoribus inuisa magnanimis.

15   Lucan, viii, 382–386:

        Inlita tela dolis, nec Martem comminus usquam
        Ausa pati virtus, sed longa tendere nervos
        Et, quo ferre velint, permittere volnera ventis
        Ensis habet vires, et gens quaecumque virorum
        Bella gerit gladiis . . .

        Their [i.e., the Parthians'] missiles are smeared
        with guile; their valour nowhere dares to face the enemy
        at close quarters, but only to draw the bow at a distance
        and suffer the winds to carry their weapons whither they will.
        Strength belongs to the sword and every manly race uses cold
        steel to fight with.

LCL, Duff, p. 465. Cf. *Fam.* i, 7, 2. On the hand crossbow of the Middle Ages, A. R. Hall in Singer, ii (1956), pp. 721–724; and Contamine (1984), *passim.* On the rapid development of firearms in the fourteenth century, Koch

(1978), pp. 200–209; Contamine, ibid., chap. 6; and the literature, note 11, above.

16   Reason expounds the traditional view of chivalry. Cf. Evans (1969), p. 140; and Gautier (1883), p. 67. On images from bowshot used by Dante, Boyde (1981), pp. 216–217, 243, 268.

100 ❖ STORED TREASURE

1   Dialogues 100–106 deal with issues of war and peace. On Petrarch's own involvement in the internecine conflicts between the Italian city states, e.g., *Fam.* xi, 8, xiv, 5, xiv, 6, xv, 7, xvii, 3, xvii, 4, xviii, 11, xviii, 16, xix, 9, xx, 3, *Sen.* xvii, 2, *Prose* (1955), p. 1148; Hortis (1874); and Wilkins (1961), pp. 98, 120–121, 136–138, 140 *et passim*.

2   I.t.: *Flaccus*

3   The only passage Reason may refer to, known to me, is Horace, *Ep.* ii, 2, 26–40:

> Luculli miles collecta viatica multis
> aerumnis, lassus dum noctu stertit, ad assem
> perdiderat: post hoc vehemens lupus, et sibi et hosti
> iratus pariter, ieiunis dentibus acer,
> praesidium regale loco deiecit, ut aiunt,
> summe munito et multarum divite rerum
> Clarus ob id factum donis ornatur honestis,
> accipit et bis dena super sestertia nummum.
> Forte sub hoc tempus castellum evertere praetor
> nescio quod cupiens hortari coepit eundem
> verbis quae timido quoque possent addere mentem:
> "i, bone, quo virtus tua te vocat, i pede fausto,
> grandia laturus meritorum praemia. quid stas?"
> Post haec ille catus, quantumvis rusticus: "ibit,
> ibit eo, quo vis, qui zonam perdidit," inquit.

> A soldier of Lucullus [commander against Mithridates 74–67 B.C.], by dint of many toils, had laid by savings, but one night, when weary and slumbering, had lost all down to the last penny. After this, furious as a wolf, angry with himself and his foe alike, and fiercely showing hungry teeth, he dislodged, they say, a royal garrison from a strongly fortified site, rich in vast treasure. Winning fame thereby, he was

decorated with gifts of honour, and received, over and above,
twenty thousand sesterces in coin. Soon after this it chanced
that the commander, wishing to storm some fort, began to urge
the man with words that might have given spirit even to a coward.
"Go, sir, whither your valour calls you. Go, good luck to you!—
to win big rewards for your merits. Why stand still?" On this
the shrewd fellow, rustic though he was, replied: "Yes, he will
go—go where you wish—he who has lost his wallet."

LCL, Fairclough, p. 427.

4   E.g., Horace, *Carm.* iii, 24; Sallust, *Catil.* x-xii; and references in Livy, Pliny,
etc., and note 5, below.

5   Cf. Lucan, i, 160–166:

Namque, ut opes nimias mundo fortuna subacto
Intulit et rebus mores cessere secundis,
Praedaque et hostiles luxum suasere rapinae,
Non auro tectisve modus, mensasque priores
Aspernata fames; cultus gestare decoros
Vix nuribus rapuere mares; fecunda virorum
Paupertas fugitur, totoque accersitur orbe
Quo gens quaeque perit . . .

For when Rome had conquered the world and Fortune
showered excess of wealth upon her, virtue was dethroned
by prosperity, and the spoil taken from the enemy lured
men to extravagance: they set no limit to their wealth
or their dwellings; greed rejected the food that once
sufficed; men seized for their use garments scarce decent
for women to wear; poverty, the mother of manhood, became
a bugbear; and from all the earth was brought the special
bane of each nation.

LCL, Duff, p. 15. Related, *DR* i, 22, note 7, i, 37, note 25, i, 42, 80–86, i, 53,
35–40, ii, 8, 6–7, ii, 9, 110–112, etc.

101 ❖ VENGEANCE

1   Cf. above, e.g., *DR* i, 45, 20–22, and 46, 122–124.
2   Cf. *Sen.* xiv, 1 (1581:374).

3   Seneca, *De ira* iii, 27, 1:

> Quanto satius est sanare iniuriam quam ulcisci!

> How much better it is to heal than to avenge an injury!

LCL, Basore, pp. 321, 323.

4   *nil soleret nisi iniurias oblivisci:* Cicero, *Pro Ligario* xii, 35. Petrarch used the quotation in one of his letters to Emperor Charles IV (*Fam.* xxiii, 9, Milan, March 21, 1362, 6), slightly varied in *Rer. mem. lib.* ii, 2, and again in *Sen.* xiv, 1 (1581: 374).

5   1492: Sume igitur
     1581: Summe igitur

6   1492 and 1581: cyneam: tarmadamque

Pliny, *Nat. hist.* vii, 24–25:

> Memoria necessarium maxime vitae bonum cui praecipua fuerit haut facile dictu est tam multis eius gloriam adeptis. Cyrus rex omnibus in exercitu suo militibus nomina reddidit, L. Scipio populo Romano, Cineas Pyrrhi regis legatus senatui et equestri ordini Romae postero die quam advenerat. Mithridates duarum et viginti gentium rex totidem linguis iura dixit, pro contione singulas sine interprete adfatus. Charmadas quidam in Graecia quae quis exegerit volumina in bibliothecis legentis modo repraesentavit.

> As to memory, the boon most necessary for life, it is not easy to say who most excelled in it, so many men having gained renown for it. King Cyrus could give their names to all the soldiers in his army, Lucius Scipio knew the names of the whole Roman people, King Pyrrhus's envoy Cineas knew those of the senate and knighthood at Rome the day after his arrival [280 B.C.]. Mithridates who was king of twenty-two races gave judgments in as many languages, in an assembly addressing each race in turn without an interpreter. A person in Greece named Charmadas recited the contents of any volumes in libraries that anyone asked him to quote, just as if he were reading them.

LCL, Rackham, pp. 563, 565. Cf. also Cicero, *Tusc. disp.* i, 24. Petrarch relates the feat of Cineas, *Rer. mem. libri* ii, 10. (A sentence immediately following the passage in Pliny's text, above, is referred to in *DR* i, 8, 41, and note 10.)

7   1492: quod adeo uis impudenter a Domino ueniam petit
     1581: quod a Deo uis impudenter a Domino ueniam petit

Cf. Matth. 7, 12 (Luc. 6, 31):

> Omnia ergo quaecumque vultis ut faciant
> vobis homines, et vos facite illis.

> All things therefore whatsoever you would that men should
> do to you, do you also to them.

Note also Tob. 4, 16.

8   1492: Ecclesiasticus doctor clamat. Indignans homo homini iram seruat
    1581: Homo homini iram seruat

Eccli. 28, 3–4:

> Homo homini reservat iram,
> et a Deo quaerit medelam.
> In hominem similem sibi non habet misericordiam
> et de peccatis suis deprecatur.

9   Eccli. 28, 1:

> qui vindicari vult, a Domino inveniet vindictam.

10   Deut. 32, 35:

> Mea est ultio, et ego retribuam in tempore.

Cf. above, *DR* i, 96, 217–218.

11   Seneca, *De ira* iii, 39, 2:

> dabimus illi spatium.

> We must give [anger] room.

12   1492: Pontius
    1581: Pontificus
13   1492: securim
    1581: secutim

Cf. Livy, ix, 1–15, esp. 3, 4–13; and Valerius Maximus, vii, 2, Ext. 17. Florus,
i, 11 summarizes the story:

> Maxime tamen nota et inlustris apud Caudinas furculas ex hac gente clades
> Veturio Postumioque consulibus accepta est. Cluso per insidias intra eum sal-
> tum exercitu, unde non posset evadere, stupens tanta occasione dux hostium
> Pontius Herennium patrem consuluit. Et ille, mitteret omnes vel occideret,
> sapienter ut senior suaserat: hic armis exutos mittere sub iugum maluit, ut nec
> amici forent beneficio et post flagitium hostes magis. Itaque et consules statim
> magnifice voluntaria deditione turpitudinem foederis dirimunt, et ultionem
> flagitans miles Papirio duce—horribile dictu—strictis ensibus per ipsam viam
> ante pugnam furit; et in congressu arsisse omnium oculos hostis auctor
> fuit. Nec prius finis caedibus datus, quam iugum et hostibus et duci capto
> reposuerunt.

> Yet a most notable and signal defeat was sustained at the hands of [the Sam-
> nite] nation at the Caudine Forks in the consulship of Veturius and Postumius
> [321 B.C.]. The Roman army having been entrapped by an ambush in that defile
> and being unable to escape, Pontius the commander of the enemies' forces,
> dumbfounded at the opportunity offered to him, asked the advice of his father
> Herennius. The latter, with the wisdom of advanced years, had advised him
> either to let them all go free or else to slay them all; Pontius preferred to strip

them of their arms and send them under the yoke, so that they were not made his friends by an act of kindness but rendered bitterer enemies by the affront put upon them. The result was that the consuls by a generous act of devotion immediately wiped out the disgrace of the treaty by voluntarily surrendering themselves; and the soldiers, under the leadership of Papirius, calling for vengeance, rushed furiously along (horrible to relate) with their swords drawn as they advanced before they came to blows, and, when the encounter took place, the enemy affirmed that the eyes of all the Romans blazed with fire. Nor was an end put to the slaughter until they retaliated by making the enemy and the captured general pass under the yoke.

LCL, Forster, pp. 53, 55. Petrarch retells it, *Rer. mem. libri* iv, 11.

14 Seneca, *De ira* iii, 42–43.

15 Eccli. 28, 6:

> Memento novissimorum, et desine inimicari.

16 1492: manus
    1581: manos

17 1492: sic clementiae testis
    1581: sic dementiae testis

18 1492: Carmilius
    1581: Carnulius

19 On Hadrian, above, *DR* i, 96, 117–119, and note 27. The Tiberius story is found in Suetonius (iii, Tiberius, 61):

> Mori volentibus vis adhibita vivendi. Nam mortem adeo leve supplicium putabat, ut *cum audisset unum e reis, Carnulum nomine, anticipasse eam, exclamaverit: "Carnulus me evasit."*

> Those who wished to die were forced to live; for [Tiberius] thought death so light a punishment that when he heard that one of the accused, Carnulus by name, had anticipated his execution, he cried: "Carnulus has given me the slip."

LCL, Rolfe, p. 381.

20 1492: promptius
    1581: pomptius

102 ❖ HOPE FOR VICTORY

1 1492: inopine
   1581: inopiae

2   *Nusquam minus quam in bello eventus respondent / Melior tutiorque est certa pax quam sperata victoria.* Both statements occur in Hannibal's speech to Scipio, Livy, xxx, 20, 20 and 19. LCL, Moore, p. 479. The two quotations appear also in *Fam.* xi, 8, 7 and 12.

3   *apertumque inter gladios iter, acri devotum classico Marti caput.* Twyne, f. 129r: and a passage through thy fooes to be made by the edge of the swoorde.

4   The wicked brothers are Eteocles and Polyneices (above, *DR* i, 84, 11–16), who *in the course of a bitter struggle, each mortally wounded the other.* (Graves [1955], ii §106, "The Seven Against Thebes," p. 18.) L. Junius Brutus, consul with Collatinus, 509 B.C.,

> Arruntem filium regis manu sua . . . occidit superque ipsum mutuo volnere expiravit, plane quasi adulterum *ad inferos* usque sequeretur.

> killed Arruns, the king's son, and fell dead on his body from a wound dealt him by his foe, as though he would pursue the adulterer even to the infernal regions.

Florus, i, 4, 8; LCL, Forster, p. 33.

5   1492: duces spe uictoriae
      1581: doces suae uictoriae

6   1492: ut pars uictrix ducem perdat
      1581: ut pax uictrix ducem perdat

103 ❖ VICTORY

1   *Consider the end results.* Cf. above, *DR* 1, 17, 35–47, and note 7, i, 94, 4–5. Note also Machaut, *Remede de Fortune* 2718–2722;

> Dois regarder la fin des choses;
> Et s'aucune foys en meschiet,
> Pour une, .c. foys bien en chiet,
> Car il n'est regle qui ne faille.
> Pour ce ce proverbe te baille,
> Que d'or en avant bien te gardes
> Que la fin des choses regardes.

But in all you plan you must be aware of how things come out; and if they come out wrong one time, they go right a hundred, because every rule has its

exception. I've offered you this proverb so that henceforth you'll be careful to
keep your eye on how things come out.

Wimsatt & Kibler (1988), pp. 318–321, 508.

2   In 480 B.C. Xerxes attacked Greece. Nepos, ii, Themist., 3:

> . . . missi sunt delecti cum Leonida, Lacedaemoniorum rege, qui Thermopy-
> las occuparent longiusque barbaros progredi non paterentur. Hi vim hostium
> non sustinuerunt eoque loco omnes interierunt.

> . . . a band of picked men was sent with Leonidas, king of the Lacedaemoni-
> ans, to hold Thermopylae and prevent any further advance of the barbarians.
> They, however, could not resist the enemy's attack, but in that pass they all
> perished.

LCL, Rolfe, p. 393. On this heroic feat, which occasioned the famous epigram
ascribed to Simonides, Herodotus, vii, 204–228, Cicero, *Tusc. disp.* i, 42, 101.

3   A remark about the Second Punic War (218–201 B.C.) in Livy, xxi, 1, 2:

> et adeo varia fortuna belli ancepsque Mars fuit ut propius periculum fuerint qui
> vicerunt.

LCL, Foster, p. 3.

4   Valerius Maximus, i, 7, 7:

> Vincit huiusce somni dirum aspectum quod insequitur. Apud Actium M.
> Antonii fractis opibus Cassius Parmensis, qui partes eius secutus fuerat,
> Athenas confugit. Ubi concubia nocte cum sollicitudinibus et curis mente
> sopita in lectulo iaceret, existimauit ad se uenire hominem ingentis magni-
> tudinis, coloris nigri, squalidum barba et capillo inmisso, interrogatumque
> quisnam esset respondisse κακὸν δαίμονα. Perterritus deinde taetro uisu et
> nomine horrendo seruos inclamauit sciscitatusque est ecquem talis habitus aut
> intrantem cubiculum aut exeuntem uidissent. Quibus adfirmantibus neminem
> illuc accessisse, iterum se quieti et somno dedit, atque eadem animo eius obu-
> ersata species est. Itaque fugato somno lumen intro ferri iussit puerosque a se
> discedere uetuit. Inter hanc noctem et supplicium capitis, quo eum Caesar
> adfecit, paruulum admodum temporis intercessit.

> A dream may indicate a terrible event soon to follow. After the defeat of
> Antony at Actium [31 B.C.], Cassius of Parma, a follower of Antony's, took
> refuge in Athens. Early in the night, as he lay in bed mentally exhausted by
> fear and worries, he imagined being approached by a man of gigantic size and
> black skin, with a filthy beard and matted hair. When asked who he was he
> answered "I am your evil spirit." Terrified by this horrible apparition and its
> dreadful name, Cassius called his servants and asked whether they had seen
> anyone like that entering or leaving his chamber. They assured him that no-
> body had come near it. But when he lay down again and fell asleep, the same
> specter appeared in his mind. He awoke, had lights brought in, and did not

allow his pages to leave him. Between that night and his execution upon orders of Caesar [Augustus] only a short period of time intervened.

In *Rer. mem. libri* iv, 56, where the story is repeated, Petrarch circumscribes the ghost's Greek by:

> ille autem nescio quid horrisonum greco murmure respondisse.

> But he responded with I know not what horrible sounding mutterings in Greek.

Cf. also, *Sen.* viii, 3 (1581: 835). The story is retold in the *Vita di Cola di Rienzo* (ca. 1358), i, 18, Wright (1975), p. 60.

5   1492: sed quo Hanno uir melior: suae rei .p. consuluerat.
    1581: sed quo Hanno Reipub. consuluerat.

Livy, xxii, 51:

> Hannibal victori cum ceteri circumfusi gratularentur suaderentque ut tanto perfunctus bello diei quod reliquum esset noctisque insequentis quietem et ipse sibi sumeret et fessis daret militibus, Maharbal praefectus equitum minime cessandum ratus, "Immo, ut quid hac pugna sit actum scias, die quinto" inquit "victor in Capitolio epulaberis. Sequere; cum equite, ut prius venisse quam venturum sciant, praecedam." Hannibali nimis laeta res est visa maiorque quam ut eam statim capere animo posset. Itaque voluntatem se laudare Maharbalis ait; ad consilium pensandum temporis opus esse. Tum Maharbal: "Non omnis nimirum eidem di dedere: vincere scis, Hannibal, victoria uti nescis." Mora eius diei satis creditur saluti fuisse urbi atque imperio.

> Hannibal's officers crowded round him with congratulations on his victory [Cannae, 216 B.C.]. The others all advised him now that he had brought so great a war to a conclusion, to repose himself and to allow his weary soldiers to repose for the remainder of the day and the following night. But Maharbal, the commander of the cavalry, held that no time should be lost. "Nay," he cried, "that you may realize what has been accomplished by this battle, in five days you shall banquet in the Capitol! Follow after; I will precede you with the cavalry, that the Romans may know that you are there before they know that you are coming!" To Hannibal the idea was too joyous and too vast for his mind at once to grasp it. And so, while praising Maharbal's goodwill, he declared that he must have time to deliberate regarding this advice. Then said Maharbal, "In very truth the gods bestow not on the same man all their gifts; you know how to gain a victory, Hannibal: you know not how to use one." That day's delay is generally believed to have saved the City and the empire.

LCL, Foster, pp. 367, 369. Also paraphrased in *Vita di Cola di Rienzo* i, 36, Wright (1975), pp. 89–90. During the Second Punic War, Hanno was the leader of the anti-Barcine party in Carthage. He urged the Punic senate to check Hannibal and advocated peace. *Africa* vii, 1–8:

Nescius extincti iuvenis ferus Hannibal instans
Bellum animo, et varios agitant sub pectore casus.
Fraternam sperabat opem, iamque affore classem
Illius ac dulces cupide sibi fingere vultus,
Fingere colloquia, et Latiis quid passus in arvis
Audire, et proprios fratri narrare labores:
Inque sibi infestos ulcisci in tempore cives,
Hannonem ante alios:

Now savage Hannibal was pondering
the varied chances of the war to come;
and unaware of his dear brother's death,
he counted on his aid. In his mind's eye
he saw the fleet already drawing near
and that beloved face; he all but heard
the words they would exchange: his brother's trials
in Latin lands, the tale of his own deeds,
and plans for punishment in time's due course
of fellow citizens hostile to them—
and Hanno first of all.

Bergin (1977), p. 142.

6   An allusion to *Nike*—Victoria, the winged goddess of victory in ancient mythology. Kravitz (1975), p. 164; Malraux (1960), p. 85.

104 ❖ DEATH OF AN ENEMY

1   1492: sit permissum si quis usque esset immortalis
      1581: sit permissum si quis usquam esset immortalis
2   1492: affectus uestri
      1581: effectus uestri
3   Cicero, *Ad Att.* xiv, 1:

>   . . . de Bruto nostro . . . Caesarem solitum dicere: "Magni refert, hic quid
> velit, sed, quicquid volt, valde volt."

>   . . . about our friend Brutus . . . Caesar used to say: "What he wants is of
> great importance, but whatever he wants, he wants it badly."

LCL, Winstedt, p. 217.

4   1492: Itaque quicquid uultis statim uultis hinc non modo
    1581: itaque quicquid uultis, hic non modo

5   *mala electio.* Related, *DR* ii, 38, 34–36, ii, 83, 287–289; and *Fam.* ii, 7, 12.

6   I.t.: Africanus

7   On Metellus lamenting Scipio, Pliny, *Nat. hist.* vii, 44, 144–145; and Valerius Maximus, iv, 1, 12. On Caesar and Pompey, ibid. v, 1, 10; and Livy, *Perioch.* 112. —Alexander,

> miserabili regis opulentissimi exitu comperto, plurimas lacrimas profudisse statimque chlamyde sibi detracta corpus operuisse et magno cum honore ad suos deferri iusisse, ut regio Persarum more curatum, monumentis maiorum inferretur.

> on learning of the wretched end of a most powerful king, . . . shed many tears, and at once taking off his cloak, he covered the body, and ordered it to be taken with great honour to his family, in order to be embalmed after the fashion of the Persian kings, and placed among the tombs of his predecessors.

Q. Curtius, v. fin; LCL, Rolfe, p. 427. Cf. *De vir. ill.* xv, Alexander, 14–15.

8   On *deus opifex,* cf. above, *DR* i, 40, note 7. Related, *DR* i, 39, notes 4 and 6. Note also Bono Giamboni, *Della miseria dell' uomo* vi, 4, Segre & Marti (1959), pp. 234–236.

9   Eccli. 8, 8:

> Noli de mortuo inimico tuo gaudere
> sciens quoniam omnes morimur
> et in gaudium nolumus venire.

105 ✥ HOPE FOR PEACE

1   *Melius est pacem servare quam sperare*—paraphrasing Livy xxx, 20, 19, as above, *DR* i, 102, 8, and note 2.

2   1492: quos expertos inueniens non laesisset
    1581: quos expertos inueniens laesisset

3   1492: si bona fide uelle coeperint
    1581: si bona fide uel coeperint

4   Four of the seven deadly sins, headed by avarice, "the sin of modern times," not pride as in the Gregorian list (Huizinga [1930], p. 32; Bloomfield [1952],

pp. 72–73)—the desire for worldly things which suggests I Tim. 6, 10: *radix enim omnium malorum est cupiditas*—for the desire of money is the root of all evils. Augustine comments: *Haec autem avaritia cupiditas porro improba voluntas est. Ergo improba voluntas, malorum omnium causa est*—Such avarice is cupidity, and cupidity is an evil will. An evil will, therefore, is the cause of all evils. *De lib. arb.* iii, 17, 48; *PL* 32, cc. 1294–1295; Burleigh (1953), p. 200. On this, Maurer (1951), pp. 90–94; and Gilson (1960), p. 119. Cf. *DR* i, 93, 14–22, ii, 13, note 36, and ii, 105, *passim*. For another incomplete list of deadly sins (*avaricia, accidia, invidia, gula, libido*), cf. *Fam.* vi, 1, 9–12.

5   1492: has in aeternum exilium pellite: pax aeterna erit
     1581: has in externum exilium pellite, pax aeterna erit

6   1492: animosque acuit: bellumque asperat pacis spes
     1581: animosque acuit bellum, atque asperat pacis spes

7   Marcus Furius Camillus defeated the Gauls 367 B.C. (Livy v, 19, 2; Florus, i, 7; *De vir, ill.* viii, 19–32). On peace talks with the Gauls, *De vir. ill.* viii, 21–22; with Carthage, Livy, xxx, 16–25, and the relevant passages in the *Africa* (e.g., vi, 397–503, and vii, 115–610), and *De vir. ill.* xxi, 7–9, etc.

8   Cf. Sallust, *Cat.* x–xiii.

9   He who predicted the Civil War is the astrologer Nigidius Figulus. The quotation is from the end of his speech in Lucan, i, 666–670:

> Inminet armorum rabies, ferrique potestas
> Confundet ius omne manu, scelerique nefando
> Nomen erit virtus, multosque exibit annos
> Hic furor. Et *superos quid prodest poscere finem?*
> Cum domino pax ista venit. . . .

> The madness of war is upon us, when the power of the sword
> shall violently upset all legality, and atrocious crime
> shall be called heroism. This frenzy will last for many years;
> and *it is useless to pray Heaven that it may end:*
> *when peace comes, a tyrant will come with it.*

LCL, Duff, p. 51.

106 ❖ PEACE AND TRUCE

1   Sallust, *Jurgurtha* xli, 2–4;

> Nam ante Carthaginem deletam populus et senatus Romanus placide modesteque inter se rem publicam tractabant, neque gloriae neque domina-

tionis certamen inter civis erat; metus hostilis in bonis artibus civitatem re-
tinebat. Sed ubi illa formido mentibus decessit, scilicet ea quae res secundae
amant, lascivia atque superbia incessere. Ita quod in advorsis rebus optaverant
otium postquam adepti sunt, asperius acerbiusque fuit.

For before the destruction of Carthage the people and the senate of Rome
together governed the republic peacefully and with moderation. There was no
strife among the citizens either for glory or for power; fear of the enemy
preserved the good morals of the state. But when the minds of the people were
relieved of that dread, wantonness and arrogance naturally arose, vices which
are fostered by prosperity. Thus the peace for which they had longed in time of
adversity, after they had gained it proved to be more curel and bitter than
adversity itself.

LCL, Rolfe, p. 223.
2   1492: imperiis
     1581: impiis
3   I.t.: Nasica
4   *Rer. mem. lib.* iv, 3:

Iam quid aliud ante oculos habebat ille "vir optimus a senatu iudicatus"
Nasica, tertio bello punico, dum a sententia Catonis Censorii, qui vir omnium
sapientissimus habebatur, acerrime constanterque dissensit et illo censente in-
exorabiliter delendam esse Carthaginem adversatus est, non quod urbem infes-
tissimam parcius odisset, sed quod patriam diligeret, cuius mores previdere se
dicebat in luxuriam abituros amoto emule urbis stimulo? Atque utinam eius
tunc consilium valuisset! Longioris evi forsitan romana felicitas fuisset, nec
hostili urbe ferro flammisque consumpta, ipsa tam brevi post tempore non
armis sed vitiis propellentibus corruisset, pace bellorum gloriam inquinante
atque orbem domitum vindicante luxuria.

Or did that [elder] Nasica, who had been judged Best Man by the senate [Ps.
Pliny the Younger, *De vir. ill.* 44, 1], have anything else before his eyes, when,
during the Third Punic War, he continually dissented sharply from the pro-
nouncements of Cato Censorius (a man everyone considered most wise) and
opposed Cato's view that Carthage was to be destroyed—this not because he
hated that foul city any less, but because he loved Rome and her moral integ-
rity, which, he was convinced he could foresee, would be lost amidst luxury,
once the fear of the rival city was removed [Florus, i, 31, 5]? O that his counsel
would have been valued then! Perhaps Rome's happiness might have lasted for
much longer, and it would not have happened that, shortly after the enemy's
city had been devastated by sword and flames, Rome herself was ruined, not
by arms, but by virulent vice, as peace defiled the glory of her wars and luxury
avenged the world she had conquered.

Cf. *Fam.* xii, 2, 5–7, where Florus, i, 31, 5 is quoted in full; and *Fam.* xiv, 5,
19. Related, Augustine, *De civ. Dei* i, 30, and ii, 18.

5   Lucius Cornelius Sulla was dictator. Velleius Paterculus, ii, 17, 1, and 11, 1:

> vir qui *neque* ad finem victoriae satis *laudari neque* post victoriam abunde *vituperari* potest . . .

> Huius legatus fuit C. Marius . . . natus agresti loco, hirtus atque horridus vitaque sanctus *quantum bello optimus, tantum pace pessimus,* immodicus gloriae, insatiabilis, impotens semperque inquietus.

> Sulla was a man to whom, up to the conclusion of his career of victory, sufficient praise can hardly be given, and for whom, after his victory, no condemnation can be adequate . . .

> Second in command [to Quintus Metellus] was Gaius Marius . . . a man of rustic birth, rough and uncouth, and austere in his life, as excellent a general as he was an evil influence in time of peace, a man of unbounded ambition, insatiable, without self-control, and always an element of unrest.

LCL, Shipley, pp. 83, 71.

6   Juvenal, vi, 290–293:

> ac* proximus urbi
> Hannibal . . .   .
> nunc patimur longae pacis mala, saevior armis
> luxuria incubuit victumque ulciscitur orbem.**

*I.t.: et. **1581: urbem. LCL, Ramsay, p. 107. Also quoted *De ocio* (1581: 301). Cf. above, *DR* i, 22, note 7.

7   Cf. *Fam.* xi, 16, 23, and xii, 2, 5–6. Related, Sallust, *Cat.* x–xiii.

8   1492: & (ut dixi) discrimina
     1591: & ut discrimina

9   Lucan, iii, 370–372:

> . . . Dabitis poenas pro pace petita,
> Et nihil esse meo discetis tutius aevo
> Quam duce me bellum.

> They shall suffer for seeking peace; they shall
> learn that in my days none are safe but those who fight under
> my banner.

LCL, Duff, p. 141.

10   Petrarch attended the ceremony affirming the truce between Milan and the Venetian league, January 8, 1355. Cf. Wilkins (1958), p. 88; and *Fam.* xix, 3.

11   *ubi & tumor paci obstat, & timor bello.* On *tumor animi,* cf. *DR* i, 49, note 2.

107 ❖ THE PAPACY

1   1492: parum grauis unius animae tibi cura uidebatur
     1581: parum grauis unius omine tibi cura uidebatur
2   Ps. 106, 23–27:

> *Qui descendunt mare in navibus,*
> *facientes operationem in aquis multis,*
> ipsi viderunt opera Domini,
> et mirabilia eius in profundo.
> Dixit, et stetit spiritus procellae,
> et exaltati sunt fluctus eius.
> *Ascendunt usque ad caelos, et descendunt usque ad abyssos;*
> *anima eorum in malis tabescebat.*
> *Turbati sunt et moti sunt sicut ebrius;*
> et omnis sapientia eorum devorata est.

> They that go down to the sea in ships,
> doing business in the great waters:
> These have seen the works of the Lord,
> and his wonders in the deep.
> He said the word, and there arose a storm of wind:
> and the waves thereof were lifted up.
> They mount up to the heavens, and they go down to the depths:
> their soul pined away with evils.
> They were troubled, and reeled like a drunken man;
> and all their wisdom was swallowed up.

On *ascensus/descensus,* above, *DR* i, 1, note 11.

3   At court, tasters *proved by mouth* that foods and drink were *fit for a king*—appetizing and free of poison. Reason's verbal irony implies that not only princely etiquette but also foul play was now to be expected in the papal household. Cf. Hale (1968), p. 122; and Cosman (1976), pp. 29–30. Note the poison scene in Malory's *Le Morte d'Arthur,* Book ix.

4   In Dante's *Div. Comm.,* Inf. xxvii, 85–88, Guido da Montefeltro refers to Pope Boniface VIII as:

> Lo principe d'i novi Farisei,
>   avendo guerra presso a Laterano,
>   e non con Saracin ne con Giudei,
> che ciascun suo nimico era Cristiano . . .

The Prince of the new Pharisees, having war near the

> Lateran—and not with Saracens or with Jews,
> for his every enemy was Christian . . .

Singleton (1970), p. 289.—For Petrarch's bitter criticism of the Avignonese papacy, cf. *Sine nomine; Rime* 114, and 136–138; etc. On this, Piur (1925); Foresti (1977), pp. 202, 271, and chaps. 13, 34, and 35; Wilkins (1955), pp. 99, 179–181, 186–192; idem (1958b); Zacour (1973), Intro.; and Coogan (1983).

5   *ut non immerito quidam summi pontifices taedio rerum victi: non supplicium aliud: quam foelicitatem illam hostibus suis optaverint.* Cf. *Rer. mem. libri* iii, 95:

> Regio simillimum pontificale verbum—tempus est enim iam ad etatem nostram descendendi—. Adrianum romanum pontificem sepe dicentem audivisse Policratus refert, qui sibi perfamiliaris fuit, nullem se de hoste suo quolibet maius supplicium optare quam ut papa fieret. Et profecto, nisi fallor, summi pontificatus sarcinam, que vulgo felix et invidiosa creditur, humeris subiisse difficillimum et gloriosum miserie genus est: hiis dico qui eam seque ab omni contagio precipitoque preservare decreverunt; reliquis enim quanto levior videtur tanto funestior status est. Videtur itaque apud utrosque formidabilis. Quod si ille fatebatur qui id honus paucis diebus pertulit, quid illis videri debet qui sub fasce senuerunt?

> It is time to come down to our present age with a papal remark that is very similar to the words of that king [*Rer. mem. libri* iii, 94; *DR* i, 96, note 51]. Policratus reports to have heard it often from Pope Adrian, whose close friend he was. The pope said that he could not wish a worse punishment for an enemy but that he should become pope. And if I am not mistaken, having to shoulder the burden of the supreme pontificate, which is commonly considered a great boon to be envied, is in fact a most difficult kind of glorious misery. I talk about those popes who are determined to keep the office and themselves free from the pitfalls of any contagion. For all the others the papacy becomes the more calamitous, the lighter they take it. Nevertheless, it looms formidable for everyone. If Adrian, who held the honor of the pontificate but for a few days, felt like this, how must the office be viewed by those who have grown old under its crushing load?

The passage refers clearly to pope Adrian V (Ottobuono de' Fieschi of Genoa),

> elected pope at Rome, in succession to Innocent V, July 11, 1276; died at Viterbo 38 days later (August 18), before he had been crowned.

Toynbee (1968), art. Adriano². Yet the words attributed to the pope paraphrase John of Salisbury, *Policrat.* viii, 23, *PL* 199, c. 814 (completed in 1159), where they are ascribed to Adrian IV (Nicholas Breakspear of England), who ruled 1154–1159. Dante seems to make the same mistake, *Div. Comm.,* Purg. xix, where a pope of the Lavagna family, i.e., Adrian V, says:

Un mese e poco più prova'io come
    pesa il gran manto a chi dal fango il guarda,
    che piuma sembran tutte l'altre some.

One month and little more, I learned how the great mantle weighs
    on him who keeps it from the mire,
    so that all other burdens seem a feather.

Singleton (1973), p. 207. On this, Billanovich, in his introduction to the edizione naz. of the *Rerum memorandarum libri* (1943), p. lxxxviii; Toynbee, ibid.; Singleton (1973), *Commentary,* pp. 459–464; and Bosco (1942), pp. 136–143.

It is interesting to note that *Fam.* ix, 5, late in 1351, to Ugolino dei Rossi, Bishop of Parma, which contains a reference to the two stories, *Rer. mem. libri* iii, 94 and 95, identifies correctly (26)

. . . hoc Hadriani quarti dictum minus vulgatum . . . quod inter philosophica nugas legi,

. . . that less well known statement of Adrian IV, which I read in the *Philosophical Trifles,*

and cites *Policrat.* viii, 23, *PL* 199, c. 814, as follows (words in italics differ from John of Salisbury's text):

Romano pontifice nemo miserabilior est, conditione eius nulla miserior, et licet nichil aliud ledat, necesse est ut citissime vel solo labore deficiat; *fatebatur* enim in ea sede tantas se miserias invenisse, ut facta collatione presentium, tota sibi precedens amaritudo iocunditas et vita felicissima *videretur.* Spinosam *dicebat* cathedram Romani Pontificis *et mantum* acutissimis usquequaque *consertum* aculeis tanteque molis ut robustissimos terat, premat et comminuat humeros; coronam et frigium clara merito videri quoniam ignea sunt . . . . *illud* sepissime *adiciens* quod cum de gradu in gradum a claustrali clerico per omnia officia in summum pontificem *ascendisset,* nichil unquam felicitatis aut tranquille quietis vite priori adiectum *esset ex* ascensu. . . . . . . 'In incude' *aiebat,* 'et malleo semper dilatavit me Dominus, sed nunc honeri quod infimitati mee imposuit, si placet, supponat dexteram, quoniam michi importabile est.'

There is no one more wretched than a Roman pope. There is no condition that is more miserable. Nothing else hurts more. It is the need to work incessantly and alone that overwhelms. He admitted that he found in the papal see such misery that, compared to it, all the bitter things that had happened to him before seemed like a great joy in a most happy life. He said that the chair of the Roman pontiff was thorny, and the papal mantle lined with the sharpest of spikes and of such weight that it exhausts, weighs down, and crushes even the strongest shoulders. Crown and miter shine brightly, because they are burning hot. . . . . . . And very often he added that as he rose step by step from a cloistered monk, through various offices, to the papacy, his advancements never added anything to the happiness and peace of his former life. . . . . . . "God," he said, "has always bent and enlarged me with His hammer [cf. Ps. 4, 2], but now His right hand must help support the load He has imposed upon my weakness, because I cannot bear it alone [cf. Matth. 23, 4, and Luc. 11, 46]."

Petrarch adds:

> Hec eisdem pene verbis ad contextum retuli, quibus ab illo scripta sunt qui ex ore loquentis audierat.

> I repeat, nearly word for word, the entire passage, which was written by one who heard directly from the pope's mouth what he said.

(26–28.) If we discount later emendation of *Fam.* ix, 5, and assume that the brief version in *Rer. mem. libri* iii, 95, echoed in our text, precedes *Fam.* ix, 5, this portion of our text would have to be dated earlier than 1351. It is, of course, possible that Petrarch adopted the text as appropriate for inclusion into *DR* i, 107, at a much later date and dispensed with further detail, since the source of the remark was not identified.

Petrarch had several opportunities for high ecclesiastical office. On this, Wilkins (1955), chap. iv.

6   In the summer of 1366, Petrarch addressed Pope Urban V in similar terms (*Sen.* vii, 1 [1581: 826]):

> Nec uero tibi fortuna blandiatur, tua nec te longe uitae spes decipiat, breuis est uita mortalium, maximeque Pontificum, seu quod senes ad hunc statum ueniunt, seu quia curarum pondus, laborque perpetuus, & negotiorum aestus necesse est uitam ipsam efficiant breuiorem.

> Neither should Fortune beguile you, nor your hope for a long life deceive you. Short is the life of mortals, shortest that of pontiffs. The fact that they are old when they reach this office, the crushing weight of their problems and never-ending toils, the withering stress of their tasks needs add up to a shorter life span for a pope.

7   Similar: *Eneas* 663–692, Yunck (1974), p. 69.
8   Claudian, *In Rufin.* i, 22–23:

> . . . . tolluntur in altum,
> ut lapsu grauiore ruant. . . .

> He is raised aloft that he may
> be hurled down in more headlong ruin.

LCL, Platnauer, p. 29. The passage is quoted in Innocent III, *De miseria cond. hum.* ii, 29, 10, Lewis (1978), p. 183.

9   In *Africa* vi, 878–879 (1581:55), Mago says:

> . . .   . finis ad alta levatis
> Est ruere . . .   .

Bergin (1977), p. 140, 1162–1163. Note also *Fam.* xiv, 1, 30. On this, Seneca, *Ep.* 19, 9, as above, *DR* i, 17, note 4; and, e.g., *Ep.* 94, 73, *Dial.* vi, 23, 4, ix, 10, 5, x, 17, and *Nat. quaest.* iv, praef. 22. Cf. also Innocent III, *De miseria cond. hum.* ii, 29, 8, quoting Lucan i, 81. —On *ex alto ruere,* often referred to by Reason, cf. *DR* i, 91, 20–26, i, 96, 79–94, ii, 5, 83–87, and *DR* i, 1, note 10.

10   I.e., *arx fidei catholice*—the stronghold of the Catholic faith (*Contra eum, Prose* [1955], p. 772; on *Arx fidei,* De Lubac, ii, 2 [1964], pp. 49, 54–56); or the papal residence in Rome or Avignon.

11   Suetonius, i, Jul. xiii:

> Deposita provinciae spe pontificatum maximum petit non sine profusissima largitione; in qua reputans magnitudinem aeris alieni, cum mane ad comitia descenderet, praedixisse matri osculanti fertur domum se nisi pontificem non reversurum.

LCL, Rolfe, p. 17.

12   1492: cui a prima aetate propositum sit regnare
1581: cui a patria errare propositum sit regnare

13   *Servorum servus diceris. Cave ne dominorum dominus fieri velis.* Compare the chiastic sally Petrarch relates in *SN* 17, Piur (1925), p. 222:

> ┌────── q ──────┐
> . . . non illepide iocans quidam ait: Roma, tibi fuerant servi
>
> (a   b)   X   (b   a)   ┌────── q ──────┐
> domini dominorum, servorum servi nunc tibi sunt domini.

> . . . someone quipped, rather cleverly: "Rome, your servants were lords of lords, now your lords are servants of servants."

Zacour (1973), pp. 100–101. *servus servorum Dei*—servant of the servants of God—is the title favored by Pope Gregory the Great (A.D. 590–604; Cayré, ii [1940], p. 237), which has been kept by his successors. Cf. John of Salisbury, *Policrat.* viii, 23, *PL* 199, c. 814. On *servus Dei,* Curtius (1953), pp. 408–409.

14   On the pope as the vicar of Christ, Previté-Orton (1952), pp. 940–945; Kantorowicz (1957a), pp. 89–90, 194–206; and Ladner (1959), p. 131, n. 66.

108 ❖ HAPPINESS

1   *Prose* (1955), pp. 636–643. Key texts for the present dialogue are Aristotle, *Eth. Nic.* i, and Boethius, *Cons. Phil.*

2   *Non foelicem faciunt ista: vel miserum: sed detegunt: ac ostendunt:* compare *Fam.* ii, 4, 12, xii, 2, 10; and *Contra quendam,* Ricci (1949), p. 349: *non format animum fortuna sed detegit*—Fortune does not shape the mind, but exposes it.

3   Sallust, *Cat.* x, 3:

> Igitur primo pecuniae, deinde imperi cupido crevit; ea quasi materies omnium malorum fuere.

> Hence the lust for money first, then for power, grew upon them; these were, I may say, the root of all evils.

LCL, Rolfe, p. 19.

4   Lucan, viii, 618–631:

> Sed postquam mucrone latus funestus Achillas
> Perfodit, nullo gemitu consensit ad ictum
> Respexitque nefas, servatque inmobile corpus,
> Seque probat moriens atque haec in pectore volvit:
> "Saecula Romanos numquam tacitura labores
> Attendunt, aevumque sequens speculatur ab omni
> Orbe ratem Phariamque fidem: nunc consule famae.
> Fata tibi longae fluxerunt prospera vitae;
> Ignorant populi, si non in morte probaris,
> An scieris adversa pati. Ne cede pudori
> Auctoremque dole fati: quacumque feriris,
> Crede manum soceri. Spargant lacerentque licebit,
> *Sum* tamen, o superi, *felix,* nullique potestas
> Hoc auferre deo.

But when murderous Achillas had driven the point through his side, he did not acknowledge the blow by any cry or take heed of the horror, but remained motionless, and tested his strength in the hour of death; and these thoughts passed through his mind: "Future ages, that will never forget the tragedy of Rome, are watching now, and from every quarter of the world time coming gazes at this boat and the treachery of Egypt; think now of fame. Through a long life the tide of your success never slackened; men do not know, unless you prove it by your death, whether you were able to endure adversity. Sink not beneath the shame, nor resent the instrument of doom: whatever the hand that slays you, believe it to be the hand of your kinsman. Though men scatter and mutilate my limbs, nevertheless, ye gods, *I am a fortunate man,* and of this no god can deprive me."

LCL, Duff, p. 483.

5   1492: *Gaudium*: Sum foelix.

> *Ratio*: Pontificatu forsan: aut Imperio: aut omnino potentia: atque opibus foelicem fieri credis. Falleris. Non foelicem faciunt ista: uel miserum: sed detegunt: ac ostendunt: & si quid facerent: miserum potius quam foelicem facerent. Sunt enim plena periculis: quibus humanarum est affixa miseriarum radix.
>
> *Gau.*: Foelix sum.
>
> *Ra.*: Opinione fortassis tua: quae quoniam falsa est: foelicitati nihil addiderit: sed miserie multum. Si quidem propriam non nosce miseriam: miseria summa est.
>
> *Gau.*: Foelix sum.
>
> *Ra.*: Hoc inter carnificum gladios magnus ille Pompeius de se praedicat: quod tamen si profundius uerum fodis nunquam fuerat: ne tum quidem: dum florentissimo in statu foelicissimus uideretur.
>
> *Ra.*: O miser qui in tot malis te foelicem speres.

1581: *Gaudium*: Sum foelix.

> *Ratio*: Pontificatu forsan, aut imperior, aut omnino potentia, atque opibus foelicem fieri credis: falleris, non foelicem faciunt ista uel miserum, sed detegunt atque ostendunt, & si quid facerent, miserum potius quam foelicem facerent: sunt enim plena periculis, quibus humanarum est affixa miseriarum radix.
>
> *G.*: Foelix sum.
>
> *R.*: O miser, qui in tot malis te foelicem speres.
>
> *G.*: Sum foelix.
>
> *R.*: Opinione fortassis tua, quae quoniam falsa est, foelicitati nihil addiderit, sed miserie multum, siquidem propriam non nosse miseriam, miseria summa est.
>
> *G.*: Foelix sum.
>
> *R.*: Hoc inter carnificum gladios magnus ille Pompeius de se praedicat, quod tamen si profundus uerum fodis, nunquam fuerat, ne tum quidem, dum florentissimo in statu foelicissimus uideretur.

6   *Prose* (1955), p. 638: *et vivis viator.* 1492, 1581: *et unus viator.*

7   *I.t.* Quintus Metellus

Cicero, *Tusc. disp.* i, 36, 86:

> Metelli sperat sibi quisque fortunam, proinde quasi aut plures fortunati sint quam infelices aut certi quidquam sit in rebus humanis aut sperare sit prudentius quam timere.

Each one hopes for himself the good fortune of Metellus, just as if more men were lucky than unlucky, or there were certainty in men's affairs or hope were wiser than apprehension.

LCL, King, p. 103. Petrarch quotes Cicero's initial phrase, *Fam.* iii, 20, 8, ix, 14, 6; and *De ocio, Prose* (1955), p. 602. Cf. also Cicero, ibid. i, 35, 85; and Valerius Maximus, vii, 1, 1. On this, *Fam.* iii, 20, 9, vi, 5, 6, and viii, 1, 2, 13–14.

8   This refers to the tribune of the commons Gaius Attinius Labeo, who, in 131 B.C., ordered Metellus to be thrown from the Tarpeian Rock and his property confiscated. Pliny, *Nat. hist.* vii, 44, 142–144, 146; Livy, *Perioch.* 59.

9   Sulla assumed the surname *Felix*—the Fortunate—after the death of his enemy, the younger Marius. Livy, xxx, 45, 6. Cf. above, *DR* i, 106, note 5. On surnames, *DR* i, 63, note 8. Alexander the Great died of a fever at Babylon 323 B.C. For the story of his poisoning, cf. *De vir. ill.* xv, Alex., 33–34, based on Curtius Rufus, x, 10, 14; and Justin xii, 13, 7–15. Note also Pseudo-Callisthenes, Wolohojian (1969), pp. 149–157. Caesar was assassinated March 15, 44 B.C. On Scipio Maior at Liternum, *DR* i, 51, 5–17, and note 2. On the younger Scipio, e.g., *DR* i, 52, note 11.

10 1492: sed foelicem negant
    1582: sed infoelicem negant

11 Suetonius ii, Aug. 61, 1:

    refeream nunc interiorem ac familiarem eius vitam quibusque moribus atque fortuna domi.

    I shall next give an account of his private and domestic life, describing his character and his fortune at home.

    LCL, Rolfe, p. 217.

12 Cf. Suetonius ii, Aug., 63–65; Pliny, *Nat. hist.* vii, 45, 147–150.

13 The all-too-true sentence is probably Eccli. 11, 30:

    Ante mortem ne laudes hominem quemquam.

    Praise not any man before death.

Quoted in Augustine, *De civ. Dei* xiii, 11. In his rebuttal on behalf of the French cardinals in Avignon, of Petrarch's second letter to Pope Urban V (*Sen.* ix, 1 [1581: 844–854], written in January 1368), Jean de Hesdin alluded to the same scriptural passage in refutation of Petrarch's claim that the pope would be happy in Italy and in Rome (1581: 1062):

    D. N. Papam esse foelicem non dubito: sed hoc esse, ut dicit, propter eius aggressum non concedo, imo firmiter credo, illam viam, quantum ad multas operationes, tam speculativas, quam practicas, & tam contemplativas, quam activas impedimentum magnum, & obicem extitisse, quoniam secundum Aristotelem ubi supra. Accidentia [non] tribulant & conturbant beatum, tristitias enim inferunt & impediunt. Si autem per foelicitatem, iuxta sententiam Boetii tertio de Consolatione intelligat statum *omnium bonorum (congregatione) perfectum,* secundum deductionem eiusdem Boetii in eodem, veram foelicitatem in ipso summo Deo esse necesse est, propter quod talis status non habitus in via, beatis in patria reservatur. Unde & iuxta Salomonis sententiam: Nemo foelix dicitur in hac vita. Mutabilitas enim fortunae mortalium, nomen foelicitatis annihilat.

I do not doubt that Our Lord the Pope is happy. But I do not agree that this is due to the move to Rome, as (Petrarch) says. To the contrary, I believe firmly that that road constitutes a great obstacle and a serious impairment for many of his activities, be they now speculative or practical, contemplative or dealing with the busy world of affairs—about which, Aristotle, as cited above [*Eth. Nic.* x, 6–8]. Accidentals do not bother and upset a happy man, but worries burden and obstruct. If then, according to Boethius' sentence in Book iii of his *Consolation* [P 2, 11, LCL, p. 228], happiness is *the perfect state in which all goods are possessed* [Green (1962), p. 43], it follows, as the same Boethius concludes, that true happiness must necessarily be placed in God, the Most High [iii, P 10, 37; LCL, p. 268]—wherefore such a state cannot be found on this, our earthly road, but is reserved for the blessed in the heavenly city. Because, in the words of Solomon, no man can be called happy in this life [Eccli. 11, 30]. The instability of the fortunes of man destroys the term happiness.

On this, Wilkins (1961), pp. 214–215, 235–236. Note also *Fam.* viii, 1, 8 *et passim,* and ii, 2, 3:

Vita est que miseros facit et beatos, quam qui usque ad extremi fugam spiritus bene egit, nullo eget amplius, felix est, securus est, in portu est.

It is life that makes people wretched or blessed, and he who has conducted it well until the flight of his last breath stands in need of nothing more, for he is happy, secure, and in port.

Bernardo (1975), p. 65. —On *nemo felix in hac vita*—No one is happy in this life—*Fam.* vi, 5, 6, viii, 2, 1, xii, 14, 6, xiii, 4, 4, xxiii, 12, 3; *Sen.* xiii, 1 (1581: 916); *De ocio,* Rotondi, pp. 53, 63–64, 74; and DR i, 10, 51–53, ii, 84, 66–74. On the related topics *respice finem,* DR i, 17, note 7; dying of joy, DR i, 23, 28, and note 13, i, 29, 39–46, and note 9 and i, 90, 39–50.

14   Lucan i, 458–459:

. . . . . . Certe populi, quos despicit Arctos,
Felices errore suo, ...

The nations under the Northern stars, for sure,
are happy in their error . . .

Quoted with the same reference *ut ille ait*—as one says—in *Contra eum, Prose* (1955), p. 772.

15   Cf. above, *DR* i, 10, 50–51, and note 19; *Var.* 61, Fracassetti, iii (1863), p. 475; *De sui ipsius, Prose* (1955), pp. 746, 748; and H. Nachod in Cassirer (1948), pp. 105–106.

16   1492: hac in parte caecissimi
     1581: ac parte caecissimi

17   Cf. Aristotle, *Eth. Nic.* i, 8; and the discussion in Boethius, *Cons. phil.*, e.g., ii. P 3.

18   Aristotle, ibid. i, 7, 1098a, 16, i, 10, 1100b, 11–22. On this Jean de Hesdin, *In Petrarcham* (1581: 1062–1063).

109   ❖   HOPEFULNESS

1   Dialogues 109–122 deal with "great expectations."

2   On Hope or Desire and Fear, the children of Prosperity and Adversity, respectively (*DR* i, Pref., 236–239), cf. above, *DR* i, 10, note 20. On contraries, above, *DR* i, 11, note 19.

3   Reason seems to allude to Terence, *Adelphoë* 386–387:

> istuc est sapere, non quod ante pedes modost
> videre sed etiam illa quae futura sunt
> prospicere.

> That is indeed wisdom, not only seeing what is in front of your nose,
> but foreseeing
> what is to come.

LCL, Sargeaunt, p. 259. The passage is identified and quoted (*Nam ut ait Comicus:* . . .) in *Sen.* vii, 1 (1581: 824). For an Ennius-Cicero quotation which is related, but in different context, see below, *DR* i, 112, 32–33, and note 6.

4   1492: et optato carcere
     1581: & optato carere

5   1492: gustu caret
     1581: gestu caret

Reason equates the purposive act of hoping with the hoped-for object, the absence and desirability of which inspires the hope for it.

6   *Magnus labor expectare*—I have been unable to locate the source of this saying.

7   Cf. above, *DR* i, 11, 52–53, and note 11.

8   1492: credulitas
     1581: crudelitas

     On deceiving oneself, note 7, above.

9   Cf. *De ocio,* Rotondi, p. 26:

> spem tenete, nemo illam vobis extorqueat,

> Hold on to hope, let no one wrest it from you.

10   Cf. above, *Dramatis personae,* note 13. —Foster (1984), p. 160, fails to consider this passage.

11   Cf. Aristotle, *Eth. Nic.* x, 7, 1177b, 31–35.

12   The Peripatetics held that there were three goods of mind, of body, and of fortune (*bona animi, corporis, et fortunae*). Epicurus stressed living modestly, honorably, wisely, and justly. The Stoics (Zeno and Chrysippus) thought that virtue alone is required for leading a happy life. Cf. Aristotle, *Eth. Nic.* i, 8; Cicero, *Tusc. disp.,* e.g., v, *passim* (see *Fam.* xviii, 14, 4; and the discussion in Boethius, *Cons. phil.* iii, and Pickering [1970], pp. 182–186). Note also Augustine, *De civ. Dei* x, 18:

> Eius enim propheta veracissimus ait: *Mihi autem adhaerere Deo bonum est.* De fine boni namque inter philosophos quaeritur, ad quod adipiscendum omnia officia referenda sunt. Nec dixit iste: Mihi autem divitiis abundare bonum est, aut insigniri purpura et sceptro vel diademate excellere, aut, quod nonnulli etiam philosophorum dicere non erubuerunt: Mihi voluptas corporis bonum est; aut quod melius velut meliores dicere visi sunt: Mihi virtus animi mei bonum est; sed: *Mihi,* inquit, *adhaerere Deo bonum est.*

> Indeed, his wholly veracious prophet says: *But for me it is good to cling to God* [Ps. 73, 28]. Now among philosophers there is argument about the supreme good, to the attainment of which all our responsible acts should be directed. And the psalmist did not say: 'For me it is good to have riches in abundance,' nor, 'to be decked out in imperial purple and have sceptre and diadem to mark my superiority,' nor, as some even of the philosophers have not blushed to say: 'For me the pleasure of the body is good [i.e., the Epicureans; cf. Cicero, *De Fin.* ii, 1, 2],' nor, as the nobler philosphers, it is thought, have said more nobly: 'For me the moral strength of my mind is good [i.e., the Stoics].' No, the psalmist said: *For me it is good to cling to God.*

LCL, Wiesen, p. 337. Cf. *Fam.* i, 8, 10, iii, 6, 2–3, vi, 2, 4, xi, 3, 10, xvi, 6, 15, xxiii, 12, 6; *Secretum* i, *Prose* (1955), pp. 32, 34; *Contra med.* iv, Ricci (1950), 97–125; *De sui ipsius, Prose* (1955), pp. 746, 748, H. Nachod in Cassirer (1948), p. 105; and above, *DR* i, Pref., note 7, i, 2, note 11. On

Petrarch's position, also J. E. Seigel in Wiener (1973), iv, p. 478; and Foster (1984), pp. 168–169.

13   Cf. Hebr. 6, 17–19:

> In quo abundantius volens Deus ostendere pollicitationis heredibus immobili-
> tatem consilii sui, interposuit jusjurandum, ut per duas res immobiles, quibus
> impossibile est mentiri Deum, fortissimum solatium habeamus, qui confugimus
> ad tenendam propositam spem; quam sicut anchoram habemus animae tutam
> ac firmam, et incedentem usque ad interiora velaminis . . .

> Wherein God, meaning more abundantly to shew to the heirs of the promise
> the immutability of his counsel, interposed an oath: That by two immutable
> things, in which it is impossible for God to lie, we may have the strongest
> comfort, who have fled for refuge to hold fast the hope set before us. Which we
> have as an anchor of the soul, sure and firm, and which entereth in even within
> the veil . . .

On the anchor is iconic emblem in pictorial representations of Hope, Ferguson (1954), p. 174. The image recurs in *Fam.* xix, 10, 5.

14   Virgil, *Aeneid* vi, 3–4:

> . . . . dente tenaci
> ancora fundabat naves . . .

15   1492: proram
      1581: pronam

16   *Secretum* i, *Prose* (1955), p. 62:

> Et ego, in mari magno sevoque ac turbido iactatus, tremulam cimbam fatis-
> centemque et rimosam ventis obluctantibus per tumidos fluctus ago. Hanc diu
> durare non posse certe scio nullamque spem salutis superesse michi video, nisi
> miseratus Omnipotens prebeat ut gubernaculum summa vi flectens antequam
> peream litus apprehendam, qui in pelago vixerim moriturus in portu.

> For I too am cast upon a wide ocean, cruel and full of storms. I sail across its
> angry waves and struggle with the wind; and the little boat I steer shivers and
> seems to be letting in the water in every part. I know well she cannot hold out
> for long, and I see I have no hope at all of safety unless the Almighty Pity put
> forth His strong right hand and guide my vessel rightly ere it be too late, and
> bring me to shore— "So that I who have lived upon the waters may die in
> port" (Seneca, *Ep.* 19, 2).

Draper (1911), pp. 39–40. Cf. Augustine, *Contra acad.* ii, 1, 1, *PL* 32, c. 919

> Quamobrem contra illos fluctus procellasque fortunae, cum obnitendum remis
> qualiumcumque virtutum, tum in primis divinum auxilium omni devotione
> atque pietate implorandum est; ut intentio constantissima bonorum studiorum
> teneat cursum suum, a quo eam nullus casus excutiat, quominus illam philo-
> sophiae tutissimus jucundissimusque portus accipiat.

Against the tides and storms of Fortune, therefore, we must strain with the oar of all our virtue—but, above all, we must implore divine help with deep devotion and piety. That the eternal goal of all honest studies maintain the right course from which nothing should divert it, so that it may reach that safest and most joyous harbor of all philosophy.

On the stormy sea of life, also Boethius, *Cons. phil.* i, P 3, 37–39, Gruber (1978), pp. 79, *4,* and 107, *11;* and Misch, iii, 2 (1976), p. 272. On the nautical metaphor, Rico (1974), pp. 104–105; and Curtius (1953), pp. 128–130.

17 In 1346 Petrarch wrote to "his Laelius" (Lello di Stefano dei Tosetti) from Vaucluse (*Fam.* iii, 19, 1–7, 11):

Adeo pertinax et fixa mortalium spes est adversus infeliciter experta, ut neque sterilitas agricolam, neque tempestas nautam, neque tectorum casus architectum, neque patremfamilias sobolis acerbus interitus deterreat ab incepto. Hinc illa communia, ut et famelicos serere et naufragos navigare et ruinis vix elapsos nova super eisdem fundamentis edificia moliri et orbos senes inter sepulcra filiorum aliis procreandis intendere videamus. Piscatores frigoribus et fame confectos hic ante oculos habeo. Mirum et prorsus incredibile, totos dies ieiuni ac nudi noctesque ad auroram insomnes agunt, cum interim vel hamos vel retia tentantium una eademque sors est: nichil agere, frustra torqueri, tempus, in aliis aliquanto forsan utilius consumendum, perdere: neque tamen obstinatis ad inceptum animis a fatali gurgite divelluntur. Usque adeo etiam amari exercitii consuetudo longior dulcis est. Infaustam arenam imo verrentes alveo, quam fugiunt egestatem inter undas et scopulos inveniunt, nunquam forte quod tantopere satagunt, reperturi. Illa quidem dictu minora, nescio an maiori admiratione digna sint. Ferarum studium, totiens vacuatis cubilibus, non lentescit; novis fetibus pariendis alendisque prioris raptu nunquam segnior tigris redit; columbe, crebri partus solatio destitute, nichilo moderatior in reliquum ardor est; philomena, postquam pastorali furto perditos natos longo gemitu et predulcibus querimoniis prosecuta est, nidum ab eodem ramo, sequentis puerperii fortunam tentatura, suspendit. Rem dicam novam tibi sed omnibus vallis huius incolis notissimam. Aquila iampridem in his montibus habitat; subulcus advena, nedum quos pascit suibus sed hirsutis etiam apris asperior, clam nido insidiatus est, neque animam suam pluris extimans quam valet, de altissima rupe, que fonti Sorgie nubibus par impendet, ancipiti fune demissus, cuius rei vel meminisse horror est, ad aeriam domum temerarius .predator accessit, et solicite genitrici, spem generis, pullos implumes abstulit. Id semel, idque iterum et iterum ausus, nil amplius aquilam movit, quam ut, nuper tristi domicilio deserto, nidum dumosamque supellectilem in alteram rupis partem parumper avexerit; illic modo sepius amisse sobolis spem refovet, nichil solito letius, ut reor; siquidem saxeus iste suus hostis, exigui lucri cupidus, vite prodigus, iam restem nodosque preparat, quibus per inane suspensus de insolito specu solitas predas agat.

Iam sensim ad minima rerum ratiocinando descendimus; nec apibus quidem prerepti mellis iniuria mellificandi dulcedinem, nec formicis sub terra latentium horreorum inundatio graniferi laboris experientiam frequentisque cursus ac recursus imminuit voluptatem; non enim desperant infeliciter tentata retentari posse felicius. Alioquin, si cum successibus rerum animorum simul spes intereat, torpebunt estus hi quos undique cernimus, actionum variarum, quotidie interpellantibus fatis, et vitam situ marcidam exitus inglorius manebit. Quod ne forte contingeret animantibus cuntis et presertim homini, dura propositique tenacia pectora data sunt. . . . . Miraris nunc quid tam longa sibi velit oratio; scilicet, unum ago: ut amicum tuum subscribas exemplorum turbe, raras et forte vanas sed firmas utique spes habentem.

Mortal hope is so pertinacious, so deep implanted against misfortune, that crop failure cannot deter the farmer from his enterprises, nor can storm restrain the sailor, nor the collapse of his house the home builder, nor the cruel death of children the paterfamilias. Thus we see the starving peasant sow his seed once more, the shipwrecked sailor put forth again, the householder emerge from ruins to build again on the same foundations, the bereaved parent look to new begettings among the very tombs of his sons. From my home I watch the fishermen, chilled and hungry. It seems almost incredible. They labor all day, stripped and fasting, and all night long until dawn, trying out their hooks and nets, with one constant result: to catch nothing, to cast in vain, to waste time that might be more usefully spent. Yet their minds are so fixed on their task that they can't be torn away from the fatal stream. The longer their harsh labors last the better they like them. Scraping the very river bottom, they find among the rocks and waters the poverty they would avoid, and never obtain what they so eagerly seek. Other cases, perhaps of less importance, may better deserve our wonder. Wild animals are never discouraged by the robbing of their dens. The tigress whose young have been ravished does not weary of bearing and rearing new offspring. The dove who has lost part of her brood lavishes no less maternal care on the remainder. The nightingale deprived of her young by a thievish shepherd mourns them long and melodiously, but she hangs her nest from the same branch to try the fortune of a new brood. Let me tell you something new to you but well known to all our valley-dwellers. We have had for some time an eagle in our hills. A common swineherd, rougher than his own beasts, nay rougher than the hirsute wild boar, has laid a plot against her and, counting his life at its true worth, has let himself down by a double rope from the lofty cliff that overhangs the Sorgue like a cloud. It horrifies me even to think of it. The bold pillager reached the eyry and robbed the solicitous mother of her fledglings, the hope of her race. He did this not once but twice or thrice, until finally the eagle left her ill-starred home and moved her bushy bedding to another part of the cliff, hoping to raise there a new family. But I think she won't be any luckier there, for her stonyhearted enemy, eager for a small gain and careless of his life, is busily knotting his ropes, with which, suspended over the void, he will seize the prey as usual in its new site.

We are gradually descending to treat of *animalculae.* Neither do bees renounce the sweetness of honey-making from the frequent loss of their stores; nor do ants who lose the fruits of their grain-bearing labors by the flooding of

their underground storehouses abdicate the pleasures of their everlasting jour-
neys to and fro. They do not despair of attempting again an enterprise that has
come to disaster. If our hopes should die with every mischance, our ardor for
high deeds would cool under the cudgeling of fate, and a life wasted in inactiv-
ity would end in inglorious death. Lest this should be the fate of all creatures
and particularly of men, we have been given stout spirits, tenacious of purpose.
[Bishop [1966], pp. 41–42.] . . . . . . And now you wonder what this long
discourse intended to show. Only one thing: that you count your friend among
the huge number who exemplify that their hopes are few and perhaps vain, but
always firm and strong.

Note also *Fam.* xviii, 16, 11.

110 ❖ EXPECTING AN INHERITANCE

1   On *captatio*—legacy hunting—Horace, *Sat.* ii, 5; Juvenal, i, 37–44, v, 137–
145, xii, 93–130; and Seneca, *Dial.* vi, Ad Marciam xix, 2, and *De benef.* vi,
38, 4. The *old man without kin* recalls Cicero, *Parad. Stoic.* v, 39:

> Hereditatis spes quid iniquitatis in serviendo non suscipit? quem nutum
> locupletis orbi senis non observat? Loquitur ad voluntatem, quidquid denun-
> tiatum est facit, assectatur assidet muneratur: quid horum est liberi, quid
> denique non servi inertis?

> The hope of a legacy—what harshness of service does it not undertake? what
> nod from a rich old man without children does it not attend to? It makes
> conversation when it suits him, executes all his commissions, follows him
> about, sits at his side, makes him presents: which of these is the action of a free
> man? which indeed does not mark an indolent slave?

LCL, Rackham, p. 291. Note also Horace, *Sat.* ii, 5, esp. 23–57, and *Ep.* i, 1,
77–79; Juvenal, vi, 38–40, xii, 98–130; and Jerome, *Ep.* 52, LCL, Wright, p.
206. Cf. Sandys (1929), pp. 186–187; and above, *DR* i, 90, 90–96.

2   Above, *DR* i, 90.

3   1492: se uicturos sperent
1581: se uictores sperent

4   *nemo tam senex: qui non possit annum vivere.* Cf. Cicero, *De sen.* vii, 24:

> nemo enim est tam senex qui se annum non putet posse vivere.

> For no one is so old as to think that he cannot live one more year.

LCL, Falconer, p. 33. —Note the exchange between *Augustinus* and *Franciscus* in *Secretum* iii, *Prose* (1955), p. 198:

Aug.: . . . . . . Qui annum habet ad vivendum, certum quiddam habet ille, scilicet modicum; qui vero sub ambiguo mortis imperio est, sub quo quidem omnes degitis mortales, nec anni, nec lucis, denique nec hore integre certus est. Annum victuro, sex licet mensibus amissis, adhuc semestre superest spatium; tibi vero, si hic perditur dies, quis sponsor est crastini? Verba sunt Ciceronis: "moriendum esse certum est et hoc ipsum incertum an hac eadem die," nec est aliquis adeo iuvenis "cui compertum sit se usque ad vesperam esse venturum." Quero igitur ex te, quero itidem ex cuntis mortalibus, qui venturis inhiantes presentia non curatis: quis scit

> an addiciant hodierne crastina vite
> tempora dii superi?

Fr.: Nullus profecto, ut pro me ipse, et pro cuntis respondeam; sed speramus annum saltem, quem nemo tam senex est ut non superesse sibi speret, quod Ciceroni placet.

Aug.: . . . . . . The man who has one year of life possesses something certain though short; whereas he who has no such promise and lies under the power of death (whose stroke may fall at any moment), which is the common lot of all men—this man, I say, is not sure of a year, a day; no, not even of one hour. He who has a year to live, if six months shall have slipped away, will still have another half-year left to run; but for you, if you lose the day that now is, who will promise you to-morrow? It is Cicero who says: "It is certain that we must die: what is uncertain is whether it will be today; and there is none so young that he can be sure he will live until the evening" (*De sen.* xx, 74, xix, 67). I ask, then, of you, and I ask it likewise of all those who stand gaping after the future and pay no heed to the present, Who knows

> if the high gods will add even one morrow
> to this your little day of life?

[Horace, *Carm.* iv, 7, 17–18.]

Fr.: If I am to answer for myself and for all: No one knows, of a truth. But let us hope for a year at least; on which, if we are still to follow Cicero, even the most aged reckons! [*De sen.* vii, 24.]

Draper (1911), pp. 174–175. On this, Rico (1974), pp. 394–395.

5   The entire sentence apears in *La Celestina* iv, 4, Marciales (1985), ii, p. 82; Simpson (1955), p. 50; and Deyermond (1961), p. 43.

6   I.t.: Gaius

7   Emperor Claudius was 51 years old when he succeeded Caligula, who died at age 29; Galba was 71 when he succeeded Nero, 31; Nerva, 68, succeeded Domitian, 45; and Pertinax, 67, Commodus, 31.

8   *elogio.* Cf. *Cod. Iust.* 3, 28, 37, §1; *Dig.* 28, 2, 14; 37, 10, 1, §9; and Suetonius, *Vita Horati,* LCL, p. 484.

9   1492: Potest nolle
      1481: Atqui potest nolle
10   *Roman de la Rose* 4803–4836:

> A rich man who thinks himself loved is more horned than an antlered stag.
> Now isn't this a great folly? It is certain that he doesn't love; and how can he
> believe that anyone loves him unless he calls himself a fool? In such a case he
> is no wise man, but a fine branched stag. By God, he who wants real friends
> must be a friend. I can prove that he doesn't love: when he has his wealth and
> thinks his friends poor, he keeps his wealth and guards it from them. He plans
> to keep it always, until his mouth is closed and wicked death has struck him
> down. For he would first let his body be carved up limb by limb before he
> allowed his wealth to leave him, so that none of it would be shared with his
> friends. Thus love has no part whatever in his situation, for how could there be
> any real friendship in a heart that knows no lawful pity? Certainly, the man
> who neither loves nor is loved is much to be blamed.

Dahlberg (1971), p. 102. On the parallels in Cicero's *De amic.,* ibid., p. 376.
Cf. above, *DR* i. 50; note 11.
11   Cf. above, *DR* i, 46, 115–116.
12   CF. *Cod. Iust.* 6, 23, 27; and Sohm & Mitteis (1931), §101, v.
13   The stories of Lucullus, disappointed by Quintus Caecilius, and of Augustus,
      disappointed by T. Marius Urbinas, are told in Valerius Maximus, vii, 8, 5 and
      6. Cf. below, *DR* ii, 62, 44–48, and note 7.
14   Pliny, *Nat. hist.* vii, 14, 61:

> Mulier post quinquagensimum annum non gignit, maiorque pars XL
> profluvium genitale sistit. Nam in viris Masinissam regem post LXXXVI annum
> generasse filium quem Methimannum appellaverit clarum est, Catonem cen-
> sorium octogesimo exacto e filia Saloni clientis sui:

> A woman does not bear children after the age of fifty, and with the majority
> menstruation ceases at 40. As for the case of men, it is well known that King
> Masinissa begot a son when over 86, whom he called Methimannus, and
> Cato the ex-censor had a son by the daughter of his client Salonius when he
> was 81:

LCL, Rackham, p. 547. Similarly, on Cato, Pseudo-Pliny the Younger, *De vir.
ill.* 47; and, on Masinissa (I.t.: Masanissa), Livy, *Perioch.* 50:

> Masinissa Numidiae rex maior nonaginta annis decessit, vir insignis. Inter cet-
> era iuvenalia opera, quae ad ultimum edidit, adeo etiam veneris usu in senecta
> viguit, ut post sextum et octogesimum annum filium genuerit.

> Masinissa King of Numidia died aged more than ninety, a distinguished man.
> Among other youthful exploits which he performed during his last years, he
> was so vigorous even sexually in his old age as to beget a son after he was
> eighty-six.

LCL, Schlesinger, p. 33,

15   A reference to the provision of *testamentum ruptum* in Roman civil law. Sohm (1931), p. 601, 2.a. On the canon law of inheritance, Berman (1983), pp. 230–237.

16   *Cato, that wisest of old men* echoes Cicero, *De amic.* ii, 9, which Petrarch quotes in *De vir. ill.* xxii, Cato, 1:

> Marci Portii Catonis Censorii laudibus plena sunt omnia; precipuum sapientie cognomen obtinuit, in qua nulli creditur cesisse. Notum est illud Lelii sapientis apud Tullium, qui de hoc Catone "aut enim nemo," inquit "quod quidem magis credo, aut si quisquam ille sapiens fuit." Neque vero apud scriptores tantum sed etiam apud gentes vulgata hec sapientie fama est; quis est enim, quamvis ex acie vulgari, qui Catonis audito nomine non intelligat sapientem?

> Everywhere the praises of Marcus Porcius Cato Censorius are plentiful. He earned the highest title of wisdom in which he was considered second to none. The remark of the wise Laelius in Cicero [above, *DR* i, 12, 75 and note 15] is widely known, who said about this Cato: "For either no man was wise—which really I think is the better view—or, if anyone, it was he." (LCL, Falconer, p. 117.) But the fame of his wisdom was well established, not only among writers, but among ordinary people. Who in the common crowd does not think of wisdom when he hears Cato's name?

Cf. also *Fam.* ii, 1, 33, and xii, 2, 7. —*Inter os atque offam* is discussed in Aulus Gellius, xiii, 18:

> Quid apud M. Catonem significent verba haec
> "inter os atque offam."

> Oratio est M. Catonis Censorii *De Aedilibus Vitio Creatis*. Ex ea oratione verba haec sunt: "Nunc ita aiunt, in segetibus, in herbis bona frumenta esse. Nolite ibi nimiam spem habere. *Saepe audivi inter os atque offam multa intervenire posse;* verumvero inter offam atque herbam, ibi vero longum intervallum est." Erucius Clarus, qui praefectus urbi et bis consul fuit, vir morum et litterarum veterum studiosissimus, ad Sulpicium Apollinarem scripsit, hominem memoriae nostrae doctissimum, quaerere sese et petere, uti sibi rescriberet quaenam esset eorum verborum sententia. Tum Apollinaris, nobis praesentibus. nam id temporis ego adulescens Romae sectabar eum discendi gratia, rescripsit Claro ut viro erudito brevissime, vetus esse proverbium "inter os et offam," idem significans quod Graecus ille παροιμιώδης versus:

> Πολλὰ μεταξὺ πέλει κύλικος καὶ χείλεος ἄκρου.

> The Meaning of Marcus Cato's Phrase "Between Mouth and Morsel."

> There is a speech by Marcus Cato Censorius *On the Improper Election of Aediles.* In that oration is this passage: "Nowadays they say that the standing

grain, still in the blade, is a good harvest. Do not count too much upon it. *I have often heard that many things may come* inter os atque offam, *or 'between the mouth and the morsel'*; but there certainly is a long distance between a morsel and the blade." Erucius Clarus, who was prefect of the city and twice consul, a man deeply interested in the customs and literature of early days, wrote to Sulpicius Apollinaris, the most learned man within my memory, begging and entreating that he would write him the meaning of those words. Then, in my presence, for at that time I was a young man in Rome and was in attendance upon him for purposes of instruction, Apollinaris replied to Clarus very briefly, as was natural when writing to a man of learning, that "between mouth and morsel" was an old proverb, meaning the same as the poetic Greek adage:

'Twixt cup and lip there's many a slip.

LCL, Rolfe, p. 459. The story is also referred to in *Rer. mem. lib.* iii, 39, 6–7. Note also *Fam.* vii, 11, 3:

Inter cogitatus atque actus magnus quidam, ut vulgo dicitur, mons est.

Between will and deed there is, as the saying goes, a high mountain.

17   1492: rotetur
1581: roretur

For another reference to the instability of money because of its roundness, above, *DR* i, 27, note 3.

111 ❖ ALCHEMY

1   The main alchemical belief was that the base metals, such as copper, lead, tin, and iron, were impure or unripe forms of a single metallic substance which in its pure and fully ripened state appeared as gold. It followed that if a base metal could be suitably purified or ripened it would be converted into gold, and the principal efforts of the practical alchemists were directed to the accomplishment of this transmutation.

E. J. Holmyard in Singer, ii (1956), p. 731. Cf. Thorndike, iii (1935); P. Brunet in Daumas (1957), esp. pp. 345–349; the many references in Sarton (1975);

and A. C. Debus in Wiener (1973), i, pp. 27–34. Note *Roman de la Rose* 16065–16148, Dahlberg (1971), pp. 272–273; the materials on Chaucer, *Canterbury Tales,* The Canon's Yeoman's Prologue and Tale, collected by J. W. Spargo in Bryan & Dempster (1958), pp. 695–698; Kittredge (1910); Coogan (1971); and the remarks in Boyde (1981), pp. 60–62. On our dialogue, Lippmann (1913); and *Isis* 5, p. 503.

2   Due to the "outburst of Latin alchemy after 1300" (Thorndike, iii [1934], chap. 3), Petrarch may well have been acquainted with some of the literature, among it, perhaps, Vincent of Beauvais, *Speculum naturale,* Book viii, and the *Preciosa margarita novella* of 1330 by Pietro Bono Lombardo of Ferrara, in which the author admits *that he has not yet penetrated to the secret* of alchemical art, *or experienced the philosopher's stone himself* (ibid., p. 151). For convenient excerpts from the English translation of the work by Wait (1894), see Grant (1974), pp. 573–536.

3   1492: ut uerum opinemini: quod optatis: falsumque quod cernitis
    1581: ut uerum opinioni quod optatis, falsumque quod cernitis

4   Cf. above, *DR* i, 16, note 2.

5   1492: miris
    1581: mitis

6   Cf. Crombie (1959), i, pp. 134–136; and Holmyard in Singer, ii (1956), chap. 21.

7   Twyne, ff. 140r–140v, translates with more than the usual gusto:

> But goe to, forasmuch as thy minde is so bent, followe it, and I tell thee before hand that thou shalt reape profite by this art, thy house shall swarme with strange gheastes, and wonderfull kindes of implementes, thou shalt have store of eaters and drinkers, and that by good reason, as beyng incensed with heate of the fire, and greedinesse of desire: there shalbe blowers, & deceivers, and mockers, every corner shal stande ful of vessels, and pottes, and basons, and pannes, & glasses of stinking waters: moreover, strange hearbes, and outlandyshe saltes, and sulphure, and stilles, and furnaces, by meanes of all whiche, in the ende thou shalt procure unto thy selfe vayne cares, follie of minde, deformitie of countenaunce, filthinesse of body, dimnesse of sight, carefulnesse and povertie, and that which is woorst of all, the name of a Jugler or Sorcerer, & a lyfe continually to be ledde in darkenesse, among the secret infamous lurkyng corners of Theeves.

8   On congealing mercury, the alchemical *prime matter,* e.g., Avicenna, *On the Formation of Minerals and Metals and the Impossibility of Alchemy;* or Albertus Magnus, *Libellus de alchimia* 13, in Grant (1974), pp. 571–572, 592. On the basic theory of mercury and sulphur, i.e., metal and nonmetal, Albertus Magnus, ibid., p. 588–589; Singer, ii (1956), pp. 42, 737; Crombie (1959), i, pp. 133, 138; Taton, i (1963), p. 519; and the literature noted in Bernal (1971), i, p. 280.

112 ❖ PROMISES OF FORTUNE-TELLERS

1 On contemporary prediction and prognosis, astrological or otherwise, Thorndike, iii (1934), with a casual treatment of Petrarch in chap. xiv. For a general
   essay on the subject, cf. Sarton ([1947], 1975), iii, 1, esp. pp. 110–134; and
   Tester (1987), chap. 5 —On the subject of this dialogue, *Sen.* i, 7, to Francesco Bruni, Venice, September/October, 1362, and iii, 1, to Boccaccio, Venice, September 7, 1363 (1581: 747–749, and 765–772). Cf. Wilkins (1958),
   pp. 75–76, 200–201, 244; and idem (1959), pp. 45, 61–62. Note also Aulus
   Gellius, xiv, 1; and Augustine, *Conf.* vii, 6.

2 On Ixion's wheel, *DR* i, 24, 48, and note 5.

3 Cf. *DR* i, 11, 52–53, and note 11, and i, 89, note 2.

4 On those who act as though they had been to heaven, *DR* i, 46, 22–24, and
   notes 9–14. Cf. Rawski (1967), pp. 175–176, n. 8.

5 I.t.: *apud Tullium*

6 Cicero, *De div.* ii, 13, 30:

   > quód est ante pedes, némo spectat, cáeli scrutantúr plagas

   "This is the third of three verses quoted by Cicero from the *Iphigenia* of
   Ennius in *De re publ.* i, 18, 30" (LCL, Falconer, pp. 402–403; Ennius, *fragm.*
   251). Related, Socrates' story about the Thracian maidservant, who chid
   Thales, the philosopher, when he fell into a well as he was looking up to
   study the stars (Plato, *Theaetetus* 174a; Diogenes Laertius, i, 34, and ii, 4).
   —The verse is also quoted in *De sui ipsius, Prose* (1955), p. 722, where it is
   described as *Democriti non ineptus iocus*—Democrit's not inept witticism.
   Petrarch probably did not know the part of Cicero's *De re publ.* that contained and identified it (Sabbadini [1905], pp. 110–111). Cf. also above, *DR* i,
   109, note 2, and i, 111, 10–11.

7 Probably referring to Cicero's argument in *De div.* ii, e.g., ii, 52, 107–108,
   and ii, 71, 146.

8 1492: a uestris iudico
   1581: a uiris iudico

9 Cicero, *De div.* i, 1, 1:

   > Vetus opinio est iam usque ab heroicis ducta temporibus, eaque et populi
   > Romani et omnium gentium firmata consensu, versari quandam inter homines
   > divinationem, quam Graeci μαντικήν appellant, id est praesensionem et scien-
   > tiam rerum futurarum. Magnifica quaedam res et salutaris, si modo est ulla,
   > quaque proxime ad deorum vim natura mortalis possit accedere. Itaque ut alia
   > nos melius multa quam Graeci, sic huic praestantissimae rei nomen nostri a
   > divis, Graeci, ut Plato interpretatur, a furore duxerunt.

There is an ancient belief, handed down to us even from mythical times and firmly established by the general agreement of the Roman people and of all nations, that divination of some kind exists among men; this the Greeks call μαντική—that is, the foresight and knowledge of future events. A really splendid and helpful thing it is—if only such a faculty exists—since by its means men may approach very near to the power of the gods. And, just as we Romans have done many other things better than the Greeks, so have we excelled them in giving to this most extraordinary gift a name, which we have derived from *divi,* a word meaning "gods," whereas, according to Plato's interpretation (*Phaedrus,* 244c), they have derived it from *furor,* a word meaning "frenzy."

LCL, Falconer, p. 223. Note also Cicero, *De leg.* ii, 13, 32; and Martianus Capella, *De nupt.* i, 6. On a Petrarchan note on μάντις, see Nolhac (1907), ii, p. 185; and Weiss (1977), pp. 178–179.

10   For Ambrose, cf. his *De exc. frat. Satyri* ii (above, DR i, 46, note 13); for Augustine, e.g., *De civ. Dei* v, 5, 7 and 8. The fourteenth-century reader of the DR may have been aware of Isidore's statement that a Christian had to reject and condemn all forms of divination (*Etym.* viii, 9, 31), as well as contemporary critical reaction such as, e.g., *Piers the Plowman, A*-Version, Passus xi, 152–161:

> Ac astronomye is hard thing and evil for to knowe:
> Geometrie and geomesie is gynful of speche.
> That thinketh werche with tho thre thriveth wel late;
> For sorcerie is the soverayn bok that to that science longith.
> Yet arn there febicchis of forellis of many menis wittes,
> Experimentis of alkenemye, of Albertis makyng,
> Nigromancie and perimansie, the pouke to reisen;
> Yif thou thenke Do-wel, deile there with nevere.
> Alle thise sciences, sikir, I my self
> Foundit hem formest folk to desceyve.

Knott (1952), p. 143. On Albert, above, DR i, 111, note 8. —The debate about divination lasted into the eighteenth century. The Jesuit Jean-François Baltus, writing in 1711 "à l'instruction & à l'édification des Fidéles," devoted an entire chapter to the "entêtement de Platon pour la Divination" and Augustine's refutation. Baltus (1711), pp. 255–267.

11   Reason uses *paronomasia per detractionem: Et quamvis divinationem improbent divini viri.* Cf. *Ad Herenn.* iv, 21; Preminger (1965), art. Pun.

12   Cicero, *De div.* ii, where Cicero, in reply to his brother Quintus, *first directs his attack against divination in general.*

Divination, he says, has no application to things perceived by the senses, which are sufficient of themselves and require no aid from divination. Nor is there any place for it in matters within the domain of science and of art. Likewise divination has no place in resolving questions in philosophy, in dialectic or in politics. And since it is of no use in any of these cases there is no use for it anywhere.

W. A. Falconer, in his edition of *De div.*, LCL, p. 220.

13   Cicero, *De div.* ii, 24, 51:

> Vetus autem illud Catonis admodum scitum est, qui *mirari se* aiebat *quod non rideret haruspex haruspicem cum vidisset.*

> But indeed, that was quite a clever remark which Cato made many years ago: 'I wonder,' said he, 'that *a soothsayer doesn't laugh when he sees another soothsayer.*'

LCL, Falconer, p. 429.

14   Fabricius (1716), chap. xii, 2, lists alphabetically some 114 *genera divinationis*—kinds of fortune-telling.

15   Cicero, *De div.* i, 53, 120:

> Eademque efficit in avibus divina mens, ut tum huc, tum illuc volent alites, tum in hac, tum in illa parte se occultent, tum a dextra, tum a sinistra parte canant oscines.

> The Divine Will accomplishes like results in the cases of birds, and causes those known as *alites,* which give omens by their flight, to fly hither and thither and disappear now here and now there, and causes those known as *oscines,* which give omens by their cries, to sing now on the left and now on the right.

LCL, Falconer, p. 355. Falconer notes that "*alites* were birds, like the eagle, hawk, and osprey, that gave omens by their flight; *oscines* were birds, like the raven, crow, and owl, that gave omens by their voices." (Ibid. p. 354, n. 1.)

16   I.t.: *Marcus Tullius.*

17   Cicero, *De div.* ii, 47, 99:

> Quam multa ego Pompeio, quam multa Crasso, quam multa huic ipsi Caesari, a Chaldaeis dicta memini, neminem eorum nisi senectute, nisi domi, nisi cum claritate esse moriturum! ut mihi permirum videatur quemquam exstare, qui etiam nunc credat eis quorum praedicta cotidie videat re et eventis refelli.

> I recall a multitude of prophecies which the Chaldeans made to Pompey, to Crassus and even to Caesar himself (now lately deceased), to the effect that no one of them would die except in old age, at home and in great glory. Hence it would seem very strange to me should anyone, especially at this time, believe in men whose predictions he sees disproved every day by actual results.

LCL, Falconer, p. 483.

18   I.t.: *Agrippe hebreo*

19   On King Deiotarus, Cicero, *De div.* i, 15, 26:

Nam quid ego hospitem nostrum, clarissimum atque optimum virum, Deiotarum regem, commemorem, qui nihil umquam nisi auspicato gerit? Qui cum ex itinere quodam proposito et constituto revertisset aquilae admonitus volatu, conclave illud, ubi erat mansurus, si ire perrexisset, proxima nocte corruit. Itaque, ut ex ipso audiebam, persaepe revertit ex itinere, cum iam progressus esset multorum dierum viam.

I need not remind you of that most famous and worthy man, our guest-friend, King Deiotarus, who never undertook any enterprise without first taking the auspices. On one occasion after he had set out on a journey for which he had made careful plans beforehand, he returned home because of the warning given him by the flight of an eagle. The room in which he would have been staying, had he continued on his road, collapsed the very next night. This is why, as he told me himself, he had time and again abandoned a journey even though he might have been travelling for many days.

LCL, Falconer, pp. 253, 255. Cf. also ibid. ii, 8, 20, and ii, 37, 78–79. On Herod Agrippa I (d. A.D. 44), Josephus, *Jewish Antiqu.* xviii, 7, 195–204, specifically referred to, below, *DR* ii, 90, 78. On Petrarch and Josephus, above, *DR* i, 69, note 40.

20   Isidore, *Etym.* xii, 7, 39:

Bubo a sono vocis conpositum nomen habet, avis feralis, onusta quidem plumis, sed gravi semper detenta pigritia: in sepulcris die noctuque versatur, et semper commorans in cavernis. De qua Ovidius:

> Foedaque fit volucris, venturi nuntia luctus,
> ignavus bubo, dirum mortalibus omen.

Denique apud augures malum portendere fertur: nam cum in urbe visa fuerit, solitudinem significare dicunt.

The owl, named after its call [bubo], is an ill-boding bird, weighed down by feathers, always grave and stolid. It stays in burial places day and night, and often dwells in caves. On it, Ovid:

> He has become a loathsome bird, prophet of woe,
> the slothful [horned] owl, a bird of evil omen to men.

[*Metam.* v, 549–550. LCL, Miller, p. 277.] Therefore the augurs hold that the owl portends evil: but if it is seen in the city, they say it signifies loneliness.

Cf. also, Statius, *Theb.* iii, 511, as in Nicole Oresme, *De config.* i, 36, Clagett (1968), p. 261; Alain de Lille, *Planctus nat., PL* 210, c. 436; *Roman de la Rose* 5976–5977, Dahlberg (1971), p. 119; Chaucer, *Parl. of Fowles,* 343 (Robinson [1933], pp. 367a, 905); and the literature listed in Janson (1952), p. 196, n. 91.

The Virgil reference is *Aeneid* iv, 462–463:

> solaque culminibus *ferali carmine* bubo
> saepe queri et longas inflectum ducere voces.

> and alone on the house-tops with *ill-boding song*
> the owl would oft complain, drawing out its lingering notes into a wail.

LCL, Fairclough, p. 427.

21   *Omen ab homine dictum nomen*—i.e., in contrast to the warnings sent by the gods. Cf. Cicero, *De div.* i, 45, 102:

> Neque solum deorum voces Pythagorei observitaverunt, sed etiam hominum, quae vocant omina. Quae maiores nostri quia valere censebant, idcirco omnibus rebus agendis, 'Quid bonum, faustum, felix, fortunatumque esset' praefabentur; rebusque divinis, quae publice fierent, ut 'faverent linguis,' imperabatur; inque feriis imperandis, ut 'litibus et iurgiis se abstinerent.' Itemque in lustranda colonia ab eo qui eam deduceret, et cum imperator exercitum, censor populum, lustraret, bonis nominibus, qui hostias ducerent, eligebantur. Quod idem in dilectu consules observant, ut primus miles fiat bono nomine.

> Nor is it only to the voices of the gods that the Pythagoreans have paid regard but also to the utterances of men which they term 'omens.' Our ancestors, too, considered such 'omens' worthy of respect, and for that reason, before entering upon any business enterprise, used to say, 'May the issue be prosperous, propitious, lucky, and successful.' At public celebrations of religious rites they gave the command, 'Guard your tongues'; and in issuing the order for the Latin festival the customary injunction was, 'Let the people refrain from strife and quarrelling.' So too, when the sacred ceremony of purification was held by one starting on an expedition to found a colony, or when the commander-in-chief was reviewing his army, or the censor was taking his census, it was the rule to choose men with names of good omen to lead the victims. Furthermore, the consuls in making a levy of troops take pains to see that the first soldier enlisted is one with a lucky name.

LCL, Falconer, pp. 333, 335. Cf. also Varro, *De lingua latina* vi, 7, 76. —Reason's figure of diction (*omen/nomen*) may be intended to express contemptuous derision.

22   Cicero, *De div.* ii, 40, 84:

> Quae si suspiciamus, pedis offensio nobis et abruptio corrigiae et sternutamenta erunt observanda.

> But if we are going to accept chance utterances of this kind as omens, we had better look out when we stumble, or break a shoe-string, or sneeze!

LCL, Falconer, p. 467. On *sternutatio,* Fabricius (1716), pp. 419–420, 428–429.

23   The statement of the centurion occurred in connection with the sack of Rome by the Gauls 390 B.C. After the Gauls departed, Livy reports a movement to

transfer the capital to Veii. Furius Camillus, the *dictator,* spoke against it. Livy, v, 55:

> Movisse eos Camillus cum alia oratione tum ea quae ad religiones pertinebat maxime dicitur; sed rem dubiam decrevit vox opportune emissa, quod cum senatus post paulo de his rebus in curia Hostilia haberetur cohortesque ex praesidiis reversentes forte agmine forum transirent, centurio in comitio exclamavit: "Signifer, statue signum; hic manebimus optime." Qua voce audita et senatus accipere se omen ex curia egressus conclamavit et plebs circumfusa adprobavit.

> The speech of Camillus is said to have moved them, particularly where he touched upon religion; but the doubtful issue was resolved by a word that was let fall in the nick of time. It was while the senate, a little later, was deliberating about these matters in the Curia Hostilia; some cohorts returning from guard-duty were marching through the Forum, and as they came to the Comitium a centurion cried out, "Standard-bearer, fix your ensign; here will be our best place to remain." Hearing this sentence the senators came out from the Curia and shouted their acceptance of the omen, and the commons gathering round them signified approval.

LCL, Foster, pp. 185, 187. The story is repeated in *De vita sol.* ii, 15, *Prose* (1955), p. 582; and *Fam.* xv, 4, 8. It is alluded to in *Sen.* vii, 1 (1581: 813). The little girl was the daughter of Lucius Paulus, Cicero, *De div.* i, 46, 103:

> L. Paulus consul iterum, cum ei bellum ut cum rege Perse gereret obtigisset, ut ea ipsa die domum ad vesperum rediit, filiolam suam Tertiam, quae tum erat admodum parva, osculans animum advertit tristiculum. 'Quid est,' inquit, 'mea Tertia? quid tristis es?' 'Mi pater,' inquit, 'Persa periit.' Tum ille arctius puellam complexus, 'Accipio,' inquit, 'mea filia, omen.' Erat autem mortuus catellus eo nomine.

> When Lucius Paulus was consul the second time, and had been chosen to wage war against King Perses, upon returning home on the evening of the day on which he had been appointed, he noticed, as he kissed his little daughter Tertia (at that time a very small child), that she was rather sad. 'What is the matter, Tertia, my dear? Why are you sad?' 'Oh! father, Persa is dead.' Paulus clasped the child in a closer embrace and said, 'Daughter, I accept that as an omen.' Now 'Persa' was the name of a little dog that had died.

LCL, Falconer, p. 335. Cf. also ibid. ii, 40, 83; and Boccaccio, *De casib.,* Hall (1962), f. 53v.

24   *animas et ingenia vestra.* Cf. above, *DR* i, 7, note 1.

25   Petrarch annotated his copy of Leontius' Latin version of Homer's *Iliad* (Wilkins [1961], p. 216), at xii, 237–243, where Hector says:

> But you: you tell me to put my trust in birds, who spread wide their wings. I care nothing for them, I think nothing of these, nor whether they go by on our

right against dawn and sunrise or go by to the left against the glooming mist
and the darkness. No, let us put our trust in the counsel of great Zeus, he who
is lord over all mortal men and all the immortals. One bird sign is best: to fight
in defense of our country . . .

(Lattimore [1951], p. 264). *Vir fortis spernit auguria*—a brave man rejects
auguries. Nolhac (1907), ii, p. 182.

113 ❖ GLAD TIDINGS

1   Virgil, *Aeneid* iv, 175:

> mobilitate viget, viresque acquirit eundo.

LCL, Fairclough, p. 407.
2   Cf. above, *DR* i, 23, 16–18.

114 ❖ EXPECTING FAMILY AND FRIENDS

1   1492: si uixisti
    1581: si uidisti
2   I.t.: Marcus Marcellus
3   Livy, *Perioch.* 115;

> M. Marcello consulari senatu rogante reditum concessit; quo *beneficio* eius
> Marcellus frui non potuit, a Cn. Magio cliente suo Athenis occisus.

> [Caesar] permitted the return of the ex-consul Marcus Marcellus, at the request
> of the senate; Marcellus was unable to profit by this *kindness* of Caesar's, since
> he was killed at Athens by *his client* Gnaeus Magius [46 B.C.].

LCL, Schlesinger, p. 145. On this, Toynbee (1968), art. Marcello. Note the
shocked reaction of Cicero in *Ad fam.* iv, 12, 2; also idem, *Ad Att.* xiii, 10, 3;
and Valerius Maximus, ix, 11, 4. Cf. *Sen.* viii, 3, as below, *DR* ii, Pref., note
91; and *Fam.* ii, 3, 10, below, *DR* ii, 67, note 10.
4   Cicero, *De off.* ii, 5, 16:

> Est Dicaearchi liber de interitu hominum, Peripatetici magni et copiosi, qui
> collectis ceteris causis eluvionis, pestilentiae, vastitatis, beluarum etiam repen-

tinae multitudinis, quarum impetu docet *quaedam hominum genera* esse consumpta, deinde comparat, quanto plures deleti sint homines hominum impetu, id est bellis aut seditionibus, quam omni reliqua calamitate.

There is a book by Dicaearchus on "The Destruction of Human Life." He was a famous and eloquent Peripatetic, and he gathered together all the other causes of destruction—floods, epidemics, famines, and sudden incursions of wild animals in myriads, by whose assaults, he informs us, *whole tribes of men* have been wiped out. And then he proceeds to show by way of comparison how many more men have been destroyed by the assaults of men—that is, by wars or revolutions—than by any and all other sorts of calamity.

LCL, Miller, pp. 183, 185.

5   1492: Mors quam dixi
1581: mox quam dixi

6   I follow Twyne, f. 144r–144v, whose text may have read *ita ut deum paulo minus adorarent*. Both 1492 and 1581 read *ita ut eum*.

7

Ad divorcia rheni
pervasi hostiles depopulatus agros.
Dum tibi Roma decus aeternaque sudo trophaea.
Hister paccatis levior ibit aquis.

1581 reads *Persuasi, hostes depopulatos agros . . . ludo trophaea*. Cf. *CIL,* i², and vi, no. 1207; and Suetonius, v, Claud., i, 1–5, etc. Nolhac (1907), ii, p. 64, n. 2, notes that the verses, which Petrarch thought referred to Drusus, were still extant during the sixteenth century at S. Giovanni in Laterano, the oldest of the Roman basilicas.

8   Reference seems to be to Agrippa (Suetonius, ii, Aug., 65, 1 *et passim*) and to Tiberius (Suetonius, iii, Tiberius, 7, 3; Seneca, *Dial.* xi, 15, 5).

9   9 B.C. Livy, *Perioch.* 142:

Ipse ex fractura, equo super crus eius conlapso, XXX die, quam id acciderat, mortuus. Corpus a Nerone fratre, qui nuntio valetudinis evocatus raptim adcucurrerat, Romam pervectum et in tumulo C. Iulii reconditum. Laudatus est a Caesare Augusto vitrico, et supremis eius plures honores dati.

Drusus himself died of a broken leg, sustained when his horse fell on it, on the thirtieth day after the accident. His body was conveyed to Rome by his brother [Tiberius] Nero, who had arrived posthaste on news of his illness; burial was in the tomb of Gaius Julius. The eulogy was pronounced by Caesar Augustus, his stepfather, and many distinctions were conferred on him at his funeral.

LCL, Schlesinger, pp. 167, 169.

10   Reason's account, lines 60–71, is a paraphrase of Suetonius, iv, Caligula, 6, 1–2.

11   Cf. above, *DR* i, 32, note 4.

12   1492: fors
1581: sors

13   Cf. *Trionfi,* Tr. fame ii, 134–138. On Arthurian lore and the *Tavola Ritonda* (Marti [1959], pp. 663–735), e.g., Gardner (1930); Cecchi & Sapegno (1965), i, pp. 584–586, 620; and Fisher (1966), and the literature cited there, pp. 22–23. In *De vulg. el.* i, 10, 2, Dante refers to *Arturi regis ambages pulcerrime*—the delightful adventures of King Arthur. Boccaccio summarizes them in *De casibus,* Hall (1962), ff. 98v–99v. On Arthur and his knights in Italian medieval art, Mâle (1978), pp. 268–270. On Arthur's messianic return, also Leach (1949), art. Arthur; Percy-Wheatley (1927), iii, pp. 27–28; and Fazio degli Uberti, *Il Dittamondo* iv, 24, 46–51 (Corsi [1952], i, p. 323):

> Seguitò poi il suo figliuolo Artú
> lo qual fu franco, largo e temperato
> quanto alcun altro nel suo tempo o piú.
>   Tanto da' suoi fu temuto e amato,
> che lungamente dopo la sua morte
> che dovesse tornare fu aspettato.

Twyne, f. 145v, omits Reason's deprecatory remark about the fact that "the *Britaines* looke for the comming of king Arthure." He may have known that, as late as 1485, Caxton's edition of Sir Thomas Malory's *Le Morte Darthur* (Spisak [1983], p. 592; Senior [1981], p. 339) reported the inscription above King Arthur's grave:

HIC IACET ARTHURUS, REX QUONDAM REXQUE FUTURUS

Here lies Arthur, the Once and Future King.

On Nero's return, *Sen.* vi, 6, to Zanobi da Strada, 1358 (1581: 809; Rossi [1930], pp. 224–227; Wilkins [1958], pp. 173–174; idem [1959], pp. 305–306):

> Credo ego iam mundi finem instare, crebrescunt ecce prodigia, iam Antichristum aduentare, iam quod quidam suspicati sunt Neronem uiuere, audiemus & reliqua fieri, quae illius turbinis futura praeambula nobis a patribus nunciatum est.

> I do believe the end of the world is close at hand already; just look, the portents are increasing: already we hear that the Antichrist is approaching, already that, as some think, Nero is alive, and that the other tokens are occurring, which, the fathers have told us, are harbingers of the whirlwind to come [cf. Ier. 30, 23].

Another apocalyptic remark, *Send back Nero, I pray, send back Domitian!* occurs in *SN* 6, Piur (1925), p. 188, Zacour (1973), p. 62; note also *Met.* iii,

23, 20–23. —On the identification of the Antichrist of Judaeo-Christian apoc-
alypticism (Apoc. 13 and 17; ii Thess. 2, 1–11, etc.) with Nero as resurrected
persecutor, based, perhaps, on Suetonius, vi, Nero, 57, or Tacitus, *Hist.* ii, 8,
cf., e.g., Lactantius, *Div. inst.* vii, 16, *PL* 6, cc. 790–793, and Jos. Isaeus,
Notae, ibid., c. 1008; idem, *Lib. de mort. persecut.* ii, *PL* 7, cc. 197–198, and
Notae, Steph. Baluzius, cc. 303–304, Joh. Columbus, c. 395; Sulpicius
Severus, *Dial.* ii, 15 (i, 41; McGinn [1979], p. 52); *Sacra hist.* ii, 29; Augustine,
De civ. Dei xx, 19. The Antichrist myth was also associated with Domitian
(McGinn [1979], pp. 66–67, 84). On the apocalyptic traditions in the Middle
Ages, McCall (1979), esp. pp. 161–164, 225–227; and McGinn, ibid., and the
literature cited there.

14   Cf. above, *DR* i, 85, note 1.

115 ✢ EXPECTING BETTER TIMES

1   *bonarumque artium studiis*—cf. Cicero, *De inv.* i, 25, 36:

> Studium est autem animi assidua et vehementer ad aliquam rem applicata
> magna cum voluptate occupatio, ut philosophiae, poeticae, geometricae,
> litterarum.

> *Interest* is unremitting mental activity ardently devoted to some subject and
> accompanied by intense pleasure, for example interest in philosophy, poetry,
> geometry, literature.

LCL, Hubbell, pp. 73, 75.

2   Cf. *Fam.* xx, 4, 28; *Sen.* iii, 9 (1581: 779); and above, *DR* i, 21, 64–73.
3   Reason seems to refer to Horace, *Carm.* iii, 6, 45–48:

> damnosa quid non imminuit dies?
> aetas parentum, peior avis, tulit
>   nos nequiores, mox daturos
>   progeniem vitiosiorem.

> What do the ravages of time not injure!
> Our parents' age, worse than our grandsires',
> has brought forth us less worthy and destined soon to
> yield an offspring still more wicked.

LCL, Bennett, p. 203. Petrarch cited the passage in *Fam.* ii, 10, 4; and in
Contra eum (1581: 1078). Cf. also Seneca, *Thyestes* 133–135; Seneca Rhetor,
Controv. i, Pref. 7; *Fam.* ii, 10, xx, 1, *passim,* and viii, 10, 12 (= *Fam.* xiii, 6,

10), xi, 7, 1; *Sen.* iii, 1, xi, 16, xiii, 14 (1581: 767, 894, 929); SN 6, Piur (1925), pp. 187–191; *Trionfi,* Tr. cup. i, 17, *Rime* (1951), p. 481; and *DR* ii, 28, 59–61, ii, 96, 22–28, and note 2, ii, 130, 22–23, and note 4. The topic "things were so much better in former times" recurs in Augustine, *Sermo Caillau 2*, 92 (*PL* Supplem. 2, c. 441), which is included in today's Catholic Office of Reading for Wednesday, 20th Week, Ord. time.

4   *Omnem aetatem de moribus suis questam*—also quoted in *Fam.* xx, i (to Neri Morando, Milan, July 1355), 3. As pointed out by Bosco (*Le Familiari,* Ediz. naz., iv, p. 4), this appears to be a paraphrase of Seneca, *De benef.* i, 10, 1:

> Sed longius nos impetus evehit provocante materia; itaque sic finiamus, ne in nostro saeculo culpa subsidat. Hoc maiores nostri questi sunt, hoc nos querimur, hoc posteri nostri querentur, eversos mores, regnare nequitiam, in deterius res humanas et omne nefas labi.

> But, because the subject is alluring, my ardour has carried me too far; and so let me close by showing that it is not our generation only that is beset by this fault. The complaint our ancestors made, the complaint we make, the complaint our posterity will make, is that mortality is overturned, that wickedness holds sway, and that human affairs and every sin are tending toward the worse.

LCL, Basore, p. 31. Note also, idem, *Ep.* 97, 1. An earlier reminiscence occurs in Walter Map, *De nug. cur.* iv, 5:

> Omnibus seculis sua displicuit modernitas, et quevis etas a prima preteritam sibi pretulit . . .

> Every century has disliked its own modernity; every age, from the first onwards, has preferred the previous one to itself.

James et al. (1983), p. 313. On *modernitas,* above. *DR* i, Pref., note 21.

5   Cf. *Fam.* ii, 3, 28, xv, 7, 21; and *DR* ii, 104, 36–43, and 118, 45–51.

116 ✤ A PRINCELY VISIT

1   On *sperare/metuere, DR* i, 10, note 20; contraries, *DR* i, 11, note 19; *in utranque partem*—on either side—*DR* i, 11, 29. Note *Fam.* iv, 12, 28, xi, 3, 9, as below, *DR* ii, 114, note 48, xv, 5, 8, xvii, 3, 17, xx, 12, 2; *Sen.* ix, 1 (1581: 845); and *DR* ii, 128, 24–26.

2   On the phenomena of thunder and lightning, Aristotle, *Meteor.* ii, 9, Barnes

(1984), i, pp. 596–597; Cicero, *De div.* ii, 19, 44–45; Pliny, *Nat. hist.* ii, 55, 142; Wallace (1972), pp. 44–47; and Boyde (1981), pp. 78, 321, 324.

3   Cf. above, *DR* i, 89, note 2.

117 ❖ HOPE FOR FAME AFTER DEATH

1   Dialogues 117–119 deal with fame and posterity. Cf. *Trionfi,* esp. Tr. temp. and Tr. aetern., and Bernardo (1962), pp. 65–70 *et passim.* —On this dialogue, note *Secretum* iii, *Prose* (1955), pp. 188–214; *Fam.* i, 2; and the opening of *Posteritati, Sen.* xviii, 1, *Prose* (1955), p. 2. Note also Quinones (1972), chap. 3.

2   For Seneca's prophecy, cf., e.g., his *Ep.* 21, 5, and 79, esp. 17–18. Reason's reference to Statius paraphrases the concluding verses of his *Thebaid* xii, 810–819:

> Durabisne procul dominoque legere superstes,
> o mihi bissenos multum vigilata per annos
> Thebai? Iam certe *praesens tibi Fama benignum*
> *stravit iter coepitque novam monstrare futuris.*
> Iam te magnanimus dignatur noscere Caesar,
> Itala iam studio discit memoratque iuventus.
> vive, precor; nec tu divinam Aeneida tempta,
> sed longe sequere et vestigia semper adora.
> Mox, tibi si quis adhuc praetendit nubila livor,
> occidet, et meriti post me referentur honores.

> Wilt thou endure in the time to come, O my
> *Thebaid,* for twelve years object of my wakeful toil,
> wilt thou survive thy master and be read? Of a truth
> *already present Fame hath paved thee a friendly road,*
> *and begun to hold thee up, young as thou art, to future ages.*
> Already great-hearted Caesar deigns to know thee, and the
> youth of Italy eagerly learns and recounts thy verse.
> O live, I pray! nor rival the divine *Aeneid,* but follow
> afar and ever venerate its footsteps. Soon, if any envy
> as yet o'erclouds thee, it shall pass away, and, after
> I am gone, thy well-won honours shall be duly paid.

LCL, Mozley, p. 505. Ovid often predicted fame for his poems. In view of the fact that his *Tristia* were very popular in the Middle Ages—Albertino Mussato composed a cento from the *Tristia* (Sabbadini [1914], pp. 111–112)—it is likely that our text alludes to *Tristia* iv, 10, 115–130:

ergo quod vivo durisque laboribus obsto,
  nec me sollicitae taedia lucis habent,
gratia, Musa, tibi: nam tu solacia praebes,
  tu curae requies, tu medicina venis.
Tu dux et comes es, tu nos abducis ab Histro,
  in medioque mihi das Helicone locum;
tu mihi, quod rarum est, vivo sublime dedisti
  nomen, ab exequiis quod dare fama solet.
Nec, qui detractat praesentia, Livor iniquo
  ullum de nostris dente momordit opus.
Nam tulerint magnos cum saecula nostra poetas,
  non fuit ingenio fama maligna meo,
cumque ego praeponam multos mihi, non minor illis
  dicor et in toto plurimus orbe legor.
Si quid habent igitur vatum praesagia veri,
  protinus ut moriar, non ero, terra, tuus.
Sive favore tuli, sive hanc ego carmine famam,
  iure tibi grates, candide lector, ago.

So then this living of mine, this stand against the hardness of my sufferings, this bare will to view the daylight's woes, I owe, my Muse, to thee! For thou dost lend me comfort, thou dost come as rest, as balm, to my sorrow. Thou art both guide and comrade: thou leadest me far from Hister and grantest me a place in Helicon's midst; thou hast given me while yet alive (how rare the boon!) a lofty name—the name which renown is wont to give only after death. Nor has jealousy, that detractor of the present, attacked with malignant tooth any work of mine. For although this age of ours has brought forth mighty poets, fame has not been grudging to my genius, and though I place many before myself, report calls me not their inferior and throughout the world I am most read of all. If then there be truth in poets' prophecies, even though I die forthwith, I shall not, O earth, be thine. But whether through favour or by very poetry I have gained this fame, 'tis right, kind reader, that I render thanks to thee.

LCL, Wheeler, pp. 205, 207. But note the concluding lines of the *Metamorphoses,* xv, 871–879:

Iamque opus exegi, quod nec Iovis ira nec ignis
nec poterit ferrum nec edax abolere vetustas.
Cum volet, illa dies, quae nil nisi corporis huius
ius habet, incerti spatium mihi finiat aevi:
parte tamen meliore mei super alta perennis
astra ferar, nomenque erit indelebile nostrum,

> quaque patet domitis Romana potentia terris,
> ore legar populi, perque omnia saecula fama,
> siquid habent veri vatum praesagia, vivam.

And now my work is done, which neither the wrath of Jove, nor fire, nor sword, nor the gnawing tooth of time shall ever be able to undo. When it will, let that day come which has no power save over this mortal frame, and end the span of my uncertain years. Still in my better part I shall be borne immortal far beyond the lofty stars and I shall have an undying name. Wherever Rome's power extends over the conquered world, I shall have mention on men's lips, and, if the prophecies of bards have any truth, through all the ages shall I live in fame.

LCL, Miller, p. 427.

3 1492: et scripserunt: nec quod sibi promiserant impleuerunt
1581: & scripserunt, nec quod sibi promiserunt

4 Cf. *DR* i, 16, note 3, and ii, 35, note 1.

5 Cf. above, *DR* i, 96, 270–272, and 11, note 20.

6 Cicero was murdered by Antony's agents December 7, 43 B.C. Pursued by Antipater, Demosthenes took poison 322 B.C. Socrates was sentenced to death 399 B.C., after a trial reported in the Apologies of Plato and of Xenophon. His death is described in Plato's *Phaedo*. For the stories of Zeno of Elea and Zeno of Citium, the Stoic, cf. Valerius Maximum, iii, 3, Ext. 2 and 3. Note also Boethius, *Cons. phil.* i, P 3, 31–34. —Androgeus, son of the Cretan king Minos and Pasiphaë,

> visited Athens, and won every contest in the All Athenian Games. But King Aegeus knew of his friendship for the fifty rebellious sons of Pallas and fearing that he might persuade his father Minos to support these in an open revolt, conspired with the Megareans to have him ambushed at Onoë on the way to Thebes, where he was about to compete in certain funeral games. Androgeus defended himself with courage, and a fierce battle ensued in which he was killed.

Graves (1955), i, 90.h. Cf. Boccaccio, *De casibus* (Hall [1962]), f. 4v. The annual sacrifice to the Minotaur of seven youths and seven maidens, above, *DR* i, 27, note 10, was imposed by Minos in retribution for the death of Androgeus. Graves, ibid., 98.c. —Reason advocates Seneca's *licit sapere sine pompa, sine invidia*—a man may be wise without parade and without arousing enmity (*Ep.* 103, 5; LCL, Gummere, p. 189).

7 I.t.: Oete

8 1492: aureum uellus arietis
1581: aureum, uelut arietis

9 Cf. Graves (1955), ii, esp. 148g, and 152. Reason's mythology is somewhat deficient. But note Boccaccio, *De casib.* (Hall [1962]), f. 4r.

10   1492: si notitia comes esset
       1581: si noxia comes esset
11   On this, Boethius, *Cons. phil.* iii, P 8, 17–31, as above, *DR* i, 2, note 8;
       Secretum, Proem., and ii, *Prose* (1955), pp. 22, 88, 154 (as above, *DR* i, 69,
       note 14); and *DR* i, 1, 81, i, 42, 2, i, 55, 21, also, i, 86, 17–20, i, 40, note 4.

118 ❖ GLORY EARNED BY BUILDING

1   On this dialogue, *Fam.* vi, 2; and *Africa* viii (Bergin [1977], pp. 213–217). Cf.
      the *Mirabilia mundi,* the *Mirabilia Urbis Romae,* and related texts (Fazio degli
      Uberti, *Il dittamondo* ii, 31, Corsi [1952], i, pp. 177–180; Manitius, iii, [1931],
      pp. 244–253; Nichols [1889], and this informative discussion in Gregorovius,
      viii, 7, 2 and 3, i [1926], pp. 1215–1230; Rawski [1967], p. 204, n. 52; Alsop
      [1982], pp. 558–559, nn. 36, 71; and Krautheimer [1980], pp. 198–199,
      354–355, nn. for pp. 189 f, 198 f). On the city of Rome after Constantine,
      Krautheimer, ibid., esp. pp. 187–190, and chap. 10; and Gregorovius (1926).
      On Petrarch's interest in the ruins of ancient Rome, Baxandall (1971), p. 59;
      Krautheimer (1956/1982), chap. xix; and Martellotti (1983), chap. 2.
2   On the topic *ubi sunt*—where are they now?—above, *DR* i, 15, note 49.
3   In contradistinction to the Great Babylon, Apoc. 17, 5, this is Babylon the
      Small, the Western Babylon, i.e., the Papal Court at Avignon, of *Sine nomine*
      (e.g., viii, Zacour [1973], p. 67; cf. also pp. 22–23). *Rime* 115, 1–4:

> De l'empia Babilonia ond' è fugita
> ognivergogna, ond' ogni bene è fori,
> albergo di dolor, madre d'errori,
> son fuggito io per allungar la vita.

> From that dire Babylon, from where is run
> Away all shame, from where all good is gone,
> Dwelling of misery, mother of strife,
> I fled to lengthen the course of my life.

Armi (1946), p. 173. On the topic, also Coogan (1983).
4   Those seven great works, the Seven Wonders of the World, are the pyramids
      near Memphis in Egypt; the hanging gardens of Semiramis at Babylon; the
      tomb of Mausolus at Halicarnassus; the temple of Artemis/Diana at Ephesus;
      the colossal statue of Helios at Rhodes; the chryselephantine statue of Zeus/

Jupiter by Phidias at Olympia; and the Pharos lighthouse at Alexandria—or, in some lists, the walls of Babylon, or the palace of Cyrus. Many variations were adopted by later authors. Cf. Cottrell (1959); and Omont (1882). On the Golden House of Nero, above, *DR* i, 96, 145–169 *et seq.*

5   I.t.: *balneum Antonianum* —On *Antonius* for *Antoninus*, Martellotti (1983), pp. 121–122, 156.

6   *& septizonium Severi: et eiusdem thermae severianae.* Cf. *Hist. Aug.*, Severus, xix, 5:

> Opera publica praecipua eius exstant Septizonium et Thermae Severianae.

> The principal public works of his now in existence are the Septizonium and the Baths of Severus.

LCL, Magie, p. 417.

7   1492: atrium libertatis
     1581: artium libertatis

8   1492: Munacii Plancii
     1581: Munacii & Plancii

9   I.t.: *Balbi Cornelii*

10   On the baths of Diocletian and Caracalla Antoninus, Krautheimer (1980), pp. 28, 189. On Abbot Suger's plan to bring to Saint-Denis columns from the *thermae* of Diocletian, Panofsky (1946), pp. 90–91; and Krautheimer, ibid., p. 188. On the shrine of Marius, Cicero, *De div.* i, 28, 59; and the note in Falconer's LCL edition, p. 288. On the Septizonium and the *thermae* of Alexander Severus, *Hist. Aug,* Severus xix, 5, and xxiv, 3–5, Geta, vii, 2; and Krautheimer, ibid., pp. 252, 322. Cf. also the entries in Platner & Ashby (1929); and Billanovich (1981), pp. 133–135. On *the heart of the matter,* i.e., the public works of Augustus (Boardman [1986], pp. 771–780), Suetonius ii, 29:

> Publica opera plurima exstruxit, e quibus vel praecipua: forum cum aede Martis Ultoris, templum Apollinis in Palatio, aedem Tonantis Iovis in Capitolio. . . . . . . Templum Apollinis in ea parte Palatinae domus excitavit, quam fulmine ictam desiderari a deo haruspices pronuntiarant; addidit porticus cum bibliotheca Latina Graecaque, quo loco iam senior saepe etiam senatum habuit decuriasque iudicum recognovit. Tonanti Iovi aedem consecravit liberatus periculo, cum expeditione Cantabrica per nocturnum iter lecticam eius fulgur praestrinxisset servumque praelucentem exanimasset. Quaedam etiam opera sub nomine alieno, nepotum scilicet et uxoris sororisque fecit, ut porticum basilicamque Gai et Luci, item porticus Liviae et Octaviae theatrumque Marcelli. Sed et ceteros principes viros saepe hortatus est, ut pro facultate quisque monimentis vel novis vel refectis et excultis urbem adornarent. Multaque a multis tunc extructa sunt, sicut a Marcio Philippo aedes Herculis Musarum, a L. Cornificio aedes Dianae, ab Asinio Pollione atrium Libertatis, a

Munatio Planco aedes Saturni, a Cornelio Balbo theatrum, a Statilio Tauro amphitheatrum, a M. vero Agrippa complura et egregia.

He built many public works, in particular the following: his forum with the temple of Mars the Avenger [24 B.C.], the temple of Apollo on the Palatine [28 B.C.], and the fane of Jupiter the Thunderer on the Capitol [22 B.C.]. . . .   . . . He reared the temple of Apollo in that part of his house on the Palatine for which the soothsayers declared that the god had shown desire by striking it with lightning. He joined to it colonnades with Latin and Greek libraries, and when he was getting to be an old man he often held meetings of the senate there as well, and revised the lists of jurors. He dedicated the shrine to Jupiter the Thunderer because of a narrow escape; for on his Cantabrian expedition during a march by night, a flash of lightning grazed his litter and struck the slave dead who was carrying a torch before him. He constructed some works too in the name of others, his grandsons and nephew to wit, his wife and sister, such as the colonnade and basilica of Gaius and Lucius [12 B.C.]; the colonnades of Livia and Octavia [33 and 15 B.C.], and the theatre of Marcellus (13 B.C.). More than that, he often urged other prominent men to adorn the city with new monuments or to restore and embellish old ones, each according to his means. And many such works were built at that time by many men; for example, the temple of Hercules and the Muses by Marcius Philippus, the temple of Diana by Lucius Cornificius, the Hall of Liberty by Asinius Pollio, the temple of Saturn by Munatius Plancus, a theatre by Cornelius Balbus, and amphitheatre by Statilius Taurus, and by Marcus Agrippa in particular many magnificent structures.

LCL, Rolfe, pp. 167, 169. On the porticus of Octavia and the theater of Marcellus in medieval Rome, Krautheimer, ibid., pp. 157, 243, 251, 283, 299, 305.

11   Original structure by Marcus Agrippa (27 B.C.), rebuilt by Hadrian.

In A.D. 609 Emperor Phocas presented the building to Pope Boniface IV, who dedicated it to the Virgin. It became S. Maria della Rotonda and thus the marvellous structure survived the ruin of the centuries.

Curtius (1950), p. 76. Cf. also Burckhardt (1935), pp. 18–21; and Krautheimer (1980), pp. 72–73, 143 et passim. Twyne, f. 149r. translates, perhaps with an eye on Protestant readers, "except one only, whiche is the Temple of *Pantheon* made by *Agrippa*," and omits the rest.

12   Suetonius, ii, *Aug.*, 28, 3:

Urbem neque pro maiestate imperii ornatam et inundationibus incendiisque obnoxiam excoluit adeo, *ut iure sit gloriatus marmoream se relinquere, quam latericiam accepisset.*

Since the city was not adorned as the dignity of the empire demanded, and was exposed to flood and fire, he so beautified it *that he could justly boast that he found it built of brick and left it in marble.*

LCL, Rolfe, p. 167. Also quoted in Aurelius Victor, *Epit.* i, 19, Pichlmayr (1911), p. 135.

119 ❖ GLORY FROM THE COMPANY WE KEEP

1 *Likeness attracts* —cf. *DR* i, 66, note 2, and i, 94, 15–17.
2 Cf., e.g., Petrarch's admonition of Giacomo dal Verme to imitate his father Luchino, who had died in Constantinople, *Sen.* viii, 5 (1581: 839; Wilkins [1959], pp. 114–115, 118–119).
3 I.e., the *artes mechanicae,* below, *DR* ii, Pref., note 74.
4 Cf. above, *DR* i, 29, note 17.

120 ❖ ALL KINDS OF HOPE

1 I.t.: *res*
2 On the oxymoron, *DR* i, 69, note 2.
3 In *DR* i, 109, Hope is described as female.
4 Cf. above, *DR* i, 11, note 16, and i, 44, 106.

121 ❖ HOPE FOR PEACE OF MIND

1 1492: contraque tuam spem tantopere niteris
   1581: contraque tuam spem tanto poeniteris
2 Similar, *Sen.* viii, 6 (1581: 839); and *DR* i, 5, 16–19, and ii, 6, 17–19.

122 ❖ HOPE FOR LIFE ETERNAL

1   Cicero, *De off.* i, 5, 15, based on Aristotle, *Eth. Nic.* vi, 13, 1144b, 30–35:

> Quae quattuor quamquam inter se colligata atque implicata sunt, tamen ex
> singulis certa officiorum genera nascuntur . . .

> Although these four are connected and interwoven, still it is in each one con-
> sidered singly that certain definite kinds of moral duties have their origin . . .

LCL, Miller, p. 17. Note also Cicero, ibid. i, 20; *De fin.* v, 23, 66; *Tusc. disp.*
14, iii, 8, 16–18, above, *DR* i, Pref., note 27; and *Var.* 50, as above, *Dramat*
personae, note 23. The Christian fathers shared this view. Cf. Ambrose,
Luc. V, super 6, 20, *PL* 15, c. 1738; Augustine, *De trin.* vi, 4, *PL* 42, c. 92
Gregory, *Moral.* xxii, 1, *PL* 7, c. 212. On this, Abelard, *Sic et non* 137, 1
Boyer-McKeon, p. 467; Thomas Aquinas, *Summa theol.* i, II, Q 65.a.1; ar
Pegis (1945) ii, pp. 495–496.

2   On this, above, *Dramatis personae,* note 13.

3   Cf. *Var.* 64, Fracassetti, iii (1863), p. 480; and *DR* i, 16–18.

4   Isidore, *Etym.* i, 6, 1–2:

> Partes orationis primus Aristoteles duas tradidit, nomen et verbum; deinde
> Donatus octo definivit. Sed omnes ad illa duo principalia revertentur, id est, ac
> nomen et verbum, quae significant personam et actum. Reliquae adpendice
> sunt et ex his originem trahunt. . . .   . . . Adverbium de nomine nascitur, ι
> 'doctus, docte.'

> Aristotle was the first to differentiate between two parts of language, noun an
> verb [*De interp.* 1–3]; later, Donatus defined eight [*Ars minor,* Keil (1864), i
> pp. 355–366]. But all these are based upon the principal two, that is, noun ar
> verb, which signify person and act. What remains are additions which deriv
> from the noun, as in *doctus*—a learned man—*docte*—learnedly.

On this, Fontaine (1959), i, chap. 3, esp. pp. 109–111. On *infallible judge*
DR i, 36, 14–20; and *Var.* 64, Fracassetti, iii (1863), p. 480:

> Non te superficies rerum fallit; solerter introspicis, et suum pretium reb
> ponis.

> You are not duped by the surface of things. You examine them more careful
> and assess them according to their worth.

5   1492: de se sperari amant
    1581: de se separari amant

6   Cf. above, *DR* i, 57, 5.

7   In the Latin text of *DR* i, 122, Hope's eight statements exhibit this intercalated pattern:

Spero aeternam vitam	1	
Aeternam vitam spero	2	
		α
Vitam spero aeternam	3	
Spero vitam aeternam	β	4
Vitam aeternam spero	5	
Spero vitam aeternam	4	
aeternam vitam spero	2	$1/α$
Spero aeternam vitam	1	

END OF NOTES TO BOOK I

DATE DUE

Demco, Inc. 38-293